P9-ELS-677

The Joy Of C

Chirasak Thasanatorn

THE
JOY
OF
C

Programming in C, Second Edition

Lawrence H. Miller
The Aerospace Corporation

Alexander E. Quilici
University of Hawaii at Manoa

John Wiley & Sons, Inc.
New York □ Chichester □ Brisbane □ Toronto □ Singapore

Another one for our families and friends

Acquisitions Editor: Steven Elliot
Production Supervisor: Charlotte Hyland
Cover Designer: Michael Jung
Book Designer: Maddy Lesure
Manufacturing Manager: Andrea Price
Copy Editing Supervisor: Elizabeth Swain

Copyright ©1986, 1993 by John Wiley & Sons, Inc.

All rights reserved. Published simultaneously in Canada.

Reproduction or translation of any part of this work beyond that permitted by Sections 107 or 108 of the 1976 United States Copyright Act without the permission of the copyright owner is unlawful. Requests for permission or further information should be addressed to the Permissions Department, John Wiley & Sons, Inc.

Recognizing the importance of preserving what has been written, it is a policy of John Wiley & Sons, Inc. to have books of enduring value published in the United States printed on acid-free paper, and we exert our best efforts to that end.

The programs presented in this book have been included solely for their instructional value. They have been carefully tested but are not guaranteed for any particular purpose. The publisher does not offer any warranties or representations, nor does it accept any liabilities with respect to the programs.

Library of Congress Cataloging-in-Publication Data

Miller, Lawrence H.
  The Joy Of C / Lawrence H. Miller, Alexander E. Quilici.
    p.   cm.
  Includes index.
  ISBN 0-471-51333-4 (pbk.)
  1. C (Computer program language) I. Quilici, Alexander E.
  II. Title.
  QA76.73.C15M54   1993
  005.13'3–dc20
                                                        92-23091
                                                        CIP

Printed in the United States of America
10 9 8 7 6 5

PREFACE

C is a powerful programming language. It provides a variety of features that help us write clear, concise programs that are portable, efficient, and easy to maintain. But C also has a reputation for being hard to learn and even harder to master. Its conciseness and complexity can overwhelm all but the most experienced programmer. Many programmers, in fact, wind up avoiding many of its most important features and missing out on the true pleasures of programming in C.

The Joy Of C is intended to be a step-by-step companion in your journey from novice to expert C programmer. It's a life-raft that will keep you from slowly sinking into a sea of confusion, and a gentle guru that will guide you along the path to becoming a true C master. You'll find this book useful as a self-study guide to C if:

- *You've programmed in other high-level languages such as BASIC, FORTRAN, or Pascal and now want to program in C.* We don't start from scratch and try to teach you how to program. Instead, we assume some prior programming experience and expend much of our effort describing and investigating C's unique and unfamiliar features.[1] We've also carefully chosen our examples, wherever possible picking programs similar to those you're likely to have seen written in another language, thus easing the transition to programming in C.

- *You've programmed in C but you don't yet feel as though you've mastered it.* We cover the language completely, delving deeply into many issues that are often casually examined or completely avoided. You can't be a proficient C programmer without knowing how to put together large programs, how to produce portable and efficient code, or how to use pointers to effectively organize and access data—topics we emphasize rather than ignore.

- *You're familiar with C but not ANSI C.* The ANSI C standard adds many useful features to the original C definition and implementation, including function prototypes, generic pointers, implicit string concatenation, an improved preprocessor, and additional library functions and header files. We don't simply relegate these features to an appendix, nor do we just briefly touch on them as interesting extensions. Instead, we thoroughly examine and exploit these features as integral parts of the language.

---

[1] In particular, we assume that you're fairly familiar with the basic concepts underlying computer programming and that you've previously written programs using variables, arithmetic, decisions, and loops.

- *You're planning on eventually learning C++.* C++ is an object-oriented programming language that's based on C. It's rapidly gaining in popularity and looks to be the language of the future. Unfortunately, it's all but impossible to learn C++ unless you're completely comfortable with C. We've tried to smooth your likely transition to C++ by including a special chapter on the basics of C++ programming. It redoes some of our earlier C examples in C++ so that you can get a good feel for some of the key differences between the two languages.

- *You're looking for examples of real-world C programs or are interested in obtaining a set of useful programming tools.* We provide over 200 useful programs and functions, including a base converter, a histogram producer, an electronic address book, a C program cross-referencer, various sorting and searching programs, and more. We also provide implementations of useful libraries such as sets, queues, stacks, lists, and trees. All of these programs have been written, compiled, and executed using a variety of ANSI C compilers on everything from small personal computers to powerful workstations to large mainframes.

Special Features

This book has grown out of almost a decade of teaching C courses to a wide range of students—from first-year computer science and electrical engineering majors to life-long assembly language programmers, from casual computer users who've never programmed before to competent C hackers fine-tuning their skills. And we've concluded that there are several ways to ease the often difficult process of mastering a programming language, all of which we've incorporated here:

- *We provide complete, useful programs.* Our examples don't merely illustrate language features, they illustrate them in a realistic way as part of a useful function or program. And our examples are complete—we avoid potentially confusing program fragments and ensure that every function comes with a main program that shows how to call it and how to use its return value. As a result, you won't have to puzzle for hours over how a particular piece of code might actually be used.

- *We provide non-trivial example programs.* Almost every chapter ends with a case study, a significant, real-world application that cements the concepts covered in the chapter. We often construct these case studies from functions and programs written and explained earlier in the text, reinforcing these examples and providing realistic demonstrations of how bigger programs are built from smaller pieces. As a result, you won't be left wondering how non-trivial programs are actually written, and you won't be stuck starting your own programming projects from scratch.

- *We provide multiple versions of our example programs.* Our approach to presenting most of C's constructs is to gradually rewrite and extend our earlier examples. We usually begin with a simple, straightforward function or program and then gradually improve it, showing how we can use various language features to make it more concise or efficient, or more powerful and useful. We've resisted the strong temptation to immediately take advantage of extremely useful but potentially confusing language features. As a result, you won't have to struggle with simultaneously trying to understand a new program and new language features, and you'll come to a deep understanding of exactly why and when certain features are useful.

- *We provide pictorial descriptions of data structures and algorithms.* Numerous illustrations help clarify complex concepts such as pointers, arrays, and dynamic allocation. These pictures simplify seemingly complicated data structures and algorithms and ensure that our explanations are easy to follow. As a result, you won't have to rely on closing your eyes and trying to visualize what pointers, arrays, or structures actually look like, or exactly how a particular searching algorithm really works.

- *We highlight potential trouble spots and likely errors.* C comes loaded with language constructs that can lead to complete chaos when they're not used carefully or their fine points are forgotten. And most C programmers seem to make the same set of mistakes when first learning the language. We address both of these problems by liberally sprinkling over 60 warnings and reminders throughout the text, each set in boldface and in a gray-shaded box. As a result, you can use these boxes both as a checklist of mistakes to avoid when writing your programs, and as a list of likely bugs when trying to debug programs you've written.

- *We provide end-of-chapter summaries.* Each chapter concludes with a short section summarizing its key points. Often these summaries list the most important language features covered in the chapter, along with a few crucial details of their use. As a result, you can use these summaries as a checklist of the topics we expect you to have learned from reading the chapter.

- *We provide plenty of programming exercises.* Each chapter ends with a set of programming exercises, each carefully designed to provide practice in using the particular language features discussed in the chapter. There are over 300 exercises in the text as a whole, spanning a wide range of difficulty. Some are simply modifications to our example programs that make them more robust, more efficient, more concise, more useable, or more user-friendly. Others range from small programs to sizeable programming projects, many of which are useful programs in their own right. As a result, you'll obtain important practice in using these features by writing functions or programs that you'll find useful later on.

- *We provide a disk containing the source files for all of our example programs.* All you have to do is compile, link, and execute them. If you're having trouble understanding a particular example, you can easily explore its behavior by executing it within a debugger or modifying it to produce useful tracing information. As a result, you won't waste hours and hours typing in the sample programs and can instead spend that time trying to better understand their behavior.

Organization

We divide the text into five parts. Part I is a gentle tutorial introduction to C. Part II is a detailed discussion of fundamental C features: its basic data types, operators, statements, functions, and storage classes. Part III addresses advanced data types, such as pointers, strings, structures, multidimensional arrays, and arrays of pointers. Part IV looks at advanced program structure, including advanced use of functions, the preprocessor, generic functions, and complex declarations. Part V deals with real-world issues, including external files, advanced data structures, portability and efficiency, and moving from programming in C to programming in C++.

Part I: A Gentle Introduction to C

Chapter 1 presents a pair of introductory programs: one is a variant on the traditional "Hello World" example, the other is a program to do several simple financial calculations. Together, these programs introduce the basics of producing output, declaring variables, performing arithmetic, and the process of compiling and linking C programs. • *Chapter 2* provides a series of different versions of a program that computes the interest accumulating in a bank account—and uses them to introduce the basic C data types, statements, and functions.

Part II: The Basics

Chapter 3 describes integer and floating point numbers, the basic arithmetic operators, the idea of data type conversions, and the most important functions in the math library. Its case study is a program to convert values in bases between 2 and 10. • *Chapter 4* covers the character data type, emphasizing character input and output, character testing, and the intimate connection between characters and integers. Its case study extends the earlier base conversion program to handle bases larger than 10. • *Chapter 5* addresses operators, paying special attention to the shorthand assignment and bitwise operators and highlighting often unexpected features such as integer division or lazy evaluation. Its case study is a pair of programs to compress and uncompress files. • *Chapter 6* studies statements, showing the most appropriate uses for each, and concludes with a case study that prints its input in octal, one byte at a time. • *Chapter 7* introduces arrays, using an input reversal program to illustrate how to use them and pass them as parameters. It also provides several functions for searching and sorting arrays. Its case study is a histogram producer. • *Chapter 8* focuses on program structure, discussing the differences between local and global variables, and presenting C's storage classes. Its case study is a useful package that implements sets.

Part III: Advanced Data Types

Chapter 9 presents pointers and arrays, emphasizing the relationships between them and introducing the notion of dynamic allocation. Its case study implements dynamically allocated sets. • *Chapter 10* presents strings, showing how to construct them from the input and introducing the standard string functions. Its case study is a useful tool to detect duplicate lines in its input. • *Chapter 11* studies structures, unions, and

enumerated types, including arrays of structures and structures whose fields are allocated dynamically. Its case study is a simple electronic address book.   • *Chapter 12* discusses multidimensional arrays, showing how we can use pointers to access them efficiently. It dramatically illustrates their use in an implementation of the Game of Life.
• *Chapter 13* presents arrays of pointers, showing how we can use dynamic allocation to initialize them, and how we can use them to access command-line arguments. Its case study is a string sorting program that takes advantage of both.

Part IV: Advanced Program Structure

Chapter 14 discusses advanced details of functions, covering the closely related topics of simulating call-by-reference parameter passing, pointers to functions, and functions that can take variable numbers of arguments. Its case study is a recursive implementation of binary search.   • *Chapter 15* presents the preprocessor, describing how we can use it to make our programs easier to read and debug, as well as more efficient. Its case study reimplements the earlier set package using macros.   • *Chapter 16* grapples with generic functions, showing how to use the standard library's generic sorting and searching functions, and then implementing several simpler generic functions. Its case study is an implementation of the standard library's binary search function.   •
Chapter 17 covers complex declarations, showing several examples using complex types, and then focusing on how to construct and understand these declarations. Its case study is a program to translate English type descriptions into C declarations.

Part V: Real-World Programming Issues

Chapter 18 explains external files, providing complete coverage of the standard I/O library, bringing together the ideas of the chapter in an externally stored address book for names, addresses, and phone numbers.   • *Chapter 19* discusses dynamic data structures, such as linked lists, trees, stacks, and queues. Its case study combines most of them in a C program cross-referencer.   • *Chapter 20* presents common portability problems and suggests some solutions. It concludes with a case study that implements a set of functions for portably managing console displays and performing immediate character input.   • *Chapter 21* examines efficiency, including techniques for making our programs run faster or take up less space. Its case study provides fast functions for allocating fixed-size blocks of memory and for reading in an array of integers.   •
Chapter 22 discusses some C++ features useful to C programmers, such as references and function overloading, and briefly looks at how C++ extends C into the world of object-oriented programming.

Appendices

Appendix A shows how to compile and link C programs.   • *Appendix B* discusses input/output redirection.   • *Appendix C* provides the missing details of C libraries discussed earlier in the text.   • *Appendix D* examines different numbering systems.
• *Appendix E* provides the ASCII and EBCDIC character sets.

Using This Book As A Textbook

We've taught a wide variety of classes using prepublication drafts of this text. These courses have included both semester courses at the university and state college level, as well as numerous short courses for programmers in industry. Here's how we've used the text for various one-semester C courses:

Introduction To C Programming for students who've taken at least one course in another programming language. In this type of course we usually cover Parts I, II, and III in order, and then use any remaining time to squeeze in as much of Chapters 14, 15, and 18 as possible. How much of these later chapters we can actually cover depends significantly on what programming languages the students have previously used. We tend to cover them in great detail when the students know Pascal and to skim them when the students come from a FORTRAN or BASIC background. We find that using the text for this type of course requires no supplementary material.

Advanced C Programming for students who've done some programming in C. In these courses we usually skip Part I and fly through Part II, using it mostly as a quick refresher, covering it in at most 2-3 weeks. We then spend the vast majority of our time covering Parts III, IV, and V, at a rate of about one chapter a week. We also usually try to spend a week or so on the standard library functions discussed in Appendix C. If we're short on time, we're most likely to cut out parts of Chapter 19 and all of Chapter 22. Again, we find no supplementary material is necessary, although we occasionally spend several weeks toward the end of the semester discussing how to do operating system calls in C.

Introduction To Programming Using C for students with no previous programming experience. In these courses, we spend the first 4-5 weeks thoroughly covering Part I, usually at the rate of around one example program per day. We then spend the next 5-6 weeks covering Part II, and the balance of the semester covering as much as possible of Part III, skipping the more difficult material in Chapters 12 and 13. We find that this sort of course requires significant supplementary material while covering Part I, primarily on the basics of how to write a program and how a computer works.[2]

Our primary goal has been to write a single stand-alone guide to programming in C. We've tried to produce a text that introductory students would want to keep after finishing the course. We're aware that most introductory courses are likely to cover no more than two-thirds of this text, but we've included the additional material anyways, since it's very useful for those students who plan on really programming in C once the semester is over. To this end, we've been careful to ensure that the entire text is suitable for self-study, especially the chapters on the more advanced topics. A nice side effect is that the text can easily be used as a supplement for other software-related courses, such as Operating Systems, Programming Languages, or Data Structures.

---

[2]The necessary supplementary material is available with the instructor's manual.

Another goal was to make life easier for instructors using the text. To this end, we've provided an instructor's manual containing solutions to all of the exercises, additional exercises and programming projects, and some sample exams. The instructor's manual also comes with a complete set of transparency masters for all of the programs, tables, and illustrations in the text, as well as the supplementary material we use when we teach C programming to students who've never before programmed. And the instructor's manual comes with instructions for obtaining the programs in the text for machines other than the PC.

We welcome comments on the text, both from instructors and students. We can currently be reached over the internet at **joyofc@wiliki.eng.hawaii.edu** or through John Wiley and Sons.

Acknowledgments

Contributions by several of our friends and colleagues have greatly improved the quality of this text. We're deeply indebted to Robert Quilici for painstakingly plowing through our prepublication drafts, unearthing plenty of problems with our programs and explanations. And we're grateful to David Smallberg for his always perceptive comments and criticisms, and to Dorab Patel for his invaluable wizardry with formatting.

The reviewers of earlier versions of our manuscript made many wonderful suggestions that we have incorporated into this text. We want to extend a special thanks to Thomas Crowe (Arizona State University), Edmund Deaton (San Diego State University), Joyce Harris (DeAnza College), Gary Huckabay (Cameron University), Henry Ruston (Polytechnic University), Wayne Staats (North Carolina State University), and Jieming Zhu (Wichita State University). In addition, we also owe our thanks to the many students at UCLA, the University of Hawaii at Manoa, and at a whole host of corporations who have used our earlier C textbooks or suffered through the initial drafts of this manuscript. Their many questions and suggestions have improved this text immensely.

We would like to thank the University of Hawaii's Electrical Engineering Department and The Aerospace Corporation for the generous use of their resources and their allowing us the time to produce this work. We would also like to thank the people at John Wiley and Sons, especially Steven Elliot, our extremely patient and helpful editor.

This text has also benefited from the sharp eyes of the instructors and students who have used its early printings. Manny Feliciano, Jim Heavener, Joy Higa, Richard O'Keefe, Derek Oyama, Lee Tokuda, Brian Weaver, and John Witherspoon have helped us root out a variety of embarassing errors.

And finally, we're grateful for all of the encouragement and support given to us by our families and friends—especially Rita Grant-Miller, Daphne Borromeo, Tammy Merriweather, Irene Borromeo, and Doris Perl.

Alex Quilici
Honolulu, Hawaii

Larry Miller
Los Angeles, California

June, 1993

Contents

Part II   THE BASICS   41

Part I

A GENTLE INTRODUCTION TO C

1 GETTING

STARTED

WITH C

This chapter is a gentle introduction to C. We begin with a pair of simple programs: one prints a welcoming message, the other calculates the actual cost of purchasing a set of items. We describe these programs in great detail and provide several variants of each. Along the way we introduce the basics of C program organization, the process of compilation and linking, and several fundamental language features: the `printf` function for performing formatted output, variable declaration and assignment, and the arithmetic operators.

1.1 A FIRST C PROGRAM

Figure 1.1 contains a very simple C program. When compiled and run, it prints the message:

```
Welcome to the Joy of C!
```

Let's dive right into this program to see exactly how it works.

Comments

Our example program, like most C programs, starts with a *comment* that describes what it does.

```
/*
 * A program that prints a welcoming message.
 */
```

A comment begins with a `/*` and ends with a `*/` and can go anywhere blank spaces can occur—at the end of a line, at the beginning, or even in the middle. For readability, however, we usually place comments only at the end of lines or on lines by themselves, as we've done here.

What does the compiler do with our comments? It simply ignores them. That's because comments are directed at the program's reader, not the compiler. In general,

```
/*
 * A program that prints a welcoming message.
 */

main()
{
  printf("Welcome to the Joy of C!\n");
}
```

Figure 1.1   (welcome.c)   A program to print a welcome message.

we use comments to answer questions that are likely to arise about the program, such as what it does or how it works. Although at first comments may seem to be a luxury rather than a necessity, they're not. It can be difficult to understand another person's program unless they've been kind enough to comment it liberally. In fact, it can even be difficult to understand your own programs after you've put them aside for awhile, unless you were careful to sprinkle helpful comments throughout your code. Don't be afraid to shower a program with comments!

The main Program

After the initial comment, the remainder of the program defines a single function named **main**. C's functions are analogous to Pascal's procedures and FORTRAN's and BASIC's subroutines—they simply package together and name a collection of statements. We execute these statements by *calling* the function. When a C program starts up, **main** is always the first function called, so every program must have a **main**.

Function definitions have two parts: a header and a body. At a minimum, the header provides the function's name, followed by a pair of parentheses, as in **main**'s header.

```
main()
```

The function's body contains the statements to execute when the function is called. We enclose these statements in braces (**{** and **}**) to group them with the function header. In this case, **main**'s body consists of a single **printf** statement to be executed when the function is called.

The printf Statement

Now, we've arrived at the heart of our program: the single call to the **printf** function that does all the work.

```
printf("Welcome to the Joy of C!\n");
```

printf is a predefined output function. *Predefined* means that it has been written and compiled for you, and is linked together with your program after it compiles. C does all input and output through a set of predefined functions that together compose the standard input/output (I/O) library.

We call a function by following its name with a list of *parameters*, which we enclose in parentheses. In this case, we provide **printf** with a single string parameter (a list of characters between double quotation marks), and it writes those characters to the standard output. The standard output is usually the terminal (or computer monitor or window) from which you invoked the program. Most operating systems actually let us change where the standard output goes, but we have to do something special before we run the program, a topic discussed in Appendix B.

There are a couple of details we've ignored. One is the semicolon following our **printf**. In C, whenever a statement consists solely of a call to function, as does our **printf**, we need to end it with a single semicolon. The other is the **\n** at the end of the formatting string. The backslash indicates a special character. **\n** is the newline character; writing a **\n** causes further output to start on the next line. Without it, output continues on the same line. In our example, we write the newline so that when our program finishes, the cursor is sitting on the line following our welcome message.

1.2   COMPILING AND RUNNING C PROGRAMS

The previous sections have presented several different versions of a single C program. But how do we actually arrive at an executable program, one that when run, produces our earlier output? We have to go through several steps, shown in Figure 1.2:

1. Enter the program into a source file, usually with an *interactive text editor*.

2. Provide this program to the *compiler*, which takes it and produces an *object module*.

3. Give this object module to the *linker*, which produces an executable program.

The *object module* contains compiled code, along with references to any functions, such as **printf**, that the code uses but doesn't define. These references are called *externals*. Before a program can be executed, the compiled versions of these external functions must be linked together with the object module. That's the job of the *linker*. It looks for definitions of these externals in a standard location that contains a library of precompiled standard functions, and links them together with the object module to produce a runnable program.

The process of turning C source into executable code sounds simple enough, but the particular details of it vary widely from system to system. Appendix A discusses how to compile and run programs using the most popular compilers.

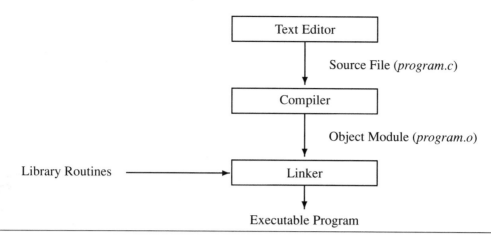

Figure 1.2   The process of building, compiling, and executing a C program.

1.3	**IMPROVING OUR INITIAL PROGRAM**

Our first C program actually has several sloppy coding practices. Although the program will execute and appear to work correctly, many compilers will warn us about possible flaws and many experienced C programmers will shake their heads sadly when they examine our code.

Figure 1.3 contains an improved version of our initial example. What did we have to fix and how did we fix it?

Function Prototypes and Include Files

The first problem is that we originally failed to provide a *function prototype* for **printf**. Among other things, a function prototype describes the types of parameters the function expects. **printf**'s prototype, for example, indicates that its first parameter must be a string of characters.

Why do we need to provide this information? One reason is so that the compiler can make sure we call the function with the correct parameters. If we accidentally provide **printf** with a number as its first parameter, rather than a string, we want the compiler to point out the error.

Every C programming environment provides a collection of *header files* that contain prototypes for their predefined functions. The file stdio.h, for example, contains prototypes for all of the input and output functions, including **printf**. To use these prototypes, we need to *include* this file, which we do with the line:

```
#include <stdio.h>
```

```
/*
 * An improved version of our program to print a welcoming message.
 */
#include <stdio.h>

main()
{
  printf("Welcome to the Joy of C!\n");
  return 0;
}
```

return "0" when run is successful.

Figure 1.3   (welcome2.c)   An improved version of our initial program to print a welcoming message.

Lines beginning with a **#** are special. These lines are handled by the *preprocessor*, a special part of the compiler that processes C programs before the "real" compiler sees them. When we invoke the compiler on a source file, it automatically passes that source file through the preprocessor, and then works with the result. The line above instructs the preprocessor to include the contents of the file named stdio.h in the program it passes to the compiler (the angle brackets around the name tell the preprocessor this is a special system header file). The compiler sees only the contents of the included file and not the **#include** itself. Including stdio.h provides the necessary prototype for **printf**.

> **When you use a predefined function, be sure to include the appropriate header file.**

Return Values

The second problem is that we ignored **main**'s return value. In C, as in most programming languages, a function can return a value to its caller once it finishes executing. **main** is expected to return a value indicating whether or not the program failed. But who is **main**'s caller? And what value should **main** return?

main's caller is whatever program invoked it, which is normally the operating system command interpreter. Fortunately, most command interpreters ignore **main**'s return value. But not all of them. Some print an error message based on this return value; this means our sloppiness could lead to an error message's being written when it shouldn't. It's also possible that our C programs will be run from *command scripts*: programs that are written in a special language and that use other programs as their basic building blocks. These programs often test **main**'s return value to determine what action to take next.

By convention, programs return 0 when they succeed and some other value when they fail. This behavior may seem strange, but the rationale behind it is sensible. Usually there is only a single way to succeed and many different ways to fail (mistakes in the input, a full disk, and so on), so we use specific nonzero values to indicate the cause of the program's failure, if any.

We don't expect our welcoming program to fail, so we would like **main** to always return 0 to its caller. We do so with the new statement

```
return 0;
```

at the end of **main**, following the **printf**. The **return** statement terminates the function containing it and returns the specified value to that function's caller. Here, it does what we want: terminates **main** and returns 0 to its caller.

> *Always return a value from* **main** *indicating whether the program succeeded or failed.*

1.4   A SECOND C PROGRAM

Let's take a look at a more realistic C program. Figure 1.4 computes the actual cost of a set of items, given a list price per item, a percentage discount, and a sales tax rate. Here is its output when we used it to compute the actual cost of buying 23 compact disks, given that each CD is $13.95, we get an 18% discount for buying more than 20, and the state sales tax is 7.5%:

```
List price per item: 13.950000
List price of 23 items: 320.850000
Price after 18.000000% discount: 263.097000
Sales tax at 7.500000%: 19.732275
Total cost: 282.829275
```

This program begins the same way our earlier programs did: with a comment describing what it does and a **#include** for stdio.h. But our **main** program is not nearly as simple as before: it now includes variable declarations, assignment statements, and a more complex form of **printf**.

Variable Declarations

Variables are named locations for storing values. Each variable can store a single value of a particular type. C forces us to declare the type of every variable before we can use it. These variable declarations appear at the beginning of a function and specify the variable's name, storage requirements, and internal representation. Here, the first declaration tells the compiler that **items** is an **int**, an abbreviation for the word *integer*.

```
int    items;              /* # of items bought */
```

The next specifies that **list_price** is a **double**, which is short for the phrase "double precision *floating point*".

```
double list_price;         /* list price of item */
```

```c
/*
 * Compute the actual cost of buying 23 items at $13.95.  We assume an
 * 18% discount rate and a 7.5% sales tax.
 */
#include <stdio.h>

main()
{
    int    items;                       /* # of items bought */
    double list_price;                  /* list price of item */
    double discount_rate;               /* discount percentage */
    double sales_tax_rate;              /* sales tax percentage */
    double total_price;                 /* total price of all items */
    double discount_price;              /* discount price of all items */
    double sales_tax;                   /* amount of sales tax */
    double final_cost;                  /* cost including sales tax */

    items = 23;
    list_price = 13.95;
    discount_rate = .18;
    sales_tax_rate = .075;

    total_price = items * list_price;
    discount_price = total_price - total_price * discount_rate;
    sales_tax = discount_price * sales_tax_rate;
    final_cost = discount_price + sales_tax;

    printf("List price per item: %f\n", list_price);
    printf("List price of %i items: %f\n", items, total_price);
    printf("Price after %f%% discount: %f\n",
           discount_rate * 100, discount_price);
    printf("Sales tax at %f%%: %f\n",
           sales_tax_rate * 100, sales_tax);
    printf("Total cost: %f\n", final_cost);

    return 0;
}
```

Figure 1.4   (price.c)   Compute the actual cost to purchase a set of items.

The others declare several more variables, all of which are **double**s. In these declarations, the underscore is part of the variable name just as if it were a letter. Using it helps make our variable names easy to understand.

Why are there these different types? We use integers when we need exact "whole" numbers, since their representation is exact within the range of integers that a given word size can represent. We also use them when speed of arithmetic operations is important, since most operations are faster with integers than with floating point numbers. In C, an **int** is at least 16 bits, with 1 bit used for the sign; this means that we can *safely* use an **int** to store values between $-32,767$ and $+32,767$ (that is, between $-2^{15} + 1$ and $+2^{15} - 1$). That seems like a small range of values, and it is. But C provides other types we can use when we need to store larger integral values.

In our example, we use **items** to store the number of items we're going to buy. That number is always whole (we can't buy half a CD) and always small (we can't afford to buy 30,000 compact disks), so we can safely use an **int** to store it.

Floating point numbers, or reals, are numbers with a decimal point. We use them when we need to store fractional values or very large numbers. They differ from integers in that their representations are only approximate and not exact. Their accuracy and range varies from machine to machine, but a **double** has at least 10 significant decimal digits of precision and can hold positive or negative values between 10^{-38} and 10^{+38}. In many machines, however, the number of significant digits, and the maximum exponent, are much larger.

In our example, all of our **double** variables are used to hold either monetary amounts or percentages. Since all of these quantities potentially involve a fraction, we have to use floating point values rather than integers to store them.[1]

It's a pain to declare all our variables. Many other languages rely on naming conventions to declare variables implicitly. Why doesn't C? Primarily because explicit declarations at the beginning of a function make the program more readable. We don't have to remember strange, often unintuitive naming conventions. And we can get an idea of the types of data a function manipulates without having to read all the way through it.

Assignment Statements

Most of the work in this program is done with a series of *assignment statements*. An assignment statement puts a value into a variable. **main**'s first few assignments store the number of items we want to purchase, the price of each item, the discount rate, and the sales tax rate.

```
items = 23;
list_price = 13.95;
discount_rate = .18;
sales_tax_rate = .075;
```

They work as one might expect. The first assigns the value 23 to the variable **items**, the second assigns the value 13.95 to the variable **list_price**, the third sets **discount_rate** to .18, and the last sets **sales_tax_rate** to .075.

After we've stored our initial values, we need to perform a set of calculations:

total list price = list price of an item × number of items
total discount amount = total price of all items × discount rate

---

[1] Actually, using real numbers to store monetary amounts is cheating! That's because we usually want exact arithmetic for dollars and cents, but once dollar amounts get into the tens of thousands, we run up against the floating point precision limits of some machines. Solving this problem is tricky. It usually involves storing the dollars and cents in separate integer variables, doing arithmetic separately on the dollars and cents, and then combining the results.

total discounted price = total price of all items − total discount amount
total sales tax = total discounted price × sales tax rate
actual cost of all items = total discounted price + total sales tax

We do so with a series of assignment statements. These statements make use of several *arithmetic operators*. C provides the usual **+** (addition), **−** (subtraction), ***** (multiplication), and **/** (division), along with several others, which we will introduce later. ***** and **/** have higher precedence than **+** and **−**. That means C performs multiplication and division before addition and subtraction. As with most other programming languages, however, we can use parentheses to change the order of evaluation.

The first assignment statement computes the total list price. It multiplies the number of items by the price of an item and stores the result in **total_price**.

```
total_price = items * list_price;
```

As with **printf**, we have to follow assignment statements with a semicolon.

The second computes the total discounted price. This computation takes two steps. We compute the total discount amount by multiplying the total list price by the discount rate. And we then subtract this discount amount from the total price. Since we're not really interested in the dollar savings, we don't bother storing the discount amount.

```
discount_price = total_price - total_price * discount_rate;
```

This assignment works correctly because C performs multiplications and divisions before additions and subtractions. It does not subtract **total_price** from itself and then multiply the result by the discount_rate (again giving 0).

The last two assignments are straightforward, computing and storing the sales tax amount, and then adding it to the discounted price to give us the actual cost.

```
sales_tax = discount_price * sales_tax_rate;
final_cost = discount_price + sales_tax;
```

Formatted Output with `printf`

The last few statements in the program display the results of all these calculations. As you might expect, we use **printf**, but now we take advantage of its ability to perform *formatted output*. Formatted output means that we provide the format in which **printf** writes a set of values. We specify the format as **printf**'s first parameter, called *the formatting control string*. **printf** then writes its other parameters to the standard output, according to this specification.

By default, **printf** writes anything in the formatting control string (between the quotation marks) as is. We took advantage of that feature to display our first program's welcoming message. But there's also an exception. When **printf** encounters a **%**, it takes **%** to be the start of a description of how to write a value. **printf** expects the **%** to be followed by a letter specifying the value's type. **%i** or **%d** indicates a base 10 (or decimal) integer, and **%f** a floating point value.

Consider what happens with the first two **printf** statements in our example:

```
printf("List price per item: %f\n", list_price);
printf("List price of %i items: %f\n", items, total_price);
```

The first **printf** writes the string

```
List price per item:
```

followed by a space. It then encounters the **%f**, which causes it to write the value of **list_price**, and ends by writing the newline. The second **printf** is similar except that when it encounters the **%i** it writes the value of **items**, and when it encounters the **%f**, it writes the value of **total_price**.

There's no limit to the number of values we display with a single **printf**; we simply provide a formatting control for each and follow **printf** with a comma-separated parameter list.

> *Make sure there's a one-to-one correspondence between the formatting instructions and values to print.*

It's not a terrible error to provide more values to write than formatting codes; any extra values will simply be ignored. It's much worse to provide too few values or values of the wrong type. That's likely to cause your program to terminate early or produce output consisting of bizarre values.

The next few **printf**s are a bit trickier.

```
printf("Price after %f%% discount: %f\n",
       discount_rate * 100, discount_price);
printf("Sales tax at %f%%: %f\n",
       sales_tax_rate * 100, sales_tax);
```

When we write the discount and sales tax rates, we want to follow them with a percent sign. But we can't simply put a **%** in our formatting string, since a **%** indicates that a formatting code follows. The trick is that to write a percent sign, we use two of them, **%%**.

As these **printf**'s illustrate, we're not restricted to passing variables as parameters. We are also free to provide an expression, as we do here. When we do, C simply computes its value and passes it on to the function.

1.5   IMPROVING OUR SECOND PROGRAM

As with our first example, our cost computing program has several problems. The first is stylistic: the various values we need to compute prices are buried in the program, making them somewhat difficult to modify.[2] The other is aesthetic: quite frankly, this program's output is ugly. The dollar amounts, for example, have six places after the decimal, rather than the two we would prefer.

---

[2]Of course, it would be even better to have the program read these values from its input. We'll see how to do that in the next chapter.

```
/*
 * An improved version of our cost-computing program.
 */
#include <stdio.h>

#define ITEMS           23
#define LIST_PRICE      13.95
#define DISCOUNT_RATE    .18
#define SALES_TAX_RATE   .075

main()
{
  double discount_price;         /* discounted price of item */
  double total_price;            /* total price of all items */
  double sales_tax;              /* amount of sales tax */
  double final_cost;             /* cost including sales tax */

  total_price = ITEMS * LIST_PRICE;
  discount_price = total_price - total_price * DISCOUNT_RATE;
  sales_tax = discount_price * SALES_TAX_RATE;
  final_cost = discount_price + sales_tax;

  printf("List price per item:\t\t%7.2f\n", LIST_PRICE);
  printf("List price of %i items:\t\t%7.2f\n", ITEMS, total_price);
  printf("Price after %.1f%% discount:\t%7.2f\n",
         DISCOUNT_RATE * 100, discount_price);
  printf("Sales tax at %.1f%%:\t\t%7.2f\n",
         SALES_TAX_RATE * 100, sales_tax);
  printf("Total cost:\t\t\t%7.2f\n", final_cost);

  return 0;
}
```

Figure 1.5   (price2.c) An improved version of our program to compute the cost of a set of items.

Figure 1.5 contains a revised version of this program that fixes these difficulties. Here is its much prettier output:[3]

```
List price per item:          13.95
Total price of 23 items:      320.85
Price after 18.0% discount:   263.10
Sales tax at 7.5%:             19.73
Total cost:                   282.83
```

Let's see what changes we had to make.

---

[3]This program makes use of tab stops. These tab stops are usually set by using an operating system command. This output was produced with tab stops every 8 columns (the usual default). Your output may vary if your tab stops are set differently.

Defining Constants

Our first change is that we now use a new preprocessor statement, **#define**, to define four *constants*: **ITEMS** is the number of items we want to buy (23), **LIST_PRICE** is the list price of an individual item (13.95), **DISCOUNT_RATE** is our discount (.18), and **SALES_TAX_RATE** is the sales tax (.075).

```
#define ITEMS               23
#define LIST_PRICE          13.95
#define DISCOUNT_RATE        .18
#define SALES_TAX_RATE       .075
```

#define gives a name to a value. Its syntax—that is, the way the statement is constructed—is simple. The keyword **#define** starts in column one, and is followed by a *NAME* and a *VALUE*. (We use italics as in *NAME* or *VALUE* to indicate generic symbols; the programmer provides the actual name and its value.)

```
#define NAME  VALUE
```

NAME doesn't have to be all uppercase letters, but we usually restrict ourselves to uppercase names for our constants so that they stand out when reading the program. There is also no syntactic limitation on where we can place our **#define**s, other than that they must begin in the first column. Despite this freedom, we usually place them near the beginning of a program, usually immediately following any **#include**s.

#define's semantics—that is, what the statement actually does—are more complex. When the preprocessor encounters a **#define**, it associates the value with the name. Then, whenever the name occurs later in the program, the preprocessor replaces it with its corresponding value.[4]

After the preprocessor has finished its replacements, it passes the program to the compiler proper; this means the compiler never sees the names in the **#define**s. In our program, the preprocessor replaces each use of **LIST_PRICE** with its defined value, 13.95, and performs a similar action for the other three defined constants. By using **#define** for our constants, we no longer have to declare variables to hold them, and we highlight which values in our program can be easily changed. This results in a program that's easier to read and easier to change.

Using Field Widths with printf

The other change we've made to our program is in how we display values. Now we display dollar amounts with two places after the decimal point, and percentages with one, and we line up all of the amounts.

Normally, **%i** and **%d** use just enough space to print the entire value, and **%f** prints floating point values with exactly six digits after the decimal point and however many digits are necessary preceding it. We change these defaults by providing an optional field width and precision, as in our first **printf**.

---

[4]In fact, **#define** isn't restricted to replacing names with values. It's actually a general mechanism for replacing a name with a string of characters. Later chapters discuss **#define** in more detail.

```
printf("List price per item:\t\t%7.2f\n", LIST_PRICE);
```

Here, to write the value of **LIST_PRICE**, we use **%7.2f**, which tells the compiler that we want floating point output, with seven places in all and two places to the right of the decimal point. That is, as xxxx.xx, with the x's replaced by the digits in **LIST_PRICE**.

It's possible that our field width will be too large or too small for the value we're printing. If the field width is too large, **printf** simply *right*-justifies the number within the field. That's the case above, where **LIST_PRICE** is 13.95 and therefore requires only two digits before the decimal point. The result is a pair of leading blanks. If the field width is too small, such as where we use **%3.2f** to write our list price of 13.95, **printf** stretches the field so that it's just large enough to write the entire value. We get the same behavior if we leave off the field width entirely, as in **%.2f**. We take advantage of that in later **printf**s to guarantee that the discount and sales tax amounts do not have leading blanks:

```
printf("Price after %.1f%% discount:\t%7.2f\n",
        DISCOUNT_RATE * 100, discount_price);
printf("Sales tax at %.1f%%:\t\t%7.2f\n",
        SALES_TAX_RATE * 100, sales_tax);
```

Perhaps you've noticed that **\t** pops up in most of these **printf**s. The **\t** is a tab character. It behaves like **\n**, except that instead of placing the cursor on the beginning of the next line, it places the cursor at the next tab stop. Usually there are tab stops every eight characters, so by writing tab characters, we can line up all the dollar amounts on one of these tab stops.

printf is actually more powerful than we've let on, and we'll present more of its capabilities later. But because **printf** is so powerful, there are times when it is inefficient and there are better ways to produce output. We'll discuss these methods later, along with other functions in the standard I/O library. Appendix C supplies a more complete description of **printf**'s formatting codes.

Program Layout

C is a free-format language—there are few restrictions on the format of C programs. This means we can lay out our programs any way we choose. There is nothing to prevent us from placing most of our example program on a single, lengthy line. But we didn't, for an obvious reason: the program would have been completely unreadable. Figure 1.6 is an example. It's a new version of Figure 1.5 without any indentation or whitespace. On top of that, we didn't bother to use defined constants or descriptive variable names. The result is a program that's an eyesore to look at and a headache to try to understand.

White space and consistent indentation make our programs easier to understand, so we take care to indent our statements consistently and to place spaces around operators. You don't have to mimic our formatting style, but try to ensure that whatever style you choose is consistent and readable.

```
/*
 * A very messy version of our cost-computing program.
 */
#include <stdio.h>
main() {double dp;double tp;double st;double fc;
tp=23*13.95;dp=tp-tp*.18;st=dp*.075;fc=dp+st;
printf("List price per item:\t\t%7.2f\n",13.95);
printf("List price of %i items:\t\t%7.2f\n",23,tp);
printf("Price after %.1f%% discount:\t%7.2f\n",.18*100,dp);
printf("Sales tax at %.1f%%:\t%7.2f\n",.075*100,st);
printf("Total cost:\t\t\t%7.2f\n",fc);return 0;}
```

Figure 1.6　(messy.c)　A much less readable version of our program to compute costs.

A Word to the Wise

The only way to really learn a programming language is to program in it. And the best way to start programming is to take existing programs and modify them. To this end, each chapter in this text ends with exercises. They fall into three categories: The first set suggests interesting modifications to the programs presented in the chapter. The second set suggests writing from scratch simple programs that require a small subset of the features discussed in the chapter. And the last set suggests more sizeable programming projects involving most of the topics covered in the chapter. Do several exercises from each category before moving on to the next chapter.

SUMMARY

- A C program consists of several parts:

  preprocessor statements

  main()
  {
  　declarations

  　statements
  }

- Anything between a **/*** and ***/** is treated as a comment and ignored by the compiler.

- All C programs are run through a preprocessor before they are passed to the compiler proper. Preprocessor statements are lines starting with a **#**. There are preprocessor statements to include system header files (**#include**) and to give symbolic names to constants (**#define**).

- We declare variables by providing a type (**int** for integers or **double** for floating point numbers) and a name. We assign values to variables using the = operator.

- C provides the usual arithmetic operators: **+** for addition, **–** for subtraction, ***** for multiplication, and **/** for division. The precedence of ***** and **/** is higher than that of **+** and **–**.

- We perform output by calling the **printf** library function.

  printf("*format string*", *expression-1*, *expression-2*, ...**);**

  It uses special formatting codes in its first parameter to determine how to display subsequent parameters.

- **main** uses the **return** statement to provide an indication of success or failure. By convention, a 0 indicates success, and anything else indicates failure.

EXERCISES

√ **1–1** Compile and run our initial welcoming program (Figure 1.1) on your computer. Does your compiler warn you about its sloppy coding practices?

√ **1–2** Modify our improved welcoming program (Figure 1.3) to print a different message:

  This is my first C program.

√ **1–3** Modify our improved welcoming program (Figure 1.3) to print the welcome message several times, rather than just once.

√ **1–4** Experiment with making various errors in entering the programs in this chapter. What happens if you add an extra semicolon after the **main()**? Leave out the parentheses? Place an extra semicolon after the **printf**? Leave off the semicolon? Start keeping a list of different error messages and their underlying causes.

1–5 Modify our initial price-computing program (Figure 1.4) to compute the price of 25 gallons of gas at $1.29 per gallon with a 3% discount and a 5% sales tax.

1–6 Repeat the previous exercise for the improved price-computing program (Figure 1.5).

1–7 If your system doesn't have 8 characters per tab stop, make appropriate changes to the improved price-computing program (Figure 1.5) so that its output lines up correctly anyway.

√ **1–8** Write a simple program to print the following message five times.

  I will heed the programming advice in the text.

1–9 Write a program to compute and print the actual cost of a new Mercedes two-seater convertible. Assume that the sticker price is $89,950, that the dealer will discount the car 12%, that there's a 10% luxury tax on the amount over $30,000, and that the state sales tax is 8.75%.

1–10 Write a program to determine the list price of a car, when you know the actual cost is $12,200, the sales tax was 5.5%, and the discount was 11%.

1–11 Write a program to print your net income after taxes, assuming your gross salary is $78,000, you have to pay 7.5% in social security on the first $58,000 of income, your federal tax is $3000 plus 28% of all income over $30,000, and that your state tax is 10% of your gross.

1–12 Extend the program in the previous exercise to also print the total amount paid in taxes, as well as the percentage of the gross salary that amount represents.

2 GETTING
COMFORTABLE
WITH C

This chapter continues our tutorial introduction to C. We concentrate on a single C program, one that computes interest accumulating in a bank account over time. We describe how this program works and provide several different extensions. We use these variants to introduce C's `while` and `for` loops, `if` statement, and predefined `scanf` input function, as well as to show how to write your own, simple functions. By the chapter's end you'll have been exposed to a wide variety of C's features, and should feel comfortable writing small but useful C programs.

2.1 A PROGRAM TO COMPUTE SIMPLE INTEREST

Let's take a look at a new C program. The program in Figure 2.1 calculates and prints the interest accumulating in a bank account over a 7-year period, assuming an initial deposit of $5000 and a simple interest rate of 6 percent. Here's the output that results when we compile and run it.

```
Interest Rate:        6.00%
Starting Balance: 5000.00$

Year      Balance
   1    $ 5300.00
   2    $ 5618.00
   3    $ 5955.08
   4    $ 6312.38
   5    $ 6691.13
   6    $ 7092.60
   7    $ 7518.15
```

This output includes the interest rate and the account balance at the beginning of each year in the period. The program uses a simple interest rate compounding formula to do its calculations.

> balance at year's end =
>   balance at year's start + (balance at year's start × interest rate)

```
/*
 * Generate a table showing interest accumulation.
 */
#include <stdio.h>

#define PRINCIPAL   5000.00           /* start with $5000 */
#define INTRATE        0.06           /* interest rate of 6% */
#define PERIOD         7              /* over 7-year period */

main()
{
  double balance;                     /* balance at year's end */
  int    year;                        /* year of period */

  printf("Interest Rate:    %7.2f%%\n", INTRATE * 100);
  printf("Starting Balance: %7.2f$\n\n", PRINCIPAL);
  printf("Year      Balance\n");
  balance = PRINCIPAL;
  year = 1;
  while (year <= PERIOD)
  {
    balance = balance + balance * INTRATE;
    printf("%4i   $ %7.2f\n", year, balance);
    year = year + 1;
  }
  return 0;                           /* assume program worked! */
}
```

Figure 2.1   (intrate.c)   A program to calculate accumulated interest.

Comments and Preprocessor Commands

Most C programs start the same way: with a comment that says what it does, some **#include**s to obtain prototypes for any predefined functions it uses, and some constant definitions. This program is no different. It begins with a comment, includes stdio.h to obtain **printf**'s prototype, and defines three constants: **PRINCIPAL** is the initial bank balance (5000), **INTRATE** is the interest rate (.06), and **PERIOD** is the number of years our money will remain in the bank (7).

The main Program

As in our earlier programs, the function **main** follows the constant definitions. Its first few lines should seem familiar. They declare several variables: **balance** is a **double** to hold the current bank balance, and **year** is an **int** to hold the current year in the period.

```
double balance;                     /* balance at year's end */
int    year;                        /* year of period */
```

After these variable declarations come several **printf** statements to write our interest rate, starting balance, and column headings:

```
printf("Interest Rate:    %7.2f%%\n", INTRATE * 100);
printf("Starting Balance: %7.2f$\n\n", PRINCIPAL);
printf("Year     Balance\n");
```

The first prints the annual interest rate we're assuming, multiplied by a hundred to make it a percentage rather than a fraction. The second displays the starting balance. The last writes the labels for the columns of years and balances.

Finally, these **printf**s are followed by a pair of assignment statements.

```
balance = PRINCIPAL;
year = 1;
```

The first assigns **PRINCIPAL** to **balance**, setting the current balance to the starting balance. The second sets **year** to 1, setting the current year of the period to the first year of the period. So far, there's been nothing all that new.

The while Loop

Now, however, we encounter a new construct, the **while** loop, which the program uses to compute the ending balance for each of the years in the period:

```
while (year <= PERIOD)
{
  balance = balance + balance * INTRATE;
  printf("%4i   $ %7.2f\n", year, balance);
  year = year + 1;
}
```

while is a mechanism for repeating a statement or a group of statements. Its syntax is

> **while** (*expression*)
>   *statement*

A **while** evaluates the *expression* in parentheses and, if the condition is true, executes *statement*. It repeats the process until the condition is false, when it skips to the statement that follows it.

Here, as long as **year** is less than or equal to **PERIOD**, we execute the three statements:

```
balance = balance + balance * INTRATE;
printf("%4i   $ %7.2f\n", year, balance);
year = year + 1;
```

Because **while** expects only a single statement, we have to group these statements together with **{** and **}**. The first statement in the group updates **balance**, the second prints it, and the last updates **year**. Each time through the loop **year** increases by one, and the loop exits when **year** is finally greater than **PERIOD**.

The test in this **while** loop uses one of C's *relational operators*, **<=**, which tests whether a value is less than or equal to another value (**<=**). There are also operators to test for inequality (! =), equality (==), less than (<), greater than (>), and greater than or equal to (>=).

2.2   DEALING WITH COMPILE ERRORS

Learning a new programming language can be difficult, so it's likely that your first few C programs will not compile successfully the first time. Figure 2.2 contains a version of our interest rate program that illustrates several common mistakes. Figure 2.3 shows the error messages one popular compiler produces when we compile this file.[1]

Compiler error messages usually include the type of error, the file and line number where the error occurred, and a description of the mistake made. In general, there are two types of errors. The first type (**Error**, in our compiler) indicates a serious problem. So serious, in fact, that no object module is created. In our example, the serious errors are the missing semicolon after the first **printf**, and the incorrect assignment operator in the statement to update **year**. The other type of error (**Warning**, in our compiler) indicates a potential problem—but not one serious enough to terminate compilation early. As long as there are no **Error**s, the program will compile, even with warnings. The warnings above were generated because we didn't initialize **balance** before using it (so its initial value would be whatever value is in the memory location assigned to it). This occurred because we forgot the statement assigning **PRINCIPAL** to **balance**.

> *Do not take compiler warning messages lightly.*

Compiler warnings inevitably indicate some programming mistake or faulty assumption, and failing to take heed of them often leads to disastrous results. Here's the output we got when we fixed our syntax errors and ran our program without fixing the source of the warnings.

```
Interest Rate:          6.00%
Starting Balance: 5000.00$

Year      Balance
   1    $      0.00
   2    $      0.00
   3    $      0.00
   4    $      0.00
   5    $      0.00
   6    $      0.00
   7    $      0.00
```

The balance is incorrectly 0.00 at the end of each year. The problem arises because we didn't initialize **balance** before we tried to print its value, and on our machine it happened to be initialized to zero.

---

[1]This output comes from Turbo C, version 2.0, and has been edited slightly.

```
/*
 * Generate a table showing interest accumulation.
 */
#include <stdio.h>

#define PRINCIPAL  5000.00              /* start with $5000 */
#define INTRATE       0.06              /* interest rate of 6% */
#define PERIOD        7                 /* over 7-year period */

main()
{
  double balance;                       /* balance at year's end */
  int    year;                          /* year of period */

  printf("Interest Rate:    %7.2f%%\n", INTRATE * 100) ;
  printf("Starting Balance: %7.2f$\n\n", PRINCIPAL);
  printf("Year      Balance\n");
  year = 1;
  while (year <= PERIOD)
  {
    balance = balance + balance * INTRATE;        balance not initialized
    printf("%4i    $ %7.2f\n", year, balance);
    year := year + 1;
  }
  return 0;                             /* assume program worked! */
}
```

Figure 2.2   (oops.c)   A less-than-perfect version of our interest rate program.

```
Compiling oops.c:

Error oops.c 16: Statement missing ; in main
Warning oops.c 21: Possible use of 'balance' before definition in main
Warning oops.c 21: Possible use of 'balance' before definition in main
Error oops.c 23: Expression syntax in main

*** 2 errors in Compile ***
```

Figure 2.3   Sample output from compiling our erroneous interest rate program.

```
/*
 * Generate a table showing interest accumulation.
 */
#include <stdio.h>

#define PRINCIPAL   5000.00              /* start with $5000 */
#define INTRATE        0.06              /* interest rate of 6% */
#define PERIOD         7                 /* over 7-year period */

main()
{
  double balance;                        /* balance at year's end */
  int    year;                           /* year of period */

  printf("Interest Rate:    %7.2f%%\n", INTRATE * 100);
  printf("Starting Balance: %7.2f$\n\n", PRINCIPAL);
  printf("Year      Balance\n");
  balance = PRINCIPAL;
  for (year = 1; year <= PERIOD; year = year + 1)
  {
    balance = balance + balance * INTRATE;
    printf("%4i  $ %7.2f\n", year, balance);
  }
  return 0;                              /* assume program worked! */
}
```

Figure 2.4   (intrate2.c)   A version of our interest rate program that uses a **for** rather than a **while**.

2.3   A MORE COMPACT INTEREST COMPUTING PROGRAM

Figure 2.4 contains a slight variant on our initial interest rate computing program. Our previous version used a **while** loop to update the balance.

```
year = 1;
while (year <= PERIOD)
{
  balance = balance + balance * INTRATE;
  printf("%4i  $ %7.2f\n", year, balance);
  year = year + 1;
}
```

Now we use another looping construct, the **for** loop.

```
for (year = 1; year <= PERIOD; year = year + 1)
{
  balance = balance + balance * INTRATE;
  printf("%4i  $ %7.2f\n", year, balance);
}
```

We make this change because the **for** leads to a more concise, more readable program, even though both loops are appropriate.

Most programming languages have a construct that allows us to initialize a loop index to some starting value, increment or decrement it each time through the loop, and terminate the loop when some stopping condition is met. C's **for** loop is similar but much more general. Its basic form is:

> **for** (*Start* ; *Test* ; *Action*)
>   *statement*

Start, *Test*, and *Action* can be any C expressions. As with the **while**, a loop body containing multiple statements must be surrounded by braces.

The **for** begins by evaluating *Start*, which usually initializes a counter. Then it evaluates *Test*, which usually tests a counter's value. It exits the loop if the condition checked is false. Otherwise, it executes *statement*, evaluates *Action*, and repeats the cycle. *Action* usually increments the counter controlling the loop.

Our **for** initializes **year** to 1 and then tests to see whether it's less than or equal to **PERIOD**. If it is, it executes the loop body (printing the current balance and computing the next balance), increments **year**, and does the test again. The loop exits when **year** is greater than **PERIOD**.

2.4   EXTENDING OUR INTEREST PROGRAM TO READ VALUES

Let's make our interest accumulation program more flexible. Rather than hard-wiring the initial balance (**PRINCIPAL**), the interest rate (**INTRATE**), and the number of years (**PERIOD**), we'll obtain these values from an interactive user. Figure 2.5 contains the new version of the program. Here's a sample run:

```
Enter interest rate, principal and period: .04 1000 7
Interest Rate:       4.00%
Starting Balance: 1000.00$

Year      Balance
   1    $ 1040.00
   2    $ 1081.60
   3    $ 1124.86
   4    $ 1169.86
   5    $ 1216.65
   6    $ 1265.32
   7    $ 1315.93
```

Using scanf

To read input, we use a new standard I/O library function, **scanf**, the input analog to **printf**. **scanf** reads formatted input from the *standard input*, which is usually the keyboard.

```
/*
 * Generate a table showing interest accumulation.  Now the user
 * provides the initial interest rate, balance, and principal.
 */
#include <stdio.h>

main()
{
  double intrate;                            /* interest rate */
  double balance;                            /* balance at year's end */
  int    year;                               /* year of period */
  int    period;                             /* length of period */

  printf("Enter interest rate, principal, and period: ");
  scanf("%lf %lf %i", &intrate, &balance, &period);
  printf("Interest Rate:    %7.2f%%\n", intrate * 100);
  printf("Starting Balance: %7.2f$\n\n", balance);
  printf("Year      Balance\n");
  for (year = 1; year <= period; year = year + 1)
  {
    balance = balance + balance * intrate;
    printf("%4i   $ %7.2f\n", year, balance);
  }
  return 0;                                  /* assume program worked! */
}
```

Figure 2.5   (intrate3.c)   An interest rate program that gets user input.

---

scanf's arguments are a formatting control string, enclosed in quotation marks, and a list of locations where values are to be stored. The control string uses conventions just similar enough to those of **printf** to cause confusion. As expected, we can use %i and %d to read a base 10 **int**. But rather than using %f to read a **double**, we must use %1f, which stands for "long float", a double-precision floating point value.

scanf works its way through the control string, and whenever it encounters a field specification, such as %i or %1f, it skips space characters, such as blanks, tabs, and line boundaries, and simply looks for the next appropriate character. It ignores space characters in the control string, but expects any other characters that appear in the control string to appear in its input as well.

The program in Figure 2.5 begins by using **printf** to write a prompt requesting the starting balance, interest rate, and period. It then uses **scanf** to obtain their values from the user.

```
printf("Enter interest rate, principal, and period: ");
scanf("%lf %lf %i", &intrate, &balance, &period);
```

scanf reads two floating point values and an integer from the program's input. Because scanf automatically ignores intervening white space, the input values can be widely separated and do not even have to be on the same line.

There's one little detail we've so far ignored. We don't simply provide **scanf** a list of variable names. **scanf** expects to be passed a variable's address rather than its name. To obtain a variable's address, we simply precede its name with the address-of operator **&**. Forgetting the address operator **&** causes strange and unforgiving behavior (we'll see why when we consider how function parameters work).

> *Remember to precede any variables passed to* scanf *with an* &.

Handling Input Errors

Our current interest accumulator has one major flaw: it doesn't say anything if it isn't given the two **double**s and an **int** that it expects. In fact, it quietly produces incorrect results. This behavior is obviously undesirable, since the user could accidentally provide three floating point values instead of two, provide letters rather than numbers, or possibly provide no input at all. At the very least, invalid input should result in an error message.

We can easily correct this problem: it turns out that **scanf** returns a useful value—either the number of values it correctly read from the input or the special value **EOF**, a constant (defined in stdio.h) that indicates that the end of the input has been reached. When the input is coming from the keyboard, the user signals the end of input by typing a special, system-dependent character.[2]

We can determine whether an error has occurred by comparing the number of values correctly read (returned by **scanf**) with the expected number. Since we are reading three values, **scanf** should return three. Any other return value indicates an input error or the end of the input. In either case, the program should print a simple message and terminate. Figure 2.6 shows a version that does just this. For valid input, it produces the same output as the previous version. But for invalid input, such as providing a name rather than the expected numeric values, it lets us know there's a problem:

```
Enter interest rate, principal, and period: alex
Error: Expected three numeric input values.
```

The if Statement

We can test **scanf**'s return value by using an **if** statement:

```
if (expression)
    true-statement ;
else
    false-statement ;
```

---

[2]Usually **EOF** is defined as −1, although its value is system-dependent. By default, on UNIX systems the EOF character is a control-*D*. On MS-DOS, it's a control-*Z* at the beginning of the line and immediately followed by a carriage return.

```
/*
 * A new version of our interest computing program that verifies
 * it received the expected input values.
 */
#include <stdio.h>

main()
{
  double intrate;                              /* interest rate */
  double balance;                              /* balance at year's end */
  int    year;                                 /* year of period */
  int    period;                               /* length of period */
  int    status;                               /* did program fail? */

  printf("Enter interest rate, principal, and period: ");
  if (scanf("%lf %lf %i", &intrate, &balance, &period) != 3)
  {
    printf("Error: Expected three numeric input values.\n");
    status = 1;                                /* record program failed */
  }
  else
  {
    printf("Interest Rate:    %7.2f%%\n", intrate * 100);
    printf("Starting Balance: %7.2f$\n\n", balance);
    printf("Year      Balance\n");
    for (year = 1; year <= period; year = year + 1)
    {
      balance = balance + balance * intrate;
      printf("%4i   $ %7.2f\n", year, balance);
    }
    status = 0;                                /* record program success */
  }
  return status;                               /* return program status */
}
```

(handwritten annotations: "inequality" pointing to `!= 3`; "if not true" bracketing the first block; "true" bracketing the else block)

Figure 2.6   (intrate4.c) A new version of our interest accumulator that verifies it read its input successfully.

if evaluates the expression in parentheses and, if the condition is true, executes *true-statement*. If the condition is false, it executes *false-statement*. Like Pascal, the **else** and the *false-statement* are optional. If we omit them and the condition is false, *true-statement* is simply skipped. Unlike Pascal, there is no **then** keyword, and *expression* must be surrounded with parentheses. As with **while**, we need to surround multiple statements with braces when they appear in places where C requires a single statement.

In Figure 2.6, we expect **scanf** to return 3. We test **scanf**'s return value using the test-for-inequality operator, (**!=**). If the test is true, it means that **scanf** did not return 3, and we execute the group of statements immediately following it, which writes an error message and records that an error occurred by setting a flag variable, **status**, to 1. But if the test is false, **scanf** did return 3, and we execute the group of statements following the **else**, writing the heading and computing the balances for the various years. These statements are essentially the body of our earlier interest rate program, except that we now have an additional statement that records that no error occurred by setting **status** to zero. After the **if**, **main** concludes by returning **status**.

The Assignment Operator

To explore the effects of more than one interest rate, principal, or period, we're now stuck with repeatedly running our interest computing program. We would much rather run it just once.

Figure 2.7 is a new version of this program that lets us enter more than one interest rate, principal, and period. The key change is that we now wrap the process of writing the headings and computing the year-ending balances in a **while** loop.

```
while ((n = scanf("%lf %lf %i", ...)) == 3)
{
    compute and print balances
}
```

This loop test is tricky. What exactly is it doing?

The idea is to keep processing input as long as we can successfully read three new values (the interest rate, starting balance, and period). There are two possible reasons why we might fail: we hit the end of the input or there's an error in the input. In either case, we want to leave the loop, which we can do by testing whether or not **scanf**'s return value is 3, the number of values we expect to read. But if an error occurred, we also want to write a message at the end of the loop, so we need a way to distinguish between errors and end of file.

The trick is to record **scanf**'s return value in a variable before comparing it with 3 to determine whether to exit the loop.

```
(n = scanf("%lf %lf %i", &intrate, &balance, &period)) == 3
```

After the loop exits, that variable can then be compared against **EOF** to determine whether an error occurred.

This whole scheme works because assignment, **=**, is actually an operator; it assigns a value to a variable and then returns the value assigned. In this case, after **scanf** reads the input values, its return value is assigned to **n**. After that assignment, this value is compared with 3 to determine if the loop should exit.

Assignment as an operator is a powerful feature, but it has several potential pitfalls. It can make our programs harder to understand, since an embedded assignment can make a single expression do several different things. Above, we manage to read input, save a function's return value, and determine whether to exit the loop, all in a single expression. It also has very low precedence, which usually gets us into trouble if we don't surround its use with parentheses.

> *Make sure to parenthesize any assignment you embed in a larger expression.*

```c
/*
 * An interest rate program that repeatedly reads input values.
 */
#include <stdio.h>

main()
{
  double intrate;                          /* interest rate */
  double balance;                          /* balance at year's end */
  int    year;                             /* year of period */
  int    period;                           /* length of period */
  int    status;                           /* did program fail? */
  int    n;                                /* number of values read */

  printf("Enter interest rate, principal, and period: ");
  while ((n = scanf("%lf %lf %i", &intrate, &balance, &period)) == 3)
  {
    printf("Interest Rate:    %7.2f%%\n", intrate * 100);
    printf("Starting Balance: %7.2f$\n\n", balance);
    printf("Year     Balance\n");
    for (year = 1; year <= period; year = year + 1)
    {
      balance = balance + balance * intrate;
      printf("%4i    $ %7.2f\n", year, balance);
    }
    printf("\nEnter interest rate, principal, and period: ");
  }
  if (n != EOF)
  {
    printf("Error: Expected three numeric input values.\n");
    status = 1;
  }
  else
    status = 0;
  return status;                           /* return program status */
}
```

Figure 2.7   (intrate5.c) A version of our interest computing program that allows us to enter more than one set of input values.

Some Problems with Using scanf

scanf is a useful function, but less useful than it may at first appear. One problem is that we usually can use it only when we can assume that the input is correct, as when our input has been generated by another program. Why? Because scanf simply quits reading input at the first unexpected character and there's no simple way to use it to skip over illegal input. Another problem has to do with efficiency. Since scanf can read an arbitrary number of values of differing types, its underlying implementation is often large and cumbersome.

In subsequent chapters we'll look at low-level input in detail and develop solutions to these problems. In fact, we'll end up writing our own special-purpose versions of **scanf**. The methods we use are brief and surprisingly simple, and they substantially reduce the running times of our programs and the size of our compiled code.

2.5 DEFINING OUR OWN FUNCTIONS

A C program is simply a collection of one or more functions (including **main**), some predefined and others user-defined. So far, **main** is the only function we've written. But when we write larger programs, we need to break them into smaller, more manageable pieces. Functions are the mechanism that lets us do so. We can create common, single purpose routines and use them from the main program, without the main program's having to know how they actually accomplish their task. In fact, we have already used functions that were prewritten and compiled for us, such as **printf** and **scanf**, without knowing what they look like internally.

Figure 2.8 is a final variant of our interest rate program that shows how to create and use our own functions. This program uses two new functions: **display_values** writes the interest rate and starting balance, and **year_end_balance** computes a year's ending balance, given the year's starting balance and the annual interest rate. Unlike **scanf** and **printf**, these functions have not already been written for us and placed in a library, so we are forced to create them ourselves. Although simple, these functions demonstrate the different aspects of function use and will guide you in writing your own functions.

Because we thought you might be getting bored with seeing version after version of the interest rate program, this version has a slight twist: it now compounds the interest monthly rather than annually. And because we wanted this entire program to fit on a single page of the text, we've eliminated the error checking and reading of multiple input values from the previous version. Here is some sample input and output for the program.

```
Enter interest rate, principal, and period: .04 1000 7
Interest Rate:      4.00%
Starting Balance: 1000.00$

Year      Balance
   1    $ 1040.74
   2    $ 1083.14
   3    $ 1127.27
   4    $ 1173.20
   5    $ 1221.00
   6    $ 1270.74
   7    $ 1322.51
```

```
/*
 * A new version of our interest rate program that compounds
 * interest monthly, rather than yearly.
 */
#include <stdio.h>

main()
{
    void    display_values(double yrly_pct, double start_bal);
    double  year_end_balance(double intrate, double monthly_bal);

    int     period;                     /* length of period */
    int     year;                       /* year of period */
    double  balance;                    /* balance at end of year */
    double  intrate;                    /* interest rate */

    printf("Enter interest rate, principal, and period: ");
    scanf("%lf %lf %i", &intrate, &balance, &period);
    display_values(intrate * 100, balance);
    printf("Year     Balance\n");
    for (year = 1; year <= period; year = year + 1)
    {
        balance = year_end_balance(intrate, balance);
        printf("%4i   $ %7.2f\n", year, balance);
    }
    return 0;                           /* assume program succeeded */
}

/* Print the initial interest rate and starting balance */

void display_values(double yrly_pct, double start_bal)
{
    printf("Interest Rate:    %7.2f%%\n", yrly_pct);
    printf("Starting Balance: %7.2f$\n\n", start_bal);
}

/* Compute a year's ending balance, compounding interest monthly */

double year_end_balance(double intrate, double monthly_bal)
{
    int     month;                      /* current month */
    double  monthly_intrate;            /* % interest per month */

    monthly_intrate = intrate / 12;
    for (month = 0; month < 12; month = month + 1)
        monthly_bal = monthly_bal * monthly_intrate + monthly_bal;
    return monthly_bal;
}
```

Figure 2.8   (intrate6.c)   One final variant of our interest rate computing program. This time we define several functions and compound interest monthly, rather than annually.

Creating Functions

We create a function by specifying its parameters, the type of value that the function returns, the function's local variables, and the code executed when the function is called.

i.e. double

```
return-type function-name (parm-1, parm-2, ... , parm-N)
{
    local declarations
    statements
}
```

We precede the function's name with the type of value it returns, such as **int** or **double**. If we omit the return type, the compiler assumes that the function returns an **int**. (In fact, that's what we've been doing with **main**.) There is also a special type, **void**, for functions such as **display_values** that never return a useful value. These **void** functions behave like a procedure in languages like Pascal or a subroutine in FORTRAN.

We follow the function's name with a parenthesized *parameter* list, a list of variable declarations that specify each parameter's name and type. When we have a function that takes no parameters, we specify a parameter list of **void** or simply leave the list empty, as we've done with **main**.

Finally, we follow the parameter list with the function's body. This is where we declare any variables local to the function (such as loop counters and array indexes). These *local variables* can be accessed only within that function. The statements executed when the function is called follow these declarations. We must supply the braces surrounding the function's body even if it contains no variable declarations or statements.

Now that we've abstractly discussed function definitions, let's examine the two functions we've defined—**display_values** and **year_end_balance**—and see how we call and use them from the **main** program.

Defining Functions

display_values takes two parameters: **yrly_pct** is the annual interest rate (but expressed as a percentage such as 4.0 rather than as a fraction such as 0.04), and **start_bal** is the starting balance to display. We declare these parameters in the function header; both variables are **double**s.

```
void display_values(double yrly_pct, double start_bal)
{
    . . .
}
```

Because **display_values** simply writes the interest rate and starting balance, and doesn't return any value, its return type is **void**.

year_end_balance also has two parameters: **intrate** is the yearly interest rate (but as a fraction like 0.04, not a percentage like 4.0), and **monthly_bal** is the balance for the first month of the year. As with **display_values**, both of its parameters are **double**s.

```
double year_end_balance(double intrate, double monthly_bal)
{
  ...
}
```

Unlike `display_values`, however, `year_end_balance` does return a useful value: the year's final balance, a `double`.

Calling Functions

We actually execute the functions we create by *calling* them. A function calls another function by specifying its name and providing a list of values, the functions *actual* parameters or *arguments*. `main` calls `display_values` with two arguments: `intrate * 100`, the yearly interest rate expressed as a percentage, and `balance`, the current balance just read from the user.

```
display_values(intrate * 100, balance);
```

Similarly, each time through the `for` loop, `main` calls `year_end_balance` with two parameters: `intrate`, the annual interest rate, and `balance`, the current balance.

```
balance = year_end_balance(intrate, balance);
```

When we call a function, C assigns its argument values to its formal parameters and executes the function's statements until it encounters a return (or ending brace). This parameter-passing mechanism is known as *call by value* because each argument's *value* is *copied* and given to the function. In fact, we tend to think of a function's formal parameters as local variables that happen to be conveniently initialized when the function is called. When we call `display_values`, for example, C computes the value of `intrate * 100` and assigns it to the parameter `yrly_pct` and assigns the value of `balance` to the other parameter `start_bal`. Similarly, when we call `year_end_balance`, C assigns the value of `intrate` in `main` to the parameter `intrate` and assigns the value of `balance` in `main` to the parameter `monthly_bal`.

> *Changes to a function's parameters do not affect its arguments.*

In Figure 2.8, for example, even though `year_end_balance` repeatedly modifies `monthly_bal`, it doesn't affect `balance`, the value passed to it. This behavior has its good points and bad points. Score one point because it makes it hard for functions to *accidentally* change values in their callers. This helps keep our programs modular and eases debugging. Score another point because it lets us pass constants and expressions, such as `intrate * 100`, to functions without having to store them in temporary variables first. But take away a point because it's now hard for functions to *intentionally* change values in their callers. They can do so only indirectly through addresses (as does `scanf`, for example).

Return Values

After C executes a function, it substitutes its return value, if any, for the function call. In this way, the called function can pass a single value back to its caller. To do so, it uses the **return** statement:

> **return** *expression*;

A **return** evaluates *expression*, exits the function, and returns its value to the function's caller. You should think of a function's return value as replacing the function's call. In Figure 2.8, **year_end_balance** returns **monthly_bal**, which at that point contains the monthly balance for the last month of the year.

```
return monthly_bal;
```

When **year_end_balance** returns, its value replaces the call to it in **main**,

```
balance = year_end_balance(intrate, balance);
```

so **balance** is assigned the value of **monthly_bal**.

It may seem strange to pass **balance** as a parameter and then assign it the function's return value. But there's no easier way to update it. We've already seen that call by value means that changing **monthly_bal**'s value doesn't affect **balance**. And changing **monthly_bal**'s name to **balance** isn't a simpler alternative: the function's formal parameters are distinct, local variables, so all we would be doing is creating two different variables named **balance**, one in **main** and the other in **year_end_balance**, just as we've done with **intrate**.

Just because a function returns a value, however, we're not obligated to do anything with it. Had we not cared what the new balance was, we could have simply ignored **year_end_balance**'s return value, with a call such as:

```
year_end_balance(intrate, balance);
```

But doing so here is silly, since the only reason we're calling **year_end_balance** is to compute the new balance. Ignoring a function's return value is really only sensible when the function has a useful side effect. It's reasonable, for example, to ignore **scanf**'s return value in **main**, since we're assuming that the input was read successfully.

```
scanf("%lf %lf %i", &intrate, &balance, &period);
```

Providing Function Prototypes

As usual, **main** starts with a set of declarations, but this time two of them are new:

```
void    display_values(double yrly_pct, double start_bal);
double  year_end_balance(double intrate, double monthly_bal);
```

These declarations, called *function prototypes*, look like the function headers. You should be wondering why we need them. After all, don't we provide the same information when we define the function?

The problem is that we often define functions after we define their callers, as we did here, defining **display_values** and **year_end_balance** after **main**. But to process function calls, the compiler needs to know the expected type of the function's arguments and return value. These declarations tell the compiler how **display_values** and **year_end_balance** are supposed to be called; they describe the types of their return values and parameters. Without them, how could the compiler check whether we were passing the right arguments to the function or using its return value correctly? The compiler needs the above declaration to detect common mistakes such as passing an incorrect number of arguments to **year_end_balance** or trying to use **display_values**'s return value.

> *Make sure to provide a prototype for every function you call.*

So what happens if we don't provide a prototype? If we've defined the function before its caller, we're fine. That's because the compiler can get the necessary type information from the function's definition. But if we haven't, the compiler assumes that the function has some unknown set of arguments and returns an **int**. That assumption can lead to trouble. It means that the compiler won't be able to do type checking on our function calls. And it often leads to "type mismatch" error messages at the point where we define the function we were calling. Life is much simpler if we always provide a prototype.

 To verify that a function call is reasonable, the compiler actually need not know the parameter names, only their types. In the prototypes we can omit the names entirely or include different names—the names we supply are *dummies*, so they need not correspond in any way to the names used as the function's parameters or function arguments when it is called. We usually take the trouble to provide names, since they help document what the function does. But there's no reason why we couldn't have also written the above prototypes this way:

```
void    display_values(double, double);
double  year_end_balance(double, double);
```

2.6   SEPARATE COMPILATION

Our programs have so far resided in individual files. But C also allows us to spread a program's source over a set of files. We can compile each file separately and link at a later time, or compile and link all at one time.

Figure 2.9 shows what happens when we compile a program composed of several source files. Each source file compiles into an *object module* containing its machine language code, along with a list of its references to external functions and variables. The *linker* then creates an executable file from these object modules by filling in external references and adding any referenced library functions.

Figures 2.10 and 2.11 show how we can divide our latest example program into a pair of files. The first file, irmain.c, contains **main**. The other file, irfuncs.c,

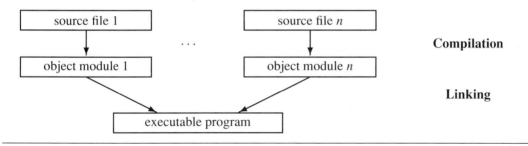

Figure 2.9 The process of separate compilation and linking.

```
/*
 * The main program of our separately compilable interest rate program.
 */
#include <stdio.h>

main()
{
  void    display_values(double yrly_pct, double start_bal);
  double  year_end_balance(double intrate, double monthly_bal);

  int     period;                        /* length of period */
  int     year;                          /* year of period */
  double  balance;                       /* balance at end of year */
  double  intrate;                       /* interest rate */

  printf("Enter interest rate, principal, and period: ");
  scanf("%lf %lf %i", &intrate, &balance, &period);
  display_values(intrate * 100, balance);
  printf("Year     Balance\n");
  for (year = 1; year <= period; year = year + 1)
  {
    balance = year_end_balance(intrate, balance);
    printf("%4i   $ %7.2f\n", year, balance);
  }
  return 0;                              /* assume program succeeded */
}
```

Figure 2.10 (irmain.c) The function **main** of our latest interest-computing program.

```
/*
 * The functions for our separately compilable interest rate program.
 *   display_values - print initial interest rate and starting balance.
 *   year_end_balance - compute year's ending balance, compounding
 *      interest monthly.
 */
#include <stdio.h>

void display_values(double yrly_pct, double start_bal)
{
  printf("Interest Rate:    %7.2f%%\n", yrly_pct);
  printf("Starting Balance: %7.2f$\n\n", start_bal);
}

double year_end_balance(double intrate, double monthly_bal)
{
  int     month;
  double  monthly_intrate;

  monthly_intrate = intrate / 12;
  for (month = 0; month < 12; month = month + 1)
    monthly_bal = monthly_bal * monthly_intrate + monthly_bal;
  return monthly_bal;
}
```

Figure 2.11   (irfuncs.c)   The functions to display the interest rate and starting balance and to compute the year's ending balance.

contains the functions **display_values** and **year_end_balance**. There are several advantages to this organization. One is that we can use these functions in other programs as well. We need only compile them once, and then they can be linked together with whatever programs find them useful. The other is that it speeds program development and debugging. When we update one of our functions—perhaps to fix a newly discovered mistake—there's no need to recompile the source file containing **main**. We simply recompile irfuncs.c and link the resulting object module with the object module originally compiled from irmain.c.

Which commands and options we use to compile and link files separately varies from system to system. The overall process, however, is the same. We first invoke the compiler individually on each of the source files that make up our program. This process usually involves using a special command option or menu selection to tell the compiler not to invoke the linker after creating the object module. Once we've created all the necessary object modules, we then invoke the linker to tie them together. So to put the interest rate program together, we would compile irfuncs.c and irmain.c into object modules and then link those object modules together. Appendix A shows how we can separately compile and link files using some of the more popular compilers.

SUMMARY

- C provides the **while** and **for** looping constructs. The **while** repeatedly tests an expression and, if it's true, executes the body of the loop. The **for** allows us to initialize a variable before going through the loop and to update it each time we finish executing the loop body.

- C provides a variety of operators for doing comparisons (==, !=, <, <=, >, >=) and taking an address (**&**).

- We perform formatted input with the predefined **scanf** function.

    scanf(*"format string"*, *address-1*, *address-2*, ...)

- We make decisions using the **if** statement.

- We can define our own functions by providing the function's return value, parameters, and statements to be executed when the program is called.

- We can divide our programs into multiple source files, compile them separately, and then link the resulting object modules together. *To link: cc intmain.o intfuncs.o*

EXERCISES *cc -c intmain.c ⟹ intmain.o* / *cc -c intfuncs.c ⟹ intfuncs.o*

2–1 Compile and run this chapter's interest rate programs on your computer. Try separately compiling, linking, and executing Figures 2.10 and 2.11.

2–2 Fix the errors but not the warnings in our erroneous interest rate program (Figure 2.2). What output does the program produce on your machine?

2–3 Modify Chapter 1's final welcoming program (Figure 1.3) to print the welcoming message over and over, one per line, until it fills the entire screen (that's usually 24 lines on most terminals or PCs in text mode).

2–4 Rewrite Chapter 1's final cost computing program (Figure 1.5) to read any values it needs, rather than defining them as constants.

2–5 The interest rate programs in this chapter write the starting balance followed by a $. Pick one of them and modify it to write the $ first.

2–6 Modify the final version of the interest rate program (Figures 2.10 and 2.11) to verify that the balance and interest rate are both positive numbers. Write appropriate error messages if either is not.

2–7 Modify the final version of the interest rate program (Figures 2.10 and 2.11) to allow more than one interest rate, period, and balance to be entered.

2–8 Modify the final version of the interest rate program (Figures 2.10 and 2.11) to compute the interest daily rather than monthly.

comma (,) = 44
space ( ) = 32

2-9   Modify the error-checking version of the interest rate program (Figure 2.7) to expect input values separated by a comma. What happens when the user separates the numbers by spaces instead? *must 1/0 c to read comma*

2-10   Write a program to print the integers between **M** and **N**, inclusive, where **M** and **N** are program constants. With an **M** of 1 and an **N** of 5, it should write the numbers 1, 2, 3, 4, and 5. Assume **M** is less than **N**.

2-11   Rewrite the program from the previous exercise to print the values in reverse order. That is, with an **M** of 1 and an **N** of 5, its output is 5, 4, 3, 2, and 1.

2-12   Write a small program to print the sum of the integers between **M** and **N**, inclusive, where **M** and **N** are program constants. With an **M** of 1 and an **N** of 100, your program should print 5050.

2-13   Rewrite the program from the previous exercise to use **scanf** to read the two limiting values. Also modify it to behave sensibly even if $M \geq N$.

2-14   Write a program to print the sum of its input values. Assume the values are **int**s. What happens if the total sum is too large to fit in an **int**? Rewrite the program in the previous exercise to work with **double**s.

2-15   Write a program to print the largest and smallest values in its input. The program should behave reasonably even when there are no input values.

2-16   Write a program that reads two values, **min** and **max**, and then reads the remainder of its input, counting the values less than **min** and those greater than **max**. When the program is done reading its input, it prints these two counts.

2-17   Write a program to print a multiplication table for the integers 1 through 12. The table should have 12 rows of 12 columns. The first row of the table contains the values of $1 \times 1, 1 \times 2, \ldots, 1 \times 12$, the second row of the table contains the values of $2 \times 1, 2 \times 2, \ldots, 2 \times 12$, and so on.

2-18   Write a program to print a table of powers. The program should read three values: a **base** and two exponents **min** and **max**. Assume the input values are positive integers. The program should print $base^n$ for $min \leq n \leq max$. With a **base** of 2, a **min** of 0, and a **max** of 4, the program's output should be:

```
Base  Exp  Result
   2    0       1
   2    1       2
   2    2       4
   2    3       8
   2    4      16
```

2-19   Modify the previous exercise to allow negative powers. The result must now be a floating point value.

Part II

THE BASICS

3 NUMBERS

This chapter delves into the details of C's numerical data types and arithmetic operators. We begin with the rules for composing identifiers and then move on to the various integer and real data types. We show how to create numerical constants and declare numerical variables and how to read and print these values. Along the way we study the range of values each type can hold, and when each type is most appropriate. After looking at the numerical data types, we introduce C's arithmetic operators and examine conversions between different data types. The chapter concludes with a case study that converts decimal numbers to other bases.

3.1   IDENTIFIERS AND NAMING CONVENTIONS

Variable and function names are known as *identifiers*. But not every combination of characters is a legal identifier. First, identifiers consist only of lowercase and uppercase letters, digits, and underscores (_)—no other characters are allowed. Second, the first character must be a letter or an underscore—it can't be a digit. Though legal, we avoid names beginning with an underscore, as they are "reserved for the implementation." That is, they exist (as the name of a system-provided library function, for example), but the lowly programmer is not supposed to create new ones. Finally, there's a set of keywords that are reserved, so we can't use them as identifiers. Table 3.1 lists the standard keywords.[1] In addition, all names in the standard libraries are reserved. That means, for example, that we can't legally write our own function named **printf**.

Case is significant in identifiers: **var** refers to a different identifier than **Var**, which refers to a different identifier than **VAR**. C's keywords must be in lower-case, so an identifier like **INT** or **Double** is perfectly legal, though perhaps more than a little confusing.

There is no limit on the length of an identifier. There is, however, a limit to the number of significant characters. Originally, only the first 8 characters were significant, implying that **var_name1** and **var_name2** referred to the same identifier. Now things have improved significantly, and we're guaranteed that at least the first 31 characters are significant in an internal name, such as a local variable. But for an external name, such as a function call, only the first 6 characters are guaranteed to be significant, and case differences may be ignored. That's problematic, since it means that in some implementations any function name starting with **display_** (such as **display_values**)

[handwritten: - internal fn 31 char.]

[handwritten: - External fn 1st 6 Characters]

---

[1] Each implementation may have a few additional reserved words; some of the more common ones we've run into include **asm**, **far**, **fortran**, **huge**, **near**, and **pascal**.

auto	break	case	char	const	continue	default	do
double	else	enum	extern	float	for	goto	if
int	long	register	return	short	signed	sizeof	static
struct	switch	typedef	union	unsigned	void		volatile	while

Table 3.1   C's reserved words.

INTEGER TYPE	BITS	RANGE
short	16	$-32,767$ to $+32,767$
int	16	$-32,767$ to $+32,767$
long	32	$-2,147,483,6487$ to $+2,147,483,647$
unsigned short	16	0 to $65,535$
unsigned int	16	0 to $65,535$
unsigned long	32	0 to $4,294,967,295$

3 classes {short, int, long}

Table 3.2   The *minimum* sizes and values of the integer data types. Their specific values can vary on different machines, but they're required to be greater than or equal to these values in magnitude.

refers to the same function. Fortunately, most implementations don't have this painful restriction. For readability, most of the programs in this book assume that external names are no different from internal names. In a later chapter on portability, however, we show an easy way to relax this assumption.

3.2   INTEGERS

Integers are whole numbers. There are three classes of integers: **short int**, **int**, and **long int**, in both **signed** and **unsigned** forms. We can write **short int** and **long int** more concisely as **short** and **long**, respectively.

These classes vary in size and efficiency of use. Table 3.2 lists the minimum sizes and ranges of these values. On most systems, a **short** is 16 bits, an **int** is either 16 or 32 bits, and a **long** is 32 bits. The language, however, only guarantees that **int**s and **short**s will be at least 16 bits, that **long**s will be at least 32, and that a **short** is not going to be larger than an **int**, which is not going to be larger than a **long**.

Why do we have all of these different classes? Because they all have different uses. **int**s occupy one word of storage and are generally the most efficient data type to use. **long**s provide a portable way to store values that require more than 16 bits, but often are much slower than **int**s when used to perform arithmetic. And **short**s provide a portable way to save space when a variable's value always falls within a small range. To keep things simple, however, we usually try to avoid **short**s unless our program is running out of space and to avoid **int**s unless it's running out of time.

CONSTANT		VALUE	DESCRIPTION
INT_MAX		+32767	largest value of an **int**
INT_MIN		-32767	smallest value of an **int**
LONG_MAX		+2147483647L	largest value of a **long**
LONG_MIN		-2147483647L	smallest of a **long**
SHRT_MAX		+32767	largest value of a **short**
SHRT_MIN		-32767	smallest value of a **short**
UINT_MAX		65535U	largest value of an **unsigned int**
ULONG_MAX		4294967295UL	largest value of an **unsigned long**
USHRT_MAX		65535U	largest value of an **unsigned short**

[handwritten: get info of these from limits.h]

Table 3.3 Constants for ranges of integer types (found in the system header file limits.h). The specific values on your machine are required to be greater than or equal to these values in magnitude.

> *When efficiency isn't crucial, make all integer variables* **longs**.

Integers can be either signed or unsigned. Signed integers use 1 bit for the sign of the number. A **signed int** (or just **int**, the default) uses 1 bit for the sign and 15 bits for the magnitude on 16-bit machines or 31 bits for the magnitude on 32-bit machines. Unsigned integers have no sign bit and use all the bits for the magnitude, doubling the range of values they can represent. When a variable will only hold nonnegative values, as in a loop counter or an array index, making it unsigned increases the range of values it can hold. We declare unsigned integers with **unsigned int** (or simply, **unsigned**), **unsigned short**, and **unsigned long**.

The range of values on a particular implementation can be determined using the standard header file limits.h, which contains constants defined for the smallest and largest values of each of the integer types (among other things). All we have to do is include this header file and print the appropriate constants. Table 3.3 lists the more important constants in that file, what they mean, and their smallest acceptable values. The next section explains the notation used for these constants in more detail.

Integer Constants

[handwritten: decimal base 10]
[handwritten: octal base 8]
[handwritten: hexadecimal → base 16]

Integer constants are expressed as a string of digits. We can have decimal (base 10), octal (base 8), and hexadecimal (base 16) integers (Appendix D describes the octal and hexadecimal number systems). A leading zero indicates an octal number; a leading '0x' or '0X' indicates a hexadecimal (hex for short). Regardless of how the value is specified, it is stored in its binary equivalent. For example, the decimal value **63**, the octal value **077**, and the hex value **0x3f** are all stored as 0...0111111.

All constants in C have a type. By default, if the constant fits in an **int**, it's of type **int**, just as we might expect. So **63** is always an **int**, as are **077** and **0x3f**. If the value doesn't fit in an **int**, there are two cases to consider: decimal, and octal or

[handwritten: Decimal Octal Hex]
[handwritten: 63 ⟷ 077 ⟷ 0x3f]

Constant Value	Bits in an `int`	Constant Type
1000	16 or 32	`int`
100000	16	`long`
100000	32	`int`
2500000000	16 or 32	`unsigned long`
0x7FFF	16	`int`
0xFFFF	16 or 32	`unsigned int`
0x7FFFFFFF	16	`long`
0x7FFFFFFF	32	`int`
0xFFFFFFFF	16	`unsigned long`
0xFFFFFFFF	32	`unsigned int`

Table 3.4   Some example integer constants and their types. A constant's type depends on the number of bits in the underlying type on the particular machine being used.

decimal ⇒ long
⇒ unsigned long.

octal or hex ⇒ unsigned int
⇒ long
⇒ unsigned long

No short constant!

hex. If it's decimal, it's automatically treated as a **long** or as an **unsigned long** if it's too large for a **long**. And if it's octal or hex, it has the first type it fits in from among **unsigned int**, **long**, or **unsigned long**. Table 3.4 shows some values and their types.

These rules are complex and we would rather not worry about them. C provides several suffixes that let us specify the particular type we want. A suffix of **l** or **L** forces the constant to be a **long** (that is, to take at least 32 bits), so **255L** and **0xFFL** both are **long** constants. We force a constant to be treated as **unsigned** with a suffix of **u** or **U**, so **255U** is an **unsigned int**. Finally, we can force a constant to be an **unsigned long** by combining the suffixes for **unsigned** and **long**. **100000ul** is an **unsigned long** constant. There are no **short** constants.

C provides us with a unary minus operator, –, which we can use to change the sign of our constants.[2] As expected, **-15** gives us negative **15**.

Reading and Writing Integers

We read and write integers with **scanf** and **printf**; Table 3.5 shows the appropriate formatting codes.

Using an incorrect formatting code may cause strange results. The little program in Figure 3.1 provides an example of what can go wrong. It writes an **unsigned long** as both an **unsigned long** and as a **long**.

```
printf("%lu %li\n", value, value);
```

When we run it on a machine with 32-bit **long**s, we get this output.

```
2500000000 -1794967296
25000 25000
```

---

[2]As an extension to ANSI C, many compilers also provide a unary plus operator, **+**.

for short

TYPE	READING WITH scanf	PRINTING WITH printf
short *h*	%hd or %hi	%d or %i
int *l*	%d or %i	%d or %i
long	%ld or %li	%ld or %li
unsigned short	%hu	%u
unsigned int	%u	%u
unsigned long	%lu	%lu
octal short	%ho	%o
octal int	%o	%o
octal long	%lo	%lo
hex short	%hx	%x
hex int	%x	%x
hex long	%lx	%lx

Table 3.5 Common formatting codes for reading and printing integers.

The first value is the expected result when we write 2500000000, and the other is a strange, signed value. The problem is that when we write a value with %li, it's taken as a **signed long**, and since this value's leftmost bit is on, it's taken as a negative value. But when we write it with %lu, the leftmost bit isn't treated as a sign and we get the value we expect. There's no problem when we write 25000, since its leftmost bit is off.

> *Make sure your formatting codes correspond to the types of the values that you're trying to read or write.*

3.3 REALS

Reals, or floating point numbers, are stored differently than integers. Internally, they are broken into a fraction and an exponent. The number of bits for each is machine-dependent, but a typical representation for a 32-bit real uses 23 bits plus a sign bit for the fraction and 8 bits for the exponent, as shown below. Bit 0 is the sign of the fraction, bits 1 through 8 are the exponent, and bits 9 through 31 contain the fraction.[3]

0	1 ··· 8	9 ··· 31
SIGN	EXPONENT	FRACTION

---

[3] The value of the exponent is usually encoded using an "excess" notation. The trick is that an "excess" amount is added to the exponent's value before storing it, guaranteeing that the stored value is positive. That excess is then subtracted when the value is retrieved. Fortunately, we almost never have to worry about these low-level details.

```
/*
 * Write a large and a small unsigned value as signed.
 */
#include <stdio.h>

int main()
{
  unsigned long value;

  /* write a large value as both an unsigned long and a long */

  value = 2500000000ul;
  printf("%lu %li\n", value, value);

  /* write a small value as both an unsigned long and a long */

  value = 25000ul;
  printf("%lu %li\n", value, value);

  return 0;
}
```

Figure 3.1 (converr.c) A program to write a large unsigned value as both unsigned and signed. It comes out negative when written as signed.

FLOATING POINT	'e' NOTATION	SCIENTIFIC NOTATION
12.45	1.245e1	1.245×10^1
−211.0	−2.110e2	$−2.110 \times 10^2$
0.0056	5.600e-3	5.600×10^{-3}
−0.000123	−1.230e-4	$−1.230 \times 10^{-4}$
1000000.0	1e6	1.000×10^6

Table 3.6 Some examples of scientific notation.

We normally write real numbers with a decimal point, as in 13.45 or -211.0, but we can also write them in 'e' notation, giving both a fraction and a base 10 exponent. 'e' notation is similar to scientific notation, except that the letter 'e' replaces the times sign and the base. Table 3.6 provides several examples.

There are three types of real values: **double**, which we've already seen, **float**, and **long double**. A **double** provides at least 10 significant digits and usually requires 64 bits of storage. A **float** provides at least 6 significant digits and usually requires 32 bits of storage. And a **long double** potentially provides even more significant digits and a larger range of values. Many implementations, however, treat **double**s and **long double**s as synonyms.

[handwritten margin notes: Real (3 Types) — double 10 significant — long double — float 6 signr digits]

print values from float.h

CONSTANT	VALUE	DESCRIPTION
FLT_DIG	6	decimal digits of precision for **float**
FLT_EPSILON	1E-5	smallest x such that $1.0 + x \neq 1.0$
FLT_MAX	1E+37	largest **float**
FLT_MIN	1E-37	smallest **float**
FLT_MAX_10_EXP	+37	largest integer power of 10 in a **float**
FLT_MIN_10_EXP	-37	smallest integer power of 10 in a **float**
DBL_DIG	10	decimal digits of precision for **double**
DBL_EPSILON	1E-9	smallest x such that $1.0 + x \neq 1.0$
DBL_MAX	1E37	largest **double**
DBL_MIN	1E-37	smallest **double**
DBL_MAX_10_EXP	+37	largest integer power of 10 in a **double**
DBL_MIN_10_EXP	-37	smallest integer power of 10 in a **double**
LDBL_DIG	10	decimal digits of precision for **long double**
LDBL_EPSILON	1E-9	smallest x such that $1.0 + x \neq 1.0$
LDBL_MAX	1E37	largest **long double**
LDBL_MIN	1E-37	smallest **long double**
LDBL_MAX_10_EXP	+37	largest integer power of 10 in a **long double**
LDBL_MIN_10_EXP	-37	smallest integer power of 10 in a **long double**
FLT_RADIX	2	radix of exponent representation
FLT_ROUNDS	0	addition rounds toward nearest value (1), toward zero (0), toward $+\infty$ (2), toward $-\infty$ (3), or indeterminate (-1)
FLT_GUARD	0	guard digits are used (1) or not used (0) for multiplication
FLT_NORMALIZE	0	floating values must be normalized (1) or need not be (0)

Table 3.7 The *minimum* values of some important floating point constants (found in the system header file float.h). Their actual values must be greater than or equal to these values in magnitude.

Why are there all of these types? We use **float**s when we need to save storage or want to avoid the overhead of double precision operations. We use **double**s when we need more significant digits and we're less concerned with storage. And we use **long double**s when our implementation provides even more significant digits or a wider range of values for them. As with integers, we try to keep things simple and use only one type.

> *Unless efficiency is a major concern, make all of your floating point variables* **double***s.*

For reals, as with integers, there's a header file that contains constants for their implementation-defined limits. This header file is float.h. Table 3.7 lists its important constants, their minimum values (if any), and their purpose.

By default, any real constant is a **double**. To have **float** constants, we follow

```
/*
 * Compute the area of a circle.
 */
#include <stdio.h>

#define  PI   3.1415926            /* our favorite constant! */

int main()
{
  double radius;                    /* user entered radius of a circle */
  double area;                      /* computed area of that circle */

  printf("Enter radius: ");
  if (scanf("%lf", &radius) == 1)
  {
    area = PI * radius * radius;
    printf("Area in floating point notation: %f\n", area);
    printf("Area in exponential notation:    %e\n", area);
    printf("Area in smallest notation:       %g\n", area);
  }
  else
    printf("Error: expected numeric radius.\n");
  return 0;                         /* always return success */
}
```

Figure 3.2 (area.c) A program to compute the area of a circle..

%lf double
%f float
%LF long double
%e exponential
%g whichever

the number with an 'f' or 'F', as in **3.1415926F**. To have **long double** constants, we follow it with an 'l' or 'L', as in **3.1415926L**.

As with integers, we use **scanf** to read reals and **printf** to print them. With **scanf**, **%f** indicates a **float**, **%lf** a **double**, and **%LF** a **long double**. With **printf**, **%f** indicates a **float** or **double**, and **%LF** indicates a **long double**. If we need output in 'e' notation (1.3e4 instead of 13000), we use **%e** instead of **%f**. If we want whichever form can be displayed in the fewest characters, we use **%g**.

Figure 3.2 is a short program that uses the simple formula

$$area = \pi \times radius^2$$

to compute the area of a circle, given its radius. It uses **double**s for all of its calculations and prints its answer in several different formats. Here's an example run:

```
Enter radius: 34.5
Area in floating point notation: 3739.280592
Area in exponential notation:    3.739281e+03
Area in smallest notation:       3739.28
```

3.4 ARITHMETIC OPERATORS

% remainder of int div (handwritten margin note)

C has only a small set of integer and real data types and only a few arithmetic operators we can use on them. These operators are: + (addition), - (subtraction), * (multiplication), / (division), and % (remaindering—for integers only). All these operators take two operands, and except for %, operate on both integer and real operands. They associate (are evaluated) left to right, with *, /, and % having higher precedence than either + or -. This means that

```
balance = balance + balance * INTRATE;
```

is evaluated as though it were written as

```
balance = balance + (balance * INTRATE);
```

Signed Integer Arithmetic

Integer arithmetic is always exact within the limits of the number of values that can be represented within the integral data type used—so you don't have to worry about precision problems. Unfortunately, you do have to worry about overflow, which leads to severe headaches, since C provides no run-time indication that a signed integer overflow has occurred.

overflow ⇒ undefined (handwritten margin note)

Officially, the result of an overflow is undefined. In reality, the arithmetic usually takes place and gives an incorrect result. On most machines, adding 1 to the largest positive number yields the largest negative value, and conversely, subtracting 1 from the largest negative value yields the largest positive value (both operations cause the sign bit to change). Overflow can also be caused by multiplying two large numbers together, regardless of their signs. While it is possible to detect overflow after the fact—perhaps by noting that adding two positive numbers produced a negative result—it is better to try and avoid any overflow in the first place. Use data types appropriate to the range of values the result *might* cover. If you are adding two **int**s and their result might not fit in an **int**, use **long**s instead. As an alternative, use a **double** and then test to see if the result is greater than **INT_MAX**.

> *Avoid overflows during signed integer arithmetic by carefully choosing your data types.*

Integer addition, subtraction, and multiplication (both operands are integers) behave just like in other programming languages or your home calculator. Integer division (both operands are integers) produces a *truncated* result. That is, it simply throws away the real part of the result: **10/3** is 3, as is **17/5**. This truncation means that "fractional" division of integers always returns zero: **1/3**, for example, evaluates to 0, as does **25/26**. The direction of truncation is machine-dependent for negative numbers. As you might expect, you should avoid dividing by zero.

```
/*
 * Display largest unsigned int and the numbers following it.
 */
#include <stdio.h>
#include <limits.h>                /* for UINT_MAX */

int main()
{
  unsigned int i;

  i = UINT_MAX;
  printf("Largest unsigned int: %u\n", i);
  printf("Largest plus one:     %u\n", i+1);
  printf("Largest plus two:     %u\n", i+2);
  return 0;
}
```

Figure 3.3   (unsign.c) A program that adds several values to the largest unsigned integer.

The remaindering operator, %, takes two integer operands and returns the remainder when the first is divided by the second: **5%3**, for example, is 2, and **1%3 is 1.** For positive integers, this is the familiar modulus operation. The sign of the result is machine-dependent for negative numbers. For this reason, % is best used only with positive values. Regardless of the sign of **a** and **b**, however, **(a/b) * b + a%b** will always equal **a** (assuming, of course, that **a/b** is possible).

Unsigned Integer Arithmetic

Unsigned integer arithmetic is similar to signed integer arithmetic, except that there are no negative results and no overflow. Instead, all unsigned integer arithmetic takes place modulo 2^n, where n is the number of bits in the unsigned operands. This means that adding 1 to the largest unsigned value gives zero, and conversely, subtracting 1 from zero gives the largest unsigned value. Figure 3.3 contains a program that illustrates unsigned arithmetic. It simply adds 1 and 2 to the largest possible **unsigned int**. Its output, on a 16-bit machine, is:

```
Largest unsigned int: 65535
Largest plus one:     0
Largest plus two:     1
```

To obtain the largest **unsigned int**, we include the standard header file limits.h, which contains its value in the constant **UINT_MAX**.

Floating Point Arithmetic

Significance
float ⇒ 6 digits
double ⇒ 14

Floating point arithmetic is an approximation of the correct result, since floating point values are rounded or truncated to the number of significant digits allowable in the representation. Typically, this is 6 digits for **float**s and 14 digits for **double**s. Both overflow and underflow can occur with real arithmetic; the action taken is machine dependent. For example, adding to the largest possible **float** will produce overflow, and dividing the smallest possible **float** by a large value will cause underflow. The hardware of most machines traps floating point overflow, causing a run-time error and termination of the program. Technically, the result of floating point underflow is undefined, although it usually gives us a zero result.

Floating point differs from integer division in that the real part of the result is not thrown away. As long as either operand of **/** is real, floating point division is used. That means **1.0/3.0**, **1/3.0**, and **1.0/3** all give the result **0.333333**.

Arithmetic Functions

C has a sparse set of arithmetic operators when compared with many other languages. Where, for example, is FORTRAN's exponentiation operator? How do we obtain a floating point remainder? And how do we obtain an absolute value?

C's philosophy is to keep the language small and to have standard library functions that perform any missing operations. It's easy to write a **power** function to compute x^y, assuming that **x** is a **double** and that **y** is an **int**. Figure 3.4 contains **power**, and Figure 3.5 contains a main program that uses it to read **x**, **y** pairs (without checking for input errors), compute x^y, and print the result. Here's some example input and output:

```
3.567 4
3.567^4 = 161.887
1.2 20
1.2^20 = 38.3376
1.2 40
1.2^40 = 1469.77
3.4 20
3.4^20 = 4.26166e+10
```

Many other functions, such as **sin** and **cos**, aren't as easy to write, and most of us have little desire to write them ourselves. Fortunately, C comes complete with a large library of math functions. Table 3.8 provides a brief description of the more commonly used ones. The appendices provide a more complete description of this library and a discussion of how these functions indicate errors in their arguments or results.

#include < math.h >
math lib.

Here, however, we'll be content to use just one of them: **pow**. This function is a generalization of **power** that takes two **double** arguments and returns the first raised to the power of the second. To use it, all we have to do is include the math library header file, math.h, and call **pow** with appropriate arguments. Figure 3.6 is a rewrite of Figure 3.5, which uses the math library **pow** to compute the same results. The **main** programs are almost identical except that when we call **pow**, we can pass it a **double** exponent, whereas **power** is restricted to processing an **int** exponent.

```
/*
 * A function to compute x to the y.
 */
double power(double x, int exp)
{
  double p;                              /* power computed so far */

  p = 1;
  if (exp > 0)
    while (exp > 0)                      /* positive exponent */
    {
      p = p * x;
      exp = exp - 1;
    }
  else
    while (exp < 0)                      /* negative exponent */
    {
      p = p / x;
      exp = exp + 1;
    }
  return p;
}
```

Figure 3.4   (power.c) A simple function to compute integer exponents.

```
/*
 * Using our own function to compute exponents (no error checking).
 */
#include <stdio.h>

int main()
{
  double power(double base, int exp);
  double x;                              /* user-supplied base */
  int    y;                              /* user-supplied exponent */

  while (scanf("%lf %i", &x, &y) == 2)
    printf("%g^%i = %g\n", x, y, power(x, y));
  return 0;
}
```

Figure 3.5   (usepower.c) A main program using our **power** function. It's restricted to **int** exponents.

FUNCTION	COMPUTES	RESTRICTIONS
`exp(x)`	e^x	
`ldexp(x,n)`	$x \times 2^n$	
`log(x)`	$\log_e x$	$x > 0$
`log10(x)`	$\log_{10} x$	$x > 0$
`pow(x,y)`	x^y	$x \neq 0$ if $y \leq 0$, and $x > 0$ if y not integer
`sqrt(x)`	$\sqrt{x}$	$x \geq 0$
`ceil(x)`	nearest whole number $\geq x$	
`floor(x)`	nearest whole number $\leq x$	
`fabs(x)`	$|x|$ (absolute value)	
`fmod(x,y)`	real remainder of x/y	$y \neq 0$
`sin(x)`	sine of x in radians	
`cos(x)`	cosine of x in radians	
`tan(x)`	tangent of x in radians	
`asin(x)`	$\sin^{-1} x$, in range $[-\pi/2, \pi/2]$	$-1 \leq x \leq 1$
`acos(x)`	$\cos^{-1} x$, in range $[0, \pi]$	$-1 \leq x \leq 1$
`atan(x)`	$\tan^{-1} x$, in range $[-\pi/2, \pi/2]$	
`atan2(x,y)`	$\tan^{-1} x/y$, in range $[-\pi, \pi]$	$x \neq 0$ and $y \neq 0$
`sinh(x)`	hyperbolic sine of x	
`cosh(x)`	hyperbolic cosine of x	
`tanh(x)`	hyperbolic tangent of x	

Table 3.8 The most frequently used math library functions. **x** and **y** are **double**s; **n** is an **int**. All angles are expressed in radians. All functions return a **double**.

```
/*
 * Using the math library to compute exponents (no error checking).
 */
#include <stdio.h>
#include <math.h>

int main()
{
  double x;                              /* user-supplied base */
  double y;                              /* user-supplied exponent */

  while (scanf("%lf %lf", &x, &y) == 2)
    printf("%g^%g = %g\n", x, y, pow(x, y));
  return 0;
}
```

Figure 3.6 (usepow.c) A program using **pow** to compute exponents. It's not restricted to **int** exponents.

3.5 TYPE CONVERSIONS

mixed types operation
⇒ automatic type
conversion

Our discussion of arithmetic operators has ignored an important question: What happens when an operator's operands are not both the same type? This occurred, for example, in our **power** function when we assigned an **int** (**1**) to a **double** (**p**). It also happened in Chapter 2's **year_end_balance** function (Figure 2.11) when we sneakily divided a **double** (**intrate**) by an **int** (**12**). In these cases, automatic type conversions occurred. There are two types of automatic conversions: *assignment* and *arithmetic*.

Assignment Conversions

convert to type
on left-hand side.

Whenever we assign one value to another, C automatically converts the assigned value to the type on the left-hand side of the assignment, if possible. Sometimes these conversions involve truncating a value or changing its internal representation, as when we assign an **int** to a **double**.

These automatic *assignment conversions* are convenient. In **power**, we assigned a **1** to the **double p**, and it was automatically converted to **1.0** before the assignment took place. But these conversions can cause problems when we assign a value of one type to a value with a shorter type. Consider the program shown in Figure 3.7. It first multiplies two **long**s together, assigns them to an **int**, and prints the result. And then it assigns a large negative **long** to the same **int** and prints that result. Here's its strange output when run on a machine with 16-bit **int**s and 32-bit **long**s.[4]

```
First answer: -7936
Second answer: 1980
```

How did multiplying two positive values give a negative result? And how did assigning a negative value give a positive result? When we multiply the two **long**s, we obtain the correct result, 100,000,000 in this case. But when we assign this value to an **int**, only its least significant bits were actually assigned (because we ran this on a machine with 16-bit **int**s and 32-bit **long**s). The same thing happens when we assign the negative **long** to the **int**, as shown below.

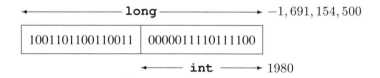

The sign bit (the leftmost bit) is on in the **long** and off in the **int**.

> *Avoid converting from a longer type to a shorter type.*

---

[4]This program produces the expected output on machines where **int**s and **long**s are the same size.

```
/*
 * Example of automatic conversions: multiplying two longs together
 * and storing them in an int.
 */
#include <stdio.h>

int main()
{
  int answer;
  long i;
  long j;

  i = 10000;
  j = 10000;
  answer = i * j;
  printf("First answer: %i\n", answer);
  answer = -1691154500L;
  printf("Second answer: %i\n", answer);
  return 0;
}
```

Figure 3.7   (conex.c) A program illustrating potential problems with automatic conversions.

Converting from a longer type to a shorter type usually leads to loss of significance or, worse, meaningless results. Fortunately, most compilers will produce a warning when we try to assign a value from a larger type to a shorter type.

Assignment conversions actually happen in two places other than explicit assignment. The first occurs whenever we call a function with arguments that differ in type from those of its prototype. The other occurs when the expression in a function's **return** statement differs in type from that of the function's return type.

Figure 3.8 illustrates both of these conversions with a pair of functions, **round** and **trunc**, and a simple **main** program to call them. **round** and **trunc** do the obvious things: **round(10.6)** returns **11**, **round(10.2)** returns **10**, and both **trunc(10.6)** and **trunc(10.2)** return **10**.

How do these functions work? **round** simply adds **0.5** to its **double** argument and returns the result. But because **round** is defined to return an **int**, that result is automatically converted to an **int** before it returns. **trunc** does even less work. We define it to take an **int**, rather than a **double**. Since we provide a prototype before calling it, the **double** we pass it is automatically converted to an **int** before **trunc** is called. **trunc** then simply returns that converted value.

There are actually even simpler ways to round and truncate variables. We'll see those in the next section.

round ⇒ add 0.5 to the result

```
/*
 * The round and trunc functions and a minimal test program using them.
 *    round - round a value up or down (for positive values only).
 *    trunc - get rid of fractional part of value.
 */
#include <stdio.h>

int main()
{
  int    round(double);
  double trunc(int);
  double x;

  printf("Enter a series of positive real numbers, followed by EOF\n");
  while (scanf("%lf", &x) == 1)
    printf("value=%f,rounded=%i,truncated=%f\n", x, round(x), trunc(x));
  return 0;
}

int round(double value)
{
  return value + 0.5;
}

double trunc(int value)
{
  return value;
}
```

Figure 3.8 (round.c) Taking advantage of assignment conversions to implement **round** and **trunc**. **round** works correctly only with positive values.

Arithmetic Conversions

In addition to assignment conversions, C performs the following conversions whenever it evaluates expressions, such as when it performs arithmetic or compares values:

1. If either operand is a **long double**, convert the other to a **long double**.

2. Otherwise, if either operand is a **double**, convert the other to a **double**.

3. Otherwise, if either operand is a **float**, convert the other to a **float**.

4. Otherwise, convert any **short** (or **char**, discussed in the next chapter) operand to an **int** if it fits in an **int** or an **unsigned int** if it doesn't. Then, if either operand is an **unsigned long**, convert the other to an **unsigned long**.

5. Otherwise, if one operand is a **long** and the other is an **unsigned int**, convert the **unsigned int** to a **long** if it fits in a **long**, or convert them both to **unsigned long**s if it doesn't.

FROM	TO	REPRESENTATION CHANGE
`short`	`int`	none
`float`	`double`	pad mantissa with 0s
`signed int`	`signed long`	sign-extended high word
`unsigned int`	`unsigned long`	zero-fill high word
`long`	`int`	truncate high word
`signed long`	`unsigned long`	none
`signed int`	`unsigned int`	none
`unsigned int`	`signed int`	none

Table 3.9   What may happen when we convert one type to another. Most conversions from a longer to a shorter type produce undefined results.

6. Otherwise, if either operand is a **long**, convert the other to a **long**.

7. Otherwise, if one operand is an **unsigned int**, convert the other to an **unsigned int**.

8. Otherwise, both operands must be of type **int**, so no additional conversion takes place.

These rules may seem complicated, but essentially all C does is convert the value of the operand with the smaller type to the type of the other operand. So, for example, if we multiply an **int** by a **double**, C will convert the **int**'s value to a **double** and the multiplication will then take place in double precision.

Table 3.9 gives an idea of what happens during some of these conversions, assuming a machine with 16-bit **int**s, 32-bit **long**s, 32-bit **float**s, and 64-bit **double**s.

Casts

As we've just discovered, C performs some type conversions automatically. At times, however, we want to force a type conversion in a way that is different from the automatic conversion. We call such a process *casting* a value. We specify a cast by giving a type in parentheses followed by the expression to be cast:

(*type*) *expression*

The cast causes the result of the expression to be converted to the specified type.

Casts eliminate the need for truncation and rounding functions. We can replace **trunc** with a cast to an **int**.

    (int) x

This expression turns **x**'s value into an **int** by truncation. If **x** is **12.7**, the expression's value is **12**. We can replace **round** by adding 0.5 to the value and then casting the entire expression to an **int**.

```
/*
 * Compute average of its input values.
 */
#include <stdio.h>

int main()
{
    int     next;                   /* next input value */
    long    sum;                    /* running total */
    int     n;                      /* number of input values */
    int     result;                 /* did we read another value? */
    double  avg;                    /* average of input values */

    sum = 0;
    n = 0;
    while ((result = scanf("%i", &next)) == 1)      use ^D to terminate
    {
        sum = sum + next;
        n = n + 1;                 ──────  or  n += 1 ;
    }
    if (result != EOF)
        printf("Warning: bad input after reading %i values\n", n);
    if (n == 0)
        avg = 0.0;
    else
        avg = (double) sum / n;
    printf("Average of %i values is %f.\n", n, avg);

    return 0;
}
```

Figure 3.9 (avg.c) A program to compute the average of its input values.

```
        (int) (x + 0.5);
```

If **x** is 12.7, adding 0.5 to it yields 13.2; casting this to an **int** truncates the result to 13. Of course, the variable or expression being cast is not changed; a cast simply returns a value of the cast type. The cast operator has high precedence, so we had to parenthesize the expression to be cast. Had we failed to do so, as in

```
        (int) x + 0.5;
```

the result would have been **12.5** instead.

Another typical use of a cast is in forcing division to return a real number when both operands are **int**s. Figure 3.9 is a program to average a series of integers (assuming that there are less than **INT_MAX** of them). Here is some sample input and output for the program (we hit the EOF character after entering five values):

use ^D to terminate ⇒ EOF

97 76 85 91 98
Average of 5 values is 89.400000.

This program accumulates a total in an integer variable **sum**, and a count of the number of values read in the integer **n**. We compute the average with:

```
avg = (double) sum / n;
```

Casting **sum** to a **double** causes the division to be carried out as floating point division. Without the cast, integer division is performed, since both **sum** and **n** are integers.

Our final uses of the cast are for a different purpose. We mentioned before that it's a bad idea to convert a longer type to a shorter type. But sometimes we know it's a safe conversion. Assuming that **i** and **j** are **int**s and **l** is a **long**,

```
i = l % j;
```

is safe. That's because $0 \le i \le j - 1$, which fits safely in an **int**. The problem here is that many compilers would give a warning; after all, we are assigning a **long** result to an **int**. But we know it's safe, and we can tell the compiler and the program's reader we know that by casting the resulting **long** to an **int**.

```
i = (int) (l % j);
```

Doing this cast turns off any compiler warnings about unsafe conversions.

Another similar situation occurs when we want to ignore a function's return value. In many of our earlier programs, for example, we didn't do anything with **scanf**'s return value.

```
scanf("%lf", &radius);
```

It's better style to cast **scanf**'s return value to **void**. Some compilers will give a warning here, fearing that we're accidentally throwing away a useful value. To turn off those warnings, we can cast the function's return value to **void**.

cast to void

```
(void) scanf("%lf", &radius);
```

A cast to **void** simply states that we know we're ignoring the value returned by the function and not simply overlooking it by mistake.

3.6   CASE STUDY—A BASE CONVERSION PROGRAM

This section is optional!

We conclude this chapter with a program that converts an input value from base 10 to a user-selectable base between 2 and 10. The program repeatedly reads value/base pairs from the user, converts the value into that base, and prints the result. Like many of our earlier programs, it stops when it encounters an error in the input or the end of file. Figure 3.10 contains the main program, and Figure 3.11 contains the function it uses to convert and display the value. Here is some sample input and output, in which we gave the program the value 175 and determined its value in each of the bases 2 through 9:

```
175 2
175 in base 10 is 10101111 in base 2
175 3
175 in base 10 is 20111 in base 3
175 4
175 in base 10 is 2233 in base 4
175 5
175 in base 10 is 1200 in base 5
175 6
175 in base 10 is 451 in base 6
175 7
175 in base 10 is 340 in base 7
175 8
175 in base 10 is 257 in base 8
175 9
175 in base 10 is 214 in base 9
```

How do we convert a base 10 value v to a value in another base b? We work left to right, producing the most significant digit in b first and the least significant digit last. As a result, the overall algorithm is a bit unnatural:

1. Set k to the number of digits the result will have.

2. While $k \geq 0$,

    (a) Display $v/(b^{k-1})$ (this is the most significant remaining digit).

    (b) Set v to $v\%(b^{k-1})$ (this is the remaining part of the base 10 value to display).

    (c) Subtract 1 from k (this is the number of digits in the result we still have to display).

To see how this algorithm works, consider converting 175 to its value in octal (base 8). The most significant digit in the result is $175/(8^2)$, which is $175/64$ or 2. The remaining value to display is $175\%64$ or 47. Now we repeat the cycle and compute the next most significant digit as $47/(8^1)$, which is $47/8$ or 5. The remaining value to display is $47\%8$ or 7. So the least significant digit in the result is $7/(8^0)$, or 7, and we're finished. Our final result is 257_8. We can test this result by calculating $2 \times 8^2 + 5 \times 8^1 + 7 \times 8^0$, which is 175, as it should be.

There are actually several problems with directly implementing this algorithm. One is that it assumes we magically know how many digits are in the result. It turns out there's a simple formula we can use: the number of digits needed to display a positive value v in base b is $\lfloor \log_b v \rfloor + 1$. The math library provides the **floor** function, but doesn't provide any function to compute $\log_b v$. Fortunately, however, the math library does provide the function **log10**, and $\log_b v$ is equivalent to $\log_{10} v / \log_{10} b$.

Another problem is that it's inefficient: we have to compute an exponent (a power of b) each time through the loop. Fortunately, we can solve this problem by calculating b^{k-1} before we enter the loop and storing it in a variable **divisor**. Then instead of using k to index the loop, we can just use **divisor**, dividing it by the base each time and stopping once it reaches 0.

```c
/*
 * Convert base 10 values into values in a specified base between 2
 * and 10.  If the base is invalid, the program uses a default base.
 */
#include <stdio.h>

#define MINBASE   2                     /* smallest destination base */
#define MAXBASE   10                    /* largest destination base */

int main()
{
  void display_value_in_base(long value, int base);
  long value;                           /* next input value */
  int  newbase;                         /* base to convert it to */
  int  n;                               /* number of values read in */
  int  status;                          /* did program succeed? */

  while ((n = scanf("%li %i", &value, &newbase)) == 2)
  {
    if (value < 0)
    {
      printf("Error: %li is negative (ignoring -).\n", value);
      value = -value;
    }
    if (newbase < MINBASE)
    {
      printf("Error: %i invalid base (using %i).\n", newbase, MINBASE);
      newbase = MINBASE;
    }
    if (newbase > MAXBASE)
    {
      printf("Error: %i invalid base (using %i).\n", newbase, MAXBASE);
      newbase = MAXBASE;
    }
    printf("%li in base 10 is ", value);
    display_value_in_base(value, newbase);
    printf(" in base %i\n", newbase);
  }

  if (n != EOF)
  {
    printf("Error: Expected pair of integer values.\n");
    status = 1;
  }
  else
    status = 0;
  return status;
}
```

Figure 3.10   (convert.c)   A program to convert from base 10 to other bases.

```
/*
 * Display a value in a specified base between 2 and 10.
 */
#include <stdio.h>
#include <math.h>

void display_value_in_base(long v, int b)
{
  int  k;                               /* digits needed in result */
  long divisor;                         /* initially b^(# of digits - 1) */

  if (v == 0)                           /* zero is the same in any base */
    printf("0");
  else
  {
    k = floor(log10(v)/log10(b)) + 1;
    divisor = pow(b, k - 1);            /* first divisor is b^(k - 1) */

    /* Run through value, calculating and displaying the value of each
       of the digits in the new base (left to right */

    while (divisor >= 1)
    {
      printf("%i", v / divisor);
      v = v % divisor;
      divisor = divisor / b;
    }
  }
}
```

Figure 3.11   (convfunc.c)   A function to print a base 10 value in another base.

SUMMARY

- C provides several different types of whole numbers: **int**s, **short**s, and **long**s, in both **signed** and **unsigned** variations. We use **short**s to save space, **int**s to save time, and **long**s to prevent portability problems.

- C allows several different types of integer constants: decimal (begins with a digit other than zero), octal (begins with a 0), and hex (begins with 0x), **long** (trailed by **l** or **L**) and **unsigned** (trailed by **u** or **U**).

- C provides several different types of real numbers: **float**s, **double**s, and **long double**s. We use **float**s to save space, **double**s to maximize precision, and **long double**s to take advantage of the extra range and precision provided by some machines.

- C provides only the arithmetic operators **+**, **−**, *****, **/**, and **%**. Operators common to other languages are often found as functions in the math library.

- C performs automatic conversions whenever we mix types in arithmetic expressions, assignments, or function calls (when we've provided a prototype).

- We can use the cast operator (a type surrounded by parentheses) to request specific conversions.

EXERCISES

3–1 Modify the **round** function in Figure 3.8 to work correctly for negative numbers.

3–2 The program to average a collection of values (Figure 3.9) produces incorrect results if the number of values is greater than **INT_MAX**, if any input value is greater than **INT_MAX**, or if the sum is greater than **LONG_MAX**. Rewrite the program to avoid these problems. *change int → long int.*

3–3 Modify the programs that compute exponents (Figures 3.5 and 3.6) to print a prompt before reading each input value. Then modify the program to compute averages (Figure 3.9) to print a single prompt before reading any input values.

3–4 Modify the program using the **power** function (Figure 3.5) to display powers in bases other base 10. That is, the program should prompt for a base and then print the powers it computes in that base.

3–5 Use the routines in our base converter (Figures 3.10 and 3.11) to write a program that reads a pair of values and prints a table of all the values between them in bases 2 through 10.

3–6 Rewrite any of Chapter 2's interest computing programs to use the interest computing formula

$$balance\ at\ end\ of\ period =$$
$$balance\ at\ start\ of\ period \times (1.0 + monthly\ interest\ rate)^{months}$$

This formula assumes that the interest is compounded monthly, rather than annually as we did our earlier programs.

3–7 Write a program that reads in a integral value and prints all powers from 1 until n, where n is the last power that can be computed without causing overflow.

3–8 Write a program to print the ranges of each of C's numeric data types.

3–9 Write a program to determine whether a particular year is a leap year. Assume that a year is a leap year if it's divisible evenly by 4 or 400, but not by 100.

3–10 Write a program to read two points and print out the distance between them. Given two points $(x1, y1)$ and $(x2, y2)$, the distance between them is

$$\sqrt{(x1 - x2)^2 + (y1 - y2)^2}$$

3–11 Write a program to read Fahrenheit temperatures and print them in Celsius. The formula is $°C = (5/9)(°F - 32)$.

3–12 Write a program to read Celsius temperatures and print them in Fahrenheit.

3–13 The math library **sin**, **cos**, and **tan** functions expect their argument to be an angle in radians. Write a program to read an angle in degrees and print its **sin**, **cos**, and **tan**. Convert from degrees to radians by multiplying by $\pi/180$.

3–14 Write a program to read the coefficients a, b and c of a quadratic equation and print its roots: the values of x such that $ax^2 + bx + c = 0$. The roots are given by

$$\frac{-b \pm \sqrt{b^2 - 4ac}}{2a}$$

3–15 Write a program to print a table of logs. Its input is a range of values and an increment. Its output is $\log_e x$ and $\log_{10} x$ for each x in the specified range.

4 CHARACTERS

This chapter discusses characters, the one basic data type we've so far ignored. As with integers and reals, we study how to create character constants and define character variables, and we examine the range of values they can hold and present several different ways to read and print them. As part of this discussion, we introduce C's library functions for efficient character-at-a-time input and output and for testing whether a character falls into a particular class, such as uppercase or lowercase. Along the way, we'll also study what happens when we convert back and forth between characters and integers and discover that characters are little more than a special type of integer. The chapter concludes by extending the previous chapter's base conversion program to handle conversions from any base to any other base.

4.1 REPRESENTING AND STORING CHARACTERS

We usually think of characters as letters of the alphabet, but they encompass more than that. There are characters for digits and punctuation, as well as for special actions such as ringing a *bell* or causing a *form feed*.

Internally, every character is represented by a small integer. What characters are available and how they are represented internally depends on the machine on which the program runs. The most common character sets are ASCII (American Standard Code for Information Interchange) and EBCDIC (Extended Binary Coded Decimal Interchange Code). ASCII is the character set used on most personal, micro, and minicomputers, as well as several large mainframes, while EBCDIC is used on large IBM mainframes. There are 128 ASCII and 256 EBCDIC characters. That means ASCII characters are 7 bits (values between 0 to 127) but are usually put into an 8-bit byte, whereas EBCDIC requires the full 8 bits (values between 0 and 255). Appendix E describes both of these character sets.

We obtain character variables by declaring them to be of type **char**:

```
char c;
```

The **char** type corresponds to a single byte and can hold the representation for a single character, stored internally as an 8-bit integer (on most machines). In fact, as we'll see shortly, **char**s are just a special case of C's integral data types.

CODE	CHARACTER	ASCII HEX VALUE
\0	null character	0
\a	audible alert	0x07
\b	backspace	0x08
\f	form feed	0x0C
\n	newline	0x0A
\r	carriage return	0x0D
\t	horizontal tab	0x09
\v	vertical tab	0x0B
\'	single quote	0x27
\"	double quote	0x22
\\	backslash	0x5C
\?	question mark	0x3F
\ddd	up to 3-digit octal value	
\xddd	up to 3-digit hexadecimal value	

Table 4.1 Characters available using backslash escape sequences.

Character Constants

Just as we can have numeric constants, we can have character constants. We create one by placing a character between quotation marks, as in `'A'`, `'z'`, `'7'`, or `'?'`. Character constants are stored as their value in the machine's character set.

Some characters aren't printable, or perform special actions when they're displayed. We represent these characters with *escape sequences*, a backslash (\) followed by a special character, an octal number, or a hex number. Table 4.1 provides a complete list of these escape sequences.

Without knowing it, we've already been using one of them: `\n` to obtain a newline. As another example, we can produce a bell by writing a `\a`.

```
printf("Wake up!\a\n");
```

Why are there the `\'`, `\"`, and `\?` escape sequences? We use `\'` when we want to have a single quote as a character constant, as in `'\''`. We use `\"` when we want to have a double quote inside a quoted string of characters, as in **printf**'s formatting control string.

```
printf("How do like \"The Joy of C\" so far\?\n");
```

The need for `\?` is more difficult to explain. In many places, such as large parts of Europe, their character sets don't include some special punctuation characters, such as the curly braces (`{` and `}`), square brackets (`[` and `]`), and a few others. C programs can be written with these deficient character sets using the *trigraphs* listed in Table 4.2. A *trigraph* is a three-character sequence beginning with a pair of question marks that stands for a particular character. Whenever the preprocessor encounters a trigraph, it

TRIGRAPH	CHARACTER
??=	=
??/	\
??'	^
??{	[
??}	]
??!	|
??<	{
??>	}
??-	~

Table 4.2   Trigraphs and the characters they represent.

substitutes that character. So to prevent pairs of question marks being accidentally interpreted as the beginning of a trigraph, we make use of **\?**.

The last two codes in Table 4.1—the *****ddd* and **\x***ddd*—don't look like characters at all, but exist because we need a flexible mechanism to specify all available characters, including ones that don't print. Following a backslash by one to three octal digits (0 through 7) specifies a single character based on its octal representation. So, on ASCII machines, we can also ring a bell by writing a **\007**.

A backslash followed by an **x** or **X**, followed by one to three hexadecimal digits (**0** through **9**, **A** through **F**, **a** through **f**), specifies a single character based on its hexadecimal representation. We can make our code more obscure by writing **\x3F** instead of **\?**, though we probably wouldn't want to do so.

```
printf("Huh\x3F\n");
```

Formatted Reading and Writing of Characters

We can read a value into a character with **scanf** using the **%c** formatting code:

```
scanf("%c", &c);
```

Unlike other formatting codes, **%c** doesn't cause **scanf** to ignore leading white-space. If the next character in the input is a blank, tab, or newline, that's what we read. We can write a character with **printf** in a similar way:

```
printf("%c", c);
```

Figure 4.1 puts everything together in a little program that prints several bells to obtain the user's attention, asks a question, and then prints the response.

```
/*
 * Example program using the various character codes.
 */
#include <stdio.h>

#define MAXBEEP 10

int main()
{
  int  i;                              /* index to write beeps */
  char c;                              /* character we read */

  for (i = 0; i < MAXBEEP; i = i + 1)  /* lots of beeps */
    printf("Wake up!\a\n");
  printf("Are you awake yet\?\?\? ");  /* query user */
  if (scanf("%c", &c) == 1)            /* obtain response */
  {
    printf("You responded with a '%c'\n", c);
    if (c == 'y')
      printf("We're glad you're awake!\n");
    else
      printf("Well, we tried!\n");
  }
  else                                 /* couldn't read character */
    printf("Huh\x3F\n");
  return 0;
}
```

or i++

Figure 4.1 (wakeup.c) An example program using the various character codes.

4.2   CHARACTERS VERSUS INTEGERS

Because characters are stored in an integer representation, we're allowed to treat them as small integers. In fact, **char**s *are* simply 1-byte integers, and C automatically converts back and forth between **char**s and **int**s whenever it's necessary, as in assignments, arithmetic expressions, or comparisons. Unlike languages such as Pascal, we don't need built-in functions to explicitly convert between characters and integers.

> *Automatic conversions between characters and integers are safe only with legal integer representations in the machine's character set.*

To illustrate a safe conversion, let's consider a common problem: converting an uppercase character into lowercase. Suppose we have a **char** variable **lower** that contains a character between **'a'** and **'z'**, and we want to assign its corresponding uppercase character to another **char** variable **upper**. That is, if **lower** is **'q'**, we want to assign `'Q'` to **upper**. Here's how we do it, assuming that we're using the ASCII character set.

```
upper = (lower - 'a') + 'A'
```

Convert between upper & lower case character

This assignment seems strange—are we doing arithmetic with characters? Actually, we're not. C converts all **char**s to **int**s and then operates on these **int**s. After the calculations it converts the resulting **int** to a **char** and assigns it to **upper**.

The expression converts from lowercase to uppercase by computing the difference between the ASCII code for the lowercase character in **lower** and the ASCII code for `'a'`. This difference will be 0 for `'a'`, 1 for `'b'`, 2 for `'c'`, and so on. We then add this difference to the code for `'A'`, which gives us the code for the corresponding uppercase character. Of course, this technique assumes that the lowercase and uppercase letters are contiguous, which is true of ASCII, but not of EBCDIC. We'll see a more portable way to do this conversion in a little while.

These automatic conversions also allow us to print **char**s as integers, and vice versa. When we write a **char** as an **int**, we see its character set representation. And when we write an **int** as a **char**, we see the character with that integer representation. So assuming that **c** is a **char**,

```
printf("%4i\t%4o\t%c\n", c, c, c);
```

displays **c**'s internal representation in both decimal and octal and then displays the character **c** contains.

Signed versus Unsigned Characters

The integral types—**short**, **int**, and **long**—are **signed** by default. But what about **char**s—are they **signed** or **unsigned**? That is, what values do **char**s store? -128 to 127? Or 0 to 255?

> *Whether* **char** *is* **signed** *or* **unsigned** *is implementation-defined.*

The only thing we're guaranteed is that a legitimate character in the machine's character is always treated as nonnegative. EBCDIC uses all 8 bits to represent characters, so with it we're guaranteed to have **unsigned char**s. ASCII requires only 7 bits, however, so some implementations may have **char** default to **signed char**, and others to **unsigned char**. As with integers, we can precede **char** with **signed** or **unsigned** to explicitly request a particular type. Table 4.3 lists the constants in limits.h that we can use to determine the range of the various types on our machines.

Why do we care whether **char**s are **signed** or **unsigned**? Most of the time we don't. It really matters only when we're on ASCII machines and put a value into a **char** that's outside the legal character set (less than 0 or greater than 127). The program in Figure 4.2 illustrates this distinction. It runs through all the ASCII characters and prints their decimal, octal, and character values. But be careful if you run it, as some of the nonprinting characters do strange things such as erasing the screen or causing a form feed. We've tried to mediate these effects by placing each character on a separate line.

CONSTANT	VALUE	DESCRIPTION
CHAR_BIT	8	maximum number of bits in a byte
CHAR_MAX	127	maximum value of a **char**
CHAR_MIN	0	minimum value of a **char**
SCHAR_MAX	+127	maximum value of a **signed char**
SCHAR_MIN	−127	minimum value of a **signed char**
UCHAR_MAX	255	maximum value of an **unsigned char**

Table 4.3 Constants for ranges of character types (found in the header file limits.h). The specific values on your machine are required to be greater than or equal to these in magnitude.

Even so, you might consider running this program with its output redirected into a file and then examining it with a text editor.

Figure 4.2 uses a variable **c** to run through the character set. We initially set it to 0 and keep incrementing it until we've printed all the characters. We know the loop is complete when **c** is one greater than the last ASCII character (128). What type should **c** have? One possibility is **char**, but then we're in trouble if **char** defaults to **signed**. That's because the largest **signed char** is 127, and we would have an overflow, which would cause **c** to become negative. But we're safe with **c** as an **unsigned char**.

Of course, we could have eliminated worrying about this whole problem simply by declaring **c** as an **int**. In fact, we need to make that change to process EBCDIC with our program, since there are 256 EBCDIC characters, and 257 doesn't fit into an **unsigned char**. We've really just used **unsigned char** here to make a point, not because it's the best way to do things. In fact, C's automatic conversions and I/O functions that return integers make **char** variables less useful than one might think, and we ordinarily use them only with arrays of characters, a topic covered in later chapters.

Extended Character Sets

Some implementations have extended character sets that don't fit into a single byte. One use for these character sets is Asian languages, which often have an enormous number of different characters. C provides an additional character type, **wchar_t** (*wide character type*), for characters in these extended character sets. **wchar_t** is a synonym for an implementation-dependent integral type. To use it, we need to include a new standard header file, stddef.h, that provides definitions for several useful data types. We can use **wchar_t** just as we use **char**, with one exception: we write constants with a preceding **L**. So **L'q'** is a constant of type **wchar_t**. Most of us, however, will be able to get by quite comfortably without ever using **wchar_t**.

```
/*
 * Print character set in decimal, octal, and character (ASCII only).
 */
#include <stdio.h>
#include <limits.h>

int main()
{
  unsigned char c;

  for (c = 0; c <= SCHAR_MAX; c = c + 1)
    printf("%4i\t%4o\t%c\n", c, c, c);
  return 0;
}
```

from lib = 127

Figure 4.2 (charset.c) A program to print the local character set.

4.3   CHARACTER INPUT AND OUTPUT

Just as there are prewritten routines for formatted input and output of numerical and string data, there are predefined functions for character input and output. The two character-equivalent functions of **scanf** and **printf** are **getchar** and **putchar**, respectively.

scanf ⇒ getchar
printf ⇒ putchar
one character at a time.

getchar reads the next character in the standard input. It takes no arguments and returns the character's integer representation. Like **scanf**, **getchar** returns **EOF** if it encounters the end-of-file character. As we saw earlier, **EOF** is usually −1, a value that does not represent a legal character. That's why **getchar** returns an **int** rather than a **char**: it must be able to return any normal character, plus **EOF**, which must be a value outside the machine's character set. Because **getchar** returns an **int**, we usually store its return value into an **int** variable, rather than a **char**.

*getchar returns
in integer.*

putchar is a similar function for writing a character. It takes the integer representation for a character in the machine's character set and writes it as a character to the standard output. We get machine-dependent results if the number does not represent a legal character, although most machines simply use its least significant bits (equivalent to the local character representation). **putchar** returns the character it wrote, or **EOF** if for some reason it fails.

Figure 4.3 uses **getchar** and **putchar** in a program to copy its input to its output. Figure 4.4 shows sample input and output for the program. At first glance, this program seems utterly useless. But Appendix B shows how with input and output redirection we can use it to display and copy files.

The program simply reads characters with **getchar** and writes them with **putchar**, stopping when **getchar** returns **EOF**. We include stdio.h because it contains the definitions of **getchar**, **putchar**, and **EOF**. Because **getchar** can return either a legitimate character or **EOF**, we declare the variable **c**, which holds the character we're

```
/*
 * Copy the input to the output.
 */
#include <stdio.h>

int main()
{
  int c;                                    /* next character */

  while ((c = getchar()) != EOF)
    putchar(c);
  return 0;
}
```

(handwritten annotations: return integer · read one character at a time store in buffer until we hit *)*

Figure 4.3 (display.c) A program to copy its standard input to its standard output.

```
Don't you just love
Don't you just love
programming in C?
programming in C?
We thought so!
We thought so!
```

Figure 4.4 Sample input and output for character-copying program. The output is written only when an entire input line has been read.

reading or writing, as an **int**. The loop test is especially compact because we take advantage of the assignment operator's ability to return the value it assigned:

```
while ((c = getchar()) != EOF)
```

This reads a character, stores it into **c**, and then compares it with **EOF** to determine whether to go through the loop.

Look carefully at the output in Figure 4.4. Do you notice something strange? You should: The input characters aren't printed until after an entire line has been read. How can this be when we're reading a character at a time? Shouldn't each character be printed right after it is input?

The reason for this behavior is that standard I/O library functions such as **getchar** and **scanf** *buffer* their input. In other words, when we read from the keyboard, the operating system collects characters in a special location until we type a carriage return or hit the enter key. It does something similar when we read from a file, except that it reads a larger chunk of characters each time. All **getchar** does is return the next character in the buffer. This buffering is also done when we do output to a file. When we write to a file, the operating system collects characters and writes them to the file

(handwritten: input buffer / read full line until encounter)

```
/*
 * Copy input to output, giving each line a number.
 */
#include <stdio.h>

int main()
{
  int  c;                           /* current and */
  int  lastch;                      /*   previous characters */
  long lineno;                      /* lines printed so far */

  lineno = 0;
  lastch = '\n';
  while ((c = getchar()) != EOF)
  {
    if (lastch == '\n')
    {                               /* hit end of line */
      lineno = lineno + 1;
      printf("%8li ", lineno);
    }
    putchar(c);
    lastch = c;
  }
  return 0;
}
```

Figure 4.5   (lineno.c) A program to line number its input.

in large groups. And when we write to the standard output, our output is usually only written when the buffer is full (normal buffering), when we write a newline, or when we request input. Buffering allows us to use backspace to edit our input and makes input and output more efficient.[1]

We can extend our character-copying program to perform more complex input transformations. The program in Figure 4.5 prints each input line preceded with a line number. Like Figure 4.3, this program reads one character at a time until it reaches the end of the input, writing each character onto its output. But this program also remembers the last character read. Whenever it is about to print a character, it first checks whether the preceding character it wrote was a newline (**\n**). If it is, it means that it's at the beginning of a new line, and so it prints the line number before writing the next character. Figure 4.6 shows the output of running the line numbering program on itself.

Because **getchar** buffers its input, it isn't well suited for interactive programs such as editors or menu-driven interfaces. These programs need to read a character as soon as the user types it—without waiting for a carriage return. An interactive screen editor shouldn't make the user type a carriage return after entering an editor command.

---

[1]There are no unbuffered I/O operations in the standard I/O library. That doesn't mean you can't do real character at a time I/O, you just have to do it using operating-system specific routines, not standard portable ones.

```
 1 /*
 2  * Copy input to output, giving each line a number.
 3  */
 4 #include <stdio.h>
 5
 6 int main()
 7 {
 8   int  c;                              /* current and */
 9   int  lastch;                         /*    previous characters */
10   long lineno;                         /* lines printed so far */
11
12   lineno = 0;
13   lastch = '\n';
14   while ((c = getchar()) != EOF)
15   {
16     if (lastch == '\n')
17     {                                  /* hit end of line */
18       lineno = lineno + 1;
19       printf("%8li ", lineno);
20     }
21     putchar(c);
22     lastch = c;
23   }
24   return 0;
25 }
```

Figure 4.6   The output of running the line numbering program on itself.

Similarly, an interactive data base interface shouldn't force the user to enter a carriage return after making a menu selection. In fact, we usually don't want buffering whenever we read input from the keyboard or write output to the display.

Unfortunately, obtaining unbuffered input is often a chore, as there's no standard library function that does this for us. That's because turning the buffering on and off generally involves complicated interactions between C and the operating system.[2]

Fortunately, many implementations of C provide special functions for reading characters immediately that hide all the nasty interactions with the operating system. These functions, however, aren't portable and they're not part of standard C. However, because they're so useful, we'll see how to use them in a later chapter on portability.

---

[2]On UNIX systems, for example, it takes at least two complex system calls to set things up so that we can access characters as soon as they're typed. In fact, in Chapter 20's discussion on portability we show how to obtain unbuffered input and output on both UNIX and MS-DOS systems. That discussion also shows how to manage unbuffered input and output in a portable way.

< ctype.h >

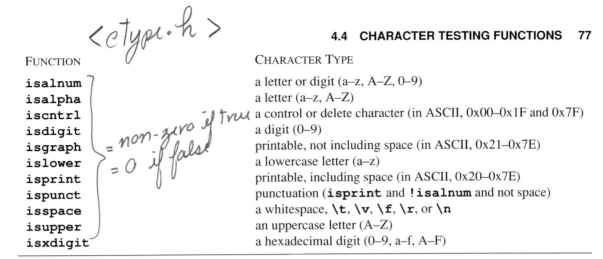

FUNCTION	CHARACTER TYPE
isalnum	a letter or digit (a–z, A–Z, 0–9)
isalpha	a letter (a–z, A–Z)
iscntrl	a control or delete character (in ASCII, 0x00–0x1F and 0x7F)
isdigit	a digit (0–9)
isgraph	printable, not including space (in ASCII, 0x21–0x7E)
islower	a lowercase letter (a–z)
isprint	printable, including space (in ASCII, 0x20–0x7E)
ispunct	punctuation (**isprint** and **!isalnum** and not space)
isspace	a whitespace, **\t**, **\v**, **\f**, **\r**, or **\n**
isupper	an uppercase letter (A–Z)
isxdigit	a hexadecimal digit (0–9, a–f, A–F)

= non-zero if true
= 0 if false

Table 4.4   The character testing functions defined in ctype.h.

Check character type.

4.4   CHARACTER TESTING FUNCTIONS

When we read a character, we often need to know what type of character we have. Is it an uppercase letter—or lowercase? A digit? Is it printable—or is it a control character? And so on.

One way to find out this information is to check whether the character falls within a particular range of characters. We could determine whether **c** is a lowercase letter by checking whether both **c >= 'a'** and **c <= 'z'** are true. But this method works only when the lowercase letters are contiguous within the local character set. Unfortunately, while this is true of ASCII, it is not true of EBCDIC. If we want our program to work regardless of the underlying character set, we need another method. Fortunately, C provides a set of functions that we can use to perform these comparisons. Table 4.4 lists these functions. To use them, we include another system-supplied header file, ctype.h.

Each of these functions takes an **int**, which must be a valid character in the character set or **EOF**, and returns a nonzero value if it falls into the given class and false (zero) if it doesn't. For example, we can use **islower** to portably determine whether a character is lowercase:

testing fn
returns
- nonzero ⇒ true
- 0 ⇒ false

        islower(c) != 0   *determines whether a character is lowercase*

And we can verify that a character is not an uppercase letter in a similar way.

        isupper(c) == 0   *determines whether a character is not an uppercase*

In Figure 4.7, we use one of these functions in a program that writes its input onto its output, one word per line. A word is defined as a group of letters. The input

        this is 1 short line!

```
/*
 * Break input into words (groups of letters).
 */
#include <stdio.h>
#include <ctype.h>

#define YES   1
#define NO    0

int main()
{
  int c;                        /* next input character */
  int word;                     /* flag: are we dealing with a word? */

  word = NO;
  while ((c = getchar()) != EOF)
    if (isalpha(c) != 0)
      {                         /* it's a letter */
        putchar(c);             /* write it and note we're in word */
        word = YES;
      }
    else                        /* it's not a letter */
      if (word == YES)          /* write a newline if we were in word */
      {
        putchar('\n');
        word = NO;
      }
  return 0;
}
```

Figure 4.7   (brkwd.c)   A program to print its input onto its output, one word per line.

produces the output

```
this
is
short
line
```

This program is yet another extension to our earlier character-copier. It reads its input one character at a time, writes any character that is part of a word, and writes a newline when it reaches the end of a word. To test whether a character is part of a word, we use **isalpha**.

There are two other useful routines available in the character-type library, **tolower** and **toupper**. Both take a character and return a character. **tolower** converts an uppercase character to its lower case equivalent. If the character isn't uppercase, **tolower** simply returns it. **toupper** is similar, except it converts a lowercase character to uppercase.

The program in Figure 4.8 uses **tolower** in a function called **yesorno** that

```
/*
 * Print a prompt and then get a yes or no answer using "yesorno".
 */
#include <stdio.h>
#include <ctype.h>

#define YES 1
#define NO  0

int main()
{
  int yesorno(void);

  printf("Enter a YES or NO answer: ");
  if (yesorno() == YES)
    printf("That was a YES!\n");
  else
    printf("That was a NO!\n");
  return 0;
}
```

[handwritten annotation: use only once in main if compile together with fn.]

```
int yesorno(void)
{
  int c;                              /* holds input character */
  int answer;                         /* holds YES or NO answer */

  c = getchar();
  if (tolower(c) == 'y')
    answer = YES;                     /* YES for 'Y' or 'y' */
  else
    answer = NO;                      /* NO for anything else */
  if (c != EOF)
    while (c != '\n')                 /* skip other characters on line */
      c = getchar();
  return answer;
}
```

[handwritten annotation: fn]

[handwritten annotation: if c = y, it return y c = Y, it returns y]

[handwritten annotation: keep reading until \n]

Figure 4.8 (yesorno.c) A function to get a yes or no answer from the user and a program that uses it.

gets a "yes" or "no" response from its user. A "yes" is any response beginning with an uppercase or lowercase '**y**'; anything else is a "no" (including the end-of-file character). We take the user's input character, and if it's a letter, we map into lowercase to make the test a little simpler. We then skip the remaining characters on the input line. We do this because the input is buffered, so the user has to enter a newline character before we see any of the input. That means there's a newline waiting to be read, so we read it, along with any extra characters that might precede it.[3]

---

[3]This program subtly assumes that all input lines end with a newline, and not with an end-of-file character. That's a safe bet when the input comes from the terminal, but dangerous

4.5   CONVERTING CHARACTERS INTO NUMBERS

We often want to read characters and convert them into integers. Our first thought is to use **scanf**—but unfortunately it handles input errors poorly. An alternative is to read characters one at a time and to convert them into a single integer ourselves. This type of input scanning is important in many different programming problems; the efficiency we gain by writing our own scanners, plus the better error control, is well worth the effort.

Figure 4.9 contains a program to read a single digit from the user and then print its value. Here's some sample input and output:

```
Select an entry: 8
Enter a value between 0 and 5: what?
Enter a value between 0 and 5: 4
You chose 4!
```

This program uses the function **get_base10_dig**, a variant of **yesorno** that obtains a single digit from the user and returns its numeric value. **get_base10_dig** takes a single parameter, the largest acceptable input value. So the call

```
get_base10_dig(5)
```

indicates that the user must enter a digit between 0 and 5. If we've displayed a menu with several entries, **get_base10_dig** is a convenient way to obtain the user's choice.

Figure 4.10 contains **get_base10_dig**. It uses a new function, **get_first**, to read an input line and return its first character, and **isdigit** to verify that it is indeed a digit. As you might expect, **get_first** works by using **getchar** to read the individual characters, skipping over extra input characters until it hits the line-ending newline (as did **yesorno**).

get_base10_dig then converts the character to its integer equivalent and verifies that the resulting value is acceptable. If it isn't, **get_base10_dig** writes an error message and repeats the process until it gets one of the desired digits. If for some reason the user enters the end-of-file character, **get_base10_dig** returns **EOF**.

To perform the conversion, we need not know the character's internal representation. We use a similar technique to the one we used earlier to convert from a lowercase character to an uppercase one. To convert a digit character to an integer, we simply subtract the character **' 0 '** from it.

```
value = c - '0'
```
zero

(This assumes that all digits are represented by contiguous codes, which is the case with both ASCII and EBCDIC.) For example, in ASCII, the code for **' 7 '** is 55 and the code for **' 0 '** is 48; the subtraction yields the integer value 7.

Examine **get_base10_dig** closely and you'll see that it does something new: it has a pair of **return** statements, rather than just one. The first exits the **while** loop—and the function—if it successfully converted a digit's value. The other is at the function's end and returns **EOF** if the user enters the end of file. C allows us to have as

---

if it's been redirected to come from a file. We'll see how to fix that problem in later chapters, but the remaining programs in this chapter share this minor flaw.

```
/*
 * Program illustrating converting a character to a number.
 */
#include <stdio.h>

#define MAX_DIGIT    5          /* largest possible input value */

int main()
{
  int get_base10_dig(int max);
  int digvalue;                 /* value of user-entered digit */

  printf("Select an entry: ");
  if ((digvalue = get_base10_dig(MAX_DIGIT)) != EOF)
    printf("You chose %i!\n", digvalue);
  return 0;
}
```

Figure 4.9   (getdigmn.c) A program to read a digit from the user and print its value.

have as many return statements as one wants.

many **return** statements as we want in a function, although we usually avoid taking advantage of this feature. That's because multiple **return**s tend to make a function hard to read, since we're then forced to figure out which circumstances caused which exit. Here, however, we've made an exception, since there are really two completely different circumstances when we want to leave the function: we've found a value, or we know we'll never find a value.

get_base10_dig is useful, but it's not general—it handles only single-digit numbers. Figure 4.11 contains **get_base10_num**, which extends it to read and convert a *sequence* of characters. The function uses **getchar** to read characters, and **isdigit** to determine whether the character is a digit. As each character is read, it's checked to determine whether it's a digit. If it is, **get_base10_num** updates a sum representing the value of the sequence by multiplying the current sum by 10 and then adding the digit the new character represents:

```
sum = 10 * sum + (c - '0');
```

It may not be immediately clear why this conversion works. The basic idea is that the value of an n-digit number is the value of the first $n - 1$ digits times 10, plus the value of the nth digit. So 34 is 3 (the value of its first digit) times 10, plus 4 (the value of its second digit). And 345 is 34 (the value of its first two digits) times 10, plus 5 (the value of its third digit). Since we're reading numbers one digit at a time, each time we encounter a new digit we must multiply the current value by 10 and add the new digit.

How does **get_base10_num** know when to stop converting? The trick is that it stops as soon as it hits a character that's not a digit. It then checks whether that character is a newline and, if it is, returns the value of the sequence. Otherwise, it skips over the rest of the line and returns −1 to indicate an error.

```
/*
 * Functions to read a character and convert it to a number.
 *   get_base10_dig - get a digit between 0 and "max" from user.
 *   get_first - read an input line, returning its first character.
 */
#include <stdio.h>
#include <ctype.h>

int get_base10_dig(int max)
{
  int get_first(void);
  int c;                        /* character that might be a digit */
  int value;                    /* value of character as number */

  while ((c = get_first()) != EOF)              return values
  {
    if (isdigit(c) != 0)
      if ((value = c - '0') <= max)
        return value;           /* return value of character */
    printf("Enter a value between 0 and %i: ", max);
  }
  return c;    —    return EOF
}                                 fn

int get_first(void)
{
  int first;                    /* first character on line */
  int junk;                     /* holds other characters */

  if ((first = getchar()) != EOF)
  {
    junk = first;               /* skip remaining characters */
    while (junk != '\n')
      junk = getchar();
  }
  return first;
}
```

Figure 4.10   (getdig.c)   Read a digit from the user and compute its integer value.

Reading numerical data one character at a time and doing our own conversions may seem wasteful when we already have **scanf**, but it isn't. **scanf** has several problems: it compiles into a large amount of runnable code, and it is often slower than using our own conversions. More importantly, **scanf** makes error handling difficult by telling us only how many values it correctly converted, and providing no information about why a failure might have occurred. To provide suitable error messages or error recovery when a failure occurs, we still have to deal with the input one character at a time.

```c
/*
 * Read a line's worth of characters and convert them into a number,
 * one character at a time.  It only works for positive numbers.  It's
 * an error if the line contains anything other than digits.
 */
#include <stdio.h>
#include <ctype.h>

int main()
{
  long get_base10_num(void);
  long val;                             /* input value read */

  printf("Enter a number: ");
  if ((val = get_base10_num()) == -1)
    printf("You didn't enter a number.\n");
  else
    printf("You entered %li\n", val);
  return 0;
}

long get_base10_num(void)
{
  int  c;                               /* next input character */
  long sum;                             /* running total */

  if ((c = getchar()) == EOF)           /* EOF is error */
    sum = -1;
  else
  {
    if (isdigit(c) == 0)                /* not digit, so its an error */
      sum = -1;
    else
    {                                   /* in number, convert it */
      sum = 0;
      while (isdigit(c) != 0)
      {
        sum = 10L * sum + (c - '0');    /* convert value */
        c = getchar();
      }
      if (c != '\n')                    /* not ending with a newline? */
        sum = -1;                       /* then it's an error */
    }
    while (c != '\n')                   /* skip rest of line */
      c = getchar();
  }

  return sum;
}
```

Figure 4.11   (getnum.c)   Read a group of characters and turn them into a single integer.

| **4.6** | **CASE STUDY—A MORE GENERAL BASE CONVERTER** |

*This section
is optional!*

We conclude this chapter with a more general version of the base converting program we wrote in the last chapter. This version differs in that it's not restricted to converting decimal numbers into other bases. Instead, it lets us convert from any base to any base, from binary through base 36. Bases larger than 10 use letters as placeholders for their digits—a is 10, b is 11, c is 12, all the way up through z, which is 35. For more information on different bases, see Appendix D, which describes the octal and hexadecimal numbering systems.

Figure 4.12 contains the main program. It reads the desired input and output bases, and then reads a sequence of values in the input base, displaying those values in the desired output base. It terminates reading the input when an invalid value is entered or it encounters the end-of-file character. Here's one example run of the program:

```
Enter initial base: 16
Enter target base: 2
Enter number to convert: FFFF
FFFF in base 16 is 1111111111111111 in base 2.
Enter another base 16 number to convert: A8B4
A8B4 in base 16 is 1010100010110100 in base 2.
Enter another base 16 number to convert: 8EF5
8EF5 in base 16 is 1000111011110101 in base 2.
Enter another base 16 number to convert:
```

The program makes use of several other source files and borrows heavily from what we've written before.

It reads its input values using a pair of functions. The first, **get_baseN_num**, is a variant on **get_base10_num** that reads a value in any base, up to base 36, rather than just up to base 10. Like the original, however, it still returns a base 10 value. The other, **get_base**, reads in the input and output bases using **get_baseN_num** and then does some error checking to ensure the specified bases are reasonable. Figure 4.13 contains **get_base** and Figure 4.14 contains **get_baseN_num**.

How does **get_baseN_num** differ from **get_base10_num**? One change is that it now takes the base of the input number as a parameter, rather than having base 10 hardwired into its code. Another change is that it makes use of a new function, **todecimal**, to turn a character into its appropriate base 10 value. That is, if the input character is an 'f', **todecimal** returns 15. Before we knew we had a digit, so we converted it simply by subtracting '0'. Now the conversion is more complex, since letters are legitimate digits in bases greater than 10. When we have a letter, we have to subtract 'a' from it and then add 10. This conversion is, of course, ASCII-dependent.

todecimal actually takes a pair of parameters: the character to convert and a base. That way it can ensure that the character is a legitimate digit in the specified base before attempting the conversion. It returns −1 if there's an error.

We still use **display_value_in_base** to convert the number from base 10 to the output base—with one change. Now we have to convert values other than 0 through 9 to an appropriate character. If we're displaying a base 16 number and one of its digits is a 15, we write an 'F' rather than 15. To do this conversion, we

```
/*
 * Convert from any base to any other base.
 */
#include <stdio.h>

#define   MINBASE    2              /* smallest base */
#define   MAXBASE   36              /* largest base */

int main()
{
  void display_value_in_base(long v, int b);
  long get_baseN_num(int b);
  int  get_base(int minbase, int maxbase);
  int  base;                        /* initial base */
  int  newbase;                     /* final base*/
  long num;                         /* initial value, in base 10 */

  printf("Enter initial base: ");   /* grab initial base (in base 10) */
  if ((base = get_base(MINBASE, MAXBASE)) != -1)
  {
    printf("Enter target base: ");               /* grab target base */
    if ((newbase = get_base(MINBASE, MAXBASE)) != -1)
    {
      printf("Enter number to convert: ");       /* grab number */
      while ((num = get_baseN_num(base)) != -1)
      {
        display_value_in_base(num, base);
        printf(" in base %i is ", base);
        display_value_in_base(num, newbase);
        printf(" in base %i.\n", newbase);
        printf("Enter another base %i number to convert: ", base);
      }
      putchar('\n');
    }
  }
  return 0;
}
```

Figure 4.12   (convert.c)   The main program for our more general base converter program.

Convert # to char.

use another new function, **tochar**, which takes an **int** and returns the appropriate
character to display. It uses a technique that's similar to what we showed for converting
lowercase characters to uppercase. And, as in **todecimal**, **tochar** is now ASCII-
dependent. We'll provide more portable versions of these functions in later chapters.
Figure 4.15 contains **todecimal** and **tochar**, Figure 4.16 contains the new version
of **display_value_in_base**.

```
/*
 * Read in the base using get_baseN_num.
 */
#include <stdio.h>

int get_base(int minbase, int maxbase)
{
  long get_baseN_num(int b);
  long base;

  if ((base = get_baseN_num(10)) == -1)
    printf("Error: nonnumeric base detected\n");
  else
  {
    if (base < minbase)                 /* set to smallest if too small */
    {
      printf("Error: Smallest base is %i.\n", minbase);
      base = -1;
    }
    if (base > maxbase)                 /* set to largest if too large */
    {
      printf("Error: Largest base is %i.\n", maxbase);
      base = -1;
    }
  }
  return (int) base;            /* cast tells compiler not to complain */
}
```

Figure 4.13   (getbase.c)   A function to read in a base and perform some basic error checking on it.

SUMMARY

- C provides a special integral type, **char**, for holding the integer representations of characters.

- C automatically converts back and forth between **char**s and **int**s.

- C provides character constants, a character enclosed in single quotes, as well as escape sequences to identify special characters.

- The standard library contains a pair of functions for doing I/O a character at a time: **getchar** reads the next character in the standard input, and **putchar** writes a character onto the standard output.

- The library also provides a set of character testing functions used to determine whether a particular character has certain properties, such as being a lower- or uppercase letter.

- Reading numerical data a character at a time and doing our own conversions allows us to improve on **scanf**'s error handling abilities.

```
/*
 * Read a base N number, one character at a time.
 */
#include <stdio.h>

long get_baseN_num(int base)
{
  int  todecimal(int c, int b);
  int  c;                            /* next input character */
  int  value;                        /* decimal value of next char */
  long sum;                          /* running total */

  if ((c = getchar()) == EOF)        /* EOF is error */
    sum = -1;
  else
  {
    if ((value = todecimal(c, base)) == -1)
      sum = -1;                      /* not a digit in desired base */
    else
    {                                /* in number, update it */
      sum = 0;
      while (value != -1)
      {                              /* valid next digit in base */
        sum = base * sum + value;    /* update number */
        c = getchar();
        value = todecimal(c, base);
      }
      if (c != '\n')
        sum = -1;                    /* indicate error! */
    }
    while (c != '\n')                /* skip rest of line */
      c = getchar();
  }
  return sum;
}
```

Figure 4.14   (getbasen.c)   A function that reads a value in a specified base.

EXERCISES

4–1 Modify the character set printing program (Figure 4.2) to avoid printing control characters.

4–2 Make two changes to the program that prints its input onto its output one line at a time (Figure 4.3). It should now print its output in lower case, and it should strip out any digits and punctuation characters.

4–3 Modify the line numbering program (Figure 4.5) to avoid numbering blank lines (it counts them, but doesn't display a number in front of them).

```
/*
 * Functions to convert digits to and from characters (ASCII ONLY).
 *     todecimal - convert char to equivalent decimal number.
 *     tochar - convert decimal number to equivalent character.
 */
#include <ctype.h>

int todecimal(int c, int base)
{
  int value;

  value = -1;                           /* simplify later error handling */
  if (isdigit(c))
    value = c - '0';
  if (islower(c))
    value = c - 'a' + 10;
  if (isupper(c))
    value = c - 'A' + 10;
  if (value != -1)                      /* if we got a value */
    if (value >= base)                  /* make sure it's legal for base */
      value = -1;
  return value;
}

int tochar(int value)
{
  int c;

  if (value < 10)
    c = '0' + value;
  else
    c = 'A' + value - 10;
  return c;
}
```

Figure 4.15   (convchar.c)   Functions for converting characters to and from decimal values.

4–4   Modify the line numbering program (Figure 4.5) to number pages. That is, place a line with "PAGE *N*" at the beginning of each page, with a blank line between the page-numbering line and the next line of the output. Assume that a page has a maximum of 66 lines (use a constant **PAGE_LEN**).

4–5   The one-word-per-line program (Figure 4.7) uses a definition of a word that will break a line such as

```
    #include <ctype.h>
```

into:

```
/*
 * Display a value in a specified base between 2 and 36.
 */
#include <stdio.h>
#include <math.h>

void display_value_in_base(long v, int b)
{
  int tochar(int value);            /* addition since Chapter 3 */
  int  k;                           /* digits needed in result */
  long divisor;                     /* initially b^(# of digits - 1) */

  if (v == 0)                       /* zero is the same in any base */
    printf("0");
  else
  {
    k = floor(log10(v)/log10(b)) + 1;
    divisor = pow(b, k - 1);        /* first divisor: b^(k - 1) */

    /* Run through value, calculating and displaying the value of each
       of the digits in the new base (left to right) */

    while (divisor >= 1)
    {
      putchar(tochar((int)(v / divisor)));  /* changed from Chapter 3 */
      v = v % divisor;
      divisor = divisor / b;
    }
  }
}
```

Figure 4.16 (convfunc.c) Function for displaying a value in a specified base.

```
include
ctype
h
```

Modify this program to recognize special C characters such as **#**, **<**, **>**, and **.** as part of a word. Handling **.** is tricky—it should be part of a word only if it's surrounded by letters.

4–6 Modify **get_base10_dig** (Figure 4.10) to verify that there is nothing but trailing spaces after the digit. Any other characters should result in an error message.

4–7 Modify **get_base10_num** (Figure 4.11) so that it reads and converts real numbers (that is, numbers containing a decimal point) instead of integers. Extend the function to handle numbers in scientific notation as well.

4–8 Modify **get_base10_num** (Figure 4.11) to allow a **+** or **–** before the number.

4–9 The function `get_base10_num` (Figure 4.11) requires that the first character the user enters be a valid digit. Modify it to allow leading blanks or tabs before the digit and trailing blanks or tabs after the digit.

4–10 Modify any version of Chapter 2's interest rate program to use the extension to `get_base10_num` you wrote in the previous exercise instead of `scanf`.

4–11 The conversion in `todecimal` (Figure 4.15) depends on the ordering of lowercase letters—it works for ASCII but not for EBCDIC. Modify it so that it works with any character set encoding scheme.

4–12 Write a program that eliminates all blank lines from its input.

4–13 Write a program that reads a single character and prints its integer equivalent. Then write a program that reads an integer and prints its character equivalent. Be sure to do appropriate error/range checking.

4–14 Write a program to read an `int` and print its octal, decimal, hexadecimal, and unsigned decimal equivalents.

4–15 Write a program to print the decimal, octal, and hex values of the characters that have special escape sequences.

4–16 Write a program that prints the number of control characters in its input.

4–17 Write a program to count the number of words, lines, and characters in its input. A word is any sequence of non-white space characters.

4–18 Write a program to print each number found in its input on a line by itself, preceded by the line number on which it was located. A number is simply a sequence of digits.

4–19 Write a function, `getletter`, that reads an upper- or lowercase letter between minimum and maximum letters provided as arguments.

5 OPERATORS

This chapter takes a long look at C's rich set of operators. We examine more closely the operators we've already introduced, and we introduce the operators we previously ignored. We pay special attention to the operators that have no analog in most other programming languages, such as the shorthand assignment and bit-manipulation operators. Many of C's operators are just similar enough to those of other programming languages to cause problems, so we spend much of our time on their caveats and quirks. The chapter concludes with a case study: a pair of programs that compress and uncompress their input.

5.1 OPERATORS, OPERANDS, AND PRECEDENCE

Much of a programming language's power derives from the operators it provides. And C provides a wide selection of operators. Table 5.1 summarizes them, their relative precedence, and the operations they perform. The table is organized in order of decreasing precedence. As in most programming languages, we can use parentheses to override the default order of evaluation.

There are two properties most operators hold. First, they expect their operands to share the same type and will perform the arithmetic conversions we described earlier if they don't. There are a few operators that require specific types of operands, but unless we point out otherwise, assume an operator works with any integral or real data type. Second, most operators don't impose an order of evaluation on their operands. When we multiply two expressions together, there's no guarantee that the operand on the left will be evaluated before the operand on the right. That rarely matters—we need to worry about the order of evaluation only when it involves a side effect, such as a function call. There are several operators that do impose an order of evaluation, but again, unless we point out otherwise, assume an operator's operands aren't evaluated in any particular order.

The remainder of this chapter describes the operators in Table 5.1, although we do skip several of them. We ignore the arithmetic and type-casting operators, since we've already discussed them in some detail. And we skip over the structure, array, and pointer accessing operators, since we devote the better part of several later chapters to them.

[handwritten margin note: ① Operator expects operands to share the same type.]

OPERATOR	DESCRIPTION
`x[i]`, `f(x)`	array subscripting and function call
`.`, `->`	direct and indirect structure field selection
`++`, `--`	postfix increment/decrement
`++`, `--`	prefix increment/decrement
`sizeof`, (*type*)	size of a variable or type (in bytes), cast to *type*
`-`, `!`, `~`	unary minus, logical and bitwise NOT
`&`, `*`	address of and dereferencing
`*`, `/`, `%`	multiply, divide, modulus
`+`, `-`	addition, subtraction
`>>`, `<<`	right, left shift
`<`, `>`, `<=`, `>=`	test for inequality *relational*
`==`, `!=`	test for equality, inequality *relational*
`&`	bitwise AND
`^`	bitwise XOR (exclusive OR)
`|`	bitwise OR
`&&`	logical AND
`||` *true*	logical OR
`?:` *false*	conditional operator
`=`	assignment
`+=`, `-=`, `*=`, `/=`, `%=`	add to, subtract from, multiply to, divide by, assign remainder
`<<=`, `>>=`, `^=`, `&=`, `|=`	shift right and left, assign bitwise XOR, AND, OR
`,`	sequential expression evaluation

Table 5.1 C's operators and their precedence. All operators within a set of lines have equal precedence.

5.2   THE RELATIONAL OPERATORS

return 1 if true 0 if false

We use relational operators to test whether a particular relationship holds between two values. There are relational operators to compare values for equality (`==`), inequality (`!=`), greater than (`>`), less than (`<`), greater than or equal (`>=`), and less than or equal (`<=`). A relational operator returns an **int**: 1 (true) if the relation holds, 0 (false) if it doesn't. They return **int**s because the statements that perform tests, such as **if** or **while**, don't actually test whether the test is true or false. Instead, they test whether it evaluates to something other than 1 (true) or 0 (false).

As a result, we never need to explicitly check whether values are zero. Figure 5.1 avoids doing so in a new version of our earlier program to display its input, one word per line. We've rewritten the **if** that tests whether the next character is a letter,

```
if (isalpha(c) != 0)
```

⟸ *if (isalpha(c))*

more compactly as:

```c
/*
 * Break input into words (groups of letters).
 */
#include <stdio.h>
#include <ctype.h>

#define YES  1
#define NO   0

int main()
{
    int c;                      /* next input character */
    int word;                   /* flag: are we dealing with a word? */

    word = NO;
    while ((c = getchar()) != EOF)
        if (isalpha(c))
        {                       /* it's a letter */
            putchar(c);         /* write it and note we're in word */
            word = YES;
        }
        else                    /* it's not a letter */
            if (word)           /* write a newline if we were in word */
            {
                putchar('\n');
                word = NO;
            }
    return 0;
}
```

→ if word == 1

Figure 5.1 (brkwd.c) A more compact program to break its input into one word per line. We've eliminated all explicit comparisons with zero.

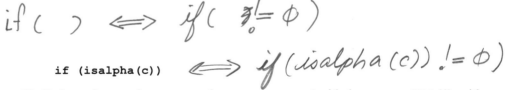

$$\text{if ( )} \iff \text{if (} \neq \emptyset \text{)}$$

$$\texttt{if (isalpha(c))} \iff \text{if (isalpha(c)) != } \emptyset \text{)}$$

Similarly, we've rewritten our test that compares **word** with the constant **YES** (1), with

```
if (word == YES)
```

more simply as:

```
if (word)
```

That's because **word** has to be either **YES** (1) or **NO** (0). If it's not 0, which is what we're testing for here, we know it's 1.

We can write compact code by using the relational operators to test the result of an assignment—but we have to be careful. That's because the relational operators have higher precedence than assignment. In our loop to read input characters, we had to parenthesize the assignment:

relational operator has higher precedence than assignments handwritten: ! = φ)

```
(c = getchar()) != EOF
```

What happens if we leave off the parentheses?

```
c = getchar() != EOF        /* OOPS! */
```

Looking at Table 5.1, we see that `!=` has higher precedence than `=`. That means we assign to `c` the result of comparing the newly read character with **EOF**. So `c` will be 0 or 1, depending on whether or not we read **EOF**, and **putchar** would write whatever character has an internal representation of \001, which is probably something unprintable.

> *Don't forget to parenthesize assignments when using the relational operators to compare their results.*

In fact, it's generally a good idea to parenthesize the operands of relational operators, since they fall in the middle of the precedence hierarchy.

Figure 5.2 contains another common mistake made by novice C programmers. Can you spot it? The program is a new version of our earlier program to print the average of its input values. The problem is in the `if` statement that protects against dividing by zero.

```
if (n = 0)
  avg = 0.0
else
  avg = (double) sum / n;
```

Our mistake is that we used the assignment operator, `=`, rather than the test-for-equality operator, `==`. This expression now mistakenly assigns 0 to `n`, which the `if` then treats as false. The result is that we *always* do the division by zero we were trying to prevent!

> *Watch out for accidentally using = to test for equality.*

5.3   THE LOGICAL OPERATORS

handwritten: logical AND && / logical OR || / return / 1 = true / 0 = false

We often need to combine relational tests in a single expression. To do so, we use the logical operators: logical AND (`&&`), logical OR (`||`), and logical negation (`!`). Like the relational operators, these return an `int`, 1 (true) or 0 (false). Table 5.2 shows how they determine what's true and false. Logical AND and OR interpret nonzero operands as true and zero operands as false. An expression such as `x && y` will evaluate to true only if both `x` and `y` aren't zero. Similarly, an expression such as `x || y` will evaluate to true if either `x` or `y` isn't zero. Logical negation returns 1 if its operand is zero, and zero otherwise.

Figure 5.3 uses them both in a new version of our **yesorno** function. Now we use `||` to check whether the next input character is an upper- or lowercase 'y', rather than first using **tolower** to convert the input character to lowercase:

```
/*
 * Compute average of its input values.
 */
#include <stdio.h>

int main()
{
  int    next;                           /* next input value */
  long   sum;                            /* running total */
  int    n;                              /* number of input values */
  int    result;                         /* did we read another value? */
  double avg;                            /* average of input values */

  sum = 0;
  n = 0;
  while ((result = scanf("%i", &next)) == 1)
  {
    sum = sum + next;
    n = n + 1;
  }
  if (result != EOF)
    printf("Warning: bad input after reading %i values\n", n);
  if (n = 0)                             /* MISTAKE! */
    avg = 0.0;
  else
    avg = (double) sum / n;
  printf("Average of %i values is %f.\n", n, avg);

  return 0;
}
```

Figure 5.2   (avg.c)   A buggy version of our Chapter 3 program to compute the average of its input values.

Operands		Result	
Op1	Op2	&&	||
nonzero	nonzero	1	1
nonzero	zero	0	1
zero	nonzero	0	1
zero	zero	0	0

Table 5.2   Results of using the logical operators.

```
/*
 * Print a prompt and then get a yes or no answer using "yesorno".
 */
#include <stdio.h>
#include <ctype.h>

#define YES 1
#define NO  0

int main()
{
  int yesorno(void);

  printf("Enter a YES or NO answer: ");
  if (yesorno() == YES)
    printf("That was a YES!\n");
  else
    printf("That was a NO!\n");
  return 0;
}

int yesorno(void)
{
  int c;                            /* holds input character */
  int answer;                       /* holds YES or NO answer */

  if ((c = getchar()) == 'y' || c == 'Y')
    answer = YES;                   /* YES for 'Y' or 'y' */
  else
    answer = NO;                    /* NO for anything else */
  while (c != EOF && c != '\n')     /* skip other characters on line */
    c = getchar();
  return answer;
}
```

Figure 5.3 (yesorno.c) A new and improved version of Chapter 4's **yesorno** function..

```
    if ((c = getchar()) == 'y' || (c == 'Y'))
```

And in our loop to skip the remaining characters on a line, we now enter the loop only if the character we read is not **EOF** and is not a newline.

```
    while (c != EOF && c != '\n')
```

Doing so guarantees that our program doesn't go into an infinite loop if for some reason the input has an end of file without a preceding newline.

The logical operators **&&** and **||** associate left to right, and their precedence is low, so we rarely need to parenthesize when we combine them with the relational operators. As we might expect, the expression

```
/*
 * Print a prompt and then get a yes or no answer using "yesorno".
 */
#include <stdio.h>
#include <ctype.h>

int main()
{
  int yesorno(void);

  printf("Enter a YES or NO answer: ");
  if (yesorno())
    printf("That was a YES!\n");
  else
    printf("That was a NO!\n");
  return 0;
}

int yesorno(void)
{
  int c;                          /* holds input character */
  int answer;                     /* holds YES or NO answer */

  answer = (c = getchar()) == 'y' || c == 'Y';
  while (c != EOF && c != '\n')    /* skip other characters on line */
    c = getchar();
  return answer;                  /* 1 for 'Y' or 'y', otherwise 0 */
}
```

logical and

or

Figure 5.4 (yesorno2.c) An even more concise version of our **yesorno** function. It takes advantage of the assignment operator and the integer return values of the logical operators.

```
            c != '\n' && c != EOF
```

is evaluated as though we wrote

```
            (c != '\n') && (c != EOF)
```

Figure 5.4 shows how this **yesorno** program can be written even more compactly. We now compute the function's return value with a single assignment:

```
    answer = (c = getchar()) == 'y' || c == 'Y';
```

answer = 1 if satisfy
= 0 if not satisfy

Like the relational operators, the logical operators return 1 for true and 0 for false. What this assignment does is read a character, store it into **c**, and then place a 1 into **answer** if it's a 'y' or a 'Y' and a 0 otherwise. By taking advantage of this feature, we've eliminated entirely the need for the special constants **YES** and **NO**, shrinking our program considerably.

We have to be careful when we combine logical operators. The program in Figure 5.5

```
/*
 * Break input into words (letter followed by letters or digits).
 */
#include <stdio.h>
#include <ctype.h>

#define YES   1
#define NO    0

int main()
{
  int c;                          /* next input character */
  int word;                       /* flag: are we dealing with a word? */

  word = NO;
  while ((c = getchar()) != EOF)
    if (isalpha(c) || word && isdigit(c))
    {                             /* it's a letter */
      putchar(c);                 /* write it and note we're in word */
      word = YES;
    }
    else                          /* it's not a letter */
      if (word)                   /* write a newline if we were in word */
      {
        putchar('\n');
        word = NO;
      }
  return 0;
}
```

Figure 5.5   (brkwd2.c) An extension to our program to write words one per line. Now a word can include digits, as long as it begins with a letter.

revises Figure 5.1 to allow words to contain digits as well as letters, so long as the first character is still a letter. For example, the input

```
w8 4 me 2go with you.
```

produces

```
w8
me
go
with
you
```

as its output. This program now contains a more complex test to determine whether the character we read is part of a word:

```
if (isalpha(c) || word && isdigit(c))
```

Because the precedence of `&&` is higher than that of `||`, this test actually evaluates as though it were written as:

```
if (isalpha(c) || (word && isdigit(c)))
```

That is, this expression is true if `c` is a letter, or if `c` is a digit and we're already in a word. That's very different than if it were evaluated as:

```
if ((isalpha(c) || word) && isdigit(c))
```

Because combining logical operators can be confusing, it's a good idea to surround their use with parentheses.

It's possible that `&&` and `||` may never evaluate one of their operands. The reason is that we often know their value after evaluating only the first operand—eliminating the need to evaluate the other operand. In C, if we have a series of clauses connected by logical AND, the first false one terminates the evaluation. Consider the logical AND in our earlier test:

```
while (c != '\n' && c != EOF)
    c = getchar();
```

The clause `c != \n` is evaluated first. If it's false, the entire logical expression is false, regardless of the value of the second clause—so the second clause is not evaluated. More to the point, `c` isn't compared with **EOF**. That's not all that important here, but we'll take advantage of this feature frequently in later programs.

Logical OR, `||`, is similar: the first true clause terminates the evaluation of all succeeding clauses. Here,

```
answer = (c = getchar()) == 'y' || c == 'Y';
```

`c` is not compared with 'Y' when `c` is 'y'.

> *Unlike the relational operators, `&&` and `||` impose an order of evaluation on their operands.*

Logical NOT, `!`, takes one operand, which it always evaluates. Figure 5.6 uses it in a program to shrink its input by deleting all leading and trailing whitespace and by turning other groups of whitespace into a single blank. The `!` appears in this test:

```
while (!isspace(c))
```

`isspace(c)` returns a 1 if `c` is a whitespace character and a 0 otherwise. The `!` in front of it turns the 1 into a 0 and the 0 into a 1. The result is that we enter the loop only if `c` is not a whitespace character.

Logical negation has high precedence, so we have to be careful to parenthesize its operand when it contains other operators. Those cases are rare, however, since we can often eliminate the need for logical negation entirely by carefully rewriting our tests.

```
/*
 * Removes leading and trailing whitespace from its input and turns runs
 * of whitespace into a single blank.  Assumes lines end with a newline.
 */
#include <stdio.h>
#include <ctype.h>

int main()
{
  int c;                                    /* next input character */

  while ((c = getchar()) != EOF)
  {                 /* each pass through loop takes care of one input line */
    while (isspace(c) && c != '\n')
      c = getchar();                        /* skip leading spaces */
    while (c != '\n')
    {                                       /* process any words */
      while (!isspace(c))
      {                                     /* dump out word */
        putchar(c);
        c = getchar();
      }
      while (isspace(c) && c != '\n')       /* skip trailing spaces */
        c = getchar();
      if (c != '\n')                        /* not trailing, write space */
        putchar(' ');
    }
    putchar('\n');                          /* trailing, write newline */
  }
  return 0;
}
```

Figure 5.6   (shrink.c) A program to shrink its input by removing whitespace.

5.4   BITWISE OPERATORS

The operators we've seen so far are found in most high-level programming languages. There are also less-common operators for accessing bits. We can shift bits left (<<) or right (>>), invert bits (~), and do bitwise AND (&), OR (|), and XOR (^). All of these operators require integral operands. In fact, we usually restrict our use of them to **unsigned** operands.

These operators let us deal with the details of the machine, and they help us write more efficient programs. We must often set specific bits to request various hardware operations, such as direct writing to and from a disk. When these operations complete, they often set status bits to tell us whether they succeeded or failed. We use the bitwise operators to set and examine these bits. In addition, we can often use these operators to store our data compactly and to provide fast versions of some numerical operations.

Bit Shifts

The left (`<<`) and right (`>>`) shift operators take an operand and return its value shifted left or right by a specified number of bits. The operand itself is not affected. The form of the operators is *op* `>>` *n* and *op* `<<` *n*. *n* should be a positive integer less than the number of bits in the variable being shifted.

For left shifts, 0 bits are shifted in from the right. For right shifts on **unsigned** values or nonnegative signed values, 0 bits are shifted in from the left. But for negative values, the value of the shifted-in bits is implementation-defined: it may be either 0 or 1.[1] As an example,

```
y = x << 1;
```

takes **x**'s value, shifts it 1 bit to the *left*, and assigns it to **y**. The result is that **y** is assigned **x** $\times$ 2. In general, shifting to the left *n* places is the same as multiplying by 2^n. Similarly,

```
y = x >> 1;
```

takes **x**'s value, shifts it 1 bit to the *right*, and assigns it to **y**. The result is that **y** is assigned **x** / 2. In general, shifting to the right *n* places is the same as dividing by 2^n. Assuming **x** is 6, here is what **x** looks like, shifted left by 1 bit and right by 1 bit:

x	x << 1	x >> 1
`0...0 0110`	`0...0 1100`	`0...0 0011`
6	12	3

When we do a *left* shift, we replace the vacated bits on the right with zero. But when we do a *right* shift, the replacement for the vacated bits on the left depends on the variable's type. If the variable is unsigned, the replacement bits are zero. If it's signed, the replacement bits *usually* share the sign bit's value (sign extension). But it's possible that on some machines zeros are shifted in for signed values, which would have the (most likely undesired) effect of changing the sign of the value.

> *Whenever possible, avoid right shifts on signed values.*

Bitwise Logical Operators

There are three bitwise logical operators that take a pair of operands: bitwise AND (`&`), bitwise OR (`|`), and bitwise XOR (`^`). They work on their operands bit by bit, setting each bit in the result. Table 5.3 shows the results of these operators: bitwise AND is one only when both bits are one, bitwise OR is one if either operand is one, and bitwise XOR (exclusive OR) is one if exactly one of the bits is one. AND is sometimes called

---

[1]The term *implementation-defined* means that each compiler is free to do whatever it wants, but what it does must be documented.

OPERANDS		RESULTS		
OP1	OP2	&	|	^
1	1	1	1	0
1	0	0	1	1
0	1	0	1	1
0	0	0	0	0

Table 5.3   Results of using the bitwise operators.

EXPRESSION	BINARY VALUE			
A:	1001	0110	0001	0001
B:	0001	1010	1101	1001
A & B:	0001	0010	0001	0001
A | B:	1001	1110	1101	1001
A ^ B:	1000	1100	1100	1000
~A:	0110	1001	1110	1110
~B:	1110	0101	0010	0110

Table 5.4   An example of the bitwise logical operators

the "both" or "all" function, OR the "either" or "any" function, and XOR the "odd" or "only one" function.

There's one other bitwise logical operator: bitwise NOT (~). It takes only one operand and returns its value with each of its bits inverted—any 1 bit becomes zero, and any zero bit becomes 1. That means, for example, that ~0 is an integer with all 1 bits. Table 5.4 shows an example of these bitwise operators. It highlights one key difference between the logical and the bitwise logical operators. Although && and || always return 0 or 1, there's no such restriction on their bitwise logical counterparts.

We use these bitwise operators primarily to test and set individual bits or groups of bits in a word. This ability is often needed to manipulate devices that use individual bits as controlling signals or status indications. When manipulating bits, we create a *mask* that selects particular bits. A mask is simply an integer with only those bits we are interested in turned on, as in

```
#define OURBIT  0x80        /* bit 7: (...00 1000 0000) */
```

Given this mask, we can turn on the desired bit in an integer **x** with

```
x = x | OURBIT                    /* turn on bit 7 */
```

On the other hand, we can turn off that bit with

```
x = x & ~OURBIT                   /* turn off bit 7 */
```

This works because ~OURBIT is a word with all bits on except for the one in which we're interested. When we do the AND we're turning off that bit and keeping all the other bits the same.

x:	0...0 1100 1011
~OURBIT:	1...1 0111 1111
X & ~OURBIT:	0...0 0100 1011

Finally, we can test whether our bit is on or off with

```
x & OURBIT              /* nonzero if bit on */
```

The expression returns a non-zero value if the bit is on, and zero if it's off.

The bitwise operators have very low precedence. Bitwise & and |, for example, have lower precedence than the relational operators. That means to be safe, we generally parenthesize all uses of bitwise operators that are part of more complicated expressions.

> *Parenthesize all uses of the bitwise operators in larger expressions.*

Figure 5.7 uses these operators in a function **print_binary** to print an integer's value in binary. It takes two parameters: **x** is the value we want to print in binary (**unsigned int**), and **nbits** is the number of bits in an **int**. It works by running through the bits in **x**, going from left (bit n) to right (bit 0). To print bit **i**, it first shifts **x**'s value **i** bits to the right, making the value's rightmost bit the one we're interested in. It then turns off the other bits by ANDing the result of the shift with a word with just the rightmost bit on.

```
printf("%i", (x >> i) & 01);
```

print_binary assumes we know how many bits are in **int**. To figure that out, it uses a function **int_bits**. The trick we use is to start with an **int** with just its rightmost bit on. We then keep shifting it to the left, a bit at a time, and count how many shifts we can do before the bit disappears off the left end. That count's final value is the number of bits in an **int**. This technique is clever, but it's actually not the easiest way to determine how many bits a particular type has. We'll see a better way later in the chapter.

Why did we write a new function rather than simply using our earlier base-converting functions? For the special case of printing values in binary, the bit-shifting operators result in a simpler, more efficient function.

```
/*
 * A pair of useful bit-manipulating functions.
 *     int_bits - returns number of bits in an unsigned int.
 *     print_binary - prints an unsigned int in binary.
 */
#include <stdio.h>

int int_bits(void)
{
  int x;                                     /* word being shifted */
  int i;                                     /* count of shifts */

  i = 0;
  for (x = 1; x != 0; x = x << 1)
    i = i + 1;
  return i;
}

void print_binary(unsigned int x, int nbits)
{
  int i;                                     /* index of desired bits */

  for (i = nbits - 1; i >= 0; i = i - 1)
    printf("%i", (x >> i) & 01);
  putchar('\n');
}
```

Figure 5.7 (prbin.c) Print the underlying binary representation of an **unsigned int**.

Figure 5.8 is a program that uses **print_binary** and **int_bits** to show what happens to an input value when we shift it to the right, to the left, and when we turn various bits on and off. Here's some sample input and output for the program when run on a machine with 16-bit **int**s.

```
Enter value: 15487
In binary: 0011110001111111
15487 >> 1 = 7743: 0001111000111111
15487 << 1 = 30974: 0111100011111110
Bit 7 was off, now on = 15615: 0011110011111111
```

Getting and Setting Bits

Sometimes it seems as though there's an operator for everything. But that impression is misleading. There are many useful operations for which no built-in operator exists. One important example is accessing a bit or group of bits within a word. We can create our own mask and then do a bitwise AND or OR to access them, but that's painful. What we really want is an easy way to specify the bits of interest and have the appropriate

```
/*
 * Program illustrating some basic bit-manipulating operations.
 */
#include <stdio.h>

#define OURBIT   0x80                        /* bit 7: (...00 1000 0000) */

int main()
{
  int        int_bits(void);
  void       print_binary(unsigned value, int intbits);
  int        nbits;                          /* bits in an int */
  unsigned value;                            /* input value */
  unsigned x;                                /* modified input value */

  nbits = int_bits();                        /* get # of bits in an int */
  printf("Enter value: ");                   /* get value to display */
  scanf("%u", &value);                       /* assume no errors */

  printf("In binary: ");
  print_binary(value, nbits);                /* display in binary */
  x = value >> 1;
  printf("%u >> 1 = %u: ", value, x);        /* show right shifted */
  print_binary(x, nbits);
  x = value << 1;                            /* show left shifted */
  printf("%u << 1 = %u: ", value, x);
  print_binary(x, nbits);

  if ((value & OURBIT) != 0)                 /* show with bit 7 off and on */
    printf("Bit 7 was on, now off = %u: ", x = value & ~ OURBIT);
  else
    printf("Bit 7 was off, now on = %u: ", x = value | OURBIT);
  print_binary(x, nbits);
  return 0;
}
```

Figure 5.8   (useprbin.c) A program that uses **print_binary** to illustrate the bit-shifting operators.

masks created for us automatically.

Figure 5.9 contains implementations of a set of functions for accessing bits that let us do just that. **getbit** and **setbit** get or set the value of the **n**th bit within a word. **getbits** and **setbits** are similar, but work with a group of **k** bits, starting at position **n** within a word. All of these functions assume the *rightmost* bit in the word is bit number zero. Figures 5.10 and 5.11 show exactly what happens with the calls **getbits(word,3,2)** and **setbits(word,2,5,16)**, respectively. Table 5.5 shows the results of a variety of example calls, given a variable **word** whose value is 181 (0...10110101).

```
/*
 * Functions to get and set bit values.  All assume suitable parameters.
 *    getbit:  get value of bit n in word.
 *    setbit:  return value with bit n set to v (0 or 1).
 *    getbits: get value of k bits at position n in word.
 *    setbits: return value with k bits starting at bit n assigned v.
 */

unsigned getbit(unsigned word, int n)
{
  return (word >> n) & 01;
}

unsigned setbit(unsigned word, int n, unsigned v)
{
  if (v != 0)
    return word | (01 << n);      /* turn on the bit */
  else
    return word & ~(01 << n);     /* turn off the bit */
}

unsigned getbits(unsigned word, int n, int k)
{
  return (word & (~(~0 << k) << n)) >> n;
}

unsigned setbits(unsigned word, int n, int k, unsigned v)
{
  return (word & ~(~(~0 << k) << n)) | (v << n);
}
```

Figure 5.9   (bits.c)   Functions to determine and set the value of bits in a word.

CALL	RETURN VALUE	BIT PATTERN		
getbit(word, 1)	0	0...0	0000	0000
getbit(word, 2)	1	0...0	0000	0001
setbit(word, 3, 1)	189	0...0	1011	1101
setbit(word, 4, 0)	165	0...0	1010	0101
getbits(word, 3, 2)	2	0...0	0000	0010
getbits(word, 0, 4)	5	0...0	0000	0101
setbits(word, 2, 5, 16)	193	0...0	1100	0001
setbits(word, 0, 4, 7)	183	0...0	1011	0111

Table 5.5   The results of some example calls of our bit-manipulating functions. These assume **word** is 181 or 0...0 1011 0101 in binary.

Build mask (**n**=3, **k**=2)

all ones (˜0):

1111111111111111

k zeros (<< **k**):

1111111111111100

invert:

0000000000000011

shift (<< **n**):

0000000000011000

AND with **word** and shift

word:

0000000010110101

after AND:

0000000000010000

after shift (>> **n**):

0000000000000010

Figure 5.10 How **getbits(word,3,2)** builds and uses a mask to get a group of bits within a word.

Build mask (**n**=2, **k**=5)

earlier mask:

0000000001111100

inverted:

1111111110000011

AND with **word**, OR with shifted value

word:

0000000010110101

after AND:

0000000010000001

shifted value:

0000000001000000

after OR:

0000000011000001

Figure 5.11 How **setbits(word,2,5,16)** builds and uses a mask to set a group of bits within a word.

Figure 5.12 provides a main program that uses these functions to store several integers—representing an employee's sex, age, marital status, and years employed—into an **unsigned short**, as shown below. By compressing this information into a single word, we make the most efficient use of our available memory.

15 ⋯ 14	13 ⋯ 7	6	5 ⋯ 0
STATUS	AGE	SEX	YEARS

How do these functions work? **getbit** shifts **word** *right* **n** places, so that the rightmost bit, bit 0, holds the desired bit value. As with **print_binary**, it then ANDs the entire word with a mask containing a single 1 in its rightmost bit, effectively turning off all of **word**'s other bits.

setbit behaves differently depending on whether it is turning on or turning off the desired bit. To turn on the **n**th bit, **setbit** ORs the word with a mask containing a single 1 in the **n**th position. It is easy to create this mask: **setbit** simply shifts a 1 *left* **n** places. To turn off the **n**th bit, **setbit** ANDs the word with a mask containing a single 0 in the **n**th position, the negation of the mask above.

We could write **getbits** and **setbits** on top of repeated calls to **getbit** or **setbit**—which is acceptable if we don't care how quickly our program runs. Instead, however, both functions work by creating a mask that isolates the desired group of bits. They do so by taking a word of all 1s (~**0**), shifting it left **k** places, and inverting it bitwise. This results in a group of 1 bits in the **k** rightmost bits of the mask. Then they shift this group left **n** places, which puts them in the correct place.

getbits simply ANDs this mask with the word, shifts the result right **n** places, and returns the desired bits. **setbits** is more complex. It ANDs the *negation* of the mask to turn off the relevant bits, and then ORs the word with the new value shifted left **n** places.

Using Exclusive OR

We have used all of the bitwise operators except exclusive OR. One use for it is in data encryption. Encrypting a file makes its contents unreadable while preserving the information it contains. And one of the simplest ways to encrypt text is to exclusive OR the text with a lengthy key. If the text is larger than the key (which is usually the case), just cycle through the key repeatedly until the entire file has been encrypted. The nice aspect of this scheme is that we use the same method and the same key to decrypt the encrypted version of the file: we just take the exclusive OR with the key one more time.

As an example, suppose we have an 8-bit piece of data to be encrypted and an 8-bit key. Taking the exclusive OR with the key produces the encrypted data.

```
DATA (ASCII 'P')    0101  0000
KEY                 0001  0010
DATA xor KEY        0100  0010    (encrypted data)
```

Taking the exclusive OR with the key again produces the original data.

```
/*
 * Pack employee information into a single word (no error checking).
 */
#include <stdio.h>

#define SINGLE     0          /* codes for marital status */
#define MARRIED    1
#define SEPARATED  2
#define DIVORCED   3
#define MALE       1          /* codes for sex */
#define FEMALE     0
#define MSBIT      14         /* starting bit for marital status */
#define MSBITS     2          /* number of marital status bits */
#define AGEBIT     7          /* starting bit for age */
#define AGEBITS    7          /* number of bits for age */
#define SEXBIT     6          /* bit number for sex */
#define YRSBIT     0          /* starting bit for employed years */
#define YRSBITS    6          /* number of bits for years */

int main()
{
  unsigned getbit(unsigned word, int n);
  unsigned setbit(unsigned word, int n, unsigned v);
  unsigned getbits(unsigned word, int n, int k);
  unsigned setbits(unsigned word, int n, int k, unsigned v);
  unsigned mstat, sex, age, years;
  unsigned short info;             /* holds info on one person */

  info = 0;                        /* all bits off initially */
  printf("male=%i, female=%i? ", MALE, FEMALE);
  scanf("%u", &sex);
  info = setbit(info, SEXBIT, sex);
  printf("age? ");
  scanf("%u", &age);
  info = setbits(info, AGEBIT, AGEBITS, age);
  printf("single=%u, married=%u, separated=%u, divorced=%u? ",
         SINGLE, MARRIED, SEPARATED, DIVORCED);
  scanf("%u", &mstat);
  info = setbits(info, MSBIT, MSBITS, mstat);
  printf("years employed? ");
  scanf("%u", &years);
  info = setbits(info, YRSBIT, YRSBITS, years);
  printf("Sex: %u\n", getbit(info, SEXBIT));
  printf("Age: %u\n", getbits(info, AGEBIT, AGEBITS));
  printf("Marital status: %u\n", getbits(info, MSBIT, MSBITS));
  printf("Years employed: %u\n", getbits(info, YRSBIT, YRSBITS));
  return 0;
}
```

Figure 5.12 (usebits.c) A program that uses the bit-shifting operators to store employee information efficiently.

```
/*
 * Encrypt the standard input using a built-in encryption key (0xABCD).
 */
#include <stdio.h>
#include <limits.h>

#define MAXKEY    4L      /* length of the key (4 bytes) */
#define HIGHBIT   0x80    /* mask to access high bit only */

int main()
{
  unsigned long key;        /* the encryption key */
  unsigned char keybyte;    /* the next byte in the key */
  int           c;          /* next character */
  unsigned long j;          /* character count */

  key = 0xABCD;             /* hex key: byte 1 = 10, byte 2 = 11, etc. */
  j = 0;
  while ((c = getchar()) != EOF)
  {
    keybyte = (unsigned char) (key >> ((int) (j % MAXKEY) * CHAR_BIT));
    putchar(c ^ (keybyte | HIGHBIT));
    j = j + 1;
  }
  return 0;
}
```

Figure 5.13   (encrypt.c) A program to encrypt a file, using exclusive OR with a built-in key.

DATA xor KEY	0100 0010	(encrypted data)
KEY	0001 0010	
DATA	0101 0000	

Figure 5.13 contains a program that encrypts (or decrypts) its input. It's virtually identical to our earlier character-copying program, except that instead of copying each character directly to the output (via **putchar**), we take the exclusive OR of the current character with the next character of the key. This is actually a bit tricky, since we store the key in a single 4-byte **unsigned long**. To grab the next character, we need to shift the key over 1 byte. The bit-shifting operators, however, require the number of bits to shift, not the number of bytes. Fortunately, the system header file limits.h contains a constant **CHAR_BIT** that represents the number of bits in a byte, so we shift **CHAR_BIT** bits × the number of the byte we want.

There's actually one more tricky detail. Before we do the exclusive OR, we turn on the high bit in the key character. That's because it turns out that many systems use a special control character, such as a *control*-Z, to indicate the end of the file, and this pattern can result from doing an exclusive OR with a key character—but only if its high bit is off. Turning it on prevents a potentially nasty problem.

To simplify the structure of the program, we've built the key into it. In a more secure encryption program, of course, the key would be provided independently by the program's user.

5.5 ASSIGNMENT OPERATORS

We have seen that in C, unlike most other programming languages, assignment not only assigns the result of an expression to a variable but also returns this value. One benefit is that we can assign values during tests, as in our now familiar loop to read the input one character at a time.

```
while ((c = getchar()) != EOF)
    putchar(c);
```

Another benefit is that we can use assignment operators more than once in a single statement. We can initialize more than one variable to some initial value (say, 0) with

```
sum = i = 0;
```
right to left

The assignment operator associates right to left, so this multiple assignment is equivalent to

```
sum = (i = 0);
```

Shorthand Assignment Operators

C doesn't just provide a single assignment operator—it provides an entire collection. These operators have the form

> *lhs op = rhs*

where *lhs* is the left-hand side of the assignment, *rhs* is an expression, and *op* is any one of C's arithmetic or bit-shift operators (so the shorthand operators are `+=`, `-=`, `*=`, `/=`, `%=`, `&=`, `>>=`, `<<=`, `&=`, `|=`, and `^=`). The shorthand form is equivalent to

shorthand op operators

> *lhs = lhs op (rhs)*

with *lhs* evaluated once. Like `=`, the shorthand assignment operators return the value assigned, and we can use them in other expressions.

These shorthand operators are mostly for convenience—they save a large amount of typing. In fact, the shorthand operators are so convenient that after using them for just a little while, you'll find it hard to program in any language that doesn't have them. With the shorthand operators, for example, we can multiply **p** by **x** with

```
p *= x;
```
$\Rightarrow p = p * x$

a terse equivalent of

```
/*
 * Compute powers, more concise version.
 */
double power(double x, int exp)
{
  double p;

  p = 1.0;
  if (exp > 0)                            /* positive exponent */
    while (exp > 0)
    {
      p *= x;
      exp -= 1;
    }
  else                                    /* negative exponent */
    while (exp < 0)
    {
      p /= x;
      exp += 1;
    }
  return p;
}
```

Figure 5.14   (power.c)   Chapter 3's **power** made concise using shorthand assignment operators.

```
p = p * x;
```

Similarly, we can divide **p** by **x** with

```
p /= x;          ⟹  p = p/x
```

the shorthand for

```
p = p / x;
```

Figure 5.14 uses almost all of the shorthand arithmetic operators in a new version of our earlier **power** function.

These operators not only save typing, they lead to more concise, and perhaps surprisingly, more readable code. To see why, consider the assignment

```
balance = balance + balance * intrate;
```

We can write this assignment more concisely using an assignment operator:

```
balance += balance * intrate;
```

The latter is more likely to be correct because we have to type **balance** once less, lowering the chance of typing a different name by mistake. And it's more readable because it makes it clear that the point of this multiplication is to add it to **balance**.

```
/*
 * Most concise version of our power computing function.
 */
double power(double x, int exp)
{
  double p;

  p = 1.0;
  if (exp > 0)                                /* positive exponent */
    while (exp > 0)
    {
      p *= x;
      exp--;
    }
  else                                        /* negative exponent */
    while (exp < 0)
    {
      p /= x;
      exp++;
    }
  return p;
}
```

Figure 5.15 (power2.c) Our most concise version of **power**.

Postfix and Prefix Assignment

C also provides two special sets of shorthand operators for the common operations of incrementing and decrementing by 1: **++** adds 1 to its operand and **--** subtracts 1 from its operand. There are two forms of these operators, *prefix* (preceding its operand) and *postfix* (following its operand).

The form doesn't matter, *so long as the operator and its operand are not part of a larger expression.* By itself, **exp++** or **++exp** is equivalent to **exp += 1**, and **exp--** or **--exp** is equivalent to **exp -= 1**. Figure 5.15 uses these operators to write our most concise version of **power**. The function is now significantly more compact than the original version, without suffering any significant loss in readability. Here, we wrote it using the postfix form, but we could have written it using the prefix form as well.

We can use postfix and prefix operators as a piece of a more complicated expression. The problem is that it then makes a big difference which form we use. When we use **++** as a postfix operator, it first evaluates the operand, provides its value to the rest of the statement or expression, and then adds 1 to it. As a prefix operator, it does the additions first and makes the new value of the variable available to the expression. Prefix and postfix **--** behave similarly to **++**, except that they decrement their operand.

In Figures 5.16 and 5.17, we have two new versions of the previous chapter's line numbering program. The first initializes **lineno** to zero and uses

```
printf("%6i ", ++lineno);
```

```
/*
 * Copy input to output, giving each line a number.
 */
#include <stdio.h>

int main()
{
  int  c;                           /* current and */
  int  lastch;                      /*   previous characters */
  long lineno;                      /* lines printed so far */

  lineno = 0;  lastch = '\n';
  while ((c = getchar()) != EOF)
  {
    if (lastch == '\n')             /* hit end of line */
      printf("%8li ", ++lineno);
    putchar(c);
    lastch = c;
  }
  return 0;
}
```

Figure 5.16   (lineno.c) Our line numbering program made more concise with prefix increment.

```
/*
 * Copy input to output, giving each line a number.
 */
#include <stdio.h>

int main()
{
  int  c;                           /* current and */
  int  lastch;                      /*   previous characters */
  long lineno;                      /* lines printed so far */

  lineno = 1;  lastch = '\n';
  while ((c = getchar()) != EOF)
  {
    if (lastch == '\n')             /* hit end of line */
      printf("%8li ", lineno++);
    putchar(c);
    lastch = c;
  }
  return 0;
}
```

Figure 5.17   (lineno2.c) Our line numbering program made more concise with postfix increment.

to print it. This increments **lineno** *before* passing its value to **printf**. It's equivalent to the two statements:

```
++lineno;
printf("%6i", lineno);
```

increment by 1 and then starts using

The second version initializes **lineno** to 1 and uses

```
printf("%6i", lineno++);
```

to print it. This increments **lineno** *after* passing its value to **printf**. It's equivalent to

```
printf("%6i", lineno);
lineno++;
```

start with lineno and then increment by 1.

We also use these forms frequently when accessing arrays, and we'll see several examples in the next few chapters.

5.6   OTHER OPERATORS

There are three other operators of interest, the comma operator (**,**), the **sizeof** operator, and the conditional operator (**?:**). None of these have analogs in other high-level languages like Pascal or BASIC.

The Comma Operator

C treats a comma-separated list of expressions as a single expression and evaluates it left to right, returning the value of the rightmost expression as the expression's value.

One use for the comma operator is to eliminate embedded assignments from tests. Figure 5.18 uses it in a new version of the previous chapter's program to copy its input on its output. We can rewrite

```
while ((c=getchar()) != EOF)
    putchar(c);
```

as

left to right

```
while (c = getchar(), c != EOF)
    putchar(c);
```

The latter separates reading the character from testing for end of file. Because the comma operator evaluates left to right, the rightmost expression's value (here, the test for end of file) controls the **while**'s execution. Either method is acceptable, and we find ourselves using them interchangeably; use the one you find easiest to read.

Another use is to allow us to prompt for input in the same expression in which we read it. Figure 5.19 is a version of our earlier program to read x, y pairs and display x^y. This time we prompt for each x, y pair.

```
/*
 * Copy the input to the output.
 */
#include <stdio.h>

int main()
{
  int c;                                     /* next input character */

  while (c = getchar(), c != EOF)
    putchar(c);
  return 0;
}
```

Figure 5.18   (display.c)   A new version of our earlier character-copying program.

```
/*
 * Using our own function to compute exponents.
 */
#include <stdio.h>

int main()
{
  double power(double base, int exp);
  double x;                               /* user-supplied base */
  int    y;                               /* user-supplied exponent */

  while (printf("Enter x,y: "), scanf("%lf %i", &x, &y) == 2)
    printf("%g^%i = %g\n", x, y, power(x, y));
  return 0;
}
```

Figure 5.19   (usepower.c)   A new version of our earlier exponent computing program.

```
Enter x,y: 10 4
10^4 = 10000
Enter x,y: 2.5 8
2.5^8 = 1525.88
Enter x,y:
```

To do so, we use the comma operator in the test expression of the **while**.

```
while (printf("Enter x,y: "), scanf("%lf %i", &x, &y) == 2)
```

What happens is that C evaluates the first expression, the **printf**, which writes the prompt. C then evaluates the second expression, the **scanf**, which reads the input values. Finally, it compares **scanf**'s return value with 2 and returns the result as the value of the entire expression.

Yet another use is to provide multiple expressions where the language allows only one, such as in a **for** loop. We'll see examples of this in the next chapter.

The comma operator has the lowest precedence of any of C's operators, so we can safely use it to turn any list of expressions into a single statement. Don't do so, however, unless the expressions are closely related, or the program will become harder to understand and maintain.

> *The comma separating parameters in function calls is not a comma operator and does not guarantee left-to-right evaluation.*

The comma in function calls is simply a syntactic separator, not an operator. The order of evaluation of the arguments of function calls is implementation-dependent (unspecified); sometimes it's right to left, other times it's left to right, or it may even be completely random.

The **sizeof** Operator   *# include < stddef.h >*

sizeof returns the number of bytes necessary to store an object with the type of its operand. The operand can either be a type, which must be enclosed in parentheses, or an expression, which is usually a variable or constant. By definition, **sizeof(char)** is 1.

sizeof is unique because it's evaluated at compile time, not run time. In fact, it actually doesn't evaluate its operand; it simply figures out what type it is, how much room it requires, and then replaces itself with a constant.

What's the type of **sizeof**'s return value? Obviously, it's an unsigned integer—no data type in C requires less than 1 byte—but which unsigned integer? That depends on the implementation; what **sizeof** returns is a value of type **size_t**, which is defined in the system header file stddef.h. Whenever we store the result of a **sizeof** in our programs, we need to include this header file.

Figure 5.20 is a program that uses **sizeof** to compute and print the size of several different data types, including the standard types **short**, **int**, and **long**. Before printing an object's size, we cast **sizeof**'s return value to an **unsigned long**. That way we're safe regardless of what type **sizeof** returns. We didn't bother to print the size of a **char**, since by definition that is 1 byte. Here is the program's output when we ran it on a 16-bit machine.

```
short:    2
int:      2
long:     4
float:    4
double:   8
```

```
/*
 * Print the sizes of various types.
 */
#include <stdio.h>
#include <stddef.h>

int main()
{
    printf("short:    \t%lu\n", (unsigned long) sizeof(short));
    printf("int:      \t%lu\n", (unsigned long) sizeof(int));
    printf("long:     \t%lu\n", (unsigned long) sizeof(long));
    printf("float:    \t%lu\n", (unsigned long) sizeof(float));
    printf("double:   \t%lu\n", (unsigned long) sizeof(double));
    return 0;
}
```

Figure 5.20   (sizeof.c)   A program that prints the sizes of the basic data types.

The Conditional Operator

The final operator is the *conditional operator*, which is an **if** statement in disguise.

> *expression* **?** *true-expression* **:** *false-expression*

It first evaluates *expression*, and if it is true (nonzero), it then evaluates and returns *true-expression*. Otherwise, it evaluates and returns *false-expression*. No matter what, it only evaluates one of *true-expression* and *false-expression*.

The conditional operator provides a convenient shorthand for **if** statements that decide which of two values a particular variable should be assigned. Figure 5.21 uses it in a more concise version of Chapter 3's program to compute the average of its input values. Originally, we had an **if** statement to protect against dividing by zero when there were no input values.

```
if (n == 0)
    avg = 0.0;
else
    avg = (double) sum / n;
```

But with the conditional operator we can turn this **if** into a single assignment statement.

```
avg = (n == 0) ? 0.0 : (double) sum / n;
```

Conditional operator
? true : false

It's not necessary to parenthesize the test, but doing so is a good idea, since the parentheses help distinguish the test from the values returned.

Using conditional operators leads to programs that are more concise and possibly more efficient. Unfortunately, it's easy to go overboard with them, which leads to programs that are definitely less readable. Anything with more than a single nested conditional operator is better written using **if**s. Should you decide, despite our warn-

```
/*
 * Compute average of its input values.
 */
#include <stdio.h>

int main()
{
  int    next;                       /* next input value */
  long   sum;                        /* running total */
  int    n;                          /* number of input values */
  int    result;                     /* did we read another value? */
  double avg;                        /* average of input values */

  sum = n = 0;
  while ((result = scanf("%i", &next)) == 1)
  {
    sum += next;
    n++;
  }
  if (result != EOF)
    printf("Warning: bad input after reading %i values\n", n);
  avg = (n == 0) ? 0.0 : (double) sum / n;
  printf("Average of %i values is %f.\n", n, avg);
  return 0;
}
```

Figure 5.21 (avg2.c) A more concise version of our earlier program to compute the average of its input values.

ings, to use nested conditional operators, you can make them more readable by not only parenthesizing the expressions tested by the conditional operators, but also by wrapping parentheses around the nested conditional operators themselves. Again, you don't have to do that, but it's a good habit to get into since it protects against possible precedence problems.

> *Avoid writing nested conditional operators.*

5.7 CASE STUDY—DATA COMPRESSION

This section is optional!

We conclude this chapter with a pair of programs to compress and uncompress their input. Data compression reduces the amount of storage needed to hold a particular piece of information, such as a file, saving disk space and lessening the time required to copy or move the file.

There are all sorts of techniques for file compression that vary greatly in complexity and efficiency. We've chosen one of the simplest, called run length encoding: simply replace any sequence of identical bytes (or characters) with 2 bytes, one containing the repeated byte and the other containing the length of the sequence. With this method, for example, a group of eight blanks becomes a single blank followed by an 8. Since many files, programs, image data, and so on, have frequent runs of duplicated characters, this encoding scheme can provide substantial savings.

Unfortunately, this scheme also has a problem: What do we do with a single byte surrounded by different characters? We certainly don't want to replace it with 2 bytes (the character and a count of one), as the file would grow rather than shrink. Ideally, in fact, we would like to simply leave it alone. But then how do we tell whether a particular byte is a character or a count? One possibility is to precede the count by a special character that means "here comes a character/count pair," an approach that takes 1 *byte* per sequence. We can do better, however, if we assume that our input is ASCII characters. Then there is an alternative that takes a single *bit* per sequence. ASCII characters take 7 bits and C characters are stored in 8-bit bytes, so we can use the extra (high order) bit to identify groups. Of course, this means our compression program only works with text files and cannot be used to compress binary files, such as object modules.

Figure 5.22 contains compress, a program that implements this compression scheme. The assumption is that the program will be run with its standard input redirected to the file to be compressed, and its standard output redirected into some other file. It reads groups of identical characters, a character at a time, counting the characters in the group. As long as the group is larger than some minimum that makes it worthwhile to compress (in our case, three or more characters), the program writes the repeated character once, first turning its high-order bit on, and follows it with the count. The program simply writes shorter groups directly.

We have to uncompress a compressed file to access its original contents. Figure 5.23 contains uncmprss, a program to accomplish this task. It reads a character at a time and examines the character's high-order bit. If the bit is off, it simply writes the character. Otherwise, the bit is on, and the next byte must be the count. It reads the count, and then writes that many characters (with their high bit turned off).

We ran compress on a collection of source programs and achieved space savings ranging from 10 to 20 percent. While this is commendable—we now have more available disk space and our files transmit faster over phone lines—other, more complex methods do much better. Most of these work by creating a frequency distribution of characters in the file, and using varying length bit strings to encode the different characters.

SUMMARY

- C provides relational operators for testing whether one value is equal (==), not equal (!=), less than (<), greater than (>), less than or equal (<=), or greater than or equal (>=) another value.

- C provides logical operators for combining relational expressions: && ANDs the results of the expressions and || ORs them. Both make use of short-circuit evaluation. There is one other logical operator, !, that inverts the logical value of an expression.

```c
/*
 * Simple data-compression program (assumes ASCII characters).
 */
#include <stdio.h>
#include <limits.h>

#define MINSIZE   3              /* smallest group to compress */
#define HIGHBIT 0x80             /* high bit indicates compressed char */

int main()
{
  int c;                        /* last character read */
  int newc;                     /* new character read */
  int cntc;                     /* count of last character */

  c = getchar();
  while (c != EOF)
  {
    cntc = 1;                   /* count occurrences of c */
    while (cntc < UCHAR_MAX && (newc = getchar()) == c)
      cntc++;
    if (cntc >= MINSIZE)
    {                           /* write count (high bit on) */
      putchar(c | HIGHBIT);
      putchar(cntc);
    }
    else                        /* write chars (high bit off) */
      while (cntc-- > 0)
        putchar(c & ~HIGHBIT);
    c = newc;
  }
  return 0;
}
```

Figure 5.22 (compress.c) A program to compress its input.

- C provides operators for shifting bits (<< and >>), inverting bits (~), and doing logical operations on bits (&, |, and ^).

- C provides a set of shorthand assignment operators. There are both arithmetic shorthand operators (+=, -=, *=, /=, and %=) and bitwise operators (&=, |=, <<=, >>=, and ^=). These operators often lead to more readable and efficient code.

- C provides increment (++) and decrement (--) operators, in both prefix and postfix forms. As prefix operators, the operation happens before the value is used. As postfix operators, the operation happens after the value is used.

- C provides a conditional operator (?:) for selecting between a pair of expressions, a comma operator (,) for sequentially evaluating a list of expressions, and a **sizeof** operator for determining the number of bytes in a variable or type.

```
/*
 * Simple uncompress program.
 */
#include <stdio.h>

#define HIGHBIT    0x80        /* high bit on indicates compressed char */

int main()
{
  int getcount(int c);
  int c;                        /* new character read */
  int cntc;                     /* count of times char should appear */

  while ((c = getchar()) != EOF && (cntc = getcount(c)) != 0)
    while (cntc-- > 0)
      putchar(c & ~HIGHBIT);
  return 0;
}

int getcount(int c)             /* determine # of times to write char */
{
  if (! (c & HIGHBIT))
    return 1;                               /* once - not compressed */
  return ((c = getchar()) == EOF) ? 0   /* zero - EOF followed char */
                                  : c;  /* next char is count */
}
```

Figure 5.23   (uncmprss.c)   A program to uncompress its input.

EXERCISES

5–1 Modify the file shrinking program (Figure 5.6) to eliminate completely any lines containing nothing but whitespace (this includes lines consisting only of a newline).

5–2 Modify Chapter 2's interest-computing programs to take advantage of C's shortcut operators. Does this change make those programs more or less readable?

5–3 Rewrite Chapter 4's base converter to take advantage of shortcut operators. Does this change make this program more or less readable?

5–4 Modify the data-packing program (Figure 5.9) to check for input errors such as entering a value other 0 or 1 for the person's sex.

5–5 Modify the data-packing program (Figure 5.9) to read a series of values and compute the average age and average length of employment. Then modify it to print all female employees before any male employee. Finally, modify it to print only the unmarried employees.

5–6 In the encryption program (Figure 5.13), j will eventually overflow on very large files. Is this a problem? If so, how can it be fixed?

5–7 Our compression program (Figure 5.22) is restricted to ASCII characters because we use the high bit to indicate compressed strings. Write a new version that instead indicates sequences by preceding them with an extra byte, one that contains a null character. Your program should work on any input, even one with null characters. Of course, you have to modify the uncompression program (Figure 5.23) to understand this new scheme.

Write a program that verifies that every character in its input is an ASCII character. A non-ASCII character (a character with its high-order bit set) causes an error message containing its octal code and position in the file (line number and character). We can use this program to verify that a file contains only ASCII characters before trying to compress it with our compression program (Figure 5.22).

5–8 Write a pair of functions, **bits_on** and **bits_off**, that return the number of bits that are on and off in a word. Use the shorthand bit-manipulating operators.

5–9 Write a function, **invbits**, that inverts a group of bits within a word. **invbits** should be passed a word, the position (from the right) of a group of bits within the word, and the number of bits to invert.

5–10 Write expressions that return the smaller and larger of two values.

5–11 Write expressions that return the smallest and largest of three values.

5–12 Write a program to produce a sales report. The input is in the form of a product code (an **int**), a sales price (a **double**), and a number of units sold (an **int**). Print the total sales and units sold for each product, along with the average price per unit. Also print the total sales of all products. Assume the products are grouped together by sales code.

5–13 Extend your solution to the previous exercise to print the highest and lowest sales item by volume and by units.

5–14 Write a concise program to compute student grade point averages (GPAs). Its input is a list of grades ('A', 'B', 'C', 'D', or 'F'). Each grade is separated by spaces. Each input line contains the grades for a single student. When computing a student's GPA, an A is worth 4 points, a B is worth 3 points, and so on. Here's some sample input and output:

```
A A A A
4.0
A C B
3.0
B B B B A
3.2
```

5–15 Extend the program in the previous exercise to print the average GPA.

5–16 Write a concise program to extract all the integers from its input. It should print each integer it detects on a line by itself. The input

```
w8 4 me 2 finish 2!
```

should result in the output

8
4
2
2

5–17 Extend the program in the previous exercise to recognize and print floating point numbers as well.

5–18 Write a program to compress its input data. Each input line contains a child's age (between 3 and 18), grade in school (between 0 and 12), sex (either 'M' or 'F'), and grade point average (a number between 0.0 (all F's) and 4.0 (all A's). Assume the GPA has exactly one digit after the decimal point. Your program should convert each input line into a single 16-bit integer. Its output is the integers that result.

6 STATEMENTS

This chapter covers C's rather small set of statements. We present the fine points of the statements we have already used and describe in detail those we have so far overlooked. While doing so, we improve and extend many of the programs we wrote in earlier chapters, and we write new programs to simulate a simple calculator and to print various breakdowns of input characters. The chapter concludes by tying several topics together in a program that prints an octal dump of its input.

6.1 EXPRESSION STATEMENTS

C's simplest statement is the *expression statement*, an expression followed by a semi-colon:

> *expression*;

We can use it anywhere C's syntax requires a statement. Both assignment statements and function calls, such as

```
lineno = 0;
```

and

```
printf("%6i ", ++lineno);
```

are merely expression statements and not special statement types, as in FORTRAN, BASIC, and Pascal.

An expression statement executes by evaluating the expression and throwing away the result. To be useful, it must have a side effect, such as invoking a function or changing a variable's value. The legal but useless expression statement

```
p * x;
```

multiplies `p`'s value by `x`'s value but does nothing with the result. Why would we ever write such a silly statement? Simply because of a typo—we probably meant to write `*=` instead of `*`. Fortunately, many compilers will warn us about this sort of statement.[1]

> *Watch out for accidentally writing syntactically legal expression statements that accomplish nothing.*

---
[1] The warning is usually something along the lines of "Statement has no effect at line ...".

```
/*
 * Break input into words (letter followed by letters or digits).
 */
#include <stdio.h>
#include <ctype.h>

#define YES   1
#define NO    0

int main()
{
  int c;                        /* next input character */
  int word;                     /* flag: are we dealing with a word? */

  word = NO;
  while ((c = getchar()) != EOF)
    if (isalpha(c) || (word && isdigit(c)))     /* write letter */
      putchar(c), word = YES;
    else
      if (word)                 /* write newline if we were in word */
        putchar('\n'), word = NO;
  return 0;
}
```

Figure 6.1 (brkwd.c) A terse version of our program to print its input onto its output, one word per line. All its compound statements have been replaced with expression statements.

6.2   **COMPOUND STATEMENTS**

A *compound statement* or *block* is a group of statements surrounded by braces.

```
{
    statement
    . . .
    statement
}
```

As with expression statements, we can place compound statements anywhere C's syntax requires a statement. But unlike expression statements, we *don't* follow compound statements with a semicolon.

Whenever we have a compound statement composed entirely of expression statements, we can use the comma operator to rewrite it as a single, more compact expression statement. Figure 6.1 does so several times in a new version of our earlier program that writes its input on the output, one word per line. In one place, for example, we replaced the compound statement

```
{
    putchar(c);
    word = YES;
}
```

with the more compact expression statement

```
putchar(c), word = YES;
```
but not readable

Are changes like this one worth it? They certainly lead to more compact programs, but at a cost: the program is now less readable and harder to modify and debug. In general, leave compound statements alone unless they consist of closely related expression statements or unless the lines saved make the function fit on a single page, aiding readability.

6.3   SIMPLE DECISIONS—THE IF

We've already seen the **if** statement. There is, however, one common combination of **if**s that we haven't seen: the *nested if*, one **if** inside another, as in this **if** that converts military time (**mhour**), a 24-hour clock, to standard time (**stdhour**).

```
if (mhour <= 12)
  if (mhour == 0)
    stdhour = 12;              /* midnight */
  else
    stdhour = mhour;           /* AM */
else
  stdhour = mhour - 12;        /* PM */
```

The idea is that if the hour is less than or equal to 12, it's left alone, unless it's 0, in which case it's converted to 12. If the hour is greater than 12, it's converted by subtracting 12 from it.

Nested **if**s aren't a big deal unless the inner **if** doesn't have an **else**. Consider this mistaken alternative to the previous **if**:

belongs to the closest if statement

```
stdhour = mhour;               /* assume AM */
if (mhour <= 12)
  if (mhour == 0)
    stdhour = 12;              /* midnight */
  else
    stdhour = mhour - 12;      /* PM */
```

To which **if** does the **else** belong? From the indentation, we might assume the outer. But the compiler ignores the indentation and simply assumes that any **else** attaches to the closest nonterminated **if**. So, despite this program's misleading indentation, the **else** associates with the *inner* **if** and the program does the time conversion incorrectly. We avoid the problem by placing the inner **if** in braces:

```
/*
 * Convert military time to standard time.  No error checking.
 */
#include <stdio.h>

int main()
{
  unsigned int mhour;                /* input: military hour */
  unsigned int min;                  /* input: military minutes */
  unsigned int stdhour;              /* standard hour */

  while (printf("Enter military time (as xx:xx): "),
         scanf("%u:%u", &mhour, &min) == 2)
  {
    stdhour = mhour;                         /* assume AM */
    if (mhour <= 12)
    {
      if (mhour == 0)
        stdhour = 12;                        /* midnight */
    }
    else
      stdhour = mhour - 12;         /* PM */
    printf("Standard time: %u:%02u\n", stdhour, min);
  }
  return 0;
}
```

Figure 6.2   (mtime.c) Convert military time to standard time.

```
    stdhour = mhour;                 /* assume AM */
    if (mhour <= 12)
    {
      if (mhour == 0)
        stdhour = 12;                /* midnight */
    }
    else
      stdhour = mhour - 12;          /* PM */
```

Figure 6.2 is a short program using this fragment. It reads in military time and prints standard time. Here's some sample input and output:

```
Enter military time (as xx:xx): 21:15
Standard time: 9:15
Enter military time (as xx:xx): 13:05
Standard time: 1:05
Enter military time (as xx:xx): 12:05
Standard time: 12:05
Enter military time (as xx:xx): 0:05
Standard time: 12:05
```

To print the minutes, we make use of a new feature of `printf`: if a field width begins with a leading zero, then the field is filled with zeros rather than blanks. So we write the hours and minutes with

```
printf("Standard time: %u:%02u\n", stdhour, min);
```

This writes the minutes in a field two digits wide, padded with leading zeros instead of blanks.

6.4   MULTIWAY DECISIONS—THE ELSE-IF

There's one other interesting form of `if`—the `else-if`:

```
if (first-expression)
    first-statement
else if (second-expression)
    second-statement
    . . .
else if (final-expression)
    final-statement
else
    default-statement
```

if expression other than zero, execute exp. statement below

final else & default statement is optional

The final `else` and *default-statement* are optional.

So far we've used `if`s to select one of two alternatives. The `else-if` comes in handy when we want to decide among many alternatives. It evaluates each expression in turn until one evaluates to something other than zero and then executes the statement associated with that expression. If all the expressions evaluate to zero, it executes the *default-statement* if any. In either case, control then passes to the statement following the `else-if`. Of course, `else-if` really isn't a special statement; it's simply a common way of writing `if`s in which the statement associated with each `else` happens to be another `if`:

```
if (first-expression)
    first-statement
else
    if (second-expression)
        second-statement
    else
        . . .
        if (final-expression)
            final-statement
        else
            default-statement
```

Figure 6.3 provides an example. It's a program that counts the number of characters in its input that fall into different classes, such as white space, letters, digits, punctuation, and so on. Here's its output when we run it with its source file as its input (using redirection):

```
/*
 * Print counts of various types of characters appearing in the input.
 */
#include <stdio.h>
#include <ctype.h>

#define  CNT_WIDTH  11    /* field width for displaying counts */

int main()
{
  double        pct(unsigned long count, unsigned long total);
  int           c;                      /* next input character */
  unsigned long spaces;                 /* white space characters */
  unsigned long letters;                /* a-z, A-Z */
  unsigned long digits;                 /* 0-9 */
  unsigned long puncts;                 /* punctuation characters */
  unsigned long others;                 /* anything else */
  unsigned long t;                      /* total characters */

  spaces = letters = digits = puncts = others = 0;
  while ((c = getchar()) != EOF)
    if (isspace(c))
      spaces++;                         /* whitespace */
    else if (isalpha(c))
      letters++;                        /* upper- or lowercase letter */
    else if (isdigit(c))
      digits++;                         /* digit */
    else if (ispunct(c))
      puncts++;                         /* punctuation */
    else
      others++;

  t = spaces + letters + digits + puncts + others;
  printf("Total   %*lu\n\n", CNT_WIDTH, t);
  if (t != 0)
  {
    printf("spaces  %*lu %5.1f%%\n", CNT_WIDTH, spaces, pct(spaces, t));
    printf("letters %*lu %5.1f%%\n", CNT_WIDTH, letters, pct(letters, t));
    printf("digits  %*lu %5.1f%%\n", CNT_WIDTH, digits, pct(digits, t));
    printf("puncts  %*lu %5.1f%%\n", CNT_WIDTH, puncts, pct(puncts, t));
    printf("others  %*lu %5.1f%%\n", CNT_WIDTH, others, pct(others, t));
  }
  return 0;
}

double pct(unsigned long count, unsigned long total)
{
  return count * 100.0 / total;         /* compute/return percentage */
}
```

no semi-colon (annotation on the `while ((c = getchar()) != EOF)` line)

Figure 6.3   (countem.c) A program to print a breakdown of the different types of characters in its input.

```
Total           1766

spaces           576   32.6%
letters          905   51.2%
digits            21    1.2%
puncts           264   14.9%
others             0    0.0%
```

From running this program on our files, we've discovered that C programs are typically about 50% letters, 25-35% spaces, and around 15% punctuation; executables are 75% control characters; and input files to text formatting programs are 70% letters, 10% punctuation. But what is this program useful for—other than giving us something to do when we're bored? We use an extended version of it to make educated guesses about the contents of files, based on the percentage breakdown of their input characters.

The program reads its input one character at a time. It uses a single **else-if** to determine the type of character we have and to update the appropriate counter.

```
if (isspace(c))
    spaces++;                    /* whitespace */
else if (isalpha(c))
    letters++;                   /* upper- or lowercase letter */
else if (isdigit(c))
    digits++;                    /* digit */
else if (ispunct(c))
    puncts++;                    /* punctuation */
else
    others++;
```

The **else-if** checks if the character is whitespace, a letter, a digit, or a punctuation character, stopping as soon as it falls into one of those classes. Then it updates the appropriate counter and exits. If the character doesn't fall into one of these classes, it updates the default counter, **others**. We're careful to make all of these counters **unsigned long**, since files can easily have more characters than we can count with an **int**.

To display the counters, we take advantage of another new feature of **printf**.

```
printf("Total    %*lu\n\n", CNT_WIDTH, t);
```

If the field width is a *, as in %*lu, we must supply two parameters, not just one. The first parameter is the desired field width, and the second is the value to write. Here, since **CNT_WIDTH** is 11, it means we're writing **t** in a field that's 11 digits wide.

6.5 MULTIWAY DECISIONS—THE SWITCH

Occasionally we have an **else-if** that tests for different values of the same expression. We might, for example, have an **else-if** that compares a single-letter, user-entered command with the program's legal commands to determine which action to take. But there's a better way: the **switch** statement.

— when statements
executed, it passes
to next following
statements,

— use "break" to exit
the enclosing switch.

```
switch (expression)
{
    case case-label-1 :
                                    statement-list
    case case-label-2 :
                                    statement-list
        . . .
    case case-label-n :
                                    statement-list
    default:
                                    statement-list
}
```

switch works by evaluating *expression*, passing control to the case labeled with its value (or to **default** if there is no such case), and executing the case's *statement list*. There are several restrictions on the labels. They have to be expressions that the compiler can evaluate to an integer constant, and all of the labels within a single **switch** must be unique, although they can appear in any order. Each case's *statement-list* can contain zero or more statements; there is no need to put braces around them.

After executing these statements, control automatically passes through to the next label. This falling through is almost always undesirable, so we usually place a **break** statement at the end of each **case**'s statement list. A **break** exits the enclosing **switch**.[2]

Figure 6.4 illustrates **switch** with a simple calculator program. Its input is a series of triplets containing a floating point operand, a single-character operator (such as **+**, **-**, *****, or **/**), and another floating point operand. The calculator prints the result of applying the operator to its operands. Here's some sample input and output for the calculator program:

```
35.6+23.9
59.500000
67/69
0.971014
87.12-56.11
31.010000
10*15
150.000000
1/0
Warning: division by zero.
0.000000
```

We use **scanf** to read the operand-operator-operand triplets. Because **scanf** doesn't automatically skip white space before single characters, there can be no spaces between the operator and its operands (eliminating this restriction is left as an exercise). The program simply quits if the user enters bad input.

Most of the program is a giant **switch** that selects the appropriate action for the user-entered operator. There is one case for each legal operator, along with a default case

---

[2]Unless the **break** is within a loop within a **switch**, but we'll worry about that possibility later in the chapter

```
/*
 * Simple calculator program.
 */
#include <stdio.h>

int main()
{
  int    vals;                                /* scanf return value */
  double op1;                                 /* the operand on the right */
  double op2;                                 /* the operand on the left */
  char   operator;                            /* operator */
  double result;                              /* result */

  while ((vals = scanf("%lf%c%lf", &op1, &operator, &op2)) == 3)
  {
    switch(operator)
    {
      case '+':
        result = op1 + op2;
        break;
      case '-':
        result = op1 - op2;
        break;
      case '*':
        result = op1 * op2;
        break;
      case '/':
        if (op2 != 0.0)                       /* watch out for divide by 0 */
          result = op1 / op2;
        else
        {
          printf("Warning: division by zero.\n");
          result = 0.0;
        }
        break;
      default:
        printf("Unknown operator: %c\n", operator);
        result = 0.0;                         /* default result */
        break;
    }
    printf("%f\n", result);
  }

  if (vals != EOF)
    printf("Error detected in the input: program terminated.\n");

  return vals != EOF;                         /* 0 only if read all values */
}
```

Figure 6.4 (calc.c) A simple calculator program that illustrates **switch**.

that prints an error message for any invalid operator. We end the actions for each case with a **break** statement; without it, control would automatically pass to the following case. We don't need the **break** after the **default**—it's there solely as a defensive measure to prevent an accidental fall-through if we add more case labels later.

> *Don't forget to place a **break** at the end of each case to prevent accidentally falling through.*

This automatic falling through cases leads to serious problems when we forget the **break**. But it's useful when we want numerous cases to select the same action. Figure 6.5 takes advantage of it in a program to provide a breakdown by group (quotes, brackets, and the usual delimiters) of the punctuation characters in its input. Here's the output when we run the program on itself.

```
Quotes          41
Brackets        28
Delimiters      51
Others        1171
```

The program has one counter for each group, and a **switch** to select the counter to be updated. Each character within a group has a case label, with all labels for a group placed above the single statement that increments its counter. When control passes to the label for any character in the group, it falls through to the statement updating the group's counter.

Falling through cases is appropriate only when the same action occurs for many different constants. Don't use it to execute statements in one case followed by statements in another.

6.6   LOOPS

stop when expression = 0.

C provides three looping mechanisms: **while**, **do-while**, and **for**. We're already well acquainted with **while**, and we've been introduced to **for**. **do-while** is similar to **while**, except that it's guaranteed to execute its body at least once.

- while ⇒ test and execute.

- do-while ⇒ execute and test

The do-while Statement

Unlike the **while**, which tests before it executes its body, the **do-while** tests afterward.

```
do
  statement
while (expression);
```

stop when expression = 0

A **do-while** repeatedly executes *statement* and evaluates *expression*. As with the **while**, the cycle comes to an end when *expression* evaluates to zero. But unlike the **while**, *statement* is always executed at least once.

```
/*
 * Count various types of punctuation characters.
 */
#include <stdio.h>

#define  CNT_WIDTH  11   /* field width for displaying counts */

int main()
{
  int     c;                      /* next input character */
  unsigned long quotes;           /* counts quotation marks */
  unsigned long brackets;         /* counts parens/brackets */
  unsigned long delims;           /* counts punctuation */
  unsigned long others;           /* counts everything else */

  quotes = brackets = delims = others = 0L;
  while ((c = getchar()) != EOF)
    switch(c)
    {
      case '\'':
      case '"':
      case '`':
        quotes++;                 /* single and double quotes */
        break;
      case '(':
      case ')':
      case '{':
      case '}':
      case '[':
      case ']':
        brackets++;               /* punctuation brackets */
        break;
      case ',':
      case '.':
      case ';':
      case ':':
      case '!':
      case '?':
        delims++;                 /* nonpunctuation chars */
        break;
      default:
        others++;
    }
  printf("Quotes     %*lu\n", CNT_WIDTH, quotes);
  printf("Brackets   %*lu\n", CNT_WIDTH, brackets);
  printf("Delimiters %*lu\n", CNT_WIDTH, delims);
  printf("Others     %*lu\n", CNT_WIDTH, others);
  return 0;
}
```

Figure 6.5 (countpct.c) A program to count special input characters.

Figure 6.6 uses **do-while** in a new version of our earlier **yesorno** function. Originally, **yesorno** took anything other than a 'y' or a 'Y' as a "no". This new version instead forces the user to enter an appropriate answer. The heart of **yesorno** is a single **do-while**. It keeps reading input lines until it finds one whose first character is appropriate. We use a **do-while** because we know we have to read at least one line of input.

The **for** Statement

any legal expressions

The last looping construct is the **for** statement:

```
for (Start ; Test ; Action )
    statement
```

We've seen that a **for** evaluates *Start* and then enters a cycle of evaluating *Test*, executing *statement*, and evaluating *Action*. The cycle terminates when *Test* evaluates to zero.

Usually, *Start* and *Action* are assignments or function calls and *Test* is a relational test—but all expressions are arbitrary and optional. *Arbitrary* means that we can fill them with any legal expression—we're not restricted to simply updating and testing a variable. *Optional* means that we can omit an expression whenever we want.

a missing test is taken to be nonzero ⇒ infinite loop.

We usually omit both *Test* and *Action* when we want to write an infinite loop. That's because a missing *Test* is taken to be nonzero, which means that such a loop is infinite and we expect to exit it with a **return** or some other *jump* statement (which we discuss in subsequent sections). So,

```
for(;;)
    statement
```

infinite loop

will execute *statement* forever.

use return or jump statement to visit.

> Remember that we need the semicolons in the **for** even when we leave out the expressions.

Figure 6.7 uses an infinite **for** in another version of **yesorno**. It repeatedly reads a character, skips the remaining characters on the input line, and writes an error message. We leave the loop (by returning from the function) only when the first character is an appropriate answer or an end of file.

Usually we omit *Start* because we've already done any needed initializations before entering the loop, such as when the loop index is passed as a parameter. Figure 6.8 does so in an even more concise version of our earlier **power** function. Because the exponent **exp** is passed as a parameter, there's no need to initialize it:

```
for (; exp > 0; exp--)
    p *= x;
```

Start, *Test*, and *Action* are truly arbitrary expressions and are in no way limited to the simple testing or updating of index variables. Figure 6.9 is a new version of our line

```
/*
 * Print prompt and then get a yes or no answer using "yesorno".
 */
#include <stdio.h>
#include <ctype.h>

#define YES 1
#define NO  0
#define BAD (-1)

int main()
{
  int yesorno(void);

  printf("Enter a YES or NO answer: ");
  switch (yesorno())
  {
    case YES: printf("YES!\n");
              break;
    case NO:  printf("NO!\n");
              break;
    default:  printf("EOF!\n");
  }
  return 0;
}

int yesorno(void)
{
  int c;                              /* holds input character */
  int answer;                         /* holds YES or NO answer */

  do
  {
    answer = BAD;
    switch (c = tolower(getchar()))
    {
      case EOF:                           /* nothing to do */
                break;
      case 'y': answer = YES;
                break;
      case 'n': answer = NO;
                break;
      default:  printf("Please answer with a YES or NO: ");
    }
    while (c != '\n' && c != EOF)
        c = getchar();                /* skip rest of line */
  }
  while (answer == BAD && c != EOF);
  return answer;
}
```

Figure 6.6   (yesorno.c) A new way to get a yes or no answer from the user.

```
/*
 * Print prompt and then get a yes or no answer using "yesorno".
 */
#include <stdio.h>
#include <ctype.h>

#define YES 1
#define NO  0

int main()
{
  int yesorno(void);

  printf("Enter a YES or NO answer: ");
  (yesorno() == YES) ? printf("YES!\n") : printf("NO!\n");
  return 0;
}

int yesorno(void)
{
  int answer;                          /* holds input character */
  int c;                               /* for skipping characters */

  for (;;)
  {
    if ((answer = tolower(getchar())) == EOF)
      return NO;                       /* EOF is NO */
    c = answer;
    while (c != '\n' && c != EOF)
      c = getchar();
    if (answer == 'y' || answer == 'n')
      return (answer == 'y') ? YES : NO;
    printf("Please answer with a YES or NO: ");
  }
}
```

Figure 6.7   (yesorno2.c) A version of **yesorno** that uses an infinite **for**.

numbering program, rewritten to take full advantage of this feature. Almost all of the program fits in a simple **for**:

```
for (lastch = '\n'; (c = getchar()) != EOF; putchar(lastch = c))
  if (lastch == '\n')                /* hit end of line */
    printf("%8li ", ++lineno);
```

Here, *Start* initializes **lastch**, the variable that holds the last character written. *Test* reads a new character and verifies that it's not end of file. And *Action* remembers this character and writes it out. All that's left in the body of the loop is to write out line numbers at the beginning of each new line.

```
/*
 * Compute powers, more concise version.
 */
double power(double x, int exp)
{
  double p;

  p = 1.0;
  if (exp > 0)                          /* positive exponent */
    for (; exp > 0; exp--)
      p *= x;
  else                                  /* negative exponent */
    for (; exp < 0; exp++)
      p /= x;
  return p;
}
```

Figure 6.8 (power.c) A very concise version of **power**.

```
/*
 * Copy input to output, giving each line a number.
 */
#include <stdio.h>

int main()
{
  int  c;                    /* current and */
  int  lastch;               /*    previous characters */
  long lineno;               /* lines printed so far */

  lineno = 0;
  for (lastch = '\n'; (c = getchar()) != EOF; putchar(lastch = c))
    if (lastch == '\n')            /* hit end of line */
      printf("%8li ", ++lineno);
  return 0;
}
```

Example for use 'for' statement

Figure 6.9 (lineno.c) Yet another version of our line numbering program.

```
/*
 * Compute average of its input values with no error checking.
 */
#include <stdio.h>

int main()
{
  int     next;                        /* next input value */
  long    sum;                         /* running total */
  int     n;                           /* number of input values */
  double  avg;                         /* average of input values */

  for (sum=n=0; scanf("%i", &next) == 1; sum += next, n++)
    ;
  avg = (n == 0) ? 0.0 : (double) sum / n;
  printf("Average of %i values is %f.\n", n, avg);
  return 0;
}
```

Figure 6.10   (avg.c)   An input averaging program that uses a **for** with an empty loop body.

Selection to use
'for' or 'while'

The **for** is more general than the **while**, so you may be wondering when each is appropriate. We use **for** when our loop control statements are simple and related. We use **while** when an equivalent **for** would contain unrelated computations or would omit both *Start* and *Action*. When in doubt, write the code for both and use the more readable one.

6.7   **THE NULL STATEMENT**   *place holder, it does nothing.*

C has a statement that does nothing: a lone semicolon with no preceding expression is a *null statement*. It's merely a placeholder that we use when the syntax requires a statement but we don't need to do any action. This situation occurs most frequently when side effects in a loop's control expression obviate the need for the loop body.

Figure 6.10, a new version of our program to average its input, takes advantage of this feature in the **for** loop to sum the input:

```
for (sum=n=0; scanf("%i", &next) == 1; sum += next, n++)
  ;                          /* compute total of input values */
```

By using the comma operator, we're able to turn the two statements that were in the body of the loop into a single expression, which then becomes the *Action* of the loop. This leaves the body of the loop empty, allowing us to use a null statement as its body.

> *Avoid placing a null statement on the same line as a* **for** *or a* **while**.

It's legal, and it makes the program more compact, but it also makes the program more difficult to decipher. It's far too easy for the program's reader to ignore the semicolon at the end of the line and mistake the following lines for the loop's body. Always place the null statement on a line by itself, indented slightly and followed by a comment. Failing to do so makes it hard to find mistakes like the one in this loop:

```
while (scanf("%i", next) == 1);
    printf("%i\n", next);
```

[handwritten: print only when loop exits]

[handwritten: while does not require ; therefore ; represents null statement]

It was supposed to echo each value it read. But it doesn't. The semicolon on the line containing the **while** is a null statement that forms the loop's body. What was meant to be the loop body,

```
printf("%i\n", next);
```

executes only after the loop exits, printing the value of the last number read.

6.8   JUMP STATEMENTS

[handwritten: break; continue; goto]

Statements ordinarily execute sequentially. Several statements alter this normal flow of control: **break**, **continue**, and **goto**. These *jump* statements violate some of the basic principles of structured programming and should be used with care.[3] In fact, many programmers avoid these statements like the plague, since they are always unavoidable and their abuse leads to impenetrable programs. Carefully used, however, they can simplify otherwise complex code, and contribute to making our programs more readable.

The break Statement *[handwritten: (break the nearest loop)]*

We've already used **break** to exit a **switch**. But **break** actually exits the nearest enclosing **for**, **while**, and **do-while**, as well.

Figure 6.11 provides an example of **break**. It contains a new version of Chapter 5's program to prompt for and read x, y pairs and then compute x^y. The program uses a loop that reads values until the end of file is reached:

```
while (printf("Enter x,y: "), (r = scanf(...)) != EOF)
```

Ostensibly, the **while** takes us through the entire set of input values. But the first thing in the body of the loop is a check to determine whether **scanf** actually read two values successfully. If there was a problem, we print an error message and use **break** to exit the loop and pass control to the statement following it.

---

[3]When it appears in the middle of a function, the **return** statement also alters the normal flow of control. At the end of a function, however, **return** is necessary, since it's the only way for a function to provide a value to its caller.

```
/*
 * Using our own function to compute exponents.
 */
#include <stdio.h>

int main()
{
  double power(double base, int exp);
  double x;                              /* user-supplied base */
  int    y;                              /* user-supplied exponent */
  int    r;                              /* scanf return value */

  while (printf("Enter x,y: "), (r = scanf("%lf %i", &x, &y)) != EOF)
  {
    if (r != 2)
    {
      printf("Error: Didn't read two input values.\n");
      break;
    }
    printf("%g^%i = %g\n", x, y, power(x, y));
  }
  return r == EOF;
}
```

Figure 6.11   (usepower.c) Our main program for **power** rewritten to handle errors using **break**.

```
if (r != 2)
{
  printf("Error: Didn't read two input values.\n");
  break;
}
```

In this case, that statement is the return from **main**.

Why write it this way? Simply because using **break** highlights failing to read a pair of input values as a special case. In general, we can use **break** to simplify a loop's test by separating out special cases or error conditions.

The continue Statement   *(cleap over the rest of the loop)*

continue;

A **continue** skips the rest of the loop body and causes the loop test to be immediately evaluated (except in the **for**, which evaluates *Action* first).

When do we use **continue**? Usually, to help prevent excessive nesting within a loop. Figure 6.12 uses **continue** in a slight revision of our earlier program to convert from military time to standard time. Now the program prints an error message if it encounters an invalid input (such as an hour field that's greater than 23 or a minutes field that's larger than 59). It then uses a **continue** to skip further processing of that input.

```
/*
 * Convert military time to standard time, now with error checking.
 */
#include <stdio.h>

int main()
{
  unsigned int mhour;              /* input: military hour */
  unsigned int min;               /* input: military minutes */
  unsigned int stdhour;           /* standard hour */

  while (printf("Enter military time (as xx:xx): "),
         scanf("%u:%u", &mhour, &min) == 2)
  {
    if (mhour >= 24 || min >= 60)
    {
      printf("Error: military time is from 0:00 to 23:59\n");
      continue;
    }
    stdhour = mhour;                      /* assume AM */
    if (mhour <= 12)
    {
      if (mhour == 0)
        stdhour = 12;                     /* midnight */
    }
    else
      stdhour = mhour - 12;       /* PM */
    printf("Standard time: %u:%02u\n", stdhour, min);
  }
  return 0;
}
```

jump to here

Figure 6.12 (mtime2.c) A version of our program to convert from military time to standard time that uses a `continue`.

```
if (mhour >= 24 || min >= 60)
{
  printf("Error: military time is from 0:00 to 23:59\n");
  continue;
}
```

use of continue

This `continue` is actually somewhat silly, since we can eliminate it simply by adding an `else` to our `if`. In fact, we can always avoid using a `continue` by adding an `else` and making the code to be skipped a separate function. We use it only when we check for errors at the beginning of a loop and find it convenient to leap over the rest of the loop body if an error occurs.

> *Avoid* `continue` *except when checking for error conditions at the top of a loop.*

The `goto` Statement

goto

The **goto** is the final jump statement. It simply transfers control to a labeled statement:

```
goto label
    . . .
label: statement
```

A *label* has the same syntax as an identifier and must be in the same function as the **goto**. If we want a label at the end of the function, we need to follow it with a null statement (but in that case we should probably be using a **return** rather than a **goto**).

One reasonable use of a **goto** is to rapidly bail out of nested loops when an error occurs.

```
for (...)
  for (...)
  {
    ...
    if (error condition) goto error;
    ...
  }
  ...
error:
  printf("Serious error detected -- bailing out\n");
```

When the error condition occurs, control simply transfers to the label **error** and the error message is printed. To see why **goto** is useful in this situation, consider trying to avoid it. We can't use **break** because it only exits a single loop. We could let a boolean variable note the error condition and then test its value each time through the loop, or we could make the code fragment containing the loops a function that returns a special value when an error condition occurs—but these alternatives seem to be more work than they're worth.

The above **goto** is reasonable, but in general the fewer **goto**s in your programs, the better. Most compilers generate less efficient code for loops implemented with **goto** instead of the structured loop constructs. In addition, rampant **goto**s render a program unreadable. **goto**s are scarce in well-written programs, and we haven't needed any in the programs in this book.

> *Avoid* **goto**s *whenever possible.*

6.9   CASE STUDY—OCTAL DUMP

*This section
is optional!*

We end this chapter with a program to print an octal dump of its input. The input

```
this is      a test
```

(which has two invisible tab characters between the "is" and the "a") produces

```
000000  164 t   150 h   151 i   163 s
000004  040     151 i   163 s   011 \t
000008  011 \t  141 a   040     164 t
000012  145 e   163 s   164 t   012 \n
```

The program reads the input one character at a time, writing it in octal and as a character if it is printable. It displays special characters, such as tabs and form feeds, as escape sequences. An octal dump is useful for displaying binary files, as well as for text files containing strange characters.

Figure 6.13 contains the entire octal dump program, which happens to use several of the special features of C's statements discussed in this chapter. The **main** program handles reading the characters and keeping track of when it's time to go to the next line of output. It uses a function **print_char** to actually display the character's octal and text representations. To print the count of characters and to print each character's octal representation, we again use the ability of **printf** to provide leading zeros instead of blanks.

SUMMARY

- C provides expression statements (any expression followed by a colon) and compound statements (any set of statements surrounded by braces).

- C provides an **if** statement for doing different actions if an expression is true or false.

- C provides a **switch** statement for selecting an action based on different values of a single expression.

- C provides three looping constants: **while**, which tests before the loop body; **for**, which also lets us specify actions to perform before we enter the loop and each time we complete the loop body; and **do-while**, which tests after the loop body.

- C provides several control-flow altering statements: **break**, **continue**, and **goto**. **break** exits the nearest enclosing loop or **switch**, **continue** skips the rest of a loop, and **goto** transfers control to an arbitrary label. These statements should be avoided if at all possible.

- Finally, C provides a **return** statement, which generally should appear only at the end of a function.

```c
/*
 * Dump input in octal (and character if printable).
 */
#include <stdio.h>
#include <ctype.h>

#define MAXCHARS  4                         /* max # of chars on a line */

int main()
{
  void          print_char(int c);
  int           c;                          /* next character */
  int           linecnt;                    /* # of chars on line */
  unsigned long inpcnt;                      /* # of chars in input */

  for (linecnt = 0, inpcnt = 0; (c = getchar()) != EOF; inpcnt++)
  {
    if (linecnt++ == 0)
      printf("%06li  ", inpcnt);
    else
      printf("   ");
    print_char(c);
    if (linecnt == MAXCHARS)
    {
      putchar('\n');
      linecnt = 0;
    }
  }
  if (linecnt > 0)                          /* finish up last line */
    putchar('\n');
  return 0;
}

void print_char(int c)
{
  printf("%03o ", c);              /* write octal code for character */
  switch (c)                       /* write escape sequence or char */
  {
    case '\a':  printf("\\a");   break;
    case '\b':  printf("\\b");   break;
    case '\f':  printf("\\f");   break;
    case '\n':  printf("\\n");   break;
    case '\r':  printf("\\r");   break;
    case '\t':  printf("\\t");   break;
    case '\v':  printf("\\v");   break;
    default:    printf("%c ", isprint(c) ? c : ' ');
  }
}
```

Figure 6.13   (octdump.c)   A program to produce an octal dump of its input.

EXERCISES

6–1   Rewrite our military time to standard time conversion program (Figure 6.2) to use the conditional operator.

6–2   Extend our military time to standard time conversion program (Figure 6.2) to also print "AM", "PM", "Noon", or "Midnight".

6–3   Modify our character counting program (Figure 6.3) to print the number of upper- and lowercase characters in its input and to print the number of vowels and the number of consonants.

6–4   Modify the calculator program (Figure 6.4) to include various synonyms for the existing operators (such as **a** for **+**, **s** for **-**, **m** for *****, and **d** for **/**), along with two additional operators, **%** (remainder) and **^** (exponentiation).

6–5   Rewrite the calculator (Figure 6.4) to use an **else-if** instead of a **switch**. Which version is more readable? Which version makes it easier to add synonyms for operators?

6–6   Modify the calculator (Figure 6.4) to allow the operands to be preceded and followed by an arbitrary amount of white space and to try to recover from input errors.

6–7   Rewrite our **break** and **continue** examples (Figures 6.11 and 6.12) without using a **continue** or **break**.

6–8   Rewrite a **while**, a **do-while**, and a **for** using only **if**s and **goto**s. Are the **goto** versions more or less readable than the standard loop constructs? You better say less readable!

6–9   Many programmers work in hex rather than octal. Modify the octal dump program (Figure 6.13) to produce a hex dump instead.

6–10   Modify the octal dump program (Figure 6.13) to print control characters in the form **^X**. For example, a *control-G* prints as **^G**.

6–11   Using nested **if**s, write a function **min3** that returns the smallest of three **int** values passed to it as parameters. Also, write a function **max3** that returns the largest of its three **int** parameters.

6–12   Write a program that prints the line numbers of those lines in its input that are over 80 characters long (those lines that are too big to fit on the typical terminal screen). Modify the program so that it also prints the length of those lines.

6–13   Write a program that prints the line numbers of those lines that contain only white space characters. Modify this program so that it also prints the line number of any line containing control characters, along with any control characters that line contains.

6–14   Write a simple program to aid in balancing a checkbook. The program's input is single-letter commands followed by an amount. The legal commands are **d** (deposit), **c** (check), **s** (service charge), **w** (withdrawal), and **b** (set starting balance). The program should print the balance after each transaction. Make sure your program is well behaved even when the input is in error.

6–15 Write a simple program to assign grades. The program's input is a test score and its output is a letter grade. Assume the traditional grading scale: 90-100 is an 'A', 80-89 is a 'B', 70-79 is a 'C', 60-69 is a 'D', and 0-59 is an 'F'. Make sure your program checks for input errors.

6–16 Modify the grading program from the previous exercise to read a series of scores for each student rather than a single score. Each input line now contains the scores for a single student. Print the average score and the final grade.

6–17 Modify the grading program from the previous exercise to expect each score to be followed by a weight. Make sure all the weights for a particular student add up to 100. Now the program prints both the weighted average and the final grade.

6–18 Write a program that prints all the prime numbers between 1 and 1000. A prime number is exactly divisible only by 1 and itself.

6–19 Write a program to determine whether a series of purchases come in over or under a budget. The program starts by reading a budget and a sales tax rate. It then reads a series of input lines containing the price of an item, the number purchased, and a discount rate. The program computes and prints the cost of each item. After reading all the input, it then prints the total cost and how it compared to the budget.

7 ARRAYS

This chapter introduces arrays. Our focus is on how to declare arrays and access their elements and on the mechanics of passing them as parameters. We introduce arrays with a program that reverses its input and show how to pass them as parameters by rewriting this program, building it on top of a pair of user-defined functions. We further illustrate the use of arrays by writing several useful functions: one reads values into an array until a sentinel is encountered, another searches an array for a particular value, and the last reads values into an array using a technique known as insertion sort. The chapter concludes with a case study that makes use of almost all the C features we've seen so far: a program that produces a histogram of its input.

7.1   USING ARRAYS—A PROGRAM TO REVERSE ITS INPUT

Figure 7.1 is a program to reverse its input. It reads all of its input values and then writes them in reverse order; the last value read is the first one written. If the program's input is:

```
10 20 18 24 68 1 19
```

its output is:

```
19
1
68
24
18
20
10
```

Reversing the input may seem senseless, but we can use this program to take values sorted in ascending order and print them in descending order. This program introduces the *array*, a convenient method for storing a large table of values.

An array is a named collection of values, all of which have the same underlying type. C supports arrays of any of its data types. We declare an array by giving the type of its elements, its name, and the number of elements. The declaration

```
int table[MAXVALS];
```

declares **table** to be an array, consisting of **MAXVALS int**s (100 in Figure 7.1).

```
/*
 * Read values and print them in reverse order.
 */
#include <stdio.h>

#define MAXVALS 100          /* max number of values we can reverse */

int main()
{
  int table[MAXVALS];        /* array to hold input values */
  int n;                     /* number of values in "table" */
  int i;                     /* index used in writing values */
  int next;                  /* next input value */
  int r;                     /* return code from trying to read values */

  for (n = 0; (r = scanf("%i", &next)) != EOF; n++)
  {
    if (r != 1)              /* bad return from scanf */
    {
      printf("Input error after reading %i values.\n", n);
      break;
    }
    if (n == MAXVALS)        /* no room to store this value */
    {
      printf("No more room after reading %i values.\n", n);
      break;
    }
    table[n] = next;
  }

  for (i = n - 1; i >= 0; i--)
    printf("%i\n", table[i]);
  return 0;
}
```

read until EOF

Figure 7.1   (revint.c) A program that prints its input in reverse order, one value per line.

We access an array element by following the array's name with an index enclosed in square brackets. An index is any expression that can be interpreted as an integer. Arrays are indexed from 0, so in this example we can access `table[0]` through `table[99]`.

> *Arrays are indexed starting with 0, not with 1 as in many other programming languages.*

There is no run-time array bounds checking, unlike languages such as Pascal, where an illegal array access terminates the program. C programmers are responsible for doing their own bounds checking in their program. If we don't, and we attempt to access an invalid location, such as `table[100]`, neither the compiler nor the run-time environment will complain.[1]

Figure 7.1 reverses its input by reading values into an array and then printing the array in reverse order. A single **for** loop controls the reading of the program's input values.

```
for (n = 0; (r = scanf("%i", &next)) != EOF; n++)
{
  if (r != 1)              /* bad return from scanf */
  {
    printf("Input error after reading %i values.\n", n);
    break;
  }
  if (n == MAXVALS)        /* no room to store this value */
  {
    printf("No more room after reading %i values.\n", n);
    break;
  }
  table[n] = next;
}
```

The idea is that ideally we want to read values into the array until we encounter **EOF**. Unfortunately, several things can go wrong: we can have an error in the input, and we can run out of room in the array. So we read each input value in a temporary variable, **next**, and then check for both of these conditions before storing the value into the next available array element. If we didn't have the first test and an error occurred, we would be storing garbage into the array. If we didn't have the second test and we ran out of room, we would be storing a value in the nonexistent memory location, `table[100]`.

> *Make sure any value used as array subscript is a legal array subscript.*

The program concludes with a **for** loop that prints **table**'s elements in reverse order.

```
for (i = n - 1; i >= 0; i--)
  printf("%i\n", table[i]);
```

We use **i** to index through **table**'s elements backward from its last element to its first. The loop is straightforward, with one subtlety. Even though **n** is the number of array elements, when we initialize **i** as the index of **table**'s last element, we initialize it to **n-1**, not **n**. We do this because arrays are indexed from 0, not 1. We want to ensure we access only `table[0]` through `table[n-1]`. In fact, `table[n]` is not a value we've read into the array.

---

[1] C officially describes the results of an access outside an array's bounds as *undefined*. That means the program is allowed to do *anything*, from writing a reasonable error message to crashing the system. In this case, we're likely to access or modify the value at the memory location immediately following our table, which is likely to be the location reserved for another variable. This type of error can be incredibly hard to track down, even in small programs like this one.

7.2 PASSING ARRAYS AS PARAMETERS

We can pass arrays as parameters, but the details are more complex than with the data types we've passed before. To illustrate this process, we rewrite our input reversal program to use two new functions, `table_fill` and `table_print_rev`. `table_fill` reads data into an array and counts the number of elements read. We pass it the array to fill and the number of values it can hold. It returns the number of elements read. `table_print_rev` prints an array in reverse order. We pass it the array to print and the number of values it contains. Figure 7.2 contains the new input reversing program, showing how the functions are defined and how they are called.

It's straightforward to pass an array to a function: all we do is provide its name. The heart of the **main** program is two function calls. The first passes the array **table** and the number of elements it can hold to `table_fill`, and the second passes the array and the number of values actually read into it to `table_print_rev`.

```
n = table_fill(table, MAXVALS);
table_print_rev(table, n);
```

Now let's look at how these functions work.

A Function to Read Values into an Array

`table_fill` takes two parameters: the array where the input values are to go (**a**) and the maximum number of values to read (**max**). As usual, we declare these parameters in the function header; **a** is an array of integers and **max** is an integer.

```
int table_fill(int a[], int max)
{
   ...
}
```

With array parameters we leave out the size of the array. We'll see why shortly.

Two things happen when we execute `table_fill`: it reads values into the array **a**, and it keeps track of the number of values read in a local variable **cnt**. When it finishes, **a** contains values at **a[0]** through **a[cnt-1]**. There's a problem though: because **cnt** is local, no other function, such as **main** or `table_print_rev` can access it. `table_fill` therefore returns **cnt**'s value (the number of values read into **a**), so that the main program can use it.

At this point alarm bells should be ringing. Aren't we expecting `table_fill` to read values into an array that's located in **main**? How is this possible if C always passes parameters using call by value?

It's possible because we've kept something hidden: an occurrence of an array name doesn't really refer to the entire array. In fact, an array name is merely an address, the address of the array's first element. When we pass **table** to `table_fill` what we're really passing is the address of **table[0]**, **&table[0]**. And it's that address that's copied into **a** and used in subsequent subscript calculations. Within `table_fill`, accessing **a[cnt]** is really accessing **table[cnt]**. So when within `table_fill`, we change **a[cnt]** with the assignment

```
/*
 * Read values and print them in reverse order.  This time uses:
 *    table_fill - reads values into an array.
 *    table_print_rev - prints the array in reverse order.
 */
#include <stdio.h>

#define MAXVALS 100          /* max number of values we can reverse */

int main()
{
  int  table_fill(int a[], int max);
  void table_print_rev(int a[], int max);
  int  table[MAXVALS];       /* array to hold input values */
  int  n;                    /* number of values in "table" */

  n = table_fill(table, MAXVALS);
  table_print_rev(table, n);        pass the address of array, i.e.
  return 0;                                location of table [0].
}
```

```
int table_fill(int a[], int max)
{
  int next;                  /* next input value */
  int r;        local.       /* return from trying to read values */
  int cnt;   no. of values   /* count of values read */
             read into a
  for (cnt = 0; (r = scanf("%i", &next)) != EOF; cnt++)
  {
    if (r != 1)              /* bad return from scanf */
    {
      printf("Error in the input after reading %i values.\n", cnt);
      break;
    }
    if (cnt == max)          /* no room to store this value */
    {
      printf("No more room in array after reading %i values.\n", cnt);
      break;
    }
    a[cnt] = next;           /* save element in array */
  }
  return cnt;
}
```

```
void table_print_rev(int a[], int n)
{
  int i;                          /* index used in writing values */

  for (i = n - 1; i >= 0; i--)
    printf("%i\n", a[i]);
}
```

Figure 7.2   (revint2.c) A new version of our input reversal program.

```
    a[cnt] = next;
```

we change `table[count]` in `main`.

> *Changing an array parameter changes the corresponding array argument.*

Now we can better understand the parameter list in `table_fill`'s header:

```
int table_fill(int a[], int max)
```

The first parameter, **a**, is described as an array (of some unknown number) of **int**s. We don't give a size because **a** really isn't an array at all—it's just a copy of the address of the array's first element.

Passing an address rather than the entire array can be a bit bewildering, but it has one nice benefit: functions aren't tuned to a particular size array. We can, for example, use `table_fill` to read in any size array of integers. It doesn't matter if the array has 10 or 100 or even 1000 elements. When we declare an array parameter, we need only declare that it's an array of a particular type, but can omit how many elements it contains. Of course, these functions do need to know how many elements are actually in the particular arrays they are passed. But we can easily supply that information in an additional parameter, as we did with `table_fill`.

You might think that an alternative to passing an array as a parameter would be to somehow have `table_fill` return an array. However, C does not allow functions to return arrays.

The function `table_print_rev` is similar to `table_fill`. It takes two arguments, the array to print and the number of values in the array, and its header follows the same format as `table_fill`:

```
table_print_rev(int a[], int max)
```

And like `table_fill`, it's a general function. We can use it to print any size array of integers in reverse order.

Arrays and Function Prototypes

Before we called `table_fill` and `table_print_rev` from `main`, we supplied prototypes for them.

```
int table_fill(int a[], int size);
void table_print_rev(int a[], int items);
```

We mentioned earlier that with function prototypes only the type information is important, not the names, which allows us to leave the names out. With arrays, however, doing so makes the prototypes especially ugly and hard to understand.

```
int table_fill(int [], int);
void table_print_rev(int [], int);
```

In C, the type information is everything in the type declaration without the variable name. So these declarations say that **table_fill** and **table_print_rev** take two parameters: an **int** array of any size and an **int**. When our prototypes involve arrays, we generally provide a dummy name to keep them readable.

Arrays and the `sizeof` Operator

In Chapter 5, we introduced the **sizeof** operator as a mechanism for determining how many bytes a particular variable requires. We can also use it with arrays. On a 16-bit machine, modifying Figure 7.2 by inserting this statement before the call to **table_fill**

```
printf("Table requires %lu bytes.\n",
       (unsigned long) sizeof(table));
```

causes the program to print

```
Table requires 200 bytes.
```

The 200 is the number of elements in **table** (100) × the number of bytes per element (2).

> **sizeof** *returns the number of bytes in the array, not the number of elements.*

You might think that **sizeof** gives us a way to calculate the number of elements in an array parameter, allowing us to avoid passing that information explicitly as an additional argument. But it doesn't. The reason is that taking **sizeof** of an array parameter gives the number of bytes in the address that's actually passed, not in the entire array. Although inconvenient, this behavior makes sense because **sizeof** is a compile-time operator, so it has no way of knowing how many items are actually passed at run time.

7.3   SOME EXAMPLE PROGRAMS USING ARRAYS

Arrays will play a role in the vast majority of programs you write. The most frequent operations we perform on arrays are reading values into them, searching them for a value, putting them into sorted order, and printing them. This section contains a pair of example programs that illustrate these common operations. The first reads values into an array and then uses sequential search to determine whether or not it contains certain values. The second reads values into an array, using a special technique called insertion sort. Both of these examples work only with arrays of **int**, but you can use them as a model for similar functions that work with other types of arrays.

```
/*
 * Search table for the target value, returning its position.
 */
#include <stdio.h>

#define MAXVALS   10                     /* max # of entries in table */
#define SENTINEL   0                     /* terminating input value */

int main()
{
  int table_search(int a[], int n, int target);
  int table_fill_sentinel(int a[], int n, int termval);
  int table[MAXVALS];                    /* table of values */
  int target;                            /* value to find */
  int found;                             /* target position */
  int n;                                 /* number of items */
  int r;                                 /* scanf return value */

  n = table_fill_sentinel(table, MAXVALS, SENTINEL);
  while ((r = scanf("%i", &target)) == 1)
    if ((found = table_search(table, n, target)) != -1)
      printf("Found %i as element %i.\n", target, found);
    else
      printf("Didn't find %i.\n", target);
  if (r != EOF)
    printf("Illegal value to search for.\n");
  return 0;
}
```

Figure 7.3   (usetable.c)   A program to read values into an array and then search it for particular values.

Searching an Array with Sequential Search

Figure 7.3 contains our first example. It reads values into an array until encountering a zero, then determines whether subsequent input values are in the array. Here's some sample input and output:

```
10 45 67 16 0
67
Found 67 as element 2.
10
Found 10 as element 0.
76
Didn't find 76.
```

We've already seen how to read values into an array until we encounter end of file or run out of room. But we can't use **table_fill** here, since we need to read additional values after filling the array. Instead, we have to write a new function that reads values into the array only until the user enters a special value indicating the end of the input.

```
/*
 * Read values into an array until a sentinel value is read.
 */
#include <stdio.h>

int table_fill_sentinel(int a[], int max, int sentinel)
{
  int next;                       /* next input value */
  int r;                          /* return from trying to read values */
  int cnt;                        /* count of values read */

  cnt = 0;
  while ((r = scanf("%i", &next)) == 1 && next != sentinel)
  {
    if (cnt == max)               /* no room to store this value */
    {
      printf("Array full after reading %i values.\n", cnt);
      break;
    }
    a[cnt++] = next;              /* save element in array */
  }
  if (r == EOF)                   /* never saw sentinel */
    printf("End of file before encountering %i\n", sentinel);
  else if (r != 1)                /* bad return from scanf */
    printf("Error in the input after reading %i values.\n", cnt);
  return cnt;
}
```

(handwritten annotations: "what does the input string look like?", "incrementing cnt by 1")

Figure 7.4   (tabsent.c)   A function to fill an array until a sentinel is reached.

That value is called a *sentinel*.

Figure 7.4 contains `table_fill_sentinel`, our new input reading function. It's similar to `table_fill`, but with several key differences. One is that it takes an extra parameter: the sentinel indicating the end of the input. The other is that it now prints an error message if it encounters `EOF`. We're still careful to check for whether there's an error in the input or the array is full and to place the value we read into the array only after we're sure it's safe to do so.

Once we fill the array, we need to search the array for subsequent input values. To do so, we use a new function, `table_search`, shown in Figure 7.5. It takes three parameters: the array to search, the number of elements actually in the array, and the target value we're trying to find. It works by simply running through the array, comparing each array element with the target. It returns the index of the matching element, or −1 if a matching element isn't found. For small arrays, searching the entire array for the target value is sufficiently fast. For large arrays, however, this sequential search method is likely to be too slow, since on average it's going to examine half of the elements in the array. Fortunately, we'll soon see a much more efficient approach we can use for large sorted arrays.

```
/*
 * A function to search for a target in an array of integers.
 */
int table_search(int a[], int n, int target)
{
  int i;

  for (i = 0; i < n && a[i] != target; i++)
    ;                                        /* search for matching value */
  return (i != n) ? i : -1;
}
```
← return -1 if no matching is found

Figure 7.5 (tabsrch.c) A function to perform sequential search on an array.

Sorting an Array with Insertion Sort

The other example of using arrays is a sorting program. This program reads integers, keeps them sorted in an array (in ascending order), and prints the array when it is done reading. The program reads from its standard input and writes to its standard output, but we can use redirection to use it to sort a file.

The program in Figure 7.6 uses a sorting technique known as *insertion sort*; it is easy to understand and to program, and usually works with little debugging effort. Its drawback is that it is not the fastest sorting routine; the computing time increases as the *square* of the number of values to be sorted. Double the number of values and the computing time goes up by a factor of 4; triple the number and the computing time goes up by a factor of 9. Even so, insertion sort is suitable when we have to sort fewer than 50 to 100 values.

Insertion sort works by assuming that the array is already sorted and its job is to take each new value and insert it into the appropriate place in the array. We compare the new value with the last, "largest" element in the array. If the new value is smaller than the largest, we shift the largest over one place in the array and compare the new value with the next largest value. When the new number is finally larger than some value in the array, we have found the appropriate place to insert it. If the new value is smaller than every value in the array, it goes into the first position. The entire operation can be characterized as "compare, shift; compare, shift; ..." until we find the appropriate place. Figure 7.7 illustrates the technique.

We use two functions to implement insertion sort: **table_insert** places a value in its correct place in the array, and **table_print** prints the array.

table_insert needs to determine where the new element should go and put it there. To insert a value in the array, we compare it with each array element, starting with the largest, or last, element and shifting values one place whenever it is smaller than the element we are comparing. Eventually, it will be greater than or equal to some array element, or we will have reached the start of the array. In either case we insert it into the newly created hole. Finding the place for the new element is accomplished with a single **for** loop, whose body consists of a single statement:

```
/*
 * Read values and sort them using "insertion sort."  It uses:
 *    table_insert - place value in correct place in array.
 *    table_print - print array containing "num" items in sorted order.
 */
#include <stdio.h>

#define  MAXVALS  100                    /* max # of values to sort */

int main()
{
  void table_insert(int [], int, int);
  void table_print(int [], int);
  int  table[MAXVALS];                   /* table of values */
  int  n;                                /* number of values in table */
  int  r;                                /* value returned by scanf */
  int  v;                                /* current value */

  for (n = 0; (r = scanf("%i", &v)) != EOF; table_insert(table, n++, v))
  {
    if (r != 1)
    {
      printf("Input error after reading %i values\n", n);
      break;
    }
    if (n == MAXVALS)
    {
      printf("Table full after reading %i values\n", n);
      break;
    }
  }
  table_print(table, n);
  return 0;
}

void table_insert(int a[], int num, int val)
{
  int pos;

  for (pos = num; pos > 0 && val < a[pos-1]; pos--)
    a[pos] = a[pos-1];
  a[pos] = val;
}

void table_print(int a[], int num)
{
  int i;

  for (i = 0; i < num; i++)
    printf("%i\n", a[i]);
}
```

Figure 7.6   (isort.c) A program to sort integers using insertion sort.

```
table
  [0]   [1]   [2]   [3]   [4]   [5]              val     pos
 ┌─────┬─────┬─────┬─────┬─────┬─────┐         ┌─────┐ ┌─────┐
 │  2  │  7  │  9  │ 18  │ 21  │     │  · · ·  │  8  │ │  5  │
 └─────┴─────┴─────┴─────┴─────┴─────┘         └─────┘ └─────┘
```

(*a*) The value is smaller than `table[pos-1]`, copy, decrement `pos`.

```
table
  [0]   [1]   [2]   [3]   [4]   [5]              val     pos
 ┌─────┬─────┬─────┬─────┬─────┬─────┐         ┌─────┐ ┌─────┐
 │  2  │  7  │  9  │ 18  │ 21  │ 21  │  · · ·  │  8  │ │  4  │
 └─────┴─────┴─────┴─────┴─────┴─────┘         └─────┘ └─────┘
```

(*b*) The value is smaller than `table[pos-1]`, copy, decrement `pos`.

```
table
  [0]   [1]   [2]   [3]   [4]   [5]              val     pos
 ┌─────┬─────┬─────┬─────┬─────┬─────┐         ┌─────┐ ┌─────┐
 │  2  │  7  │  9  │ 18  │ 18  │ 21  │  · · ·  │  8  │ │  3  │
 └─────┴─────┴─────┴─────┴─────┴─────┘         └─────┘ └─────┘
```

(*c*) The value is smaller than `table[pos-1]`, copy, decrement `pos`.

```
table
  [0]   [1]   [2]   [3]   [4]   [5]              val     pos
 ┌─────┬─────┬─────┬─────┬─────┬─────┐         ┌─────┐ ┌─────┐
 │  2  │  7  │  9  │  9  │ 18  │ 21  │  · · ·  │  8  │ │  2  │
 └─────┴─────┴─────┴─────┴─────┴─────┘         └─────┘ └─────┘
```

(*d*) Compare value with `table[pos-1]`, value is bigger, install at `table[pos]`.

```
table
  [0]   [1]   [2]   [3]   [4]   [5]
 ┌─────┬─────┬─────┬─────┬─────┬─────┐
 │  2  │  7  │  8  │  9  │ 18  │ 21  │  · · ·
 └─────┴─────┴─────┴─────┴─────┴─────┘
```

(*e*) The final array.

Figure 7.7 Stages in insertion sort. The new value is eventually put between the 7 and the 9.

```
for (pos = num; pos > 0 && val < a[pos - 1]; pos--)
    a[pos] = a[pos - 1];
```

A great deal is taking place within this **for** loop; we suggest trying to work through it by hand to see its effect.

table_print is almost identical to **table_print_rev**; the only difference is in the order in which the table is printed. Like **table_print_rev**, **table_print** is passed the number of elements in the array it is printing, so it also works for any size array.

7.4 CASE STUDY—A HISTOGRAM PRODUCER

This section is optional!

All of the examples of arrays in this chapter have manipulated them sequentially. This chapter concludes with a program that uses them in a more random access way. This program produces a histogram of its input. A histogram is a way to visualize a frequency distribution using a set of bars, with each bar's length representing the relative frequency of a group of values. Figure 7.8 shows a sample histogram generated from the data in Figure 7.9.

The usual approach to generating histograms is to maintain an array whose elements count the values falling within each range. After reading and counting the input values, the bars can be generated by writing one asterisk (or other desired character) for each value that falls within that range. There are two tricky parts: mapping the input value to the appropriate counter within the array and producing reasonable output when one group has a large number of values.

To keep things simple, we assume that each group of values (or *bucket*) has one counter and that every bucket is the same size. Given an input value, we can map it to the appropriate counter by subtracting the smallest value from it and dividing the result by the size of a bucket. If we have a data value of 45, a minimum value of 0, and 10 values per bucket, we should update bucket number 4.

Our other worry is how to produce reasonable output, even if there are more values in a bucket than there are columns available on the output device. The trick is to scale the output so that the row with the most asterisks covers the available width, and the other rows are proportionally shorter. It's possible, however, that this scaling will cause a row with proportionally few values to appear as though it has none. To fix that, we write at least one asterisk for each row that has one or more values. We also write an exact count at every row's end.

The histogram program is broken into several different files. Figure 7.10 contains **main** and the function **fill_buckets**, which reads the input values and updates the appropriate counter. Figure 7.11 contains **print_histogram**, which writes the histogram, after first scaling the counters to determine how many asterisks to print. Finally, the histogram program uses a set of generally useful utility functions such as **inrange**, **min**, **max**, and **put_n_chars**. Since we want to use these functions in other programs, we've placed them in a separate file, shown in Figure 7.12.

SUMMARY

- C provides arrays whose size must be specified at compile time.

- Arrays are indexed from 0, and access outside defined bounds produces *undefined* behavior.

- When we pass an array to a function, only the address of its first element is copied, not the entire array. There's no need to specify the number of elements.

```
  0-   4  |
  5-   9  |
 10-  14  |***                                (3)
 15-  19  |
 20-  24  |*                                  (1)
 25-  29  |
 30-  34  |
 35-  39  |
 40-  44  |
 45-  49  |*                                  (1)
 50-  54  |
 55-  59  |*****                              (5)
 60-  64  |**                                 (2)
 65-  69  |*********                          (9)
 70-  74  |*********************             (21)
 75-  79  |****************                  (16)
 80-  84  |*******                            (7)
 85-  89  |******                             (6)
 90-  94  |**                                 (2)
 95-  99  |*                                  (1)
100-100  |*****                              (5)
```

Figure 7.8   Sample histogram output.

```
89   87   56   89   67   78   79   80   85   97  100  100   23   45   12   14   87
88   84   84   84   84   77   77   72   73   68   69   69  100  100   11   75   71
71   72   79   84   71   72   70   74   75   73   71   79   72   55   55   68   65
67   72   71   75   73   71   74   71   71   78   79   80  100   91   92   66   61
61   57   57   65   71   74   78   78   78   78   78
```

Figure 7.9   Sample histogram input.

- Unlike the other variables we've seen, changes to array parameters affect the passed array.

- Some common operations on arrays are to read values into them, search for a value, sort the array, and print the values they contain.

EXERCISES

7–1   Modify the programs in this chapter to work with **double**s.

7–2   Modify the insertion sort program (Figure 7.6) to sort its input in descending rather than ascending order. Also, modify it to count and print the number of elements moved. For

```c
/*
 * Produce a histogram of its input values.
 */
#include <stdio.h>

#define NUMBCKTS    21              /* reasonable number of buckets  */
#define MINVAL       0              /* range of values is 0-100      */
#define MAXVAL     100              /*    (assumption is test scores) */

int main()
{
  void          fill_buckets(unsigned long buckets[],
                             int bucket_size, int numbuckets,
                             int minval, int maxval);
  void          print_histogram(unsigned long buckets[],
                             int bucket_size, int numbuckets,
                             int minval, int maxval);
  unsigned long buckets[NUMBCKTS];
  int           bucket_size;

  bucket_size = (MAXVAL - MINVAL) / (NUMBCKTS - 1);
  fill_buckets(buckets, bucket_size, NUMBCKTS, MINVAL, MAXVAL);
  print_histogram(buckets, bucket_size, NUMBCKTS, MINVAL, MAXVAL);
  return 0;
}

/* Place each input value in an appropriate bucket */

void fill_buckets(unsigned long buckets[],
                  int bucket_size, int numbuckets,
                  int minval, int maxval)
{
  int inrange(int min, int max, int value);
  int next;                              /* next input value */
  int r;                                 /* scanf return value */
  int i;                                 /* index */

  for (i = 0; i < numbuckets; i++)       /* zero out buckets */
    buckets[i] = 0;
  while ((r = scanf("%i", &next)) != EOF)
    if (r != 1)
    {
      printf("Error while reading input values\n");
      break;
    }
    else if (!inrange(minval, maxval, next))
      printf("Out of range input value: %i\n", next);
    else
      buckets[(next - minval) / bucket_size]++;
}
```

Figure 7.10   (histo.c) The main program for our histogram producer.

```
/*
 * Print the histogram.
 */
#include <stdio.h>

#define MAXMARKS  25                       /* maximum marks per bucket */
#define MARKER    '*'                      /* marker for values */

void print_histogram(unsigned long buckets[],
                      int bucketsize, int numbuckets,
                      int minval, int maxval)
{
  int           min(int x, int y);
  int           max(int x, int y);
  void          put_n_chars(char c, int n);
  unsigned long table_max(unsigned long a[], int n);
  int           b;                      /* bucket index */
  int           bmin;                   /* smallest value in a bucket */
  int           bmax;                   /* largest value in a bucket */
  double        scale;                  /* scaling factor */
  int           marks;                  /* # of marks to write on line */
  unsigned long most;                   /* # of marks in largest bucket */

  most = table_max(buckets, numbuckets);
  scale = (most > MAXMARKS) ? (double) MAXMARKS / most : 1.0;
  for (b = 0, bmin = minval; b < numbuckets; b++, bmin = bmax + 1)
    {                                   /* print each row to scale */
    bmax = min(bmin + bucketsize - 1, maxval);
    marks = (buckets[b] > 0) ? max(buckets[b] * scale, 1) : 0;
    printf("%3i-%3i |", bmin, bmax);        /* write label */
    put_n_chars(MARKER, marks);             /* write markers */
    put_n_chars(' ', MAXMARKS - marks);     /* write spaces */
    if (buckets[b])                         /* write count */
      printf(" (%lu)", buckets[b]);
    putchar('\n');
    }
}

unsigned long table_max(unsigned long a[], int n)
{
  int           i;
  unsigned long largest;                    /* largest count */

  for (largest = 0, i = 0; i < n; i++)
    if (a[i] > largest)
      largest = a[i];
  return largest;
}
```

Figure 7.11   (histoout.c)   The function to print the histogram.

```
/*
 * Some useful utility functions.
 *    min - returns smaller of two values.
 *    max - returns larger of two values.
 *    inrange - check whether one value is between two others.
 *    put_n_chars - write a character "n" times.
 */
#include <stdio.h>

int min(int x, int y)
{
  return (x < y) ? x : y;
}

int max(int x, int y)
{
  return (x > y) ? x : y;
}

int inrange(int min, int max, int v)
{
  return v >= min && v <= max;
}

void put_n_chars(char c, int n)
{
  while (n-- > 0)
    putchar(c);
}
```

Figure 7.12   (utils.c) Some generally useful utility functions.

a random set of n input values, there should be somewhere between 0 and $n(n + 1)/2$ exchanges.

7–3 Modify the insertion sort program (Figure 7.6) to first find the appropriate place to insert the new value and then shift everything after it one place before inserting the value.

7–4 Rewrite the histogram program (Figures 7.10 and 7.11) to read its input using **get_base10_num** (Figure 4.11) rather than **scanf**.

7–5 Modify the histogram program (Figures 7.10 and 7.11) to read the minimum and maximum values, bucket size, and number of rows per bar. Obviously there needs to be some internal maximum bucket count; the program should verify that the desired bucket count is not too large.

7–6 Write a function, **table_init**, that sets every element of an array of integers to a particular value. The function takes three parameters: the array, its size, and the initial value.

7–7 Write a function, **table_average**, that computes and returns the average of the first n elements in an array of **int**s. Test it with a small program that uses **table_fill** to fill the array with values.

7–8   Write a function to determine whether an array of **int**s is symmetrical. That is, its first element is the same as its last element, its second element is the same as its next-to-last element, and so on.

7–9   Write a function, **get_base10_nums**, that reads values from a single input line, stopping when a **\n** is read. It takes two arguments. The first tells it how many values to read, and the second is an array in which to place those values. Use blanks and tabs to delimit numbers.

7–10   One way to avoid overflow is to use an array to represent the numbers, with one integer in the array corresponding to one digit in the number. Write a function, **add_bignum**, that adds two numbers represented by digit arrays, and fills in a third digit array with the result. Also write its counterpart, **sub_bignum**, that subtracts two numbers represented by digit arrays.

7–11   Extend your solution to the previous exercise to include two additional functions, **mult_bignum** and **div_bignum**, which multiply and divide two numbers represented by digit arrays.

7–12   Write a program that reads its input into an array and then uses selection sort to sort the array. In selection sort, we first find the largest element in the array and exchange it with the first array element's value; then we find the next largest element in the array and exchange it with the second array element's value; and so on, until the array is sorted.

7–13   Write a program that uses insertion sort to sort an array in place.

7–14   Write a program that reads values from its input and counts the occurrences of each unique value in the input. Assume the values are between 1 and 100. Once the input has been read, write each value and the number of its occurrences. Ignore values that didn't appear in the input.

7–15   Rewrite the program from the previous exercise so that there's no limit on the number or range of the input values. You'll need to keep two arrays, one containing the input values and the other containing their corresponding counts.

7–16   Write a program that prints the 10 smallest values in its input. Extend the program to print the 10 largest values.

7–17   Write a program that reads test scores into an array. Once it's read the scores, have it print the mean (the average score), median (the score that half the students are less than and the other half are better than), and mode (the score the most students had).

7–18   Extend the program in the previous exercise to print the scores in sorted order.

7–19   Write a program that reads pairs of values and prints them, both sorted by the first value and sorted by the second. One use of this program would be to read student ID numbers and test scores and then print them sorted by student numbers and student scores.

8 PROGRAM STRUCTURE

Our previous programs have had a simple structure. This chapter deals with more complex program organizations. We finish up our description of variables local to particular functions and introduce variables accessible by any function. While discussing variables, we present the storage classes that control their lifetime, location, and visibility. We then show how header files simplify accessing variables and functions visible only within a single file and how we can have variables and functions visible only within a single file. This chapter concludes with a case study: an initial implementation of a set data type.

8.1 LOCAL VARIABLES

Local variables are those declared within a function body. We've so far ignored two of their most useful features. First, there's a short cut for declaring more than one variable with the same type. Second, we're able to provide an initial value whenever we declare a variable. And third, we're not restricted to declaring local variables only at the start of functions.

Concise Variable Declarations

So far, we have declared each variable by preceding it with a type and following it with a semicolon, even if the variables had the same type:

```
int next;              /* next input value */
int n;                 /* number of input values */
```

However, there's a short cut, and Figure 8.1 takes advantage of it in a slightly more concise version of our earlier program to compute the average of its input values. C lets us factor out common type information and then connect the declarations up with commas, instead of separating them with semicolons.

```
int next, n;                   /* next input, number of inputs */
```

The obvious advantage to this more concise form is a lot less typing, since we don't have to repeat the type in every variable declaration. But there are disadvantages as

```
/*
 * Compute average of its input values with no error checking.
 */
#include <stdio.h>

int main()
{
  int    next, n;                      /* next input, number of inputs */
  long   sum = 0;                      /* running total */
  double avg;                          /* average of input values */

  for (n = 0; scanf("%i", &next) == 1; n++)
    sum += next;
  avg = (n == 0) ? 0.0 : (double) sum / n;
  printf("Average of %i values is %f.\n", n, avg);
  return 0;
}
```

Figure 8.1   (avg.c)   A more concise version of our program to compute the sum of its input values.

well. One is that we now have no obvious place to comment on what the variable does, unless we place names on separate lines and lose some of the conciseness.

```
    int next,                      /* next input */
        n;                         /* number of inputs */
```

The other is that it's not as easy to change a variable's type. For this reason, we generally prefer the more verbose form, unless we happen to be declaring a few temporary variables.

Initializing Local Variables

What's the default initial value of local variables we don't initialize explicitly? You might guess zero, since that's the value they would have in many other languages, but you would be wrong. Instead, they simply start with whatever was previously in the memory location allocated for them—usually garbage.

> *Don't count on local variables automatically being initialized to zero.*

To prevent hard-to-find problems, we must explicitly initialize all our local variables before we use them.[1] Conveniently, we can initialize a local variable when we declare it. All we have to do is follow its name with an equal sign and an arbitrary expression. We took advantage of this in Figure 8.1 when we declared **sum**:

---

[1]Some compilers generate code that sets local variables to zero but the language has no such requirement; if a program depends on this behavior, it may fail when we compile it on another machine or compiler or even when we use different compiler options.

```
long sum = 0;
```

This declares **sum** as an integer and then initializes it to zero. It's essentially the equivalent of a declaration immediately followed by an assignment.

```
long sum;

sum = 0;
```

These initializations take place each time the function containing them executes. Here, that's just once, when **main** is first called.

We aren't restricted to initializing variables to zero. We can, in fact, initialize them with any legal C expression, which means that we can include function calls, parameters, and already-declared local variables. We'll use this feature frequently in subsequent programs.

We initialize arrays by supplying a brace-enclosed, comma-separated list of expressions. The values in this list become the initial values of the corresponding array elements. There's one restriction, however: the initial values for the array elements must be computable at compile time, so they can't involve other variables or functions. As an example,

```
int days[12] = {31, 28, 31, 30, 31, 30, 31, 31, 30, 31, 30, 31};
```

declares **days** as an array of 12 **int**s and initializes **days[0]** to 31, **days[1]** to 28, and so on. When we provide initial values, we don't have to explicitly specify how many items an array has—the compiler will allocate just enough space for the initialized elements. So

```
int days[] = {31, 28, 31, 30, 31, 30, 31, 31, 30, 31, 30, 31};
```

is equivalent to the previous declaration.

> *Make sure the array size you provide is large enough to hold the initial elements.*

This declaration of **days**,

```
int days[10] = {31, 28, 31, 30, 31, 30, 31, 31, 30, 31, 30, 31};
```

will result in a compiler error message, since we're specifying more than 10 values. If our specified array size is larger than the number of elements, the extra elements remain uninitialized.

```
int days[13] = {31, 28, 31, 30, 31, 30, 31, 31, 30, 31, 30, 31};
```

Here, the extra element **days[12]** is given no initial value. Unfortunately, there's no convenient way to initialize only selected elements.

Figure 8.2 takes advantage of the initialization of arrays with a little program to read dates (month, day, and year) and to print the day of the year. Here's some sample input and output for the program:

```
Enter date (month day year): 6 24 1988
176
Enter date (month day year): 6 24 1991
175
Enter date (month day year): 2 19 1990
50
Enter date (month day year): 4 7 1992
98
Enter date (month day year): 1 1 1992
1
Enter date (month day year): 12 31 1991
365
Enter date (month day year): 12 31 1992
366
```

Most of the work is done by the function **daycalc**, which takes a date and returns the corresponding day of the year. It uses **days** to hold the number of days in each month. Given a date, it runs through the table summing the entries, until it reaches the entry for the given month. It then adds the provided days and adds one more day if the specified year is a leap year.

Declaring Variables within Blocks

We've seen that we can declare and initialize local variables at the beginning of any function. But we can also declare and initialize local variables at the beginning of any statement group or *block*. These variables are initialized each time we enter the block. This feature is useful whenever we need a variable in only a small part of a function, such as a loop index, or a temporary variable to hold the result of a calculation.

Figure 8.3 provides an example in a new version of Figure 8.1. Like the previous version, it uses a variable **avg** to hold the average of the input values. Now, however, we declare **avg** in a block following the loop to read the input values:

```
{ /* compute and print input avg */
  double avg = (n == 0) ? 0.0 : (double) sum / n;

  printf("Average of %i values is %f.\n", n, avg);
}
```

We initialize **avg** at the same time we declare it, using the same expression to protect against dividing by zero we used in earlier versions of the program.

Why not simply declare **avg** at the beginning of the function? By declaring variables only within the small portion of the program where they are needed, we lessen the chances of accidentally using or changing them in other places. Of course, this program is relatively small, so it's probably not worth the extra effort to declare variables right where they are used. But in a larger function, declaring variables local to particular blocks can greatly improve the program's readability and maintainability.

Local variables do not have a long lifetime: they live only from block entry to block exit. When we enter a block, space is reserved for its local variables. When we exit the block, this space is freed. As a result, the next time we enter a block its local variables

```
/*
 * Given month, day, year, return day of year (no error checking).
 *   daycalc - calculate day or year, given month, day, and year.
 *   leapyear - returns 1 if current year a leap year, 0 otherwise.
 */
#include <stdio.h>

int main()
{
  int daycalc(int month, int day, int year);
  int month, day, year;                        /* current input date */

  while (printf("Enter date (month day year): "),
         scanf("%i %i %i", &month, &day, &year) == 3)
    printf("%i\n", daycalc(month,day,year));
  return 0;
}

int daycalc(int month, int day, int year)
{
  int leapyear(int year);
  int days[] = {31, 28, 31, 30, 31, 30, 31, 31, 30, 31, 30, 31};
  int i;
  int total = day + (month > 2 && leapyear(year));

  for (i = 0; i < month - 1; total += days[i++])
    ;                                 /* sum days in preceding months */
  return total;
}

int leapyear(int year)
{
  return year % 4 == 0 && year % 100 != 0 || year % 400 == 0;
}
```

Figure 8.2   (daycalc.c) A program to determine on which day of the year a particular date falls.

may not even use the same physical memory locations—so we can't count on them still having the values they had before.

Local variables have limited visibility, only from the point of their declaration until the end of the block in which they are declared. We can't directly access a local variable outside of the block in which it's declared. Trying to access **avg** before or after the block computing and printing the average results in an error message from the compiler.

```c
/*
 * Compute average of its input values with no error checking.
 */
#include <stdio.h>

int main()
{
  int    next, n;                   /* next input, number of inputs */
  long   sum = 0;                   /* running total */

  for (n = 0; scanf("%i", &next) == 1; n++)
    sum += next;
  { /* compute and print input average */
    double avg = (n == 0) ? 0.0 : (double) sum / n;

    printf("Average of %i values is %f.\n", n, avg);
  }
  return 0;
}
```

Figure 8.3   (avg2.c) Yet another version of our program to compute the average of its input values.

8.2   GLOBAL VARIABLES

So far we have declared variables only at the beginning of blocks. But we can also declare variables outside any function, anywhere in the source file. These *global* variables are visible from their declaration until the end of the file. That means that functions can access these variables—which resemble the global variables of Pascal and the common variables of FORTRAN—simply by referring to them by name, without our needing to pass them as parameters. Global variables differ from local variables in several other ways as well: they exist throughout the life of the program, rather than just the life of a block, and they start off at zero by default, rather than at some unknown value.

Figure 8.4 uses global variables in a program that counts occurrences of each unique character in its input. Figure 8.5 shows its output with the input

```
this is a test
```

assuming that there are two invisible tab characters between the words "is" and "a".

How does this program work? It reads each new character and uses it as an index into a table of counters, **charcnts**.

```
while (c = getchar(), c != EOF)
    charcnts[c++];
```

There is one entry in this table for each character code, from 0 to the number of possible character codes on the machine (**UCHAR_MAX**, from limits.h). The counters themselves are **unsigned long**s.

global variable
initial value is
always zero.
(default)

Declare before
main()

```
/*
 * A program to count different characters in its input.
 */
#include <stdio.h>
#include <ctype.h>
#include <limits.h>

unsigned long charcnts[UCHAR_MAX + 1];        /* 0..UCHAR_MAX */

int main()
{
  void print_counters(void);
  int  c;

  while(c = getchar(), c != EOF)
    charcnts[c]++;
  print_counters();
  return 0;
}

void print_counters(void)
{
  int i;

  for (i = 0; i < UCHAR_MAX; i++)
    if (charcnts[i])                      /* write count only when nonzero */
    {
      printf("\\%03o ", i);
      isprint(i) ? printf("(%c)", i) : printf("   ");
      printf(": %lu\n", charcnts[i]);
    }
}
```

declare global variable. before main() or before fn. that uses it.

see p: 179 for the purpose of this declaration.

Figure 8.4 (charcnt.c) A program to count different characters in its input.

```
\011    : 2
\012    : 1
\040 ( ): 2
\141 (a): 1
\145 (e): 1
\150 (h): 1
\151 (i): 2
\163 (s): 3
\164 (t): 3
```

Figure 8.5 Some output from running our character counter.

```
unsigned long charcnts[UCHAR_MAX + 1];
```

Once the program has read its entire input, it uses **print_counters** to run through **charcnts** and print each of the counts.

```
for (i = 0; i < UCHAR_MAX; i++)
  if (charcnts[i])                    implicit test against zero.
  {
    printf("\\%03o ", i);
    isprint(i) ? printf("(%c)"", i) : printf("   ");
    printf(": %lu\n", charcnts[i]);
  }
```

This loop takes advantage of several subtle C features. The first is an implicit test against 0 in the **if** statement. If the count is zero, we don't print any information about that character. The second is the use of the **%03o** formatting code, which writes the character's value in a field three digits wide, padded with zeros rather than blanks. The last is the use of the conditional operator to select which **printf** we use. If the character is printable, we write the character, but if it isn't, we write blanks instead.

Since that table is declared outside of any function, it's a global variable, and both **main** and **print_counters** can use it simply by referring to it by name.

Since global variables start at zero, we don't bother to initialize the elements in **charcnts**. This implicit initialization is convenient and countless programs take advantage of it. Of course, we can also explicitly initialize global variables in the same way we initialize their local counterparts, with one exception: the initializing expression must evaluate to a constant at compile time. That means it cannot make use of function calls or references to other variables. There's also one other difference: if we provide a global array size larger than the number of initializing values, the other values are taken to be zero. So the declaration

```
unsigned long charcnts[UCHAR_MAX + 1] = {0};
```

explicitly initializes the first element to zero; the others are zero by default. Sometimes we use this form to make explicit our reliance on the array's elements starting with zero.

We used global variables here because they saved us from having to explicitly initialize the table. It also simplifies the call to **print_counters**, since we don't have to provide any parameters. There's a cost though: our program is now less general, since **print_counters** now only works with a particular global array named **charcnts**.

> *Avoid global variables wherever possible.*

Global variables obscure the connections between functions, decreasing readability and modular independence. Any of a program's functions can easily change a global variable, leading to subtle errors when the change is accidental. When using global variables, consider carefully the trade-off between readability and convenience. A little extra effort to avoid globals and to have all functions communicate through parameters increases modularity and aids readability. We try to use globals only for tables or for variables shared between routines when it is inconvenient to pass them as parameters.

8.3 STORAGE CLASSES

auto
register
static
extern

We've seen that every variable has a type, such as `int`, `double`, and so on. But what we haven't seen yet is that every variable also has a *storage class*. A variable's storage class provides information about its visibility, lifetime, and location. So far, we've been relying on the compiler's default storage classes. There are, however, several explicit storage class specifiers: `auto`, `register`, `static`, and `extern`. We can explicitly provide a storage class simply by preceding a variable's declaration with one of these keywords.

The Storage Class `auto`

Our local variables have the default storage class `auto`. The name `auto` derives from their *automatic* creation and removal on block entry and exit. We can use the keyword `auto` to make the storage class of a local variable explicit, but no one does, since a declaration such as

```
{
    auto int x, y;
      . . .
}
```

is exactly equivalent to

```
{
    int x, y;
      . . .
}
```

The Storage Class `register`

Automatic variables are stored in memory. We can suggest to the compiler that specific variables are stored in the machine's high-speed registers by declaring them with the storage class `register`. The declaration

```
register int i;
```

declares `i` as a `register` variable. Making frequently accessed variables `register` usually leads to faster and slightly smaller programs. But `register` is really only a hint, and the compiler is free to ignore our advice.

There are several restrictions on `register` variables. First, we can only declare local variables and function parameters to be `register`, not global variables. Second, since a machine register is usually a single word, many compilers only allow those variables that fit into a single word to be placed in registers. This means that we can normally only place integers or addresses into registers, although the actual types vary from machine to machine. Third, a `register` variable is not kept in memory, so we can't take its address with `&`. That means, for example, that we can't use `scanf` to read a value directly into a `register` variable. And finally, most machines have

```
/*
 * Faster version of array searching function.
 */
int table_search(int a[], register int n, register int t)
{
  register int i;

  for (i = 0; i < n && a[i] != t; i++)
    ;                                       /* search for matching value */
  return (i != n) ? i : -1;
}
```

Figure 8.6 (tabsrch.c) A new version of the previous chapter's table-searching function. It takes advantage of **register** declarations.

only a few registers available to user programs, as few as two or three. If we declare a **register** variable that isn't of the right type, or if there aren't enough registers, the compiler simply ignores our advice.

Figure 8.6 uses **register** in a new version of our earlier function to search a table of **int**s. This time we place into registers any variable that is accessed each time we go through a loop, such as an index variable or other variable tested to determine whether to go through the loop. The exception is the table we're searching, since we can't declare an array as **register**.

When we call a function with **register** parameters, we aren't required to supply the **register** as part of its prototype. Even though the function **table_search** declares **n** and **t** as **register** parameters,

```
int table_search(int a[], register int n, register int t)
```

we can still use its earlier prototype:

```
int table_search(int a[], int n, int t)
```

C also allows us one other shortcut. The declaration

```
register i;
```

is a terse equivalent to

```
register int i;
```

Since there are usually few available registers, carefully select the variables you place in them—if you don't, the compiler will select them for you. Then place into registers the most often used variables in the functions that take the most time. In our example, there are several other tricks that make a much bigger difference in efficiency than using **register**.

The Storage Class `static`

Local variables live only as long as the block in which they reside. But that may not be what we want when we need a local variable to retain its value between function calls. Suppose, for example, that we want to modify a function to print a message that includes the number of times it is called. This might be useful when debugging: any output the function produces is then labeled by the call that produced it. To do so, however, the function must somehow maintain a count that it updates each time we call it. One approach is to use a global variable to hold the count, but then the count can be modified by any function.

Figure 8.7 shows our first attempt at writing this function. We simply use a local variable `cnt`, initialized to zero when we declare it,

```
int cnt = 0;
```

and we increment it each time the function is called. Unfortunately, it doesn't work, since `cnt` is initialized to zero *every* time we call `testfunc`. No matter how many times we call it, it still writes a 1.

The trick to fixing this problem is to give `cnt` the storage class `static`,

```
static int cnt = 0;
```

as we've done in Figure 8.8. A `static` local variable lives as long as the program containing it does. Space for it is allocated and initialized once, conceptually at compile time. The rules for `static` initialization are the same as for globals: they start at zero by default, but we can provide an initializing expression or list of items if the variable is an array.

In the new version of `testfunc`, `cnt` is assigned a zero when the program starts. Each time we call `testfunc`, it increments and prints `cnt`. Since `cnt` is `static`, its value is preserved across calls. So the first time we call `testfunc`, it writes a 1, the next time a 2, and so on.

Figure 8.9 provides a more realistic use of `static` variables. It's a little program that line numbers its input and writes a page number on the top of every page. This program is broken into several pieces: a `main` program that reads a character at a time, and a function `dumpchar` to print each character, keeping track of the number of lines and pages written, and writing a page number at the top of every new page. The idea behind `dumpchar` is to encapsulate all line numbering and page handling in a single function, so that the main program worries only about reading and writing characters. `dumpchar` keeps the page number and line numbers in `static` variables, `pageno` and `lineno` so that their values remain between successive calls to it. They are initialized to zero once, before we ever call `dumpchar`. Because `static` and global variables are initialized to zero by default, explicitly setting them to zero is not necessary, but for readability we do so anyway.

The Storage Class `extern`

In our character counting program, we conveniently defined the global table `charcnts` before either of the functions `main` and `print_counters` that used it.

```
/*
 * Keep a count of times function is called (buggy version).
 */
#include <stdio.h>

int main()
{
  void testfunc(void);

  testfunc(); testfunc(); testfunc();
  return 0;
}

void testfunc(void)
{
  int cnt = 0;

  printf("testfunc call #%i\n", ++cnt);
}
```

Figure 8.7 (tstfnc1.c) An incorrect try at counting function calls. No matter how many times we call it, it always writes a 1.

```
/*
 * Keep a count of times function is called (working version).
 */
#include <stdio.h>

int main()
{
  void testfunc(void);

  testfunc(); testfunc(); testfunc();
  return 0;
}

void testfunc(void)
{
  static int cnt = 0;

  printf("testfunc call #%i\n", ++cnt);
}
```

it initializes to zero only at first time of call, will not set to zero the subsequent times of calls.

Figure 8.8 (tstfnc2.c) Correct version of a function that counts and prints the number of times it's called.

```
/*
 * Print lines with automatic page and line numbering.
 */
#include <stdio.h>

#define PAGELEN  60                                /* page length */

int main()
{
    void dumpchar(int c);
    int   c;                                       /* next input character */

    for (; (c = getchar()) != EOF; dumpchar(c))
        ;
    return 0;
}

void dumpchar(int c)
{
    static int pageno = 0;            /* current page number */
    static int lastch = '\n';         /* last char read */
    static int lineno = 0;            /* current line number */

    if (lastch == '\n')                            /* beginning of line */
    {
        if (lineno % PAGELEN == 0)
            printf("\fPage: %i\n\n", ++pageno);    /* new page */
        printf("%6i ", ++lineno);
    }
    putchar(lastch = c);
}
```

[handwritten annotation: initialize only once @ beginning]

Figure 8.9 (pagenum.c) A program to page number its input.

```
unsigned long charcnts[UCHAR_MAX + 1];
```

This definition does two things. It allocates storage for the table, and it provides the type information necessary to access the table simply by referring to it by name.

If **charcnts** is defined later in the file or in another file, we need some other mechanism to provide the necessary type information to the functions accessing it. To do so, we declare each global variable within the functions using it, preceded by the storage class specifier **extern** (but without size information for arrays):

[handwritten annotation: Declare global variable inside the function]

```
extern unsigned long charcnts[];
```

This *external declaration* tells the compiler the type of the variable and that the compiler should assume space for it is allocated elsewhere. Because external declarations don't allocate space, we need not provide bounds for the array.

Figures 8.10 and 8.11 contain a new version of our character counting program that's

```
/*
 * A program to count the different characters in its input.  This
 * time it uses global variables to hold the counts.
 */
#include <stdio.h>
#include <limits.h>

unsigned long charcnts[UCHAR_MAX + 1];             /* 0..UCHAR_MAX */
int           chars = UCHAR_MAX + 1;

int main()
{
  void print_counters(void);
  int  c;

  while(c = getchar(), c != EOF)
    charcnts[c]++;
  print_counters();
  return 0;
}
```

Figure 8.10 (charcnt1.c) The main program of our character counting program. It defines global variables for the table of counts and the number of items in that table.

split into a pair of files. In charcnt1.c, we define the array of counters, **charcnts**, and the **main** program. We also define a new global, **chars**, which holds the number of items in the array. In prcnt1.c, we define **print_counters**, the function used to display the table. To access the globals defined in the other file, it contains a pair of external declarations:

```
extern unsigned long charcnts[];
extern int           chars;
```

These declarations leave the linker to resolve the references. Similarly, **main** provides an external declaration for the function **print_counters**, leaving the linker to fill in that reference as well.

An **extern** within a function provides type information to just that one function. We can provide the type information to all functions within a file by placing external declarations before any of them. We've done so in the new version of our character-counting program shown in Figures 8.12 and 8.13.

> *Define a global variable exactly once and use external declarations everywhere else.*

A global definition (where we don't preface the variable's type with **extern**) allocates storage. But we can declare a global as often as needed, since a global

```
/*
 * Function to print the character counts.
 */
#include <stdio.h>
#include <ctype.h>

void print_counters(void)
{
  extern unsigned long charcnts[];          /* table of counts */
  extern int          chars;                /* entries in table */
  int                 i;

  for (i = 0; i < chars; i++)
    if (charcnts[i])                        /* write count only when nonzero */
    {
      printf("\\%03o ", i);
      isprint(i) ? printf("(%c)", i) : printf("   ");
      printf(": %lu\n", charcnts[i]);
    }
}
```

Handwritten annotations:

Required in fn. because we split main() and fn. into 2 separate files. declare global variables within the fn. i.e. comes after fn. void print_counter(void) statement.

no sign declared.

Figure 8.11 (prcnt1.c) The function to print the table of character counts. It uses external declarations to access the table and the count of items in it.

declaration merely provides type information and doesn't allocate any storage. We don't need these declarations, however, if the global variable is defined before the functions that use it. That's because a global variable definition also declares the variable's type.

The distinction between *definition* and *declaration* also applies to functions. We *define* a function when we specify its parameters and function body, which causes the compiler to allocate space for the function's code and provides type information for its parameters. We *declare* a function when we provide a prototype, but we don't need the **extern**, since functions are external by default. The declaration

```
    void print_counters(void);
```

is equivalent to

```
    extern void print_counters(void);
```

Function declarations outside of any function work the same way as variable declarations outside of any function—they provide the necessary type information to all functions in the source file. So if we supply prototypes once, at the top of the source file, we don't have to supply them within each of the functions. Of course, a function definition also supplies that type information, which means we can avoid providing prototypes by defining a function before any of the functions that use them.

What happens when we fail to provide the necessary external declarations? If we don't declare a global variable, the compiler complains about its being undefined the first time it encounters it. Here, that means failing to declare **charcnts** results in an

```
/*
 * A new version of our character counting program.
 */
#include <stdio.h>
#include <limits.h>

unsigned long charcnts[UCHAR_MAX + 1];   /* 0..UCHAR_MAX-1 */
int           chars = UCHAR_MAX + 1;

void print_counters(void);

int main()
{
  int c;

  while(c = getchar(), c != EOF)
    charcnts[c]++;
  print_counters();
  return 0;
}
```

Figure 8.12   (charcnt2.c)   A simpler version of our character counting program.

```
/*
 * A new version of the function to print the character counts.
 */
#include <stdio.h>
#include <ctype.h>

extern unsigned long charcnts[];   /* table of counts */
extern int           chars;        /* entries in table */

void print_counters(void)
{
  int i;

  for (i = 0; i < chars; i++)
    if (charcnts[i])       /* write count only when nonzero */
    {
      printf("\\%03o ", i);
      isprint(i) ? printf("(%c)", i) : printf("    ");
      printf(": %lu\n", charcnts[i]);
    }
}
```

Figure 8.13   (prcnt2.c)   A simpler version of the function to print the table of character counts.

"undefined variable" error the first time we use it. With a function, however, the compiler assumes it returns an `int`, and that it knows nothing about its arguments, which means that it can't do any type checking or assignment conversions of its parameters. Here, that's not a problem, although we generally want those features. We provide prototypes for *all* our functions, even those that take no arguments and return `int`.

8.4   TYPE QUALIFIERS

Storage classes provide information about a variable's lifetime and visibility. *Type qualifiers* provide additional information about how the variable is going to be used. There are two type qualifiers: `const` and `volatile`. We use them by placing one of these keywords in front of the variable's type.

`const` informs the compiler that a particular object is not supposed to change. For example,

```
const int PAGELEN = 60;
```

declares `PAGELEN` as an `int` and tells the compiler that its value should remain constant throughout its lifetime. This causes the compiler to forbid any assignments to `PAGELEN` (including trying to increment or decrement it), except for the initializing declaration. This means we have to provide initial values for objects declared as `const`.

We can also use `const` to declare constant arrays; that is, arrays whose elements won't be modified. Our earlier function `daycalc` could be improved with a new declaration for `days`.

```
const int days[] =
            {31, 28, 31, 30, 31, 30, 31, 31, 30, 31, 30, 31};
```

It's now an error to attempt to change an element of `days`, as in

```
days[1] = 29;
```

We aren't limited to declaring array variables as `const`; we can also use `const` to indicate that a function doesn't change its array parameters. We do so in Figure 8.14, a new version of our earlier character counting program. This time we have the array of counters as a local variable, rather than as a global, and pass it to the function `print_counters` to print. The function doesn't modify the array it's passed, so we've now defined it to take a constant array of integers:

```
void print_counters(const unsigned long charcnts[])
```

When we create a function with a `const` parameter, the function's prototype must also declare that parameter as `const`.

We're allowed to pass a non-`const` array to a function expecting a `const` array; C simply treats the array as a `const` inside the function. The array, `charcnts`, we pass `print_counters` is not a `const` array. But the compiler will warn us if we pass a `const` array when the corresponding array parameter hasn't been declared as `const`, as in

```
/*
 * One final version of the character counting program.
 */
#include <stdio.h>
#include <ctype.h>
#include <limits.h>

int main()
{
  void    print_counters(const unsigned long charcnts[]);
  static unsigned long charcnts[UCHAR_MAX + 1];      /* 0..UCHAR_MAX */
  int     c;

  while(c = getchar(), c != EOF)
    charcnts[c]++;
  print_counters(charcnts);
  return 0;
}

void print_counters(const unsigned long charcnts[])
{
  int i;

  for (i = 0; i < UCHAR_MAX; i++)
    if (charcnts[i])                        /* write count only when nonzero */
    {
      printf("\\%03o ", i);
      isprint(i) ? printf("(%c)", i) : printf("   ");
      printf(": %lu\n", charcnts[i]);
    }
}
```

Figure 8.14   (charcnt3.c) Yet another version of our character counting program. This time we're careful to make sure the array is passed to **print_counters** as a constant.

```
            n = table_fill(days, 12);
```

We prefer **const** to **#define** for defining named constants, since it allows us to easily limit the constant's scope. **const** also allows the compiler to flag as an error any attempt to assign a value to that variable. In fact, it lets the compiler put the object in read-only memory. Not all implementations do, of course, which means we get machine-dependent results when we modify a **const**.

const, however, doesn't completely eliminate the need for **#define**. We can't use a **const** in any expression that must be evaluated at compile time, such as a subscript in an array declaration or an initializing expression for a global variable. In Chapter 7's array manipulating programs, for example, we defined the number of elements in **table** with

```
#define MAXVALS 100
```

We can't replace that definition with

```
const int MAXVALS = 100;
```

The other type qualifier, **volatile**, is the opposite of **const**. It means that the value could change at any time and that the compiler should be aware of this when doing optimizations. We use **volatile** only when we have a variable that's being updated by external sources, such as operating system functions or interrupt routines.

8.5   HEADER FILES

We've seen how to use explicit external declarations to access variables and functions defined in other files. Another approach is to put those declarations into header files.

We'll illustrate the difference between these approaches with a pair of multi-file versions of our earlier **yesorno** program: the first using explicit declarations, the second using a header file. Figure 8.15 is a source file that contains the **yesorno** function and a pair of global constants, **YES** and **NO**, that it returns. Figure 8.16 is useyn1.c, the **main** function that uses **yesorno** to obtain a yes or no answer from its user. Since **main** calls **yesorno**, it must provide its prototype,

```
int yesorno(void);
```

along with external declarations for the constants **YES** and **NO**.

```
extern const int YES, NO;
```

The problem with this approach is that every function (or source file) using **yesorno** must provide these declarations.

A better approach is to put these declarations into a header file, which we then include in any source file calling **yesorno**. Figure 8.17 is this header file, yesorno.h. Figure 8.18 is useyn2.c, a file containing a new version of the main program using **yesorno** that simply includes this header file.

We now use a slightly different form of **#include**.

```
#include "yesorno.h"
```

We surround yesorno.h by quotation marks instead of angle brackets to indicate that it is our own include file, and not one that is system-supplied. That way the preprocessor will search our files first, before searching the standard system locations for it.

At this point, it should be clear why we include yesorno.h in useyn2.c—it needs the prototypes and constants to call **yesorno** correctly. But we should also include it in yesorno.c. Doing so ensures that its prototype matches its definition. By including yesorno.h in yesorno.c, we guarantee that the compiler will catch any inconsistencies. If we don't, it's possible that the prototype we include in **main** won't match the function's actual definition, leading to hard-to-find errors.

```
/*
 * Get a yes or no answer from the user.
 */
#include <stdio.h>
#include <ctype.h>

const int YES = 1, NO = 0;

int yesorno(void)
{
  int answer;                                /* holds input character */

  while ((answer = tolower(getchar())) != EOF)
  {
    int junk = answer;                       /* for skipping characters */

    while (junk != '\n' && junk != EOF)
      junk = getchar();                      /* skip until end of line */
    if (answer == 'y' || answer == 'n')
      return (answer == 'y') ? YES : NO;
    printf("Please answer with a YES or NO!\n");
  }
  return NO;
}
```

Figure 8.15   (yesorno.c)   Our **yesorno** function.

```
/*
 * Main program using yes or no.
 */
#include <stdio.h>

int main()
{
  int                yesorno(void);
  extern const int YES, NO;

  printf("Enter a YES or NO answer: ");
  (yesorno() == YES) ? printf("YES!\n") : printf("NO!\n");
  return 0;
}
```

Figure 8.16   (useyn1.c)   A main program accessing **yesorno** using explicit external declarations.

```
/*
 * Prototypes and constants for "yesorno".
 */
extern const int YES;
extern const int NO;

int yesorno(void);
```

Figure 8.17 (yesorno.h) A header file defining a prototype for **yesorno** and providing external declarations for the constants it uses.

```
/*
 * Main program using yes or no.
 */
#include <stdio.h>
#include "yesorno.h"                          /* for yesorno prototype */

int main()
{
  printf("Enter a YES or NO answer: ");
  (yesorno() == YES) ? printf("YES!\n") : printf("NO!\n");
  return 0;
}
```

Figure 8.18 (useyn2.c) A main program accessing **yesorno** using a header file. This is substantially less effort than providing the necessary declarations explicitly.

8.6   PRIVATE VARIABLES AND FUNCTIONS

So far, we've had two types of variables: local variables accessible only within a function, and global variables accessible to any function, even one in a different file. For modularity, however, we sometimes want to have variables and functions that are accessible only to the functions within a single file, not by functions in other files.

We'll illustrate these *private* globals with a program that computes the average time riders must wait for a bus. Its input describes the time that either a person or bus arrived at the bus stop, and consists of triplets of integers. The first integer is a code (0 indicates a person, 1 a bus), the second is the arrival time, and the third indicates how many people arrived or how many seats were available on the bus. The program's output identifies the arrivals and prints the total number of riders and the average waiting time. Here's some sample input and output for the program:

```
0 2 2
2 people arrived at time 2
0 6 1
1 people arrived at time 6
0 7 4
4 people arrived at time 7
1 7 5
Bus arrived at time 7 (5 seats)
0 8 2
2 people arrived at time 8
0 8 9
9 people arrived at time 8
1 15 13
Bus arrived at time 15 (13 seats)
18 riders waited 104, average wait 5.78
```

Implementing Queues

The program simulates a line of people waiting for a bus. When a person arrives, it saves their arrival time. When a bus arrives, it lets those who have waited the longest onto the bus first and updates a count of the total waiting time. We use a queue to store these arrival times. A queue is a "first-in, first-out" data structure that behaves like a line for a movie: the people who arrive first are at the front, and those who arrive last are at the back. We implement three queue operations: **enqueue** adds an item to the rear of the queue, **dequeue** takes an item off the front of the queue, and **emptyqueue** returns nonzero if the queue is empty. Queues are generally useful, so we place these functions in a separate file, queues.c, and provide a header file, queues.h, that contains their prototypes. Figure 8.19 contains queues.h and Figure 8.20 contains queues.c.

How can we implement a queue? The simplest way is as an array and a count. Adding an item is easy: we increment the count and add the item to the array's end. But deleting an item is difficult: not only do we have to decrement the count, but we also have to shift all array elements over one place. Alternatively, we can maintain two indices into the array: **f** indexes its first item, and **r** indexes its last. Adding an element is still easy: we increment **r** and place a value at the location it indexes. But now deleting an item is also easy: we simply increment **f** and return the item it indexed.

The queue operations are straightforward, although we've ignored something: the queue is actually a moving subsection of the array. After enqueueing three items and dequeueing two of them, the first item in the queue is actually the third item in the array. This queue movement means that whenever **f** or **r** index the array's last element, updating either should cause the index being updated to index the array's first element. To handle this case, **enqueue** and **dequeue** both use a function **next** to return the appropriate index value.

How and where should we declare the queue and its indices? All of the functions in queues.c use them, so we must declare them outside of any of these functions. The problem is that functions in other files can also access these globals. All they have to do is provide an appropriate external declaration.

```
/*
 * Prototypes for our queue functions.
 */
void enqueue(int item);              /* add item to queue */
int  dequeue(void);                  /* take item away from queue */
int  emptyqueue(void);               /* is queue empty? */
```

Figure 8.19 (queues.h) The header file for the queues package.

```
/*
 * Simple queue manager, no error checking.
 */
#include "queues.h"                  /* queue prototypes */

#define MAXQUEUE 100                 /* number of queue items */

static int queue[MAXQUEUE];          /* the queue itself */
static int f, r;                     /* indices to queue front and end */

static int next(int i);

void enqueue(int item)               /* add item to end of queue */
{
  queue[r] = item;
  r = next(r);
}

int dequeue(void)                    /* delete first item in queue */
{
  int temp = queue[f];

  f = next(f);
  return temp;
}

int emptyqueue(void)                 /* is queue empty? */
{
  return f == r;
}

/* PRIVATE: returns index to next item, handling wraparound */

static int next(int i)
{
  return (i + 1 < MAXQUEUE) ? i + 1 : 0;
}
```

Figure 8.20 (queues.c) The source file for managing queues.

```
extern int queue[], f, r;
```

We would prefer to have these variables visible only to the functions implementing the queue operators, not to the entire outside world. That's because we want to be able to change how we implement queues without having to worry about whether some function, somewhere, takes advantage of our particular implementation. But how can we limit access to the queue variables to the single source file in which they're defined?

The trick is to declare those variables as **static**.

```
static int queue[MAXQUEUE];
static int f, r;
```

static variables and functions are not made available to the linker. Since the linker doesn't know about them, it can't resolve any external references to them made in other files. That means only the queue-handling functions can access **queue**, **f**, and **r**. For the same reason, we also declare the function **next** to be **static**. That way it can't be called directly from functions in other files, preventing accidental name conflicts and keeping outside functions from sneakily accessing the queue.

We've placed **next**'s prototype before any of its callers. Unfortunately, we're not allowed to place prototypes for **static** functions inside other functions, so the only other alternative would be to define **next** before defining its callers.

Implementing Our Bus Stop Simulator

Besides queues.c and queues.h, our program consists of files containing definitions for global variables and other functions (wait.c and handle.c), external declarations for the global variables (wait.h), and prototypes for the other functions (handle.h).

wait.c contains the **main** program and definitions for two global counters: one for the total number of riders, another for the total number of minutes they've waited.

```
unsigned long riders;
unsigned long waiting;
```

main handles reading the input, invokes the functions **person** or **bus** to process each new arrival, and prints the final statistics.

handle.c contains **person** and **bus**. These functions handle the arrival of new riders or busses by using **enqueue** and **dequeue** to add or delete arrival times from the queue. They also update the counts of riders and the total waiting time. That means these counters have to be accessed in two source files: wait.c, where we define and print them, and handle.c, where we update them.

One way to share these variables among files is to include external declarations for the counters in **person** and **bus**, the functions that access them. That's similar to what we did in our character-counting program. But, in general, a better to way to share globals in a set of source files is to define them in one file and to create a header file that provides their external declarations. We then include this header file whenever we reference the globals.

wait.h is the header file that contains the needed external declarations:

```
extern unsigned long riders;
extern unsigned long waiting;
```

We include this header file in both places that refer to these globals: wait.c and handle.c. In a small program with only a few globals, it's not clear how we're better off with the added complications of a header file. But in larger programs it's much easier to include a header file than it is to explicitly provide the external declarations. In addition, by including the header file in the source file defining the globals, we guarantee our external declarations are correct.

handle.h is the final file in our program. It contains the prototypes for **person** and **bus**. We include this file in both source files. In wait.c, it supplies the prototypes we need to successfully call the functions. In handle.c, it causes the compiler to make sure our prototypes match our function definitions.

Figure 8.21 contains wait.c, Figure 8.22 contains wait.h, Figure 8.23 contains handle.c, and Figure 8.24 contains handle.h. To make the executable program, we need to link together the object modules for queues.c, wait.c, and handle.c.

8.7 CASE STUDY—ABSTRACT DATA TYPES

This section is optional!

One possible criticism of C compared with other high-level languages is its lack of a "set" data type. A set is simply an unordered collection of values, without duplications, with certain operations defined on it. Some of the more common operations are adding and deleting values and testing to determine if a value is in a set. We conclude this chapter by implementing these set operations and a program that uses them.

We implement sets as an *abstract data type* by creating a **SET** data type and functions for the various set operations. Programs using sets know only the names of these operations, restrictions on their use, and the order and expected type of their parameters. To hide the details of their implementation from their users, we package the set operations in a single module we compile separately. This allows us to change the implementation or add operations without having to rewrite the programs using them.

The concept of an abstract data type shouldn't seem strange. We have been using **float**s and **double**s without knowing either their internal representation or the implementation details of operators such as + or /.

Implementing Sets

We implement sets as a bit array, one bit per set element. C doesn't provide bit arrays, but we can simulate them using an array of **unsigned short**s. To access the bit corresponding to a given set element, we have to determine its location: the array element that contains the bit, and where that bit is located within that array element. We do so by dividing the set element by the number of bits in an **unsigned short**; the remainder is the bit's position within the array element. Figure 8.25 shows a sample computation. With this representation, the set operations are simple. We add an element to a set by turning on the bit it indexes and delete it by turning that bit off. And we check membership by examining the bit's value.

```c
/*
 * Compute average waiting time of riders of a bus.
 */
#include <stdio.h>
#include "wait.h"
#include "handle.h"

unsigned long riders;                   /* total riders */
unsigned long waiters;                  /* total waiting time */

int main()
{
  int   code,                           /* transaction code */
        time,                           /* event time */
        count;                          /* room on bus, people at stop */

  while (scanf("%i %i %i", &code, &time, &count) == 3)
    switch(code)
    {
      case 0:  person(time, count);
               break;
      case 1:  bus(time, count);
               break;
      default: printf("Invalid code of %i\n", code);
               break;
    }
  if (riders == 0)
    printf("No riders ever showed up.\n");
  else
    printf("%lu riders waited %lu, average wait %.2f\n",
            riders, waiters, (double) waiters / riders);
  return 0;
}
```

Figure 8.21   (wait.c) The main program for bus simulator.

```c
/*
 * Declarations for shared counters.
 */
extern unsigned long riders;            /* people on bus */
extern unsigned long waiters;           /* people waiting for bus */
```

Figure 8.22   (wait.h) Definitions of shared counters of bus riders and people waiting for a bus.

```
/*
 * Functions to update riders and waiting time.
 *    person - add a new set of riders to a bus stop.
 *    bus - take away a set of riders from a bus stop.
 */
#include <stdio.h>
#include "queues.h"
#include "wait.h"
#include "handle.h"

void person(int time, int newpeople)
{
  riders += newpeople;
  printf("%i people arrived at time %i\n", newpeople, time);
  while (newpeople--)
    enqueue(time);
}

void bus(int time, int capacity)
{
  printf("Bus arrived at time %i (%i seats)\n", time, capacity);
  while (capacity-- && !emptyqueue())
    waiters += time - dequeue();
}
```

Figure 8.23 (handle.c) The functions to handle updating counters.

```
/*
 * Prototypes for functions to update appropriate counters.
 */
void person(int time, int persons);
void bus(int time, int capacity);
```

Figure 8.24 (handle.h) The prototypes for the functions to handle updating counters.

The Set Type and Its Operations

Programs using sets don't have to know that they are implemented as a bit array. In fact, we want programs to be able to declare a **SET** type as if the language provided one. To do so, we use a new C facility, **typedef**, which allows us to define synonyms for existing types. A **typedef** looks like a variable declaration except that we replace the variable name with the name of the new type. We can define **integer** as a synonym for **int** with

```
typedef int integer;
```

Defining our **SET** data type is a little more complex:

[0]	[1]	[2]	[3]	[4]
0 · · · 15	16 · · · 31	32 · · · 47	48 · · · 63	64 · · · 79	· · ·

(*a*) Element 69 is in word 4 (69 / 16).

4

0111101010001111

(*b*) Element 69 is bit 5 in word 4 (69 % 16). This bit is 0, so 69 isn't in the set.

Figure 8.25 Locating the bit representing a set element, here 69. First we select the array element and then the bit within it.

study for mat.

```
typedef unsigned short SET[MAXELEMS/US_BITS];
```

This **typedef** makes **SET** a synonym for an array of **unsigned shorts**. The number of elements in the array is the number of items in the set divided by the number of bits in an **unsigned short**.

We can then use these types as if they are built-in types such as **int** or **double**. The declaration

```
SET s;
```

declares **s** as an array of **unsigned shorts**. **typedef**s usually appear outside of any function and are in effect from the **typedef** until the end of the file.

Figure 8.26 shows the header file sets.h, in which we've defined the **SET** type, as well as the prototypes for the set operations. As expected, we have to include sets.h in all files containing functions that manipulate sets.

Figure 8.27 is the file sets.c, containing the set operations: initializing a set (setting all entries in the representation to 0), adding an element to a set (turning its bit on), deleting an element from a set (turning its bit off), and determining whether an element is a member of a set (checking whether its bit is on).

We build the basic set operations on top of a pair of functions: **word** returns the index of the array element containing the desired set element, and **bit** returns its bit position within that **unsigned short**. Because these functions are internal to the **SET** type's implementation, we keep them hidden by declaring them as **static**.[2]

Most of the set operations modify the **SET** passed to them (since a **SET** is an array, they can modify its elements). The sole exception is **set_member**, so we've made its **SET** parameter a **const** to protect against accidental change.

---

[2]We've placed the **static** functions in the file before the definition of their callers. This eliminates the need to provide prototypes for them. We've done that simply to shrink the program's size.

```
/*
 * Definitions to use "sets" of integers.
 */
#define US_BITS    16              /* bits in unsigned short */
#define MAXELEMS   512             /* set items, must be multiple of 16 */

typedef unsigned short SET[MAXELEMS/US_BITS];

extern void set_init(SET s);
extern void set_add(SET s, int e);
extern void set_delete(SET s, int e);
extern int  set_member(const SET s, int e);
```

Figure 8.26 (sets.h) The header file for sets.

Using Sets

Figure 8.28 uses sets in a program that partitions its input into values that appear once and those that appear many times. We could use this program to verify that no identification number appears more than once. Figure 8.29 shows the program's output for the input:

```
8 99 99 245 0 99 501 99 309 17 410 17
```

The program uses two sets: **unique** contains the values appearing once, and **dup** contains the duplicates. When the program starts, we declare variables with the **SET** type.

```
SET unique, dup;
```

The program reads each value and checks whether it is a member of **unique**. If it is, we remove it from **unique** and add it to **dup**. Otherwise, we simply add it to **unique**. When finished, we print the members of these two sets. To print a set, we run through all possible set values, printing those values that are set members.

The program uses two new functions built on top of the existing **SET** operations. **set_switch** moves an element from one set to another, modifying both of the **SET**s passed to it. **set_print** runs through a set, printing all of its elements. It doesn't modify the **SET** passed to it, so we've made that **SET** a **const**.

Some Notes on Abstract Data Types

This example illustrates two important points. The first is that we should separate the details of a function or data type's implementation from those of its use. The program in Figure 8.28 would be considerably more complex and consequently harder to understand if it also contained the definition of each of the set operations. We can understand how it works without knowing that sets are implemented as bit arrays. That program would also be much harder to change. By implementing sets as a separate module, we've made

```
/*
 * The functions to handle sets.
 */
#include "sets.h"

static int word(int elem)
{
  return elem / US_BITS;                    /* word # containing element */
}

static int bit(int elem)
{
  return elem % US_BITS;                    /* bit # containing element */
}

void set_init(SET s)                        /* initialize set to empty */
{
  int i;

  for (i = 0; i < MAXELEMS / US_BITS; s[i++] = 0)
    ;
}

void set_add(SET s, int elem)               /* add element to set */
{
  s[word(elem)] |= 1 << bit(elem);
}

void set_delete(SET s, int elem)            /* delete element from set */
{
  s[word(elem)] &= ~(1 << bit(elem));
}

int set_member(const SET s, int elem)    /* is element in set? */
{
  return ((unsigned) s[word(elem)] >> bit(elem)) & 01;
}
```

Figure 8.27 (sets.c) An implementation of a simple sets package.

it easy to change the internal implementation of sets without having to make changes in the programs using it.

The other point is that wherever possible, we should build our programs on top of functions we have already written. We should create modules, like our sets, that can easily be used by new programs. Doing so effectively adds features to the language, allowing us to build programs much more quickly than we could if we had to start from scratch each time.

```
/*
 * Identify duplicates in the input.
 */
#include <stdio.h>
#include "sets.h"                    /* for SETs */

int main()
{
  void set_print(const SET s);
  void set_switch(SET news, SET olds, int elem);
  SET  unique, dup;                  /* unique and duplicate elements */
  int  r, inp;                       /* scanf return, input value */

  set_init(unique);  set_init(dup);
  while ((r = scanf("%i", &inp)) != EOF)
  {
    if (r != 1)
    {
      printf("Value in error.\n");
      break;
    }
    if (inp < 0 || inp >= MAXELEMS)
    {
      printf("Value out of range.\n");
      continue;
    }
    if (set_member(unique, inp))
      set_switch(dup, unique, inp);
    else if (!set_member(dup, inp))
      set_add(unique, inp);
  }
  printf("Unique values\n");  set_print(unique);
  printf("Duplicate values\n");  set_print(dup);
  return 0;
}

void set_switch(SET new, SET old, int value)
{
  set_delete(old, value);  set_add(new, value);
}

void set_print(const SET set)
{
  int i;                             /* next potential element */

  for (i = 0; i < MAXELEMS; i++)
    if (set_member(set, i))
      printf("%i\n", i);
}
```

Figure 8.28 (usesets.c) A program to check for duplicate input values.

```
Unique values
0
8
245
309
410
501
Duplicate values
17
99
```

Figure 8.29   Sample output for our program to use sets.

SUMMARY

- C lets us declare variables in any block. These variables have visibility only within that block and exist only throughout the life of the block.

- C also lets us declare variables outside of any function. These variables are visible throughout the remainder of the source file. They can also be accessed from other files through the use of external declarations.

- C lets us initialize variables when we declare them. With local variables, we can provide any expression. With global variables, we're restricted to those expressions that are evaluable at compile time.

- C allows us to specify that variables are constants. When we do so, we must initialize them when we declare them.

- We can place external declarations and constant definitions in header files that are included by the modules requiring them.

- We can have variables and functions local to a single source file by declaring them outside of any function and prefacing them with the storage class **static**.

- We implement abstract data types by defining the operations in a single source file and putting their external declarations in a header file. This way the functions using the data type aren't privy to the details of their implementation.

EXERCISES

8–1   Modify the programs in this chapter to limit the scope of any index variables used. Does this make those loops more readable? Does this make these program more or less compact?

8–2 Rewrite several programs from earlier chapters to initialize variables where they're declared and **const** where appropriate. Does this make these programs more or less readable?

8–3 Modify our program to calculate the day of the year (Figure 8.2) to do error checking on its input. It should make sure that the month is between 1 and 12 and that the day of the month is legal for that month.

8–4 Our bus stop simulator (Figures 8.21 and 8.22) doesn't print a count of how many people are left waiting at the bus station when the program ends. This can be fixed by adding and using a new queue-handling function, **queuelen**, which returns the number of items in the queue.

8–5 Another problem with our bus stop simulator (Figures 8.21 and 8.22) is that it doesn't behave sensibly if the arrival times aren't increasing in sequential order. Fix the program so that it does something reasonable instead.

8–6 Modify the final character counting program (Figure 8.14) to break its output into groups corresponding to the different *ctype* categories. For example, it should have one group for lowercase letters, another for uppercase letters, another for digits, and so on.

8–7 Modify our earlier histogram program (Figure 7.10) to use registers where appropriate. Does it make a noticeable difference in program speed?

8–8 Rewrite our earlier histogram program (Figure 7.10) to use global variables for the bucket array, the bucket size, and the number of buckets. Use header files rather than explicit declarations.

8–9 With our queue-handling functions (Figures 8.19 and 8.20), what happens when we add items to an already full queue? What about deleting an item from an empty queue? Modify these functions to return an appropriate value if we attempt one of these operations.

8–10 Our implementation of sets (Figures 8.26 and 8.27) is incomplete. Other common set operations include union and intersection. **set_union** is a function that takes two sets and returns a set containing all the items in either of those two sets. **set_inter** is similar, but returns a set containing the items that are in both of those sets. Implement these operations.

8–11 Our implementation of sets (Figures 8.26 and 8.27) isn't particularly space-efficient for sets containing only a few elements. An alternative is to use sorted arrays of **int**s rather than bit arrays. Now when we add an element to the set, we place it in its correct place in the array. We check for membership by searching the array. And we delete an element by shifting array items. Implement sets using sorted arrays.

8–12 The difference of two sets is defined as the elements in the first set that are not also present in the second set. Write a function, **set_diff**, that places the difference of two sets into a third set.

8–13 Write a function, **set_print_elems**, that prints the elements of a set in traditional set notation. A set containing the elements 3, 7, and 14, should print as {**3, 7, 14**}. Can this be implemented without adding set operations?

8–14 Write a program to print the calendar for a particular month. Its input should be a pair of integers: the number of the month and the number of the day of the week of the first day of the month (0 for Sunday, 1 for Monday, and so on).

8–15 A stack is the reverse of a queue: The first thing placed on it is the last thing taken off, just like a stack of cafeteria trays. Stacks generally have a small set of operations: **stack_push** adds an item to a stack, **stack_pop** takes an item off, **stack_top** returns the top item, and **stack_empty** returns nonzero if the stack is empty. Write these operations.

8–16 Use the stack operations created in the previous exercise to write a program to reverse its input.

8–17 Use the stack operations to write a program that prints out the location in the input of any unbalanced parentheses. That is, if it detects that a left parenthesis has no matching right parenthesis, it should print its position in the input (character number is sufficient).

Part III

ADVANCED DATA TYPES

9 POINTERS

AND

ARRAYS

We can use arrays in C in the same way we use arrays in other languages. But doing so ignores some of their most important features and leads to slower, less powerful programs. This chapter shows how to take full advantage of C arrays. We introduce pointers, a data type that can hold addresses, and study how to use them to traverse arrays efficiently. And we introduce dynamically allocated arrays, arrays for which space is allocated at run time rather than compile time. The chapter concludes with a new implementation of sets, this time with dynamically allocated sets of varying sizes.

9.1   POINTERS

A *pointer* is simply the address of a memory location. Whenever we declare a variable, as in

        int i;

the compiler reserves a memory location for it. The compiler might, for example, set aside memory location 10000 for i. When we subsequently refer to i, we are really referring to this location. Assigning zero to i with

        i = 0;

places a 0 in memory location 10000. We say that 10000 is i's address or, in other words, a *pointer* to i. In C, we can access a value directly by providing its name or indirectly through a pointer. We will soon see how this indirect pointer access allows us to traverse arrays more efficiently and to manipulate dynamically allocated arrays. And in later chapters, we'll see how we can use pointers to simulate call-by-reference parameter passing and to write functions that work with many different data types.

call by value
call by reference.

Declaring and Obtaining Pointers

Pointers are a basic data type. We can declare pointer variables, variables that contain addresses (or pointers to) other values. We have to declare a pointer as pointing to a value of a particular type, such as an `int`, a `double`, a `char`, and so on. We must do so because when we access a value through a pointer, the compiler needs to know the value's type.

We declare a variable as a pointer to a particular type with

```
type *name;
```

This declares *name* as a pointer to *type*. The following declares `iptr` as a "pointer to int," `fptr` as a "pointer to `float`," `cptr` as a "pointer to `char`," and `dptr` as a "pointer to `double`."

```
int    *iptr;        /* pointer to int */
float  *fptr;        /* pointer to float */
char   *cptr;        /* pointer to char */
double *dptr;        /* pointer to double */
```

[handwritten: ＊ declares as pointer]

Each of these declarations allocates space for the named pointer variable, but doesn't make it point to anything. To do so, we use a new operator, `&`, that returns the address of its operand. We can initialize `iptr` to point to `i` with

```
iptr = &i;
```
[handwritten: ⟹ iptr to point to i]

[handwritten: iptr points to address of "i"]

Assuming `i` is stored in memory location 10000, after this assignment `iptr` contains the address 10000, a pointer to `i`.

Dereferencing Pointer Variables

Once we have made a pointer point to something, we access the pointed-to value using the indirection operator `*`, a process called *dereferencing*. In the example above, `*iptr` is `i`. Since `i` is 0, so is `*iptr`.

Because `iptr` is of type "pointer to int," `*iptr` is of type `int`, and we can use it anywhere an `int` variable can occur, such as in assignments. So,

```
n = *iptr;
```

assigns to `n` whatever `iptr` points to (zero in this example),

```
*iptr = j;
```
[handwritten: put j into pointed location]

assigns `j`'s value to whatever `iptr` points to (`i` in this case), and

```
*iptr = *iptr + 10;
```

adds 10 to whatever `*iptr` points to. Figure 9.1 illustrates what's going on with these assignments.

[handwritten: assign to n the pointed value by ＊iptr.]

[handwritten: Fig 9.1]

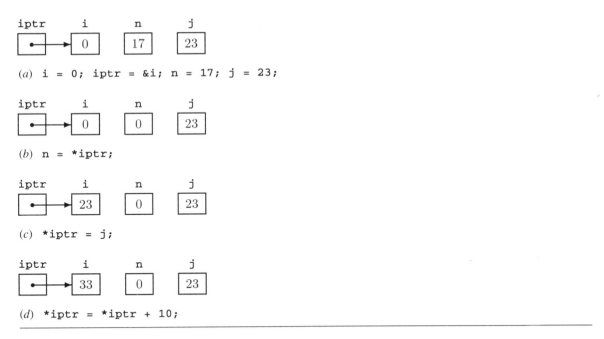

Figure 9.1 Examples of indirectly accessing values through a pointer.

The Generic Pointer Type

Figure 9.2 is a short program that plays around with pointers. Here's its output when we run it on our machine:

```
Addresses: &i=FFB6 &n=FFB8 &j=FFBA
Initial values: iptr=0000 i=0 n=17 j=23
Later values: iptr=FFB6 i=0 n=0 j=23
Final values: iptr=FFB6 i=33 n=0 j=23
```

Among other things, it prints the values of several pointers, as well as what they point to. To do so, we use a new **printf** formatting code, **%p**, that writes a pointer's value in hexadecimal. But how does **%p** know what type of pointer we're passing to it? That's an issue because there are many types of pointers, and these pointers can vary in size. On some machines, for example, a pointer to a **char** takes up two words, whereas a pointer to an **int** takes only one. **printf** needs to know the type of pointer to know how many bytes to write.

The trick is that **%p** always expects the same type of pointer—a pointer to **void**. A pointer to **void** is a *generic* pointer: it is simply an address, but not the address of any particular type of object. So to print a pointer, we first cast it to a pointer to **void**, which we then pass to **printf**:

use '/:p in printf to write a pointer value in hexadecimal.

```
/*
 * Examples of assigning, following, and printing pointers.
 */
#include <stdio.h>

int main()
{
  int *iptr = NULL;
  int i = 0;                             /* some useful value */
  int n = 17;                            /* another value */
  int j = 23;                            /* still another value */

  printf("Addresses: ");                 /* display addresses: */
  printf("&i=%p", (void *) &i);          /*   i's address */
  printf(" &n=%p", (void *) &n);         /*   n's address */
  printf(" &j=%p\n", (void *) &j);       /*   j's address */

  printf("Initial values: ");            /* display initial values */
  printf("iptr=%p i=%i n=%i j=%i\n", (void *) iptr, i, n, j);
  iptr = &i;                             /* place i's address in iptr */
  n = *iptr;                             /* place i's value into n */

  printf("Later values: ");              /* display changed values */
  printf("iptr=%p i=%i n=%i j=%i\n", (void *) iptr, i, n, j);

  *iptr = j;                             /* place j's value in i */
  *iptr = *iptr + 10;                    /* update i */
  printf("Final values: ");
  printf("iptr=%p i=%i n=%i j=%i\n", (void *) iptr, i, n, j);
  return 0;
}
```

cast it to void.

Figure 9.2 (ptrex.c) A program that declares, assigns to, dereferences, and prints pointers.

```
        printf("&i=%p\n", (void *) &i);
```

This works because we're guaranteed that a generic pointer is large enough to safely hold a pointer to *any* type of object and that we can cast any pointer type to and from a pointer to **void** without loss of information.[1] The drawback, of course, is that we can't do operations, such as dereferencing a generic pointer, that need to know the size of the pointed-to thing.

Generic pointers are a very powerful tool that we'll explore in much greater detail later in this chapter.

---

[1]On many machines, all pointers are the same size, so a cast from one type of pointer to another doesn't really do anything—but not on *all* machines. We need the cast to ensure the maximum portability of our program.

constant NULL defined in <stddef.h>

The Null Pointer

There's one pointer we can't follow. It's illegal to dereference a pointer with the value 0, and doing so usually causes a run-time error that terminates the program.[2] We use such a pointer as a placeholder to indicate explicitly that a pointer variable doesn't point anywhere. In fact, we use it so frequently that there's a special constant **NULL**, defined in the system header file stddef.h, that's exactly equivalent to the constant 0.

Local pointer variables, like other local variables, are not automatically initialized. In fact, they start off with a random value—whatever happens to be in the memory location reserved for the pointer—and could therefore point anywhere. Following these pointers will likely lead us into areas of memory into which we don't want to go. On the other hand, global and **static** pointers are initialized, but to zero, which we've just seen is illegal to dereference. So ***iptr** is meaningless until **iptr** has been made to point to something, regardless of whether **iptr** is global or local.

> *Don't dereference a pointer variable until you've assigned it an address.*

initialize all pointers to NULL

One way to prevent problems with using uninitialized pointer variables is to initialize all of them to **NULL**. Of course, we still need to initialize them to some other value before we follow them, but this way we're less likely to damage some random memory location. We'll see other uses for **NULL** later in the chapter.

9.2   TRAVERSING ARRAYS USING POINTERS

In C, arrays and pointers are intimately intertwined. When we declare an array, the compiler not only allocates a block of storage large enough to hold the array, but also defines the array's name as a (constant) pointer to its first (zeroth) element.

Figure 9.3 shows what happens when we declare **t** to be an array of 100 **int**s with

```
int t[100];
```

*int t[100];
t ⇒ address of t[0]
t = &t[0];*

The compiler first allocates 100 contiguous storage locations, each holding a single **int**. It then defines **t** as the address of its zeroth element. Since array indexing begins with 0, **t** is equivalent to **&t[0]**. Here, **t** is the constant 1000, the location where **t[0]** is stored.

There are two ways to access array elements. One is through the direct array indexing we've been using in earlier array-manipulating programs. To access an array element, we provide the array name and a bracket-enclosed index. Arrays are indexed beginning at zero, so in **t** we can legally access elements between **t[0]** and **t[99]**. To traverse the array, we can use an index variable that runs through the possible index values.

We use this traditional array indexing in a program to read its input into a table, compute the average, and then print the number of items in the table less than and greater than the average. If the program's input is:

---

[2]Officially dereferencing such a pointer causes *undefined* behavior, but it's always a programming mistake.

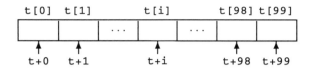

Figure 9.3 What happens when we declare an array. Here we declared **t** as an array containing 100 **int**s.

```
10 40 20 30 30 100 20 10 20 20
```

its output is:

```
There are 10 values.
The average is 30.
There are 2 values above average.
There are 6 values below average.
```

We divide the program into several source files. Figure 9.4 contains the main program, along with a pair of functions to read the table and print the values greater than, less than, or equal to the average. Figure 9.5 contains the function **table_average**, which uses traditional indexing to sum an array of integers:

to sum up values in array using traditional indexing

```
for (i = 0; i < n; i++)
    sum += a[i]
```

Traditional array indexing is simple to use, easy to understand, and similar to the way we process arrays in other languages. But there's another, often more efficient way to traverse arrays: accessing array elements indirectly through pointers. We can do so because C provides pointer arithmetic—the ability to add integers to or subtract integers from a pointer. We're now going to rewrite this program to use pointers rather than array subscripting.

Pointer Arithmetic *(add, and subtract only)*

In C, pointer arithmetic is automatically done in units of the pointer's underlying base type. That is, adding 1 to a pointer to an array element gives a pointer to the next element—regardless of whether we have an array of **int**s, an array of **double**s, or an array of any other type. In the declaration for **t**, an array of **int**s, **t** is a pointer to its first element (**&t[0]**). That means **t + 1** is a pointer to its second element (**&t[1]**), **t + 2** is a pointer to its third element (**&t[2]**), and so on. In general, **t + i** is the address of element **t[i]**.

t = pointer
t+i is the address of t[i]

Since **t + i** is the address of **t[i]**, ***(t + i)** is equivalent to **t[i]**. So we can initialize **t[3]** to 0 with array indexing,

```
t[3] = 0;
```

```
/*
 * Compute average and print interesting counts.  Uses:
 *   table_fill - reads in table entries (same table_fill as before).
 *   table_avg_cnts - compute average statistics.
 */
#include <stdio.h>

#define MAXVALS 100

int main()
{
  int    table_fill(int a[], int max);
  void   table_avg_cnts(int a[], int n, double avg);
  double table_average(int a[], int n);
  int    t[MAXVALS];
  int    n   = table_fill(t, MAXVALS);
  double avg = table_average(t, n);

  printf("There are %i values.\n", n);
  printf("The average is %g.\n", avg);
  table_avg_cnts(t, n, avg);
  return 0;
}

int table_fill(int a[], int max)
{
  int count = 0;

  for (; count < max; count++)
    if (scanf("%i", &a[count]) != 1)
      break;                             /* kick out on error */
  return count;
}

void table_avg_cnts(int a[], int n, double avg)
{
  int i;                                 /* index */
  int above = 0;                         /* above average */
  int below = 0;                         /* below average */

  for (i = 0; i < n; i++)
    if (a[i] > avg)
      above++;
    else if (a[i] < avg)
      below++;
  printf("There are %i values above average.\n", above);
  printf("There are %i values below average.\n", below);
}
```

Figure 9.4   (useavg.c) Our average computing and printing program.

```
/*
 * Compute average of an array, array subscripting version.
 */
double table_average(int a[], int n)
{
  double sum = 0.0;                          /* running total */
  int    i;                                  /* count of items */

  for (i = 0; i < n; i++)
    sum += a[i];
  return (n != 0) ? sum / n : 0.0;
}
```

Figure 9.5   (avg.c) Compute average of an array.

or with pointer indexing,

$$*(t + 3) = 0; \quad \Leftarrow \text{ initialize } t[3] = 0$$

In fact, the compiler converts array subscripts into pointer dereferences—$t[i]$ *becomes* $*(t + i)$. Why are these equivalent? Because in the pointer dereference, $*(t + i)$, the addition $t + i$ is carried out in $\texttt{sizeof(int)}$ increments. Selecting the *i*th element of an array involves calculating its address, given the array's base address (the location of $t[0]$). When we write $t[3]$, C multiplies the index (3) by the size of an $\texttt{int}$ and adds the result to the base address of the array. In our example, assuming t is 1000 and $\texttt{int}$s are 2 bytes long, the computation results in an address of 1006, which is where we find $t[3]$.

What have we gained with all this pointer manipulation? So far it may seem that we've simply discovered a more complicated way to access array elements. But consider the new version of $\textbf{table\_average}$ shown in Figure 9.6. It uses a pointer, $\textbf{ptr}$, to traverse the array rather than an array index.

```
ptr = a;
for (i = 0; i < n; i++)
{
    sum += *ptr;
    ptr++;              adding 1 to ptr
}
```

We access the individual elements with $\textbf{*ptr}$, rather than through an array subscript. And we traverse the array by simply adding 1 to $\textbf{ptr}$ each time we go through the loop. This works because incrementing a pointer makes it point to the next array element.

Why is this pointer-accessing method potentially faster? The main reason is that we eliminate an address computation. When we write $t[i]$, the compiler turns it into $*(t + i)$, which requires an addition (and possibly a multiplication) to locate the desired element. In the pointer version, the pointer is incremented each time we go through the loop—which can often be done as part of the machine instruction that

```
/*
 * Compute average of an array, pointer version.
 */
double table_average(int a[], int n)
{
  double sum = 0.0;                       /* running total */
  int     i;                              /* count of items */
  int    *ptr;                            /* traversing pointer */

  ptr = a;
  for (i = 0; i < n; i++)
  {
    sum += *ptr;
    ptr++;
  }
  return (n != 0) ? sum / n : 0.0;
}
```

[handwritten annotations: "a which is a name of array, i.e. &a[0]."; "? assign a to pointer ptr"; "?"]

Figure 9.6 (avg2.c) A pointer version of `table_average`.

dereferences the pointer—and no other calculation is necessary. Perhaps surprisingly, we're able to improve this loop even more. We'll show how in the next section.

There is one final form of pointer arithmetic: subtracting two pointers. We use this most frequently to calculate the subscript of a pointed-to array element. That's because the result of subtracting a pointer q from a pointer p is j such that $p + j$ gives q (that is, the number of elements between them). So if p is $\&t[0]$ and q is $\&t[3]$, $q - p$ is 3. Of course, this operation gives a portable result only if both operands point to the same array.

[handwritten left margin: "subtracting 2 pointers to calculate the subscript of a pointed-to-array element."; "Pointer Arithmetics 1) pointer ± integer 2) pointer - pointer2"]

> *The only legal arithmetic operators on pointers are adding or subtracting an integer, or subtracting one pointer from another.*

We can't add, multiply, or divide two pointers, and we can't multiply or divide a pointer by an `int`. This restriction is occasionally irritating. Suppose we need the value of the middle element in an array of **n** elements (the element halfway between the array's first and last element). We can easily find it using array indexing: it's `t[n/2]`. And we might think that we could also easily find it using pointer arithmetic (assuming `minptr` points to the array's first element and `maxptr` points to its last element):

```
* ((minptr + maxptr) / 2)
```

[handwritten: "2 pointer variables."]

But this fails because we can't legally *add* pointers. Fortunately, we can legally *subtract* pointers, so we can instead use

```
* (minptr + (maxptr - minptr) / 2)
```

[handwritten: "This is ok"; "becomes integer and thus add to the pointer minptr"]

Although this may look like pointer addition, it's not. Subtracting two pointers yields an integer, as does dividing an integer by 2. And adding an integer to a pointer gives a pointer. We'll make use of this computation in a later chapter when we present an implementation of binary search.

Pointer Comparison

Pointers can be compared. We can test whether a pointer is equal (`==`), not equal (`!=`), less than (`<`), less than or equal (`<=`), greater than (`>`), or greater than or equal (`>=`) to another.

Two pointers are equal only if they point to the same location. One pointer is less than another if it points to a lower location in memory, so `&t[3]` is less than `&t[5]`. Conversely, one pointer is greater than another if it points to a higher location in memory, so `&t[5]` is greater than `&t[3]`.

Where different arrays reside in memory is machine dependent and is likely to vary from implementation to implementation.[3] That means it's not portable to compare pointers into different arrays.

> *Don't compare pointers that don't access the same array.*

Figure 9.7 shows how we can use pointer comparisons to write **table_average** more efficiently. This loop is more efficient because it no longer tests a counter to determine when the array has been traversed. Instead, we compare the indexing pointer with a pointer to just past the array's last element. When they're equal, we leave the loop. We declare and initialize the ending pointer with

```
int *endptr = a + n;
```

which is identical to the separate declaration and assignment

```
int *endptr;

endptr = a + n;
```
assign address?

That is, it assigns `a + n` to `endptr`, not to what `endptr` points to.

Having a pointer to just past the last element seems strange. But we're guaranteed that a pointer to *one* element past the end of an array is legal. It's not legal to follow that pointer; the guarantee is merely that the *address* is legal. Even so, why didn't we just have a pointer to the last element, not one past it? The main reason is that we want our pointer traversal of an array to resemble our array subscripting traversal. With array subscripting, we stopped the loop when the index was 1 more than the index of the array's last element.

---

[3]On the PC, for example, different arrays may be stored in different memory segments. Two pointers could compare equal when they point to completely different locations.

```
/*
 * Compute average of an array, concise pointer version.
 */
double table_average(int a[], int n)
{
  double sum = 0.0;                        /* running total */
  int    *ptr;                             /* traversing pointer */
  int    *endptr = a + n;                  /* pointer to just past end */

  for (ptr = a; ptr < endptr; ptr++)
    sum += *ptr;
  return (n != 0) ? sum / n : 0.0;
}
```

same as endptr = a + n;

Figure 9.7 (avg3.c) A more concise pointer version of `table_average`.

> *Don't assume that a pointer to the element just before the start of an array is legal.*

That becomes important when we're traversing an array in reverse order. Figures 9.8 and 9.9 do so in a pointer version of Chapter 7's input reversal program. As before, we read the array with `table_fill` and print it in reverse order with `table_print_rev`. To print an array backward, we run a pointer from its last element through its first. The obvious solution is to have a pointer to the last element and to keep decrementing as long as it's greater than or equal to the first element's address:

```
for (ptr = &a[num-1]; ptr >= a; ptr--)
  printf("%i\n", *ptr);
```

But this solution has a problem: the loop terminates only when `ptr` becomes less than `a`. And that's not guaranteed to be a legal address, which means the comparison may fail. We must take a different approach: test whether `ptr` is greater than `a`, and decrement it before we dereference it.

```
ptr = &a[num];
while (ptr-- > a)
  printf("%i\n", *ptr);
```

Concise Pointer Loops

We haven't been writing our loops as concisely as we could. We can, for example, rewrite `table_average`'s loop to sum up `a`'s values (assuming `ptr` and `endptr` have been initialized appropriately) as

Main Program

```
/*
 * Pointer version of input-reversal program.
 */
#define MAXVALS   100                         /* max values in table */

int main()
{
  int  table_fill(int a[], int max);
  void table_print_rev(int a[], int num);
  int  t[MAXVALS];                            /* input values*/
  int  n = table_fill(t, MAXVALS);

  table_print_rev(t, n);
  return 0;
}
```

Figure 9.8   (revtab.c)   The main program of our input reverser.

Function Routine

Fn. Routine

```
/*
 * Pointer versions of table-handling functions.
 *    table_fill - read values into table.
 *    table_print_rev - print values in reverse order.
 */
#include <stdio.h>

int table_fill(int a[], int max)
{
  int *ptr = a;                    /* pointer to first element */
  int *endptr = ptr + max;         /* pointer to just past last element */

  for (ptr = a; ptr < endptr; ptr++)
    if (scanf("%i", ptr) != 1)
      break;
  return ptr - a;                  /* # of values read successfully */
}

void table_print_rev(int a[], int num)
{
  int *ptr = a + num;              /* pointer to just past last element */

  while (ptr-- > a)
    printf("%i\n", *ptr);
}
```

Figure 9.9   (table.c)   Pointer versions of the table-handling routines.

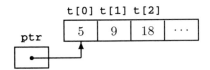

(a) Initial assignment: `ptr = &t[0]` (or equivalently, `ptr=t`).

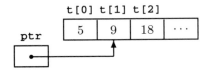

(b) `*ptr++` increments `ptr` and returns 5, so `v = *ptr++` sets `v` to 5.

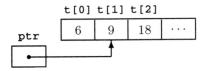

(c) `(*ptr)++` increments `t[1]` and returns 9, so `v = (*ptr)++` sets `v` to 9.

Figure 9.10   The difference between `*ptr++` and `(*ptr)++`.

*[handwritten annotation:] *ptr++ ⟹ obtains pointed value and then increment the pointer*
*(*ptr)++ ⟹ increment the pointed value.*

```
while (ptr < endptr)
    sum += *ptr++;
```

Because of the precedence and evaluation order of `*` and `++`, `*ptr++` means "obtain the value that `ptr` points to (`*ptr`), return the value, and then increment the pointer." This differs from `(*ptr)++`, which simply increments the value pointed to by `ptr`, after returning its original value, as shown in Figure 9.10. The result is that

```
sum += *ptr++;
```

*[handwritten annotation:] *--ptr*
*[handwritten annotation:] *++ptr*

is equivalent to

```
sum += *ptr;
ptr++;
```

Similarly, `*ptr--` decrements the pointer after returning the pointed-to value. The prefix forms increment (`*++ptr`) or decrement (`*--ptr`) the pointer and return whatever value it then points to.

Pointers and Other Types of Arrays

Pointers can be used to traverse an array of any type. Figures 9.11 and 9.12 take advantage of pointer arithmetic in a version of our input reversal program that assumes

```
/*
 * Input-reversal program using pointers.  For doubles, not ints.
 */
#define MAXVALS 100

int main()
{
  int     dbl_table_fill(double d[], int max);
  void    dbl_table_print_rev(double d[], int num);
  double  table[MAXVALS];
  int     n = dbl_table_fill(table, MAXVALS);

  dbl_table_print_rev(table, n);
  return 0;
}
```

Figure 9.11   (drevtab.c) A program to reverse its input doubles.

```
/*
 * Table-handling functions using pointers.  For doubles, not ints.
 *   dbl_table_fill - read values into table.
 *   dbl_table_print_rev - print table in reverse order.
 */
#include <stdio.h>

int dbl_table_fill(double a[], int max)
{
  double *ptr = a;                   /* pointer to first element */
  double *endptr = ptr + max;        /* pointer to just after last element */

  for (ptr = a; ptr < endptr; ptr++)
    if (scanf("%lf", ptr) != 1)
      break;
  return ptr - a;                    /* # of values read successfully */
}

void dbl_table_print_rev(double a[], int num)
{
  double *ptr = a + num;

  while (ptr-- > a)
    printf("%f\n", *ptr);
}
```

Figure 9.12   (dtable.c) Functions to fill and print in reverse order an array of doubles.

```
/*
 * Function to compute average of array, most concise version.
 */
double table_average(int *ptr, int n)
{
  double sum = 0.0;
  int  *endptr = ptr + n;    /* pointer to just past last element */

  while (ptr < endptr)
    sum += *ptr++;
  return (n != 0) ? sum / n : 0.0;
}
```

Figure 9.13   (avg4.c) The most concise version of our function to find the average of an array.

our input values are **double**s rather than **int**s. The program works because pointer arithmetic for references to an element in an array of **double**s is done in terms of **double**s, units of 8 bytes (assuming 8-byte **double**s). We did little more than change all of the pointer and function declarations.

9.3   ARRAY PARAMETERS AND POINTERS

We saw earlier that when we pass an array parameter, we really only pass the address of its first element—or, in other words, a pointer. This means that a function header or prototype, such as

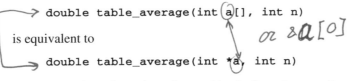

```
        double table_average(int a[], int n)
```
is equivalent to

or &a[0]

```
        double table_average(int *a, int n)
```

We can use these forms interchangeably. In fact, the compiler automatically translates any array parameter into a pointer parameter.

We don't explicitly declare an array parameter's size, so functions that process arrays need to know how many array elements to process. That means that when we pass an array, we usually also pass the number of elements in the array, **n** in **table_average**.[4] Figure 9.13, shows a pointer version of **table_average**.

One benefit of an array's being passed as a pointer is that we can pass the address of any array element. This effectively allows us to pass only part of an array. We can compute the average of **k** elements of **t**, starting with **t[i]**, with either

```
        avg = table_average(&t[i], k);
```

---

[4]We cannot use **sizeof** in **table_average** because **sizeof**(*a pointer*) returns the size of the pointer, not of the entire array.

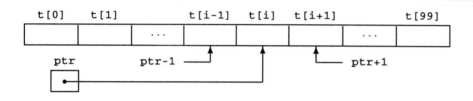

```
  t[0]    t[1]            t[i-1]   t[i]   t[i+1]            t[99]
┌──────┬──────┬──────┬──────┬──────┬──────┬──────┬──────┐
│      │      │ ...  │      │      │      │ ...  │      │
└──────┴──────┴──────┴──────┴──────┴──────┴──────┴──────┘
   ptr           ptr-1 ─┐  ↑      ↑     ↑
                        └──┘      │     └── ptr+1
   ┌──────┐                       │
   │  •───┼───────────────────────┘
   └──────┘
```

Figure 9.14   Passing part of an array. We can still access the entire array.

or the equivalent

```
        avg = table_average(t + i, k);
```

In both cases we pass `t[i]`'s address. Figure 9.14 shows how `table_average` can still access any element of `t` through appropriate negative or positive offsets of `ptr`.

> *Don't pass an array element to a function expecting an array parameter.*

A function expecting an array must be passed an array name or an element's address. The call

```
        avg = table_average(t[i], k);          /* wrong! */
```

is a serious mistake, since `table_average` expects a pointer and instead receives an `int`. So as long as you provided a prototype, the compiler should catch this error for you.

9.4   CONSTANTS AND POINTERS

Just as we have integer and real variables that are constants, we can also have pointers to constants and constant pointers. The declaration

```
const int *ptr;
```

declares `ptr` to be a pointer to a constant `int`. That means that although we can modify `ptr`, we can't modify what it points to. An operation such as

```
        *ptr = 0;
```

is illegal. One use for `ptr` would be to traverse a constant array, perhaps to print each of its elements.

We can assign a pointer to a non-`const` to a pointer to a `const` of the same basic type. So if we have an `int *`, we can assign it to a `const int *`. But we need a cast to assign the other way. We can't simply assign a `const int *` to an `int *`. Even with the cast, however, we're courting danger, as we can now modify a value originally declared to be constant.[5]

The syntax for declaring pointers that are constants is strange:

```
int *const endptr = ptr + max;
```

This makes `endptr` a constant pointer to an `int` and initializes it with the address `ptr + max`. We can't modify a constant pointer, so we must initialize constant pointers when we declare them. We can, however, modify what they point to.

Finally, we can declare a constant pointer to a constant item. This happens most frequently when we pass an array to a function that uses a pointer to traverse it and doesn't change its items. This declaration

```
const int *const firstptr = a;
```

declares `firstptr` as a constant pointer to a constant integer. That means we can neither modify `firstptr`, nor modify the value it points to. Since the pointer itself is constant, we must initialize it when we declare it.

The syntax for declaring constants seems tricky. Just remember that if the pointer is constant, place the `const` immediately preceding the identifier. And if the pointed-to object is constant, place the `const` before that object's type.

Figures 9.15 and 9.16 contain a new version of our program to reverse its input, modified to use `const` for its pointer parameters and local variables.

9.5   GENERIC POINTERS AND POINTER CONVERSIONS

We often find ourselves wanting to copy one array into another. The obvious way to do it is to simply assign one array name to another.

```
double f[MAXVALS], g[MAXVALS];

    f = g;                              /* illegal! */
```

The only problem is that this assignment doesn't work. In fact, it doesn't even compile. It's an illegal assignment because we're trying to modify a constant. The name of an array is a *constant* pointer to its first element, so `f` is a constant address. Even if it weren't a constant, however, we would still only be modifying a pointer, and not the pointed-to elements. To copy one array into another, we're stuck with running through the arrays and copying one element at a time.

While we could write a loop to do this copy ourselves, there's a library function, `memcpy`, that we can use instead. It simply copies a block of bytes from one location to another, so we can use it to copy arrays containing elements of any type. In fact, the standard libraries provide a set of easy-to-use functions that perform tasks such as

---

[5]One common use of this conversion, however, is to write search functions that treat the array they're searching as a constant but return a non-`const` pointer to the matching array element. That way their caller can use this pointer to modify the array without doing a cast.

```
/*
 * Pointer version of input-reversal program, using constants.
 */
#define MAXVALS    100                    /* max values in "table" */

int main()
{
  int  table_fill(int *ptr, int max);
  void table_print_rev(const int a[], int num);
  int  t[MAXVALS];                        /* table for input values*/
  int  n = table_fill(t, MAXVALS);

  table_print_rev(t, n);
  return 0;
}
```

Figure 9.15   (revtab2.c)   A version of our reverse program modified to use **const** pointers.

```
/*
 * Pointer versions of table-handling functions:
 *    table_fill - read values into table.
 *    table_print_rev - print values in reverse order.
 */
#include <stdio.h>

int table_fill(int *ptr, int max)
{
  int *const firstptr = ptr;       /* pointer to first element */
  int *const endptr = ptr + max;   /* pointer to just past end */

  for ( ; ptr < endptr; ptr++)
    if (scanf("%i", ptr) != 1)
      break;
  return ptr - firstptr;           /* # of values read successfully */
}

void table_print_rev(const int a[], int num)
{
  const int *const firstptr = a;
  const int *ptr;

  ptr = firstptr + num;
  while (ptr-- > firstptr)
    printf("%i\n", *ptr);
}
```

Figure 9.16   (table2.c)   Versions of **table_fill** and **table_print_rev** that use **const** pointers.

FUNCTION	WHAT IT DOES
`void *memcpy(d,s,n)`	Copy **n** bytes from the location pointed to by **s** into the location pointed to by **d**. Returns **d**. It shouldn't be used when the memory locations overlap.
`void *memmove(d,s,n)`	Exactly like **memcpy** except that the memory locations may overlap.
`int memcmp(s1,s2,n)`	Compare the first **n** bytes in **s1** with the first **n** bytes in **s2**. Returns a negative value if **s1** < **s2**, zero if they're equal, and a positive value if **s1** > **s2**.
`void *memchr(s,c,n)`	Find the first occurrence of **c** in the first **n** bytes of **s**. Returns a pointer to the character if found, or the null pointer otherwise.
`void *memset(d,c,n)`	Copy the byte **c** into the first **n** locations pointed to by **d**. Returns **d**.

[handwritten: to work w/ any types of pointers]

Table 9.1 Functions that access blocks of bytes. **d** is a pointer to a **void**; **s**, **s1**, and **s2** are pointers to **const void**; **n** is a **size_t**; and **c** is an **int** cast to an **unsigned char** for comparison purposes.

[handwritten: — need #include < string.h >]

copying, searching, or initializing blocks of bytes. Figure 9.1 lists these functions. To use these functions, we need to include the standard header file string.h.

To copy one array into another, we pass **memcpy** pointers to the first element of the arrays, along with the number of *bytes* we want to copy. **memcpy** copies its second argument into its first, 1 byte at a time. So we can copy **g** into **f** with

[handwritten: copy g[ ] to f[ ]]

```
memcpy(f, g, sizeof(g));
```

[handwritten: give # of bytes in g[ ] array]

f and **g** are pointers to the first elements of those arrays, and since **g** is declared as an array, **sizeof(g)** is the number of bytes in that array.[6]

How can we implement a function like **memcpy** that doesn't care what type of pointers we pass to it? The trick is that we declare **memcpy**'s two pointer parameters as pointers to **void** (declared as **void ***). Pointers to **void** differ from other pointers in several ways. Ordinarily, there are no automatic conversions between pointers. To assign a pointer of one type to a pointer of another type, we're forced to insert an explicit cast. But we can assign any pointer to and from a pointer to **void** without a cast. That's what happens when we call **memcpy**: the pointers we pass are automatically converted to pointers to **void**.

The other difference is that we can't dereference a pointer to **void** or do pointer arithmetic with it. We first have to convert it to some other pointer type. **memcpy** treats the pointer it's passed as a pointer to a byte and goes through the blocks of bytes it's passed, copying 1 byte at a time.

Figure 9.17 shows one possible implementation of **memcpy**, called **ourmemcpy** to prevent name conflicts with the standard library function. We also provide a main program that uses it to copy an array of **double**s.

[handwritten: pointer to void can not be dereferenced.]

We've declared the two pointer parameters **xptr** and **yptr** as pointers to **void**, so it's illegal to dereference them with ***xptr** or ***yptr**. Before we can access the bytes

___

[6]The call **memcpy(f, g, MAXVALS)** is incorrect. Why? Because the third argument is in *bytes*, not *elements*.

```
/*
 * One possible implementation of memcpy, along with a program that
 * uses it to copy one array into another.
 */
#include <stdio.h>
#define MAXVALS 10              /* number of items in array */

typedef unsigned char BYTE;    /* BYTE's a synonym for unsigned char */

int main()
{
    void ourmemcpy(void *xptr, const void *yptr, size_t n);
    double f[MAXVALS];
    double g[MAXVALS] = {7.5, 4.5, 5.4, 9.8, 9.5, 8.2, 9.1, 9.9, 4.5, 6.3};
    int    i;

    ourmemcpy(f, g, sizeof(g));            /* copy g into f */
    for (i = 0; i < MAXVALS; i++)          /* print f to see result */
        printf("f[%i]=%f\n", i, f[i]);
    return 0;
}

void ourmemcpy(void *xptr, const void *yptr, size_t n)
{
    BYTE       *destptr;
    const BYTE *srcptr;
    const BYTE *endptr;

    destptr = xptr;
    srcptr = yptr;
    endptr = srcptr + n;
    while (srcptr < endptr)
        *destptr++ = *srcptr++;
}
```

Figure 9.17 (memcpy.c) One possible implementation of **memcpy**, called **ourmemcpy** to prevent name conflicts.

Definition of BYTE

to which they point, we must turn them into pointers to bytes (**unsigned char**s). That's easy to do: we simply assign them to variables declared as pointers to **BYTE** (a typedef to **unsigned char**).

```
    BYTE       *destptr;
    const BYTE *srcptr;

    destptr = xptr;
    srcptr = yptr;
```

There are a couple of subtleties about **memcpy**. First, it returns the generic pointer passed as a first argument. So far, however, we've simply ignored this return value.

size_t is a type

Second, the parameter holding the number of bytes to copy has type `size_t`. That's because we usually pass it the result of doing `sizeof` on the array we're copying. And third, we can't use `memcpy` if the copied arrays overlap. That situation arises when we copy one part of an array to earlier or later in the array. In these situations, we need to use a separate function, `memmove`, that's identical to `memcpy`, except that it *always* works correctly. Why are there two functions? Because sometimes we want `memcpy`'s efficiency and other times we want `memmove`'s generality.

9.6   DYNAMICALLY ALLOCATING ARRAYS

Many languages let us specify an array's size at run time. This feature is convenient, since we don't always know at compile time exactly how many elements an array should have. But the problem is that the arrays we allocate at compile time often turn out to be much too big, which wastes space, or much too small, which makes our programs fail.

Unfortunately, C requires the number of items in an array to be known at compile time. Luckily, there are several library functions we can use to get around this restriction. Table 9.2 lists these functions and provides brief descriptions. The two we use most frequently are `malloc` (for "memory allocation"), which allocates storage space from a system-maintained pool of memory, and `free`, which returns the space allocated by `malloc` to this pool for reuse later. The idea is that we can use `malloc` to allocate space for an array and `free` to return it. Prototypes for these functions are defined in the system header file stdlib.h, which must be included to use them.

< stdlib.h >

Allocating Storage with `malloc`

no. of bytes

Library fn: malloc

`malloc` is passed a single argument (type `size_t`) specifying the number of bytes to allocate. It allocates a block of bytes of at least the desired size and returns a pointer to it, or `NULL` if a large enough chunk could not be found. For example, we've declared `tptr` as a pointer to a `double`; we can allocate an array large enough for `n` `double`s with

determine # of bytes/double

```
tptr = malloc(n * sizeof(double));
if (tptr = NULL)
{
    printf("Couldn't allocate %i elements\n", n);
    return 1;   /* out of memory error, quit */
}
```

declare as a pointer

`malloc` allocates bytes, not integers. If we want to allocate an array of 100 integers, we can't simply pass it 100. Instead, we must pass it the number of bytes an array of 100 `double`s requires, the size of a `double` times 100.

We can use `malloc` to allocate space for an array of any type. `malloc` simply returns a pointer to the first byte in a block of bytes and guarantees that the returned block satisfies the alignment considerations for all of C's data types. This returned pointer is a pointer to `void`, so we have to place it into a pointer to a `double` before we can actually follow it to access the elements in the allocated array. There's no need

#include <stdlib.h>

FUNCTION	WHAT IT DOES
`void *calloc(n,size)`	Allocates space for **n** items, each of **size** bytes. Sets the allocated space to zero. Returns a pointer to the beginning of the allocated space, or **NULL** if the space can't be allocated.
`void free(p)`	Allows allocated space pointed to by **p** to be allocated again.
`void *malloc(size)`	Allocate space for **size** bytes. Doesn't initialize the allocated space. Returns a pointer to the beginning of the allocated space, or **NULL** if the space can't be allocated.
`void *realloc(p,size)`	Changes the space allocated by **p** to be **size** bytes. Returns a pointer to the beginning of the allocated space, or **NULL** if the space can't be allocated. The contents of the space pointed to by **p** are unchanged.

memory allocation

Table 9.2   Functions for managing dynamically allocated storage. **n** and **size** are both **size_t**, and **p** is a pointer to **void**.

for a cast, though, since C does the appropriate automatic conversion when we do the assignment.

Figure 9.18 uses **malloc** and **free** in one final variant of our input reversing program. This version expects its input to be broken into groups, with each group preceded by a count of the items in it. The program reads and reverses each of these groups. Unlike most of our earlier versions, however, it expects **double**s as its input values, not **int**s. Here's some sample input and output:

```
4 19.8 35.5 25.3 45.5
45.500000
25.300000
35.500000
19.800000
3 15.4 20.2 12.6
12.600000
20.200000
15.400000
```

Problems with using malloc (3 problems)

①

How can the program read and reverse a group? It needs to read the group into an array large enough to hold it and then print this array in reverse order. After the program reads the group's size, it uses **malloc** to allocate a large enough array. It then uses **dbl_table_fill** to fill it and **dbl_table_print_rev** to print it in reverse order. Once the program is done with a group, it uses **free** to release the group's storage, so it can be reused for the next group.

malloc is a powerful function, but we have to be careful when we use it. One problem arises when we run out of memory. If there isn't enough memory to honor our request, **malloc** will fail and will return **NULL** instead of a legitimate pointer. That means it's crucial to check whether the pointer **malloc** returned is **NULL** before using it.

```
/*
 * Read and reverse groups within the input.
 */
#include <stdio.h>
#include <stddef.h>                    /* definition of NULL */
#include <stdlib.h>                    /* definition of malloc */

int main()
{
  int      dbl_table_fill(double a[], int max);
  void     dbl_table_print_rev(double a[], int n);
  double *tptr;                        /* holds the input array */
  int      n;                          /* elements in group, table */
  int      res;                        /* scanf result */

  while ((res = scanf("%i", &n)) == 1)
  {
    tptr = malloc(n * sizeof(double));
    if (tptr == NULL)
    {
      printf("Couldn't allocate %i elements\n", n);
      return 1;   /* out of memory error, quit */
    }
    dbl_table_print_rev(tptr, dbl_table_fill(tptr, n));
    free(tptr);
  }
  if (res != EOF)
    printf("Couldn't read all elements\n");
  return res == EOF;
}
```

Figure 9.18 (grprev.c) A program to reverse groups within its input.

> *Don't assume* malloc *will always succeed.*

② Another problem arises if we fail to initialize the storage malloc allocates. This space starts off with whatever happens to be in memory at the time it's allocated. That means we have to be careful to initialize it ourselves. There is, however, a variant of malloc that allocates the storage and fills it with zeros. This function, calloc, takes two arguments rather than one. The first is the number of items (an unsigned int); the second is the size of each item (a size_t). Like malloc, it returns a pointer to the first byte in the storage it allocated.

> *Don't assume the storage* malloc *provides is initialized to zero.*

③ One final problem arises if we modify the pointer **malloc** returns. If we increment that pointer, for example, it no longer points to the beginning of the storage we allocated, and we can no longer pass that pointer to **free** to return that storage. We're best off treating that pointer like a constant, just as if it were the name of an array.

[handwritten margin note: treats the pointer malloc returns like a constant]

> **Don't modify the pointer returned by malloc.**

Deallocating Storage with free

free takes a pointer ... allocated by **malloc** or **calloc** and makes ... storage available ... We can return the array **tptr** allocated above with

    free(tptr);

Be... **free** can be ... of bytes allocated by **malloc**, its argument ... declared as a pointer to ... don't have to cast **tptr**, as it's automatically ... pointer in ... call to **free**.

There ... common ... that occur when first using dynamic allocation ... to deallocate storage that wasn't originally obtained from **malloc** ... global variables. This causes general chaos, since **free** assumes ... storage obtained from **malloc**. Another is to try to access ... deallocated with **free**. Some implementations will let us get away with this ... possible that storage has already been reallocated elsewhere.

[handwritten margin note: 'free' is used to free storage obtained from 'malloc' only]

> ... from malloc, *and don't access the stor-*

9.7   CASE STUDY—DYNAMICALLY ALLOCATED SETS

This section is optional!

This chapter concludes with a case study—we extend our sets package from the previous chapter to allow varying sizes. Surprisingly, we need only make a few changes to our earlier version. Figure 9.19 above... our new version of sets.h, and Figure 9.20 shows our new version of sets.c.

First, we need to add two new functions: **set_create** creates a new set capable of handling a specified number of elements; **set_destroy** gets rid of a set once we no longer need it. **set_create** dynamically allocates the storage needed for a **SET**; **set_destroy** releases it. Their prototypes are

    SET set_create(unsigned int n);
    void set_destroy(SET s);

Since we want sets to start out empty, we use **calloc** to allocate storage rather than **malloc**. This guarantees that all bytes used for the set are initially zero.

```
/*
 * Improved definitions to use "sets" of integers.
 */
typedef void *SET;

extern SET    set_create(unsigned int n);
extern void   set_destroy(SET s);
extern void   set_add(SET s, int e);
extern void   set_delete(SET s, int e);
extern int    set_member(const SET s, int e);
```

Figure 9.19   (sets.h)   The revised header file for sets.

Second, we need to redeclare **SET** as a pointer, rather than as a fixed-size array. Specifically, we define **SET** as a pointer to **void**. That way we keep the details of what a **SET** actually is hidden from its callers. They don't need to know that a **SET** is a dynamically allocated array of **unsigned short**s. Unfortunately, this complicates the functions implementing sets, since they now have to cast the **SET** pointer to a pointer to an **unsigned short** before dereferencing it.

And third, we have to modify the other set functions, the ones that access the individual set elements. They're still passed a **SET**, but now they have to cast it into a pointer to an **unsigned short**, so that they can dereference it to get to the bits representing the set values.

To redo our earlier program that printed the unique and duplicate values in its input, we have only to make two minor changes. There is no longer a constant **MAXELEMS** defined in **sets.h**, so we now define it appropriately in the programs that use sets. And it's no longer sufficient to simply declare **SET** variables. Now we need to call **set_create** to actually allocate space for the **SET** elements. Figure 9.21 shows a revised version of that earlier program.

SUMMARY

- C provides pointers, a data type that can hold addresses. We obtain pointers with **&** and obtain the value they point to with *****.

- There is a generic pointer type, **void ***, that can contain any type of pointer. But before we can make use of that pointer, we must cast it to another type.

- We can add or subtract an integer and a pointer, and we can subtract one pointer from another. The arithmetic takes place in units of the pointed-to type. We can also compare two pointers, so long as they point to the same array.

- To print a pointer, we cast it to **void *** and use **printf**'s **%p** formatting code.

```
/*
 * Functions to handle dynamically allocated sets.
 */
#include <stdlib.h>
#include "sets.h"

#define US_BITS 16

typedef unsigned short USHORT;

static int word(int elem);
static int bit(int elem);

SET set_create(unsigned int n)                /* create an empty set */
{
  return calloc((n / US_BITS) + ((n % US_BITS) != 0), sizeof(USHORT));
}

void set_destroy(SET s)                       /* get rid of a set */
{
  free(s);
}

void set_add(SET s, int elem)                 /* add element to set */
{
  * ((USHORT *) s + word(elem)) |= 1 << bit(elem);
}

void set_delete(SET s, int elem)              /* delete element from set */
{
  * ((USHORT *) s + word(elem)) &= ~(1 << bit(elem));
}

int set_member(const SET s, int elem)    /* is item in set? */
{
  const unsigned int temp = * ((const USHORT *) s + word(elem));

  return (temp >> bit(elem)) & 01;
}

static int word(int elem)
{
  return elem / US_BITS;                      /* word # containing element */
}

static int bit(int elem)
{
  return elem % US_BITS;                      /* bit # representing element */
}
```

Figure 9.20   (sets.c) The revised source for the set operations.

```
/*
 * Identify duplicates in the input.
 */
#include <stdio.h>
#include "sets.h"                          /* for SETs */

int main()
{
  void  set_print(const SET s, int max);
  void  set_switch(SET news, SET olds, int elem);
  const int MAXELEMS = 512;                /* # of set elements */
  SET   unique = set_create(MAXELEMS),     /* unique and */
        dup    = set_create(MAXELEMS);     /*   duplicate sets */
  int   r, inp;                            /* scanf return, input value */

  while ((r = scanf("%i", &inp)) != EOF)
  {
    if (r != 1)
    {
      printf("Value in error.\n");
      break;
    }
    if (inp < 0 || inp >= MAXELEMS)
    {
      printf("Value out of range.\n");
      continue;
    }
    if (set_member(unique, inp))
      set_switch(dup, unique, inp);
    else if (!set_member(dup, inp))
      set_add(unique, inp);
  }
  printf("Unique values\n");  set_print(unique, MAXELEMS);
  printf("Duplicate values\n");  set_print(dup, MAXELEMS);
  return 0;
}

void set_switch(SET new, SET old, int value)
{
  set_delete(old, value);  set_add(new, value);
}

void set_print(const SET set, int max)
{
  int i;                                   /* next potential element */

  for (i = 0; i < max; i++)
    if (set_member(set, i))
      printf("%i\n", i);
}
```

Figure 9.21   (usesets.c)   The revised program to use the set operations.

- We can combine pointer arithmetic and comparisons to traverse arrays more efficiently than with array subscripting. Pointer arithmetic takes place in units of the pointed-to type.

- C has several library functions to manage dynamic memory allocation: **malloc**, which allocates a chunk of memory; **calloc**, which allocates and sets to zero a chunk of memory; and **free**, which returns a chunk of memory.

EXERCISES

9–1 Rewrite all of Chapter 7's programs and functions to use pointers to traverse their arrays.

9–2 Add error checking to the final version of **table_fill** (Figure 9.16).

9–3 Rewrite **table_search** (Figure 7.5) to use pointers to search backward from the end of the array rather than forward from the front.

9–4 Rewrite Chapter 8's queue manipulating functions (Figure 8.20) to use pointers rather than array indexing. Then extend it to allocate the queues dynamically.

9–5 Modify the group reversal program to allocate more space only if the existing array is too small.

9–6 Write **table_reverse**, a function to reverse an array in place. First write it using array subscripting, and then using pointers.

9–7 Write **table_delete**, a function that deletes all occurrences of a particular item from an array of **int**s. It does the delete by shifting array elements. First write it using array subscripting, and then using pointers.

9–8 Write **calloc**, assuming **malloc** exists.

9–9 Write **memmove**, the variant of **memcpy** that can handle an overlap between the copy's source and destination.

9–10 Write **table_diff**, a function that compares two arrays of integers and returns the subscript of the first place they differ. If the arrays are the same, the function returns -1. First, write it using array subscripting, and then using pointers.

9–11 Write **table_sym**, a function that tests whether an array of **int**s is symmetrical. That is, it returns a 1 if the array would print the same forward and backward, and a zero otherwise. Use pointers. How concise a function can you create?

9–12 Write **table_max**, a function to find the largest value in an array. Use pointers to traverse the array.

9–13 Write **table_dup**, a function to create a dynamically allocated copy of an existing array of **int**s. It takes the name of the array it's copying and the number of elements in the array.

9–14 Write **table_dump**, a function that prints all of the elements in an array and their addresses, one per line.

10 STRINGS

This chapter presents strings, a special type of array of characters. We introduce string constants and variables and examine the close relationship strings have with pointers. We present the standard library functions for manipulating strings and provide array subscripting and pointer indexing implementations of several of the more commonly used ones. We also present an implementation of a useful function for reading an input line into a string and rework several of our earlier programs to use it. We conclude with a case study: a program that strips consecutive duplicate lines from its input.

10.1   STRING CONSTANTS

A *string* is simply an array of characters, terminated with an extra character, the null character, `'\0'`. We can create a *constant* string by enclosing a group of characters in double quotation marks.

```
"Enter YES or NO: "
```

C folds consecutive constant strings into a single string, so

```
"Enter " "YES " "or" " NO: "
```

is equivalent to the string above. We take advantage of this automatic folding when we have to store strings too long to fit on a single line.

When the compiler sees a constant string, it tacks on a terminating null character, allocates space for the string, and returns a pointer to its first character. Typically, we assign this pointer to a pointer variable.

```
char *q = "Enter YES or NO: ";
```

This declares `q` as a pointer to a character and initializes `q` to point to the first character in our constant string.

The result is that `q` points to a string containing 18 characters: the 17 between the double quotation marks, and the final null character inserted by the compiler.

expect string with 0 termination.

Why does the compiler insert the terminating null? Primarily to make it easier for us to pass strings to functions—we don't have to pass their length. C has a library of useful string functions, all of which expect a string to be null-terminated. We can, for example, print a string using **printf**'s **%s** format without explicitly supplying its length.

string constant has type "pointer to character"

A string constant has type "pointer to **char**", and a value equal to a pointer to its first character. That means we can use a constant string anywhere we can use a pointer to a **char**. We can, for example, separate the variable declaration from the assignment.

```
char *q;
```

q

```
q = "Enter YES or NO: ";
```

And we can pass strings as function arguments, as we've been doing all along with **printf**.

```
printf("That wasn't a valid response\n");
```

One thing we can't do is change the characters within a string constant. For the pointer **q** above, it's illegal to do

```
q[5] = 'x';
```

This restriction arises because compilers are free to place string constants in read-only memory and to merge duplicate string constants.

Figure 10.1 takes advantage of string constants in a new version of **yesorno** that is passed a prompt to write. Figure 10.2 is a main program that uses it.

10.2 STRING VARIABLES

So far our strings have been constants, for which the compiler allocates space. But we can also create strings by allocating an array and then providing the individual characters ourselves.

initialize string variables 3 ways:

①
```
char q[18] = {'E', 'n', 't', 'e', 'r', ' ', 'Y', 'E', 'S',
              ' ', 'o', 'r', ' ', 'N', 'O', ':', ' ', '\0'};
```

This declares **q** as an array of 18 characters and then initializes those characters from the list we provide. When we take this approach, we have to be careful to explicitly provide the trailing null. The advantage to allocating the array ourselves is that we can then change the characters within it.

> *Don't forget to supply the trailing null character when creating a string.*

Listing all the characters is somewhat tedious, especially for large arrays. Fortunately, there's a special shortcut for initializing character arrays: we simply surround the initial characters by double quotes, just as if they were a string constant.

②
```
char q[18] = "Enter YES or NO: "
```

17 characters

```
/*
 * Obtain a yes or no answer from the user, prompting for response.
 */
#include <stdio.h>
#include <ctype.h>

static const int YES = 1;           /* can be any nonzero value */
static const int NO = 0;            /* shouldn't be changed from zero */

int yesorno(const char *prompt)
{
  int answer, junk;

  while (printf(prompt), (answer = tolower(getchar())) != EOF)
  {
    for (junk = answer; junk != '\n' && junk != EOF; junk = getchar())
      ;                             /* skip extra characters on line */
    if (answer == 'y')
      return YES;
    if (answer == 'n')
      return NO;
    printf("That's not a reasonable answer.\n");
  }
  return NO;
}
```

Figure 10.1 (yesorno.c) A new version of **yesorno** that's passed a prompt to write.

```
/*
 * Main program using our new "yesorno" function.
 */
#include <stdio.h>

int main()
{
  int   yesorno(const char *prompt);
  char *q;                                      /* question for user */

  q = "Enter YES or NO: ";
  printf("%s!\n", yesorno(q) ? "YES" : "NO");
  return 0;
}
```

Figure 10.2 (ynmain.c) A new main program that uses **yesorno**.

But this isn't a real string constant, even though it looks like one. That is, its value is not an address. When we declare an array and provide a string constant as its initial value, the constant is simply a shorthand to save us from having to provide the entire list of characters and the trailing null. As with other arrays, we can omit the subscript and the compiler will allocate just enough space for the elements we provide. This declaration

(3)
```
char q[] = "Enter YES or NO: "
```

is exactly equivalent to the one above.

> **We can't simply assign one character string to another, just as we couldn't assign arrays.**

Although it seems as if the following set of declarations and assignments should work, they don't.

```
char   *q = "Enter YES or NO: ";
char   qcopy[100];
    . . .
qcopy = q;
```

The reason is that even though **qcopy** is indeed a pointer to the first character location in the array, it is a *constant*. Its value, the address of **qcopy[0]**, may not change. If we really want to copy the characters in **q** into **qcopy**, we have to do so one at a time. Luckily, as we'll see shortly, there's a standard library function to do this operation for us.

10.3   BUILDING STRINGS FROM THE INPUT

We often want to build strings from a program's input instead of creating them at compile time. Figure 10.3 contains a new version of our line-numbering program that needs this ability. It works a line at a time, rather than a character at a time. It reads each line into a string and then prints the line number and the string. To do this, it makes use of a new function: getline.

Figure 10.4 contains **getline**. It reads a line of input, with a maximum length of **max** characters, into a character array **line**. The string passed to **getline** must be large enough to hold **max** + 1 characters (the characters on the line, plus the trailing null).

How does **getline** work? It repeatedly reads characters and places them into the array **line**. It stops when it encounters the end of the input line (a **\n**) or finds that the array is full. It does *not* place the newline character into the array. But it does terminate the string with a null. Since there must be room for this extra null character, **getline** stops filling the array after it has read **max** characters—but it continues reading until it hits the end-of-line character, effectively ignoring any other characters on the line. This guarantees that the next time the function is called, it begins reading characters from the start of a new line. **getline** returns the number of characters it placed in the string, not counting the added null character, or **-1** when it reaches end of file.

[handwritten margin notes:]

getline
- return no. of characters placed in the string
or -1 when reaches EOF

getline fills the array until reaching max. but continue reading until the end of line character.

```
/*
 * Line number its input, one line at a time.
 */
#include <stdio.h>

#define MAXLEN   80                    /* longest line */

int main()
{
  int         getline(char line[], int max);
  char        line[MAXLEN + 1];        /* input line (plus \0) */
  unsigned long lines = 0L;            /* line count */

  while (getline(line, MAXLEN) != -1)
    printf("%6lu %s\n", ++lines, line);
  return 0;
}
```

Figure 10.3   (lineno.c) A version of our line-numbering program that reads its input a line at a time.

```
/*
 * Read a single input line into an array.
 */
#include <stdio.h>

int getline(char line[], int max)
{
  int c;                               /* current character */
  int i = 0;                           /* character count */

  while ((c = getchar()) != '\n' && c != EOF)
    if (i < max)
      line[i++] = c;
  line[i] = '\0';                      /* terminate with null */
  return (c == EOF) ? -1 : i;
}
```

Figure 10.4   (getline.c) The function `getline`, which reads an input line into a string.

#include <string.h> (handwritten)

NAME	WHAT IT DOES
char *strcat(s1,s2)	Concatenates **s2** to the end of **s1**, returning **s1**.
char *strncat(s1,s2,n)	Concatenates at most **n** characters from **s2** to the end of **s1**, returning **s1**.
char *strcpy(s1,s2)	Copies **s2** to **s1**, including the null character, returning **s1**.
char *strncpy(s1,s2,n)	Copies at most **n** characters from **s2** to **s1**, returning **s1**. If it stops copying before the null, the null isn't added to **s2**.
int strcmp(s1,s2)	Compares **s1** and **s2**, returning less than 0, 0, or greater than 0, depending on whether **s1** is less than, equal to, or greater than **s2**, respectively.
int strncmp(s1,s2,n)	Compares at most n characters; same return as **strcmp**.
size_t strlen(s)	Returns number of characters in **s**, *not* counting trailing null.
char *strchr(s,c)	Returns a pointer to the first occurrence of **c** in **s**, or **NULL**.
char *strrchr(s,c)	Returns a pointer to the last occurrence of **c** in **s**, or **NULL**.
char *strstr(s1, s2)	Returns a pointer to the first occurrence of the string **s2** in **s1**.
size_t strspn(s1,s2)	Returns length of prefix of **s1** consisting of characters in **s2**.
size_t strcspn(s1,s2)	Returns length of prefix of **s1** consisting characters not in **s2**.
char *strpbrk(s1,s2)	Returns pointer to first occurrence in **s1** of any character in **s2**, or **NULL** if it's in the string.

(handwritten margin notes: "link together", "lib fn", "expect string to terminate with \0")

Table 10.1   Commonly used standard string functions (**s**, **s1**, and **s2** are pointers to **char** for comparison purposes; **c** is an **int** treated as a **char**, and **n** is a **size_t**). We need to include string.h to obtain their prototypes.

10.4   STRING FUNCTIONS FROM THE STANDARD LIBRARY

C provides no operators that work on strings directly, such as string assignment, string comparison, or string concatenation. Instead, we have to rely on a set of standard string library functions. Table 10.1 lists the string-handling functions we use most frequently. The standard library actually contains several other functions, but we leave the more obscure and more complicated functions for Appendix C.

All of these functions expect the strings they're passed to be terminated with a null character. Our programs will fail miserably when we pass these functions character arrays without the terminating null. If we use the **%s** format to **printf** and mistakenly provide it with a character array that's not null-terminated, it will display whatever characters it finds in the memory following the array, stopping only when it finally encounters a null or gets a memory error.

> *Make sure to null-terminate any character arrays you pass the standard string functions.*

In addition, the copying and concatenating functions expect sufficient room in the destination string to contain the result. They also shouldn't be used on overlapping strings.

Using the Standard String Functions

Figure 10.5 is a small program that uses several of these standard I/O library functions. It reads input lines containing people's names and converts them to a last name, first name format. For the input:

```
Alex Quilici
Larry Miller
```

it produces the output:

```
Quilici, Alex
Miller, Larry
```

The program also does a little error checking, making sure that each input line fits the format it expects.

How does this program work? It begins by reading the input line into a character array, **inpline**. It then locates the blank separating the first and last names, copies the characters after the blank (the last name) into another character array **newname**, appends a comma and a blank to **newname**, and finally copies the characters preceding the blank (the first name) onto the end of this array. After all this work it prints **newname**.

We make heavy use of the string library functions. First, we use **strchr** to locate the separating blank.

```
blankptr = strchr(inpline, ' ')
```

char *strchr(s, c)
strlen

strchr takes a string and a character and returns a pointer to the first occurrence of that character in the string. It returns **NULL** if it can't find the character. We use **strlen** to make sure that we have a last name following the separating blank.

```
strlen(blankptr + 1) == 0
```

strlen takes a string and returns the number of characters in it, *not counting the trailing* **'\0'**. Here, we make sure there is at least one character following the blank and preceding the trailing null. Figure 10.6 shows the end result of performing these calls.

Once we've gotten a pointer to the blank, we start constructing the new name. We first use **strcpy** to copy the characters after the blank into **newname**.

strcpy

```
strcpy(newname, blankptr + 1);   /* grab last name */
```

strcpy takes two arguments, both strings, and copies the second into the first, returning a pointer to its first argument. Here, we pass **blankptr + 1** because we want to start copying with the character after the blank.

strcpy assumes that the second string is null terminated and that the first string is large enough. Here, that's a safe assumption, since the string we're copying into

Sample of Usage of String Functions from Lib

```c
/*
 * Name conversion program
 */
#include <stdio.h>
#include <string.h>
#include <stddef.h>

#define MAXLEN     80

int main()
{
  int    getline(char line[], int maxlen);
  char   inpline[MAXLEN + 1];               /* input line */
  int    len;                               /* length of input line */
  char   newname[MAXLEN + 1];               /* converted input name */
  char *blankptr;                           /* pointer to blank separator */

  while ((len = getline(inpline, MAXLEN)) != -1)
    if (len == 0 || (blankptr = strchr(inpline, ' ')) == NULL ||
        strlen(blankptr + 1) == 0)
      printf("ERROR: bad format input line\n");
    else
    {                                       /* split into two strings */
      strcpy(newname, blankptr + 1);        /* make last name first */
      strcat(newname, ", ");                /* append comma */
      *blankptr = '\0';
      strcat(newname, inpline);             /* put first name last */
      printf("%s\n", newname);              /* write new name */
    }
  return 0;
}
```

Figure 10.5   (convnam.c)   Convert names from first name/last name to last name/first name.

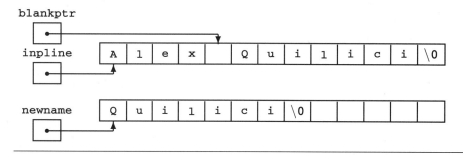

Figure 10.6   The pointers after finding the blank separating the names and copying the last name.

(**newname**) is at least as large as the string we're copying from (**inpline**). The order of **strcpy**'s arguments may seem strange, but it is intended to mimic assignment.

After we've copied the last name, we need to append a comma and a blank to it. To do that, we use one other standard string function: **strcat**.

strcat( )

```
strcat(newname, ", ");          /* append comma */
```

strcat copies its second argument onto the end of its first argument, overwriting the terminating null. It terminates the entire string with a null character. Like **strcpy**, **strcat** assumes there's enough room for all the characters it appends.

Finally, we again use **strcat** to copy the first name onto the end of **newname**.

```
*blankptr = '\0';          ⟶  replace separating blank with \0
strcat(newname, inpline);       for use in copying the first-name
                                               string.
```

Both **strcat** and **strcpy** copy characters until they hit a null. Since we want to copy only the characters before the separating blank, we replace it with a null before calling **strcat**.

Figure 10.7 is an improved version of our name conversion program. This time we allow more varied input—we let one or more blanks and tabs precede, separate, and follow the names. This makes our program considerably more complex. We now have to search for where the first and last name begin. The first name can be preceded by blanks and tabs. To locate it, we use a new function: **strspn**.

```
fnameptr = inpline + strspn(inpline, Spaces);
```

strspn ( )

strspn takes two arguments, both strings. It returns the length of the longest prefix of the first argument that contains only characters found in its second argument. Here, we want the length of the prefix containing only blanks and tabs (the contents of a global constant **Spaces**). We obtain a pointer to the beginning of the name by adding the number of these leading blanks to **inpline**, the address of the beginning of the string.

Our next task is to find the blank following the first name. We do that using **strcspn**:

```
blankptr = fnamelen + strcspn(fnameptr, Spaces);
```

strcspn ( )

strcspn is similar to **strspn**. The difference is that it returns the length of the longest prefix not containing any of the characters in its second argument. Here, we're trying to determine the number of nonblanks or tabs, since those characters constitute the characters in the first name.

We use these functions again to obtain pointers to the beginning and end of the last name. Once we have pointers to the first and last names and their lengths, we can start building the converted name, again using **strcpy** and **strcat**. Figure 10.8 shows the pointers that result.

Figure 10.9 implements a new version of the **yesorno** function. This version improves the most recent version by allowing the user to enter entire words such as "yes" or "no" instead of single letter responses. To compare the user's response with the various "yes" or "no" responses, we use one final library function: **strcmp**.

```
/*
 * Name conversion program, more free-format version.
 */
#include <stdio.h>
#include <string.h>
#include <stddef.h>

#define MAXLEN   80                     /* longest input line */

const char *const Spaces = " \t";

int main()
{
  int    getline(char line[], int maxline);
  char   inpline[MAXLEN + 1];           /* input line */
  int    len;                           /* input line length */
  char   newname[MAXLEN + 1];           /* final converted name */
  char *fnameptr;                       /* ptr to first name */
  char *lnameptr;                       /* ptr to last name */
  char *blankptr;                       /* ptr to separating blank */
  char *followptr;                      /* ptr to char after last name */
  char *finalptr;                       /* ptr to end of trailing blanks */

  while ((len = getline(inpline, MAXLEN)) != -1)
    if (len == 0)
      printf("ERROR: empty input line\n");
    else
    {                                   /* compute needed pointers */
      fnameptr = inpline + strspn(inpline, Spaces);
      blankptr = fnameptr + strcspn(fnameptr, Spaces);
      lnameptr = blankptr + strspn(blankptr, Spaces);
      followptr = lnameptr + strcspn(lnameptr, Spaces);
      finalptr = followptr + strspn(followptr, Spaces);

      if (fnameptr == blankptr || blankptr == lnameptr ||
        lnameptr == followptr || finalptr != inpline + len)
        printf("ERROR: not exactly two names on input line\n");
      else
      {                                 /* do the actual conversion */
        *followptr = '\0';              /* delete trailing blanks */
        *blankptr = '\0';               /* separate into two strings */
        strcpy(newname, lnameptr);
        strcat(newname, ", ");
        strcat(newname, fnameptr);
        printf("%s\n", newname);        /* display new name */
      }
    }
  return 0;
}
```

Figure 10.7 (convnam2.c) An improved version of our name conversion program.

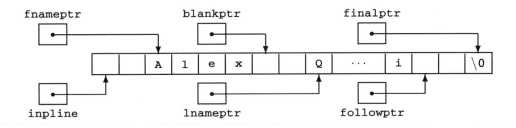

Figure 10.8 The pointers to the beginning and end of the first and last names.

```
/*
 * Obtain a yesorno answer, allowing multicharacter responses.
 */
#include <stdio.h>
#include <string.h>

#define MAXLEN   80

static const int YES = 1;
static const int NO = 0;

int yesorno(const char *prompt)
{
  int  getline(char line[], int max);
  char line[MAXLEN + 1];                      /* input line */

  while (printf(prompt), getline(line, MAXLEN) != -1)
  {
    if (strcmp(line, "yes") == 0 || strcmp(line, "YES") == 0)
      return YES;
    if (strcmp(line, "no") == 0 || strcmp(line, "NO") == 0)
      return NO;
    printf("That's not a reasonable answer.\n");
  }
  return NO;
}
```

Figure 10.9 (yesorno2.c) An even better version of our old **yesorno** function.

```
if (strcmp(line, "yes") == 0 || strcmp(line, "YES") == 0)
  return YES;
if (strcmp(line, "no") == 0 || strcmp(line, "NO") == 0)
  return NO;
printf("That's not a reasonable answer\n");
```

strcmp takes two strings and returns a negative value if the first is alphabetically less than the second, zero if they are equal, and a positive value if the first is alphabetically greater than the second. Here, we use it to compare the user's input line with various reasonable positive and negative responses.

Implementing the Standard String Functions

Why does C provide all of these different string functions? It's not because they're difficult to write. In fact, most of these functions are short and simple. The real power of the standard string library is that it implements frequently used routines, simplifying our job of program construction.

Figure 10.10 shows one way to write functions like **strcpy**, **strcmp**, and **strlen**.[1] The actual code, however, differs from one machine to another. **strcpy** works by walking through the two strings, copying the next character in the second into the next character in the first. It stops when it hits the terminating null.

strcmp is similar, but as it walks through the two strings it compares the corresponding characters. It stops if the characters differ, because that means one of the strings is alphabetically less than the other. And it stops if the characters are the same but null, because that means the strings are the same. **strcmp** returns the difference between the characters. Subtracting two characters yields zero if they are the same, a negative value when the first is alphabetically less than the second, and a positive value when it is greater.

strlen is the simplest of the group. It simply walks through its single string argument, counting characters and stopping when it hits the null. It returns the count of characters it visited.

Additional String Functions

The standard I/O library provides two functions, extensions to **printf** and **scanf**, that allow output to and input from a string. These functions are **sprintf** and **sscanf**, respectively. Both take a string for input or output, a control string, and a list of variables. As with **scanf**, **sscanf** returns the number of values correctly converted.

We can use **sscanf** together with **getline** to avoid some of the problems associated with illegal input using **scanf**. We can read an entire input line using **getline** and then use **sscanf** to extract the values of the variables: Figure 10.11 is a new version of our earlier calculator program that reads the operands and operators using

---

[1]We're not supposed to redefine library functions. In fact, most compilers warn us if we do. But we've redefined these functions so that you can easily link our implementations in with other programs in this chapter.

```
/*
 * Implementations of several standard string functions
 */
#include <stddef.h>

char *strcpy(char d[], const char s[])          /* copy "s" -> "d" */
{
  int i;

  for (i = 0; (d[i] = s[i]) != '\0'; i++)
    ;
  return d;
}

int strcmp(const char s[], const char t[])      /* compare "s" and "t" */
{
  int i;

  for (i = 0; s[i] == t[i] && s[i] != '\0'; i++)
    ;
  return s[i] - t[i];
}

size_t strlen(const char s[])                   /* length of "s"? */
{
  size_t i;

  for (i = 0; s[i] != '\0'; i++)
    ;
  return i;
}
```

Figure 10.10   (string.c) Implementations of several of the standard string library functions.

this technique. This method automatically ignores input lines containing invalid or missing data items, so we no longer have to quit the first time we encounter bad data.

We can use **sprintf** to build strings without having to resort to **strcpy** and **strcat**. We can rewrite this sequence from our name converting program

```
strcpy(newname, blankptr + 1);
strcat(newname, ", ");
*blankptr = '\0';
strcat(newname, inpline);
```

more compactly with **sprintf**.

```
*blankptr = '\0';
sprintf(newname, "%s, %s", blankptr + 1, inpline);
```

Figure 10.12 provides one final example of these string functions in action. It's a new

```c
/*
 * Simple calculator program (uses getline) to read its input.
 */
#include <stdio.h>

#define MAXLEN 80

int main()
{
  int    getline(char line[], int max);
  double op1, op2;                          /* operands */
  char   operator;                          /* operator */
  double result;                            /* result */
  char   inpline[MAXLEN + 1];               /* to hold input line */

  while (getline(inpline, MAXLEN) != -1)
  {
    if (sscanf(inpline, "%lf%c%lf", &op1, &operator, &op2) != 3)
    {
      printf("Input line in error.\n");
      continue;
    }
    switch(operator)
    {
      case '+':
        result = op1 + op2;
        break;
      case '-':
        result = op1 - op2;
        break;
      case '*':
        result = op1 * op2;
        break;
      case '/':
        if (op2 != 0.0)            /* watch out for divide by 0 */
          result = op1 / op2;
        else
        {
          printf("Warning: division by zero.\n");
          result = 0.0;
        }
        break;
      default:
        printf("Unknown operator: %c\n", operator);
        continue;
    }
    printf("%f\n", result);
  }
  return 0;
}
```

Figure 10.11 (calc.c) A new version of the calculator program that reads one line of input at a time.

```
/*
 * Counts various types of punctuation characters.
 */
#include <stdio.h>
#include <ctype.h>
#include <string.h>
#include <stddef.h>

const char *const Puncts     = ",.;:!?";
const char *const Brackets   = "(){}[]";
const char *const Quotes     = "'\"";
const int         PrintWidth = 11;            /* width of counter */

int main()
{
  int           c;
  unsigned long quotes = 0,
                brackets = 0,
                delims = 0,
                others = 0;

  while ((c = getchar()) != EOF)
    if (strchr(Quotes, c) != NULL)
      quotes++;                               /* single & double quotes */
    else if (strchr(Brackets, c) != NULL)
      brackets++;                             /* punctuation brackets */
    else if (strchr(Puncts, c) != NULL)
      delims++;                               /* usual punctuation */
    else
      others++;                               /* other characters */
  printf("Quotes     %*lu\n", PrintWidth, quotes);
  printf("Brackets   %*lu\n", PrintWidth, brackets);
  printf("Delimiters %*lu\n", PrintWidth, delims);
  printf("Other      %*lu\n", PrintWidth, others);
  return 0;
}
```

Figure 10.12 (countpct.c) A new version of our earlier program to count quotation, bracket, and punctuation characters in its input.

version of our earlier program to count the occurrences of various punctuation characters. The old version was a giant **switch** statement. Now, however, we have one string for each category of punctuation, and we do table lookup to determine which counter to update. This version is considerably more compact and more easily extensible, but at a cost. All the string searching it does is likely to make it run much more slowly than our original version.

```
/*
 * Read input line into an array, pointer version.
 */
#include <stdio.h>
```

```
int getline(char *ptr, int max)
{
  int           c;                       /* current character */
  char *const startptr = ptr;            /* pointer to line start */
  char *const endptr   = ptr + max;      /* pointer to line end */

  while ((c = getchar ()) != '\n' && c != EOF)
    if (ptr < endptr)
      *ptr++ = c;
  *ptr = '\0';                           /* terminate with null */
  return (c == EOF) ? -1 : ptr - startptr;
}
```

Figure 10.13 (getline2.c) Pointer version of `getline`.

10.5   USING POINTERS TO TRAVERSE STRINGS

Strings are simply arrays, so we can process them using pointers. Figure 10.13 provides a new version of `getline` that uses a pointer, `ptr`, to traverse the string. As it reads each character, it places the character into the location pointed to by `ptr` and then increments `ptr`. This version of `getline` also uses two other pointers: `startptr`, which points to the first character in the array, and `endptr`, which points to the last. We compare `ptr` with `endptr` to determine whether there is still room in the array. When we've read a line, we subtract `startptr` from `ptr` to determine how many characters we read. Figure 10.14 shows the relationship between all of these pointers.

Figure 10.15 shows how to rewrite our earlier versions of `strcpy`, `strcmp`, and `strlen` to use pointers. Our original version of `strcpy` used an array index `i` to walk through the strings `source` and `dest`. But we can also write the function to treat these strings as pointers (initialized to the first element of the respective arrays) rather than as arrays. When we do so, we access the elements indirectly through pointers rather than directly through array indexes. We use `dest` and `source` to traverse the destination and source strings, respectively. Each pass through the loop begins by placing the character to which `source` points in the location to which `dest` points. We then compare this character with `\0` to see if we've reached the end of the string. If we haven't, we increment both pointers and continue the loop. `strcmp` and `strlen` use similar techniques.

What advantage do we gain by accessing storage through pointers rather than through array indexing? The answer, in most computers, is speed. We ran both the original array version and the pointer version of `strcpy` on several different computers, copying a string of 15,000 characters. On the average, the pointer versions are about 50% faster!

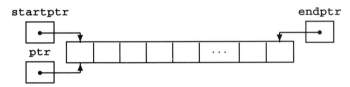

(*a*) The pointers when **getline** starts up.

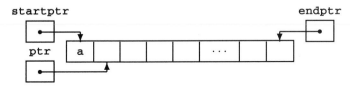

(*b*) The pointers after reading one character.

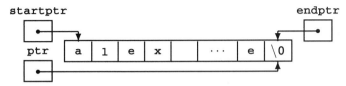

(*c*) The pointers after reading the input line "alex was here".

Figure 10.14 Pointers used in **getline**.

<table>
<tr><td>**10.6**</td><td>**CASE STUDY—ELIMINATING DUPLICATE LINES**</td></tr>
</table>

This section is optional!

To further illustrate strings, we will write a program (called uniq) that takes text as input and copies it to its output, minus any lines that are the same as the line they follow. If the input consists of the lines

```
C
C
is
a
wonderful
wonderful
wonderful
wonderful
language
language
```

we want the output to be

```
/*
 * Pointer versions of our string functions
 */
#include <stddef.h>

char *strcpy(char *dptr, const char *sptr)
{
  char *const startptr = dptr;        /* save starting pointer */

  for (; (*dptr = *sptr) != '\0'; dptr++, sptr++)
    ;
  return startptr;
}

int strcmp(const char *sptr, const char *tptr)
{
  for (; *sptr == *tptr && *sptr != '\0'; sptr++, tptr++)
    ;
  return *sptr - *tptr;               /* difference of two chars */
}

size_t strlen(const char *ptr)
{
  const char *const startptr = ptr;

  for (; *ptr != '\0'; ptr++)
    ;
  return ptr - startptr;
}
```

Figure 10.15   (string2.c) Pointer versions of some of the string library functions.

```
      c
      is
      a
      wonderful
      language
```

When is this program useful? We used a variation, suggested in the exercises, to create a list of the number of different words that appear in this book. We first broke the input into individual words, one per line (using a program we wrote earlier), then sorted these lines (using a program we'll see in a later chapter), and finally ran uniq.

uniq is a useful program created from small, already existing pieces. It uses getline, strcmp, and strcpy, each of which we have already written. It processes its input a line at a time, using strcmp to compare the current and previous input lines. If they differ, it prints the current line and copies the current line into the previous one using strcpy. The process ends when we've read all the input (getline returns -1). Figure 10.16 contains uniq.

```
/*
 * Strip consecutive duplicate lines from the input.
 */
#include <stdio.h>
#include <string.h>

#define MAXLEN      80                            /* longest input line */
#define FALSE        0
#define TRUE         1

int main()
{
   int   getline(char *buf, int bufsize);
   char curr[MAXLEN + 1],                         /* current line */
        prev[MAXLEN + 1];                         /* previous line */
   int   first = TRUE;

   for (; getline(curr, MAXLEN) != -1; strcpy(prev, curr))
     if (first || strcmp(prev, curr) != 0)
     {
       printf("%s\n", curr);
       first = FALSE;
     }
   return 0;
}
```

Figure 10.16   (uniq.c) A program to remove duplicate lines from its input.

SUMMARY

- A string is an array of characters, terminated with the null character, '\0'. When we create a string, we must provide the terminating null ourselves.

- We initialize strings by declaring an array and providing a list of characters, or by declaring a pointer and assigning it to a string constant.

- We can easily write a function to read an input line into a string. This allows us to easily recover from input errors.

- Since strings are arrays, we can run through them using either array subscripting or pointer indexing.

- C provides a large library of functions for manipulating strings. To use them, we need to include string.h. They all expect the string to be null-terminated.

EXERCISES

10–1 Modify Chapter 7's insertion sort program (Figure 7.6) to read its input with **getline** and **sscanf**. It should expect one value per line and report errors for any input lines not containing exactly one value.

10–2 Modify **yesorno** (Figure 10.1) to accept both upper- and lowercase responses and responses surrounded by leading or trailing spaces.

10–3 Write a variation of uniq (Figure 10.16) that prints only duplicated lines and, then, only the first occurrence of each repetition.

10–4 Write a variation of uniq (Figure 10.16) that prints one instance of each line, preceded by a count of the number of times the line is repeated.

10–5 Write **putline**, a function that takes a string and writes it and a trailing newline. Use **putchar** rather than **printf**.

10–6 Write compact pointer versions of the other string library functions we used in this chapter. Are these more efficient than straightforward array versions?

10–7 Write **stoi** (for string to integer), a function that takes a null-terminated string (array of **char**) and converts the characters to an integer.

10–8 Write **itos**, a function that takes an integer and a character array and converts the integer into characters and places them into the array.

10–9 Implement **strchr**, **strrchr**, **strspn**, and **strspcn**.

10–10 Using pointers and avoiding unnecessary local variables, write a function, **rmchr**, that takes a string and a character as arguments, removing all occurrences of the character from the string. **rmchr** should not leave holes in the string. What should **rmchr** return?

10–11 Write a function, **rmstr**, that takes two strings as arguments, removing all occurrences of any characters in the second string from the first string. Like **rmchr**, **rmstr** should not leave holes in the string. What should **rmstr** return?

10–12 Write a function **question** that takes a string and writes the string, followed by a question mark and a space. Use **putchar** rather than **printf**.

10–13 Write a function **palstr** that determines whether or not a string is a palindrome (reads the same forward and backward).

10–14 Write a function **strrev** to reverse a string in place.

10–15 Write the functions **strup** and **strlow** that turn a string into all upper- or lowercase characters, respectively.

11 CONSTRUCTED TYPES

Arrays are the only type of data structure we have used so far. But arrays are limited—all their elements must share the same underlying type. This chapter examines three new ways to represent collections of values: structures, unions, and enumerated types. We introduce structures and show how they group different values in a single variable. We introduce unions and show how they allow us to have a single variable whose value varies in type. And finally, we introduce enumerated types and show how they provide a convenient way to define a set of constants. The chapter concludes with a small data base program for storing employee names and phone numbers that comes complete with a menu-driven front end.

11.1   STRUCTURES

Sometimes we want to combine data of different types into a single variable. We might, for example, want a variable to hold all the information on a particular employee: the employee's name, employee number, phone number, and age. Unfortunately, we can't use an array because array elements all share the same underlying type. Instead, we must use a structure, which is similar to a Pascal record.

Defining Structure Types

The first step in using a structure is to define a structure type. We do so by following the keyword **struct** with the name of the structure type (called the *structure tag*) and declarations for each of the items it contains (called *fields* or *members*). We define a structure type to hold our employee information with

```
struct employee                    tag.
{
    long number;                   /* employee number */
    char name[MAXNAME];            /* first and last name */
    char phone[MAXDIGITS];         /* at least xxx-xxx-xxxx\0 */
    int age;                       /* age */
};
```

field

This declares a new type, **struct employee**, consisting of four fields: **number** (a **long**), **name** (an array of **MAXNAME** characters), **phone** (another array of characters), and **age** (a single **int**). Field names are in a special "name class" kept separate from variable names, so we can have field names that are the same as existing variable names, and we can use the same field name in different structure definitions without fear of conflict.

The fields within a structure can have any legal type, which means they themselves can be structures. The following

```
struct date                        /* to hold a single date */
{
    int month, day, year;
};

struct period                      /* to hold two dates */
{
    struct date start;             /* the starting date */
    struct date end;               /* the ending date */
};
```

defines a **date** structure type containing three integers, one each for the month, day, and year, and a **period** structure type that contains a starting and ending date.

Where do these structure type definitions go? Typically, we place them in our source file, outside any function, and preceding any of the functions that make use of them. A structure definition is like a **typedef**; it's known from the point of definition until the end of the source file. As with external declarations, if we need a structure type in more than one source file, we can place its definition in a header file.

Declaring Structure Variables

Once we've defined the structure type, we can declare variables with that type as if it were one of C's built-in data types. For example,

```
struct employee emp;
```

declares a single variable, **emp**, with type **struct employee**. This forces the compiler to allocate at least enough storage for **emp** to hold the four fields within a **struct employee**. Similarly,

```
struct period x;
```

declares a variable **x** with two fields, **start** and **end**, each of which is a structure containing three integers. We can use structure variables like any others: we can assign to them, pass them to functions, and so on.

As a shortcut, we can combine declaring a variable with defining a type. That's because a structure type definition can go anywhere a type can appear.

```
struct date { int month, day, year; } d;
```

This declaration combines defining a new type, **struct date**, and declaring a variable **d** with that type. If we only need the structure type in this one place, we can omit the structure tag.

```
struct { int month, day, year; } d;
```

We usually use this form only when we have a nested structure or when we combine it with **typedef**.

```
typedef struct { int month, day, year; } DATE;
```

This defines a type **DATE** that's synonymous with a structure containing the three **int** fields **month**, **day**, and **year**. We can then declare variables with the type **DATE**:

```
DATE birthday;          /* month, day, and year of birth */
```

Accessing Structure Fields

Although it is convenient to treat a structure variable as a single unit, we also need a way to access its individual fields. To access a field, we follow the structure name with the field selection operator, **.**, and the name of the desired field. Assuming that we've declared **emp** as a **struct employee**, we can assign values to **emp**'s fields with

```
emp.number = 1001;
emp.age = 26;
strcpy(emp.name, "merriweather, tammy");
strcpy(emp.phone, "818-555-5741");
```

The result is shown below.

	number	name	phone	age
emp	1001	merriweather, tammy\0	818-555-5741\0	26

The dot operator associates left to right. With **x** declared as a **struct period**, **x.start.month** refers to the month field within the start field of **x**. We can initialize **x**'s fields with

```
x.start.month = 7;
x.start.day   = 20;
x.start.year  = 1981;
x.end.month   = 7;
x.end.day     = 30;
x.end.year    = 1984;
```

Initializing Structures at Compile Time

Like other data types, we can initialize structures when we declare them. As far as initialization goes, structures obey the same set of rules as arrays. We initialize the fields of a structure by following the structure's declaration with a list containing values for each of its fields. As with arrays, these values must be evaluable at compile time. We could initialize **emp** at compile time with *initialize struct*

```
struct employee emp =
{
    1001,                            /* number */
    "merriweather, tammy",           /* name */
    "818-555-5741",                  /* phone */
    26                               /* age */
};
```

This initializes the **number** field to **1001**, the **name** field to "**merriweather, tammy**," the **phone** field to "**818-555-5741**", and the **age** field to **26**. Since the values for the **name** and **phone** fields are string constants, they are automatically terminated with a null character.

When we have fields that are themselves structures, we enclose the values of their fields in brackets.

```
struct period x = { {7,20,1981}, {7,30,1984} };
```
← can be omitted if data is complete.

We can omit the brackets surrounding a field when we provide all of its elements, but leaving them in clarifies which values are going to what fields.

Structures and Functions

We can pass structures as arguments to functions. Unlike array names, however, which are always pointers to the start of the array, structure names are not pointers. When we pass a structure, C copies the entire structure and assigns it to its corresponding parameter. As a result, when we change a structure parameter inside a function, we don't affect its corresponding argument.

Actually, we usually pass pointers to structures, rather than structures themselves. Why? Simply because it's faster to pass a pointer: only the pointer has to be copied, not the entire structure.

Figure 11.1 illustrates both methods in a small program that declares, initializes, and prints the fields of several **struct employee**s. We initialize the fields in the first employee, **emp**, by assigning them values at run time, and we print it by passing the entire structure to a function **write_emp**.

```
write_emp(emp);
```

We initialize the other employee, **other_emp**, at compile time rather than run time. We print **other_emp** by passing its address to a function **print_emp**.

```
print_emp(&other_emp);
```

The **printf** statements within **print_emp** must dereference the pointer to the structure and then select the appropriate field. Assuming **ep** is a pointer to the structure, one way to do this is

```
printf("Employee: %li\n", (*ep).number);
```

Why the parentheses? The selection operator binds tighter (has higher precedence) than dereferencing. Without the parentheses, as in ***ep.number**, we're trying to

```
/*
 * Display employee information.  Uses:
 *    write_emp - write employee given a structure.
 *    print_emp - write employee given pointer to the structure.
 */
#include <stdio.h>
#include <string.h>

#define MAXNAME   40                    /* longest name */
#define MAXDIGITS 27                    /* longest phone */

struct employee
{
  long number;                          /* employee number */
  char name[MAXNAME];                   /* first and last name */
  char phone[MAXDIGITS];                /* at least xxx-xxx-xxxx\0 */
  int  age;                             /* age */
};

int main()
{
  void write_emp(struct employee e);
  void print_emp(struct employee *p);
  struct employee emp;
  struct employee other_emp = {1023, "perl, doris", "213-555-6917", 26};

  emp.number = 1001;
  emp.age = 26;
  strcpy(emp.name, "merriweather, tammy");
  strcpy(emp.phone, "818-555-5741");
  write_emp(emp);                       /* write the first employee */
  print_emp(&other_emp);                /* write the second employee */
  return 0;
}

void write_emp(struct employee e)
{
  printf("Employee: %li\n", e.number);
  printf("Name:     %s\n",  e.name);
  printf("Age:      %i\n",  e.age);
  printf("Phone:    %s\n",  e.phone);
}

void print_emp(struct employee *ep)
{
  printf("Employee: %li\n", ep->number);
  printf("Name:     %s\n",  ep->name);
  printf("Age:      %i\n",  ep->age);
  printf("Phone:    %s\n",  ep->phone);
}
```

[handwritten annotations: "pass the structure data to fn", "pass pointer to the structure data to fn.", "pass the pointer."]

Figure 11.1 (prstruct.c) Initialize and print a structure one field at a time.

*dereferencing the
pointer to the structure*

$\Rightarrow$ *symbol*

$\rightarrow$

dereference the value of a field in the structure (which makes no sense in this case, as the field isn't a pointer).

Dereferencing a pointer to a structure and selecting one of its fields is such a common operation that C provides a special shorthand operator for it, a right arrow, made up of a minus sign and a "greater than" symbol: `->`. We can use this operator to write the `printf` statements in `print_emp` more concisely:

```
printf("Employee: %li\n", ep->number);
```

Not only can we pass structures to functions, but we can return them as well. We rarely do, however, for the same reason we rarely pass structures to functions: it's too slow. We return pointers to structures instead.

Structures and Operators

Only a few operators apply to structure variables. We've already used `&` to take a structure's address. Another, `sizeof`, determines the number of bytes used by the structure. We could compute the size of a `struct employee` by taking the size of a variable with that type

```
sizeof(emp)
```

or by taking the size of the structure type itself

```
sizeof(struct employee)
```

You might think that we could also compute the size by summing up the sizes of each of the structure's fields:

```
sizeof(emp.number) + sizeof(emp.name) +
    sizeof(emp.phone) + sizeof(emp.age)
```

*Operators

1) sizeof ( )

2) assignment
   = (assignment)*

But we don't get the same result. Why? Because each data type has alignment restrictions, which may force the compiler to leave "holes" in a structure so that it can satisfy all the alignment constraints of the various fields within the structure. Although a `char` can start on a byte or word boundary, `int`s, `long`s, and other data types can usually begin only on a word boundary. In our structure, the 27-byte array containing the phone number ends on a byte boundary, so the single byte that follows it and precedes the age field (which must start on a word boundary) is likely to be left unused.

> *Don't assume the size of a structure is the sum of the size of its fields.*

There's only one other operator we can apply to structures: `=` (assignment), which copies the contents of one structure into another.

```
struct date old_date, date;

old_date = date;
```

This assignment is equivalent to

```
old_date.day = date.day;
old_date.month = date.month;
old_date.year = date.year;
```

There are no operators for comparing structures, so we're stuck with writing functions to perform these types of comparisons. Figures 11.2 and 11.3 provide a set of functions for comparing **struct date**s, along with their prototypes, and Figure 11.4 is an example program using them.

> *We're not allowed to compare structures directly.*

Arrays of Structures

Earlier we mentioned that we can have arrays of any type. That includes structures. One use for an array of structures would be to store a table of personnel records.

```
#define SIZE 100

struct employee emptab[SIZE];
```

This declares an array of 100 elements, with each element in the array a **struct employee** containing **number**, **name**, **phone**, and **age** fields. Figure 11.5 shows what this array looks like.

emptab is an array of structures, so we use the usual array-accessing methods to reach individual records and then the dot field selection operator to reach their fields. We can, for example, assign a value to **emptab[1]** with

```
emptab[1].number = 1023;
emptab[1].age = 26;
strcpy(emptab[1].name, "perl, doris");
strcpy(emptab[1].phone, "213-555-6917");
```

We can also initialize a global or static array of structures when we declare it. The following declares and initializes **emptab**. We don't provide a size for the array, so the compiler determines it from the number of items we provide, seven in this case.

```
struct employee emptab[] =
{
  {1001, "merriweather, tammy", "818-555-5741", 26},
  {1023, "perl, doris",          "213-555-6917", 26},
  {1033, "pham, gisele",         "714-555-2559", 29},
  {1036, "borromeo, daphne",     "818-555-2042", 22},
  {1039, "borromeo, irene",      "213-555-2718", 26},
  {1047, "goebel, diane",        "213-555-4854", 26},
  {1048, "ockert, veronica",     "213-555-4741", 29}
};
```

initialize array of structures

We can index an array of structures in the same way we index any other array—either by array subscripting or by using pointers.

```
/*
 * Provides DATE type and prototypes for functions that compare DATEs.
 */
typedef struct
{
  int month,
      day,
      year;
} DATE;

int date_equal(const DATE *xptr, const DATE *yptr);
int date_lt(const DATE *xptr, const DATE *yptr);
int date_gt(const DATE *xptr, const DATE *yptr);
```

Figure 11.2   (date.h) Prototypes for functions to compare dates.

```
/*
 * Functions for comparing dates.
 *    date_equal - are two dates the same?
 *    date_lt - is the first date before the second?
 *    date_gt - is the first date after the second?
 */
#include "date.h"                              /* date type and prototypes */

int date_equal(const DATE *xptr, const DATE *yptr)
{
  return xptr->year  == yptr->year  &&
         xptr->month == yptr->month &&
         xptr->day   == yptr->day;
}

int date_lt(const DATE *xptr, const DATE *yptr)
{
  if (xptr->year < yptr->year)
    return 1;
  if (xptr->year > yptr->year)
    return 0;
  return (xptr->month < yptr->month ||
         (xptr->month == yptr->month && xptr->day < yptr->day));
}

int date_gt(const DATE *xptr, const DATE *yptr)
{
  return !date_lt(xptr, yptr) && !date_equal(xptr, yptr);
}
```

Figure 11.3   (date.c) Functions for comparing dates.

```
/*
 * A program to test our date comparison routines.  Uses:
 *    cmpdates - compare two dates and print message describing results.
 *    datestr - convert date to string format for output.
 */
#include <stdio.h>
#include "date.h"

#define MONTH_CHARS    2        /* number of chars in a month */
#define DAY_CHARS      2        /* number of chars in a day */
#define YEAR_CHARS     4        /* number of chars in a year */

int main()
{
  void cmpdates(const DATE *ptr1, const DATE *ptr2);
  DATE day1 = {10,4,1965};
  DATE day2 = {10,18,1963};
  DATE day3 = day1;
  DATE day4 = {6,24,1963};

  cmpdates(&day1,&day2);              /* lots of test cases */
  cmpdates(&day1,&day3);
  cmpdates(&day2,&day1);
  cmpdates(&day4,&day2);
  cmpdates(&day2,&day4);
  return 0;
}

void cmpdates(const DATE *d1ptr, const DATE *d2ptr)
{
  char *datestr(const DATE *ptr);

  printf("Comparing %s ", datestr(d1ptr));
  printf("with %s: ", datestr(d2ptr));
  if (date_lt(d1ptr,d2ptr))
    printf("it's earlier.\n");
  if (date_gt(d1ptr,d2ptr))
    printf("it's later.\n");
  if (date_equal(d1ptr,d2ptr))
    printf("they're the same.\n");
}

char *datestr(const DATE *dptr)
{
  static char d[MONTH_CHARS + DAY_CHARS + YEAR_CHARS + 3];

  sprintf(d, "%0*i/%0*i/%*i", MONTH_CHARS, dptr->month,
                              DAY_CHARS,   dptr->day,
                              YEAR_CHARS,  dptr->year);
  return d;                           /* ptr to first character of date */
}
```

Figure 11.4 (datetest.c) A main program to test our date comparison routines.

1001	merriweather, tammy\0	818-555-5741\0	26
1023	perl, doris\0	213-555-6917\0	26
1033	pham, gisele\0	714-555-2559\0	29
1036	borromeo, daphne\0	818-555-2042\0	22
1039	borromeo, irene\0	818-555-2718\0	26
1048	goebel, diane\0	213-555-4854\0	26
1047	ockert, veronica\0	213-555-4741\0	29

Figure 11.5 Array of **struct employee**s showing the contents of an individual element.

We illustrate arrays of structures with a program that initializes and prints an array of **struct employee**s. The program has three parts. Figure 11.6 is a header file that defines a **struct employee**. Figure 11.7 is a main program that initializes the array and then calls the function **print_emps** to print each of the names. And Figure 11.8 is an array-subscripting version of **print_emps**.

print_emps takes two arguments—the address of the first element to print and the number of items we want to print. So to use **print_emps** we need to know how many items are in the array. But how can we figure this out automatically? We do so the same way we figure out how many items are in any other array—we divide the total number of bytes in the array by the number of bytes in an individual item. So we can print the entire table with

```
print_emps(emptab, sizeof(emptab)/sizeof(emptab[0]));
```

or

```
print_emps(emptab, sizeof(emptab)/sizeof(struct employee));
```

The former is more concise but the latter is more readable.

Figure 11.9 shows an alternative version of **print_emps** that uses pointer indexing rather than array subscripting. We can use pointer indexing because pointer arithmetic is always done in units of the pointed-to type, so incrementing a pointer to a structure causes it to point to the next structure in the array.

11.2 BITFIELDS (*fields specified in terms of their size in bits*)

So far, the integer fields in our structures have been at least one word in size. But this wastes space when we are dealing with integers requiring less than 16 bits. Fortunately, C lets us specify the number of bits required by an integer field, which lets us pack several different fields into a single word, saving space. Fields specified in terms of their size in bits are called *bitfields*.

```
/*
 * Define a struct employee.
 */
#define MAXNAME     40
#define MAXDIGITS   27

struct employee                     /* same definition as before */
{
  long number;                      /* employee number */
  char name[MAXNAME];               /* first and last name */
  char phone[MAXDIGITS];            /* at least xxx-xxx-xxxx\0 */
  int  age;                         /* age */
};
```

Figure 11.6 (premps.h) Header file defining the `struct employee` type.

```
/*
 * Print the name field of each element in a structure.
 */
#include <stdio.h>
#include "premps.h"

int main()
{
  void print_emps(struct employee table[], int);
  struct employee emptab[] =
  {
    {1001, "merriweather, tammy", "818-555-5741", 24},
    {1023, "perl, doris",         "213-555-6917", 24},
    {1033, "pham, gisele",        "714-555-2559", 28},
    {1036, "borromeo, daphne",    "818-555-2042", 22},
    {1039, "borromeo, irene",     "213-555-2718", 24},
    {1047, "goebel, diane",       "213-555-4854", 24},
    {1048, "ockert, veronica",    "213-555-4741", 27}
  };

  print_emps(emptab,sizeof(emptab)/sizeof(emptab[0]));
  return 0;
}
```

Figure 11.7 (premps.c) A program to print an array of `struct employee`s.

```
/*
 * Array printing function, using array subscripting.
 */
#include <stdio.h>
#include "premps.h"                    /* for structure definition */

void print_emps(struct employee table[], int n)
{
  int i;                              /* array index */

  for (i = 0; i < n; i++)
    printf("Name: %s\n", table[i].name);
}
```

Figure 11.8   (premps1.c) A function **print_emps** to print an array of structures using array indexing.

```
/*
 * Better array printing functions, using pointer indexing.
 */
#include <stdio.h>
#include "premps.h"

void print_emps(struct employee *ptr, int n)
{
  struct employee *endptr = ptr + n;

  for (; ptr < endptr; ptr++)
    printf("Name: %s\n", ptr->name);
}
```

Figure 11.9   (premps2.c) A version of **print_emps** that uses pointer indexing.

How to declare bitfield.

How do we declare bitfields? In the same way we declare any other structure field, with one exception and one restriction. The exception is that we must follow the field's name with a colon and the number of bits we need. The restriction is that bitfields must be signed or unsigned **int**s, from 1 to the number of bits in an **int**. Signed bitfields use the leftmost bit as the sign bit. For portability, we explicitly state whether we want a **signed** or **unsigned** bitfield.

We can represent our **date** structure more compactly as a set of bitfields. That's because we really only need to store months between 1 and 12, days between 1 and 31, and years between 0 and 99 (assuming years are an offset into this century).

(handwritten: 7-bit field)

```
struct date
{
    unsigned int year  : 7;    /* year is 7 bits */
    unsigned int day   : 5;    /* day is 5 bits */
    unsigned int month : 4;    /* month is 4 bits */
};
```

(handwritten left margin: declare bitfields)

This declares a structure with three bitfields: **year**, **day**, and **month**, as shown below.

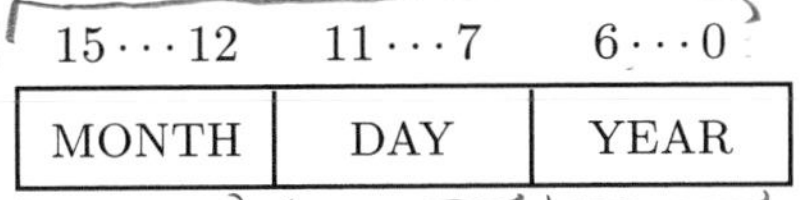

(handwritten: 16 bits)

(handwritten left margin: assume left → right allocation.)

15 ⋯ 12	11 ⋯ 7	6 ⋯ 0
MONTH	DAY	YEAR

(handwritten: ⟸ machine dependent·)

(handwritten under table: 4   5   7)

The entire structure fits in a single 16-bit word. **year** takes up 7 bits, **day** takes up 5 bits, and **month** takes up 4 bits.

It's machine dependent whether fields are allocated right to left or left to right within a word. Our picture above assumes that it's left to right, but that's not always the case. That means we can't use bitfields for data that's to be transferred from machine to machine. Instead, we're stuck using the bit-shifting operators we saw earlier.

> **Don't assume fields are allocated in a particular way.**

The name of a bitfield is optional; an anonymous bitfield simply uses up space. A bitfield with no name and a size of zero causes the following field to be aligned on a word boundary.

How do we access bitfields? In the same way we access any other structure field: by using the **.** and **->** operators.

(handwritten left margin: accessing bitfield)

```
struct date bday;       /* holds a birthday */
    . . .
bday.month = 6;  bday.day = 24;  bday.year = 63;
```

Essentially, bitfields behave as extremely small integers, and we can use them anywhere we can use an integral type, although there are several exceptions.

One restriction is that we can't take the address of a bitfield. This restriction arises because the vast majority of machines aren't bit-addressable. Practically, this means that we can't use **scanf** to read values into a bitfield. Instead, we have to read into a temporary variable and then assign its value to the bitfield.

The other restriction is that we can't apply **sizeof** to a bitfield. That would be silly to do, anyway, since we explicitly declare how many bits we want. But the restriction also arises because **sizeof** returns an integer number of bytes an object takes.

Figure 11.10 uses bitfields in a new version of our Chapter 5 program to pack employee information in a single word. We prefer the simplicity of using bitfields to the complexity of using our earlier bit-manipulating functions. But this doesn't mean that those functions are useless. They're still convenient when we don't know at compile time which combinations of bits we need to access, or we have to pack data in a portable way.

```c
/*
 * New version of our earlier program to pack employee info
 * into a single word.  This time we use bitfields.
 */
#include <stdio.h>

#define SINGLE     0                /* marital status flags */
#define MARRIED    1
#define SEPARATED  2
#define DIVORCED   3
#define MALE       1                /* sex */
#define FEMALE     0

struct emp
{
  unsigned int mstat : 2;          /* marital status */
  unsigned int age   : 7;          /* employee age */
  unsigned int sex   : 1;          /* male or female */
  unsigned int years : 6;          /* years employeed */
};

int main()
{
  unsigned int mstat, sex, age, years;
  struct emp info;                 /* holds info on one person */

  printf("male=%i, female=%i\? ", MALE, FEMALE);
  scanf("%i", &sex);
  info.sex = sex;

  printf("age\? ");
  scanf("%i", &age);
  info.age = age;

  printf("single=%i, married=%i, separated=%i, divorced=%i\? ",
          SINGLE, MARRIED, SEPARATED, DIVORCED);
  scanf("%i", &mstat);
  info.mstat = mstat;

  printf("years employed\? ");
  scanf("%i", &years);
  info.years = years;

  printf("Here's the info:\n");
  printf("Sex: %i\n", info.sex);
  printf("Age: %i\n", info.age);
  printf("Marital status: %i\n", info.mstat);
  printf("Years employed: %i\n", info.years);
  return 0;
}
```

Figure 11.10   (wordemp.c) A new version of our earlier program to pack employee information in a single word.

11.3   **UNIONS** *(store values of different types in a single location)*

Structures allow us to package different types of values as a single unit. But we also often want to store values of different types in a single location. The mechanism that allows us to do this is called a *union*. A union may contain one of many different types of values, but can store only one value at a time.

We declare and use **union**s in the same way we declare and use **struct**s. To declare a union type, we follow the keyword **union** with an optional union name and the alternative names and types it may hold. For example, we can declare a union type that can hold either an **int** or a **double** with

declare union:

```
union number
{
    int     i;
    double d;
};
```

Once we've declared a union type, we can declare variables with that type.

```
union number x;
```

This declares a variable **x**, with type **union number**, which may contain either an **int** or a **double**. As with structures we can combine the type definition with the variable declaration.

shorthand declaration

```
union number
{
    int     i;
    double d;
} x;
```

With **union**s we usually only do so when they're a field within a structure.

We can initialize a union when we declare it by following it with a brace-enclosed initializing expression.

initialize union

```
union number x = {69};
```

The expression is evaluated and assigned to the first field of the union.

How do we access a union's individual fields? As with structures, we use the dot operator. To assign to the **int** field of **x** we use **x.i**

accessing values in the union:

```
x.i = 1234;
```

and to assign to the **double** field we use **x.d**

```
x.d = -123.345;
```

We can also access the fields of a union indirectly though a pointer, using the **->** operator.

accessing using pointer

```
union number *xptr;
    ...
xptr = &x;
xptr->d = 98.76;
```

double

What does a union look like internally? It's allocated enough storage to hold its largest field. The variable **x**, a **union number**, is allocated space sufficient for a **double** at all times, as shown below. That means, however, that a union may contain only one value (here, either an **int** or a **double**) at a time.

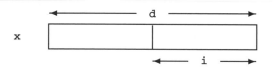

That means we should never assign to one field of a union and then retrieve from another. A series of operations such as

```
x.d = 45.67;                    /* assign a float */
printf("%d\n", x.i);            /* print field as int */
```

retrieve from the union the last field we assign.

is likely to produce results that differ from machine to machine. Whenever we retrieve a field from a union, it should be the last field we assigned.

> *Don't assign to one field of a union and then retrieve from another.*

Figure 11.11 puts all of these operations together in a little program that first assigns an integer into a union and prints it, and then assigns a floating point value into the same union and prints it. The program finishes by erroneously assigning a new floating point value to the union and printing it as an integer, a machine-dependent operation. Here are the results of running this program on our machine:

```
69
1234
-123.345000
98.760000
1078384066
```

As a more realistic use of unions, we will now write a function, **getvalue**, that prints a prompt and obtains a value—either an **int**, a **double**, or a string—from the user. The idea is that we pass **getvalue** a prompt string and an indication of the type of value we want to read. It returns us a pointer to a union that can contain either an **int**, a **double**, or a pointer.

How does **getvalue** work? It reads a line of input and fills an internal, **static** union with the desired type. If the type is numeric, **getvalue** uses **sscanf** to translate the characters it reads into the desired type. If the type is a string, **getvalue** uses **malloc** to allocate sufficient storage for it. That **union** must be **static** because the function returns a pointer to it. If there's a problem, such as the user entering a value of an inappropriate type or the end-of-file character, **getvalue** returns **NULL**.

Figure 11.12 is getvalue.h, which defines the union type and provides a prototype for **getvalue**. Figure 11.13 is getvalue.c, which defines the function itself. And Figure 11.14 is a short main program that uses **getvalue** to read a person's name, age, and salary.

```
/*
 * Program to test basic union operations.
 */
#include <stdio.h>

union number                            /* define the union type */
{
  int i;
  double d;
};

int main()
{
  union number x = {69};                /* a union and a pointer to it */
  union number *xptr;

  printf("%i\n", x.i);                  /* print the initial value */
  x.i = 1234;
  printf("%i\n", x.i);                  /* print the int we put in it */
  x.d = -123.345;
  printf("%f\n", x.d);                  /* print the double we put in it */
  xptr = &x;
  xptr->d = 98.76;
  printf("%f\n", xptr->d);              /* access it through the pointer */
  x.d = 45.67;
  printf("%i\n", x.i);                  /* oops: print the double as int */
  return 0;
}
```

Figure 11.11 (union.c) A program illustrating the basic union operations.

11.4 ENUMERATED TYPES (*used to specify possible values*)

Sometimes we know a variable will have only one of a small set of values. In the function **getvalue**, for example, we know that the type should only hold the constants **INTEGER**, **REAL**, or **STRING**. In these situations, we can use an *enumerated type* to specify the possible values.

We define an enumerated type by giving the keyword **enum** followed by an optional *type designator* and a brace-enclosed list of identifiers. So

declare →

```
enum itype {INTEGER, REAL, STRING};      /* input types */
```

defines an enumerated type, **enum itype**, that has three possible values: **INTEGER**, **REAL**, and **STRING**. Internally, these are defined as constants with an integer value equal to their position in the list: **INTEGER** is zero, **REAL** is 1, and **STRING** is 2. Of course, we could have defined these as constants with **#define**s or **const**, but we find **enum**s more convenient to use.

We are allowed to assign specific integer values to the items in an enumerated type.

```
/*
 * Define types for getvalue.
 */
#define MAXLEN 80                    /* longest input line */

#define INTEGER 0
#define REAL    1
#define STRING  2

union value                          /* can hold a long, double, or char */
{
  int    i;
  double d;
  char   *s;
};

union value *getvalue(const char *prompt, int type);
```

Figure 11.12   (getvalue.h) Header file for `getvalue`.

We do so by following the item with an equal sign and a value. The default value for any item is 1 more than the value of the item preceding it. So   *real ⇒ 1*

```
    enum itype {STRING = 2, INTEGER = 0, REAL};
```

assigns **STRING** a 2, **INTEGER** a zero, and **REAL** a 1, just like before.

All we've done so far is declare an enumerated type. We declare variables with that type in the same way we declared structures and unions.

declare

```
    enum itype type;
```

This declares a variable, `type`, that can only hold a value of **INTEGER**, **REAL**, or **STRING**.

The distinction between enumerated types and integers is a fuzzy one. Essentially, we can use any enumerated type as if it were an integer. We don't need to cast it to and from **int**. So why use enumerated types at all? Why not simply use integers instead? Because enumerated types highlight variables that only hold one of a limited set of values, contributing to more readable programs. Even when we don't care about readability, we can still use them as a convenient way to define integer constants. And some compilers will warn us when we stick inappropriate values in an enumerated type, lessening the chance of error.

"why use enum"

We can easily change `getvalue` to use enumerated types. All we have to do is change its header so that the parameter controlling what we try to read is an **enum itype** instead of an **int**. And we have to modify the header file to define this type and to provide a revised prototype for `getvalue`. We'll actually make these revisions as part of a larger program in the next section.

```
/*
 * Read a value from the user.
 */
#include <stdio.h>
#include <string.h>
#include <stddef.h>
#include <stdlib.h>
#include "getvalue.h"

union value *getvalue(const char *prompt, int type)
{
  int getline(char *buf, int bufsize);
  static union value v;
  char line[MAXLEN + 1];
  int len;

  printf("%s", prompt);
  if ((len=getline(line, MAXLEN)) == -1)
    return NULL;
  switch(type)
  {
    case INTEGER:  if (sscanf(line, "%i", &v.i) != 1)
                     return NULL;
                   break;
    case REAL:     if (sscanf(line, "%lf", &v.d) != 1)
                     return NULL;
                   break;
    case STRING:   if ((v.s = malloc(len + 1)) == NULL)
                     return NULL;
                   strcpy(v.s, line);
                   break;
    default:       return NULL;
  }
  return &v;         /* succeeded */
}
```

Figure 11.13   (getvalue.c)   A function to read different types of data.

11.5   CASE STUDY—A DATA BASE APPLICATION

*This section
is optional!*

This chapter concludes with a small program to manage a data base of employee records. Its users can interactively add, delete, and print records, accessing the desired record by providing the corresponding employee number. When the program finishes, it prints the resulting table. The program has a simple menu-driven interface, one that we'll extend in later chapters. Figure 11.15 shows a sample session with the program.

```
/*
 * A program that uses getvalue (quits on first error).
 */
#include <stdio.h>
#include <stddef.h>
#include "getvalue.h"

int main()
{
  union value *uptr;            /* return value from getvalue */
  char        *name;            /* holds name */
  int         age;             /* holds age */
  double      salary;          /* holds salary */
  int         status;          /* did program succeed? */

  if ((uptr=getvalue("Enter name: ", STRING)) == NULL)
  {
    printf("Couldn't get name\n");
    status = 1;                 /* name failure! */
  }
  else
  {
    name = uptr->s;            /* save name before getting age */
    if ((uptr=getvalue("Enter age: ", INTEGER)) == NULL)
    {
      printf("Couldn't get age\n");
      status = 1;               /* age failure! */
    }
    else
    {
      age = uptr->i;           /* save age before getting salary */
      if ((uptr=getvalue("Enter salary: ", REAL)) == NULL)
      {
        printf("Couldn't get salary\n");
        status = 1;             /* salary failure! */
      }
      else
      {
        salary = uptr->d;
        printf("Name: %s, Age: %i, Salary: %7.2f\n",
               name, age, salary);
        status = 0;
      }
    }
  }
  return status;
}
```

Figure 11.14 (useit.c) A main program that uses our **getvalue** function.

```
Main Menu
   (1) Add
   (2) Delete
   (3) Print
   (0) Quit
Enter choice: 1
Add employee number? 10
Employee name: Alex Quilici
Employee phone: 808-555-2115
Employee age: 30
   ...
Enter choice: 1
Add employee number? 5
Employee name: Larry Miller
Employee phone: 213-555-2738
Employee age: 42
   ...
Enter choice: 1
Add employee number? 29
Employee name: Tony Quilici
Employee phone: 408-555-7764
Employee age: 28
   ...
Enter choice: 2
Delete employee number? 29
   ...
Enter choice: 0

10, Alex Quilici, 30, 808-555-2115
5, Larry Miller, 42, 213-555-2738
2 employees
```

Figure 11.15   Some sample input and output for our data base program.

Storing the Data Base

How do we store the data base? It's kept as an array of **struct employee**s—but now the structure's definition is more general.

```
typedef struct employee          /* one personnel record */
{
   long number;
   char *name;
   char *phone;
   int age;
} EMPLOYEE;
```

The employee **name** and **phone** numbers are now pointers to **char** rather than arrays of **char**. This means that when we add a record we have to dynamically allocate the space for these fields. When we delete a record, we deallocate this space. We find

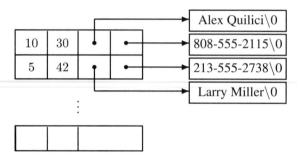

Figure 11.16 Diagram of the array after reading in and allocating several records.

this extra effort worthwhile, since it allows us to have arbitrarily long names and phone numbers without wasting storage.

To keep things simple, we don't bother to keep the array in sorted order. Instead, we add a new record by placing it after the last record, and we delete an existing record by replacing it with the last record. This organization allows us to quickly insert or delete a record, but slows searching—on the average we'll examine half of the items in the array. Figure 11.16 shows how the sample data base is stored.

The Data Base Program

We break the data base program into several different files.

Figure 11.17 contains db.h, which defines the **struct employee** data type and uses a **typedef** to define a type **EMPLOYEE** that's a shorthand for it. It also supplies the external declarations for the database and prototypes for the functions that manage it. Figure 11.18 contains db.c, the main program that prints the menu, obtains the user's choice, and calls the functions that actually access and update the data base. It also contains the definition of the data base itself.

Figures 11.19 and 11.20 contain update.c and display.c, respectively. These files define the functions that update and display the database. These functions utilize several utility functions to look up items in a table and print an appropriate message depending on whether or not we actually wanted to find the item. Figure 11.21 contains find.h, which defines the prototypes for these utilities, and Figure 11.22 contains find.c, which defines the utilities themselves.

The remaining parts of the program are concerned with reading the input. Figures 11.23 and 11.24 contain the files inp.h and inp.c, which together supply the functions we use for reading input values and their prototypes. These functions, **getlong** and **getstr**, repeatedly prompt for and read input values until they encounter an appropriate value, writing error messages for any inappropriate input values. They are built on top of our earlier **getvalue** function, which in turn was built on top of another earlier function, **getline**. However, this time we've revised **getvalue**

```
/*
 * Prototypes for data base functions, externals for table.
 */
#define MAXEMPS   100

typedef struct employee                 /* one personnel record */
{
  long number;
  char *name;
  char *phone;
  int  age;
} EMPLOYEE;

extern EMPLOYEE EmployeeTable[];         /* all personnel records */
extern int        Employees;            /* count of employees */

void AddEntry(void);
void DeleteEntry(void);
void PrintEntry(void);
void PrintEntries(void);
```

Figure 11.17 (db.h) The external declarations for the employee database and the operations on it.

to take an enumerated type describing the type of item we want to read, and we've extended it to read **long**s instead of **int**s. Figure 11.25 contains the revised header file for **getvalue**, and Figure 11.26 contains its new implementation.

Obviously our data base program is far too simplistic to be suitable for any real-world application. The individual records aren't kept in any particular order, so finding a desired record can be time-consuming. And the data base is kept in memory, which means it must be reentered every time we run the program. But we'll soon provide mechanisms for fixing these problems. Later chapters look at alternative data structures for storing tables and for dealing with external files.

SUMMARY

- Structures allow us to combine data of different types into a single variable.

- Unions allow us to store different types in the same variable location.

- Enumerated types allow us to have a variable whose values fall within a specific list of values, and provide a nice shortcut for defining a set of constants.

- We can have arrays of any of these types, and we can use pointers to traverse them.

- The only operations we're allowed to perform on a structure are accessing its fields, assigning it to another structure, taking its address, and determining its size.

```
/*
 * Program to manage an employee data base.
 */
#include <stdio.h>
#include "db.h"
#include "inp.h"

EMPLOYEE EmployeeTable[MAXEMPS];            /* table of employees */
int      Employees;                        /* count of employees */

int main()
{
  for (;;)
  {
    printf("Main Menu\n"
           "   (1) Add\n"
           "   (2) Delete\n"
           "   (3) Print\n"
           "   (0) Quit\n");
    switch ((int) getlong("Enter choice? "))
    {
      case 0:  PrintEntries();
               return 0;
      case 1:  AddEntry();
               break;
      case 2:  DeleteEntry();
               break;
      case 3:  PrintEntry();
               break;
      default: printf("Bad choice.\n");
    }
  }
}
```

Figure 11.18   (db.c) The main program and the definitions of the employee database.

- We can specify fields in a structure to have a particular size in bits, which allows us to lessen our program's need for space.

EXERCISES

11–1   Rewrite the functions to compare and print dates (Figures 11.3 and 11.4) to work with a date stored as a collection of bitfields.

11–2   Modify a **struct employee** so that the phone number is stored as a structure, with separate fields for the area code, the local prefix, and the final four digits. Change the

```
/*
 * Operations to update the database.
 *    AddEntry - add a new entry to the employee table.
 *    DeleteEntry - deleter an entry from the employee table.
 */
#include <stdio.h>
#include <stdlib.h>
#include "find.h"
#include "inp.h"

void AddEntry(void)
{
  EMPLOYEE *empptr;
  long     newnum;

  if (Employees == MAXEMPS)
    printf("Employee table is full.\n");
  else
  {
    newnum = getlong("Add employee number? ");
    if ((empptr = dont_find_employee(newnum)) == NULL)
    {                                  /* add at end of table */
      empptr = &EmployeeTable[Employees++];
      empptr->number = newnum;
      empptr->name  = getstr("Employee name: ");
      empptr->phone = getstr("Employee phone: ");
      empptr->age   = (int) getlong("Employee age: ");
    }
  }
}

void DeleteEntry(void)
{
  EMPLOYEE *empptr;
  long     empnum;

  if (Employees == 0)
    printf("Employee table is empty.\n");
  else
  {
    empnum = getlong("Delete employee number? ");
    if ((empptr = find_employee(empnum)) != NULL)
    {                                  /* replace with last employee */
      free(empptr->name);
      free(empptr->phone);
      *empptr = EmployeeTable[--Employees];
    }
  }
}
```

Figure 11.19   (update.c)   The functions to update the employee database.

```
/*
 * Functions to display entries in the employee data base.
 *    PrintEntry - print a single table entry.
 *    PrintEntries - print all table entries.
 */
#include <stdio.h>
#include "inp.h"
#include "find.h"

void PrintEntry(void)
{
  const EMPLOYEE *empptr;
  long            empnum;

  if (Employees == 0)
    printf("Employee table is empty.\n");
  else
  {
    empnum = getlong("Print employee number? ");
    if ((empptr = find_employee(empnum)) != NULL)
      printf("Employee #%li\n\tName: %s\n\tAge: %i\n\tPhone: %s\n",
             empptr->number, empptr->name,
             empptr->age, empptr->phone);
  }
}

void PrintEntries(void)
{
  const EMPLOYEE *ptr           = EmployeeTable;
  const EMPLOYEE *const endptr = ptr + Employees;

  for (; ptr < endptr; ptr++)
    printf("%li, %s, %i, %s\n",
           ptr->number, ptr->name, ptr->age, ptr->phone);
  printf("%i employee%s\n", Employees, Employees == 1 ? "" : "s");
}
```

Figure 11.20   (display.c)   The functions to display the employee database.

```
/*
 * Prototypes for lookup functions.
 */
#include "db.h"

EMPLOYEE *find_employee(long employee_number);
EMPLOYEE *dont_find_employee(long employee_number);
```

Figure 11.21   (find.h)   The prototypes for the functions to search the employee database.

```
/*
 * Functions to search employee table.
 *    find_employee - write error message if employee not found.
 *    dont_find_employee - write error message if employee found.
 */
#include <stdio.h>
#include "find.h"

static const EMPLOYEE *lookup(long target)
{
  const EMPLOYEE *ptr           = EmployeeTable;
  const EMPLOYEE *const endptr = ptr + Employees;

  for (; ptr < endptr; ptr++)              /* find employee in table */
    if (ptr->number == target)
      return ptr;
  return (EMPLOYEE *) NULL;
}

EMPLOYEE *find_employee(long employee_number)
{
  const EMPLOYEE *const temp = lookup(employee_number);

  if (temp == NULL)
    printf("There is no such employee.\n");
  return (EMPLOYEE *) temp;
}

EMPLOYEE *dont_find_employee(long employee_number)
{
  const EMPLOYEE *const temp = lookup(employee_number);

  if (temp != NULL)
    printf("There is an employee with that number.\n");
  return (EMPLOYEE *) temp;
}
```

Figure 11.22   (find.c)   The functions for searching the employee database.

```
/*
 * Prototypes for functions built on top of getvalue.
 */
#include "getval2.h"

long getlong(const char *prompt);
char *getstr(const char *prompt);
```

Figure 11.23   (inp.h)   Nice interface on top of `getvalue`.

```c
/*
 * Nice interface on top of getvalue.
 */
#include <stdio.h>
#include <stddef.h>
#include "inp.h"

long getlong(const char *prompt)     /* prompt for and read a long */
{
  union value *up;

  while ((up = getvalue(prompt, LONG)) == NULL)
    printf("Bad input.  Expected an integer.\n");
  return up->i;
}

char *getstr(const char *prompt)     /* prompt for and read a string */
{
  union value *up;

  while ((up = getvalue(prompt, STRING)) == NULL)
    printf("Bad input.  Expected a string.\n");
  return up->s;
}
```

Figure 11.24   (inp.c) Nice interface on top of **getvalue**.

```c
/*
 * Define types for getvalue.
 */
#define MAXLEN 80                /* longest input line */

enum  itype {LONG, REAL, STRING};

union value                      /* can hold a long, double, or char */
{
  long   i;
  double d;
  char   *s;
};

union value *getvalue(const char *prompt, enum itype valtype);
```

Figure 11.25   (getval2.h) A new header file for **getvalue** that uses enumerated types.

```
/*
 * Read a value from the user.
 */
#include <stdio.h>
#include <string.h>
#include <stddef.h>
#include <stdlib.h>
#include "getval2.h"

union value *getvalue(const char *prompt, enum itype type)
{
  int    getline(char *buf, int bufsize);
  static union value v;
  char   line[MAXLEN + 1];
  int    len;

  printf("%s", prompt);
  if ((len=getline(line, MAXLEN)) == -1)
    return NULL;
  switch(type)
  {
    case LONG:     if (sscanf(line, "%li", &v.i) != 1)
                     return NULL;
                   break;
    case REAL:     if (sscanf(line, "%lf", &v.d) != 1)
                     return NULL;
                   break;
    case STRING:   if ((v.s = malloc(len + 1)) == NULL)
                     return NULL;
                   strcpy(v.s, line);
                   break;
    default:       return NULL;
  }
  return &v;                                    /* succeeded */
}
```

Figure 11.26   (getval2.c) A new implementation of **getvalue** that uses enumerated types.

functions that print the employee table (Figures 11.8 and 11.9) to work correctly with this modified declaration.

11–3 Extend **getvalue** (Figures 11.25 and 11.26) to read values of other types such as **short** and **float**.

11–4 Write a program to read and sort an array of **struct employee**s. Sort by employee name.

11–5 Repeat the previous exercise working with an array of **struct date**s. Then write a function to search an array of **struct date**s for a particular date.

11–6 Define a structure type, **struct point**, for two-dimensional space coordinates (consisting of real values of x and y). Write a function, **distance**, that computes the distance between two **struct points**.

11–7   Define a structure type, **struct rational**, for rational numbers (consisting of the integer values x and y). Write functions for rational arithmetic.

11–8   Create a **union** with one field for each of C's basic data types. Store various values in the **union** and print each of the fields.

11–9   Write functions to read a date, to print a date in a nice format, to determine if a date is valid, and to determine the number of days between two **struct date**s.

11–10   How can we define a **boolean** enumerated type? Is using an enumerated **boolean** type preferable to using **typedef** or **#define**?

11–11   Define an enumerated type for the days of the week. Write functions to retrieve the next and previous days.

11–12   Write a function that is passed an array of **enum_itypes** describing the expected values on an input line and an array of **union**s that can hold these values. The function reads the values and sticks them in the array. How should errors be indicated?

11–13   Write a new version of the employee data base functions that maintains the data base in sorted order.

11–14   Write a program to handle a data base of events. An event includes the name of the event and its corresponding date. Provide operations to add, delete, and print events.

11–15   Write a program to manage a little black book. Each entry should include the person's name, address (broken into street number, street name, and apartment number), city, state, zip code, and phone number (broken into area code, prefix, and suffix). Allow the retrieval of all phone numbers in a given city, state, or zip code, as well as by specifying the person's name. Also provide a way to print the entire data base.

11–16   Write a program to manage a data base of information about an individual Compact Disc collection. Each entry includes the name of the group, the name of the CD, the year it was released, the price paid for it, and the total playing time. Allow the user to search for all the CDs released by a given group or for all the information on a particular CD. The user should also be able to print the data base sorted by group name, by playing time, by year of release, or by price paid. Finally, allow the user to print aggregate information: the total cost of the collection, the number of CDs, the number of different groups, and so on.

12 ARRAYS

OF

ARRAYS

So far our programs have needed only simple, one-dimensional arrays. This chapter introduces arrays of arrays, concentrating on how we can use pointers to gain performance improvements. We present several programs that manipulate these arrays using traditional subscripting and then rewrite them more efficiently using pointers. We conclude by implementing the Game of Life, once with array subscripting and once using pointers. This chapter contains much detail, but studying it carefully will result in faster programs and a thorough understanding of several important fine points of the language.

12.1 TWO-DIMENSIONAL ARRAYS

We can have arrays of any type, even arrays whose elements are themselves arrays. These more complex arrays correspond to the multidimensional arrays found in other languages. We can, for example, treat an array whose elements are arrays of integers as a two-dimensional array of integers.

How do we declare an array of arrays? The declaration

```
#define   MAX_STUDENTS   10
#define   MAX_TESTS       3

int   scores[MAX_STUDENTS][MAX_TESTS];
```

makes `scores` an array of 10 elements, with each element an array of 3 `int`s. That means `scores` contains a total of 30 `int`s and corresponds to a traditional two-dimensional array containing 10 rows of 3 columns each. One use of `scores` is to hold test scores for students in a class. Each row corresponds to the test scores for a particular student, each column corresponds to the scores for a particular test. In this case, that means that we have up to 10 students who have taken up to 3 tests.

We access a particular `int` within `scores` by specifying its row and column, which we do by using double sets of brackets. The first index selects the row, and the second selects the column within that row. Each dimension of the array can be indexed

scores[0][0]	scores[0][1]	scores[0][2]
scores[1][0]	scores[1][1]	scores[1][2]
scores[2][0]	scores[2][1]	scores[2][2]
scores[3][0]	scores[3][1]	scores[3][2]
scores[4][0]	scores[4][1]	scores[4][2]
scores[5][0]	scores[5][1]	scores[5][2]
scores[6][0]	scores[6][1]	scores[6][2]
scores[7][0]	scores[7][1]	scores[7][2]
scores[8][0]	scores[8][1]	scores[8][2]
scores[9][0]	scores[9][1]	scores[9][2]

Figure 12.1 How we index two-dimensional arrays.

from zero to its maximum size minus 1, so the legal indexes for **scores** range from **scores[0][0]** to **scores[9][2]**. Figure 12.1 illustrates this two-dimensional array indexing.

We illustrate this array accessing with a simple program that reads items into a two-dimensional array and then prints the array elements. Two functions do most of the work. **read_scores** reads the items into the array, and **print_scores** prints them, one row per line. Each input line contains a single score, with all of the scores for a given student preceding those of the next. Each output line contains the test scores for a particular student. Both functions use two variables, **student** and **test**, to index the array; **student** selects the row and **test** selects the element within that row.

Figure 12.2 is the header file, ioscores.h, that contains the prototypes for these functions. Figure 12.3 is the source file, ioscores.c, that contains the functions themselves. And Figure 12.4 is a main program using them.

read_scores and **print_scores** are straightforward—except for their first parameter declaration.[1]

```
int s[][MAX_TESTS]
```

Why is there a single subscript? As we saw in earlier chapters, when we pass an array, the compiler need only know the size of its elements, not how many elements it has. Here, the compiler needs to know that we're passing an array, each of whose elements is an array of **MAX_TESTS int**s. But it has no need to know how many of those elements we're passing. In general, with two-dimensional arrays this means that we need only tell the compiler how many columns the array has, but not how many rows.

---

[1]It's reasonable to expect that **print_scores** would declare its array parameter as **const**. But to keep our example programs as simple as possible, we're ignoring that issue until this chapter's case study.

```
/*
 * Prototypes for score manipulating functions.
 */
#define MAX_TESTS 3

extern int read_scores(int s[][MAX_TESTS], int maxrow);
extern void print_scores(int s[][MAX_TESTS], int maxrow);
```

dummy.

Figure 12.2 (ioscores.h) Header file containing the prototypes for our input and output functions.

```
/*
 * Functions to read and print a 2-d array of student test scores.
 *    read_scores - read scores into array, one input score per line.
 *    print_scores - write scores from array, one line per student.
 */
#include <stdio.h>
#include "ioscores.h"

#define  MAXLEN   80

int read_scores(int s[][MAX_TESTS], int maxrow)
{
  int  getline(char *buf, int len);
  int  student, test;                  /* our indices */
  char line[MAXLEN + 1];

  for (student = 0; student < maxrow; student++)
    for (test = 0; test < MAX_TESTS; test++)
      if (getline(line, MAXLEN) == -1 ||
            sscanf(line, "%i", &s[student][test]) != 1)
        return -student;               /* negative indicates problem */
  return maxrow;                        /* successfully read all scores */
}

void print_scores(int s[][MAX_TESTS], int maxrow)
{
  int student, test;                   /* our indices */

  for (student = 0; student < maxrow ; student++)
    for (test = 0; test < MAX_TESTS; test++)
      printf("%i%c", s[student][test],
                (test != MAX_TESTS - 1) ? ' ' : '\n');
}
```

Figure 12.3 (ioscores.c) Reading and printing test scores using conventional array subscripting.

```
/*
 * Read and print student scores.
 */
#include <stdio.h>
#include "ioscores.h"

#define MAX_STUDENTS 10

int main()
{
  int scores[MAX_STUDENTS][MAX_TESTS];

  if (read_scores(scores, MAX_STUDENTS) == MAX_STUDENTS)
    print_scores(scores, MAX_STUDENTS);
  else
    printf("Couldn't read all students successfully\n");
  return 0;
}
```

Figure 12.4   (tstscrs.c) A main program that uses **read_scores** and **print_scores**.

Unfortunately, there's no way to avoid telling the compiler how many items are in each row. That means any function we write works with a particular two-dimensional array: one whose rows have a particular number of items of a particular type. We can't write functions that can be passed two-dimensional arrays with varying length rows. That's why we put the definition of **MAX_TESTS** in ioscores.h, along with the prototypes for **read_scores** and **print_scores**. Both functions work only with two-dimensional arrays with **MAX_TESTS** columns.

As with all other arrays, when we pass an array of arrays as a parameter, we're really only passing a pointer to its first element. **read_scores** takes advantage of that feature in filling the array we pass it. But, as we'll soon see, with two-dimensional arrays we're passing a pointer to its first *row*, not to its first element.

Initializing Two-Dimensional Arrays

Because two-dimensional arrays are really just arrays of arrays, we can initialize them in the same way we initialize their one-dimensional counterparts: by following their declaration with a list of values enclosed in braces. For example,

```
int scores[10][3] = {{90, 75, 85}, {99, 99, 95},
                      {65, 69, 66}, {100, 100, 100},
                      {56, 60, 70}, {78, 85, 90},
                      {87, 82, 97}, {65, 80, 70},
                      {75, 78, 56}, {80, 80, 100}};
```

initializes the items in **scores**' first row to 90, 75, and 85; the items in **scores**' second row to 99, 99, and 95; and so on. Figure 12.5 shows the resulting array.

scores[0][0]

90	75	85
99	99	95
65	69	66
100	100	100
56	60	70
78	85	90
87	82	97
65	80	70
75	78	56
80	80	100

scores[9][2]

Figure 12.5   The resulting initialized two-dimensional array.

We're allowed to eliminate the braces surrounding the values in each row, so

```
int scores[10][3] =
    {90, 75, 85, 99, 99, 95, 65, 69, 66, 100, 100, 100,
     56, 60, 70, 78, 85, 90, 87, 82, 97, 65,  80,  70,
     75, 78, 56, 80, 80, 100};
```

is a terse equivalent to the initialization above. But there's a problem with this form: it's not immediately apparent which values go with which elements. We prefer the more readable but longer form.

What happens if we don't supply all the elements in the initialization list? In **static** and global arrays the missing elements start off as zero; in automatic arrays they start off with an unknown and unpredictable value. The declaration

```
static int scores[10][3] =
    {{90, 75}, {99, 99}, {65, 69}, {100, 100}, {56, 60},
     {78, 85}, {87, 82}, {65, 80}, {75, 78},   {80, 80}};
```

explicitly initializes the first two elements of each row and implicitly initializes the last element in each row to zero. Unfortunately, there's no way to initialize only selected rows. The simplest way to skip over rows that don't require initialization is to initialize their first element to zero.

Since the compiler can determine the size and structure of an array from the values we provide, we don't have to specify its first dimension (the number of rows). We can rewrite our initial declaration of **scores** as

```
int scores[][3] = {{90, 75, 85}, {99, 99, 95},
                    {65, 69, 66}, {100, 100, 100},
                    {56, 60, 70}, {78, 85, 90},
                    {87, 82, 97}, {65, 80, 70},
                    {75, 78, 56}, {80, 80, 100}};
```

Storing Two-Dimensional Arrays

All arrays in C have their elements stored sequentially in memory. With two-dimensional arrays that means the elements of the first row are stored consecutively in memory, followed by the elements of the second row, and so on. Figure 12.6 shows how **scores** is stored.

When we refer to an array element, as with **scores[7][2]**, the compiler finds its location from the two subscripts and its knowledge of the number of columns in each row and of the location of the first item in the array. Using our earlier declaration of **scores** and assuming that **scores** starts at location 1000, we find **scores[7][2]** at

&scores[0][0] + words for 3×7 elements in rows 0 through 6
    + words for the 2 elements preceding it in row 7

or, in other words, $1000 + 21 \times$ **sizeof(int)** $+ 2 \times$ **sizeof(int)**, which is 1046 (assuming 2-byte **int**s). In general, we find **scores[i][j]** at

&scores[0][0] + $i \times$ **MAX_TESTS** + $j \times$ **sizeof(int)**

Why do we care about the internal layout of two-dimensional arrays? Because it allows us to traverse them with pointers as though they were giant one-dimensional arrays, which leads to more efficient programs.

Figure 12.7 contains a small program that calls two different functions to initialize to some value (5, in this case) all of the elements in a large two-dimensional array. The first function, **twod_init**, takes three parameters: a two-dimensional array with **MAXCOLS** columns in each row, the number of rows in the array, and the value with which to initialize each of its elements. It uses two indices, **row** and **col**, and straightforward two-dimensional array subscripting. To obtain some data on its execution time, we had the program initialize the array 50 times. On our workstation that took approximately $\frac{7}{10}$ of a second.

The other function, **table_init**, much more quickly accomplishes this task. It's designed to initialize every item in a one-dimensional array to a particular value. It expects to be passed pointers to the array's first and last **int**s, along with the initializing value. It then uses pointers to traverse the array. We call **table_init** with

table_init(&t[0][0], &t[MAXROWS - 1][MAXCOLS - 1], 5);

&t[0][0] and &t[MAXROWS - 1][MAXCOLS - 1] are pointers to the first and last **int**s in our two-dimensional array.

When we ran this version, it took approximately $\frac{2}{10}$ of a second to perform the same task, which is slightly less than one-third the time of the first version, a significant savings. Why is it so much faster? Before, we did two-dimensional array subscripting each time we wanted to access an element. That subscripting potentially involves a great deal of arithmetic: a multiplication to locate the element's row and an addition to find the item's column. Now, however, we're treating the two-dimensional array as a one-dimensional array and using a pointer to traverse it, which eliminates the arithmetic involved in computing an array element's location. In general, whenever we traverse

scores[0][0]		scores[0][2]			scores[9][0]		scores[9][2]	
90	75	85	99	· · ·	56	80	80	100
	scores[0][1]		scores[1][0]		scores[8][2]		scores[9][1]	

Figure 12.6 Internal representation of **scores**.

```
/*
 * A program that uses two different ways to initialize a 2-d array.
 *    twod_init - initialize a two-d array using array subscripting.
 *    table_init - initialize a two-d array using pointers.
 */
#include <stdio.h>

#define ITERATIONS  50
#define MAXROWS     150
#define MAXCOLS     200

int main()
{
  void twod_init(int table[][MAXCOLS], int rows, int value);
  void table_init(int *ptr, int *endptr, int value);
  int t[MAXROWS][MAXCOLS];                /* table to initialize */
  int i;                                  /* count */

  for (i = 0; i < ITERATIONS; i++)        /* first try slow way */
    twod_init(t, MAXROWS, 5);
  for (i = 0; i < ITERATIONS; i++)        /* then try faster way */
    table_init(&t[0][0], &t[MAXROWS - 1][MAXCOLS - 1], 5);
  return 0;
}

void twod_init(int table[][MAXCOLS], int rows, int value)
{
  int row, col;

  for (row = 0; row < rows; row++)
    for (col = 0; col < MAXCOLS; col++)
      table[row][col] = value;
}

void table_init(int *ptr, int *endptr, int value)
{
  for (; ptr < endptr; *ptr++ = value)
    ;
}
```

Figure 12.7 (init2d.c) Initializing a two-d array using array subscripting and pointer indexing.

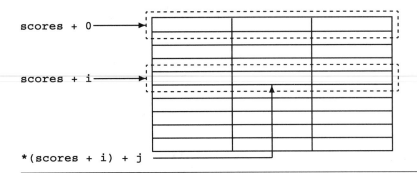

Figure 12.8 Using `*(*(scores + i) + j)` to access `scores[i][j]`. Here `i` is 4 and `j` is 2.

sequentially a segment of a two-dimensional array, we should pretend that segment is a one-dimensional array and traverse it using pointers. We will take this approach in several other examples in this chapter.

12.2 POINTERS AND TWO-DIMENSIONAL ARRAYS

The name of an array of arrays, like the name of a one-dimensional array, is the address of the array's first element. For these arrays, however, that first element is not simply an `int` or a `double`, but is itself an array. What that means is that the name of a two-dimensional array of `int`s is not a pointer to its first `int` but to its first row. That's why earlier we passed `&t[0][0]` to `twod_init`, rather than simply passing it `t`. Although both pointers refer to the same address, they have different types. `&t[0][0]` is a pointer to an `int`, and `t` is a pointer to an array of `int`s.

Why is this distinction important? Because, as we discovered earlier, any array access is automatically converted to an equivalent pointer expression. Whenever we use two subscripts to reference an element in a two-dimensional array, C converts the array access into an equivalent pointer expression. `scores[i][j]`, for example, is converted into the equivalent pointer expression

```
*(*(scores + i) + j)
```

Figure 12.8 shows how this extremely bizarre-looking expression obtains the value of `scores[i][j]`. The rest of this section clarifies why this expression works and how we can use pointers to efficiently traverse two-dimensional arrays.

Traversing Columns

We illustrate the relationship between pointers and two-dimensional arrays with a simple function, `test_avg`, that computes the average of the values in a given column of an array. The call

```
/*
 * Print average on each test.  For simplicity, the initial scores
 * are hard-coded into the array rather than read.
 */
#include <stdio.h>
#include "ioscores.h"

int main()
{
  double test_avg(int s[][MAX_TESTS], int rows, int n);
  int scores[][MAX_TESTS] = {{90, 75, 85}, {99, 99, 95},
                             {65, 69, 66}, {100, 100, 100},
                             {56, 60, 70}, {78, 85, 90},
                             {87, 82, 97}, {65, 80, 70},
                             {75, 78, 56}, {80, 80, 100}};
  const int n = sizeof(scores) / (sizeof(int) * MAX_TESTS);
  int i;

  for (i = 0; i < MAX_TESTS; i++)
    printf("Average on test %i is %.2f\n", i, test_avg(scores, n, i));
  return 0;
}
```

Figure 12.9 (usetest.c) A program to use **test_avg** to compute the average of each of the columns.

```
test_avg(scores, MAX_STUDENTS, i)
```

returns the average of the ith column in the first **MAX_STUDENTS** rows, which is the average score on a particular test. **test_avg** works correctly only if i is less than **MAX_TESTS**, but to simplify things, we don't bother with error checking.

Figure 12.9 contains a main program that uses **test_avg** to compute the average of each of the columns in an array. Here's the program's output:

```
Average on test 0 is 79.50
Average on test 1 is 80.80
Average on test 2 is 82.90
```

Rather than using a defined constant, we computes the number of students we have with

```
sizeof(scores) / (sizeof(int) * MAX_TESTS)
```

We've written two versions of **test_avg**. Figure 12.10 contains the first version, which uses array subscripting. Figure 12.11 contains the second version, which uses pointers.

> *The name of a two-dimensional array is a pointer to its first row, not its first element.*

```
/*
 * Compute the average of a column in a 2-d array using subscripting.
 */
#include "ioscores.h"

double test_avg(int s[][MAX_TESTS], int rows, int n)
{
  double sum = 0.0;                        /* column total */
  int    i;                                /* row index */

  for (i = 0; i < rows; i++)
    sum += s[i][n];
  return sum / rows;
}
```

Figure 12.10   (testavg1.c) An array-subscripting version of test_avg.

```
/*
 * Compute the average of a column in a 2-d array using pointers.
 */
#include "ioscores.h"

double test_avg(int (*rowptr)[MAX_TESTS], int rows, int n)
{
  double sum = 0.0;                        /* column total */
  int (*endptr)[MAX_TESTS];                /* will point to last row */

  for (endptr = rowptr + rows; rowptr < endptr; rowptr++)
    sum += (*rowptr)[n];
  return sum / rows;
}
```

Figure 12.11   (testavg2.c) A pointer-indexing version of test_avg.

When we declare a two-dimensional array, C automatically declares its name as a constant pointer to the array's first row. This declaration,

```
int scores[MAX_STUDENTS][MAX_TESTS];
```

allocates space for a two-dimensional array and defines **scores** as a constant pointer to its first row. So we can declare the parameter in **test_avg** as

```
int (*rowptr)[MAX_TESTS]
```

that is, as a pointer to an array of **MAX_TESTS** ints. We need the parentheses around ***rowptr** because ***** has lower precedence than **[]**. Without them, as in

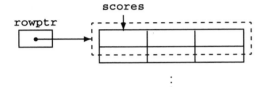

(*a*) **rowptr** starts off pointing to the first *row* in **scores**.

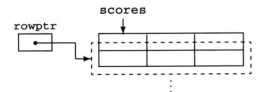

(*b*) Incrementing **rowptr** causes it to point to the next row of **scores**.

Figure 12.12   What happens when we increment a pointer to a row.

```
int *rowptr[MAX_TESTS];
```

we would be declaring **rowptr** as an array of **MAX_TESTS** elements, each a pointer to an **int**, a topic we cover in the next chapter.

Because pointer arithmetic is done in units of the pointed-to thing, incrementing a pointer to a row makes it point to the next row. This allows us to traverse a two-dimensional array by initializing a pointer (**rowptr**) to the first row of the array and incrementing the pointer (**rowptr++**) each time we need to get to the next row. Figure 12.12 illustrates this process.

But once we have a pointer to a row, how do we get at its elements? The expression (***rowptr**) **[n]** gives us the nth element in a row pointed to by **rowptr**. Figure 12.13 shows why this expression works.

> *Dereferencing a pointer to a row gives us the row itself, not its first element.*

More accurately, dereferencing a pointer to a row gives us a pointer to the row's first element. Since **rowptr** points to a particular row, ***rowptr** is a pointer to that row's first element. What's weird is that **rowptr** and ***rowptr** refer to identical addresses. The difference is their type: **rowptr** is a pointer to an array of **int**s, but ***rowptr** is a pointer to the first **int** in that array (the row). That difference in type means that **rowptr + n** is a pointer to the nth row past **rowptr**, whereas ***rowptr + n** is a pointer to the nth column in the array pointed to by **rowptr**. We can use ***rowptr** as

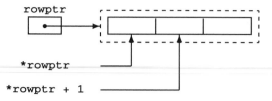

Figure 12.13   How we access an element through a pointer to a row.

though it were the name of an array (the array containing the **MAX_TESTS** elements in that row), which means that (***rowptr**) **[n]** accesses the nth element in the row.

We compiled and ran both versions of **test_avg** on several different computers. On the average, the pointer version took less than two-thirds the time of the straightforward array-subscripting version. Why is there so much improvement? Normally when we do a two-dimensional array access, such as **scores[i][j]**, to locate the desired element, the compiler must do the complicated address calculation we saw earlier. This calculation first figures out which row the element is in and then where it is in that row. But when we use the row pointer, the compiler already knows which row the element is in, eliminating a major portion of the address calculation. Later exercises suggest ways to improve this function even further.

Traversing Rows

We can use pointers to process rows as well as columns. Figure 12.14 is a program that uses a new function, **student_avg**, to compute the average of a row. Figures 12.15 and 12.16 contain array-subscripting and pointer-indexing versions of **student_avg**, respectively. Here's the program's output when run on a sample set of student scores:

        83.33 97.67 66.67 100.00 62.00 84.33 88.67 71.67 69.67 86.67

When we use pointers, we traverse a row of a two-dimensional array just as we traverse a one-dimensional array: We initialize a pointer to the row's first element and increment it until it points to the row's last element. Again we find a large performance improvement. The pointer version takes less than one-third the time of the array-subscripting version. Why? Because we now access the various elements within a row simply by incrementing a pointer—completely eliminating any address calculations.

Accessing Rows

We just wrote a specialized function to compute the average of a row within a two-dimensional array. But we could just as well have used our earlier function, **table_average** (from Chapter 9), that we wrote to compute the average of a one-dimensional array. All we have to do is pass it the address of the first element in the

```
/*
 * Read scores and print average for each student.  As before,
 * for simplicity the test scores are hard-coded, not read.
 */
#include <stdio.h>
#include "ioscores.h"

int main()
{
  double student_avg(int s[][MAX_TESTS], int n);
  int i;
  int scores[][MAX_TESTS] = {{90, 75, 85}, {99, 99, 95},
                             {65, 69, 66}, {100, 100, 100},
                             {56, 60, 70}, {78, 85, 90},
                             {87, 82, 97}, {65, 80, 70},
                             {75, 78, 56}, {80, 80, 100}};
  int n = sizeof(scores) / (sizeof(int) * MAX_TESTS);

  printf("Student\t   Average\n");
  for (i = 0; i < n; i++)
    printf("%4i\t%10.2f\n", i, student_avg(scores, i));
  return 0;
}
```

Figure 12.14   (userow.c) A program that prints the average of each of the rows in a two-dimensional array.

```
/*
 * Compute row average using array subscripting.
 */
#include "ioscores.h"

double student_avg(int s[][MAX_TESTS], int n)
{
  int i = 0;                              /* index to next row */
  long sum = 0L;                          /* total so far */

  for (; i < MAX_TESTS; sum += s[n][i++])
    ;
  return (double) sum / MAX_TESTS;
}
```

Figure 12.15   (rowavg1.c) An array-subscripting version of **student_avg**.

```
/*
 * Compute row average using pointer indexing.
 */
#include "ioscores.h"

double student_avg(int s[][MAX_TESTS], int n)
{
  const int *colptr = &s[n][0];                  /* ptr to first item */
  const int *const endptr = colptr + MAX_TESTS;  /* ptr to last item */
  long sum = 0L;                                  /* total so far */

  for (; colptr < endptr; sum += *colptr++)
    ;
  return (double) sum / MAX_TESTS;
}
```

Figure 12.16 (rowavg2.c) A pointer-indexing version of **student_avg**. It obtains a pointer to the first element in a row and uses it to traverse the row.

desired row, along with the number of elements in that row. To sum up the values in row 5, for example, we use

```
table_average(&scores[5][0], MAX_TESTS)
```

There is, however, an even more concise way to provide the address of the first element in a row. We simply follow the array name with a single subscript: the row number. We can rewrite the call above as

```
table_average(scores[5], MAX_TESTS)
```

There are two ways to understand how this works. The first relies on remembering that a two-dimensional array is really an array of arrays. So when we access **scores[i]**, we're accessing the **i**th element in **scores**, which happens to be an array of **int**s. The other way is to remember that C turns any array access into a pointer expression. **scores[i]** is turned into ***(scores + i)**. Adding **i** to **scores** gives us a pointer to the **i**th row, dereferencing it gives us a pointer to the first element in the **i**th row. So **scores[i]** is exactly equivalent to **&scores[i][0]**. Use whichever form you find most understandable.

Figure 12.17 contains a new version of our earlier program to compute the average student score. This version uses **table_average**. The primary advantage of this version is that it uses an existing function that works with one-dimensional arrays of any size, rather than requiring a special function that only works with rows in two-dimensional arrays of a particular size.

```
/*
 * Print average for each student, using our earlier table_average
 * function (again, scores are hard-coded rather than read).
 */
#include <stdio.h>
#include "ioscores.h"

int main()
{
  double table_average(int *ptr, int n);
  int i;
  int scores[][MAX_TESTS] = {90, 75, 85, 99, 99, 95, 65, 69, 66, 100,
                             100, 100, 56, 60, 70, 78, 85, 90, 87, 82,
                             97, 65, 80, 70, 75, 78, 56, 80, 80, 100};
  const int n = sizeof(scores) / (sizeof(int) * MAX_TESTS);

  printf("Student\t  Average\n");
  for (i = 0; i < n; i++)
    printf("%4i\t%10.2f\n", i, table_average(scores[i], MAX_TESTS));
  return 0;
}
```

Figure 12.17 (avgtab.c) A second version of our program to print average student scores.

12.3   MULTIDIMENSIONAL ARRAYS

It turns out that C also allows three- and higher-dimensional arrays. We declare, initialize, and subscript these as we do two-dimensional arrays. For example,

```
#define MAX_CLASSES   2
#define MAX_STUDENTS 10
#define MAX_TESTS     3

int classes[MAX_CLASSES][MAX_STUDENTS][MAX_TESTS];
```

declares an array of 2 elements, each of which is itself an array of 10 elements, each of which is an array of three ints. This corresponds to a three-dimensional array holding 60 ints organized into 2 two-dimensional arrays of 10 rows and 3 columns each. We could use it to store the test scores for students in two different classes, with each of the two-dimensional arrays holding the scores for the students in one class. As you may have guessed, the name of a three-dimensional array is a constant pointer to the first two-dimensional array inside it.

We access the elements of a three-dimensional array using three subscripts, so classes[0][1][2] refers to the third column of the second row of the first two-dimensional array, or, in plain English, the third test score of the second student in the first class.

```
/*
 * Read and print student scores, one student per line.
 */
#include <stdio.h>
#include "ioclass.h"                /* for read_scores/write_scores */

#define MAX_CLASSES  2

int main()
{
  int classes[MAX_CLASSES][MAX_STUDENTS][MAX_TESTS];

  if (read_classes(classes, MAX_CLASSES) == MAX_CLASSES)
    print_classes(classes, MAX_CLASSES);
  else
    printf("Couldn't read all classes successfully\n");
  return 0;
}
```

Figure 12.18 (classes.c) A program to read and print three-dimensional arrays.

N-Dimensional Arrays and Parameters

When we declare an N-dimensional array parameter, we must supply all dimensions except the first, regardless of what N actually is. This is because when we pass an N-dimensional array as a parameter, we really pass a pointer to its first element (the first $N - 1$ dimensional array it contains).

Figure 12.18 provides an example with a program that reads values into **classes** and then prints them. To do so, it makes use of the two functions **read_classes** and **print_classes**. Figure 12.19 contains their prototypes, and Figure 12.20 contains the function themselves.

Both functions are passed two parameters: a three-dimensional array and the number of two-dimensional arrays it contains. The functions expect to be passed **classes**, but since we're really only passing a pointer, we can declare the prototypes using either array indexing notation

```
void print_classes(int c[][MAX_STUDENTS][MAX_TESTS], int n)
```

or pointer notation

```
void print_classes(int (*ptr)[MAX_STUDENTS][MAX_TESTS], int n)
```

The latter form declares **ptr** as a pointer to a two-dimensional array. But because **read_classes** and **print_classes** use array indexing to process **classes**, we've used the first form.

```
/*
 * Prototypes for functions to read and print class scores.
 */
#include "ioscores.h"

#define MAX_STUDENTS 10

int read_classes(int c[][MAX_STUDENTS][MAX_TESTS], int n);
void print_classes(int c[][MAX_STUDENTS][MAX_TESTS], int n);
```

Figure 12.19 (ioclass.h) Header file defining prototypes for our I/O functions.

```
/*
 * Functions to read/print a 3-d array.
 *    read_classes - use read_scores to read scores for each class.
 *    print_classes - use print_scores to print scores for each class.
 */
#include <stdio.h>
#include "ioclass.h"

int read_classes(int c[][MAX_STUDENTS][MAX_TESTS], int n)
{
  int class;

  for (class = 0; class < n; class++)
    if (read_scores(c[class], MAX_STUDENTS) != MAX_STUDENTS)
      return -class;
  return class;
}

void print_classes(int classes[][MAX_STUDENTS][MAX_TESTS], int n)
{
  int class;

  for (class = 0; class < n; class++)
  {
    print_scores(classes[class], MAX_STUDENTS);
    putchar('\n');
  }
}
```

Figure 12.20 (ioclass1.c) Functions to read and print a three-dimensional array using array subscripting.

1000	x[0][1][0]	x[0][1][1]	x[0][1][2]	x[0][1][3]	*1st 2-d array*
1008	x[0][1][0]	x[0][1][1]	x[0][1][2]	x[0][1][3]	
1016	x[1][0][0]	x[1][0][1]	x[1][0][2]	x[1][0][3]	*2nd 2-d array*
1024	x[1][1][0]	x[1][1][1]	x[1][1][2]	x[1][1][3]	
1032	x[2][0][0]	x[2][0][1]	x[2][0][2]	x[2][0][3]	*3rd 2-d array*
1040	x[2][1][0]	x[2][1][1]	x[2][1][2]	x[2][1][3]	

Figure 12.21   Storage layout for a $3 \times 2 \times 4$ three-dimensional array of `int`s.

N-Dimensional Arrays and Pointers

`read_classes` uses `read_scores` to read the scores into the individual two-dimensional arrays in `classes`. It first reads the scores for the first class, then the scores for the second class, and so on. And `print_classes` does something similar, except that it uses `print_scores` to print these arrays. But both `read_scores` and `print_scores` expect a pointer to the first row in a two-dimensional array. How can we provide them with one when we're working our way through a three-dimensional array?

C treats any N-dimensional array as an array of $(N - 1)$-dimensional arrays: a two-dimensional array as an array of one-dimensional arrays, a three-dimensional array as an array of two-dimensional arrays, and so on. By treats, we mean several things. First, regardless of the number of dimensions in it, C stores any array as a single one-dimensional array. Figure 12.21 shows how three-dimensional arrays are stored: it's an array, each element of which is a two-dimensional array. Second, C defines any array name as a constant pointer to the first $(N - 1)$-dimensional array within it. `classes`, for example, is a constant pointer to its first two-dimensional array. Third, C translates any N-dimensional array into a sequence of pointer additions and dereferences, with one addition and dereference for each dimension of the array. And finally, C calculates pointer arithmetic for any N-dimensional array based on the size of the $(N - 1)$-dimensional arrays it contains.

One result of all these features is that C automatically translates `classes[i]` into `*(classes + i)`, which is a pointer to the first row in the `i`th two-dimensional array within `classes`. And that's exactly what we want to pass to `read_scores` and `print_scores`.

```
print_scores(classes[i], MAX_STUDENTS);
```

Another result is that we can use pointers to traverse any N-dimensional array—although the code can be confusing and hard to read when we traverse higher-dimensional arrays. If we have a pointer `ptr` that points to some two-dimensional array within `classes`, incrementing it with `ptr++` causes it to point to the next two-dimensional array. And because dereferencing a pointer gives a pointer to the array's first element,

```
/*
 * Pointer version of 3-d array reading and printing functions.
 *    read_classes - use read_scores to read scores for each class.
 *    print_classes - use print_scores to print scores for each class.
 */
#include <stdio.h>
#include "ioclass.h"

int read_classes(int (*ptr)[MAX_STUDENTS][MAX_TESTS], int n)
{
  int (*saveptr)[MAX_STUDENTS][MAX_TESTS] = ptr;
  int (*endptr)[MAX_STUDENTS][MAX_TESTS];

  for (endptr = ptr + n - 1; ptr <= endptr; ptr++)
    if (read_scores(*ptr, MAX_STUDENTS) != MAX_STUDENTS)
      return saveptr - ptr;    /* negative value on error */
  return ptr - saveptr;
}

void print_classes(int (*ptr)[MAX_STUDENTS][MAX_TESTS], int n)
{
  int (*endptr)[MAX_STUDENTS][MAX_TESTS];

  for (endptr = ptr + n - 1; ptr <= endptr; ptr++)
  {
    print_scores(*ptr, MAX_STUDENTS);
    putchar('\n');
  }
}
```

Figure 12.22   (ioclass2.c) Pointer-indexing versions of our I/O functions.

*twodptr is a pointer to the first row of a two-dimensional array and ****twodptr** is a pointer to its first element. Figure 12.22 provides an example, with pointer versions of **read_scores** and **print_scores**.

Initializing N-Dimensional Arrays

We can initialize any array, regardless of its dimension, by providing a brace-enclosed list of elements. If any of these elements are arrays, we can also enclose their values in braces. For example,

```
int x[3][2][4] =
  { {{ 0, 1,  2,  3}, {4, 5, 6, 7}},
    {{ 8, 9, 10, 11}, {12, 13, 14, 15}},
    {{16, 17, 18, 19}, {20, 21, 22, 23}} };
```

As with any array, we could just list the array's elements.

```
int x[3][2][4] =
  { 0,  1,  2,  3,  4,  5,  6,  7,
    8,  9, 10, 11, 12, 13, 14, 15,
   16, 17, 18, 19, 20, 21, 22, 23 };
```

For higher-dimensional arrays, we use the longer form, since it's just too easy to make a mistake and forget a desired array element.

12.4 CASE STUDY—THE GAME OF LIFE

This section is optional!

This chapter concludes with an illustration of the power of pointers. We implement the Game of Life, a simulation of population growth dynamics developed by British mathematician John Horton Conway. In Life, a board represents the world, and each cell represents a single location. A cell is either empty or contains a single inhabitant. The game uses three simple rules to model population changes:

Survival An inhabited cell remains inhabited if exactly two or three of its neighboring cells are inhabited. (A cell has eight neighbors, four adjacent orthogonally and four adjacent diagonally.)

Death An inhabited cell becomes uninhabited if fewer than two or more than three of its neighbors are inhabited.

Birth An uninhabited cell becomes inhabited if exactly three of its neighbors are inhabited.

All births and deaths occur simultaneously, together causing the creation of a new generation.

Figure 12.23 shows some sample configurations and their first few generations. Sadly, most worlds eventually become uninhabited. But don't worry—some worlds develop a stable, inhabited population, whereas others reach a dynamically stable population that oscillates between states. We usually let the game run until it results in a stable population.

An Array-Subscripting Version

life divides nicely into three separate tasks: reading an initial description of a world, computing the next generation, and displaying the next generation. Each of these corresponds to a single function, placed into its own source file. `GetWorld` reads a description of a world and records its initial inhabitants. `NextWorld` examines the current generation to determine the contents of the next generation. And `PutWorld` displays the current generation.

The world itself is a two-dimensional array of BOOLEANs; TRUE indicates an inhabited cell, and FALSE an uninhabited cell. A BOOLEAN is simply a `typedef` to `short`. For convenience and readability, we've also used `typedef` to define a type WORLD as a two-dimensional array of BOOLEANs, a type PTR_TO_WORLD as a pointer

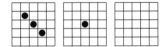

(a) A game that dies out quickly.

(b) A game that dies a little more slowly.

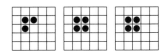

(b) A game that rapidly reaches a stable state.

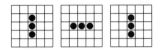

(d) A game that reaches an oscillating state.

Figure 12.23 Various worlds for the Game of Life and their population changes.

to a row within a **WORLD**, and a type **PTR_TO_CONST_WORLD** as a pointer to a row within a **WORLD** that we aren't going to change. A special header file, life.h, contains these **typedef**s, along with definitions of various useful constants for the size of the world and the characters used to display cells. To simplify counting a cell's neighbors, a **WORLD** actually includes room for an extra uninhabited border of cells. The displayable world is 20 by 78, the space available on the average display after writing a border around the world and a line identifying the current generation. Figure 12.24 contains life.h.

Figure 12.25 contains the main program, life.c. It begins by using **GetWorld** to read the initial world, and **PutWorld** to display the updated world. It then repeatedly uses **NextWorld** to calculate the contents of the next world, and **PutWorld** to display it. It stops when it has displayed the requested number of generations or the world has reached a stable state.

Figure 12.26 contains **GetWorld**. It expects the first input line to describe the desired number of rows and columns for the world, along with the number of generations to compute and display. And it expects each remaining input line to contain the row and column position of an inhabitant. **GetWorld** reads input lines with our old friend **getline** and uses **sscanf** to grab the various values. It verifies that each value is

```
/*
 * Header file for Life game.
 */
#include <stdio.h>

#define    BORDER    'X'                /* border around world */
#define    MARKER    '#'                /* occupied cell marker */
#define    MAXROW    20                 /* legal rows: 1..20 */
#define    MAXCOL    78                 /* legal columns: 1..78 */
#define    NUMROWS   22                 /* extra cells surrounding */
#define    NUMCOLS   80                 /* (simplify neighbors) */
#define    MAXLEN    80                 /* longest input line */

typedef    short BOOLEAN;
typedef    BOOLEAN WORLD[NUMROWS][NUMCOLS];

typedef    BOOLEAN (*PTR_TO_WORLD)[NUMCOLS];
typedef    const BOOLEAN (*PTR_TO_CONST_WORLD)[NUMCOLS];

#define    TRUE      1
#define    FALSE     0

extern BOOLEAN GetWorld(PTR_TO_WORLD x);
extern int NextWorld(PTR_TO_CONST_WORLD x, PTR_TO_WORLD y);
extern void PutWorld(PTR_TO_CONST_WORLD x);

extern int Rows, Cols, Gen, EndGen, Inhabs;
```

Figure 12.24   (life.h) Header file for the Game of Life program.

in range using a **static** function named **inrange** and writes an appropriate error message when one isn't.[2]

GetWorld assumes that its standard input has been redirected to come from a file, since there's likely to be too much input to enter directly. So although **GetWorld** does check for input errors, it doesn't bother to prompt for its input.

Figure 12.27 contains **NextWorld**. It computes the next generation by examining each cell of the current generation, counting how many inhabited neighbors it has, and applying the rules to see whether it is inhabited in the next generation. **NextWorld** needs to make all the changes at the same time, so it expects to be passed a pointer to another world where it can record the next generation. When it returns, the main program exchanges the next and current worlds. **NextWorld** updates a counter of inhabitants and returns a count of changes so the main program can easily determine if a generation has been annihilated or has reached a stable state.

Figure 12.28 contains the final piece of the program. **PutWorld** displays the

---

[2]We've placed the prototype for **inrange** before **GetWorld** rather than inside of it because **inrange** is a **static** function.

```
/*
 * Main program for the Game of Life.
 */
#include "life.h"

int Rows;                              /* # of rows used */
int Cols;                              /* # of columss used */
int Inhabs;                            /* # of inhabitants */
int Gen;                               /* current generation */
int EndGen;                            /* last generation */

int main()
{
  static WORLD world1,                 /* one is current world */
               world2;                 /* other is future world */
  PTR_TO_WORLD currptr = world1,       /* pointers to current and */
               nextptr = world2;       /*   future worlds */
  int          status;

  if (!GetWorld(currptr))              /* bad input */
  {
    printf("No input world or input errors -- stopping\n");
    status = 1;                        /* error exit */
  }
  else
  {
    PutWorld(currptr);                 /* write initial world */
    for (Gen = 2; Inhabs && Gen <= EndGen; Gen++)
    {
      PTR_TO_WORLD temp;

      if (!NextWorld(currptr, nextptr))
        break;                         /* no changes! */
      PutWorld(nextptr);               /* write next world */
      temp = currptr;                  /* exchange worlds */
      currptr = nextptr;
      nextptr = temp;
    }
    if (!Inhabs)
      printf("All inhabitants are dead\n");
    else if (Gen <= EndGen)
      printf("Reached stable state\n");
    else
      printf("Computed requested generations.\n");
    status = 0;
  }
  return status;
}
```

Figure 12.25   (life.c)   The main program for the Game of Life.

```
/*
 * Life input handler (quits on first error)
 */
#include <stdio.h>
#include "life.h"

static int inrange(int min, int max, int value);

BOOLEAN GetWorld(PTR_TO_WORLD world)
{
  int getline(char *ptr, int len);
  char buf[MAXLEN + 1];                     /* input line */
  int r, c;                                 /* next position */

  if (getline(buf, MAXLEN) == -1 ||
      sscanf(buf, "%i %i %i", &Rows, &Cols, &EndGen) != 3)
  {
    printf("Didn't provide ROWS, COLS, FINAL GENERATION\n");
    return FALSE;
  }

  printf("Rows=%i Cols=%i, Final Generation=%i\n",
         Rows, Cols, EndGen);

  if (!inrange(1, MAXROW, Rows))
    printf("Invalid Rows, set to %i\n", Rows = MAXROW);
  if (!inrange(1, MAXCOL, Cols))
    printf("Invalid Columns, set to %i\n", Cols = MAXCOL);
  while (getline(buf, MAXLEN) != -1)
    if (sscanf(buf, "%i %i", &r, &c) != 2)
      printf("Non-numeric cell position -- ignored\n");
    else if (!inrange(1, Rows, r) || !inrange(1, Cols, c))
      printf("%i,%i is out of range -- ignored\n", r, c);
    else if (!world[r][c])
    {
      printf("Cell %i,%i is now occupied\n", r, c);
      world[r][c] = TRUE;
      Inhabs++;
    }
  return TRUE;
}

static int inrange(int min, int max, int value)
{
  return min <= value && value <= max;
}
```

Figure 12.26 (getworld.c) A function to read the description of the world.

```
/*
 * Compute the next generation.
 */
#include "life.h"

int NextWorld(PTR_TO_CONST_WORLD curr, PTR_TO_WORLD next)
{
  int changed = 0;                      /* cells that changed */
  int r, c;                             /* row, column index */

  Inhabs = 0;
  for (r = 1; r <= Rows; r++)
    for (c = 1; c <= Cols; c++)
    {
      int neighbors =  curr[r - 1][c - 1] + curr[r - 1][c] +
                       curr[r - 1][c + 1] + curr[r + 1][c - 1] +
                       curr[r + 1][c]     + curr[r + 1][c + 1] +
                       curr[r][c - 1]     + curr[r][c + 1];

      if ((neighbors == 3) || (neighbors == 2 && curr[r][c]))
      {
        next[r][c] = TRUE;
        Inhabs++;
      }
      else
        next[r][c] = FALSE;

      changed += next[r][c] != curr[r][c];
    }
  return changed;
}
```

Figure 12.27   (nxtworld.c) Compute the next generation.

current generation. It indicates the world's border with **X**'s, inhabited cells with a **#**, and uninhabited cells with a blank.

Neither **NextWorld** nor **PutWorld** should change the world containing the current generation. We want the compiler to enforce this restriction, so these functions declare that parameter as a **PTR_TO_CONST_WORLD**, rather than simply as a **PTR_TO_WORLD**. Because the **typedef** for **PTR_TO_CONST_WORLD** indicates that the pointed-to world is a **const**, the compiler will flag as an error any attempt to change the world through that pointer. This prevents these functions from accidentally changing a cell in the world.[3]

---

[3]The disadvantage is that many compilers give us warnings when we pass non-**const** two-dimensional arrays to functions expecting **const** two-dimensional arrays. To get rid of these warnings, it's necessary to explicitly cast the problematic argument to a constant or to go out and buy a better compiler.

```
/*
 * Handle printing the generation.
 */
#include "life.h"

static void putborder(int n);

void PutWorld(PTR_TO_CONST_WORLD world)
{
  int c, r;

  printf("Generation %i out of %i\n", Gen, EndGen);
  putborder(1 + Cols + 1);
  for (r = 1; r <= Rows; r++)
  {
    putchar(BORDER);
    for (c = 1; c <= Cols; c++)
      putchar(world[r][c] ? MARKER : ' ');
    putchar(BORDER);
    putchar('\n');
  }
  putborder(1 + Cols + 1);
  putchar('\n');
}

static void putborder(int n)
{
  int i;

  for (i = 1; i <= n; i++)
    putchar(BORDER);
  putchar('\n');
}
```

Figure 12.28   (outworld.c)   Display the contents of a generation.

A New Version Using Pointers

All of the functions in the current version of Life use traditional two-dimensional array subscripting. That makes it easy to write and easy to understand—and unbearably slow. When simulating large worlds, there is an annoying pause between successive generations. So we need to speed up the program. But how?

The program spends most of its time in **NextWorld**, calculating the next generation. **NextWorld** is devoted almost entirely to traversing a two-dimensional array. Since it accesses rows sequentially within the array, and array elements sequentially within rows, we should find a performance improvement if we use pointers to traverse the array.

Figure 12.29 contains the pointers we need. The basic idea is straightforward. We traverse the current world one row at a time, using a single row pointer, **cwrptr** (which

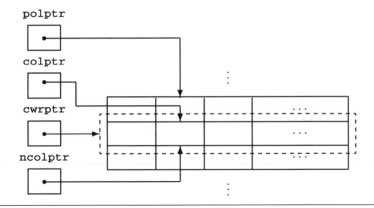

Figure 12.29 The pointers used to traverse a Life world.

stands for current world row pointer). We use another pointer, `colptr`, to process each row. The tricky part comes when we count the neighbors—we need to access elements in the rows preceding and following the one pointed to by `cwrptr`. To do this efficiently, we need two additional pointers, `pcolptr` and `ncolptr`, that point to the same column as `colptr`, but in the rows before and after it. As we traverse the current row, we increment these pointers as well.

Figure 12.30 contains the pointer version of `NextWorld`. This new version takes less than one-fifth the time of the original, an impressive savings. We leave making similar changes to `PutWorld` as an exercise for the reader.

SUMMARY

- C lets us have the elements of an array be arrays themselves.

- When we pass two-dimensional arrays as parameters, we have to specify the number of elements in each row, but not the number of rows.

- The name of a two-dimensional array is a pointer to its first element, which happens to be its first row.

- We can have pointers to rows and use them to traverse a two-dimensional array a row at a time. This lets us efficiently access a column.

- When we traverse a sequence of elements within a two-dimensional array, we can use pointers to items as if it were a one-dimensional array. This allows us to efficiently access each item in a row.

- We can often process rows of a two-dimensional array using existing functions designed to work with a one-dimensional array.

```
/*
 * Compute next generation, this time using pointers.
 */
#include "life.h"

int NextWorld(PTR_TO_CONST_WORLD curr, PTR_TO_WORLD next)
{
    PTR_TO_CONST_WORLD cwrptr = curr + 1;           /* 1st row curr world */
    PTR_TO_WORLD       nwrptr = next + 1;           /* 1st row next world */
    PTR_TO_CONST_WORLD endcwrptr = cwrptr + Rows;   /* last row curr world */
    int changed = 0;                                /* changes to world */
    int neighbors;                                  /* # of cell neighbors */

    for (Inhabs = 0; cwrptr <= endcwrptr; cwrptr++, nwrptr++)
    {
        const BOOLEAN *colptr    = cwrptr[0]  + 1;    /* current col */
        const BOOLEAN *pcolptr   = cwrptr[-1] + 1;    /* previous row */
        const BOOLEAN *ncolptr   = cwrptr[1]  + 1;    /* next row */
        const BOOLEAN *endcolptr = colptr + Cols;     /* last col */
        BOOLEAN *nxtptr          = nwrptr[0] + 1;     /* col in next */

        for (; colptr <= endcolptr; colptr++, nxtptr++, pcolptr++, ncolptr++)
        {
            neighbors =  pcolptr[-1] + pcolptr[0] + pcolptr[1] + colptr[-1] +
                         ncolptr[-1] + ncolptr[0] + ncolptr[1] + colptr[1];
            if ((neighbors == 3) || (neighbors == 2 && *colptr))
            {
                *nxtptr = TRUE;
                Inhabs++;
            }
            else
                *nxtptr = FALSE;
            changed += *nxtptr != *colptr;
        }
    }
    return changed;                                 /* nonzero if not stable */
}
```

Figure 12.30 (nxtwrld2.c) A new version of **nxtworld** that uses pointers to traverse the array.

- All of the techniques for accessing two-dimensional arrays can be generalized and used for higher-dimensional arrays.

- It's reasonable to use normal subscripting rather than pointers to traverse the elements of multidimensional arrays. Then, if the resulting programs needs to be sped up, these traverals should be rewritten to use pointers.

EXERCISES

12–1 To keep things simple, we've avoided using **const** in many of the programs in this chapter. Fix them to use **const** where it's appropriate.

12–2 Rewrite **read_scores** and **print_scores** (Figure 12.3) to use pointers.

12–3 We can improve **test_avg** (Figures 12.10 and 12.11) by treating it as a one-dimensional array and traversing it with a pointer. We initialize a pointer to the nth column and increment by **MAX_TESTS** to access the nth column of subsequent rows. Make this improvement.

12–4 Rewrite **PutWorld** (Figure 12.28) to traverse its array using pointers. Is it more efficient?

12–5 Modify life (Figure 12.25) so that it dynamically allocates space for the world. Can you make this version run even faster than ours?

12–6 Modify life (Figure 12.25) to check for an oscillating stable state in any of the last 10 generations. Use a three-dimensional array to hold the necessary generations.

12–7 Write a function to print the total values of each of the two-dimensional arrays contained in **classes** (Figure 12.18) There should be one value output for each two-dimensional array in **classes**.

12–8 Write a function, **read_student**, that reads in a student ID number, followed by the student's test scores. Use the student number to select the row in the array. Implement an appropriate error-testing and flagging mechanism.

12–9 Write a function, **print_tests**, that prints the elements of **scores**, one column per line. Each line of output contains all of the scores for a particular test.

12–10 Write a function to determine whether a particular square two-dimensional array is a magic square (all rows, columns, and diagonals add to the same value).

12–11 Write a function to determine whether a particular square two-dimensional array is an identity matrix (ones on the diagonal and zeros everywhere else). Can you write this function treating the array as though it is one-dimensional?

12–12 Write a function, **print_2d_rev**, that prints the values in a two-dimensional array in reverse order, last row first and first row last. First, write it using the usual array subscripting; then rewrite it so that the rows are indexed with a pointer. Finally, rewrite it so that all elements are indexed with pointers. Which of the three versions is the fastest?

12–13 Write a function, **sort_scores**, that takes a two-dimensional array of **int**s and a column to sort on and modifies the array so that the specified column is sorted from low to high.

12–14 Write a fast function to initialize an identity matrix. An identity matrix has ones on the diagonal and zeros everywhere else.

12–15 Write a fast function to compare a pair of two-dimensional arrays. The function should return a pointer to the first place where the arrays differ.

12–16 Write a function that dynamically allocates a two-dimensional array with the appropriate number of rows and columns. Any program using this function must declare the array it returns as a single pointer, not as a two-dimensional array.

12–17 Write a function that sums the elements in a three-dimensional array using a single pointer to traverse the array. How much faster is this than using three-dimensional subscripting?

12–18 Repeat the previous exercise for some higher-dimensional array. Can you generalize your function to work on any *N*-dimensional array? Explain why the function is substantially faster when pointers are used.

12–19 Write a function to calculate and print the average of each test by class. The order of output should be all the scores for the first test in the first class, then all the scores for the first test in the second class, and so on.

12–20 Write a library package that allows us to write to a two-dimensional array rather than the screen. The idea is that we perform numerous updates on this array (such as adding and deleting characters) and then do a library call to replace the screen with the contents of the array. Modify life so that it uses this package.

12–21 Write a program to supervise a tic-tac-toe game between two human players. It should request moves, display them, and notify them when the game is over. It should also be able to print a trace of all the moves the players made.

12–22 Write a program to play dealer in a blackjack game. Allow up to seven players.

12–23 Write a program to produce large block letters of the strings it's given as input. Represent each letter as a set of 1s and 0s in an 8 by 8 two-dimensional array. For example, an "I" would have all 1s in the top and bottom rows and 1s down the middle two columns of each row.

13 ARRAYS

OF

POINTERS

Our earlier programs have made ample use of arrays, We've seen arrays of integers, characters, and reals, as well as arrays of structures and arrays of arrays. This chapter examines another kind of array, arrays of pointers, concentrating on arrays of strings. We show how to initialize these arrays at compile time, how to construct them dynamically at run time, and how to use pointers to traverse them efficiently. We provide array subscripting and pointer indexing versions of functions to print and search arrays of strings. And we examine command-line argument processing, an important application of these arrays. The chapter concludes with an implementation of a string sorting program.

13.1   ARRAYS OF POINTERS—RAGGED ARRAYS

Two-dimensional arrays contain the same number of elements in each row. But same-size rows can be inefficient. Suppose we define a table that holds character strings for each of the days of the week.

```
char day_table[][10] =
    {
        {'m', 'o', 'n', 'd', 'a', 'y', '\0'},
        {'t', 'u', 'e', 's', 'd', 'a', 'y', '\0'},
        {'w', 'e', 'd', 'n', 'e', 's', 'd', 'a', 'y', '\0'},
        {'t', 'h', 'u', 'r', 's', 'd', 'a', 'y', '\0'},
        {'f', 'r', 'i', 'd', 'a', 'y', '\0'},
        {'s', 'a', 't', 'u', 'r', 'd', 'a', 'y', '\0'},
        {'s', 'u', 'n', 'd', 'a', 'y', '\0'}
    };
```

We have to declare each row to hold enough characters in the longest string. The problem is that we waste space in the rows containing shorter strings.

What we really want is an array whose rows can vary in length, called a *ragged array*. We can build a ragged array out of an array of pointers, making each entry in the array a pointer to a string.

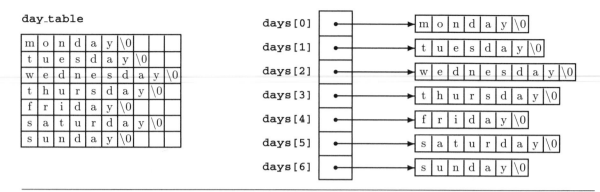

Figure 13.1   On the left is a two-dimensional array of characters with wasted space at the end of each row. On the right is an array of pointers to strings with no wasted space but with extra space used for the pointers.

We declare a d initialize a ragged array by supplying a list of character strings.

```
char *da;'s[] =
{
  "monday",  "tuesday", "wednesday", "thursday",
  "friday", "saturday", "sunday"
};
```

This declares **days** to be an array of pointers to characters.

Since we omitted the subscript from **days**, the compiler makes the array just large enough to hold the elements we supply. In this case, the compiler allocates space for an array containing seven pointers and assigns each element a pointer to the corresponding string. We access the elements of this array in exactly the same way we access the elements of an array of any other type. Figure 13.1 shows a table of days stored as a two-dimensional array and as a ragged array.

Figure 13.2 contains a program that prints a table of strings, one per line. To do so, it makes use of a function, **print_strings**, that is passed a table of character strings, along with the number of entries in the table, and prints the pointed-to strings, one per line. We're lazy, so we let the compiler calculate the number of items in **days** for us.

```
print_strings(days, sizeof(days)/sizeof(char *));
```

Figure 13.3 contains **print_strings**. It does the actual printing with **printf**, using the **%s** formatting code. The **%s** format expects a pointer to the first character of a string, which is exactly what each of the entries in **days** is.

Actually, because both the pointers **days** contains and the characters they point to are constant, we should really declare **days** with

```
const char * const days[]
```

Similarly, we should declare the **table** parameter in **print_strings** the same way.

```
/*
 * Main program that prints a table of days.
 */
#include <stdio.h>

char *days[] =
{
  "monday",  "tuesday", "wednesday", "thursday",
  "friday", "saturday", "sunday"
};

int main()
{
  void print_strings(char *table[], int n);

  print_strings(days, sizeof(days)/sizeof(char *));
  return 0;
}
```

Figure 13.2 (prdays.c) A program to print a table of days of the week, one per line.

```
/*
 * Print a table of strings, one per line.
 */
#include <stdio.h>

void print_strings(char *table[], int n)
{
  int i;

  for (i = 0; i < n; i++)
    printf("%s\n", table[i]);
}
```

Figure 13.3 (prstr1.c) Print a table of character strings, one per line, using `printf` to write the strings.

But using `const` with arrays of pointers tends to be confusing, so for now we'll just stick with our original declaration.

Accessing Individual Items

We haven't yet worried about accessing the individual items within a ragged array. In `print_strings`, for example, we simply pass a pointer to the beginning of the row (or string) we want to print. But imagine for the moment that we didn't have `printf`, and instead had to use `putchar` to write the characters. Then we would need to

```
/*
 *  Print a table of strings, one per line, using putchar.
 */
#include <stdio.h>

void print_strings(char *table[], int n)
{
  int i, j;

  for (i = 0; i < n; i++)
  {
    for (j = 0; table[i][j] != '\0'; j++)
      putchar(table[i][j]);
    putchar('\n');
  }
}
```

Figure 13.4   (prstr2.c)   Another version of our array printing function; this one uses `putchar`.

access each of the items in the string. Figure 13.4 contains a new implementation of **print_strings** written this way.

We're doing something curious in this version of **print_strings**: using two-dimensional subscripting to access individual characters in an array, even though its only a one-dimensional array. If **table** is an array of pointers to characters, **table[i][j]** refers to the **j**th character in its **i**th row. Why does this work? **table[i]** is a pointer to the first character in a string, so adding **j** to it gives a pointer to the **j**th character in the string. We can access the **j**th character with

```
*(table[i] + j)
```

which is equivalent to **table[i][j]**. Figure 13.5 provides a picture of how this expression works. More concretely, since **table[0]** is a pointer to the string **monday**, we can access the **'n'** with **table[0][2]**.

Although we can use two-dimensional accessing, we saw in the previous chapter it is better to avoid it wherever possible and use pointers instead. Figure 13.6 does just that in a new version of **print_strings**. This version uses a single pointer to a character, **ptr**, to traverse the individual strings it prints. We initialize **ptr** to point to the string's first character with

```
ptr = table[i]
```

This initialization works because each entry in **table** is a pointer to the first character in a string. Once we've assigned that pointer to **ptr**, we can traverse the string as we would traverse any other string. We dereference the pointer to access the individual characters and increment it to go on to the next one. This version takes about one-fourth the time of the previous version, making it worthwhile to try to eliminate two-dimensional array accessing wherever possible.

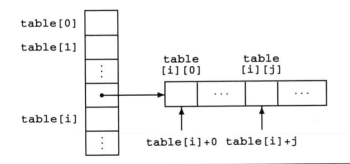

Figure 13.5 Accessing an individual character within an array of pointers to character strings.

```
/*
 * Print table of strings using pointers to traverse the string.
 */
#include <stdio.h>

void print_strings(char *table[], int n)
{
    int i;
    char *ptr;

    for (i = 0; i < n; i++)
    {
        for (ptr = table[i]; *ptr != '\0'; ptr++)
            putchar(*ptr);
        putchar('\n');
    }
}
```

Figure 13.6 (prstr3.c) A version of **print_strings** that uses a pointer to traverse the strings.

Dynamic String Allocation

Up to now, we have initialized our arrays of pointers at compile time, leaving the task of allocating space for the pointed-to strings to the compiler. We did this because we knew the contents of the table at compile time. But what about when the table's entries aren't known at compile time? We might, for example, want to write a program that sorts its input lines. The program must read its input into some kind of table in order to sort it. But what kind? Since some input lines are likely to be much longer than others, we don't want to use a two-dimensional array—it would waste too much space. Instead,

```
/*
 * Reverse input, one line at a time.
 */
#include <stdio.h>
#include <stddef.h>

#define  MAXLINES      100           /* lines to store */

int main()
{
  void print_rev_strings(char *table[], int n);
  int  read_strings(char *table[], int max);
  int  lines;                        /* input lines read */
  char *strings[MAXLINES];           /* array of pointers to strings */

  if ((lines = read_strings(strings, MAXLINES)) < 0)
    printf("Out of memory after reading %i lines\n", -lines);
  else
  {
    if (lines >= MAXLINES)
      printf("Only %i out of %i lines stored\n", MAXLINES, lines);
    print_rev_strings(strings, lines > MAXLINES ? MAXLINES : lines);
  }
  return lines < 0 || lines >= MAXLINES;
}
```

Figure 13.7   (revinp.c)   A program to reverse its input, one line at a time. It reads the input into a table of character strings and then prints that table in reverse order.

we need to read the input into an array of strings and allocate the space for each entry ourselves.

We write this sorting program at the end of the chapter. For now we illustrate run-time string allocation with a simple program, shown in Figure 13.7, to reverse its input. This program uses two functions, shown in Figure 13.8: **read_strings**, which reads its input into a table of strings, one line per string, and **print_rev_strings**, which prints the table of strings in reverse order.

read_strings takes a pair of parameters: an empty table of pointers and the maximum number of pointers that can fit in the table. It fills in the table with pointers to dynamically allocated strings containing the input lines and returns the number of lines read. **read_strings** uses **getline** to read each input line into an array **line**, and a new utility function, **makedupstr**, to make a dynamically allocated copy of **line**. If for some reason there's not enough memory to store the number of lines in the table, **read_strings** returns the negative of the lines read, leaving it to its caller to decide how to handle that situation.

makedupstr takes a pointer to a string, calls **malloc** to allocate enough storage for a copy of the string, and then uses **strcpy** to copy the string into the newly

```
/*
 * Functions to read and print string table.
 *    read_strings - read strings into table, dynamically allocating
 *       space for each string.  it indicates an out of memory error
 *       by returning the negative number of lines it successfully read.
 *    print_rev_strings - print table in reverse order.
 *    makedupstr - duplicate a single string.
 */
#include <stdio.h>
#include <string.h>
#include <stddef.h>                    /* for NULL */
#include <stdlib.h>                    /* for malloc */

#define  MAXLEN    80                  /* chars per line */

static char *makedupstr(const char *str);

int read_strings(char *table[], int max)
{
  int    getline(char *line, int n);
  int    lines;                        /* lines read */
  char   *sptr;                        /* ptr to space from malloc */
  char   line[MAXLEN + 1];             /* current input line */

  for (lines = 0; getline(line, MAXLEN) != -1; lines++)
    if (lines < max)
      if ((sptr = makedupstr(line)) != NULL)
        table[lines] = sptr;
      else
        return -lines;                 /* indicate out of memory error */
  return lines;
}

void print_rev_strings(char *table[], int n)
{
  while (--n >= 0)
    printf("%s\n", table[n]);
}

static char *makedupstr(const char *str)
{
  char *newstr = malloc(strlen(str) + 1);

  if (newstr != NULL)
    strcpy(newstr, str);
  return newstr;
}
```

Figure 13.8   (strtab.c)   Our functions to read and print tables of strings.

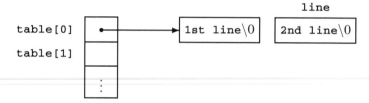

(a) The array after placing the first input line in it and reading the second input line.

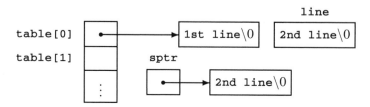

(b) The array after allocating space for the second input line and copying the line into that space.

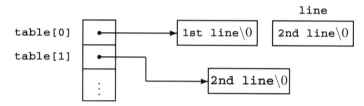

(c) The array after copying the line into that space and hooking the line into the table.

Figure 13.9   How we can build a table of strings dynamically at run time.

allocated storage. When it is all through, it returns a pointer to this newly created copy. **read_strings** takes this pointer and places it in the table. The result is that each table entry becomes a pointer to a block of storage allocated by **malloc** and containing a single input line. Figure 13.9 illustrates this process of reading a line and storing it in the table.

print_rev_strings is similar to **print_strings**, except that it prints the last element first and the first element last.

This program relies heavily on dynamic allocation, and on a small microcomputer it might easily run out of storage. What should we do when **makedupstr** (really **malloc**) fails? Unfortunately, there is no general solution, so we have to decide what to do on a case-by-case basis. Here, we take the easy way out: when **makedupstr** fails, we simply stop reading input and print an error message.

```
/*
 * Print a table of strings, one per line.
 */
#include <stdio.h>

void print_strings(char **ptr, int n)
{
  char **endptr = ptr + n;              /* ptr to just past last element */

  for (; ptr < endptr; ptr++)
    printf("%s\n", *ptr);
}
```

Figure 13.10   (prstr4.c) Yet another version of **print_strings**. This one uses a pointer to traverse the table of strings.

13.2   POINTERS AND ARRAYS OF POINTERS

In the previous section, we used normal array subscripting to traverse our arrays of pointers. We can, however, use pointers to traverse these arrays, just as we can with any other array. We do so in Figure 13.10, a new version of **print_strings**, our function to print a table of strings, one per line.

As before, we call **print_strings** by passing it an array of pointers to strings and the number of items in the array. But now we declare the array parameter differently.

```
print_strings(char **ptr, int n)
```

We've seen that when we pass an array, we are really passing a pointer to its first element. So when we pass an array of **int**s, we pass a pointer to an **int**. When we pass an array of **char**s, we pass a pointer to a **char**. And when we pass an array of pointers to characters, we pass a pointer to a pointer to a **char**, **ptr**'s type.

print_strings uses our standard method for traversing an array: We set a pointer, **ptr**, to the array's first element and keep incrementing it until it points just past the array's last element. As usual, we keep the pointer to the last element in **endptr**, which, like **ptr**, is also a pointer to a pointer to a character.

```
char **endptr = ptr + n;
```

Each time through the loop we want to pass **printf** a pointer to the first character in the next string in the table. Since **ptr** points to the string, we have to dereference it when we pass it to **printf**.

```
printf("%s\n", *ptr);
```

Figure 13.11 shows the relationship between these pointers.

As an additional example, we'll write a function, **search_strings**, to search an array of strings for a particular string. The function takes three arguments: a string to

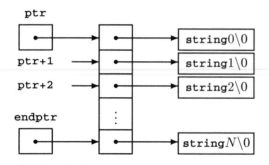

Figure 13.11   Using pointers to traverse an array of strings.

find, an array of pointers to strings, and the number of strings in the array. It returns a pointer to the matching table entry or **NULL** if no entry matches. We could, for example, use this function to determine whether an input line corresponded to one of the days of the week with

```
search_strings(line, days, 7)
```

Just like **print_strings**, it runs a pointer through a table of strings. The only difference is that now, instead of calling **printf**, it calls **strcmp**, the string library function that compares strings. Figure 13.12 contains a main program that shows how to use **search_strings**, Figure 13.13 shows an array-subscripting version of it, and Figure 13.14 shows a pointer-indexing version.

Both **print_strings** and **search_strings** simply pass a pointer to the next string to a function that processes it—they don't access the individual characters in the strings directly. But we can't always avoid doing that. Imagine once again that we don't have **printf**. Figure 13.15 is yet another version of **print_strings** that uses **putchar** to print the individual characters in the strings, this time using a pointer to traverse the array.

We access the individual characters in the string the same way we accessed individual elements when we had a row pointer. If we use a pointer **ptr** to traverse the array of strings, **(*ptr)[j]** refers to the jth character in whatever string **ptr** points to. Why? Because **ptr** points to an item in the table of pointers, ***ptr** is the value of that pointer, which means that ***ptr** is the address of the first character in the string. Adding **j** to ***ptr** gives us the address of the jth character, and dereferencing that with

```
*(*ptr + j)
```

gives us the character. This expression is equivalent to the previous one. Figure 13.16 shows what's going on here in more detail.

```
/*
 * Main program to test our string-searching function.
 */
#include <stdio.h>

#define MAXLEN 80

char *days[] =
  {"monday", "tuesday", "wednesday", "thursday",
   "friday", "saturday", "sunday"};
const int numdays = sizeof(days)/sizeof(days[0]);

int main()
{
  int        getline(char *line, int max);
  char       *search_strings(const char *target, char *t[], int n);
  const char *match;
  char       line[MAXLEN + 1];

  while (printf("Enter day of week: "), getline(line, MAXLEN) != -1)
    if ((match = search_strings(line, days, numdays)) != NULL)
      printf("%s is a day of the week\n", match);
    else
      printf("%s is not a day of the week.\n", line);
  return 0;
}
```

Figure 13.12 (testsrch.c) A main program using our string-searching function.

```
/*
 * Search table for given string, array-subscripting version.
 */
#include <stddef.h>
#include <string.h>

char *search_strings(const char *string, char *table[], int n)
{
  int i = 0;

  for (; i < n; i++)
    if (strcmp(table[i], string) == 0)
      return table[i];                    /* return pointer to match */
  return NULL;                            /* no match */
}
```

Figure 13.13 (srchstr1.c) An array subscripting version of **search_strings**.

```
/*
 * Search table for a given string, pointer-indexing version.
 */
#include <stddef.h>
#include <string.h>

char *search_strings(const char *string, char **ptr, int n)
{
  char **const endptr = ptr + n;

  for (; ptr < endptr; ptr++)
    if (strcmp(*ptr, string) == 0)
      return *ptr;                    /* return pointer to match */
  return NULL;                        /* no match */
}
```

Figure 13.14   (srchstr2.c)   A pointer indexing version of **search_strings**.

```
/*
 * Print a table of strings, one per line, using a pointer to
 * traverse the table.
 */
#include <stdio.h>

void print_strings(char **ptr, int n)
{
  char **endptr = ptr + n;       /* pointer to just past last element */
  int j;                         /* index to individual items */

  for(; ptr < endptr; ptr++)
  {
    for (j = 0; (*ptr)[j] != '\0'; j++)
      putchar((*ptr)[j]);
    putchar('\n');
  }
}
```

Figure 13.15   (prstr5.c)   Our final version of **print_strings**, which traverses the array using a pointer and accesses the characters in the strings indirectly through that pointer.

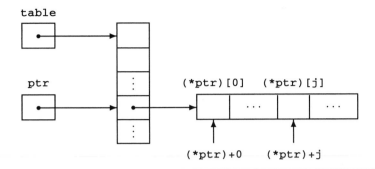

Figure 13.16 Accessing individual characters within an array of pointers to character strings when we're using a pointer to traverse them.

13.3 COMMAND-LINE ARGUMENTS

There is one important application of arrays of pointers that we haven't yet examined: they are used to store command-line arguments. When we run a program, such as the compiler or a text editor, we often provide not only the program's name but also the names of files the program will work with. The command, along with those file names, is known as a *command line*, and its individual components are *command-line arguments*.

How can a program access these arguments? It turns out that when **main** is called, it is passed two parameters that together describe the command line that invoked the program. The first is the number of arguments on the command line. The second is an array of pointers to strings containing the various arguments. Traditionally, these are called **argc** and **argv**, respectively. We declare **main**'s parameters in the same way as those of any other function.

```
int main(int argc, char *argv[])
```

By convention, **argv[0]** points to the first character of the program's name, so **argc** is always at least 1 (even so, some versions of C set the program's name to the null string). We use the other arguments to specify various program options, as well as external files the program should process. Exactly what constitutes a command-line argument varies from system to system, but individual arguments are usually delimited by white space. If you want white space within an argument, place the argument in quotes.

A Program to Echo Its Arguments

We illustrate command-line argument processing with a program called echo, which simply prints each of its arguments minus the program name. If we supply the command line

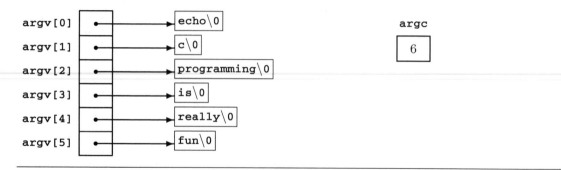

Figure 13.17   The initial values of **argc** and **argv** for our sample use of echo.

echo c programming is really fun

echo's output is

    c programming is really fun

For this command line, when **main** is called, **argc** is six and **argv** is an array of six pointers to strings, as shown in Figure 13.17.

Figure 13.18 contains a first, straightforward implementation of echo. It uses array indexing to traverse **argv** and prints each of the entries except the first (the program name). We write the arguments separated by spaces, with the last argument followed by a new line.

Figure 13.19 contains a second, trickier version. It uses a pointer to traverse **argv**. We can do this because **argv**, like any other array parameter, is really a pointer to the array's first element. We use our standard technique, setting a pointer, **argptr**, to point to the first array item in which we're interested (in this case, the one pointed to by **argv + 1**, since we want to skip the program name), repeatedly incrementing it to traverse the arguments, and stopping when it points to the end of the array.

As with other arrays, using a pointer to traverse command-line arguments makes our programs run faster—but harder to read and understand. Either method of command-line argument processing is acceptable, but you should master the pointer method, even if it isn't your favorite, as you will encounter it frequently in existing programs.

Command-Line Options

We'll illustrate the full power of command-line arguments with a program called ws, for word search. By default, ws prints all of the lines in its input that contain any of the strings provided as its arguments. So running with its source file as input and **BOOLEAN**, **TRUE**, and **FALSE** as its arguments results in its printing any line in ws.c that contains the words "BOOLEAN", "TRUE", or "FALSE".

```
/*
 * Echo arguments, using array subscripting.
 */
#include <stdio.h>

int main(int argc, char *argv[])
{
  int next;                                /* index to next argument */

  for (next = 1; next < argc; next++)
    printf("%s%c", argv[next], (next < argc - 1) ? ' ' : '\n');
  return 0;
}
```

Figure 13.18   (echo.c) Echo the program's arguments using array indexing.

```
/*
 * Echo arguments, using pointer indexing.
 */
#include <stdio.h>

int main(int argc, char *argv[])
{
  char **argptr        = argv + 1;      /* pointer to first argument */
  char **const endptr = argv + argc;    /* pointer to last argument */

  for (; argptr < endptr; argptr++)
    printf("%s%c", *argptr, (argptr < endptr - 1) ? ' ' : '\n');
  return 0;
}
```

Figure 13.19   (echo2.c) Echo the program's arguments using pointer indexing.

ws also allows some optional arguments. Traditionally, optional arguments begin with a dash ("-") or a slash ("/"), depending on which operating system you're using.[1] ws's options are -n to print only those lines that don't match, -c to print only a count of those lines that do or don't match (depending on whether -n is used with it), and -l to precede its output with a line number.

ws's design is typical of most programs that have options. The main program handles the options and a separate function handles all the real work, in this case doing the search. The two pieces communicate through constants and external variables declared in the header file. Figure 13.20 contains the header file ws.h, Figure 13.21 contains the main program, and Figure 13.22 contains the functions to do the actual searching.

---

[1]UNIX, for example, uses the dash, whereas MS-DOS uses the slash.

```
/*
 * Header file defining useful search constants and types.
 */
#include <stdio.h>
#include <string.h>

#define MAXLEN 80

typedef short BOOLEAN;

#define TRUE   1
#define FALSE  0

extern BOOLEAN PrintNumber;            /* current line number */
extern BOOLEAN PrintNoMatch;           /* print unmatched lines? */
extern BOOLEAN PrintCountOnly;         /* print match count only? */
```

Figure 13.20 (ws.h) Definitions of useful constants, types, and externals for the word-searching program.

main first processes the optional arguments. We know we're done with the optional arguments when we encounter an argument that doesn't begin with a dash. When an argument does begin with a dash, we examine the next character and set a flag to record the option's value. An unrecognized option causes us to write an error message and quit. (Our program could be improved by allowing more than one option to follow a single dash, but we leave that as an exercise.)

Once the options have been processed, we assume that any subsequent arguments are strings to process. We call a function search_input to do the searching, passing it a pointer to the first argument representing a word to find, along with the number of different words we're trying to find. It reads input lines with getline and uses a new function, find_match, to determine whether any of those words are in its input line. find_match simply runs through the various words, using strstr to see if any of them is a substring of the input line.

As before, we use pointers to process the arguments. Figure 13.23 shows the relationships between the various pointers used to process the arguments.

Command-line options are a powerful and useful idea. Many programs, however, use them to provide different and often unrelated features. These extra features are used infrequently, if at all, but they make the program significantly harder to read and debug. To avoid falling into this trap, first write a simple version of the program that performs its main task correctly. Add options only after the program has been in use for a while and it's become clear that adding certain features will make the program more useful.

```
/*
 * Search for strings provided in program's arguments.
 */
#include "ws.h"

BOOLEAN PrintNumber;                          /* line number */
BOOLEAN PrintNoMatch;                         /* print doesn't match lines */
BOOLEAN PrintCountOnly;                       /* just print match count */

int main(int argc, char *argv[])
{
  void  search_input(char *strtab[], int n);
  char **argptr         = &argv[1];     /* pointer to next real arg */
  char **const endptr   = &argv[argc];  /* pointer to past last arg */
  BOOLEAN badopt        = FALSE;        /* bad option flag */
  int     status        = 0;            /* return value */

  for (; argptr < endptr && (*argptr)[0] == '-'; argptr++)
    if ((*argptr)[1] == '\0')
      badopt = TRUE;
    else
      switch ((*argptr)[1])
        {                                       /* process next option */
          case 'c':
            PrintCountOnly = TRUE;
            break;
          case 'l':
            PrintNumber    = TRUE;
            break;
          case 'n':
            PrintNoMatch   = TRUE;
            break;
          default:
            printf("ws: bad option %c\n", (*argptr)[1]);
            badopt         = TRUE;
        }

  if (badopt || argptr >= endptr)                    /* oops */
  {
    printf("usage: ws [-c][-l][-n] patterns...\n");
    status = 1;
  }
  else
    search_input(argptr, endptr - argptr);
  return status;
}
```

Figure 13.21 (ws.c) The main part of our program to search its input for the words provided as its arguments.

```
/*
 * Do the actual search.
 *    search_input - see if any of the strings passed to it are in the
 *       program's input.
 *    find_match - find out if string is substring of any entry in table.
 *    display_line - write any matching lines.
 */
#include "ws.h"

static BOOLEAN find_match(const char *str, char *tab[], int n);
static void    display_line(const char *line, long lines);

void search_input(char *strptrs[], int n)
{
  int     getline(char *line, int maxlen);
  char    line[MAXLEN + 1];              /* holds next line */
  long    lines;                         /* count lines */
  long    matched_lines = 0L;            /* matched lines */
  BOOLEAN found;

  for (lines = 1; getline(line, MAXLEN) != -1; lines++)
  {
    found = find_match(line, strptrs, n);
    if ((found && !PrintNoMatch) || (!found && PrintNoMatch))
    {
      matched_lines++;
      if (!PrintCountOnly)
        display_line(line, lines);
    }
  }
  if (PrintCountOnly)
    printf("%li\n", matched_lines);
}

static BOOLEAN find_match(const char *str, char *tab[], int n)
{
  int i;

  for (i = 0; i < n; i++)
    if (strstr(str, tab[i]) != NULL)
      return TRUE;
  return FALSE;
}

static void display_line(const char *line, long lines)
{
  if (PrintNumber)
    printf("%li ", lines);
  printf("%s\n", line);
}
```

Figure 13.22   (wssrch.c) The functions that handle the actual searching.

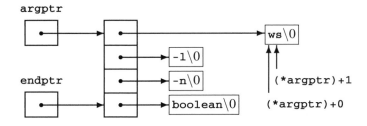

Figure 13.23   Processing the optional arguments. `argptr` points to the argument; `(*argptr)[i]` is the next character in the argument.

13.4   CASE STUDY—SORTING STRINGS

This section is optional!

We conclude this long and detailed chapter with a short but surprisingly useful program that sorts its input. To make the program more useful, we allow several options: -r reverses the sense of the sort, -bN begins sorting each string with the Nth character in the string, and -lN limits the sort to a field of N characters.

The main program, shown in Figure 13.24, consists almost entirely of function calls. It uses a new function **handle_options** to process any optional arguments. **handle_options**, shown in Figure 13.25, is similar to the main function in the searching program we wrote earlier in the chapter. It's passed pointers to the first and last entries in **argv** and uses the first pointer to traverse the argument array. When it encounters a -b or a -l, it uses **sscanf** to turn the subsequent characters into an integer. We could improve **handle_options** by making it do more error checking, as it currently ignores any unexpected characters. As before, we use a header file, shown in Figure 13.26, that defines various constants and externals shared by these files.

The program uses the function **sorted_read_strings** to read and sort the table of strings. This function, shown in Figure 13.27, extends our earlier **read_strings** function to use an insertion sort algorithm, similar to the one we used in Chapter 7. The program also uses **display_strings** to display the table in ascending or descending order. This function combines our earlier **print_strings** and **print_rev_strings** functions.

We're now careful to indicate those values that are constant and shouldn't be changed. In the prototype for **display_strings**, for example,

```
extern void display_strings(const char *const table[], int n);
```

we declare that both the pointers in **table** and the characters they point to are constants. Similarly, in the prototype for **handle_options**,

```
extern int  handle_options(const char *const *xptr,
                           const char *const *yptr);
```

we declare that **xptr** and **yptr** are pointers to constant pointers to constant characters.

```
/*
 * String sorting program.
 */
#include "sort.h"

BOOLEAN Reverse;                    /* flag: reverse sense of sort */
int     FieldCol = 0;               /* flag: starting column for sort */
int     FieldLen = MAXLEN;          /* flag: length of field to sort */

int main(int argc, char *argv[])
{
  char *strings[MAXLINES];              /* input lines */
  int   lines;                          /* count of input lines */
  int   status = 1;                     /* program return status */

  if (argc >= 1 && handle_options(argv + 1, argv + argc))
    if ((lines = sorted_read_strings(strings, MAXLINES)) < 0)
      printf("Out of memory after %i lines\n\n", -lines);
    else if (lines == MAXLINES)
      printf("More than %i lines of input\n\n", lines);
    else
    {
      display_strings(strings, lines);
      status = 0;
    }
  return status;
}
```

Figure 13.24   (sort.c) The main function of our string sorting program.

As a result, the compiler will complain if we try to modify the pointers to characters they point to or the characters themselves.

It's extra work to get our **const** declarations straight, but they're a big help in guarding against accidentally changing array elements.[2]

SUMMARY

- C allows us to have arrays of pointers, which are often called ragged arrays.

- We can initialize ragged arrays at compile time by providing a list of values or at run time by using dynamic allocation.

---

[2]In Chapter 12, we mentioned that some compilers complain when we pass non-**const** two-dimensional arrays to functions expecting **const** two-dimensional arrays. Those same compilers spit out similar warnings in similar situations involving arrays of pointers and pointers to pointers. Once again, we can either try to shut them up by using explicit casts to the constant type they expect, or we can go out and buy better compilers.

```c
/*
 * Handle various options.
 */
#include "sort.h"

int handle_options(const char *const *argptr, const char *const *endptr)
{
  BOOLEAN goodopt = TRUE;                /* flag to indicate bad option */

  for (; argptr < endptr && (*argptr)[0] == '-'; argptr++)
    if ((*argptr)[1] == '\0')
      printf("sort: missing option\n");
    else
      switch ((*argptr)[1])
        {                                /* process next option */
          case 'b':
            if (sscanf(*argptr + 2, "%i", &FieldCol) != 1)
            {
              printf("sort: invalid starting column\n");
              goodopt = FALSE;
            }
            break;
          case 'l':
            if (sscanf(*argptr + 2, "%i", &FieldLen) != 1)
            {
              printf("sort: invalid field length\n");
              goodopt = FALSE;
            }
            break;
          case 'r':
            Reverse = TRUE;              /* ignore anything after option */
            break;
          default:
            printf("sort: bad option %c\n", *argptr[1]);
            goodopt = FALSE;
        }

  if (argptr < endptr)
  {
    printf("sort: extra arguments\n");
    goodopt = FALSE;
  }

  if (!goodopt)
    printf("Usage: sort [-r] [-bNUM] [-eNUM]\n");
  return goodopt;
}
```

Figure 13.25   (sortopt.c)   The function to handle the various sort options.

```
/*
 * Define useful constants for string searcher.
 */
#include <stdio.h>
#include <stdlib.h>
#include <stddef.h>
#include <string.h>

typedef enum {FALSE, TRUE} BOOLEAN;

#define MAXLINES   1000
#define MAXLEN       80

extern BOOLEAN Reverse;
extern int     FieldCol;
extern int     FieldLen;

extern int  sorted_read_strings(char *table[], int n);
extern void display_strings(const char *const table[], int n);
extern int  handle_options(const char *const *xptr,
                           const char *const *yptr);
extern int  getline(char *line, int n);
```

Figure 13.26   (sort.h)   The definitions of constants and externals used by the sorting program.

- Although these ragged arrays are not stored as two-dimensional arrays, we can access their elements using two-dimensional array accessing.

- As with other arrays, we can use either array subscripting or pointer indexing to traverse ragged arrays.

- The arguments we type on the command line invoking the program are placed into an array of pointers **argv**. The number of arguments is placed into an integer **argc**.

EXERCISES

13–1   Rewrite the programs in this chapter to use **const** whenever it's appropriate.

13–2   Rewrite **read_strings** (Figure 13.8) to use a pointer to traverse the array. Do the same for **print_rev_strings** (also Figure 13.8).

13–3   Add a -r option to echo (Figures 13.18 and 13.19) that causes it to print its arguments in reverse order. First use array indexing; then use pointers.

13–4   Add two more options to echo (Figures 13.18 and 13.19): -n causes it to suppress the trailing newline; -s causes it to write each of its arguments on a separate line.

```
/*
 * Functions to read input strings using insertion sort.
 */
#include "sort.h"

static int linecmp(const char *x, const char *y)
{
  int i;

  for (i = 0; i < FieldCol && *x != '\0' && *y != '\0'; i++, x++, y++)
    ;
  return strncmp(x, y, FieldLen);
}

static void insert(const char *a[], const char *str, int n)
{
  int pos;

  for (pos = n; pos > 0 && linecmp(str, a[pos - 1]) < 0; pos--)
    a[pos] = a[pos - 1];
  a[pos] = str;
}

int sorted_read_strings(char *table[], int max)
{
  char *sptr;                    /* pointer to malloc-allocated space */
  char line[MAXLEN + 1];         /* current input line */
  int  lines = 0;                /* number of lines read */
  int  len;                      /* length of current line */

  for (; (len = getline(line, MAXLEN)) != -1 && lines >= 0; lines++)
    if (lines < max)
      if ((sptr = malloc(len + 1)) != NULL)
        insert(table, strcpy(sptr,line), lines);
      else
        lines = -lines;          /* indicate out of memory error */
  return lines;
}

void display_strings(const char *const table[], int n)
{
  int i;

  if (!Reverse)
    for (i = 0; i < n; i++)            /* print table in forward order */
      printf("%s\n", table[i]);
  else
    while (--n >= 0)                   /* print table in reverse order */
      printf("%s\n",table[n]);
}
```

Figure 13.27   (sortstrs.c)   The heart of our sorting program.

13–5 Add three new options to Chapter 10's uniq program. The first, **-c**, causes a count of the number of occurrences of any line of output to be printed before the line. The second, **-u**, causes only those lines that appear uniquely to be output. The last, **-d**, causes only those lines that are duplicated to appear in the output. What should uniq do when combinations of these options are specified?

13–6 Add an option to the sorting program (Figures 13.24 and 13.25) that allows it to sort numerically.

13–7 Write a function, **print_table_len**, that prints the length of each character string in a table of character strings.

13–8 Write a function, **reverse_tab**, that reverses each of the strings in a table of strings.

13–9 Write a function, **delete_tab**, that removes and returns a particular string from a table of strings.

13–10 Write a function, **tab_bytes**, that returns the total amount of bytes used by a table of strings. This size includes the space taken up by pointers and the space used up by the characters in the strings.

13–11 Write a function, **month_name**, that takes a single-integer argument and returns a pointer to the associated month name. The month names should be kept in a **static** table of character strings local to the function.

13–12 Write a program, tail, that prints the last *n* lines of its input (*n* is a program constant). Use the program in Figure 13.7 as a model. Make reasonable assumptions about the maximum line length and the maximum number of lines in the input (using the constants **MAXLEN** and **MAXLINES**, respectively). Be sure to test the return from **malloc** and do something reasonable if it fails.

13–13 Write a program to count the number of words, lines, and characters in its input. Provide options to request any subset of these counts.

13–14 Write a program that reads a sequence of numbers and writes their values out in English. Your program should work for any input value between 0 and 9999. Here's some sample input and output:

```
16
sixteen
567
five hundred sixty seven
9987
nine thousand nine hundred eighty seven
```

13–15 Write a program that reads a sequence of numeric dates and writes them out in English. The numeric date includes the month, day, and year, as well as the day of the week (with Sunday indicated with a 0 and Saturday with a 7). Here's some sample input and output:

```
4/7/92-3
Tuesday, April 7th, 1992.
12/25/92-6
Friday, December 25th, 1992.
```

Part IV

ADVANCED PROGRAM STRUCTURE

14 FUNCTIONS REVISITED

One of C's strengths is that functions are easy to define and use. This chapter discusses functions in great detail, concentrating on the aspects of parameter passing we have so far ignored. We also show how to simulate call-by-reference parameter passing and how to write functions that can take a variable number of arguments. We introduce pointers to functions and use them to pass functions as parameters. We present recursive functions, using them to compute factorials and permutations. And we discuss the difference between ANSI-C function prototypes and old-style C function declarations. The chapter concludes with a case study that implements an interesting and useful recursive algorithm, binary search.

14.1   SIMULATING CALL BY REFERENCE

We have seen that C passes parameters by value. When we call a function, C allocates space for its parameters and copies the values passed as the function's arguments. When the function returns, this space is deallocated. This means that *a function cannot change the values of its arguments*. In fact, we can treat parameters as though they are local variables, conveniently initialized by the calling function. This allows us to pass arbitrary expressions and prevents us from accidentally modifying a function's arguments.

But what do we do when we have a function like **scanf** that needs to modify a variable in its caller? Simply changing the value of a parameter doesn't work, since such changes are local. Instead, we must use **&** to pass a pointer to the variable. The function then dereferences the pointer with ***** to access or modify the variable's value.

The swap Function

Figure 14.1 contains a function **swap** that's designed to exchange the values of two integer variables. Because of *call by value*, however, this version of **swap** doesn't do what we want. It swaps the values of its parameters **x** and **y**, but does not affect the values **s** and **t** passed to it by the main program. Here's the program's unpleasant output:

```
/*
 * A program that doesn't exchange two values.
 */
#include <stdio.h>

int main()
{
  void swap(int x, int y);
  int s, t;

  s = 10; t = 20;
  printf("Before swap, s=%i, t=%i\n", s, t);
  swap(s, t);
  printf("After swap, s=%i, t=%i\n", s, t);
  return 0;
}

/* Incorrectly exchanges only values of its parameters */

void swap(int x, int y)
{
  int temp;

  temp = x;  x = y;  y = temp;
}
```

Figure 14.1   (badswap.c)   An incorrect version of swapping function along with a program that uses it.

```
Before swap, s=10, t=20
After swap, s=10, t=20
```

To get **swap** to exchange the values of variables in its calling function, we have to pass it their addresses and modify it to exchange the values indirectly through these pointers. Figure 14.2 contains a corrected version of **swap** and an example call. Now the program's more pleasing output is:

```
Before swap, s=10, t=20
After swap, s=20, t=10
```

Figure 14.3 illustrates how this new version of **swap** works, assuming that the addresses of **s** and **t** are 1000 and 2000, respectively, **s** is 5, and **t** is 10. When **swap** is called, **xptr** becomes 1000 and **yptr** becomes 2000, the addresses of **s** and **t**. The assignment **temp = *xptr** places the value in location 1000 (5) into **temp**. Similarly, ***xptr = *yptr** assigns to location 1000 the value in location 2000 (10), and ***yptr = temp** completes the exchange by placing **temp**'s contents (5) in location 2000.

```
/*
 * A program that does exchange two values.
 */
#include <stdio.h>

int main()
{
  void swap(int *xptr, int *yptr);
  int s, t;

  s = 10; t = 20;
  printf("Before swap, s=%i, t=%i\n", s, t);
  swap(&s, &t);
  printf("After swap, s=%i, t=%i\n", s, t);
  return 0;
}

/* Correctly exchanges a pair of values in caller */

void swap(int *xptr, int *yptr)
{
  int temp;

  temp = *xptr;  *xptr = *yptr;  *yptr = temp;
}
```

Figure 14.2 (swap.c) Correct version of the swapping function and a program that uses it.

Some Common Mistakes

There are several common mistakes when dealing with pointer parameters. Most of these mistakes, however, are simply type mismatches that the compiler will detect for us so long as we supply appropriate prototypes.

The first is failing to pass a pointer to a function that expects one. Doing so here, as in

```
    swap(s, t);
```

would cause **swap** to try to exchange the values in addresses 5 and 10, which is not at all what we want. For **swap** to work correctly, we must pass it the *addresses* of the variables whose values are to be exchanged, not the values themselves. Passing the variables themselves is likely to cause an addressing exception.

> *Don't fail to pass a pointer to a function that expects one.*

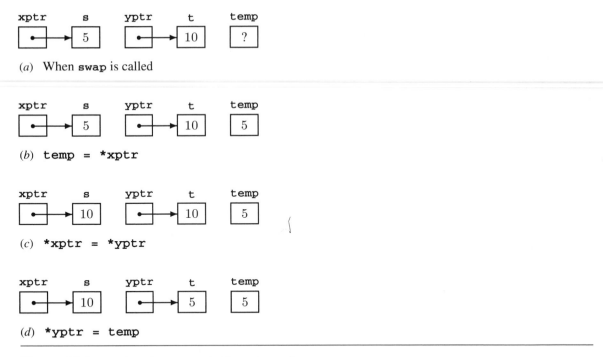

Figure 14.3   Exchanging two variables using pointers.

The second is to use a pointer as an integer in one place and as a pointer in another. One way we can avoid this problem is by first writing the function without any pointer parameters. We can then transform the appropriate parameters into pointers by renaming them to reflect their new use and then replacing all their uses with the appropriate pointer name, preceded by a *****. In fact, this is how we got the correct version of **swap** from the incorrect one. We replaced the **int** variables **x** and **y** with the pointer variables **xptr** and **yptr** and preceded all uses of these pointers with *****. Although it is not necessary for **swap**, we may have to parenthesize references through pointer variables to guarantee the desired order of evaluation.

> *Don't forget to dereference pointer parameters when you need to access their values.*

Figure 14.4 provides an example of one other common problem. It contains a function, **table_reverse**, to reverse an array in place. We have written it to use pointers to traverse the array and to use **swap** to exchange array elements. **table_reverse** uses **swap** to exchange the values pointed to by **ptr** and **lastptr**—but does so incorrectly. We are mistakenly passing the addresses of **ptr** and **lastptr** to **swap**— even though **ptr** and **lastptr** already contain the addresses of the values **swap**

```
/*
 * Reverse a table, using "swap" incorrectly.
 */
#include <stdio.h>

int main()
{
  void       table_reverse(int *ptr, int n);
  int        table[] = {56, 84, 51, 78, 11, 96, 38, 24, 35, 9};
  const int  entries = sizeof(table)/sizeof(table[0]);
  int        i;

  table_reverse(table, entries);
  for (i = 0; i < entries; i++)                    /* dump table */
    printf("%i\n", table[i]);
  return 0;
}

void table_reverse(int *ptr, int n)
{
  void swap(int *xptr, int *yptr);
  int *lastptr = ptr + n - 1;

  for (; lastptr > ptr; lastptr--, ptr++)
    swap(&ptr, &lastptr);                          /* wrong! */
}

void swap(int *xptr, int *yptr)
{
  int temp;

  temp = *xptr, *xptr = *yptr, *yptr = temp;
}
```

Figure 14.4 (oops.c) A problematic function to reverse an array in place. It uses **swap** incorrectly.

should exchange. Since we already have the pointers we need, we do not want to take their addresses. The correct call to **swap** is

```
swap(ptr, lastptr);
```

Try drawing a picture of what's happening here and trace through it by hand.

> *Don't pass a pointer's address instead of the pointer itself.*

```
/*
 * Return largest and smallest array values through pointer parameters.
 */
#include <stdio.h>
#include <limits.h>

int main()
{
  void       minmax(const int table[], int n, int *minptr, int *maxptr);
  const int table[] = {10, 56, 79, -21, 51, 5, 64, 70, 0, -10};
  const int entries = sizeof(table)/sizeof(table[0]);
  int        min, max;

  minmax(table, entries, &min, &max);
  printf("min=%i, max=%i\n", min, max);
  return 0;
}

void minmax(const int table[], int n, int *minptr, int *maxptr)
{
  int i;
  int min = INT_MAX;
  int max = INT_MIN;

  for (i = 0; i < n; i++)
    if (table[i] < min)
      min = table[i];
    else if (table[i] > max)
      max = table[i];
  *minptr = min;
  *maxptr = max;
}
```

Figure 14.5   (minmax.c) A function to find the smallest and largest values in an array, along with a main program that uses it.

Avoiding These Common Mistakes

Figure 14.5 contains **minmax**, a function that takes a table of **int**s and determines its minimum and maximum values. That means it needs some way to return both these values. One way is to directly return the minimum as its value and return the maximum indirectly through a pointer parameter. But we prefer using the same mechanism for returning both values, so we return both through pointer parameters. The problem is that having several pointer parameters increases our chances of making a mistake such as forgetting to dereference the pointer. So we want to minimize our accesses through the pointers. Our trick is to use local variables, **min** and **max**, throughout the function and only at the end of the function to return their values through the pointers.

Figure 14.6 shows another approach that seemingly eliminates the pointers entirely.

```
/*
 * Return largest and smallest array values thru another array parameter.
 */
#include <stdio.h>
#include <limits.h>

enum index {MIN, MAX};

int main()
{
  void      minmax(const int table[], int n, int results[]);
  const int table[] = {10, 56, 79, -21, 51, 5, 64, 70, 0, -10};
  const int entries = sizeof(table)/sizeof(table[0]);
  int       results[2];

  minmax(table, entries, results);
  printf("min=%i, max=%i\n", results[MIN], results[MAX]);
  return 0;
}

void minmax(const int table[], int n, int results[])
{
  int i;
  int min = INT_MAX;
  int max = INT_MIN;

  for (i = 0; i < n; i++)
    if (table[i] < min)
      min = table[i];
    else if (table[i] > max)
      max = table[i];
  results[MIN] = min;
  results[MAX] = max;
}
```

Figure 14.6 (minmax2.c) A new version of our function to find the smallest and largest values in an array, along with a main program that uses it.

We pass a two-element array to **minmax** and let it store the minimum and maximum values in the array. Of course, we're still using a pointer, but it's completely hidden. The drawback is that **main** has to refer to these values through the array, which requires subscripting and is somewhat less convenient than accessing **int** variables directly.

Figure 14.7 shows one final version of **minmax**. This time we don't pass the function an array to hold **min** and **max**. Instead, we've rewritten it to keep the array as a local, **static** variable and to return a pointer to that array. The advantages are that we have fewer parameters to worry about and that the function appears as though it's returning an array (even though it's really just returning a pointer). The main disadvantages are that we're still dealing with a pointer as the return value and that we have to refer to

```
/*
 * Return largest and smallest array values through a pointer
 * to an internal static array.
 */
#include <stdio.h>
#include <limits.h>

enum index {MIN, MAX};

int main()
{
  int        *minmax(const int table[], int n);
  const int table[] = {10, 56, 79, -21, 51, 5, 64, 70, 0, -10};
  const int entries = sizeof(table)/sizeof(table[0]);
  int        *resptr = minmax(table, entries);

  printf("min=%i, max=%i\n", resptr[MIN], resptr[MAX]);
  return 0;
}

int *minmax(const int table[], int n)
{
  static int results[2];
  int        i;
  int        min = INT_MAX;
  int        max = INT_MIN;

  for (i = 0; i < n; i++)
    if (table[i] < min)
      min = table[i];
    else if (table[i] > max)
      max = table[i];
  results[MIN] = min;
  results[MAX] = max;
  return results;
}
```

Figure 14.7   (minmax3.c) One final version of our function to find the smallest and largest values in an array, along with a main program that uses it.

the minimum and maximum values through the pointer. But returning a pointer to a **static** also makes our program more fragile. That's because it forces us to save the values if we need them and we need to call the function again.

So which approach to returning more than one value should you use? We favor just biting the bullet and using pointers, primarily because that way there are no extra arrays or array subscripting to worry about. In addition, the array approaches only makes sense when trying to return more than one value of the same type, so there are times you're going to be stuck using pointers anyways.

14.2 OLD-STYLE DECLARATIONS AND DEFINITIONS

So far, all our function calls have been preceded by a function prototype that specifies the number and types of its parameters, and the type of its return value. These prototypes let the compiler perform extensive type checking and automatic conversions. The compiler can verify that we are calling the function with the correct number of arguments, that these arguments are of the right type, and that we are using the function's return value correctly. They also let the compiler automatically convert the types of the function's arguments to the types of its formal parameters, as well as do any appropriate arithmetic and assignment conversions on the function's return value.

But C hasn't always had function prototypes. They are a new feature of ANSI-C. Earlier versions of C didn't let us specify complete prototypes when declaring functions, only their return values. They also had a slightly different syntax for defining functions. This was problematic, since without complete prototypes the compiler couldn't do type checking or automatic conversions. Even so, ANSI-C allows these *old-style* declarations and definitions—after all, there was more than a decade of C development without prototypes. Ideally, all the programs we encounter will use complete prototypes, as in our examples, but they aren't required to do so. That makes it worth taking a look at how to use pre-ANSI functions and what happens when we mix both styles.

In an old-style function definition, we provide only the parameter names, and not their types. On subsequent lines we provide variable declarations for each of the parameters.

```
return-type func-name (name-1, name-2, ..., name-n)
    parm-decl-1;
    parm-decl-2;
        ...
    parm-decl-n;
{
    function-body
}
```

Figure 14.8 contains an old-style definition of **inrange**, a function that returns zero if its last argument doesn't fall between its first two. Here's its header:

```
int inrange(min, max, value)
double min, max, value;
```

ANSI C's syntax is more compact—we don't have to list the parameter names and then provide declarations for them—but forces us to declare the type of each parameter separately.

In an old-style function prototype, we provide the function's return type, its name, and parentheses, but we don't list the parameter types.

```
return-type func-name ()
```

We need the parentheses, even if the function has no parameters, since they indicate that we are declaring a function, not just a variable. Figure 14.8 also contains an old-style

```
/*
 * A program to check if one value is between two others, using
 * old-style declarations.  But it doesn't work.
 */
#include <stdio.h>
```

```
int main()
{
  int inrange();                                  /* old-style prototype */
  int inpval;

  printf("Enter a value: ");
  scanf("%i", &inpval);
  printf("%i is %s range!\n",
         inpval, inrange(1, 100, inpval) ? "in" : "out of");
  return 0;
}

int inrange(min, max, value)
double min, max, value;                           /* old-style parameters */
{
  return value >= min && value <= max;
}
```

Figure 14.8   (inrange.c) An example of C's old-style declarations. This program doesn't work because **inrange**'s arguments aren't automatically converted.

prototype for **inrange**.

```
        int inrange();
```

There's one final difference between the styles. In ANSI-C, when a function takes no parameters, we use **void** as the parameter list in both the function header and prototype. But in pre-ANSI C, we simply leave the parameter list empty. In ANSI-C, such a declaration is taken to mean that we're providing no information about the function's parameters.

Type Checking Problems

When we use an old-style function prototype, we aren't supplying information about the types of the function's parameters. This means that there can be no assignment conversions of function arguments—the compiler has no idea what type the function expects. And it means that parameter passing works correctly only when there are no type mismatches—each argument must be the same type as its corresponding parameter. To avoid errors resulting from type mismatches, we must do any needed conversions ourselves.

> *With old-style declarations and definitions, type mismatches usually go undetected at compile time.*

The result is strange run-time behavior, not an informative compiler error message. Consider what happens when we call **inrange** as shown in Figure 14.8. Surprisingly, the "out of range" message is almost always printed, regardless of the value of **inpval** we pass to **inrange**. Why? Because **inrange** expects its parameters to be **double**s (usually 8 bytes in floating point representation) and instead receives **int**s (usually 2 or 4 bytes in two's complement representation):

```
if (inrange(1, 100, inpval))
```

As a result, on many machines, regardless of the values passed, **min** and **max** are always zero—clearly, not what we intended.

What does it take to fix this problem? We simply have to do the conversions ourselves. Here, we can correct things by making sure that all the arguments are **double**s:

```
if (inrange(1.0, 100.0, (double) inpval))
```

All floating point constants are **double**s, and the cast converts **inpval**'s value to a **double** before it is passed as a parameter.

Automatic Conversions

We don't really have to do *all* the conversions ourselves. When we don't supply a function prototype and we use old-style function definitions, C turns any **char** or **short** argument into an **int** and converts any **float** argument into a **double**. That means that we never need to declare **char**, **short**, or **float** parameters—we can declare them as **int** or **double** instead.

Figure 14.9 shows a new call to **inrange** that takes advantage of these conversions. Even though we don't bother to supply a prototype and even though **lowval**, **highval**, and **inpval** are **float**s, the function call works correctly.

```
if (inrange(lowval, highval, inpval))
```

That's because when we pass these values, they are converted automatically to **double**s.

These automatic conversions explain why **printf** has only a single formatting control code for printing real values. Effectively, **printf** is written in the old style, with an old-style function declaration. So when we pass a **float**, it's automatically converted to a **double**. That's also why we can use **%c** and **%i** to print **char**s, **short**s, and **int**s. The compiler is automatically converting these values to **int**s and using the formatting code to decide how to print them.

Do these conversions mean that we can't have **char**, **short**, or **float** parameters? After all, the automatic conversions guarantee that there's no way the value we pass is going to have one of these types. In fact, early C compilers allowed these parameter types, but quietly redeclared them. A **char** parameter, for example, became an **int**,

```
/*
 * Another version of our range-checking program that uses
 * old-style declarations.  But this one works correctly.
 */
#include <stdio.h>

int main()
{
  int inrange();                          /* old-style prototype */
  float inpval, lowval = 0.0, highval = 100.0;

  printf("Enter a value: ");
  scanf("%f", &inpval);
  printf("%f is %s range!\n",
         inpval, inrange(lowval, highval, inpval) ? "in" : "out of");
  return 0;
}

int inrange(min, max, value)
double min, max, value;                   /* old-style parameters */
{
  return value >= min && value <= max;
}
```

Figure 14.9   (inrange2.c)   Another call of `inrange` with a parameter type mismatch.

with a cast inserted wherever it was used. If we use old-style declarations, we get the same behavior with ANSI-C compilers.

Parameters and Portability

Old-style declarations and sloppy programming can lead to all sorts of problems, including programs that work on one machine but fail on another. Consider the version of `inrange` shown and invoked in Figure 14.10. This version expects `long` arguments. On 32-bit machines, `int` and `long` are usually the same size (32 bits), and the code works as expected. But we get strange results on machines where `int` is one word and `long` is two. How can we make this program work correctly on all machines? Simply use `long` constants or cast the arguments appropriately:

```
        if (!inrange(1L, 100L, (long) inpval))
```

Mixing Styles

What happens when we mix styles? That is, what happens when we use an ANSI-C function definition, but fail to provide a prototype? Or provide a complete prototype with an old-style definition?

```
/*
 * A version of our range-checking program that works sometimes,
 * but isn't portable.
 */
#include <stdio.h>

int main()
{
  int inrange();                            /* old-style prototype */
  int inpval;

  printf("Enter a value: ");
  scanf("%i", &inpval);
  printf("%i is %s range!\n",
         inpval, inrange(1, 100, inpval) ? "in" : "out of");
  return 0;
}

int inrange(min, max, value)
long min, max, value;                       /* old-style parameters */
{
  return value >= min && value <= max;
}
```

Figure 14.10 (inrange3.c) Yet another version of our range-checking function. This program isn't portable because it assumes that `long`s and `int`s are the same size.

There are two different situations to worry about. The first is *failing to provide a prototype*. In Figure 14.11, we provide an old-style prototype and a ANSI-C definition. There, we're calling **inrange** with three **float** arguments. Since we defined **inrange** to take three **float**s, there shouldn't be a problem, right? Wrong. Because we didn't provide a prototype before the call to **inrange**, C automatically converts the **float**s to **double**s. But because we used an ANSI-C definition, the function expects **float**s, not **double**s, and we get anomalous results. On typical machines, three 64-bit quantities are passed but three 32-bit values are expected within the function.[1]

The other case is *supplying a prototype with an old-style header*. Figure 14.12 shows another version of **inrange** where we provide a complete prototype but use an old-style function definition. In that case, since we provide a full prototype, when we call **inrange**, C will pass **float**s. But since we declare **inrange** using the old style, the function expects to be passed **double**s, which it will then convert to **float**s—not at all the behavior we want.

---

[1]Strictly speaking, the result is undefined, which means you've done something questionable the C compiler isn't required to catch. Some compilers will catch this error, but not if the function and prototype are placed in separate files.

```
/*
 * A disastrous version of our range-checking program.  This one
 * doesn't work at all.
 */
#include <stdio.h>
```

```
int main()
{
  int inrange();                              /* old-style prototype */
  float inpval, lowval = 1.0, highval = 100.0;

  printf("Enter a value: ");
  scanf("%f", &inpval);
  printf("%f is %s range!\n",
         inpval, inrange(lowval, highval, inpval) ? "in" : "out of");
  return 0;
}

int inrange(float min, float max, float value)
{
  return value >= min && value <= max;
}
```

Figure 14.11   (inrange4.c)   Incorrectly mixing styles by failing to use the correct prototype.

Prototypes versus Old-Style Declarations

Function prototypes help the compiler catch mismatches between numbers and types of parameters. Prototypes also have several other benefits: they help document a function's arguments, making programs that use them easier to read, and they may make programs run more efficiently, since they prevent automatic conversions of **float** arguments to **double** and of **char** arguments to **int**.

But there is one big problem with function prototypes: What do we do if we have to port programs written with them to older, pre-ANSI compilers that don't allow them? It is easy to remove all of the prototypes—but it is much more difficult to find all the places where successful parameter passing relies on the automatic conversions that prototypes make possible. When a program has to work with less sophisticated compilers, use explicit casts to ensure that the types of parameters match the function definition.[2]

---

[2]The general topic of portability—moving programs from machine to machine—is one we explore in great depth in Chapter 20. In particular, we'll see how to minimize the problems inherent in moving programs from compilers that support function prototypes to those that don't.

```
/*
 * Another disasterous version of our range-checking program.
 * This one also doesn't work at all.
 */
#include <stdio.h>

int main()
{
  int inrange(float min, float max, float value);
  float inpval, lowval = 1.0, highval = 100.0;

  printf("Enter a value: ");
  scanf("%f", &inpval);
  printf("%f is %s range!\n",
         inrange(lowval, highval, inpval) ? "in" : "out of");
  return 0;
}

int inrange(min, max, value)
float min, max, value;                       /* old-style parameters */
{
  return value >= min && value <= max;
}
```

Figure 14.12 (inrange5.c) Again incorrectly mixing styles by failing to use the correct prototype. The compiler catches the error.

14.3   PASSING VARIABLE NUMBERS OF ARGUMENTS

All functions we've written so far take a fixed number of arguments—but we've used functions, such as **scanf** and **printf**, that take a variable number of arguments. To see how these functions are written, we'll write a function, **max**, that returns the largest value in the group of values provided as its arguments. Figure 14.13 contains **max**, along with an example call.

How can **max** figure out how many arguments it was actually passed? **scanf** and **printf** figure out how many arguments they have and what their types are by examining the control string. An alternative is to supply the number of arguments as a parameter, and that's what we've done with **max**. Its first argument is the number of additional arguments. To indicate that these other arguments are arbitrary both in number and type, we use three dots (...) as the last parameter type in both the function header and the prototype.

```
        int max(int argcnt, ...)
```

Tell compiler not to complain if arguments don't match.

3 dots

To write functions with variable numbers of arguments, we need to include the system header file stdarg.h. It supplies a new data type, **va_list**, and a set of functions (macros, actually) that we use to access the undeclared arguments. The idea

```
/*
 * Illustrate variable argument "max" function.
 */
#include <stdio.h>
#include <stdarg.h>
#include <limits.h>

int main()
{
  int max(int argcnt, ...);

  printf("%i\n", max(5,1,7,3,4,2));
  printf("%i\n", max(10,87,91,18,34,65,89,99,45,99,56));
  return 0;
}

/* Return maximum value of its arguments */

int max(int argcnt, ...)
{
  va_list   argptr;              /* argument pointer */
  int       nextarg;             /* next variable argument */
  int       i;                   /* argument count */
  int       biggest = INT_MIN;   /* largest value*/

  va_start(argptr, argcnt);
  for (i = 0; i < argcnt; i++)
    if ((nextarg = va_arg(argptr, int)) > biggest)
      biggest = nextarg;
  va_end(argptr);
  return biggest;
}
```

pre-define values (handwritten annotation)

free up memory address. (handwritten annotation)

Figure 14.13   (max.c) An example function that takes a variable number of arguments.

is that we use a special pointer to traverse the arguments; these functions allow us to obtain and update that pointer.

We begin by declaring this pointer to have type **va_list**. The pointer can have any name, but we like to use **argptr**, which stands for "pointer to an argument list".

```
        va_list argptr;                    /* pointer to argument list */
```

We initialize the pointer with **va_start**, which takes two arguments. The first is the argument pointer (of type **va_list**), and the other is the name of the last parameter in the function definition (the one that appears before the three dots).

```
        va_start(argptr, argcnt);
```

This call makes **argptr** point just past **max**'s first argument, **argcnt**.

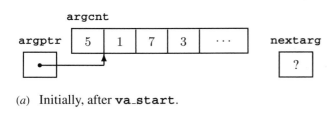

(a) Initially, after **va_start**.

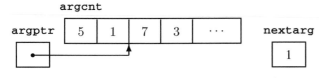

(b) After the first call to **va_arg**.

Figure 14.14 Processing **max**'s arguments.

> *Be sure to call* **va_start** *before trying to access the variable arguments.*

Now we have to run through the arguments, one at a time. We use **va_arg** to do this. It also takes two arguments, the argument pointer, **argptr**, and the *type* of the next argument.[3] It updates **argptr** to point to the next argument and then returns the value of the thing **argptr** used to point to (an item of *type*). This value is the next argument in the variable argument list. The type can be any of the C's types except **short**, **char**, and **float**, since these are automatically promoted to **int** and **double** when we don't provide their type explicitly in the function declaration. Here, *type* is always an **int**.

```
nextarg = va_arg(argptr, int)
```

Figure 14.14 illustrates this process.

When we've finished processing arguments, we call **va_end**.

```
va_end(argptr);
```

It turns out this call does nothing in many versions of C. So why do we need it? We don't if our program is only compiled with those versions of C. But on some machines with some compilers, **va_end** may reset some previously changed state information.[4] To be portable, make sure you include the **va_end** when you're done processing the arguments.

---

[3]It can take a type because it's actually a macro, not a function. We discuss macros in Chapter 15.

[4]Specifically, it may have to fix up the function call stack to allow a valid return.

Writing functions that can handle variable numbers of arguments requires extra planning and effort. But these functions are convenient—**max** would be much harder to use if we had to pass it an array of values. The functions in stdargs.h provide a clean interface to these arguments, allowing us to ignore the details of the underlying hardware and leave them to the hardworking compiler writer who has to provide these functions.

Dealing with Differing Argument Types

max only deals with **int** arguments. But functions like **printf** and **scanf** are considerably more complicated because they have to deal with many different types of arguments, and to determine their types from a control string.

Figure 14.15 shows how to write one of these functions. It contains **getinput**, a function that prompts for and reads input. **getinput** is similar to **scanf** in that it reads values according to a control string. But it has a pair of important differences: it also takes additional prompt strings as parameters, and it expects each of its input values to be on separate lines. We could, for example, use

```
getinput("sri", "Name?", name, "Salary?", &sal, "Age?", &age);
```

to prompt for and read a name, a salary, and an age. Unlike **scanf**, **getinput**'s control string is simply an array of one letter type indicators: **s** for strings, **r** for reals, and **i** for integers.

How does **getinput** work? The arguments following the control string are prompt-address pairs. For each pair, it needs to print the prompt and then read a value of the appropriate type into the corresponding address. The function begins by initializing a variable argument pointer to the argument following the control string.

```
va_start(argptr, description);
```

It then loops through the control string. For each character, it first obtains and prints the prompt.

```
printf("%s ", va_arg(argptr, char *));
```

Next, it reads the entire input line into an array **line**. And finally, it obtains the address where the value it read should go and places the value in that address. This address differs depending on the next character in the control string, so we use a **switch** to decide which type of address we have. For a **double**, we obtain the address and store the value with

```
sscanf(line, "%lf", va_arg(argptr, double *));
```

For an **int**, we do the same thing with

```
sscanf(line, "%i", va_arg(argptr, int *));
```

And for a string, we obtain the address and save the string with

```
strcpy(va_arg(argptr, char *), line);
```

```c
/*
 * A nice input fetching function.
 */
#include <stdio.h>
#include <string.h>
#include <stdarg.h>

#define  MAXLEN  80

int main()
{
  int    getinput(const char *control, ...);
  char   name[MAXLEN + 1];
  double sal;
  int    age;

  getinput("sri", "Name?", name, "Salary?", &sal, "Age?", &age);
  printf("Name: %s\nSalary: %f\nAge: %i\n", name, sal, age);
  return 0;
}

/* Get an input value according to provided formatting string */

int getinput(const char *control, ...)
{
  int         getline(char *, int);
  va_list     argptr;                      /* argument pointer */
  const char *cptr = control;              /* next char in control */
  char        line[MAXLEN + 1];            /* next input line */

  va_start(argptr, control);
  for (; *cptr != '\0'; cptr++)
  {
    printf("%s ", va_arg(argptr, char *));
    if (getline(line, MAXLEN) == -1)
      break;
    switch(*cptr)
    {                                      /* assume successful reads here */
      case 's': strcpy(va_arg(argptr, char *), line);
                break;
      case 'r': sscanf(line, "%lf", va_arg(argptr, double *));
                break;
      case 'i': sscanf(line, "%i", va_arg(argptr, int *));
                break;
    }
  }
  va_end(argptr);
  return cptr - control;                   /* successful reads */
}
```

Figure 14.15 (getinp.c) A function that uses variable numbers of arguments to help us obtain input in a clean way.

```
/*
 * Illustrates using "printf"-like debugging function.
 */
#include <stdio.h>
#include <stdarg.h>

int main()
{
  void debug(const char *funcname, const char *format, ...);
  int x = 10, y = 20;

  debug("main", "x=%i, y=%i\n", x, y);
  return 0;
}

/* Print function name, and values of variables */

void debug(const char *funcname, const char *format, ...)
{
  va_list argptr;

  printf("DEBUGGING %s: ", funcname);
  va_start(argptr, format);
  vprintf(format, argptr);    /* print various arguments */
  va_end(argptr);
}
```

Figure 14.16   (debug.c) A debugging aid that makes use of the built-in variable argument functions.

Built-in Variable Argument Functions

C provides several library functions that can be passed an argument pointer, a variable of type **va_list**. Two of these are **vprintf** and **vscanf**, which are analogous to **printf** and **scanf**, respectively.

We use these functions in the function **debug**, the simple debugging aid shown in Figure 14.16. We call it with the name of the function, a formatting string, and a list of variables. It writes the word "DEBUGGING", the function's name, and the variables' values according to the formatting string.

```
DEBUGGING main: x=10, y=20
```

Using **debug** rather than **printf** when debugging helps us obtain consistent debugging output and separates debugging statements from those that produce normal program output.

We want **debug** to take a variable number of arguments, just like **printf** does. That's because we want it to be able to write different numbers of variables in different calls. In fact, **debug** is very similar to **printf**, except that it has an additional first argument, the function name.

```
void debug(const char *funcname, const char *format, ...)
```

debug uses **printf** to write "DEBUGGING" and the function's name. It then wants to write the variable names and values according to its **format** parameter—but it doesn't want to have to process the format parameter itself. That's a lot of work, and we really don't want to duplicate **printf**, deciphering the format string and processing the various arguments. Unfortunately, however, there's no way to pass **printf** a pointer to the remaining arguments.

That's where **vprintf** comes in. **vprintf** takes a formatting string and a pointer to a variable argument list and prints each of the variables in that list appropriately.

```
vprintf(const char *format, va_list argptr);
```

debug works by obtaining the argument pointer with **va_start** and then passing it to **vprintf**.

```
va_start(argptr, format);   /* get argument pointer */
vprintf(format, argptr);    /* print rest */
```

14.4 POINTERS TO FUNCTIONS

It would be nice to be able to pass functions as parameters. To see how we could use this ability, consider a program that maintains a table of structures containing an employee's number, name, phone number, and salary. We might want to search that table for an employee record with a particular employee number or name.

There are several ways to do these searches. One is to write a pair of search functions, **search_empno** and **search_name**, each of which search the table. Figure 14.17 contains a sample declaration for the employee structure, Figure 14.18 contains the search functions, and Figure 14.19 contains a main program that uses them. The problem is that these functions duplicate code: they both have to traverse the array. The only difference between them is that one uses the **<** operator to compare an integer with the employee number field, whereas the other uses **strcmp** to compare a string with the name field. Everything else is identical.[5]

An alternate approach is to write a single search function, **empsearch**, that can search the table for any field's value. We can then build **search_empno** and **search_name** on top of it. This has the advantage that we eliminate all the unnecessary duplication of code—now only **empsearch** actually traverses the array. But how does **empsearch** know when it has found the desired table entry? We pass **empsearch** a function to perform the comparison, and we replace the direct comparison with a call to this comparison function. So **empsearch** executes this function once for each element in the table, stopping when the function returns an indication that we found a match.

---

[5]Both functions treat the array they search as a constant to prevent accidentally changing its elements. But the pointer they return isn't a constant; that way their callers can use it to update the array. The problem is that we can't directly assign a pointer to a constant to a pointer to a non-constant, which forces us to use a cast.

```
/*
 * Definition of an employee record.  Differs from Chapter 11's
 * EMPLOYEEs in that we now store a salary rather than an age.
 */
#include <stdio.h>
#include <stddef.h>

typedef struct
{
  long     number;
  char     *name;
  char     *phone;
  double   salary;
} EMPLOYEE;
```

Figure 14.17   (emp.h) Definition of an employee record.

```
/*
 * Employee table-searching functions.
 *    search_empno - find matching employee by number.
 *    search_name - find matching employee by name.
 */
#include <string.h>
#include "emp.h"

EMPLOYEE *search_empno(const EMPLOYEE *ptr, int n, long target)
{
  const EMPLOYEE *const endptr = ptr + n;

  for (; ptr < endptr; ptr++)
    if (ptr->number == target)
      return (EMPLOYEE *) ptr;
  return NULL;
}

EMPLOYEE *search_name(const EMPLOYEE *ptr, int n, char *target)
{
  const EMPLOYEE *const endptr = ptr + n;

  for (; ptr < endptr; ptr++)
    if (strcmp(ptr->name, target) == 0)
      return (EMPLOYEE *) ptr;
  return NULL;
}
```

Figure 14.18   (empsrch1.c) Simple-minded search functions.

```
/*
 * Use standard search on an array of structures.
 */
#include <string.h>
#include "emp.h"

int main()
{
  EMPLOYEE *search_empno(const EMPLOYEE tab[], int n, long target);
  EMPLOYEE *search_name(const EMPLOYEE tab[], int n, char *target);
  EMPLOYEE table[] =
            {{1001, "Daphne Borromeo",    "213-555-2134", 8.78},
             {1011, "Tammy Merriweather", "213-555-1212", 4.50},
             {1140, "Doris Perl",         "213-555-1215", 5.60},
             {2045, "Barbara Wong",       "213-555-1219", 7.80},
             {2945, "Diane Goebel",       "213-555-1245", 9.00},
             {3300, "Irene Borromeo",     "213-555-1210", 3.97},
             {4011, "Veronica Ockert",    "213-555-1212", 4.50},
             {4140, "Tony Quilici",       "213-555-1215", 5.60},
             {5045, "Brian Hight",        "213-555-1219", 7.80},
             {5945, "Gisele Pham",        "213-555-1245", 9.00}}};
  const int entries = sizeof(table)/sizeof(table[0]);
  EMPLOYEE *matchptr;

  if ((matchptr = search_empno(table, entries, 1045)) != NULL)
    printf("1045 is in record %i\n", matchptr - table);
  else
    printf("1045 wasn't found\n");
  if ((matchptr = search_name(table, entries, "Tony Quilici")) != NULL)
    printf("Tony Quilici is in record %i\n", matchptr - table);
  else
    printf("Tony Quilici wasn't found.\n");
  return 0;
}
```

Figure 14.19   (empmain.c) A main program using our searching functions.

This idea sounds great, but it has a problem: C doesn't let us pass functions as parameters or assign them to variables. But we can pass *pointers* to functions, which can be thought of as the address of the code executed when a function is called or as a pointer to a block of internal information about the function. Dereferencing a pointer to a function calls the function to which it points.

Before we show how to use pointers to functions to implement our **empsearch** function, we need to know how to declare them, how to obtain them, and how to dereference them to call a function. To declare a pointer to a function, we specify the pointed-to function's return type and its parameters. For example, the declaration *type* (***funcptr**) (*parameter-list*);

declares **funcptr** as a pointer to a function that takes parameters of the types specified in *parameter-list* and returns *type*. We need the parentheses around ***funcptr**. Without them we would be declaring it as a function returning *type*, not a pointer to a function.[6]

How do we obtain a pointer to a function? You might guess that we simply apply the address operator (**&**) to it—but that's incorrect. Instead, we simply use the function name without following it with a parenthesized parameter list. For example, assuming the declaration

```
double (*funcptr)(double, double);
```

we can use the following assignment to make **funcptr** point to the math library function **pow**.

```
funcptr = pow;
```

Before we do this assignment, however, C must know that **pow** is a function and not a variable. That means we first need to provide a prototype for **pow**. Since **pow** is the math library, we can obtain its prototype simply by including math.h.

To call the function pointed to by **funcptr**, we simply dereference it as we would any other pointer, by following it with a list of parameters. After the previous assignment,

```
(*funcptr)(14.5, 0.5)
```

is equivalent to

```
pow(14.5, 0.5)
```

calling **pow** to compute $14.5^{0.5}$. The parentheses surrounding ***funcptr** are necessary to guarantee the correct order of evaluation.[7]

All we've seen so far is how pointers to functions provide us with a longwinded way of calling functions. But they're useful. Figure 14.20 contains new versions of our earlier search functions that take advantage of them.

Our searching function, **empsearch**, takes a collection of parameters. We have to pass it the array of **EMPLOYEE**s we're searching, an **int** that holds the number of elements in the array, a pointer to the field value we're trying to find (the target), and a pointer to a comparison function (which we use to determine whether we've found the target). Its prototype seems complicated, especially its last two arguments.

---

[6]We agree this syntax is gross, but we're stuck with it. We devote a later chapter entirely to dealing with C's declaration syntax, but for now just memorize the form.

[7]Actually, there's a simpler form. We're can call a function through a pointer by using the pointer in place of the function name, as in **funcptr(14.5,0.5)**. What happens in this case is that the compiler is kind enough to automatically stick in the necessary dereference for us. Although this concise form is considerably more convenient, for now we'll use the more wordy form, since it makes the pointer dereference explicit and serves as a reminder that we're dealing with pointers to functions.

```
/*
 * New versions of our search functions.
 *    search_empno - find matching employee by number.
 *    empnocmp - employee-number comparison function.
 *    search_name - find matching employee by name.
 *    namecmp - employee-name comparison function.
 *    empsearch - actual function to search employee table.
 */
#include <string.h>
#include "emp.h"

static EMPLOYEE *empsearch(const EMPLOYEE *ptr,
                           int n,
                           const void *tarptr,
                           int (*fptr)(const void *, const EMPLOYEE *));
static int empnocmp(const void *tarptr, const EMPLOYEE *entryptr);
static int namecmp(const void *tarptr, const EMPLOYEE *entryptr);

EMPLOYEE *search_empno(EMPLOYEE *ptr, int n, long num)
{
  return empsearch(ptr, n, &num, empnocmp);
}

static int empnocmp(const void *tarptr, const EMPLOYEE *entryptr)
{
  return * (long *) tarptr != entryptr->number;
}

EMPLOYEE *search_name(const EMPLOYEE *ptr, int n, char *name)
{
  return empsearch(ptr, n, name, namecmp);
}

static int namecmp(const void *tarptr, const EMPLOYEE *entryptr)
{
  return strcmp((char *) tarptr, entryptr->name);
}

static EMPLOYEE *empsearch(const EMPLOYEE *ptr,
                           int n,
                           const void *tarptr,
                           int (*funcptr)(const void *, const EMPLOYEE *))
{
  const EMPLOYEE *const endptr = ptr + n;

  for (; ptr < endptr; ptr++)
    if ((*funcptr)(tarptr, ptr) == 0)
      return (EMPLOYEE *) ptr;
  return NULL;
}
```

Figure 14.20 (empsrch2.c) New versions of our functions to search an array of employee structures.

```
EMPLOYEE *empsearch(const EMPLOYEE *ptr,
                    int n,
                    const void *tarptr,
                    int (*fptr)(const void *, const EMPLOYEE *));
```

Declaring these last two arguments is tricky. What type should the target be? It's hard to decide, since sometimes we search for a **long** and other times we search for a string. The way out of this dilemma is to to pass **empsearch** a pointer to the target. Then we can make this pointer parameter a pointer to **void**, since that indicates a pointer to an unknown type. The final argument must be a pointer to the comparison function—but what are its parameters and what is its return value? When we call it, we need to pass it a pointer to the target and a pointer to the next table entry. That means it takes a pointer to a **void** and a pointer to an **EMPLOYEE**. Its return value must indicate whether we found a matching **EMPLOYEE**, which we can do by returning an **int**, with zero indicating a match.

We can use **empsearch** to search the table for employee number 1045 with

```
i = 1045;
matchptr = empsearch(table, entries, &i, empnocmp);
```

This call is trickier than it first appears. We can't pass the target employee number directly because **empsearch** expects a pointer. That means we have to place it in a variable and pass its address. And to pass the comparison function, we simply provide its name. We don't follow it with an argument list, since then we would be calling the function and passing its return value. But we do have to provide **empnocmp**'s prototype before calling **empsearch**. That way the compiler knows that it's a function and not an ordinary variable.

It's simpler to search the table for employee name "Tony Quilici".

```
matchptr = empsearch(table, entries, "Tony Quilici", namecmp);
```

That's because a string is already a pointer, so we don't need to do anything extra to pass it. As before, however, we don't follow the comparison function with any arguments, and we must first provide its prototype.

Actually, in our program we don't call **empsearch** directly. Instead we build our earlier functions on top of it: **search_empno** and **search_name** are simply appropriate calls to **empsearch**.

We've seen how to use **empsearch**, but what does it look like internally? It uses a pointer to traverse the array of **EMPLOYEE**s and calls our comparison function once for each employee.

```
if ((*funcptr)(tarptr, ptr) == 0)   /* do comparison */
    return (EMPLOYEE *) ptr;
```

This calls the function **funcptr** points to, passing it the pointers to the target (which is stored as a pointer to **void**) and to the next **EMPLOYEE**. The comparison functions must cast the target pointer to an appropriate type before dereferencing it and doing the actual comparison. In **empnocmp**, for example, we cast it to a pointer to a **long** before comparing what it points to against the structure's **number** field.

```
        return * (long *) tarptr != entryptr->number;
```

And in **namecmp** we cast the target to a pointer to a **char** and then use **strcmp** to compare it with the **name** field of the structure.

```
        return strcmp((char *) tarptr, entryptr->name);
```

This technique of passing pointers to functions hardly seems worth the effort. And for a simple example, like the one we've been discussing, it probably isn't. But imagine that we were using a more complex searching technique or sorting algorithm. Then using pointers to functions helps save us from duplicating a lot of complex code. In the next chapter we'll carry this technique even further to write functions that can not only search and sort based on the values of particular fields, but can actually search and sort any array, regardless of the underlying data type of its elements.

14.5   RECURSION

Many algorithms and mathematical definitions are naturally described *recursively*, that is, partially in terms of themselves. One very simple example is the mathematical definition of a factorial. The factorial of n (written $n!$) is the product of all integers between 1 and n (assuming n is nonnegative).

$$n! = \begin{cases} 1 & n = 0 \\ n \times (n-1)! & n > 0 \end{cases}$$

Some example factorials are $2! = 2$, $3! = 6$, $4! = 24$, and $5! = 120$.

Notice that to determine the factorial of any $n \geq 0$, we have to determine the factorial of $n - 1$. As with all recursive definitions, we have to know the function's value at one or more points. In this case, we know that $0!$ is 1.

Functions can call themselves recursively—which makes it easy to translate the mathematical definition of a factorial into the function **fact** that can compute a factorial. Figure 14.21 contains **fact**, along with a special version of it that prints additional information allowing us to trace the recursive calls. Figure 14.22 shows the program's output.

Figure 14.23 is another example of a recursive program. But this one isn't simply an implementation of some recursive formula. Instead, it produces the possible permutations of a string. Given **"alex"**, there are 24 permutations.

```
alex alxe aelx aexl axel axle
laex laxe leax lexa lxea lxae
elax elxa ealx eaxl exal exla
xlea xlae xela xeal xael xale
```

How do we generate these permutations? Our approach is easy to formulate recursively: *For each character in the string, exchange it with the string's first character and generate the permutations of the characters that remain.* We can implement this description in a function **permute** that takes two arguments: a string to permute, and a position within the string to start permuting. Initially, we call **permute** with

```
/*
 * Use factorial function to compute 4!.
 */
#include <stdio.h>

int main()
{
  long fact(int n);                    /* compute factorial */
  long trace_fact(int n);              /* provides tracing info */

  printf("%li\n", fact(4));            /* test it */
  printf("Here's a trace.\n");
  printf("%li\n", trace_fact(4));      /* with trace */
  return 0;
}

long fact(int n)                       /* compute N! for N >= 0 */
{
  return (n <= 1) ? 1 : n * fact(n-1);
}

long trace_fact(int n)                 /* also output tracing info */
{
  long temp;

  printf("Computing %i factorial\n", n);
  temp = (n <= 1) ? 1 : n * trace_fact(n-1);
  printf("Computed %i factorial = %li\n", n, temp);
  return temp;
}
```

Figure 14.21 (fact.c) Functions to recursively compute $n!$. One supplies tracing information, the other doesn't.

```
24
Here's a trace.
Computing 4 factorial
Computing 3 factorial
Computing 2 factorial
Computing 1 factorial
Computed 1 factorial = 1
Computed 2 factorial = 2
Computed 3 factorial = 6
Computed 4 factorial = 24
24
```

Figure 14.22 The program's output when run.

```
/*
 * Produce permutations, assuming sufficient memory.
 */
#include <stdio.h>
#include <string.h>
#include <stdlib.h>

int Len;                                /* length of string to permute */

main(int argc, char *argv[])
{
  void permute(const char *s, int pos);
  int i;

  for (i = 1; i < argc; i++)
  {
    Len = strlen(argv[i]);
    permute(argv[i], 0);
  }
  return 0;
}

/* Generate all permutations of "s" */

void permute(const char *s, int changepos)
{
  void swap(char *ptr1, char *ptr2);
  char *scopy;
  int  i;

  if (changepos < Len)
    for (i = changepos; i < Len; i++)
    {
      scopy = malloc(Len + 1);       /* assumes malloc succeeds */
      strcpy(scopy, s);
      swap(&scopy[i], &scopy[changepos]);
      permute(scopy, changepos + 1);
      free(scopy);
    }
  else
    printf("%s\n", s);
}

/* Exchange two character variables in caller */

void swap(char *p, char *q)
{
  char temp;

  temp = *p;   *p = *q;   *q = temp;
}
```

Figure 14.23 (permute.c) A program to produce permutations.

```
permute("alex", 0)
```

since we want to permute the whole string. Inside **permute** we exchange the first character with each of the subsequent characters and call permute to generate the permutations of the rest of the string. Our initial call to **permute** results in calls to **permute** with the strings **alex**, **laex**, **elax**, and **xlea**. But these calls to **permute** differ in that they start with a position of 1, rather than 0, and in that the calls they generate start with a position of 2. We print the string only when the position is past the string's end (in this case, 4), since there's nothing left to **permute** at that point.

There's one catch: when we pass a string to **permute**, we don't want **permute** to change it. But within **permute** we are actually exchanging characters in the string. If C actually passed arrays by value, we wouldn't have a problem. But it doesn't, so we're stuck simulating call by value. We do that by using **malloc** and **strcpy** to create a copy of the string that we then pass to **permute**. And we **free** this copy after the call to **permute**.

14.6   CASE STUDY—BINARY SEARCH

This section is optional!

The simplest way to search a table—and the approach we've been taking so far—is *sequential search*: We compare the value we're searching for with each table entry until we've found a match or looked through the entire table. The average successful search examines about half the table's elements—but an unsuccessful search examines them all. Although this method is reasonable for searching small unordered tables, for large *sorted* tables we can do much better. Binary search is a much faster (indeed, optimal) algorithm for searching sorted tables, which happens to be easily expressed by a recursive algorithm.

In binary search, we start by comparing the target value with the table's middle element. The table is sorted, so if the target is larger, we can ignore all values smaller than the middle element and apply binary search recursively to the table's upper half. Similarly, if the target is smaller, we apply binary search recursively to the table's lower half. We stop when we've found the target (it's equal to the middle element) or there are no values left to search.

Binary search is significantly faster than sequential search. Every time we compare the target to a table element, we no longer have to consider half of the remaining values. Roughly, its time is proportional to $\log_2 n$, where n is the number of values in the table.

We implement binary search in a function **binsearch**, shown in Figure 14.24, along with a program that uses it to search a sorted table of **int**s. We pass **binsearch** the target value and pointers to the table's first and last elements. It returns a pointer to the matching table element, or the null pointer if no such element is found.

Figure 14.25 illustrates a successful binary search on a seven-element table. Figure 14.26 illustrates an unsuccessful search on the same table. With every recursive call to **binsearch**, the pointers **minptr** and **maxptr** move toward each other. The search and recursive calls terminate when the pointers merge or the target value is found.

When we call **binsearch**, it first calculates the address of the middle element in the unsearched portion of the table (the whole table when it is first called). Because we

```
/*
 * Program using binary search for values given to it as arguments.
 */
#include <stdio.h>
#include <stddef.h>

#define MAX      100

int main(int argc, char *argv[])
{
  long *binsearch(const long *min, const long *max, long t);
  long table[MAX];                     /* table to search */
  long t;                              /* target */
  long *fndptr;                        /* pointer to item in array */
  int i;                               /* array index */

  for (i = 0; i < MAX; i++)            /* initialize table with */
    table[i] = i;                      /*    0,1,2,3,... */

  for (i = 1; i < argc; i++)
   if (sscanf(argv[i], "%li", &t) == 1)
   {
     fndptr = binsearch(&table[0], &table[MAX - 1], t);
     if (fndptr != NULL)
       printf("Found %li as element %i.\n", t, fndptr - table);
     else
       printf("Didn't find %li.\n", t);
   }
  return 0;
}

/* Use binary search to search a table of longs */

long *binsearch(const long *minptr, const long *maxptr, long target)
{
  const long *midptr = minptr + (maxptr - minptr) / 2;

  if (target == *midptr)               /* middle is target? */
    return (long *) midptr;
  if (maxptr <= minptr)                /* value's not in table? */
    return NULL;

  return (target < *midptr)            /* search correct half */
          ? binsearch(minptr, midptr - 1, target)
          : binsearch(midptr + 1, maxptr, target);
}
```

Figure 14.24   (binsrch.c)   A binary search function and a program using it.

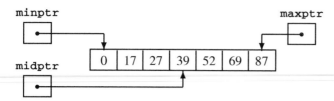

(a) At start: 39 is less than 69, so search top half of table.

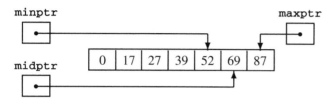

(b) After calling **binsearch** once, found it.

Figure 14.25 A successful binary search.

can't add or divide pointers, we calculate the midpoint with

```
midptr = minptr + (maxptr - minptr) / 2;
```

instead of adding the two pointers together and dividing by two. After we find the midpoint, the first thing we do is check whether the search has succeeded or failed. To do so, we compare the value pointed to by **midptr** with the target. If they're equal, we have found it, so we return **midptr**. Otherwise, we check whether the pointers are pointing to the same element. This happens only when there is one element left to search and that element isn't the target. It means the search has failed, so we return the **NULL** pointer. Otherwise, we know that there are unexamined table elements, so we recursively apply **binsearch** to the appropriate section of the table.

We can write functions such as **fact** and **binsearch** more efficiently iteratively than recursively. But using recursion often makes our functions more compact or makes them more closely reflect an algorithm or mathematical definition. Recursion is a powerful technique well worth the trouble of mastering.

SUMMARY

- We can simulate call-by-reference parameter passing by using pointers. We pass the equivalent of a call-by-reference parameter by passing its address, which the function then dereferences to access and change its value.

- We can write functions with variable numbers of arguments using the *stdargs* package.

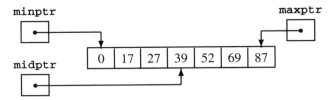

(*a*)   At start: 39 is greater than 28, so search lower half of table.

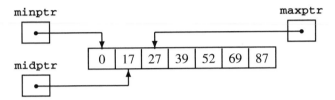

(*b*)   After calling **binsearch** once, 28 greater than 17.

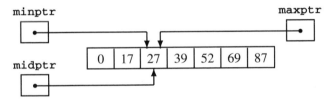

(*c*)   Call **binsearch** again, 28 not equal to 27, so we stop.

Figure 14.26   An unsuccessful binary search.

- We can write generic functions by using pointers to functions. These generic functions save us repeating the same code over and over when all that's really different is the type of data we're manipulating.

- We're allowed to have recursive functions—functions that call themselves.

- ANSI-C actually provides two styles for function declarations and definitions. The older style doesn't provide automatic type checking or conversions and is provided for backward compatibility.

EXERCISES

14–1   Compile and run our earlier table-reversing program (Figure 14.4)—the one with the incorrect version of **swap**. What happens?

14–2 Modify `getinput` (Figure 14.15) to do error checking on its input values.

14–3 Rewrite the binary search function (Figure 14.24) nonrecursively. Watch out! It's messier than it seems.

14–4 Rewrite the binary search function (Figure 14.24) using array subscripting rather than pointers. Which version is more compact? Which version is more readable?

14–5 Binary search has considerable overhead in calculating the midpoint. In fact, binary search is often slower than sequential search when searching small tables. Determine the point on your system where both searches take the same amount of time. Then write a single function that always uses the best search method.

14–6 Write a function, `stol` (for string to `long`), that takes a string and turns it into a single `long` integer. The function should return an error indication. The `long` should be returned through a pointer parameter.

14–7 Write the function `str_swap`, whose arguments are pointers to strings. The values of these pointers are swapped. When is `str_swap` useful? (Hint: `str_swap` requires pointers to pointers. Draw a picture to help you see what's going on.)

14–8 Write `min`, a variable argument function that returns its smallest argument.

14–9 Write `search`, a variable argument function that searches an array for the first occurrence of any one of a list of arguments. It returns a pointer to the desired element's position in the table, or **NULL** if no such element can be found. Its header is

```
int *search(int table[], int argcnt, ...);
```

14–10 The Fibonacci numbers are a famous mathematical sequence that can be defined recursively. For nonnegative integers

$$
fib(n) = \begin{cases} 0 & n = 0 \\ 1 & n = 1 \\ fib(n-1) + fib(n-2) & n \geq 2 \end{cases}
$$

The first 10 Fibonacci numbers are 0, 1, 1, 2, 3, 5, 8, 13, 21, and 34. Write recursive and iterative functions to compute the nth Fibonacci number and print the 20th number in this sequence. Which version is faster?

14–11 Write a function, `gentable`, to generate a table of x, y points by evaluating another function over a range of x values. `gentable` is passed a pointer to the function to plot, the starting and ending x values, the number of points to plot, and two arrays for the x and y values. For example, we can generate 1000 values of the `sin` function between 0 and 1 radians with

```
gentable(sin, 0, 1, 1000, x, y);
```

14–12 Write the rest of the function plotter you started in the previous exercise. It should take an array of points, scale it, and then plot the various points.

15 THE PREPROCESSOR

Many useful features of C aren't implemented by the compiler, but instead by a program that processes C source files before the compiler ever sees them. This chapter is a detailed discussion of that program, the C preprocessor. We introduce macros and show how they can make our programs more efficient and more readable. We examine header files in more detail and show how we can use them to effectively extend the language. And we study conditional compilation and show how it aids debugging and portability. This chapter concludes by using the preprocessor to construct a new, more efficient sets package.

15.1 PREPROCESSOR DIRECTIVES

The preprocessor reads a source file, performs various actions on it, and passes the resulting output to the C compiler. To decide what actions to perform, it looks for lines beginning with a *preprocessor directive* in column 1.

Table 15.1 lists the preprocessor directives. Some of them should be familiar; we have already used **#include** and **#define** in many of our programs.

Sometimes we want to examine the preprocessor's output, most often to help us locate problems we've introduced by erroneous preprocessor statements. There's no guarantee, but most C environments provide some way to do so. As you might expect, the details vary from system to system. Usually, we either run the preprocessor as a separate program or provide some special option to the compiler.

15.2 SIMPLE MACRO SUBSTITUTION

We've used **#define** to define various symbolic constants, such as the number of elements in an array. Doing so makes our programs easier to read and easier to change. That's because it can be difficult to decipher what a particular numeric value does, since the same value can mean different things in different places. The value 10 may be the size of an array, or it might be an interest rate or a base for number conversion. When we provide descriptive names for each unique use of a constant, we clarify its purpose and allow us to change its value throughout the program simply by changing the line defining its name.

Directive	Use
`#define`	define a macro
`#include`	include text from a file
`#undef`	undefine a macro
`#if`	test if a compile-time condition holds
`#else`	indicate alternatives if a test fails
`#elif`	combine `#else` and `#if`
`#endif`	end a preprocessor conditional (`#if`, `#ifdef`, `#ifndef`)
`#ifdef`	test if a symbol is defined
`#ifndef`	test if a symbol is not defined
`#line`	provide a line number (and optional file name) for compiler messages
`#error`	terminate processing early
`#pragma`	implementation-dependent directive

Table 15.1 C preprocessor directives and their uses.

We're not limited to using **#define** to give names to numeric constants. We can use it to give a symbolic name to any arbitrary piece of text. That's because **#define** is more powerful than we have let on—it's actually a general mechanism for text replacement. The preprocessor command line

```
#define NAME TEXT
```

instructs the preprocessor to replace all subsequent *unquoted* occurrences of *NAME* with *TEXT*. There are no restrictions on *TEXT*, but *NAME* must be an identifier. We usually write *NAME*s in uppercase to distinguish them from the variable and function names handled by the compiler. A defined name is often called a *macro*, and the process of substituting its replacement text is called *macro substitution*.

One common use for **#define** is to give symbolic names to string constants. After encountering

```
#define  DIGITS  "0123456789"
```

the preprocessor replaces each occurrence of **DIGITS** with the string constant **"0123456789"**. Figure 15.1 contains definitions of some of the more common strings we're likely to use, and Figure 15.2 uses many of those definitions in an extended version of our earlier program to count the number of various characters in its input.

Another common use is to give symbolic names to arbitrary expressions. Figure 15.3 does that in a little program to print the circumference of a circle with a radius it reads from its input. The formula for circumference is $2 * \pi * radius$. To aid readability, we define a constant **TWOPI** and use it in the expression to compute the circumference.

```
#define TWOPI  (3.1415926 * 2.0)
```

Regardless of how complex a definition we have, the preprocessor simply substitutes

```
/*
 * Generally useful, commonly used string definitions.
 */
#define DIGITS     "0123456789"
#define LOWERS     "abcdefghijklmnopqrstuvwxyz"
#define UPPERS     "ABCDEFGHIJKLMNOPQRSTUVWXYZ"
#define PUNCTS     ",.;:!?"
#define QUOTES     "''\""
#define BRACKETS   "(){}[]"
```

Figure 15.1 (comstr.h) Definitions of some common strings.

the expression for its defined name, *without evaluating it*. So it replaces

```
circumf = TWOPI * radius;
```

with

```
circumf = (3.1415926 * 2.0) * radius;
```

We can define names in terms of other names and in any order, as long as all definitions precede any use. Figure 15.4 is a new version of our circumference program that takes advantage of this ability. Rather than define **TWOPI** directly, it first defines **PI** and uses it to define **TWOPI**.

```
#define  PI     3.1415926
#define  TWOPI  (PI + PI)
```

We can get away with this because the preprocessor simply remembers the replacement text, but does not substitute for any defined names it contains. Later, when we use the name, the preprocessor substitutes the replacement text and then performs macro substitution on any defined names it contains (except for a name appearing in its own replacement text). So when the preprocessor encounters the expression to compute the circumference,

```
circumf = TWOPI * radius;
```

it first substitutes for **TWOPI**

```
circumf = (PI + PI) * radius;
```

and then for both occurrences of **PI**

```
circumf = (3.1415926 + 3.1415926) * radius;
```

Although the preprocessor doesn't evaluate expressions, using names that expand into expressions doesn't slow down our programs. Most C compilers compute the value of expressions involving only constants at compile time.

Failing to parenthesize expressions in the replacement text can cause unexpected order-of-evaluation problems. Not parenthesizing **TWOPI**'s definition,

```
/*
 * Count various types of characters.  Extension of the version
 * found in Chapter 10 that now uses defined string constants.
 */
#include <stdio.h>
#include <string.h>
#include <stddef.h>
#include "comstr.h"                          /* for string constants */

typedef unsigned long COUNTER;

const int PrintWidth = 11;                    /* counter field size */

int main()
{
  int      c;
  COUNTER quotes    = 0,
          brackets = 0,
          delims   = 0,
          digits   = 0,
          lowers   = 0,
          uppers   = 0,
          others   = 0;

  while ((c = getchar()) != EOF)
    if (strchr(DIGITS, c) != NULL)
      digits++;
    else if (strchr(LOWERS, c) != NULL)
      lowers++;
    else if (strchr(UPPERS, c) != NULL)
      uppers++;
    else if (strchr(QUOTES, c) != NULL)
      quotes++;
    else if (strchr(BRACKETS, c) != NULL)
      brackets++;
    else if (strchr(PUNCTS, c) != NULL)
      delims++;
    else
      others++;

  printf("Quotes     %*lu\n", PrintWidth, quotes);
  printf("Brackets   %*lu\n", PrintWidth, brackets);
  printf("Delimiters %*lu\n", PrintWidth, delims);
  printf("Digits     %*lu\n", PrintWidth, digits);
  printf("Lowercase  %*lu\n", PrintWidth, lowers);
  printf("Uppercase  %*lu\n", PrintWidth, uppers);
  printf("Others     %*lu\n", PrintWidth, others);

  return 0;
}
```

Figure 15.2   (cntchrs.c)   Count various types of characters.

```
/*
 * Compute the circumference of a circle.
 */
#include <stdio.h>

#define TWOPI (3.1415926 * 2.0)

int main()
{
  double radius, circumf;

  printf("Enter radius: ");
  scanf("%lf", &radius);
  circumf = TWOPI * radius;
  printf("Circumference: %g\n", circumf);
  return 0;
}
```

Figure 15.3   (circumf1.c) A program to compute the circumference of a circle.

```
/*
 * Compute the circumference of a circle.
 */
#include <stdio.h>

#define PI     3.1415926
#define TWOPI (PI + PI)

int main()
{
  double radius, circumf;

  printf("Enter radius: ");
  scanf("%lf", &radius);
  circumf = TWOPI * radius;
  printf("Circumference: %g\n", circumf);
  return 0;
}
```

Figure 15.4   (circumf2.c) A program to compute the circumference of a circle.

```
#define TWOPI  PI + PI    /* asking for trouble */
```

results in an incorrect expression to compute the circumference:

```
circumf = 3.1415926 + 3.1415926 * radius;
```

> *To avoid problems, always parenthesize the replacement text.*

Syntax errors within a definition are detected when we use the name, not when we define it. The preprocessor does no syntax checking of the results of its substitutions, leaving this task to the compiler. The incorrect definitions

```
#define PI = 3.1415926;   /* Wrong! Don't want "=" or ";" */
#define TWOPI = (2 * PI); /* Wrong! don't want "=" or ";" */
```

contain two common syntax errors: following a name with an assignment operator and ending a definition with a semicolon. Following this definition with

```
circumf = TWOPI * radius;
```

will lead to errors for the set of incorrect statements that result from the preprocessor's substitutions.

```
circumf = = (2 * = 3.1415926;); * radius;
```

> *Remember that the preprocessor doesn't know C—it blindly replaces names with replacement text.*

Syntactic Replacement

#define helps us hide confusing or error-prone parts of C's syntax. Figure 15.5 takes advantage of it in a new version of our old **yesorno** function. It uses these definitions:

```
#define FOREVER  for(;;)     /* infinite loop */
#define IS       ==          /* equality test */
#define ISNOT    !=          /* inequality test */
```

FOREVER is a more readable way to indicate an infinite loop than **for(;;)**. **IS** prevents the common mistake of using = instead of == in equality tests. And **ISNOT** prevents the Pascal programmer's mistake of using <> instead of !=.

In fact, we can actually hide enough of C's syntax to make it resemble another language, such as Pascal. We can use the definitions in Figure 15.6 to write C programs in a Pascal-like syntax, letting the preprocessor translate them into the form the compiler expects. Figure 15.7 shows a new version of our earlier power-computing functions rewritten to use these definitions.

```
/*
 * Program to print a prompt and get yes/no answer from user.
 */
#include <stdio.h>
#include <ctype.h>

#define FOREVER   for (;;)                      /* infinite loop */
#define IS        ==                            /* equality test */
#define ISNOT     !=                            /* inequality test */

int main()
{
  int yesorno(void);

  printf("Enter YES or NO answer: ");
  printf("That was a %s!\n", (yesorno()) ? "YES" : "NO");
  return 0;
}

/* Get a YES/NO answer from user */

int yesorno(void)
{
  int c;                                        /* input character */

  FOREVER
  {
    if ((c = tolower(getchar())) IS EOF || c IS 'y' || c IS 'n')
      return c IS 'y';
    while (c ISNOT '\n' && c ISNOT EOF)
      c = getchar();                            /* skip rest of line */
    printf("Please answer with a YES or NO: ");
  }
}
```

Figure 15.5 (yesorno.c) Yet another version of our **yesorno** function and a small program to use it.

Our Pascal example is cute, but the major syntactic replacement it takes advantage of has its drawbacks. First, defined names must be identifiers, so we can't redefine operators and other nonalphabetic tokens such as comment delimiters, which limits how much C syntax we can hide. Second, the compiler doesn't know about our extended syntax, so any error messages resulting from using our definitions incorrectly will correspond to C's syntax, making it hard to find these mistakes. And third, most people don't use an extended syntax, so it is hard for them to maintain programs written in one. Despite these limitations, some large programs, including a command interpreter and an object code debugger, have been written in an ALGOL-like syntax defined using the preprocessor.

```
/*
 * Definitions for Pascal-like keywords
 */
#define INTEGER     int
#define REAL        double
#define IF          if (
#define THEN        )
#define ELSE        else
#define WHILE       while (
#define DO          )
#define BEGIN       {
#define END         }
#define PROCEDURE   void
#define FUNCTION
#define RETURN      return
```

Figure 15.6   (pascal.h) Definitions used to create a Pascal-like syntax.

```
/*
 * A function to compute powers using Pascal-like keywords.
 */
#include <stdio.h>
#include "pascal.h"                              /* for Pascal keywords */

FUNCTION REAL power(REAL x, INTEGER exp)
BEGIN
  REAL p = 1;

  IF exp > 0 THEN
    WHILE exp-- > 0 DO p *= x;
  ELSE
    WHILE exp++ < 0 DO p /= x;
  RETURN p;
END
```

Figure 15.7   (power.c) Our old **power** function, rewritten using Pascal-like syntax.

15.3   MACRO SUBSTITUTION WITH PARAMETERS

So far we've defined names so that they are always replaced by the same text. There are times, however, when we want the replacement text to act like a template that's filled in differently each time we use the name. We can do this by defining a macro with parameters.

> #define *macro-name* (*name-1*, ..., *name-n*) *replacement-text*

```
/*
 * Macro replacements for our earlier bit-accessing functions.
 */
#define GETBIT(w,n)  (((unsigned int) (w) >> (n)) & 01)
#define SETBIT(w,n,v) \
        ((v == 0) ? ((unsigned int) (w) & ~(01 << (n))) \
                  : ((unsigned int) (w) |  (01 << (n))))

#define GETBITS(w,n,k) \
        (((unsigned int) (w) & (~(~0 << (k)) << (n))) >> (n))
#define SETBITS(w,n,k,v) \
        (((unsigned int) (w) & ~(~(~0 << (k)) << (n))) | ((v) << (n)))
```

Figure 15.8   (bits.h) Macros to get and set bits within a word.

Subsequent occurrences of the macro name are known as *macro calls*.

> *macro-name* (*text-1*, . . . , *text-n*)

Macro calls look like function calls but behave differently. When we call a macro, we supply its arguments, and the preprocessor performs *macro expansion*, replacing the call with macro's replacement text and then replacing the macro's parameters with its arguments.

In Chapter 5 we wrote a set of bit-accessing functions and a program that used them to pack employee information into a single word. Figure 15.8 is a header file that contains a set of macro replacements for those bit-accessing functions. GETBIT, for example, is a simple macro to return the value of an int's nth bit.

```
#define GETBIT(w, n) (((unsigned int) (w) >> (n)) & 01)
```

Once we've defined GETBIT, an expression like GETBIT(value, i) is a macro call. The preprocessor substitutes value for w and i for n in GETBIT's replacement text.

```
(((unsigned int) (value) >> (i)) & 01)
```

Why are there so many parentheses in GETBIT's definition? To prevent order-of-evaluation problems when GETBIT is expanded, we not only parenthesize the replacement text but also all occurrences of the macro's parameters.

The macro definitions in Figure 15.8 look like we might expect except for one thing: many of the lines end in a backslash.

```
#define GETBITS(w,n,k) \
        (((unsigned int) (w) & (~(~0 << (k)) << (n))) >> (n))
```

Whenever the preprocessor encounters a backslash immediately followed by a new line character, it joins the two lines together. Here, we're using the backslash so that a complicated macro can extend over multiple lines.

Figure 15.9 is a new version of our earlier bit-packing program that uses these macros. Programs using the macros are more efficient than programs using our earlier functions, since we've eliminated the considerable function call overhead associated with those simple functions. Of course, we didn't have to write macros or functions to get or set bits—we could have used the C bitwise operators directly. But using the macro aids readability without adversely affecting efficiency.

Using Macros in Macro Definitions

Our bit-shifting macros are complex and hard to understand. It would be nice if we could build them up out of smaller, more easily understood pieces. Figure 15.10 shows a new version of our bit-shifting macros that we construct on top of simpler mask-creating macros. With these definitions, when we do a macro call such as

```
SETBIT(word,2,1)
```

the preprocessor initially replaces it with

```
((1 == 0) ? SETBITOFF(word,2) : SETBITON(word,2))
```

Then it expands the macros **SETBITOFF** and **SETBITON**:

```
((1 == 0) ? (UINT(w) | ONBIT(n)) : (UINT(w) & OFFBIT(n)))
```

And finally it expands **UINT**, **OFFBIT**, and **ONBIT**, resulting in the expression we want:

```
((1 == 0) ? ((unsigned int) word & ~(01 << (2)))
          : ((unsigned int) word | (01 << (2))))
```

Some Useful Macros

Macros are much more useful than they might at first appear. That's because they can do things that functions can't. Unlike functions, they can work with many different types of arguments. Consider the macro **INRANGE**, which returns a nonzero value only if its third parameter falls between its other two parameters.

```
#define INRANGE(x,y,v) ((v) >= (x) && (v) <= (y))
```

Following this definition, the macro call **INRANGE(1, 100, i)** expands into

```
((i) >= (1) && (i) <= (100))
```

INRANGE is much more useful as a macro than as a function. Why? Because it can find the minimum of any pair of values with the same data type: ints, doubles, and so on. If we write **INRANGE** as a function, we have to specify a single type for its parameters, which means we end up writing different versions of **INRANGE** for each data type, or suffer through automatic conversions whenever we call it. We also gain efficiency by writing **INRANGE** as a macro, since macro calls are done during preprocessing instead of at run time, eliminating the overhead of a function call (argument passing, variable allocation, calling and returning from the function). Figure 15.11 provides an example

```
/*
 * Revised program to pack employee information into a single word.
 * Now uses bit macros rather than bit functions.
 */
#include <stdio.h>
#include "bits.h"

enum status {SINGLE, MARRIED, SEPARATED, DIVORCED};
enum genders {MALE, FEMALE};

#define MSBIT    0        /* marital status: bits 0-1 */
#define MSBITS   2
#define AGEBIT   2        /* age: bits 2-8 */
#define AGEBITS  7
#define SEXBIT   9        /* sex: bit 9 */
#define YRSBIT   10       /* year: bits 10-15 */
#define YRSBITS  6

int main()
{
  enum status  mstat;
  enum genders sex;
  unsigned int age, years;
  unsigned int info = 0;        /* holds info on one person */

  printf("male=%i, female=%i? ", MALE, FEMALE);
  scanf("%i", &sex);
  info = SETBIT(info, SEXBIT, sex);

  printf("age? ");
  scanf("%i", &age);
  info = SETBITS(info, AGEBIT, AGEBITS, age);

  printf("single=%i, married=%i, separated=%i, divorced=%i? ",
         SINGLE, MARRIED, SEPARATED, DIVORCED);
  scanf("%i", &mstat);
  info = SETBITS(info, MSBIT, MSBITS, mstat);

  printf("years employed? ");
  scanf("%i", &years);
  info = SETBITS(info, YRSBIT, YRSBITS, years);

  printf("Sex: %u\n", GETBIT(info, SEXBIT));
  printf("Age: %u\n", GETBITS(info, AGEBIT, AGEBITS));
  printf("Marital status: %u\n", GETBITS(info, MSBIT, MSBITS));
  printf("Years employed: %u\n", GETBITS(info, YRSBIT, YRSBITS));
  return 0;
}
```

Figure 15.9   (usebits.c) Program using our macros to get and set bits within a word.

```
/*
 * New version of our bit macros built up from simpler macros.
 *      UINT(x)             - x cast to unsigned int.
 *      ONBIT(n)            - only bit n on.
 *      OFFBIT(n)           - only bit n off.
 *      ONBITS(n,k)         - only bits n thru n+k on.
 *      OFFBITS(n,k)        - only bits n thru n+k off.
 *      SETBITON(w,n)       - turn bit n on in w.
 *      SETBITOFF(w,n)      - turn bit n off in w.
 *      GETBIT(w,n)         - value of bit n in  w.
 *      GETBITS(w,n,k)      - value of bits n thru n+k in w.
 *      SETBIT(w,n,v)       - give bit n value v in unsigned w.
 *      SETBITS(w,n,k,v)    - give bits n thru n+k value v in w.
 */
#define UINT(x)             ((unsigned int) (x))

#define ONBIT(n)            (01 << (n))
#define OFFBIT(n)           (~ ONBIT(n))
#define ONBITS(n,k)         (~(~0 << (k)) << (n))
#define OFFBITS(n,k)        (~ ONBITS(n,k))

#define SETBITON(w,n)       (UINT(w) | ONBIT(n))
#define SETBITOFF(w,n)      (UINT(w) & OFFBIT(n))

#define GETBIT(w,n)         ((UINT(w) >> (n)) & 01)
#define SETBIT(w,n,v)       (((v) == 0) ? SETBITOFF(w,n) : SETBITON(w,n))
#define GETBITS(w,n,k)      ((UINT(w) & ONBITS(n,k)) >> (n))
#define SETBITS(w,n,k,v)    ((UINT(w) & OFFBITS(n,k)) | ((v) << (n)))
```

Figure 15.10   (bits2.h)   New version of our macros to get and set bits within a word.

of **INRANGE** in an extended version of our earlier program to verify that its input values are legal. This program reads a **double** and an **int** and verifies that they fall within ranges defined by symbolic constants.

Unlike functions, macros can be passed a type as an argument. Figure 15.12 contains a header file containing a set of macros for dynamic allocation that take advantage of this feature. The first macro, **STRALLOC**, allocates an array of **n** items of type **t**, automatically computing the necessary number of bytes.

```
#define ALLOC(n, t) (malloc((n) * sizeof(t)))
```

After this definition, the call **ALLOC(MAX, int)** expands into

```
(malloc(MAX * sizeof(int)))
```

We can't write **ALLOC** as a function, since functions can't take types as arguments. The second macro, **COPY**, is similar. It copies one array into another, given pointers to the new and old arrays, the number of elements, and the type of an element.

```
/*
 * A version of our range-checking program that uses a macro.
 */
#include <stdio.h>

#define INRANGE(x,y,v)   ((v) > (x) && (v) <= (y))

#define MAXINT    1000
#define MININT       0
#define MAXDBL    9999.99
#define MINDBL   -9999.99

int main()
{
  double d;
  int    i;

  printf("Enter values: ");
  scanf("%i %lf", &i, &d);
  printf("%i is %s range!\n",
          i, INRANGE(MININT, MAXINT, i) ? "in" : "out of");
  printf("%f is %s range!\n",
          d, INRANGE(MINDBL, MAXDBL, d) ? "in" : "out of");
  return 0;
}
```

Figure 15.11   (inrange.c)   A new example of input validation.

```
/*
 * Useful macros for dynamically allocating things.
 */
#include <stdlib.h>
#include <stddef.h>
#include <string.h>

#define ALLOC(n,t)         (malloc((n) * sizeof(t)))
#define COPY(np,op,n,t)    (memcpy(np,op,(n) * sizeof(t)))
#define ZERO(p,n,t)        (memset(p,(n) * sizeof(t),0))

#define TABLEDUP(np,op,n,t) \
        (((np = ALLOC(n,t)) != NULL) ? COPY(np,op,n,t) : NULL)

#define STRALLOC(s)        (malloc(strlen(s) + 1))
#define STRDUP(ns,os)      ((ns = STRALLOC(os)) ? strcpy(ns,os) : NULL)
```

Figure 15.12   (allocs.h)   A set of macros useful for dynamically allocating things.

```
#define COPY(np,op,n,t)  (memcpy(np,op,(n) * sizeof(t))
```

The final macro, **TABLEDUP**, combines calls to these other macros to create a copy of an existing array.

```
#define TABLEDUP(np, op, n, t) \
   ((np = ALLOC(n, t)) != NULL) ? COPY(np, op, n, t) : NULL
```

It's given a pointer to fill in with a dynamically allocated array, a pointer to an existing array, the number of elements in the array, and the size of an element. Like the others, it can't be written as a function since it needs to know what kind of elements are in the arrays.

Even when we could use functions, we often use macros to make our program more readable without sacrificing efficiency. **STRALLOC** is a useful variant of **ALLOC** that automatically computes a string's length and allocates sufficient space for the string.

```
#define STRALLOC(s) (malloc(strlen(s) + 1))
```

By using **STRALLOC**, we save ourselves some typing and lessen the chance that we'll forget to allocate space for the string's trailing null character. Of course, we could write **STRALLOC** as a function, but it is much more efficient as a macro.

Figure 15.13 combines all of these macros in a little program to duplicate an array of **int**s and an array of strings. After creating the copies, it zeros out the original arrays and prints the copies.

One other important use of macros is to hide certain confusing language idioms— once again making our programs more readable without losing efficiency. The macros **STREQ**, **STRLT**, and **STRGT** hide the hideousness of **strcmp**'s return value.

```
#define STREQ(x,y) (strcmp((x),(y)) == 0)  /* equal? */
#define STRLT(x,y) (strcmp((x),(y)) < 0)   /* x < y? */
#define STRGT(x,y) (strcmp((x),(y)) > 0)   /* x > y? */
```

They test whether one string is lexicographically equal to, less than, or greater than another string. Without these macros, the program's reader must remember the meaning of the various return values of **strcmp** to understand which string comparison is being performed.

Potential Problems

Macros are useful—but they also have several potential pitfalls. One drawback is that a macro's code appears everywhere the macro is called, whereas a function's code appears only once, regardless of how many times the function is called. When minimal program size is important, write large, often-used macros as functions.

First, a macro argument, unlike a function argument, may be evaluated more than once. With our definition of **INRANGE**, the call

```
INRANGE(1, 100, i + j)
```

expands into

```
/*
 * A program using our memory allocation macros.
 */
#include <stdio.h>
#include <stddef.h>
#include <stdlib.h>
#include "allocs.h"

int main()
{
  int    table[] = {10, 87, 95, 89, 15, 45, 67, 22, 79, 32};
  char   *string = "abcdefghi";
  const int n   =   sizeof(table)/sizeof(table[0]);
  int    *newtable;
  char   *newstr;
  int    i;

  if (TABLEDUP(newtable, table, n, int) == NULL)
    printf("Integer table copy failed...\n");
  else
  {
    ZERO(table, n, int);
    for (i = 0; i < n; i++)                     /* display copied array */
      printf("%i\n", newtable[i]);
  }
  if (STRDUP(newstr, string) == NULL)
    printf("String copy failed...\n");
  else
  {
    int len=strlen(string);

    ZERO(string, len, char);
    printf("%s\n", newstr);
  }
  return 0;
}
```

Figure 15.13 (dup.c) Using macros to create copies of an array of ints and an array of strings.

$$((i + j) >= (1) \&\& (i + j) <= (100))$$

which causes two evaluations of i + j. That's not particularly troublesome—but what about when our arguments have side effects? Suppose we pass i++ instead of i + j. Then **INRANGE** expands into

$$((i++) >= (1) \&\& (i++) <= (100))$$

This ends up incrementing i twice, rather than just once.

> *Use expressions as macro arguments sparingly, and avoid them entirely
> when they contain side effects.*

Second, sloppy parenthesizing can result in incorrect orders of evaluation. Suppose
we have a macro to square its arguments, and we don't bother to parenthesize them.

```
#define SQUARE(x) (x * x) /* SLOPPY: underparenthesized */
```

This causes `SQUARE(i + j)` to expand into

```
i + j * i + j
```

which does not return $(i + j)^2$. Carefully parenthesizing eliminates potentially incorrect
orders of evaluation.

```
#define SQUARE(x) ((x) * (x))        /* correct */
```

> *Make sure to parenthesize all occurrences of the parameter inside the
> macro's replacement text.*

Macro Operators

ANSI-C provides two special operators that can appear in macro definitions: `#` and `##`.
The first, `#`, precedes a parameter name. It causes double quotes to be placed around
the argument substituted for the parameter. We use it in the macro `DUMPINT`, which
writes an `int` variable's name and value.

```
#define DUMPINT(x)  printf(#x "=%i\n", x)
```

`DUMPINT` is especially useful when debugging. The preprocessor expands the call
`DUMPINT(x)` into

```
printf("x" "=%i\n", x);
```

The preprocessor places double quotes around the **x** passed as the macro's first argument
and takes any quote that appears in it and precedes it with a backslash. The preprocessor
(or compiler) then concatenates the resulting strings into a single string.

```
printf("x=%i\n", x);
```

The other operator, `##`, turns two tokens into a single token. We use it to write
a more general macro, `DISPLAY`, that takes two arguments: the expression to print
and its type. So `DISPLAY(thing, int)` displays `thing`'s value as an `int`, and
`DISPLAY(thing, double)` displays its value as a `double`.

How does `DISPLAY` work? It expands into calls to different functions, depending
on the type of object it's displaying. `DISPLAY(i, int)`, for example, expands into
`printint("i", i)`. `DISPLAY` itself is actually quite simple.

```
/*
 * Using the preprocessor to obtain readable debugging output.
 */
#include <stdio.h>

#define DUMPINT(x)      printf(#x "=%i\n", x)
#define DISPLAY(x, t)   print ## t (#x, x)

int main()
{
  void    printint(char *name, int x);
  void    printdouble(char *name, double x);
  int     i = 69;
  double d = 3.1415926;

  DUMPINT(i);
  DISPLAY(i, int);  DISPLAY(d, double);
  return 0;
}

void printint(char *name, int x)
{
  printf("DEBUG: %s (INTEGER) = %i\n", name, x);
}

void printdouble(char *name, double x)
{
  printf("DEBUG: %s (DOUBLE) = %f (%e)\n", name, x, x);
}
```

Figure 15.14 (debugex.c) Defining and using our DISPLAY and DUMPINT macros.

```
#define DISPLAY(x, t)   print ## t (#x, x)
```

It uses **##** to concatenate its second argument onto the word **print** to form the function name. For the macro call **DISPLAY(i, int)**, the preprocessor first substitutes **i** for **x** and **int** for **t**,

```
print ## int("i", i)
```

and then concatenates the two tokens **print** and **int** together, resulting in

```
printint("i", i)
```

Figure 15.14 is a short example that displays several different variables using these macros. Here's its output:

```
i=69
DEBUG: i (INTEGER) = 69
DEBUG: d (DOUBLE) = 3.141593 (3.141593e+00)
```

Undefining a Name

Once we have defined a name, *all* subsequent occurrences are replaced with its replacement text. Sometimes, however, we want to limit a name definition's scope, either to highlight that the name is used only in a small section of the program or to allow the name to be redefined. We use the directive

```
#undef NAME
```

to undefine a defined name, which stops any further macro substitution for it. We can then use **#define** to redefine the name. Otherwise, the compiler will complain if we try to redefine a name without first undefining it.

#undef lets us select between a macro and a function to accomplish a particular task. Macros give us speed; functions save space. It's usually less harmful to have side effects in a function argument and easier to add debugging code to a function.

As a concrete example, suppose that we're including our earlier bit-accessing macros. If we decide we want **GETBITS** and **SETBITS** as functions and **GETBIT** and **SETBIT** as macros, all we have to do is undefine **GETBITS** and **SETBITS** and then link in an object module containing the function definitions.

15.4   **FILE INCLUSION**

We have been using file inclusion all along. The directive **#include** instructs the preprocessor to replace the current line with the entire contents of the specified file. If we don't provide a complete file name, the preprocessor searches for the file in various locations determined by the **#include** form used. The form

```
#include <filename>
```

has the preprocessor look in the usual system locations for the include files. We use an alternative form

```
#include "filename"
```

for include files that we create. It looks in a default directory first, and searches the other locations only if the file is not found locally. It's an error if the included file cannot be found. As you might expect, an included file can include other files, but shouldn't include itself or any file that includes it.

File inclusion allows us to create a file of useful definitions that we can include in all our programs. Definitions like those shown in Figure 15.15 require little effort to extend C in a useful way. We've explained most of these definitions and macros already, but we've also defined a pair of macros **MAX** and **MIN** that return the maximum and minimum value of their arguments, respectively, and a macro **PRINT_STRING** that writes a string on a line by itself.

```
/*
 * Our default definitions.
 */
#include <stdio.h>
#include <stddef.h>
#include <stdlib.h>
#include <string.h>
#include <ctype.h>

#define FOREVER for(;;)
#define IS       ==
#define ISNOT    !=

#define MIN(x,y)        ((x) < (y) ? (x) : (y))      /* smaller */
#define MAX(x,y)        ((x) < (y) ? (y) : (x))      /* larger */
#define INRANGE(x,y,v)  ((v) >= (x) && (v) <= (y))
#define STREQ(x,y)      (strcmp(x,y) == 0)           /* hide */
#define STRLT(x,y)      (strcmp(x,y) < 0)            /* strcmp */
#define STRGT(x,y)      (strcmp(x,y) > 0))           /* ugliness */
#define PRINT_STRING(s) (printf("%s\n", s))          /* print string */
```

Figure 15.15   (defs.h) A header file containing generally useful definitions used by many programs.

Including Data Type Definitions

File inclusion allows us to define a set of useful operations entirely within an include file. In fact, we've already done so with the bit-accessing macros we wrote earlier. We put them into the header file bits.h and then included this file when we needed these operations. If, after time, we find these macros to be generally useful, we can include bits.h from defs.h. Doing so effectively extends the language to provide additional functions we find useful, while preserving the efficiency of programs that use them.

We can, in fact, define a seemingly new data type completely within a header file. As an example, Figure 15.16 shows the include file boolean.h, which contains definitions that make it appear as though C has a Boolean data type. These definitions help us write more readable code, and make it easier to translate programs written in a language that has a Boolean type.

We use **short** to hold **BOOLEAN**s, since we need only store the two values zero (**FALSE**) and 1 (**TRUE**). For consistency with other languages, we define the constants **NOT, AND,** and **OR** as alternatives to C's equivalent logical operators. **BOOLSTR** returns a string representing the **BOOLEAN**'s value, which comes in handy when debugging. The file also makes use of several new preprocessor statements—**#if** and **#endif**—but we'll cover those in the next section.

Any program can pretend that C has **BOOLEAN**s by including boolean.h and using these definitions. We use them in Figure 15.17, a new version of our earlier program to filter duplicate input lines. Before we had these definitions in the source file, but now we just include the header file. We'd already made use of constants for **TRUE** and **FALSE**;

```
/*
 * Header file defining BOOLEAN data type.
 */
#if !defined(BOOLEAN)

#define    BOOLEAN         short
#define    TRUE            1
#define    FALSE           0
#define    NOT             !
#define    AND             &&
#define    OR              ||
#define    BOOLSTR(x)      (x) ? "TRUE" : "FALSE"

#endif
```

Figure 15.16   (boolean.h)   A header file defining a **BOOLEAN** data type.

```
/*
 * A new version of our program to strip duplicate lines.
 */
#include "defs.h"                    /* Our definitions */
#include "boolean.h"                 /* Our Boolean type */

#define MAXLEN  80                   /* longest line length */

int main()
{
  int getline(char *buf, int size);
  char    curr[MAXLEN + 1],          /* current line */
          prev[MAXLEN + 1];          /* previous line */
  BOOLEAN first = TRUE;              /* first time through? */

  for (; getline(curr, MAXLEN) ISNOT -1; strcpy(prev, curr))
    if (first OR !STREQ(prev, curr))
      {
        PRINT_STRING(curr);
        first = FALSE;
      }
  return 0;
}
```

Figure 15.17   (uniq.c)   Using the **BOOLEAN** definitions in a new version of uniq.

this version differs in that the constants are in a header file and do not have to be defined and that **first** is now a **BOOLEAN** rather than **int**. Since we've defined boolean.h ourselves, we surround the **#include** with quotes rather than angle brackets.

15.5   CONDITIONAL COMPILATION

We can use the preprocessor to select which lines of the source file are actually compiled, a process known as *conditional compilation*. Conditional compilation lets us compile a program's source into different versions, depending on our needs. The directive

```
#if  constant-expression
    first-group-of-lines
#else
    second-group-of-lines
#endif
```

evaluates *constant-expression* and compares its value with zero to determine which group of lines to process. If the expression is nonzero, the preprocessor and compiler process the *first-group-of-lines*; otherwise they process the *second-group-of-lines*. As you might expect, the **#else** and the *second-group-of-lines* is optional.

We can use a simple form of **#if** to "comment out" sections of code that contain comments. This is useful, since comments don't nest.

```
#if 0                    /* begin ignored section */
    lines-to-be-commented out
#endif                   /* end ignored section */
```

Since the **#if**'s expression is always zero, the *lines-to-be-commented-out* are always ignored.

More typically, we combine **#if** with a new preprocessor operator, **defined**, to test whether a name is known to a preprocessor. **defined** takes a *NAME* (which must be surrounded by parentheses) and returns a nonzero value only if the *NAME* is defined.

Figure 15.18 uses **#if** and **defined** in a new version of our **table_average** function. This version conditionally includes statements that provide debugging output. These statements are included only if the name **DEBUG** is defined when the function is compiled. If **DEBUG** is defined when the preprocessor evaluates the final **#if** in **table_average**, the compiler receives

```
{
    sum += *ptr;
    printf("*ptr=%i, sum=%li\n", *ptr, sum);
}
```

but doesn't see the statement between the **#else** and the **#endif**. It sees that statement,

```
sum += *ptr;
```

only if **DEBUG** is not defined.

```
/*
 * Computing the average of an array, with debugging code.
 */
#if defined(DEBUG)
#include <stdio.h>
#endif

double table_average(const int a[], int n)
{
  long       sum = 0L;
  const int *ptr = a;                  /* traversing pointer */
  const int * const endptr = a + n;   /* pointer to just past the end */

#if defined(DEBUG)
  printf("ptr=%p, endptr=%p\n", (void *) ptr, (void *) endptr);
#endif

  for ( ; ptr < endptr; ptr++)
#if defined(DEBUG)
  {
    sum += *ptr;
    printf("*ptr=%i, sum=%li\n", *ptr, sum);
  }
#else
    sum += *ptr;
#endif

  return (n != 0) ? (double) sum / n : 0.0;
}
```

Figure 15.18   (average1.c)   Table averaging routine, complete with debugging statements.

We test whether **DEBUG** is defined to decide whether to include the debugging statements. But how do we make sure **DEBUG** is defined? One way is to simply add the line

```
#define DEBUG
```

at the top of our source file when we want debugging statements. We then remove it when they are no longer necessary. Most compilers, however, provide an option to define names on the command line, and even to give them a value.

Figure 15.19 is a little program that uses **table_average** to compute the average of a small table of values. When we run it without **DEBUG** defined, it simply prints the average:

```
57.600000
```

But when we run it with **DEBUG** defined, we can see a trace of the pointer used to run through the array, as well an idea of how many values we're supposed to process:

```
/*
 * Using our table average function.
 */
#include <stdio.h>

int main()
{
  double table_average(const int a[], int n);
  const int table[] = {91, 40, 78, 23, 56};
  const int n        = sizeof(table)/sizeof(table[0]);

#if defined(DEBUG)
  printf("Averaging %i values.\n", n);
#endif
  printf("%f\n", table_average(table, n));
  return 0;
}
```

Figure 15.19   (avgmain.c) A program using our new **table_average**.

```
Averaging 5 values.
ptr=68fab31c, endptr=68fab330
*ptr=91, sum=91
*ptr=40, sum=131
*ptr=78, sum=209
*ptr=23, sum=232
*ptr=56, sum=288
57.600000
```

What are the alternatives to having the preprocessor decide whether debugging output should be produced? We could add output statements whenever we want debugging output and remove them once we've debugged the program. But then the debugging statements aren't available when we want to make changes to the program. We could use run-time tests, but then our program is larger, because the debugging statements appear in its object module even when we don't want debugging output, and slower, because the tests are done at run time, not at compile time. The preprocessor approach does have one disadvantage: The many preprocessor tests make the source less readable.

We often combine **defined** with logical negation (!) to test whether a name hasn't yet been defined. We use this most often in include files to ensure that even if the file is included more than once, any definitions it contains won't be. We did that in boolean.h, so it defines **BOOLEAN** only if it hasn't already been defined. The file's first line

```
#if !defined(BOOLEAN)
```

causes the various names contained in the file to be defined only if **BOOLEAN** is undefined. If **BOOLEAN** is already defined, we assume that the file has already been included and that we can ignore its definitions.

```
/*
 * Computing the average of an array, with debugging code.
 */
#if DEBUG > 0
#include <stdio.h>
#endif

double table_average(const int a[], int n)
{
  long      sum = 0L;
  const int *ptr = a;                  /* traversing pointer */
  const int * const endptr = a + n;  /* pointer to just past the end */

#if DEBUG > 0
  printf("ptr=%p, endptr=%p\n", (void *) ptr, (void *) endptr);
#endif

  for ( ; ptr < endptr; ptr++)
#if DEBUG > 1
    {
      sum += *ptr;
      printf("*ptr=%i, sum=%li\n", *ptr, sum);
    }
#else
    sum += *ptr;
#endif

  return (n != 0) ? (double) sum / n : 0.0;
}
```

Figure 15.20   (average2.c) Compute the average of a table, printing various pieces of useful debugging information.

Remember that **defined** tests only whether the name is defined in the preprocessor. It doesn't test whether the name of an identifier, function, or type has been declared.

One last use of **#if** is to compile things differently depending on the value of some preprocessor constant. We might, for example, want to have several types of debugging output: no output, a sketchy bit of output, and a fuller trace. We can do this by defining **DEBUG** to be 0 for no output, 1 for a dump of each function's parameters or most important variables, and 2 for additional debugging statements and then using **#if** to test for the various values of **DEBUG**. Figure 15.20 does so in a new version of **table_average**.

Other Testing Directives

There's one other directive we can use with **#if**: **#elif**. We can use it to write **#if**s of the form

```
#if test-1
    .  .  .
#else
#if test-2
    .  .  .
#endif
#endif
```

more compactly

```
#if test-1
    .  .  .
#elif test-2
    .  .  .
#endif
```

We replace any **#else** immediately followed by an **#if** with **#elif** and then remove its **#endif**.

There are also two special directives we can use for testing whether a name is defined. The line

```
#ifdef NAME
```

is equivalent to

```
#if defined(NAME)
```

and the line

```
#ifndef NAME
```

is equivalent to

```
#if !defined(NAME).
```

In practice, however, we rarely use either of these directives, since they're really just special cases of **#if**.

Predefined Names

In addition to names we define ourselves, most preprocessors also predefine some names for us. Table 15.2 contains the minimal set of names defined by any ANSI-C conforming compiler.

Figure 15.21 defines a macro **ASSERT** that uses several of these names. **ASSERT**'s argument is an expression representing a programmer assumption. If the assumption doesn't hold, it writes a message that includes the line number, and source file where the assertion was made. We can insert a call to **ASSERT** wherever a function makes a critical assumption, documenting the assumption and indicating when it fails. Invariably, a false assumption will cause our program to fail; **ASSERT** helps us find such assumptions.

NAME	VALUE OR TEST
__LINE__	current line number (an integer)
__FILE__	current file name (a string constant)
__DATE__	date source file is translated (string of the form: MMMDDYYYY)
__TIME__	time source file is translated (string of the form: HHMMSS)
__STDC__	defined if ANSI-compatible

Table 15.2 C's predefined preprocessor names.

```
/*
 * Our version of the ASSERT macro.
 */
#include <stdlib.h>

#define ASSERT(cond) \
  ((cond) || \
    printf("Assertion (" # cond ") failed (%s,%i)\n", \
           __FILE__, __LINE__), exit(1))
```

Figure 15.21 (assert.h) The definition of our **ASSERT** macro.

When **ASSERT** is called, the preprocessor replaces __LINE__ and __FILE__ with the line number and file name of the call. This way the error message indicates where the failed assumption occurred in the source file.

Figure 15.22 contains a new version of **table_average** that uses **ASSERT** to make explicit its assumption that it is passed a non-null pointer. If we accidentally pass it a null pointer, we get a useful error message.

```
Assertion (ptr != NULL) failed (average3.c,13)
```

This message was generated because the call to **ASSERT**,

```
ASSERT(ptr != NULL);
```

expands into

```
((ptr != NULL) ||
 printf("Assertion (" "ptr != NULL") failed (%s,%i)\n",
 average3.c, 13), exit(1));
```

which causes the error message that's printed when the program runs. The **ASSERT** provides some indication of where the problem lies. An error message from a failed assertion provides a better starting point for locating bugs than missing output or a potentially cryptic system message.[1]

---

[1] Our **ASSERT** macro uses **exit** to terminate the program if the assertion fails. Appendix

```
/*
 * Computes the average of an array.  Contains an assertion.
 */
#include <stdio.h>
#include "assert.h"

double table_average(const int a[], int n)
{
  long        sum = 0L;
  const int *ptr = a;                   /* traversing pointer */
  const int *const endptr = a + n;   /* pointer to just past the end */

  ASSERT(ptr != NULL);
  for ( ; ptr < endptr; ptr++)
    sum += *ptr;
  return (n != 0) ? (double) sum / n : 0.0;
}
```

Figure 15.22   (average3.c) Making an assumption explicit with the **ASSERT** macro.

ANSI-C actually provides a system header file assert.h that provides a macro
assert that behaves similarly to our **ASSERT** macro. One difference is that it writes
its error message in a slightly different format. Another is that if the symbol **NDEBUG**
is defined, none of the assertions are compiled with the program, effectively turning off
checking insertions. There's no need to worry about a conflict between our own include
file and the system's, since the double quotation marks in the **#include** guarantee that
ours will be used.

Most compilers also define a set of names that describe the particular compiler and
the operating system it's running under. A program can test these predefined names to
determine what type of environment it's running in and adjust environment dependencies
accordingly. There are several ways we can take advantage of these names. We'll present
them in detail in Chapter 20, our chapter on portability.

15.6   OTHER PREPROCESSOR DIRECTIVES

There are three other preprocessor directives. The first, **#line**, tells the preprocessor
from which input file and line, a line in its input was derived.

> **#line** *line-number* *"filename"*

#line appears most frequently in C programs that have been generated or modified
by other programs before they are seen by the preprocessor or compiler. Because line
numbers referred to in a preprocessor or compiler error message may not correspond

---

C describes **exit** in detail.

exactly to the line where the error occurred in the source file used to generate these programs, they use **#line** to make error messages refer to the correct lines in the original source file.

We use **#error** most frequently inside preprocessor conditionals. When the preprocessor encounters a **#error**,

```
#error error-message
```

it writes an error message and terminates preprocessing early. A program could use

```
#if !defined(__STDC__)
#error Requires standard C to compile
#endif
```

to terminate preprocessing unless it's being compiled by an ANSI compiler.

The final directive is **#pragma**, whose behavior differs among compilers. See your compiler manual for details.

15.7   CASE STUDY—IMPLEMENTING SETS WITH MACROS

This section is optional!

Earlier we presented a package implementing some basic set handling functions. Most of the functions were only one line long and were little more than a **return** statement of a complicated expression. That means they're good candidates for macros.

Figure 15.23 is a header file defining the macros necessary to implement sets. It's divided into several pieces. The first defines the **SET** type and a constant **US_BITS** for the number of bits in an **unsigned short**. The second defines some useful utility macros for determining an element's position within the array representing the set and the number of words needed to store the entire set. These roughly correspond to the **static** functions we had previously. Finally, the last section defines macros for each of the functions in the set package we had before, along with a new macro that switches an item from one set to another. Figure 15.24 is a new version of our program to detect duplicate input values that's written using these macros.

There are some trade-offs in using macros to implement sets. On the positive side, programs using the macro implementation will be more efficient, since they no longer suffer overhead for function calls. They'll also be easier to compile and run, since we no longer need to link in the compiled set functions. On the negative side, however, sets.h is hard to read, since the macros cram a lot of code into just a few lines. We've also defined several auxiliary names that make our macros easier to define, but we can't hide these names from the programs using our header file, which may result in various name conflicts.

SUMMARY

- All C programs are first passed through a preprocessor before the compiler ever sees them.

```
/*
 * Macro package for dynamically allocated sets.
 */
#include <stdlib.h>

typedef void *SET;
typedef unsigned short USHORT;

#define US_BITS 16                      /* Bits in unsigned short */

/* Utility macros:
 *    WORD:   index of word holding element
 *    BIT:    index of bit holding element
 *    WORDS: number of words needed to hold entire set
 */
#define WORD(e)            ((e) / US_BITS)
#define BIT(e)             ((e) % US_BITS)
#define WORDS(n)           (((n) / US_BITS) + (((n) % US_BITS) != 0))
/*
 * Macros meant for the outside world:
 *    SET_CREATE:  form a new set of n elements.
 *    SET_DESTROY: get rid of existing set.
 *    SET_ADD:     add element to an existing set.
 *    SET_MEMBER:  is item in set?
 *    SET_SWITCH:  move item from one set to another.
 */
#define SET_CREATE(n)    (calloc(WORDS(n),sizeof(USHORT)))
#define SET_DESTROY(s)   free((s))
#define SET_ADD(s,e)     (* ((USHORT *) (s) + WORD(e)) |= 1 << BIT(e))
#define SET_DELETE(s,e) (* ((USHORT *) (s) + WORD(e)) &= ~(1 << BIT(e)))
#define SET_MEMBER(s,e)  \
            (((unsigned) (* ((USHORT *) (s) + WORD(e))) >> BIT(e)) & 01)
#define SET_SWITCH(n,o,v)    (SET_DELETE(o,v),  SET_ADD(n,v))
```

Figure 15.23 (sets.h) Defining sets using macros.

- **#define** is a general mechanism for having the preprocessor substitute text for names.

- We can define names with parameters, so that the replacement text becomes a template filled in when we use the name.

- We can use **#undef** to stop substituting text for a name.

- **#include** has the preprocessor substitute the contents of the named file, which can be either a system header file or one of our own.

- **#if** (together with **#else** and **#endif**) allows us to pass different code to the compiler depending on whether a particular name is defined at compile time or what value it has.

```
/*
 * Identify duplicates in the input.
 */
#include "defs.h"
#include "sets.h"                    /* for SETs */

int main()
{
  void        set_print(const char *name, const SET s, int max);
  const int MAXELEMS = 512;                    /* # of set elements */
  SET         unique = SET_CREATE(MAXELEMS),   /* unique and */
              dup    = SET_CREATE(MAXELEMS);   /*    duplicate sets */
  int         r;                               /* scanf return */
  int         inp;                             /* input value */

  while ((r = scanf("%i", &inp)) ISNOT EOF)
  {
    if (r ISNOT 1)
    {
      printf("Value in error.\n");
      break;
    }
    if (!INRANGE(0, MAXELEMS - 1, inp))
    {
      printf("Value %i not between %i and %i\n", inp, 0, MAXELEMS - 1);
      continue;
    }
    if (SET_MEMBER(unique, inp))
      SET_SWITCH(dup, unique, inp);
    else if (!SET_MEMBER(dup, inp))
      SET_ADD(unique, inp);
  }
  set_print("Unique", unique, MAXELEMS);
  set_print("Duplicate", dup, MAXELEMS);
  return 0;
}

void set_print(const char *name, const SET set, int max)
{
  int i;                              /* next potential element */

  printf("%s values\n", name);
  for (i = 0; i < max; i++)
    if (SET_MEMBER(set, i))
      printf("%i\n", i);
}
```

Figure 15.24   (usesets.c)   Using the macro implementation of sets.

EXERCISES

15–1   Examine some of the C programs you have written. Are there complicated expressions that could be greatly simplified by using macros? Write these macros.

15–2   We've been giving our programs the value of π as a constant. It's more accurate to give it the value $2.0 \times \arctan(1.0)$. Write a constant definition for **PI** using this formula. Extend your definition into a macro **N_PI** that computes $n \times \pi$. Modify several of the programs in the text that use the value of π to use your macro rather than a constant.

What's the problem with this approach to defining π? How can we improve it?

15–3   Write the macro **DISPLAY_UL**. It takes a string, an **unsigned long**, and a field width. It prints the string and then prints the value in a field of the specified width. Modify Figure 15.2 to use it.

15–4   Repeat the previous exercise for each of C's other basic types.

15–5   Write a macro, **INDEX**, that expands into a **for** loop that indexes a variable from a minimum to a maximum.

```
INDEX(i, 1, 100) printf("This is %i\n", i);
```

expands into

```
for (i = 1; i <= 100; i++) printf("This is %i\n", i);
```

INDEX should work even if the loop bounds are expressions.

15–6   Write the macros **DIV** and **DIVMOD**. **DIV(x,y)** returns the value of x/y for nonzero values of **y**, otherwise it returns zero. **DIVMOD(d,r,x,y)** divides **x** by **y**, storing the result in **d** and the remainder in **r**.

15–7   Write a macro, **MSG(flag,msg)**, that writes the string **msg** only if **flag** is not zero.

15–8   Write a macro, **NULLPTR(type)**, that returns a null pointer correctly cast to the passed type. When is this macro useful?

15–9   Write a macro, **DEREF(ptr, type)**, that dereferences **ptr** only if it is not null. If **ptr** is null, the macro prints an error message and returns zero, cast to the appropriate type.

15–10   Write constant definitions for the maximum and minimum values of the types **short**, **int**, and **long**. These definitions should work for both 16- and 32-bit machines. Write similar constant definitions for their unsigned counterparts.

15–11   Define a header file that provides a group of functions for manipulating sets of small integers (from 0 to 31). Write macros for adding an item to the set, deleting an item from the set, testing whether an item is in the set, and taking the union and intersection of two sets.

15–12   Define a header file that provides a set of macros for traversing arrays. These include

```
INIT(array, elements, ptr, value)
```

which expands into a loop initializing each array element to a particular value,

```
FWALK(array, elements, ptr, func)
```

which expands into a loop executing a function on each array element (going from beginning to end), and

```
RWALK(array, elements, ptr, func)
```

that does the same thing but in the opposite direction.

15–13 Write a program that removes all lines beginning with an at sign (@) from C source files. This allows us to have convenient single-line comments. The program should provide #lines to ensure error messages refer to the correct lines in the original source files.

16   GENERIC

FUNCTIONS

This chapter discusses generic functions: functions that can perform a particular task on any arbitrary C data type. We introduce the built-in generic library functions for searching and sorting arrays and use them to search and sort arrays of integers, arrays of strings, and arrays of structures. We then implement our own generic functions for performing sequential search and insertion sort and show how to build a nice interface on top of them for searching and sorting specific types. The chapter concludes with a case study—an implementation of the standard library's binary search function.

16.1   GENERIC LIBRARY FUNCTIONS

A generic function is one that can perform a particular task on any underlying C data type. C's standard library provides two of these functions: **bsearch** searches an arbitrary array using the binary search technique we presented in Chapter 14, and **qsort** sorts an arbitrary array using a special sorting technique called *quicksort*. By arbitrary array, we mean an array with any type of element. We can use these functions to search and sort an array of integers, an array of strings, or even an array of structures. To use these functions, we need to include their prototypes, which are found in the system header file stdlib.h.

The bsearch Library Function

In Chapter 14 we wrote our own binary search routine, **binsearch**. It took three arguments: pointers to the first and last **long**s in the array, and a **long** to try to find. The problem with **binsearch** is that we can only use it to search a sorted array of **long**s. It's littered with dependencies on **long**s: it takes pointers to **long**s to delineate the array it's searching, it's passed a **long** to look for, it uses the less than and equality operators to compare **long**s, and it returns a pointer to a **long**. The library's **bsearch** function eliminates this restriction, but at a cost: we now have to provide it additional information about the array we want to search. Specifically, we must also pass it the size of an array element and a function to use to determine whether it has found the desired array element. Here's **bsearch**'s prototype:

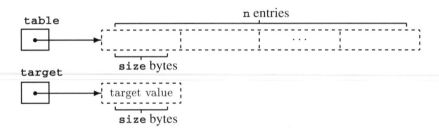

Figure 16.1 The relationship between **bsearch**'s parameters.

```
void *bsearch(const void *target,
              const void *table,
              size_t n,
              size_t size,
              int (*cmpfp)(const void *, const void *));
```

bsearch takes five arguments. The first, **target**, is a pointer to the value we're searching for. It's a pointer to **void** because **bsearch** doesn't care at all about the type of object it's trying to find—it could be an **int**, a string, a structure, and so on. As we saw earlier, we use a pointer to **void** to point to an object of unknown type. The target pointer is a **const** because we're not changing its value within the function.

The next three arguments—**table**, **n**, and **size**—describe the array we're searching. **table** is a pointer to the first element in that array. It's a **const** pointer to **void** for the same reasons as **target**: In general, **bsearch** doesn't know what sort of array it's going to be searching. **n** is an **int**, the number of elements in the array. **size** is the size of an array element. We provide this size because **bsearch** uses pointer arithmetic to traverse the array, and it must figure out where each array element begins and ends. Figure 16.1 shows the relationship between all of these parameters.

The final argument, **cmpfp**, is a pointer to a function that **bsearch** uses to determine whether a particular array element matches the target. **bsearch** calls this function each time it examines an array element, passing it a pair of pointers: one points to the target, the other to the array element it's examining. **bsearch** has no idea what types they actually point to, only how large the objects are, so it passes these as pointers to **void**. That means the comparison function must take a pair of pointers to **void**. **bsearch** expects it to return a negative value if the first pointed-to thing is smaller than the second, zero if they are equal, and a positive value if the first is larger than the second.

bsearch returns a pointer to the matching array element if it finds the value, or **NULL** otherwise. Once again, this pointer is a pointer to **void**.

Figure 16.2 uses **bsearch** to search an array of **long**s, using the call:

```
fptr = bsearch(&t, tab, MAX, sizeof(tab[0]), cmplong);
```

```
/*
 * Use generic binary search to search a table of longs.
 */
#include <stdio.h>
#include <stddef.h>
#include <stdlib.h>

#define MAX     100

int main(int argc, char *argv[])
{
  int  cmplong(const void *xptr, const void *yptr);
  long tab[MAX];                         /* array to search */
  long *ptr;                             /* ptr to found item */
  int  i;                                /* temporary index */
  long t;                                /* target */

  for (i = 0; i < MAX; i++)              /* initialize table with */
    tab[i] = i;                          /*    0,1,2,3,... */
  for (i = 1; i < argc; i++)             /* are arguments in table? */
    if (sscanf(argv[i], "%li", &t) == 1)
      if ((ptr = bsearch(&t, tab, MAX, sizeof(tab[0]), cmplong)) != NULL)
        printf("Found %li as element %i.\n", t, ptr - tab);
      else
        printf("Didn't find %li.\n", t);
  return 0;
}

/* Compare target long with table entry */

int cmplong(const void *xptr, const void *yptr)
{
  long x = * (long *) xptr;
  long y = * (long *) yptr;

  return (x == y) ? 0 : ((x < y) ? -1 : 1);
}
```

Figure 16.2   (lbsearch.c)   A program using binary search to search an array of longs.

t is a pointer to the target, **tab** is the table we're searching, **MAX** is the number of elements in **tab**, **sizeof(tab[0])** is the size of an element, and **cmplong** is the function we use to compare the target value with an array element. We precede the call to **bsearch** with a prototype for **cmplong**, so the compiler knows that it's the name of a function and not a variable.

The tricky part is writing the comparison function. It's passed two pointers to **void**, so it must cast them to pointers to **long** before following them and comparing the values to which they point.

```
/*
 * Uses generic binary search to search an array of strings.
 */
#include <stdio.h>
#include <stdlib.h>
#include <string.h>

int main(int argc, char *argv[])
{
    int    cmpstr(const void *xptr, const void *yptr);
    const char   *tab[] =
                    {"alex",    "barbi", "daphne", "diane", "doris",
                     "gisele", "irene", "sally", "tammy", "veronica"};
    const int n  = sizeof(tab)/sizeof(tab[0]);
    const char **ptr;                          /* pointer to found item */
    int    i;

    for (i = 1; i < argc; i++)
      if ((ptr = bsearch(argv[i], tab, n, sizeof(tab[0]), cmpstr)) != NULL)
        printf("Found %s in position %i\n", argv[i], ptr - tab);
      else
        printf("Couldn't find %s in table\n", argv[i]);
    return 0;
}

/* Compare target string with string in table */

int cmpstr(const void *xptr, const void *yptr)
{
    return strcmp((char *) xptr, * (char **) yptr);
}
```

Figure 16.3   (sbsearch.c) Using **bsearch** to search an array of strings.

```
            x = * (long *) xptr;
```

Taking this statement apart, we see that it converts **xptr**'s value to a pointer to a **long** and then follows it. It does the same for the other pointer parameter

```
            y = * (long *) yptr;
```

and finally compares the two **long**s and returns the result.

The nice feature of generic functions like **bsearch** is that we need only write new comparison functions to use it with different data types. Figure 16.3 uses **bsearch** to search an array of strings for a particular string. It's very similar to our previous program, except that now we're using **cmpstr** as the comparison function. As with **cmplong**, it must cast the passed pointers before doing the actual comparison. This time, however, it's comparing strings so it uses the built-in function **strcmp**, instead of the < operator.

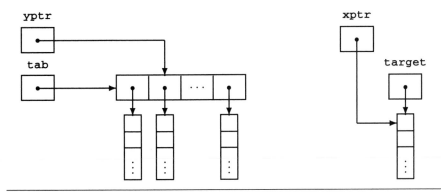

Figure 16.4 The pointers **bsearch** is passing to **cmpstr**.

```
return strcmp((char *) xptr, * (char **) yptr);
```

This call is less complex than it appears. The first parameter is simply a pointer to the target string, so **cmpstr** casts it to a pointer to a **char**. The second parameter is trickier: it's a pointer to an element in the array of strings, and since each element in the array is a pointer to a string, that means it's really a pointer to a pointer to a **char**. **cmpstr** casts it appropriately and then dereferences it to obtain the pointer it passes to **strcmp**. Figure 16.4 provides a picture of all of these pointers.

Figure 16.5 provides one final example of **bsearch**. It's a new implementation of Chapter 14's program to search an array of employees. Now, to search by employee number, it uses **bsearch**, rather than our earlier function **empsearch**.

```
bsearch(&target, tab, n, sizeof(tab[0]), empnocmp)
```

This call to **bsearch** is almost identical to the other two. Again, the only real difference lies in the comparison function, **empnocmp**, which casts the pointers appropriately and then compares the target employee number with the **number** field in the structure.

```
return * (long *) tarptr - ((EMPLOYEE *) entryptr)->number;
```

There's one caveat to using **bsearch**: it assumes that the array it's searching is sorted. Our example assumes that the table is ordered, ascending by employee number. That's fine, since we set it up that way. But more realistically we would need to sort the table on whatever field we were looking up. The next section describes a generic sorting function we can use to do just that.

> *Only use* **bsearch** *to search sorted arrays.*

```
/*
 * Using bsearch to search an array of structures.
 */
#include <stdio.h>
#include <string.h>
#include <stdlib.h>

typedef struct
{
  long number;
  char *name, *phone;
  double salary;
} EMPLOYEE;

int main(int argc, char *argv[])
{
  int empnocmp(const void *xptr, const void *yptr);
  EMPLOYEE tab[] =
            {{1001, "Daphne Borromeo",     "213-555-2134", 8.78},
             {1011, "Tammy Merriweather", "213-555-1212", 4.50},
             {1140, "Doris Perl",         "213-555-1215", 5.60},
             {2045, "Barbara Wong",       "213-555-1219", 7.80},
             {2945, "Diane Goebel",       "213-555-1235", 9.00},
             {3300, "Irene Borromeo",     "213-555-1210", 3.97},
             {4011, "Veronica Ockert",    "213-555-1214", 4.50},
             {4140, "Tony Quilici",       "213-555-1295", 5.60},
             {5045, "Brian Hight",        "213-555-6219", 7.80},
             {5945, "Gisele Pham",        "213-555-1545", 9.00}};
  const int n = sizeof(tab)/sizeof(tab[0]);
  int        i;                      /* index into values to search */
  long       target;                 /* value we're trying to find */
  EMPLOYEE   *matchptr;              /* pointer to found item */

  for (i = 1; i < argc; i++)
    if (sscanf(argv[i],"%li",&target) == 1)
      {
        matchptr = bsearch(&target, tab, n, sizeof(tab[0]), empnocmp);
        if (matchptr != NULL)
          printf("%li is in record %i\n", target, matchptr - tab);
        else
          printf("%li wasn't found\n", target);
      }
  return 0;
}

/* Comparison function for employee numbers */

int empnocmp(const void *tarptr, const void *entryptr)
{
  return * (long *) tarptr - ((EMPLOYEE *) entryptr)->number;
}
```

Figure 16.5 (ebsearch.c) Using **bsearch** to search a table of structures.

The qsort Library Function

Sorting is ubiquitous in programming. Often times we end up writing our own sort routines by rewriting routines written to handle different data types. When the items to be sorted are contained in an array, however, we can use the standard library's generic sorting routine: **qsort**.

```
void qsort(void *table,
           size_t n,
           size_t size,
           int (*cmpfp)(const void *, const void *));
```

qsort is similar to **bsearch**. It takes four parameters. The first, **table**, is the address of the first element in the array to sort. **qsort** can sort arrays of any type, so **table** is a pointer to **void**. The second, **n**, is the number of items to sort. The third, **size**, is the size of each item in bytes. The last, **cmpfp**, is a pointer to a comparison function. But this time the comparison function is passed pointers to different array elements, rather than pointers to a target and an array element. It returns the same values as before.

Figure 16.6 shows how to use **qsort** to sort an array of **long**s and an array of character strings. To sort longs, we can use the same comparison function, **cmplong**, we used with **bsearch**. That's because we originally wrote it to take a pair of addresses: the address of a table entry and the address of the target **long**.

To sort an array of character strings, however, we use a new comparison function, **cmpstrs**. We can't use our earlier **cmpstr** function because it expects to be passed a pointer to a target string and a pointer to an element. **qsort**, however, passes pointers to a pair of array elements.

Figure 16.7 provides one last example of **qsort**, using it to sort our employee records first by phone number and then by employee's first name. It uses several more comparison functions, **cmpphone** and **cmpname**. Both cast the two pointers they're passed to pointers to **EMPLOYEE**s before using **strcmp** to compare their **phone** and **name** fields, respectively.

Coding the comparison functions and getting all of the casts right may seem somewhat difficult—but it is much, much easier than writing quicksort ourselves.[1]

16.2   WRITING GENERIC FUNCTIONS

So just how are generic function like **bsearch** and **qsort** written? We'll illustrate by writing our own generic searching and sorting functions. Our functions, however, aren't going to be as elaborate or efficient as their library equivalents. That's because we search the array using sequential search and sort the array using insertion sort. These algorithms aren't as good as the ones used by the library routines; we picked them solely because their implementation is easier to understand.

---

[1] Actually, we haven't been getting the casts exactly right. Within the comparison functions, we should be casting to pointers to constants! To keep things simple, however, all our comparison functions ignore that issue.

```c
/*
 * Using quicksort to sort both an array of longs and an array of
 * character strings.
 */
#include <stdio.h>
#include <stdlib.h>
#include <string.h>

int main()
{
  int cmplong(const void *xptr, const void *yptr);
  int cmpstrs(const void *xptr, const void *yptr);
  long table[] =
          {17, 10, 89, 26, 30, 99, 78, 11, 91, 16,
           87, 45, 78, 11, 45, 98, 67, 20, 60, 8};
  char *names[] =
          {"barbi",  "irene",  "diane", "doris", "veronica",
           "gisele", "daphne", "alex",  "tammy", "sally"};
  const int nlongs = sizeof(table)/sizeof(table[0]);
  const int nnames = sizeof(names)/sizeof(names[0]);
  int i;

  /* sort and print table of longs */
  qsort(table, nlongs, sizeof(table[0]), cmplong);
  for (i = 0; i < nlongs; i++)
    printf("%li\n", table[i]);

  /* sort and print table of strings */
  qsort(names, nnames, sizeof(names[0]), cmpstrs);
  for (i = 0; i < nnames; i++)
    printf("%s\n", names[i]);
  return 0;
}

/* Compare two table longs */

int cmplong(const void *xptr, const void *yptr)
{
  long x = * (long *) xptr;
  long y = * (long *) yptr;

  return (x == y) ? 0 : ((x < y) ? -1 : 1);
}

/* Compare two table strings */

int cmpstrs(const void *xptr, const void *yptr)
{
  return strcmp(* (char **) xptr, * (char **) yptr);
}
```

Figure 16.6 (qsort1.c) Using `qsort` to sort an array of `long`s and an array of character strings.

```
/*
 * Using qsort to sort an array of structures.
 */
#include <stdio.h>
#include <string.h>
#include <stdlib.h>
#include <stddef.h>

typedef struct
{
  long number;
  char *name, *phone;
  double salary;
} EMPLOYEE;

int main()
{
  int cmpphone(const void *xptr, const void *yptr);
  int cmpname(const void *xptr, const void *yptr);
  EMPLOYEE table[] =
          {{1001, "Daphne Borromeo",      "213-555-2134", 8.78},
           {1011, "Tammy Merriweather",   "213-555-1712", 4.50},
           {1140, "Doris Perl",           "213-555-8615", 5.60},
           {2045, "Barbara Wong",         "213-555-3419", 7.80},
           {2945, "Diane Goebel",         "213-555-9035", 9.00},
           {3300, "Irene Borromeo",       "213-555-3410", 3.97},
           {4011, "Veronica Ockert",      "213-555-7814", 4.50},
           {4140, "Tony Quilici",         "213-555-3435", 5.60},
           {5045, "Brian Hight",          "213-555-6219", 7.80},
           {5945, "Gisele Pham",          "213-555-1945", 9.00}};
  const int n = sizeof(table)/sizeof(table[0]);
  int i;

  qsort(table, n, sizeof(table[0]), cmpphone);  /* sort by phone */
  for (i = 0; i < n; i++)
    printf("%s, %s\n", table[i].name, table[i].phone);
  qsort(table, n, sizeof(table[0]), cmpname);   /* sort by name */
  for (i = 0; i < n; i++)
    printf("%s, %li\n", table[i].name, table[i].number);
  return 0;
}

int cmpphone(const void *xptr, const void *yptr)
{
  return strcmp(((EMPLOYEE *) xptr)->phone, ((EMPLOYEE *) yptr)->phone);
}

int cmpname(const void *xptr, const void *yptr)
{
  return strcmp(((EMPLOYEE *) xptr)->name, ((EMPLOYEE *) yptr)->name);
}
```

Figure 16.7   (qsort2.c) Using **qsort** to sort an array of structures.

```
/*
 * Use standard sequential search on an array of integers.
 */
#include <stdio.h>

int main(int argc, char *argv[])
{
  int        *intsearch(const int *ptr, int n, int target);
  const int tab[] = {15, 78, 45, 89, 12, 16, 19, 31, 68, 90};
  const int n      = sizeof(tab)/sizeof(tab[0]);
  const int *ptr;                        /* returned pointer to element */
  int        i;                          /* index through arguments */
  int        target;                     /* value we're looking for */

  for (i = 1; i < argc; i++)
    if (sscanf(argv[i], "%i", &target) == 1)
      if ((ptr = intsearch(tab, n, target)) != NULL)
        printf("%i in tab[%i]\n", *ptr, ptr - tab);
      else
        printf("Couldn't find %i\n", target);
  return 0;
}

int *intsearch(const int *ptr, int n, int target)
{
  const int *const endptr = ptr + n;

  for (; ptr < endptr; ptr++)
    if (target == *ptr)
      return (int *) ptr;                /* found it */
  return NULL;                           /* failure, return null */
}
```

Figure 16.8   (isearch.c) Sequential search of an array of integers.

Implementing a Generic Sequential Search

To write our generic sequential search, we'll write a sequential search for ints and gradually generalize it. Figure 16.8 contains that function: intsearch. It works by running a pointer through the array, comparing the target with what the pointer points to, and stopping when they're equal. Figure 16.9 contains our generic sequential search function: search. It takes the same set of arguments as bsearch; the only difference is the algorithm it uses for the search.

The key to turning intsearch into search is to generalize all the places in intsearch that count on its being passed an array of ints.

First, we now don't know the type of array we're passed. That means the pointer to the array's starting element must now be a pointer to void, and we need an additional parameter that says how big each array element is.

```
/*
 * Generic sequential search function.
 */
#include <stddef.h>

void *search(const void *tarptr, const void *tabptr,
             int n, size_t size,
             int (*funcptr)(const void *, const void *))
{
  const char *ptr          = tabptr;
  const char *const endptr = ptr + size * n;

  for (; ptr < endptr; ptr += size)
    if (funcptr(tarptr, ptr) == 0)
      return (void *) ptr;      /* found it, return pointer */
  return NULL;                  /* failure, return null */
}
```

Figure 16.9 (search.c) Our generic sequential search function.

Second, we now have to treat the array as a large sequence of bytes. That means we need to use pointers to **char** to traverse the array rather than pointers to **int**. We make **ptr** point to the first byte in the array, and **endptr** point to the byte just past the array's end. That also means we need to include the size of an element in our pointer computations. We increment **ptr** past one array element by adding the size in bytes of an array element to it.

        ptr += size;

And we initialize **endptr** by adding the number of bytes in the array to **ptr**.

        endptr = ptr + size * n;

Finally, we can no longer use **==** to determine whether the target is in the array. Instead, we need to pass a comparison function pointers to the target and the next array element. Figure 16.10 shows how to use **search** to search an array of strings. Because **search** works just like **bsearch**, we can pass it the same comparison function, **cmpstr**, that we used earlier to search a table of strings with **bsearch**.

Implementing a Generic Insertion Sort

When writing any generic function, it helps to base it on some earlier function written for a particular type. So we would like to base our generic insertion sort on the insertion sort programs we've written in earlier chapters. In Chapter 7, for example, we wrote a program that used insertion sort to sort an array of **int**s, and in Chapter 13, we rewrote it to sort an array of strings. The problem with these earlier programs is that they combined the sorting with reading the input values. Now we want an insertion sort

```
/*
 * Use generic sequential search to search a table of strings.
 */
#include <stdio.h>
#include <stddef.h>
#include <string.h>

int main(int argc, char *argv[])
{
  int    cmpstr(const void *elptr, const void *tarptr);
  void   *search(const void *tarptr, const void *tabptr,
                 int n, size_t size,
                 int (*cmpfp)(const void *, const void *));
  const char *stab[] =
                 {"gisele", "alex",     "tammy", "irene", "diane",
                  "daphne", "veronica", "doris", "barbi", "sally"};
  const int n = sizeof(stab)/sizeof(stab[0]);
  const char  **ptr;              /* array, ptr to an item */
  int    i;                       /* temporary index */

  for (i = 1; i < argc; i++)
  {
    ptr = search(argv[i], stab, n, sizeof(stab[0]),cmpstr);
    if (ptr != NULL)
      printf("Found %s as element %i.\n", argv[i], ptr - stab);
    else
      printf("Didn't find %s.\n", argv[i]);
  }
  return 0;
}

/* Same comparison function we used for bsearch */

int cmpstr(const void *xptr, const void *yptr)
{
  return strcmp((char *) xptr, * (char **) yptr);
}
```

Figure 16.10   (ssearch.c) A program that uses generic sequential search on a table of strings.

that can sort an array in place. Figure 16.11 contains a new insertion sort function that does just that, but only for arrays of integers.

Writing a generic sort is considerably more complicated than writing a generic search. To see why, let's think about what sorting is all about. It's really just a matter of *comparing* and *copying* (exchanging out-of-order values). To write a generic sorter, we need the array to sort, a method for *comparing* values, and a method for *copying* or *exchanging* two values. We'll do the comparing with a comparison function, as we've been doing all along with the built-in searching and sorting routines and our own generic

```
/*
 * Using insertion sort to sort an existing array of ints.
 */
#include <stdio.h>
#include <stddef.h>                     /* for size_t */

int main()
{
  void   isort(int vals[], int n);
  int    table[] =
           {19, 56, 48, 99, 1, 87, 67, 14, 95, 34};
  const int n = sizeof(table)/sizeof(table[0]);
  int    i;

  isort(table, n);
  for (i = 0; i < n; i++)
    printf("%i\n", table[i]);
  return 0;
}

void isort(int vals[], int n)
{
  int i, j;
  int temp;

  for (i = 1; i < n; i++)
  {
    temp = vals[i];
    for (j = i; j > 0 && temp < vals[j-1]; j--)
      vals[j] = vals[j-1];
    vals[j] = temp;
  }
}
```

Figure 16.11   (isort1.c) Insertion sorting routine that sorts an array of ints in place.

searching routine. But now we also need a function for *copying* values. Fortunately, we don't have to provide this function to the sorting routine as a parameter. That's because if we want to copy any value from one location to another, regardless of type, all we really need to know is the locations and how many bytes to copy. Given that information, we can use **memcpy** (the standard library routine we first saw in Chapter 9) to actually do the copy.

Figure 16.12 contains our generic insertion sort routine. It takes the same set of arguments as **qsort**. We created it by making several changes to our earlier code.

One change is that we now use pointers to traverse the array, just as we did with **search**. Since we now treat the array as an array of bytes, all of these pointers are pointers to **char**. **startptr** points to the first byte, and **endptr** to the first byte just past the array's end. We initialize these in the same way we initialized their counterparts

```
/*
 * Sort integers using generic insertion sorting routine.
 *    isort - insertion sort an array of any data type.
 *    cmpint - comparison function for integers.
 */
#include <stdio.h>                              /* for printf */
#include <stddef.h>                             /* for size_t */
#include <stdlib.h>                             /* for malloc */
#include <string.h>                             /* for memcpy */

int main()
{
  void isort(void *tab, int n, size_t size,
             int (*cmpfp)(const void *, const void *));
  int  cmpint(const void *xptr, const void *yptr);
  int  table[] =
         {19, 56, 48, 99, 1, 87, 67, 14, 95, 34};
  const int n = sizeof(table)/sizeof(table[0]);
  int  i;

  isort(table, n, sizeof(int), cmpint);
  for (i = 0; i < n; i++)
    printf("%i\n", table[i]);
  return 0;
}

void isort(void *table, int n, size_t size,
           int (*cmpfp)(const void *, const void *))
{
  char *startptr      = table;                  /* ptrs to array start */
  char *const endptr = startptr + (n * size);      /* and end */
  void *const temp   = malloc(size);            /* space for 1 element */
  char *pi, *pj;                                /* loop pointers */

  for (pi = startptr + size; pi < endptr; pi += size)
  {
    memcpy(temp, pi, size);                          /* store into temp space */
    for (pj = pi; pj > startptr; pj -= size)
    {
      if (cmpfp(temp, pj - size) >= 0)
        break;
      memcpy(pj, pj - size, size);
    }
    memcpy(pj, temp, size);
  }
}

int cmpint(const void *xptr, const void *yptr)
{
  return * (int *) xptr - * (int *) yptr;
}
```

Figure 16.12   (isort2.c) Generic version of our insertion sorting routine.

in **search**. We also use two other pointers: **pi** to traverse the table, and **pj** to help us move out-of-place elements. These replace our earlier index variables **i** and **j**.

Just like before, when we do arithmetic with these pointers, we have to account for the size of an array element ourselves. So when we increment a pointer, we have to increment it by the number of bytes in an array element. That's important both when we initialize **pi** to point to the table's second element,

```
pi = startptr + size;
```

and when we move it along the array:

```
pi += size;
```

pj is similar to **pi**, but it moves backward from the current value of **pi** to the front of the array:

```
pj -= size;
```

Another change is that we now replace the comparison between array elements using < with a call to the comparison function, just as we've had to do in all our other generic routines.

There's one more catch. Our previous version exchanged variables using an assignment and a temporary variable, **temp** (which we declared as an **int**), to hold the current array element. Here, we don't know how large to make **temp** at compile time. Our only choice is to declare it as a pointer to **void**, to use **malloc** to allocate enough space for an array element, and to use **memcpy** to store an array element in it.[2] That's a pain, but that's the price we pay to play with generic functions.

Generic Functions—How Fast?

Generic functions are great—they allow us to use one routine that works with any data type. Unfortunately that power comes at a price: generic routines don't run— they crawl. We ran the two versions of insertion sort on files of **int**s and timed the programs for files of 100 and 1000 values. For 100 values, the times were similar: 0.05 seconds versus 0.07 seconds. But for 1000 values, things were much different: 0.75 seconds for the "conventional" insertion sort, versus almost 5 seconds for the generic version. Table 16.1 shows where the generic version is spending its time. Almost 30% in **memcpy** and almost a quarter million calls![3]

Despite their performance problems, we use generic routines wherever we can. Why? Simply because they're an easy way to cut down on the time we have to spend programming. Only if a generic function turns out to be a primary performance bottleneck in our program do we replace it with something that's less general but more efficient.

---

[2]To make the sorting program fit on a single page, we're a little sloppy here and don't bother to check to see whether **malloc** actually succeeded.

[3]The programs were compiled and run on an 8600 VAX using the GNU C compiler under Berkeley 4.3 UNIX. The table includes calls to two routines, **mcount** and **monstartup**, accounting for almost 25% of the program's total time. These two routines are included when execution profiling is turned on.

PERCENT TIME	TOTAL TIME (SECONDS)	NUMBER OF CALLS	TIME PER CALL (MICROSECONDS)	ROUTINE
29.6	1.47	242762	0.01	memcpy
27.2	2.82	1	1350.32	isort
21.4	3.88			mcount †
14.1	4.58	241749	0.00	cmpint
2.8	4.72			monstartup †
2.2	4.83	1001	0.11	doscan †
1.6	4.91	1000	0.08	doprnt †

Table 16.1   Execution profile for insertion sorting using a generic sort routine. The program spends almost 30% of its time in memcpy. Only routines accounting for more than 1% of the total time are shown. Routines marked with a † are C runtime routines compiled automatically with the program.

16.3   MAKING GENERIC FUNCTIONS EASIER TO USE

Generic functions such as **bsearch** and **qsort** are powerful and make our job of coding complex programs much easier. But they aren't the easiest functions in the world to use. To use **bsearch**, for example, we not only provide a target value, an array, and the number of elements in the array but also extra information describing the size of each element and the function to use to compare elements.

```
ptr = bsearch(target, tab, n, sizeof(char *), cmpstr);
```

We would prefer to hide all of this detail and to be able to perform searches with a simpler call, such as

```
ptr = SEARCH_STRINGS(target, tab, n);
```

We would also like a similar interface for using **qsort**.

By taking advantage of header files and macros, we can accomplish this quite easily. For each type we're going to search and sort, we create a header file that provides a pair of interface macros (one for searching, the other for sorting), as well as prototypes for any comparison functions we need. And we put the comparison functions in a separate source file, which we can compile separately. Once we have done that, all we have to do to search and sort is include the header file, use the macros, and link in the comparison functions.

Figure 16.13 contains a header file for searching and sorting tables of strings. Figure 16.14 contains **cmpstr** and **cmpstrs**, our string comparison functions. And Figure 16.15 is a short program that uses the macros to sort a table and then perform several searches of it. These changes make searching and sorting tables of strings a breeze.

```
/*
 * Interface for searching and sorting tables of strings.
 */
#include <stdlib.h>

#define SEARCH_STRINGS(tar,t,n)   bsearch(tar,t,n,sizeof(char *),cmpstr)
#define SORT_STRINGS(t,n)         qsort(t,n,sizeof(char *),cmpstrs)

int cmpstr(const void *xptr, const void *yptr);
int cmpstrs(const void *xptr, const void *yptr);
```

Figure 16.13 (strgens.h) Searching and sorting macros for arrays of strings.

```
/*
 * Comparison functions for strings.
 *    cmpstr - compare target string with string in table.
 *    cmpstrs - compare two strings in table.
 */
#include <string.h>

int cmpstr(const void *xptr, const void *yptr)
{
  return strcmp((char *) xptr, * (char **) yptr);
}

int cmpstrs(const void *xptr, const void *yptr)
{
  return strcmp(* (char **) xptr, * (char **) yptr);
}
```

Figure 16.14 (strgens.c) Comparison function for strings.

16.4   CASE STUDY—IMPLEMENTING BSEARCH

*This section
is optional!*

Figure 16.16 concludes the chapter with an implementation of **bsearch**. We've based
it on **binsearch**, the recursive binary search function we wrote in Chapter 14. In fact,
all **bsearch** does is set up a call to a generic version of **binsearch**.

As before, **binsearch** takes three parameters: a pointer to the table's first byte, a
pointer to just past the table's last byte, and a pointer to the target value. But we now
make the first two arguments pointers to **char**. That's because within **binsearch**
we're treating the array as an array of bytes. The last argument is a pointer to **void**,
because **binsearch** doesn't care about the target's actual type. We pass the starting
pointer and a target pointer to **bsearch**, so it can pass them unchanged to **binsearch**.
But we don't pass an ending pointer, so **bsearch** must compute it from the starting

```
/*
 * Table searching and sorting using nice interface.
 */
#include <stdio.h>
#include <stddef.h>
#include "strgens.h"

int main(int argc, char *argv[])
{
  char *tab[] =
          {"gisele", "doris",  "tammy", "tony", "daphne",
           "irene",  "vivian", "barbi", "alex", "veronica"};
  const int n  = sizeof(tab)/sizeof(tab[0]);
  char **ptr;                /* pointer to target's position in table */
  int  i;

  SORT_STRINGS(tab, n);
#if defined(DEBUG)
  for (i = 0; i < n; i++)
    printf("%i: %s\n", i, tab[i]);
#endif
  for (i = 1; i < argc; i++)
    if ((ptr = SEARCH_STRINGS(argv[i], tab, n)) == NULL)
      printf("Search failed.\n");
    else
      printf("Found %s at position %i\n", argv[i], ptr - tab);
  return 0;
}
```

Figure 16.15   (srchsort.c) Using our new interface to the generic search and sorting functions.

pointer and the size of the array.

As with our sequential search function, **binsearch** needs a comparison function to determine whether it has found the target, and it needs to know the size of an array element to do pointer arithmetic. But we aren't passing either to **binsearch**. How does **binsearch** know which comparison function to use? And how does it know how big an element is? **bsearch** places the comparison function and the array size in **static** global variables, so **binsearch** simply uses these variables. Why not pass them as parameters? Because **binsearch** is recursive, and all the recursive calls to **binsearch** use the same size and comparison function. Putting that information in global variables eliminates the unnecessary overhead of passing them as parameters.

Within **binsearch**, we have to make only a few changes from our earlier version. We use a comparison function rather than a direct comparison. And now we can no longer simply subtract or add 1 to **midptr** before we recursively call **binsearch** to search subsections of the table. Instead, we have to add or subtract the size of an element instead. There is one place we don't have to change: our computation of the **midptr** is exactly the same as before.

```
/*
 * An implementation of the library binary search.
 */
#include <stddef.h>

static int (*CmpFp)(const void *xptr, const void *yptr);
static int Size;            /* int rather than possibly unsigned size_t */

static void *
binsearch(const char *minptr, const char *maxptr, const void *tptr)
{
  const char *midptr = minptr + ((maxptr - minptr)/(Size * 2)) * Size;
  int cmpres = CmpFp(tptr, midptr);

  if (cmpres == 0)                      /* got it! */
    return (void *) midptr;
  if (maxptr <= minptr)                 /* value's not in table? */
    return NULL;
  return (cmpres < 0) ? binsearch(minptr, midptr - Size, tptr)
                      : binsearch(midptr + Size, maxptr, tptr);
}

void *bsearch(const void *tptr, const void *ptr, size_t n, size_t s,
                   int (*fp)(const void *xptr, const void *yptr))
{
  CmpFp = fp;                           /* store in globals to simplify calls */
  Size = (int) s;
  return binsearch(ptr, (char *) ptr + (n - 1) * s, tptr);
}
```

Figure 16.16 (bsearch.c) Our implementation of the library's generic binary search routine.

SUMMARY

- Generic functions are functions that can perform a particular task with any data type.

- C's standard library comes complete with a generic binary search function, **bsearch**, and a generic quicksort function, **qsort**.

- We can write our generic functions that process arrays by treating them as collections of bytes and carefully doing all of the pointer arithmetic ourselves.

- By using macros, we can write a nice interface on top of generic functions that allows us to forget the painful details of comparison functions and size computations.

EXERCISES

16–1 Write a nonrecursive, generic version of **bsearch** (Figure 16.16).

16–2 Write a program that uses binary search to search our employee table for matching names.

16–3 Write a program that uses **qsort** to sort our employee data base by salary and then by employee name.

16–4 Write a function to determine whether a generic array is already sorted.

16–5 Write a function to reverse any type of array. How can we combine this with quicksort to sort in descending order rather than ascending order?

16–6 Write a function, **traverse_array**, that will execute a pointer to a function on each element in an array of any type. Use it to print each element in a table of integers, and to print each of the records in our employee data base.

16–7 **bsearch** is said to be an order of $\log_2 n$ algorithm, where n is the number of elements in the table. Linear search (start the search from the beginning of the table and continue until either a match is found or the end of the table is reached) is order of n. Compare the search times when using **search** and **bsearch** to search tables that vary in size from 5 to 5000 elements on your own computer. Is **bsearch** always faster? If not, what is the break point in the number of elements below which linear search should be used?

16–8 There is no guarantee that **qsort** is really a "quick" sorting routine at all, only that it will order the elements in the array according to the supplied comparison function. Run **qsort** on input data sets of size 100, 200, 400, 800, and 1600 elements and plot the sorting time. A well written **qsort** will have computing time proportional to $n \times \log_2 n$. A poor sorting routine, such as our very own insertion sort, has computing time on the order of n^2.

16–9 Provide a nice interface for searching and sorting arrays of strings and arrays of **double**s.

16–10 Provide a set of functions for manipulating arrays. This set should include **walk_array**, which applies a function to every array element, and **map_array**, which is just like **walk_array**, but quits if the function it applies returns zero. Provide a nice interface for using them with arrays of **int**s and arrays of **double**s.

16–11 Write a program that reads input lines in the form of last name, first name, one name per line. Sort the input based on *two* sorting keys: last name, then first name, then print the results to the terminal. The two-key sort should yield all names in order by last name; two or more last names that are the same should then also be sorted by first name.

16–12 Write a generic table package that provides functions for adding and deleting table elements, as well as for running through the table. Then rewrite Chapter 11's employee database program to use these functions.

17 COMPLEX DECLARATIONS

This chapter discusses how to understand and construct complex type declarations. We present some types even more complex than those we've so far declared and show where we might want to use them. We provide algorithms for understanding and formulating C's type declarations—no matter how complex. And we show tricks that can help us avoid most of the material in this chapter most of the time. The chapter concludes with a case study: a program takes an abbreviated English type description and produces an appropriate C declaration for it.

17.1 SOME NEW COMPLEX TYPES

So far we've presented a bewildering collection of types—arrays of arrays, pointers to arrays, arrays of pointers, pointers to pointers, pointers to functions, functions returning pointers, and so on. And each new type declaration seems to be more complex than the last. But we're not limited to only those types we've been discussing. Despite all our efforts, we have merely skimmed the surface of the types C allows us to declare and use. We can, in fact, declare arbitrarily complex data types—we're limited only by our imagination and our ability to read and understand the resulting declarations. To give you an idea of the true power of C, we now present two new complex data types—arrays of pointers to functions, and functions returning pointers to functions.

Arrays of Pointers to Functions

Why would we ever want an array of pointers to functions? We'll use them to write a small program that repeatedly prints a menu,

```
Your choices are:
      1) Add record
      2) Delete record
      3) Print record
Or type a 0 to quit:
```

obtains the user's choice, and then executes a function corresponding to the user's choice.

The program stores a menu as an array of strings:

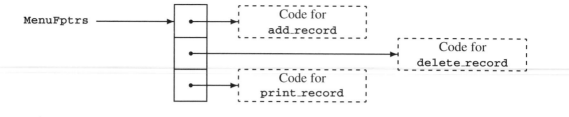

Figure 17.1   What the table of pointers to functions looks like.

```
const char *const MenuEntries[] =
{
  "Add record", "Delete record", "Print record"
};
```

And it stores the functions implementing the user's choices in an array of pointers to functions.

```
void (*MenuFptrs[])(void) =
{
  add_record, del_record, print_record
};
```

This declares **MenuFptrs** as an array of pointers to functions, each of which takes no parameters and returns no value. It also initializes the array to hold pointers to three of these functions: **add_record**, **del_record**, and **print_record**. This initialization must be preceded with their prototypes so that the compiler knows they are function names and not variable names. In general, these functions would do things such as add records to a data base, but for now they simply print a message announcing that they've been called successfully. Figure 17.1 shows this array. Figure 17.2 contains the prototypes for these functions, and Figure 17.3 contains the functions themselves.

Figure 17.4 contains the **main** program and the tables of strings and function pointers that make up the menu. **main** doesn't do much—it simply sets up the tables and calls a function, **menu_process**, to do all the real work.

Figure 17.5 contains **menu_process**. It repeatedly calls another function, **menu_choice**, to print the menu and obtain a valid user's choice. It quits when the user's choice is 0. Otherwise, the user's choice is between 1 and the number of menu entries, and **menu_process** uses it as an index into the table of function pointers.

```
fptrs[choice - 1]();    /* execute the function */
```

fptrs[choice - 1] is a pointer to a function, so supplying an argument list executes the function to which it points. The compiler automatically dereferences the pointer for us, saving us a ***** and a set of parentheses. We subtract 1 from **choice** because C arrays start at zero and the user's choice starts at 1.

```
/*
 * Prototypes for dummy functions used to test the menu.
 */
extern void add_record(void);
extern void del_record(void);
extern void print_record(void);
```

Figure 17.2   (record.h) Prototypes for dummy functions used to test **menu_process**.

```
/*
 * Dummy functions to test our menu program.
 */
#include <stdio.h>
#include "record.h"

#define ANNOUNCE(x) printf("In %s\n", x)

void add_record(void)    { ANNOUNCE("add_record"); }

void del_record(void)    { ANNOUNCE("del_record"); }

void print_record(void) { ANNOUNCE("print_record"); }
```

Figure 17.3   (record.c) Dummy functions used to test **menu_process**.

Functions That Return Pointers to Functions

Our functions so far either have returned a simple type, such as **int** or **double**, or a pointer to one of these types. There are times, however, when we want to have a function return a pointer to another function. We do so in a more sophisticated implementation of our menu program. This time the menu is an array of structures, with each structure containing a string to print and a pointer to a function to execute. And now the user selects a menu entry by typing its first few characters, not by entering a number.

Figure 17.6 contains the definition of a menu structure, Figure 17.7 contains the new version of **menu_process**, and Figure 17.8 contains the new main program.

Before, we directly indexed the menu with the user's choice: **menu_process** called **menu_choice** to print the menu and return the user's choice and then used it to index a table of function pointers. Now, however, we have **menu_choice** search the menu for a matching entry and then return its corresponding function pointer. **menu_process** then simply calls the function through this pointer. The problem is that we now must declare **menu_choice** as a function returning one of these pointers. Here is its prototype:

```
void (*menu_choice(int n, const MENU_ITEM menu[]))(void);
```

```
/*
 * Print menu and then obtain and execute the user's choice.
 */
#include <stdio.h>
#include "record.h"
```

```
const char *const MenuEntries[] =
{
   "Add record", "Delete record", "Print record"
};

void (*MenuFptrs[])(void) =
{
   add_record, del_record, print_record
};

int main()
{
   void menu_process(int, const char *const[], void (*[])(void));
   const int choices = sizeof(MenuFptrs)/sizeof(MenuFptrs[0]);

   menu_process(choices, MenuEntries, MenuFptrs);
   return 0;
}
```

Figure 17.4   (usemenu.c)   Storing a menu as an array of strings plus an array of pointers to functions.

This declares **menu_choice** as a function that takes two arguments—an **int** and an array of **MENU_ITEM**s—and returns a pointer to a function that takes no arguments and returns no value. That's a mouthful, but it's easily understandable. Just replace **menu_choice** and its parameter list with a variable, say **choiceptr**.

```
void (*choiceptr)(void);
```

That results in the familiar declaration for a pointer to a function with no parameters and no return value. And that's what **menu_choice** returns.

menu_process calls **menu_choice** just like any other function and assigns its return value to **choiceptr**.

```
choiceptr = menu_choice(n, menu)
```

And we execute the returned function simply by calling it through **choiceptr**.

```
choiceptr();
```

Once again, we take advantage of C's automatically dereferencing function pointers when we follow them with an argument list.

```
/*
 * Display menu and obtain and execute user choices.
 *    menu_process - obtain and execute user's choice.
 *    menu_choice - request and get the user's choice.
 */
#include <stdio.h>

#define MAXLEN 80

static int menu_choice(int n, const char *const items[])
{
  int  getline(char *buf, int buflen);
  int  i, num;                              /* index, selection */
  char line[MAXLEN + 1];

  printf("Your choices are:\n");
  for (i = 1; i <= n; i++)
    printf("\t%i) %s\n", i, items[i - 1]);
  printf("Or type a 0 to quit: ");
  while (getline(line, MAXLEN) != -1)
    if (sscanf(line, "%i", &num) == 1 && 0 <= num && num <= n)
      return num;
    else
      printf("Enter a value between 0 and %i: ", n);
  return 0;
}

void menu_process(int n,
                  const char *const items[],
                  void (*fptrs[])(void))
{
  int choice;                               /* holds user's choice */

  while ((choice = menu_choice(n, items)) != 0)
    fptrs[choice - 1]();
}
```

Figure 17.5 (prmenu.c) Functions to prompt the user for a menu selection and then use the user's choice to select and execute the appropriate function.

17.2   CONSTRUCTING TYPE DECLARATIONS

We've now seen some fairly complex type declarations—but how we do we construct them?

A type declaration consists of a basic type followed by a *declarator* and specifies the type of the identifier contained within the declarator. In the declaration

```
/*
 * Definition of a menu structure.
 */
typedef struct menu_item
{
  char *entry;                       /* string to write */
  void (*fptr)(void);                /* function to execute */
} MENU_ITEM;

void menu_process(int n, const MENU_ITEM tab[]);
```

Figure 17.6   (menu.h) Definition of a menu structure.

```
            double (*funcptr)(void);
```

double is the basic type, **(*funcptr)(void)** is the declarator, and **funcptr** is the identifier contained in the declarator. As we saw earlier, this declares **funcptr** as a pointer to a function that takes no arguments and returns a **double**.

The problem is to come up with the correct declarator. It's easy if we're declaring a variable with one of the basic types: it's simply a single identifier.

```
      int    i;           /* an int */
      double d;           /* a double */
```

We can declare several more complicated types by combining the identifier with a single *****, **( )**, and **[ ]**. Prefacing the identifier with ***** declares a pointer to the base type.

```
      int *iptr;          /* pointer to an int */
      char *cptr;         /* pointer to a char */
```

Following the identifier with **[ ]** declares an array of the base type.

```
      double dtab[10];    /* array of 10 doubles */
      char   ctab[10];    /* array of 10 characters */
```

We need to include a subscript only if we're defining storage and we're not following the declaration with an initialization expression. Following the identifier with a **( )**, possibly with an enclosed list of types, declares a function.

```
      int    ifunc(void); /* function returning an int */
      double dfunc(void); /* function returning a double */
```

Here, we're assuming we want to declare functions that take no parameters. Otherwise, of course, we would replace the **void** with a list of type declarations for these parameters.

We declare even more complex types, such as pointers to functions and arrays of pointers, by combining the pieces used to form the previous declarators. Now, however, we have to worry about operator precedence.

```c
/*
 * Display menu and obtain/execute user choices.
 *    menu_process - get and execute user's choice.
 *    menu_choice - read and verify choice from user.
 *    menu_search - search menu to find user's choice.
 */
#include <stdio.h>
#include <stddef.h>
#include <string.h>
#include "menu.h"

#define MAXLEN 80

static const MENU_ITEM *menu_search(const MENU_ITEM *ptr,
                                    const MENU_ITEM *endptr,
                                    const char *target)
{
  for (; ptr < endptr; ptr++)
    if (strncmp(target, ptr->entry, strlen(target)) == 0)
      return ptr;
  return NULL;
}

static void (*menu_choice(int n, const MENU_ITEM menu[]))(void)
{
  int    getline(char *buf, int buflen);
  char   line[MAXLEN + 1];
  const MENU_ITEM *ptr;
  const MENU_ITEM *const endptr = menu + n;

  printf("Your choices are:\n");
  for (ptr = menu; ptr < endptr; ptr++)
    printf("\t%s\n", ptr->entry);
  printf("Or type QUIT to quit: ");
  while (getline(line, MAXLEN) != -1 && strcmp(line, "QUIT") != 0)
  {
    if ((ptr = menu_search(menu, endptr, line)) != NULL)
      return ptr->fptr;
    printf("Select an appropriate menu entry: ", n);
  }
  return NULL;
}

void menu_process(int n, const MENU_ITEM menu[])
{
  void (*choiceptr)(void);                   /* user-selected function */

  while ((choiceptr = menu_choice(n, menu)) != NULL)
    choiceptr();                             /* execute user's choice */
}
```

Figure 17.7   (prmenu2.c)   Prompting for a menu selection and executing the corresponding function.

```
/*
 * Menu processor, rewritten to represent menus with structures.
 */
#include "menu.h"
#include "record.h"

MENU_ITEM Menu[] =
{
  {"Add record",    add_record},
  {"Delete record", del_record},
  {"Print record",  print_record}
};

int main()
{
  const int choices = sizeof(Menu)/sizeof(Menu[0]);

  menu_process(choices, Menu);
  return 0;
}
```

Figure 17.8   (usemenu2.c)   Program to use a menu defined as a structure.

The simplest combinations are an array of pointers:

```
int *iptrtab[10];     /* array of 10 pointers to int */
char *dptrtab[10];     /* array of 10 pointers to char */
```

and a function returning a pointer:

```
char *cptrfunc(void);  /* function returning ptr to char */
int  *iptrfunc(void);  /* function returning ptr to int */
```

Why are these arrays of pointers and functions returning pointers rather than pointers to arrays or pointers to functions? Because when we combine declarators, * has lower precedence than either () or []. If we want the latter types, we need to use parentheses to override the normal precedence. We declare a pointer to an array with

```
char (*crowptr)[10];   /* ptr to array of 10 characters */
int  (*irowptr)[10];   /* ptr to array of 10 integers */
```

and we declare a pointer to a function with

```
int    (*iptr)(void);  /* ptr to func returning int */
double (*dptr)(void);  /* ptr to func returning double */
```

How do we declare even more complex types? It helps to think of the English description of an identifier's type as being composed of several pieces. Each piece, except for the base type, is "an array of," "a pointer to," or "a function returning." Suppose, for example, that we want to declare an array of pointers to functions that take no arguments and return **void**. That's the type we used in the first version of our menu-processing program. We break its description into

an array of
pointers to
functions taking no arguments and returning
void

The last part of this description, **void**, is the base type of the identifier, and we can ignore it while we're trying to construct the declarator.

We compose the declarator in three steps. First, we work through the description, examining each of the remaining lines and deciding on a C declarator for a variable with that type.

```
table[]
*ptr
func(void)
```

Second, we work our way through these declarators, substituting the topmost declarator for the identifier in the declarator beneath it. So we initially substitute **table[]** for **ptr** in ***ptr**, which leaves

```
*table[]
func(void)
```

We keep repeating the process until only a single declarator remains. In this case, we have only one more substitution to do, replacing **func** with ***table[]**:

```
(*table[])(void)
```

We've done something sneaky here—we surrounded ***table[]** with parentheses. But where did they come from? As we just saw, the precedence of ***** is less than that of either **()** or **[]**, so we have to parenthesize pointer declarators whenever we substitute them into an array or function declarator.

The final step is to precede the declarator by the base type, **void** in this case.

```
void (*table[])(void)
```

And, lo and behold, this is the type declaration we used for the array of pointers in our original menu-processing program.

Let's do one more example. How can we construct the declaration for a function that takes an **int** and an array of **MENU_ITEM**s and returns a pointer to a function that takes no arguments and returns no value? That's exactly the type we used in the structure-based version of our menu-processing program.

As with any other declaration, no matter how complex, we start out with an English description.

a function taking two parameters and returning
a pointer to
a function taking no parameters and returning
void

And then we formulate the declarations for objects with each of these types.

```
func1(two-parameters)
*ptr
func2(void)
```

To keep things simple, we're ignoring the parameters of the functions for now and we'll throw them in once we've figured out the rest of the declarator.

Now we go through the same process as before, substituting the topmost declarator for the variable in the declarator following it. Here, that's substituting **func1**(*two-parameters*) for **ptr**.

```
*func1(two-parameters)
func2(void)
```

We repeat the process for the remaining declarators, this time substituting the topmost declarator for **func2**.

```
(*func1(two-parameters))(void)
```

Again, because we're substituting a pointer, we have to parenthesize it. Once we have only a single declarator left, we precede it with the base type. At this point, we can also fill in any missing parameter declarations.

```
void (*func1(int n, MENU_ITEM menu[]))(void)
```

Fortunately, this declaration matches the one we used in the previous section.

17.3   UNDERSTANDING COMPLEX TYPE DECLARATIONS

How do we understand complex type declarations? This task turns out to be considerably trickier than constructing the declaration.

We start by taking the type declaration and finding its innermost declarator. We write down its type, substitute an identifier for this innermost declarator, and repeat the process until only a single identifier remains. At that point, we have determined the identifier's type.

That sounds straightforward enough, but the hard part is locating the innermost declarator. The rule is that it's the identifier and an immediately following **[]** or **()** or, if neither of these is present, an immediately preceding *****. Once we have determined the type of the innermost declarator, we can ignore any parentheses surrounding it.

To see how this works, suppose we're suddenly confronted with this confusing type declaration.

```
void (*table[])(void)
```

First, we need to locate the innermost declarator. Here, it's **table[]** (since **[]** has higher precedence that *****), so we note that we have an array of some kind. But what kind? To find out, we substitute a variable for **table[]** and repeat the process.

```
void (*x)(void);
```

Now the innermost declarator is ***x**, so we know we have an array of pointers to something. But what's the something? We repeat the process one last time, substituting a variable for ***x** and the parentheses that surround it.

```
void y(void);
```

This leaves us with a familiar declaration: **y** is a function taking no arguments and returning **void**. So combining that with what we'd figured out before, we can see that we have an array of pointers to functions taking no arguments and returning **void**.

Here's a summary of the process. The innermost declarator is in italics.

void (**table[]*)(**void**)	*an array of*
void (*x)(**void**)	*pointers to*
void *y(void)*	*functions returning*
void *z*	**void**

We'll try the process on one more declaration. What does the declaration below declare?

```
void (*function(int x, MENU_ITEM m[]))(void)
```

To find out, we repeat the above process. The innermost declarator is

```
function(int x, MENU_ITEM m[])
```

This is a function that takes two arguments, an **int** and an array of **MENU_ITEM**s, and returns some unknown value. We replace it with a variable, resulting in a simpler declaration.

```
void (*x)(void)
```

The innermost declarator is now ***x**, which is a pointer. We replace it with a variable, which leaves a declaration we recognize:

```
void y(void);
```

This declares a function that takes no arguments and returns no value. So putting all this together, we have a function taking an **int** and an array of **MENU_ITEM**s and returning a pointer to a function taking no arguments and returning no value. We've summarized the process below.

void (**function(two-params)*)(**void**)	*a function returning*
void (*x)(**void**)	*a pointer to*
void *y(void)*	*a function returning*
void *z*	**void**

17.4   TYPE SPECIFICATIONS

When a declarator does not contain an identifier, we have a type specification rather than a variable declaration. These type specifications show up in three places: **sizeof**, function prototypes, and casts. The trick to writing a type specification is to first declare a variable of that type and then to omit the variable from the declaration.

Suppose we want to know how many bytes are required by a pointer to function taking an **int** and returning a **double**. One way to find this out is to pass an appropriate type specifier to **sizeof**. But how do we form that type specifier?

We start by declaring a variable with that type.

```
double (*fp)(int);
```

We then remove the variable to form the type specifier.

```
double (*)(int)
```

And all that remains is to add the **sizeof** operator.

```
sizeof(double (*)(int))
```

Similarly, suppose we want to write a function prototype for the **test_avg** function we wrote in Chapter 12. It takes three arguments—a pointer to an array containing three elements, and a pair of **int**s—and returns a **double**. We come up with its type specifier by first writing the declaration for a pointer to a row containing three elements as

```
int (*rowp)[3];
```

And we obtain the type specifier by removing the variable.

```
double test_avg(int (*)[3], int, int);
```

As one final example, suppose we want to pass a **NULL** pointer to a function that is expecting a table of pointers to functions taking no arguments and returning **void**. We might do so to indicate that **menu_process** is supposed to obtain choices but not execute them. (Of course, we would have to rewrite the function to test for a **NULL** pointer, but we've left that as an exercise). We can declare such an array as

```
void (*functab[])(void)
```

We obtain the type specifier by eliminating the variable.

```
void (*[])(void)
```

And we obtain the cast by wrapping parentheses around the resulting type specifier.

```
(void (*[])(void))
```

```
/*
 * Useful typedefs for menu program.
 */
typedef char *STRING;
typedef void (*PFR_VOID)(void);
typedef PFR_VOID MENU_FUNC_PTR;
```

Figure 17.9   (typedefs.h)   Useful type definitions for our menu program.

17.5   USING TYPEDEF TO AID READABILITY

The compiler can easily process these arbitrarily complex type declarations and type specifiers—but most people can't. To keep declarations readable, it is a good idea to use **typedef** when declaring types more complex than arrays of pointers and pointers to arrays.

Figure 17.9 contains several type definitions that we can use to make our menu-processing program more readable. The first is the easiest to understand:

```
typedef char *STRING;
```

As we saw earlier, to use **typedef**, we pretend we're declaring a variable with the type's name and throw **typedef** in front of it to turn that variable declaration into a type definition. So this **typedef** declares a new type **STRING** that's a synonym for a pointer to **char**.

The second is a bit more complex.

```
typedef void (*PFR_VOID)(void);
```

This **typedef** declares a type **PFR_VOID** that's a synonym for a pointer to a function that takes no arguments and returns **void**. To see why, just eliminate the **typedef**—we are then declaring a variable **PFR_VOID** with that type.

The final **typedef** simply makes **MENU_FUNC_PTR** a synonym for **PFR_VOID**.

```
typedef PFR_VOID MENU_FUNC_PTR;
```

Since these types are now identical, why do we bother to declare them both? **MENU_FUNC_PTR** describes the type's use in the program: it's the type of the functions we execute when the user chooses a menu entry. In contrast, **PFR_VOID** describes the underlying type, which makes the **typedef** easier to understand. Having both types leads a more readable program.

Figures 17.10 and 17.11 use these **typedef**s in a more readable rewrite of our original array-based menu-processing program. This version is much easier to understand than the original. We can also use these **typedef**s to rewrite our other, structure-based menu-processing program. There, we need only change the header file defining the menu structure and the functions using it. Figures 17.12 and 17.13 contain the necessary changes.

```
/*
 * Print menu and then obtain and execute the user's choice.
 */
#include <stdio.h>
#include "record.h"
#include "typedefs.h"

const STRING MenuEntries[] =
{
  "Add record", "Delete record", "Print record"
};

const MENU_FUNC_PTR MenuFptrs[] =
{
  add_record, del_record, print_record
};

int main()
{
  void menu_process(int, const STRING [], const MENU_FUNC_PTR []);
  const int choices = sizeof(MenuFptrs)/sizeof(MenuFptrs[0]);

  menu_process(choices, MenuEntries, MenuFptrs);
  return 0;
}
```

Figure 17.10   (usemenu3.c) Our original menu program rewritten more readably using type definitions.

17.6   CASE STUDY—ENGLISH TO C

*This section
is optional!*

This chapter concludes with a simple program to turn an abbreviated description of a type into an appropriate C type declaration. Here's some sample input and output from the program.

```
pf void
void (*thing)()
apf void
void (*thing[])()
fpfp void
void *(*thing())()
pfpa int
int (*(*thing)())[]
papfpa double
double (*(*(*thing)[])())[]
```

To keep things simple, we use single letter abbreviations for English type descriptions: *p* stands for "pointer to", *f* stands for "function returning", and *a* stands for "array of". So *pf* **void** is a shorthand way to write pointer to function returning **void**, and *apf* **void**

```
/*
 * Display menu and obtain and execute user choices.
 *    menu_process - obtain and execute user's choice.
 *    menu_choice - request and get the user's choice.
 */
#include <stdio.h>
#include "typedefs.h"

#define MAXLEN 80

static int menu_choice(int n, const STRING items[])
{
  int  getline(STRING buf, int buflen);
  int  i, num;                          /* index, selection */
  char line[MAXLEN + 1];

  printf("Your choices are:\n");
  for (i = 1; i <= n; i++)
    printf("\t%i) %s\n", i, items[i - 1]);
  printf("Or type a 0 to quit: ");
  while (getline(line, MAXLEN) != -1)
    if (sscanf(line, "%i", &num) == 1 && 0 <= num && num <= n)
      return num;
    else
      printf("Enter a value between 0 and %i: ", n);
  return 0;
}

void menu_process(int n,
                  const STRING items[],
                  const MENU_FUNC_PTR fptrs[])
{
  int choice;                           /* holds user's choice */

  while ((choice = menu_choice(n, items)) != 0)
    fptrs[choice - 1]();
}
```

Figure 17.11   (prmenu3.c) Menu processing functions rewritten using type definitions.

is a shortcut for array of pointers to function returning **void**. We make several other simplifications. First, we expect the input to be in the form of our sample input, but we don't bother to do any error checking. Second, we don't bother to report whether a particular type makes sense: the program will come up with a type declaration for *af* even though we aren't allowed to have an array of functions. And finally, we don't provide any mechanism for specifying what arguments a function takes. These have to be added by hand later.

Figure 17.14 contains our English-to-C translator. It simply reads a line of input

```
/*
 * Definition of a menu structure
 */
#include "typedefs.h"

typedef struct menu_item
{
  STRING entry;           /* String to write */
  MENU_FUNC_PTR fptr;     /* Function to execute */
} MENU_ITEM;

void menu_process(int, const MENU_ITEM []);
```

Figure 17.12 (menu2.h) Revised definition of a menu structure.

containing a type description and a base type and works its way through the type description, gradually building up the declarator. To do so, it uses our earlier algorithm: working left to right, declaring each item, and then wrapping it in the declaration for the item to its right. When it's all done, it prints the base type follow by the newly created declarator. Figure 17.15 contains the function that wraps the type information around the current item.

SUMMARY

- C allows us to declare arbitrarily complex data types, including types such as arrays of pointers to functions, and functions that return pointers to functions.

- These type declarations appear in numerous places, including variable declarations, function headers, and type casts.

- There are algorithms we can use both to turn an English description of a type into its declaration and to turn a declaration into its English description.

- Alternatively, we can use **typedef** to make these types considerably easier to read and declare.

EXERCISES

17–1 Modify Chapter 11's data base program to use this chapter's array-based menu-processing package.

17–2 Modify Chapter 11's data base program to use this chapter's structure-based menu-processing package.

```c
/*
 * Display menu and obtain/execute user choices.
 *    menu_process - get and execute user's choice.
 *    menu_choice - read and verify choice from user.
 *    menu_search - search menu to find user's choice.
 */
#include <stdio.h>
#include <stddef.h>
#include <string.h>
#include "menu2.h"

#define MAXLEN 80

static const MENU_ITEM *menu_search(const MENU_ITEM *ptr,
                                    const MENU_ITEM *endptr,
                                    const STRING target)
{
  for (; ptr < endptr; ptr++)
    if (strncmp(target, ptr->entry, strlen(target)) == 0)
      return ptr;
  return NULL;
}

static MENU_FUNC_PTR menu_choice(int n, const MENU_ITEM menu[])
{
  int   getline(STRING buf, int buflen);
  char  line[MAXLEN + 1];
  const MENU_ITEM *ptr;
  const MENU_ITEM *const endptr = menu + n;

  printf("Your choices are:\n");
  for (ptr = menu; ptr < endptr; ptr++)
    printf("\t%s\n", ptr->entry);
  printf("Or type QUIT to quit: ");
  while (getline(line, MAXLEN) != -1 && strcmp(line, "QUIT") != 0)
  {
    if ((ptr = menu_search(menu, endptr, line)) != NULL)
      return ptr->fptr;
    printf("Select an appropriate menu entry: ", n);
  }
  return NULL;
}

void menu_process(int n, const MENU_ITEM menu[])
{
  MENU_FUNC_PTR choiceptr;                  /* user-selected function */

  while ((choiceptr = menu_choice(n, menu)) != NULL)
    choiceptr();                            /* execute user's choice */
}
```

Figure 17.13 (prmenu4.c) More readable functions to prompt the user for a menu selection and then execute the desired function.

```
/*
 * Pseudo-English-to-C converter.
 */
#include <stdio.h>
#include <string.h>
#include <stddef.h>

#define MAXLEN     80

char declarator[MAXLEN * 5];               /* more than enough room */

int main()
{
  int  getline(char *buf, int len);
  void wrap(char *towrap, const char *frontptr, const char *backptr);
  char line[MAXLEN + 1];                    /* input line */
  char desc[MAXLEN + 1];                    /* description of type */
  char type[MAXLEN + 1];                    /* base type */
  char *descptr;                            /* ptr to next piece */

  while (getline(line, MAXLEN) != -1)
    if (sscanf(line, "%s %s\n", desc, type) != 2)
      printf("Need description and type, ie \"pfp int\"\n");
    else
    {
      strcpy(declarator, "thing");
      for (descptr = desc; *descptr != '\0'; descptr++)
        switch (*descptr)
        {
          case 'p': wrap(declarator, "*", NULL);
                    break;
          case 'f': if (*declarator != '*')
                       wrap(declarator, NULL, "()");
                    else
                       wrap(declarator, "(", ")()");
                    break;
          case 'a': if (*declarator != '*')
                       wrap(declarator, NULL, "[]");
                    else
                       wrap(declarator, "(", ")[]");
                    break;
        }
      printf("%s %s\n", type, declarator);
    }
  return 0;
}
```

Figure 17.14   (etoc.c) A program to turn English descriptions of C data types into an appropriate C declaration.

```
/*
 * Function to wrap one string inside two other strings.
 */
#include <stddef.h>
#include <string.h>

void wrap(char *string, const char *fstr, const char *bstr)
{
  char *endptr = string + strlen(string);   /* initial end */
  char *ptr = endptr;                        /* traversing ptr */
  int  flen;

  if (fstr != NULL)
  {
    flen = strlen(fstr);
    while (ptr-- > string)          /* move over to make room */
      *(ptr + flen) = *(ptr);
    while (*fstr != '\0')           /* do insert */
      *string++ = *fstr++;
    *(endptr += flen) = '\0';
  }
  if (bstr != NULL)                 /* append trailing string */
    while ((*endptr++ = *bstr++) != '\0')
      ;
}
```

Figure 17.15   (wrap.c)   A utility function to wrap type information around a declarator.

17–3 Improve our program to turn an English description of a type into its type declaration (Figure 17.14). Allow the user to specify types of the arguments of any functions by enclosing them in parentheses and appending them to the *f* indicating the function. Your program should also verify that the user's input is legal and print an appropriate error message if it isn't. You have to worry about two types of errors: an invalid letter (other than "a', 'p', or 'f') or an invalid type (there's no such type as an array of functions).

17–4 How can we declare an array of **N** elements, each a pointer to a function that returns a pointer to an **int** and takes two arguments: a **double** and a pointer to a function taking a **double** and returning a **double**?

17–5 How can we declare a pointer to a function that takes a pointer to an array of 10 **int**s and an **int** and returns a pointer to an array of 10 **int**s?

17–6 How would we declare a two-dimensional array of 10 rows of 20 elements, each of which is a pointer to a function that takes a pointer to **void** and returns no value?

17–7 How would we declare a pointer to a function that returns a pointer to a function that takes a pointer to **void** and an **int** and returns a pointer to **void**? The function takes a table of pointers to these functions, and an **int**. What might we use this type for?

17–8 Using **typedef**s, write a declaration for an array of **M LINE**s, each of which is an array of **N** chars. Write a declaration for a pointer to one of the arrays of **N** chars.

17–9 Write a function **execute** that runs through a generic array, executing a series of functions for each element. **execute** is passed a generic array, the number of elements in the array and the size of each element, along with an array of pointers to functions and the number of functions in that array. **execute** should pass each function the current array element and its size. Write this program with and without **typedef**s.

17–10 Rewrite the previous exercise to use a pointer to traverse the table of functions.

17–11 Write a program to take a C type declaration and return an English description of the type it declares.

17–12 Extend the program in the previous exercise to print English descriptions of all type declarations in a C source or header file. Make whatever simplifying assumptions you need.

Part V

C AND THE REAL WORLD

18 EXTERNAL FILES

Our earlier programs have accessed files solely through their standard input and output. But that's a severe limitation—those programs can access only one input and one output file. Fortunately, C provides a well-stocked library of functions for manipulating external files. This chapter presents most of these functions and uses them to write useful utilities to copy files, to compute a file's length, and to display a file's last few lines. We also write a small package that allows us to use "virtual arrays," data structures that behave like arrays but are actually stored in files rather than memory. The chapter concludes with an electronic address book, one that stores the addresses and phone numbers in an indexed external file.

18.1 ACCESSING EXTERNAL FILES

Up to now, whenever we've wanted one of our programs to read or write an external file, we've redirected its standard input or output. But to be able to deal with more than one file at one time, we also need a way to access external files directly. In C, we do so using a set of library functions.

Before we can access a file, we have to *open* it. Opening a file does several things. It causes the system to set up any internal data structures, such as buffers, that are necessary for processing the file. And it gives us a handle that we can use to conveniently identify the file when calling I/O library functions. We open a file with the standard I/O function **fopen**, which takes two string parameters, a file name and a mode, and returns a pointer to a **FILE**. Unlike **int** and **float**, **FILE** is not one of C's basic data types. Instead, it is usually a structure (defined in stdio.h) that contains information useful to the library routines that process files. **fopen** returns **NULL** if there is an error and the file can't be opened.

The mode specifies how we plan to use the file. The basic modes are **"r"** (open for reading), **"w"** (open for writing), and **"a"** (open for appending). So after declaring **fp** as a pointer to a file,

```
FILE *fp;
```
dichan fp as a pointer to a file.

we can use

445

file name

```
fp = fopen("phonenos", "r");   /* open phone number file */
```

to open the file **phonenos** for reading.

We can open a file for reading only if it already exists. But there is no such restriction when we open a file for writing or appending. If the file doesn't exist, it is automatically created for us. If it does exist, opening it for writing wipes out its previous contents and opening it for appending causes new writes to take place at the file's end.

> ***Don't open a file for writing unless you're sure you no longer need the data it contains.***

\r carriage return

\n line feed

wt = write only text

We can open files as either *text* or *binary*, with *text* as the default. C treats all files as a stream of bytes; the difference is how those bytes are interpreted. In some operating systems (such as MS-DOS) text files use a special combination of characters (a carriage return followed by a newline) to indicate the end of a line. When reading from a *text* file on those systems, C automatically ignores any carriage return (**\r**) that immediately precedes a line feed (**\n**). And similarly, when writing to a *text* file, C inserts a carriage return before every line feed. But for a *binary* file or on operating systems (such as UNIX) that use a newline to indicate the end of a line, C doesn't do this conversion.

To open a file as a specific type, we append a **t** or a **b** to the basic mode, as in **"rt"**, **"wt"**, or **"at"** for text files and **"rb"**, **"wb"**, and **"ab"** for binary files. In general, we use text mode when we think of the file as being divided into lines, such as in a program that prints every line containing a particular pattern. We use binary files when we don't care how the file is organized, as in a file copying program, or when we treat the file as being divided into records.

After we open a file, we can use any one of a large set of library functions to access its contents. When we're finished with a file, we use **fclose** to *close* it. This forces out any buffered output and frees up the file's **FILE** structure. **fclose** takes a single file-pointer argument and returns **EOF** if there is an error in closing the file. Because most systems have a maximum number of files that can be open simultaneously,[1] we habitually close a file as soon as we no longer need it. All files, however, are automatically closed when our program terminates.

Character File I/O

get c
put c

There are several ways to access an open file. The simplest is a character at a time, using the *macros* **getc** and **putc**, which are analogous to **getchar** and **putchar**. (There are also a couple of equivalent functions, **fgetc** and **fputc**, which we can use when the macros are undesirable.) **getc** takes a file pointer and returns the integer representation of the next character in the file, or **EOF** if it encounters an end of file. **putc** takes the integer representation of a character and a file pointer and writes the character to the file. All of these return **EOF** if an error occurs.

---

[1] On UNIX, for example, we can have at least 20 per program. On MS-DOS, we can specify the maximum number of open files by setting the *files* variable in **config.sys**.

```
/*
 * File copying utility.  Usage is: filecopy source dest.
 */
#include <stdio.h>                   from library
#include <string.h>
#include <stddef.h>

int main(int argc, char *argv[])
{
  long filecpy(const char *dest, const char *source);
  long copycnt;                     /* number of characters copied */
  int  status = 1;                  /* program return value */

  if (argc != 3)
    printf("Usage: %s source dest\n", argv[0]);
  else if ((copycnt = filecpy(argv[2], argv[1])) == -1L)    — if -1, failed
    printf("Copy failed\n");
  else
  {
    printf("Copied %li characters\n", copycnt);
    status = 0;
  }
  return status;
}
```

Figure 18.1 (filecopy.c) A program to copy one file into another. (do not care about the format)

With **getc** and **putc**, we now have the pieces to write a useful utility program to copy files. Figure 18.1 contains this program, called filecopy. It takes two file names as arguments, copying the file named by its first argument into the file named by its second. For example,

filecopy paper paper.bak

copies the contents of the file paper into the file paper.bak.

filecopy begins by verifying that it was passed three arguments (the program name and the two file names) and prints an error message if it wasn't. It then uses a function **filecpy** to perform the copy, passing it the two file names. **filecpy**, shown in Figure 18.2, opens the files, copies one into the other with **getc** and **putc**, and then closes the files. It returns the number of characters it copied or −1 if it couldn't open both files successfully.

We don't care whether the files are divided into lines, so we open both of them in binary mode. Since opening a file for writing destroys the file's contents, we are careful to do the open for writing only after the open for reading has succeeded. In this way, we destroy the previous contents of the destination file only if there is something to copy. Finally, we also take care to perform the copy only if both opens are successful.

filecpy checks for only one error, a failed open, and ignores the possibility of

```
/*
 * Actually copy one file into another.
 */
#include <stdio.h>
#include <stddef.h>

long filecpy(const char *dest, const char *source)
{
  FILE *sfp;                    /* source file pointer */
  FILE *dfp;                    /* destination file pointer */
  int  c;                       /* next input character */
  long cnt = -1L;               /* count of characters copied */

  if ((sfp = fopen(source,"rb")) == NULL)
    printf("Can't open %s for reading\n", source);
  else
  {
    if ((dfp = fopen(dest,"wb")) == NULL)
      printf("Can't open %s for writing\n", dest);
    else
    {
      for (cnt = 0L; (c = getc(sfp)) != EOF; cnt++)
        putc(c,dfp);
      fclose(dfp);
    }
    fclose(sfp);
  }
  return cnt;
}
```

Figure 18.2   (filecpy1.c)   A function `filecpy` to copy one file into another.

other errors, such as a failed read or write. Although this is standard practice, it can cause problems in the unlikely event that an I/O error does occur, and we can make our programs more robust by checking for that possibility.[2] The standard I/O output functions return **EOF** if they detect a write error, so `filecpy` should print an error message if **putc**'s return value is **EOF**. It should also check **fclose**'s return value, since output is usually buffered and it is possible that the final few characters aren't really written to the file until the file is closed.

Detecting read errors is more difficult, since **EOF** can indicate either an error or end of file. There are two library functions, **feof** and **ferror**, that help us distinguish between these two meanings. **feof** takes a file pointer and returns a nonzero value only when the end of the file has been reached. **ferror** is similar, taking a file pointer and returning nonzero only if an error has occurred in processing that file.

To keep our examples simple, we avoid the added complication of file I/O error

---

[2]Usually such failures are caused by hardware errors, but write errors can also occur when a device becomes full and there is no room for the newly written characters.

handling—but at a cost. When an error does occur, our programs may behave abnormally, without indicating any error. Typically, an unchecked input error as **EOF** prematurely terminates input processing, and an unchecked output error results in lost output. In fact, filecopy now simply prints the number of characters in the source file and relies on the user verifying that the destination file actually has this length. Production quality programs check the values returned by the standard input and output library functions and provide appropriate error indications.

Formatted File I/O

As you might have guessed, both **printf** and **scanf** have counterparts that do formatted I/O on files. **fprintf** is like **printf**, with an additional file-pointer argument that specifies the file to which we write.

> **fprintf** (*file-pointer*, *control-string*, ...)

And **fscanf** is like **scanf**, with an additional file-pointer argument that specifies the file from which we read.

> **fscanf** (*file-pointer*, *control-string*, ...)

Because of their similarity to **printf** and **scanf**, it is easy to forget to pass the file pointer to **fprintf** or **fscanf**. But if we've remembered to include stdio.h, which supplies prototypes for the various library functions, the compiler catches this error for us.

Figure 18.3 provides an example use of **fprintf** and **fscanf** in a small program to write an array to a file and then read the file back into the array. It uses two functions, **fgetints** and **fputints**. **fgetints** uses **fscanf** to read an array of integers from a file, **fputints** uses **fprintf** to write an array of integers to a file. Figure 18.4 contains their prototypes, and Figure 18.5 contains the functions.

Line-Oriented File I/O

Many programs, such as Chapter 10's uniq, most naturally process their input a line at a time. The standard I/O library provides four functions that do line-at-a-time I/O. The most general of these functions are **fgets** and **fputs**.

fgets takes three parameters: a character array, its size, and a file pointer. It reads characters into the array, stopping when it encounters a newline or finds that the array is full. Unlike our function **getline**, **fgets** includes the newline in the array. **fgets** terminates the array with a null, so it reads at most 1 less than the number of characters in the array. So the call

> **fgets(buffer, MAXLEN + 1, fp)**

reads up to **MAXLEN** characters, placing them into **buffer**. **fgets** returns **NULL** when the end of file is reached; otherwise, it returns its first argument, a pointer to a character.

```
/*
 * Read up to "max" values into "a" from file "name".
 */
#include <stdio.h>
#include "getints.h"

#define TESTFILE   "table"
#define MAX        20

int main()
{
  int table[MAX], i;
  int status = 1;

  for (i = 0; i < MAX; i++)            /* some sample values to write */
    table[i] = i;
  if (fputints(TESTFILE, table, MAX) != MAX)
    printf("Couldn't write array to file\n");
  else if (fgetints(TESTFILE, table, MAX) != MAX)
    printf("Couldn't read array from file\n");
  else
  {
    printf("Wrote and read %i ints using %s\n", MAX, TESTFILE);
    status = 0;
  }
  return status;
}
```

Figure 18.3   (fints.c)   A program to read and write arrays of integers into a file.

If the line (including the trailing newline) is too long, we can keep calling **fgets** to read the rest of the line. Unfortunately, with **fgets** there is no way to determine if the entire input line was read without examining the returned string. This makes **fgets** much less useful than it would be if it returned the line length as **getline** does.

```
    fputs("Hi Mom! Hi Dad! Send money!\n", fp);
```

writes a single line to the file specified by **fp**.

fputs takes a string and a file pointer and writes the string to the file. For example, It does not automatically terminate its output with a newline. **fputs** provides a convenient and more efficient way to print a string than **fprintf**, since it eliminates the overhead of parsing the control string. Its one drawback is that the file pointer is its last argument instead of its first argument, as with **fprintf**.

Figure 18.6 uses **fgets** and **fputs** in a new version of **filecpy**. This line-copying version produces the same result as the character-copying version, albeit somewhat slower. It's not as fast because **fgets** and **fputs** are usually built on top of **getc** and **putc** and because we have to determine the length of each line in the file.

The other two line-oriented functions, **gets** and **puts**, are closely related to **fgets**

```
/*
 * Prototypes for table reading and writing functions.
 */
int fputints(const char *name, int *ptr, int max);
int fgetints(const char *name, int *ptr, int max);
```

Figure 18.4 (getints.h) The prototypes for table-reading functions.

```
/*
 * Reading and writing arrays using formatted I/O.
 *    fgetints - read values from file into an array.
 *    fputints - write values from array into a file.
 */
#include <stdio.h>
#include "getints.h"

int fgetints(const char *name, int a[], int max)
{
  int  cnt = 0;
  FILE *fp = fopen(name, "r");

  if (fp != NULL)
  {
    for (; cnt < max && fscanf(fp, "%i", &a[cnt]) == 1; cnt++)
      ;            /* read values while there's room */
    fclose(fp);
  }
  return cnt;     /* number of values actually read */
}

int fputints(const char *name, int a[], int num)
{
  int  cnt = 0;
  FILE *fp = fopen(name, "w");

  if (fp != NULL)
  {
    for (; cnt < num; cnt++)
      fprintf(fp, "%i\n", a[cnt]);
    fclose(fp);
  }
  return cnt;            /* assumes write successful */
}
```

Figure 18.5 (getints1.c) Two functions, `fgetints` and `fputints`, for reading and writing arrays.

```
/*
 * Copy one file into another, a line at a time.
 */
#include <stdio.h>
#include <stddef.h>
#include <string.h>

#define MAXLEN   80

long filecpy(const char *dest, const char *source)
{
  FILE *sfp, *dfp;                   /* source and destination files */
  char line[MAXLEN + 1];             /* next input line */
  long cnt = -1L;                    /* count of characters written */

  if ((sfp = fopen(source,"rb")) == NULL)
    printf("Can't open %s for reading\n", source);
  else
  {
    if ((dfp = fopen(dest,"wb")) == NULL)
      printf("Can't open %s for writing\n", dest);
    else
    {
      for (cnt = 0L; fgets(line, sizeof(line), sfp) != NULL;
           cnt += strlen(line))
        fputs(line,dfp);
      fclose(dfp);
    }
    fclose(sfp);
  }
  return cnt;
}
```

Figure 18.6 (filecpy2.c) A function to copy files line by line. Surprisingly, this is slower than character by character.

and **fputs**. Unfortunately, they are also just different enough to cause confusion. **gets** takes a character array, reads a line from the standard input, places it into the array, and terminates the array with a null. It returns a pointer to the array's first character, or **NULL** if it encounters an end of file. Unlike **fgets**, **gets** does not place the terminating newline into the array. **puts** is simpler and more useful, taking a string and writing it and a trailing newline onto the standard output.

It would seem that we would use **puts** and **gets** most frequently to prompt the user for input and to read the response, as shown below.

```
puts("What's your name? ");
if (gets(name) != NULL)
  printf("Hi %s!  Do you like C?\n", name);
```

But we don't. One problem is that there is no way to limit the number of characters **gets** reads. That means the program "bombs" if the user enters more characters than the array can accommodate. And **puts** has a problem too: it automatically writes a newline after it writes the string. This means we can't use it to write prompts if we want the cursor to remain on the prompt line.

18.2   THE STANDARD FILES

When our programs start, three text files are automatically opened for us: the standard input, the standard output, and the standard error output. The corresponding file pointers are **stdin**, **stdout**, and **stderr** and are defined in stdio.h. These file pointers are constants, so we can't assign to them.

We've already been using **stdin** and **stdout**, even though we didn't know it. That is because **getchar** and **putchar** are defined as macros that expand into calls to **getc** and **putc**.

```
#define getchar()      getc(stdin)
#define putchar(c)     putc(c, stdout)
```

Similarly, we can read from the standard input with either **scanf(...)** or with **fscanf(stdin, ...)**, and we can write to the standard output with either **printf(...)** or with **fprintf(stdout, ...)**.

We haven't used **stderr** yet. **stderr** is the place where we write error messages, since they will then show up on the display, even if the standard output has been redirected. That is, **stderr** is an output file like **stdout**, but it isn't redirected when we redirect **stdout**.

We use **stderr** in the functions **fileopen** and **fileclose**. Figure 18.7 supplies their prototypes, and Figure 18.8 contains the functions themselves. **fileopen** is an extension to **fopen**, that not only opens the file for us but also writes an error message onto **stderr** if it fails. **fileclose** takes a file name and a file pointer, closing the file if it wasn't passed a **NULL** pointer, and writing an error message if necessary. These two functions simplify our file handling functions, since they take care of the messy error handling. Later in this chapter, we'll see just how convenient they are.

18.3   RANDOM FILE ACCESS

All our file processing has been sequential. That is, we started reading at the beginning of the file and read characters one after the other until we hit its end. But we are sometimes interested in only part of a file, and we want to avoid reading all the preceding data. In effect, we want to treat a file like an array, indexing any byte in the file as we would an array element. Three standard I/O functions support this random file access: **fseek**, **rewind**, and **ftell**.

fseek moves the internal file pointer, which points to the next character in the file, to a specified location within the file. It takes three arguments—a file pointer, a **long**

```
/*
 * Prototypes for fileopen/fileclose functions.
 */
#include <stdio.h>
#include <stddef.h>

extern FILE *fileopen(const char *name, const char *mode);
extern void fileclose(const char *name, FILE *fp);
```

Figure 18.7   (fileopen.h) Prototypes for our file opening and closing functions.

```
/*
 * Open/close files, with error message on failure.
 *    fileopen - open a file (built on top of fopen).
 *    fileclose - close a file (built on top of fclose).
 */
#include "fileopen.h"

FILE *fileopen(const char *name, const char *mode)
{
  FILE *fp = fopen(name, mode);               /* open the file */

  if (fp == NULL)                             /* did open fail? */
  {
    fprintf(stderr, "Can't open %s for ", name);
    switch(mode[0])
    {
      case 'r': fprintf(stderr, "reading\n");
                break;
      case 'w': fprintf(stderr, "writing\n");
                break;
      case 'a': fprintf(stderr, "appending\n");
                break;
      default:  fprintf(stderr, "some strange mode\n");
                break;
    }
  }
  return fp;
}

void fileclose(const char *name, FILE *fp)
{
  if (fp != NULL && fclose(fp) == EOF)
    fprintf(stderr, "Error closing %s\n", name);
}
```

Figure 18.8   (fileopen.c) The functions **fileopen** and **fileclose** that open and close files, printing any necessary error message onto the standard error.

offset, and an **int** specifier—and computes the new location by adding the offset to the part of the file specified by the specifier.

For text files, the offset must come from the function **ftell**, discussed below. For binary files, the offset is simply some number of bytes. In either case, however, the offset is a **long**.

The specifier must have one of three values: **SEEK_SET** (0) means the beginning of the file, **SEEK_CUR** (1) means the current position, and **SEEK_END** (2) means the end of the file. Here are some example **fseek**'s:

```
fseek(fp, 0L, SEEK_SET);   /* goto the start of the file */
fseek(fp, 0L, SEEK_CUR);   /* don't move (not too useful!) */
fseek(fp, 0L, SEEK_END);   /* goto the end of the file */
fseek(fp, n,  SEEK_SET);   /* goto the nth byte in the file */
fseek(fp, n,  SEEK_CUR);   /* skip ahead n bytes */
fseek(fp, -n, SEEK_CUR);   /* go backward n bytes */
fseek(fp, -n, SEEK_END);   /* goto n bytes before the end */
```

fseek returns −1 if there is an error, and zero otherwise. In most systems, errors include attempting to seek past the file's boundaries, as well as trying to seek on a closed file. But on some systems, such as MS-DOS, it will return a failure only if the file isn't open. We have ignored **fseek**'s return value in these examples, but by checking it we can verify that the file position was changed.

rewind is a special case **fseek** which moves the internal file pointer to the beginning of the file. That is,

```
rewind(fp)
```

is the equivalent of

```
fseek(fp, 0L, SEEK_SET)
```

except that **rewind** returns no value and clears the internal **EOF** and error indicators. A **rewind** happens implicitly during any **fopen** for reading or writing (but not, of course, during an **fopen** for appending). Any input function immediately following a **rewind** begins its reading with the file's first character. **rewind** lets a program read through a file more than once without having to repeatedly open and close the file.

The final function, **ftell**, takes a file pointer and returns a **long** containing the current offset in the file, the position of the next byte to be read or written. So an **ftell** at the beginning of the file returns the position of the file's first byte, and an **ftell** at the end of the file returns the number of bytes in the file. Typically, programs use **ftell** to save their current position in a file so that they can easily return to it later, without having to read all the intervening data.

We use **ftell** and **fseek** in two programs. Figure 18.9 prints the number of bytes in the files provided as its arguments. It uses a function **filelen** to compute each file's length. **filelen**, in turn, uses **ftell** to save the current position in the file, **fseek** to go to the end of the file, **ftell** to record that position (which is the file's length), and another **fseek** to return to the previous position within the file. We are careful to test **fseek**'s return value, because the file pointer's position doesn't change if we specify an invalid location to which to move.

```
/*
 * Find each file's length in bytes. Usage: filelen file1 ...
 */
#include <stdio.h>
#include "fileopen.h"

int main(int argc, char *argv[])
{
  long filelen(FILE *fp);
  int  i;                               /* argument length */
  long len;                             /* next file's length */
  FILE *fp;                             /* file pointer */

  for (i = 1; i < argc; i++)
  {
    if ((fp = fileopen(argv[i], "rb")) != NULL)
      if ((len = filelen(fp)) == -1)
        fprintf(stderr,"Can't compute length of %s\n", argv[i]);
      else
        printf("%s: %i\n", argv[i], len);
      fileclose(argv[i], fp);
  }
  return 0;
}

long filelen(FILE *fp)
{
  long oldpos = ftell(fp);              /* save old position */
  long length;

  if (fseek(fp, 0L, SEEK_END) == -1)    /* goto end of file */
    return -1;
  length = ftell(fp);                   /* compute length */
  return (fseek(fp, oldpos, SEEK_SET) == -1) ? -1 : length;
}
```

Figure 18.9 (filelen.c) A program to rapidly determine the size in bytes of a file.

Figure 18.10 contains a program to print the last 10 lines of each of the files specified as its arguments. It is especially useful for examining files, such as log files, in which new information is always appended to the end.

There is an especially easy way to write this program. We can use **fseek** to get to the file's end and then read the file backward until the desired number of newlines have been seen. We can read backward by first saving the current offset with **ftell**, reading a character with **getc**, and then using **fseek** to move to the character before the saved offset. Once we find the beginning of the appropriate line, we simply read and display the rest of the characters in the file. The problem with this simple-minded solution is that it is slow—we execute several library calls each time we read a character.

```
/*
 * Print last 10 lines of each file.
 */
#include "fileopen.h"

#define LAST       10               /* last 10 lines of the file */

int main(int argc, char *argv[])
{
  long findpos(FILE *fp, int lastline);
  int  i;                           /* index */
  long pos;                         /* position of newline within block */
  FILE *fp;                         /* file we're reading through */
  int  c;                           /* next character to display */

  for (i = 1; i < argc; i++)
    if ((fp = fileopen(argv[i],"rb")) != NULL)
    {
      if ((pos = findpos(fp, LAST)) == -1L
          || fseek(fp, pos, SEEK_SET) == -1)
        fprintf(stderr,"Couldn't tail %s\n", argv[i]);
      else
        while ((c = getc(fp)) != EOF)    /* display lines */
          putc(c, stdout);
      fileclose(argv[1], fp);
    }
  return 0;                         /* no special return value for error */
}
```

Figure 18.10   (tail.c)   A program to print the last 10 lines of each of the files specified as its arguments.

We improve this scheme by reading a *block* of characters each time and then counting the newlines within each block. Figure 18.11 contains the functions that actually handle reading a block and counting the newlines. The program's surprising length arises from its substantial error checking.

18.4   BLOCK INPUT AND OUTPUT *(Faster to obtain in big block)*

The standard I/O library functions we've seen so far are used to read and write characters. C also provides two functions to read and write blocks of bytes: **fread** reads an array of bytes from a file, and **fwrite** writes an array to a file. Both require four parameters: a pointer to the array's first element (a pointer to **void**), the size (in bytes) of an element, the number of elements in the array, and a file pointer. Both return the number of elements successfully read or written; zero indicates the end of file or an error.

Figure 18.12 uses **fread** and **fwrite** in new versions of the functions **fgetints** and **fputints**. Now **fgetints** reads the array with a single **fread**, and **fputints**

```
/*
 * Utility functions for tail program.
 *    findpos - locate first character in file to print.
 *    nextblock - read next block of characters in file.
 */
#include <stdio.h>

#define MAXBUF 512              /* characters in block */

long findpos(FILE *fp, int lines)
{
  int  nextblock(FILE *fp, int max, int *cnt, int target);
  int  count = 0;              /* newlines seen */
  long pos;                    /* position of desired newline in file */
  long blkend;                 /* position of last char in block */
  int  blksize;                /* # of characters within block */

  if (fseek(fp, 0L, SEEK_END) == -1)
     return -1;                /* get to end of file */

  for (blkend = ftell(fp); blkend >= 0; blkend -= MAXBUF)
  {
    blksize = (MAXBUF > blkend) ? (int) blkend : MAXBUF;
    if (fseek(fp, blkend - blksize, SEEK_SET) == -1)
       return -1;              /* couldn't go back a block - error */
    if ((pos = nextblock(fp, blksize, &count, lines)) != -1)
       return blkend - blksize + pos;
  }

  return 0L;                   /* start at beginning */
}

int nextblock(FILE *fp, int max, int *cnt, int target)
{
  char buffer[MAXBUF];                   /* to hold block */
  char *ptr    = buffer;                 /* pointer into buffer */
  char *endptr = buffer + max;           /* pointer to end of buffer */
  int  c;

  for (; ptr < endptr && (c = getc(fp)) != EOF; *ptr++ = c)
    ;                                    /* read next block */
  *ptr = '\0';
  for (; ptr >= buffer; ptr--)
    if (*ptr == '\n' && (*cnt)++ == target)
       return ptr - buffer + 1;          /* where to start reading */
  return -1;                             /* have to read another block */
}
```

Figure 18.11   (tailutls.c) Functions to determine where in the file we need to begin printing.

```
/*
 * New versions of our earlier functions to read and write arrays.
 * Now they use fread/fwrite to read/write the arrays all at once.
 */
#include "fileopen.h"
#include "getints.h"

int fgetints(const char *name, int a[], int max)
{
  FILE *fp = fileopen(name, "rb");
  int   cnt = -1;

  if (fp != NULL)
    cnt = fread((void *) a, sizeof(int), max, fp);
  fileclose(name, fp);
  return cnt;                           /* # of elements written or -1 */
}

int fputints(const char *name, int a[], int num)
{
  FILE *fp = fileopen(name, "wb");
  int   cnt = -1;

  if (fp != NULL)
    cnt = fwrite((void *) a, sizeof(int), num, fp);
  fileclose(name, fp);
  return cnt;                           /* # of elements written or -1 */
}
```

Figure 18.12   (getints2.c) New version of our functions to read and write arrays of integers.

writes the array with a single **fwrite**.

The new versions aren't exactly equivalent, however. To see why, note that our call to **fwrite** simply writes **sizeof(int)** × **num** bytes to the file, the first byte coming from **&x[0]**. And similarly, our call to **fread** reads the next **sizeof(int)** × **max** bytes from the file into the array **a**. No translation to and from ASCII characters takes place. This means the file is a binary file rather than a text file, and we are careful to specify the **rb** and **wb** modes when we open it.

fread and **fwrite** provide a convenient and efficient way to save internal tables between program runs. We often use **fwrite** to save an internal table when a program finishes and **fread** to read it the next time the program starts. This method is much more efficient than using **fprintf** and **fscanf**, but has the disadvantage that the saved table is not text and cannot be easily examined.

> **fread** *and* **fwrite** *are portable, but the files they read and write aren't.*

To see why, consider a file containing 100 **int**s written using **fwrite**. If **int**s are 2 bytes, this file takes 200 bytes. Now suppose we move the file to a machine with 4-byte **int**s, and we try to read it using **fread** and telling **fread** to read 100 **int**s. **fread** will try to read 400 bytes, which it won't be able to do. The moral: Don't use **fwrite** to create files to be transferred between machines.

18.5	## FILE UPDATING

There are three file modes we haven't yet mentioned: **r+**, **w+**, and **a+**. The trailing **+** means "open for update". When we open a file for update we are allowed to both read and write to it—with one important restriction. We can't immediately follow a read with a write or a write with a read; there must be an intervening **fseek**. Except for the ability to update, the modes have the same effects as their earlier counterparts. That is, when we open a file for **"r+"**, the file must already exist. When we open a file for **"w+"**, the file is either created or truncated. And when we open a file for **"a+"**, the file is created if it doesn't exist, and the internal file pointer moved to the end of the file.

The update modes allows us to change a file's contents without completely rewriting it. We'll show how useful this is by writing a little package that allows us to create and access an array of any type, with its elements stored in a file rather than in memory. We call such an array a *virtual* array. Virtual arrays are a convenient—but slow—way to store a large table when we have a limited amount of available memory. The package also makes it easy for us to use files as arrays without forcing us to sprinkle lots and lots of **fseek**s, **fread**s, and **fwrite**s throughout our code.

Our package lets us access these virtual arrays in the same way we access files. We first open them, which gives us a handle that we then pass to the functions that access or change an element's value. And when we are done, we close them.

How do we open a virtual array? We provide two possibilities: **va_create** and **va_open**. We use **va_create** to create a new virtual array. It takes two arguments: the name of the file in which the array is to be stored and the size in bytes of one of its elements. The function opens the file using mode **w+b**, which wipes out any previous contents and allows us to subsequently read or write the file. **va_create** returns a pointer to a **VARRAY**. A **VARRAY** is a structure, like **FILE**, that contains information needed by the other functions in our package. Specifically, it contains a file pointer, the file's name, and the size of an element.

We use the other function, **va_open**, to access an existing virtual array. Like **va_creat**, it takes a pair of arguments: the name of the file and the size in bytes of an element. Unlike **va_create**, however, **va_open** opens the file with mode **r+b**, which succeeds only if the file already exists. Like **va_create**, **va_open** returns a pointer to a **VARRAY**.

Once we've opened a virtual array, we use **va_get** and **va_put** to access or change the values of its elements. Both take similar parameters: a pointer to a **VARRAY**, the index of the desired element, and a pointer to a buffer the size of an array element. **va_get** determines the element's location within the file, uses **fseek** to move to that location, and then uses **fread** to read its value into the provided buffer. **va_put** does the opposite: It writes the contents of the buffer to the appropriate position in the

```
/*
 * Define virtual array type, prototypes, and macros.
 */
#include <stdio.h>
#include <stddef.h>
#include <stdlib.h>

typedef struct varray
{
  FILE *fp;        /* pointer to external file */
  int  size;       /* size of an element */
} VARRAY;

VARRAY *va_create(const char *name, int size);
VARRAY *va_open(const char *name, int size);

#define va_close(vaptr) ((void) fclose(vaptr->fp), free(vaptr))

#define va_entries(vaptr) \
  (fseek((vaptr)->fp, 0L, SEEK_END) == -1L \
      ? -1 : (int) (ftell((vaptr)->fp) / (vaptr)->size))

#define va_get(vaptr, i, ptr) \
  (fseek((vaptr)->fp, (long) (i) * (vaptr)->size, SEEK_SET) != -1 && \
        fread((ptr), (vaptr)->size, 1, (vaptr)->fp) == 1)

#define va_put(vaptr, i, ptr) \
  (fseek((vaptr)->fp, (long) (i) * (vaptr)->size, SEEK_SET) != -1 && \
        fwrite((ptr), (vaptr)->size, 1, (vaptr)->fp) == 1)
```

Figure 18.13 (varray.h) Header file for virtual array package.

file. Both functions (actually macros) return zero if they can't successfully access the specified array element.

There's one restriction on using **va_put**: we can use it only to assign a new value to an existing array element or to append a single new element onto the end of the array. This restriction arises because we can't use **fseek** to move the internal file pointer past the end of the file. This isn't a terrible limitation, however, since we can create and initialize the elements of a virtual array by repeatedly using **va_put**.

The package's final function, **va_close**, closes a virtual array. It takes a pointer to a **VARRAY**, closes its file, and deallocates its **VARRAY** structure.

We divide our virtual array package into two parts. Figure 18.13 is a header file that defines the **VARRAY** type and provides prototypes and macros for the various virtual array operations. Figure 18.14 contains the operations themselves. We use these virtual arrays in this chapter's case study.

```
/*
 * Operations for creating or opening a virtual array.
 */
#include "allocs.h"              /* Our memory macros (CHAP15) */
#include "varray.h"
```

```
static VARRAY *make_varray(const char *name, const char *mode, int size)
{
  FILE    *fp  = fopen(name, mode);
  VARRAY *new = (fp != NULL) ? ALLOC(1, VARRAY) : NULL;

  if (new != NULL)
  {
    new->fp = fp;
    new->size = size;
  }
  else if (fp == NULL)
    (void) fclose(fp);
  return new;
}

VARRAY *va_create(const char *name, int size)  /* create a new VARRAY */
{
  return make_varray(name, "w+b", size);
}

VARRAY *va_open(const char *name, int size)     /* open existing VARRAY */
{
  return make_varray(name, "r+b", size);
}
```

Figure 18.14　(varray.c)　Several functions for creating and opening virtual arrays.

18.6　　CASE STUDY—AN ELECTRONIC ADDRESS BOOK

This section is optional!

We bring together many of the concepts covered in this text by implementing a small indexed file containing names, addresses, and phone numbers—a computerized little black book. Our address book consists of two files, bb and bb.idx. bb is a text file that holds records that contain names, addresses, and phone numbers. The only requirements are that the first line of each record contain the person's name and that the last line of each record contain a "." on a line by itself. bb.idx is a binary file that contains a person's name and the starting position of its corresponding record in bb. We keep this index file sorted by name. Figure 18.15 shows a sample address book.

The idea is that we create and maintain bb using any ordinary text editor, but look up addresses and phone numbers using a special program. This program, lookup, doesn't simply do a slow sequential search of bb. Instead, it does a fast binary search through bb.idx to determine exactly where in bb the desired record is located and then goes

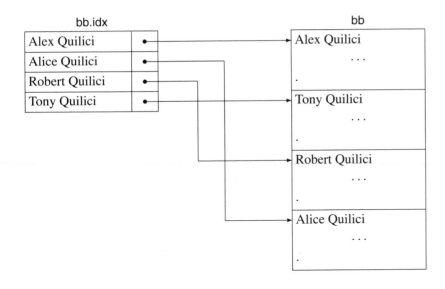

Figure 18.15   Our address book: One file contains the data and the other a sorted index.

directly to this location to retrieve it. Unlike bb, however, we don't access bb.idx directly. We construct it by running another special program. This program, index, travels through bb, building a table of names and record locations. It then sorts the table and writes it to bb.idx. To ensure that the index file is up to date, we have to run index whenever we modify the file containing the names and addresses.

Both of these programs need the definition of an index structure, so we've placed it in a header file, index.h. Figure 18.16 shows this file, which also contains constants for the address book file names, the input line length, and the end-of-record delimiter. Both programs treat the index file as a virtual array, so index.h includes varray.h.

Figures 18.17 and 18.18 contain index, which is surprisingly straightforward, despite its long length. It opens the file provided as its argument, builds the name-location table with **maketable**, sorts it with **qsort**, and then writes it to an external file with **savetable**. **savetable** uses our **VARRAY** functions to create and save this table as an external array.

lookup is also straightforward. It repeatedly prompts for names and prints the corresponding addresses and phone numbers. lookup, like index, treats the index file as a virtual array, but uses a new function, **va_search**, to look up locations. **va_search** is simply a modified version of our earlier binary search routine that uses **va_get** to access the desired record in the file.

```
/*
 * Definitions to use indexes.
 */
#include <string.h>
#include "varray.h"                      /* for external array */

#define MAXLEN      80                   /* maximum line length */
#define MAXKEY      40                   /* maximum key size */
#define INDEXFILE   "idx"                /* the index file */
#define ENDREC(x)   ((*x) == '.')        /* end of a record */
#define MAXIDX      100                  /* max number of records */

struct indexrec                          /* index record: */
{
  char key[MAXKEY];                      /*    name */
  long pos;                              /*    position */
};

typedef struct indexrec INDEX;
```

Figure 18.16   (index.h)   The address book header file.

SUMMARY

- C allows us to access external files through library functions.

- We use **fopen** to open files and **fclose** to close them. To open a file, we need to specify the file name and how we're going to use it. The three files **stdin**, **stdout**, and **stderr** are automatically opened for us.

- We can use **getc** and **putc** to do character-at-a-time I/O to files. **getchar** and **putchar** are macros defined on top of these functions.

- We can use **fgets** and **fputs** to do line-at-a-time I/O to files. These usually are slower than **getc** and **putc**, and they aren't designed to be easy to use, so we tend not to use them very much.

- We can use **fseek** to move to any byte in a file, **rewind** to move to the beginning of a file, and **ftell** to find out where in the file we actually are.

- We use **fread** and **fwrite** to read and write blocks of bytes to a file.

- There are special update modes, indicated with a "+" sign, that allow us to both read and write the same file.

```
/*
 * Create the index table for a file.
 */
#include "index.h"                            /* definition of INDEX */
#include "fileopen.h"

int main(int argc, char *argv[])
{
  int    maketable(FILE *fp, INDEX table[]);
  int    savetable(char *name, INDEX table[], int n);
  int    cmpkey(const void *, const void *);
  INDEX  itable[MAXIDX];                       /* holds index table */
  int    items;                               /* items in table */
  char   iname[MAXLEN + 1];                    /* index file name */
  FILE   *fp;                                  /* text file name */

  if (argc != 2)
  {
    fprintf(stderr,"Usage: %s file\n", argv[0]);
    return 1;                                  /* exit early, bad arguments */
  }

  if ((fp = fileopen(argv[1], "rb")) == NULL)
    return 1;                                  /* exit early, file problems */
  if ((items = maketable(fp, itable)) == -1)
  {
    fprintf(stderr,"Too many index entries\n");
    return 1;                                  /* exit early, index problems */
  }
  qsort(itable, items, sizeof(INDEX), cmpkey);
  sprintf(iname,"%s.%s", argv[1], INDEXFILE);
  if (savetable(iname, itable, items) != items)
  {
    fprintf(stderr, "Couldn't build index file\n");
    return 1;                                  /* exit early, index problems */
  }
  fileclose(argv[1], fp);

  return 0;
}

int cmpkey(const void *xptr, const void *yptr)
{
  return strcmp(((INDEX *) xptr)->key, ((INDEX *) yptr)->key);
}
```

Figure 18.17   (index.c) The program that creates the indexed address book.

```
/*
 * Functions to construct and save the index table.
 *    savetable - write index table into file.
 *    maketable - build index table from reading file.
 */
#include "index.h"

int savetable(char *name, INDEX table[], int n)
{
  int i = -1;                   /* indicates create failed error */
  VARRAY *vaptr;                /* the virtual array we create */

  if ((vaptr = va_create(name, sizeof(INDEX))) != NULL)
  {
    for (i = 0; i < n; i++)
      if (va_put(vaptr, i, &table[i]) == -1)
        break;
    va_close(vaptr);
  }
  return i;
}

int maketable(FILE *fp, INDEX table[])
{
  char line[MAXLEN + 1];        /* next line */
  long pos;                     /* record's pos in file */
  int  linecnt = 0;             /* # of lines in record */
  int  cnt = 0;                 /* count of records */
  int  last;                    /* index to last character in line */

  while (pos = ftell(fp), fgets(line,sizeof(line), fp) != NULL)
  {
    if (linecnt++ == 0)         /* add a table entry */
    {
      if (cnt == MAXIDX)
        return -1;
      last = strlen(line) - 1;          /* strip non-key chars */
      if (line[last - 1] == '\r')       /* \r\n ends line */
        line[last - 1] = '\0';
      else                              /* \n ends line */
        line[last] = '\0';
      strncpy(table[cnt].key, line, MAXKEY);
      table[cnt++].pos = pos;           /* store position */
    }
    if (ENDREC(line))
      linecnt = 0;
  }
  return cnt;
}
```

Figure 18.18 (indextab.c) The functions to build and save an index table.

```
/*
 * Look up addresses/phone numbers given name.
 */
#include "index.h"
#include "fileopen.h"

int main(int argc, char *argv[])
{
  int  findnames(FILE *fp, char *name);
  FILE *fp;                                 /* address book */
  char iname[MAXLEN + 1];                   /* index name */
  int  status = 1;                          /* return value */

  if (argc != 2)
    fprintf(stderr, "usage: %s file\n", argv[0]);
  else if ((fp = fileopen(argv[1], "rb")) != NULL)
  {
    sprintf(iname, "%s.%s", argv[1], INDEXFILE);
    if (!findnames(fp, iname))
    {
      fileclose(argv[1],fp);
      status = 0;
    }
  }
  return status;
}

int findnames(FILE *fp, char *name)
{
  long   va_search(VARRAY *ep, int first, int last, char *target);
  long   display_record(FILE *fp, long pos);
  int    getline(char *, int);
  int    entries;                           /* # of entries in file */
  VARRAY *vaptr;                            /* virtual array */
  char   line[MAXLEN + 1];                  /* user input line */
  long   pos;                               /* position of record */

  if ((vaptr = va_open(name, sizeof(INDEX))) == NULL)
  {
    fprintf(stderr,"Can't access index file %s\n", name);
    return 0;   /* oops... */
  }
  entries = va_entries(vaptr);
  while (fputs("Name? ", stdout), getline(line, MAXLEN) != -1)
    if ((pos = va_search(vaptr, 0, entries - 1, line)) == -1)
      fprintf(stderr, "Couldn't find: %s\n", line);
    else if (display_record(fp, pos) == -1)
      fprintf(stderr, "Couldn't display record at %li\n", pos);
  va_close(vaptr);
  return 1;       /* success */
}
```

Figure 18.19   (lookup.c)   Program to look up records in the address book.

```
/*
 * Get name from user, look it up, and display record.
 */
#include <string.h>
#include "index.h"

long display_record(FILE *fp, long pos)
{
  int   rval;                          /* fseek's return value */
  char line[MAXLEN + 1];               /* holds user input */

  if ((rval = fseek(fp, pos, SEEK_SET)) != -1)
    while (fgets(line, sizeof(line), fp) && !ENDREC(line))
      fputs(line,stdout);
  return rval;
}

long va_search(VARRAY *vaptr, int first, int last, char *target)
{
  int   mid = (first + last) / 2;      /* mid item */
  INDEX next;                          /* to hold record */
  int   cmp;                           /* holds comparison result */

  if (last < first || !va_get(vaptr, mid, (void *) &next))
    return -1L;                        /* not there */
  if ((cmp = strncmp(target, next.key, MAXKEY)) == 0)
    return next.pos;                   /* found it */
  return (cmp < 0)  ? va_search(vaptr, first, mid - 1, target)
                    : va_search(vaptr, mid + 1, last, target);
}
```

Figure 18.20   (find.c) Functions that actually search file for name and display record.

EXERCISES

18–1 Rewrite `filecpy` (Figure 18.2) to use `fileopen` and `fileclose` and to check for both read and write errors.

18–2 Rewrite `filecpy` to use `fread` and `fwrite`.

18–3 Make uniq (Figure 10.16) work with external files provided as command arguments. When no arguments are provided, it should use the standard input, as before.

18–4 Modify tail (Figure 18.10) to provide a command-line option that allows the user to select the number of lines to display.

18–5 Currently, when using lookup (Figure 18.19) we have to specify an entire name in order to find its address. Modify lookup to allow partial matches and to print all records matching the given name.

18–6 Modify lookup (Figure 18.19) so that it obtains the names it searches for from its command line arguments.

18–7 Modify index (Figure 18.17) and lookup (Figure 18.19) to allow fast access to records by phone number. You'll have to impose some additional structure on the file: The line containing the phone number must be easily identifiable.

18–8 Write a function, `fileapp`, that appends one file to the end of another. Can `filecpy` and `fileapp` be combined into a single function? Is this a good idea?

18–9 Implement `fgets`, `fputs`, `puts`, `gets`, `fread`, and `fwrite` using only `getc` and `putc`.

18–10 Write a function, `fgetline`, that is just like `getline` except that it reads its input from a file rather than the standard input.

18–11 Write a program to print the line number of the first byte where two files differ.

18–12 Write a program that counts the number of words, lines, and characters in each of the files supplied as its arguments.

18–13 Write a little program that prints the indexing information for the address book. It should print each entry in the index file in a readable format. It should verify that the indexed entry is indeed there and print its length in bytes. And finally, it should print some summary information, including the total number of entries in the address book and the average size of an entry.

18–14 Write a program that takes three arguments—a file name, a byte offset, and a byte count—and prints the specified bytes within the specified file.

18–15 Write a program keep that prints only certain lines in the files provided as its arguments. The lines to print are specified as options. The command

> keep -1-10 -50,52,54 *filename*

prints the first 10 lines of filename followed by lines 50, 52, and 54. keep should work with the standard input if no files are specified.

18–16 Write a program, cut, that prints only certain characters in the lines of the files provided as its arguments. As with keep, the relevant characters are provided as options. The command

> cut -1-10 -50,52 *file*

prints each line without printing its first 10 characters or characters 50 and 52.

18–17 Write a program, rev, that reverses the files provided as its arguments, one character at a time. This program is a useful April Fools' Day substitute for the DOS type and UNIX cat commands.

18–18 Write a program that allows a user to examine any specified line in a file. It should construct an index table, an array whose items hold the starting position of the corresponding line in the file. To get to the user-specified line, it uses it as an index into the table and then uses `fseek` to move to that position in the file.

18–19 Rewrite Chapter 11's program to store employee information to store its data in a file, rather than an array. The program should keep an internal index table so that it can access records quickly. When the program terminates, it writes this index table to a file. When the program starts, it begins with the existing index table.

18–20 We can speed up our array-accessing functions by keeping a cache of the most recently accessed array elements. The cache is a small in-memory array. The idea is that whenever we access an array element, we first check the cache. If the value is there, we've saved a file access. If it isn't, we access the file element as before, except that we also add it to the cache, removing whatever item has been in the cache the longest (writing it to the file if its value has changed).

18–21 Write an insertion sort that works with virtual arrays. Use any of the earlier insertion sort programs as a starting point.

18–22 Write a program to manage student grades. The program should keep these grades in a single file, with one record per student. The record should include a name, an ID number, room for 10 numeric grades, and room for a final letter grade. You should provide operations to add and delete students, to change information about a student, and to add, delete, and change grades. Index the file by student ID number. You also need to provide operations to assign grades, to print the information on various students, and to print a grading summary for the entire file.

19 LISTS AND TREES

This chapter examines two linked data structures: linked lists and binary search trees. We introduce linked lists and present a set of functions for managing ordered lists, stacks, and queues, regardless of the data stored in a list element. And we introduce binary search trees and present a set of functions for managing them. We end the chapter with a case study that uses both lists and trees—a cross referencer that produces a listing of all the words in its input, along with the line numbers on which they appear.

19.1 LINKED LISTS

Up to now we've been using arrays to store tables of values. But arrays have a pair of problems.

First, there's no easy way to maintain an array in sorted order. Instead, we're stuck with shifting array elements to make room for a new element or to close up the space used by an existing element. That's troublesome if we're constantly updating an array's elements, since when we're unlucky and have to insert or delete one of the first few elements of the array, we're going to end up moving almost all of its elements.

Second, there's no convenient and efficient way to change an array's size at run time. To do so, we're stuck with allocating a larger table and then copying our original table into it. That's an expensive operation, so we're really forced to guess accurately how many elements an array is going to need. But if we guess wrong, we're in trouble. Underestimating our storage requirements leads to our running out of space when an array fills up. And overestimating them leads to wasting space or to writing programs that may not compile on some machines because there isn't sufficient storage.

Linked lists are dynamic data structures that help us get around these problems. A linked list consists of a collection of objects called *nodes*. Each node contains two fields: a *data* field, which corresponds to an array element, and a *pointer* field, which contains a pointer to the next node in the linked list. A **NULL** pointer field marks the end of the list.

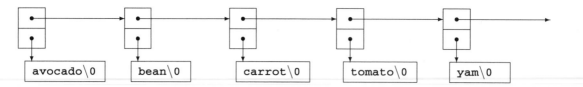

Figure 19.1   Linked list of nodes with pointers to a character string.

Figure 19.1 shows a typical linked list of strings. There, the data field is a pointer to a string, rather than the string itself. That's because strings can vary in length, and storing them this way eliminates wasted space and allows the space for the node itself to be a small fixed amount: room for the string pointer, plus room for the pointer to the next node. The trade-off is that we must now not only create nodes, but also allocate space for the string.

Linked list have a pair of advantages over arrays. We can insert an element into the list without shifting all of the elements that follow—we simply adjust the pointers appropriately. And we can have an unlimited number of values in the list—unlike with arrays, where we had to predeclare a maximum number of values. The disadvantage is that we must search the list to find the elements we want, a potentially time-consuming operation, rather than directly indexing it.

Representing Linked Lists

We can represent linked list nodes in a structure containing two fields.

```
typedef struct listnode
{
  void *dataptr;               /* ptr to node's data */
  struct listnode *nextptr;    /* ptr to next list node */
}
  LISTNODE;
```

The **dataptr** field holds a pointer to the data corresponding to the node. It's a pointer to **void** so it can hold a pointer to any type of data. **nextptr** holds the pointer to the next node in the list. To clarify and simplify the use of this structure, we use **typedef** to define **LISTNODE** as a synonym for a **listnode** structure.

Unlike array elements, we have to allocate space for each individual list node. And when we no longer need a node, it's our responsibility to free it up if we plan on reusing the storage.

Figure 19.2 is a header file defining the **LISTNODE** type, and Figure 19.3 contains definitions of a pair of functions for creating and destroying list nodes: **ln_create** and **ln_destroy**.

ln_create allocates space for a node and fills in the node's fields. It takes two arguments: a pointer to the data to be contained in this node, and a pointer to the

```
/*
 * Linked list node type and prototypes.
 */
#include <stddef.h>                   /* for NULL */
#include <stdlib.h>                   /* for malloc/free */

typedef struct listnode
{
  void *dataptr;                      /* ptr to node's data */
  struct listnode *nextptr;           /* ptr to next list node */
}
  LISTNODE;

LISTNODE *ln_create(void *dataptr, LISTNODE *nodeptr);
void ln_destroy(LISTNODE *nodeptr);
```

Figure 19.2 (lnodes.h) Definition of linked list nodes.

```
/*
 * Manage linked list nodes.
 *    ln_create - create new list node.
 *    ln_destroy - free space used by existing list node.
 */
#include "lnodes.h"                        /* node type, prototypes */

LISTNODE *ln_create(void *dataptr, LISTNODE *nodeptr)
{
  LISTNODE *nptr = malloc(sizeof(LISTNODE));

  if (nptr != NULL)
  {
    nptr->dataptr = dataptr;              /* points to data */
    nptr->nextptr = nodeptr;              /* points to next node */
  }
  return nptr;
}

void ln_destroy(LISTNODE *nptr)
{
  free(nptr);                             /* destroy node, not data */
}
```

Figure 19.3 (lnodes.c) Functions to create and destroy linked list nodes.

```
/*
 * Useful typedefs for pointers to functions that create, update,
 * compare, and access nodes in linked lists.
 */
#if !defined(POINTER_TYPEDEFS)
#define POINTER_TYPEDEFS

enum status {UPDATE, CREATE};       /* controls whether update function
                                       creates or updates list node */

typedef int   (*CMP_FPTR)(const void *, const void *);   /* comparison */
typedef void  (*ACT_FPTR)(void *);                       /* action */
typedef void *(*UPD_FPTR)(void *, enum status);          /* update */

#endif
```

Figure 19.4   (ptrfuncs.h)   Type definitions for some useful pointers to functions.

node that will follow it. It uses **malloc** to allocate space for a single **LISTNODE** and then assigns its arguments to the node's fields. **ln_create** assumes that that space has already been allocated for the data pointed to by the node and that we've already decided where in the list the node should go.

ln_destroy frees up the space used by a node. It takes one argument, a pointer to a node, which it passes to **free**. This frees the node itself, but not the data it points to. **ln_destroy** assumes that this data has already been freed.

Common Linked List Operations

We'll use linked lists to write a program that sorts strings. This requires four list-manipulating functions: **list_create** creates an empty list, **list_traverse** does an action on each data value in the list, **list_insert** inserts a new node into its correct place in the list, and **list_destroy** removes all the nodes in the list.

Although for now we're only going to manipulate lists of strings, we really want our list operations to be general enough to support lists of any data type. That way we only have to write the messy pointer manipulations once. But to do that, we'll need to pass the various list operations pointers to functions for doing things such as comparing and printing values, just as we did with our generic functions for searching and sorting arrays. To keep our programs readable, we've defined and used several type definitions for these pointers. Figure 19.4 contains these **typedef**s. Figure 19.5 provides the prototypes for our list operations, and Figure 19.6 defines the operations themselves. We now discuss each of these functions, starting with the simplest and finishing with the most complex.

```
/*
 * Definitions of list type and prototypes for list operations.
 */
#include "lnodes.h"                    /* list node and prototypes */
#include "ptrfuncs.h"                  /* pointer to function typedefs */

typedef LISTNODE *LIST;                /* list is ptr to 1st list node */

LIST list_create(void);
void list_traverse(LIST l, ACT_FPTR action);
LIST list_insert(LIST l, void *dataptr, CMP_FPTR cmp);
void list_destroy(LIST l);
LIST list_update(LIST l, void *dataptr, CMP_FPTR cmp, UPD_FPTR upd);
```

Figure 19.5 (lists.h) Definitions of list data type.

Creating an Empty List

Before we can do anything to a list, we need to create it. **list_create** takes no arguments and returns a new, empty list. We represent an empty list with a **NULL** pointer, so that's what **list_create** actually returns. We then assign this pointer to a **LIST** variable, where **LIST** is a type we've defined as a synonym for a pointer to a **LISTNODE**.

Since **list_create** is so simple, why do we bother making it a function at all? Why don't we directly assign **NULL** to the **LIST** variable and skip the overhead of a function call? Because using **list_create** contributes to making our program more readable and more maintainable. There are many reasons why we might assign **NULL** to a variable, so without the function it's not clear that we're initializing a list. Besides, it's possible that in the future we'll want a different representation for our list, such as adding a special *header* node containing a count of elements or pointers to the first and last elements. Using **list_create** helps minimize the changes to programs using lists.

Traversing an Existing List

The next operation is to run through an existing list, the task handled by **list_traverse**. When we traverse a list, we "process" each node in the list, from the first to the last. Processing a node could involve printing its data, returning the data items to the free storage pool, and so on. That means we need to tell **list_traverse** which list we're working on and what action we want to do for each list element. We do that by passing **list_traverse** a pair of arguments: a **LIST** to traverse and a pointer to a function. **list_traverse** executes the function once for each node, passing it the current node's **dataptr**.

How do we actually traverse the list? Simply by moving a pointer along the list. In particular, **list_traverse** uses a pointer called **curr** to traverse the list and uses

```
/*
 * Basic functions implementing list data type.
 *   list_create - create a new, empty list.
 *   list_traverse - do action on each list node's data.
 *   list_insert - insert new node in correct place in list.
 *   list_destroy - remove all list nodes.
 */
#include "lists.h"

LIST list_create(void)
{
  return NULL;
}

void list_traverse(LIST list, ACT_FPTR actfptr)
{
  LISTNODE *curr;                          /* ptr to current node */

  for (curr = list; curr != NULL; curr = curr->nextptr)
    actfptr(curr->dataptr);                /* do act to node's data */
}

LIST list_insert(LIST list, void *target, CMP_FPTR cmpfptr)
{
  LISTNODE *nptr;                          /* ptr to new node */
  LISTNODE *curr = list;                   /* ptr to current node */
  LISTNODE *prev = NULL;                   /* ptr to previous node */

  for (; curr != NULL; prev = curr, curr = curr->nextptr)
    if (cmpfptr(curr->dataptr, target) > 0)
      break;                               /* found place for node */
  nptr = ln_create(target, curr);
  if (prev == NULL)
    list = nptr;                           /* insert at front */
  else
    prev->nextptr = nptr;                  /* insert in middle or end */
  return list;                             /* return updated list */
}

void list_destroy(LIST list)
{
  LISTNODE *curr = list;                   /* ptr to current node */
  LISTNODE *temp;                          /* ptr to next node */

  for ( ; curr != NULL; curr = temp)
  {
    temp = curr->nextptr;
    ln_destroy(curr);
  }
}
```

Figure 19.6 (lists1.c) Our functions to create, destroy, and traverse linked lists.

`curr->dataptr` to access each node's data field. When we're done with the current node, we move `curr` along the list with the assignment

```
curr = curr->nextptr
```

We stop the traversing when `curr` finally becomes `NULL`.

> *Don't forget to make sure that all lists are properly* `NULL` *terminated.*

Forgetting to terminate a list with a `NULL` is likely to lead to disaster, just as if we forget to terminate a string with a null character.

Inserting in a Sorted Linked List

Another important operation is inserting a new element in the correct place in the list, the task handled by `list_insert`. It takes three arguments: a `LIST`, a pointer to the data item we want to insert, and a pointer to a comparison function it uses to determine where to insert this item. It returns the list with the new data item inserted in the appropriate place. `list_insert`'s caller is responsible for allocating storage for the data to be inserted in the list, and for placing a copy of that data into this storage. That means that to insert a string into the list, we have to `malloc` sufficient storage for it, copy it into this storage, and then pass `list_insert` a pointer to it. So what does `list_insert` do for us? It determines where this string belongs, creates a node whose `dataptr` field points to the storage we allocated, and hooks the node into the list. Figure 19.7 shows how it locates the correct place for a new value and how we actually insert the node.

To search the list, we use two pointers, `curr` and `prev`. We initialize `curr` to point to the list's first node and `prev` to `NULL` and move both down the list, one trailing the other. Why do we need two pointers? Because we know we've found the correct place to insert only when we've gone one node past it. That is, as we move `curr` through the list, we compare the value it points to with the value to insert. When the value we're inserting is larger, we know we should insert it in front of the current node. But since our list contains only pointers to the next node, we need to keep this *trailing link pointer*, `prev`, one node behind `curr`.

To do a comparison, `list_insert` calls the comparison function, passing it a pointer to the data item we're inserting and a pointer to the current node's `dataptr`. That function is responsible for dereferencing the passed pointers and comparing the pointed-to values. It should return zero if the values are the same, something positive if the item we're inserting is the larger value, and something negative if it's smaller.

To create a new node, we use `ln_create`, passing it a pair of pointers. The first is a pointer to its new data value—the value we used to determine where in the list we wanted to insert the new node. The other is `curr`, which points to the node that should follow the new node. We then make the previous node's `nextptr` field point to this new node and return a pointer to the beginning of the list. There is only one exception to this simple scenario: when we insert an item into the beginning of the list, there is no previous item, so we simply return a pointer to the new node, which becomes the first item in the list.

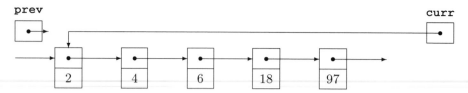

(*a*) Before searching the list.

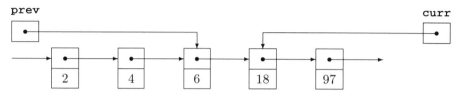

(*b*) When we find the desired node.

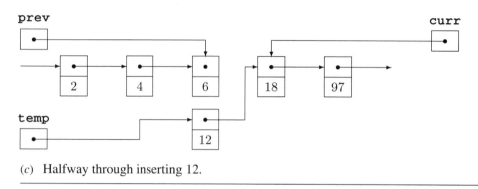

(*c*) Halfway through inserting 12.

Figure 19.7   Inserting a value into a linked list of numbers.

Destroying a Linked List

Printing a list is not the only operation that requires its traversal. Another example is deallocating all of the nodes in a list. Because we dynamically allocate linked list nodes with **malloc**, we must deallocate them with **free** once we no longer need them, so that the space they use is available for other purposes. You might think we could deallocate a list simply by **free**ing the node's first element. But we requested space a node at a time for our linked list, so we must free it a node at a time, which means that we're forced to traverse an entire list to deallocate all of its nodes.

list_destroy is a slight variant on **traverse_list** in which "process the node" becomes a call to **ln_destroy** (which calls **free**). Since they're so similar, why didn't we just use **list_traverse**, passing it **free** as the function to execute?

```
/*
 * Sort strings using generic linked lists.
 */
#include <stdio.h>
#include <string.h>
#include "lists.h"                              /* for list data type */

#define MAXLEN 80

int main()
{
  int   getline(char *line, int max);
  int   cmpstr(const void *ptr1, const void *ptr2);
  void  printstr(void *ptr);
  char  line[MAXLEN + 1];                       /* input line */
  char  *ptr;                                   /* ptr to input line copy */
  int   len;                                    /* length of input line */
  LIST  sl = list_create();                     /* list of strings */

  while ((len = getline(line, MAXLEN)) != -1)
    if ((ptr = malloc(len + 1)) != NULL)
      sl = list_insert(sl, strcpy(ptr,line), cmpstr);
    else
    {
      printf("Out of memory reading line %s\n", line);
      break;
    }
  list_traverse(sl, printstr);                  /* print elements */
  list_traverse(sl, free);                      /* free data */
  list_destroy(sl);                             /* free nodes */
  return 0;
}
```

Figure 19.8 (strlists.c) Insertion sort of input strings using linked lists.

Because that would deallocate the space used by the data in each node, not the space used by the nodes themselves.

freeing nodes in a linked list is actually a little bit tricky. We have to be careful to save a copy of the node's **nextptr** field before we **free** the node. Why? Because once we **free** something, we can't touch it again since the storage may have been marked in some way as being invalid.

Sorting Strings Using Linked Lists

Figure 19.8 puts all of these functions together in a program that uses a single linked list to sort its input lines. Figure 19.9 contains two additional functions to compare and print strings that this sorting program needs.

```
/*
 * Comparison and printing functions.
 *    cmpstr - given generic pointers, compare strings.
 *    printstr - given generic pointer, print string.
 */
#include <stdio.h>
#include <string.h>

int cmpstr(const void *xptr, const void *yptr)
{
  return strcmp((const char *) xptr, (const char *) yptr);
}

void printstr(void *ptr)
{
  printf("%s\n", (const char *) ptr);
}
```

Figure 19.9   (strfuncs.c) Comparison and printing functions for our string utilities.

list, storing it in the **LIST** variable, **sl** (for string list).

```
sl = list_create();
```

It then repeatedly uses **getline** to read the next input line, **malloc** and **strcpy** to dynamically allocate a copy of it, and **list_insert** to store the copy in the correct place in the list.

```
sl = list_insert(sl, ptr, cmpstr);
```

We pass **list_insert** the current list, a pointer to a copy of the string we want to insert, and a pointer to the comparison function **cmpstr**. **cmpstr** simply casts the passed pointers to pointers to strings and then uses **strcmp** to compare those strings. **list_insert** returns a pointer to the modified list, which we store back in **sl**.

To print the list, we use **list_traverse**, passing it **sl** and a pointer to the function **printstr**. **list_traverse** calls **printstr** once for each node, passing it a pointer to the node's data.

```
list_traverse(sl, printstr);
```

printstr simply casts the pointer into a pointer to a string and uses **printf** to write that string.

To free the list, we make two passes through it. The first uses **list_traverse** to free the node's data field—the strings we allocated before we inserted them into the list. We simply pass it **sl** and a pointer to **free**.

```
list_traverse(sl, free);
```

The second uses **list_destroy** to remove the nodes in the list. We simply pass

The second uses **list_destroy** to remove the nodes in the list. We simply pass **list_destroy** the list.

```
list_destroy(sl);
```

There are several places we can improve this program. First, we really don't need to destroy the list, since we don't need to reuse its space before we finish. So we can simply remove the calls dealing with deallocating nodes and their data. Second, we're not using the world's most efficient sorting algorithm. Although linked-list insertion sort avoids the time-consuming process of shifting data to make room for a new item, it isn't substantially faster than the array-based insertion sort. Whenever we insert a value, we still must search the list for the correct place to insert, an operation that takes time proportional to m, if there are m values in the list or array. For all n input values, this takes a total amount of time proportional to n^2. If n doubles, for example, sorting time goes up by a factor of 4.

Updating a Linked List

Our string sort always inserts an item in its correct place in the list. But how do we update an existing list item?

Suppose we want to print the number of occurrences of each word in the input. One approach is to maintain a list in which each item contains a word and a count of the number of times it appears. Whenever we see an existing word, we update its count. And whenever we see a new word, we insert it in the list with a count of zero. To do this, we need one other operation, **list_update**, shown in Figure 19.10. It takes the same arguments as **list_insert**, plus one additional argument: a pointer to a function capable of updating an existing data field or creating a new one.

Like **list_insert**, **list_update** searches the list for a place to insert the new item. But unlike **list_insert**, it also worries about whether the item is already there. If it finds the item, **list_update** calls the update function, passing it the matching node's **dataptr** and a flag telling it to update the data. The function does the update and returns a pointer to the changed data, which **list_update** stores back into **dataptr**. We use a function to perform the update, since different types of data will be updated in different ways.

If **list_update** can't find a matching node, it creates a new node and inserts it in the list, just as **list_insert** did. The one difference is that it calls the update function to create the new data item, passing it the value we were trying to find a flag telling it that we didn't find it. When we used **list_insert**, we created the new data item before we called it. But we can't do that here, since we're usually not creating a new node.

Figure 19.11 contains a program to print the number of times each input line appears. We can use it to count different words in our input by combining it with our Chapter 4 program that takes its input and prints it on the output, one word at a time. It differs from our earlier string sort in two ways. The data items are **ITEM** structures containing a word and a count, rather than strings. And it uses **list_update** to add and update list items, rather than **list_insert**.

```
/*
 * Update a list item or create it if it's not already there.
 */
#include "lists.h"

LIST list_update(LIST list, void *target, CMP_FPTR cfptr, UPD_FPTR ufptr)
{
  LISTNODE *nptr;                          /* pointer to new node */
  LISTNODE *curr;                          /* pointer to current node */
  LISTNODE *prev = NULL;                   /* pointer to previous node */
  int cmp = -1;                            /* result of list comparison */

  for (curr = list; curr != NULL; curr = curr->nextptr)
  {
    if ((cmp = cfptr(target, curr->dataptr)) <= 0)
      break;
    prev = curr;
  }
  if (cmp == 0)                            /* found it in list; do update */
    curr->dataptr = ufptr(curr->dataptr, UPDATE);
  else
  {                                        /* not in list, so create */
    nptr = ln_create(ufptr(target, CREATE), curr);
    if (prev == NULL)
      list = nptr;                         /* insert at front */
    else
      prev->nextptr = nptr;                /* insert at middle or end */
  }
  return list;                             /* return updated list */
}
```

Figure 19.10 (lists2.c) The function **list_update** for updating a linked list element.

functions to update, compare, and print items. We use **updimem** as our node updating function. It has two jobs: creating a new data item and updating an existing item. To create a new item, it **malloc**s a structure, fills in the word field with the value we were trying to find, and sets the count of appearances to **1**. To update an existing item, it simply increments its count field.

Since we're dealing with **ITEM**s rather than strings, we've had to write new comparison and printing functions: **cmpitem** determines whether an **ITEM** contains our target word, and **printitem** prints an **ITEM**'s word and count fields.

```
/*
 * Prints number of times each word appears in input, sorted by word
 * (assumes one word per input line).
 */
#include <stdio.h>
#include <string.h>
#include "items.h"

int main()
{
  int getline(char *line, int max);      /* for reading input line */
  char line[MAXLEN + 1];                 /* input line */
  LIST sl = list_create();               /* list of strings */

  while (getline(line, MAXLEN) != -1)
    if (line[0] != '\0')
      sl = list_update(sl, line, cmpitem, upditem);
  list_traverse(sl, printitem);
  return 0;
}
```

Figure 19.11   (cntwords.c) Count different words in input using a linked list to hold them.

```
/*
 * ITEM definition and prototypes.
 */
#include "lists.h"

#define  MAXLEN    80                    /* longest input line */

typedef struct item
{
  char wordtext[MAXLEN + 1];             /* text of word */
  int cnt;                               /* count of appearances */
} ITEM;

int  cmpitem(const void *ptr1, const void *ptr2);
void *upditem(void *ptr, enum status updtype);
void printitem(void *ptr);
```

Figure 19.12   (items.h) Definition of the **ITEM** type and prototypes for the functions that access it.

```
/*
 * Functions managing ITEM type.
 */
#include <stdio.h>
#include <stdlib.h>
#include <string.h>
#include "items.h"

void *upditem(void *target, enum status todo)    /* update/create item */
{
  ITEM *itemptr = target;

  if (todo == CREATE)                            /* not already there, create */
  {
    if ((itemptr = malloc(sizeof(ITEM))) == NULL)
      printf("Couldn't allocate space for item\n");
    else
    {
      strncpy(itemptr->wordtext, target, MAXLEN);
      itemptr->cnt = 1;
    }
  }
  else                                           /* already there, update */
    itemptr->cnt++;
  return itemptr;
}

int cmpitem(const void *xptr, const void *yptr)  /* compare items */
{
  return strcmp((const char *) xptr, ((ITEM *) yptr)->wordtext);
}

void printitem(void *ptr)                                /* print item */
{
  printf("%s %i\n", ((ITEM *) ptr)->wordtext, ((ITEM *) ptr)->cnt);
}
```

Figure 19.13 (items.c) The functions for updating, comparing, and printing items.

19.2   **STACKS AND QUEUES—SPECIAL PURPOSE LISTS**

We've shown how to manage ordered linked lists. But there are other useful organizations for linked lists. The most common ones are **stacks** and **queues**. Both are lists, but with restrictions. With a stack, we can only access its first element. That is, we can only put new values at the start of the list, and we can only examine and remove the value at the start of the list. And with a queue, we can only insert items at the front and remove them from the rear, as we saw when we implemented queues using an array.

We'll now show how to implement stacks and queues of any data type. They are much easier to implement than ordered lists: we don't need to do any comparisons or traversals, so we don't have to pass around any pointers to functions.

Stacks

We need to provide several stack operations: **stack_create** creates an empty stack, **stack_push** places a new item on the top of the stack, **stack_pop** removes the top item, **stack_top** returns the top item's value (without removing it), and **stack_empty** returns a nonzero value if the stack is empty. We need not implement an operation to destroy a stack, since we can do that by repeated calls to **stack_pop**.

Figure 19.14 contains the prototypes for these operations, and Figure 19.15 contains the operations themselves. To aid readability, we define a type **STACK** that's a synonym for a pointer to a **LISTNODE**.

Actually, some of our stack functions are so simple that for efficiency we've made them macros. **stack_create** takes no arguments and returns an empty **STACK**. Since an empty stack corresponds to an empty list, it simply returns a **NULL** pointer. **stack_empty** takes a **STACK** and determines whether it is empty by testing whether it is **NULL**. **stack_top** returns the **dataptr** of the first element in the **STACK**.

stack_push and **stack_pop** are slightly more complex. **stack_push** takes a **STACK** and a pointer to new data, inserts a new node at the front of the list, and returns a pointer to it. That's easy to do: it simply calls **ln_create** to create a new node, passing it a pointer to the new data item and a pointer to the front of the list. **stack_pop** takes a **STACK**, frees the first node in the list, and then returns a pointer to the next node as the new **STACK**. We have to be careful to save the first node's **nextptr** before we free the node.

Figure 19.16 reverses its input using a stack. It repeatedly reads input lines, pushing each input line onto the top of the stack. Once it hits the end of the input, it keeps printing the top stack element and popping the stack until it's empty.

Queues

There are several basic queue operations: **queue_create** creates a new queue, **enqueue** adds a new element to the end of a queue, **dequeue** removes the first element from the queue, and **queue_empty** tells us whether the queue is empty.

We could represent a queue in the same way we represent a stack: as a pointer to the first node in a linked list. **dequeue** is then just like **stack_pop**, returning the first node in the list. But then **enqueue** is prohibitively expensive, because we have to run through the entire list every time we add an item to it. A better way to represent a queue is with a pair of pointers: one to the front of a linked list and the other to the rear. Both **enqueue** and **dequeue** can do their jobs simply by changing a few pointers. Figure 19.17 shows how these functions work, Figure 19.18 contains their prototypes, and Figure 19.19 contains the functions themselves. As with stacks, we define a special type **QUEUE**, but this time it's not merely a synonym for a pointer to a **LISTNODE**. Instead, it's a pointer to a structure containing two pointers to **LISTNODE**s: **frontptr**, which points to the first node in the queue, and **rearptr**, which points to the last.

```
ltions of stack data type and prototypes.

lude "lists.h"

typedef LISTNODE *STACK;

#define stack_create()   NULL              /* create an empty stack */
#define stack_empty(s)   ((s) == NULL)     /* is stack empty? */
#define stack_top(s)     ((s)->dataptr)    /* first item on stack */

STACK stack_push(STACK s, void *dataptr);
STACK stack_pop(STACK s);
```

Figure 19.14 (stacks.h) Definitions of stack and stack prototypes.

```
/*
 * Stack operations.
 */
#include "stacks.h"                           /* STACK type and prototypes */

STACK stack_push(STACK s, void *dptr)    /* add new item to stack */
{
  return ln_create(dptr, s);
}

STACK stack_pop(STACK s)                      /* delete top item from stack */
{
  LISTNODE *topptr    = s;
  LISTNODE *secondptr = topptr->nextptr;

  ln_destroy(topptr);
  return secondptr;
}
```

Figure 19.15 (stacks.c) Definitions of stack functions.

queue_create differs from our functions to create lists and stacks in that it doesn't simply return a NULL pointer. Instead, it allocates a queue structure and returns a pointer to it. enqueue takes this pointer and a pointer to the new data item. It allocates a new node with ln_create and then updates the queue's rearptr to point to this node. If the queue is empty, it also updates the queue's frontptr. dequeue takes a pointer to the queue structure and returns the first node's dataptr. It destroys the first node and updates frontptr to point to the next node. If the queue is now empty, it also updates the queue's rearptr. We'll use these functions in our end-of-chapter case study.

```
/*
 * Reverse input strings using a stack.
 */
#include <stdio.h>
#include <string.h>
#include "stacks.h"                    /* STACK type and prototypes */

#define MAXLEN 80

int main()
{
  int   getline(char *buf, int len);
  char  line[MAXLEN + 1];              /* input line */
  char *ptr;                           /* copy of input line */
  STACK s = stack_create();            /* our stack */
  int len;

  while ((len = getline(line, MAXLEN)) != -1)
    if ((ptr = malloc(len + 1)) != NULL)
      s = stack_push(s, strcpy(ptr,line));
    else
    {
      printf("Out of memory processing line %s\n", line);
      break;
    }
  for (; !stack_empty(s); s = stack_pop(s))
  {
    printf("%s\n", ptr = stack_top(s));
    free(ptr);
  }
  return 0;
}
```

Figure 19.16 (strrev.c) Reverse input using a stack.

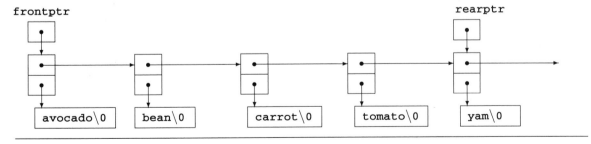

Figure 19.17 Representing a queue with pointers to first and last elements. **enqueue** adds an element at the end; **dequeue** adds an element at the beginning.

```
/*
 * Queue type and prototypes.
 */
#include "lists.h"                       /* list type and prototypes */

typedef struct queue
{
  LISTNODE *frontptr;                    /* pointer to first list node */
  LISTNODE *rearptr;                     /* pointer to last list node */
} *QUEUE;

QUEUE queue_create(void);
void  enqueue(QUEUE q, void *dataptr);
void  *dequeue(QUEUE q);

#define queue_empty(qptr) \
        ((qptr)->frontptr == NULL)    /* is queue empty? */
```

Figure 19.18   (qs.h) Definitions of the QUEUE structure and prototypes.

19.3   BINARY SEARCH TREES

In a linked list, each node contains a pointer to the next node in the list. A binary tree is an extension to lists in which each node has two pointers, where each pointer is either NULL or a pointer to a binary tree. The top node in the tree is called the *root*.

Figure 19.20 shows a particularly useful type of binary tree, a *binary search tree* (BST). In a BST, the data value at each node partitions its subtrees into two subsets. In the left subtree, every data item is smaller than the current node; in the right subtree, every data item is larger than (or equal to) the current node. We'll now use BSTs to construct another, more efficient, sorting program, called *tree sort*.

As you might expect, we can define a node in a binary tree as a structure. As with lists, we store a pointer to the data. But unlike lists we store two pointers in each node, not just one. Figure 19.21 shows the definition of a tree node, and Figure 19.22 provides the functions, tn_create and tn_destroy, for creating and destroying them.

Binary Search Tree Operations

We implement the same operations for trees that we did for lists: **tree_create** creates an empty tree, **tree_insert** inserts a new item in its correct place in the tree, **tree_update** updates an existing item or adds it if it's not there, **tree_traverse** runs through a tree in sorted order, and **tree_destroy** frees up the nodes used by the tree. Figure 19.23 provides the prototypes for these functions, and Figures 19.24 and 19.25 provide the functions themselves.

```
/*
 * Queue-manipulating functions.
 */
#include "qs.h"                          /* QUEUE type and prototypes */

QUEUE queue_create(void)                 /* create new, empty queue */
{
  QUEUE qptr = malloc(sizeof(struct queue));

  if (qptr != NULL)
    qptr->frontptr = qptr->rearptr = NULL;
  return qptr;
}

void enqueue(QUEUE qptr, void *ptr)      /* add item to rear of queue */
{
  LISTNODE *nptr = ln_create(ptr, NULL);

  if (qptr->frontptr == NULL)            /* empty queue */
    qptr->frontptr = nptr;
  else                                   /* nonempty queue */
    qptr->rearptr->nextptr = nptr;
  qptr->rearptr = nptr;
}

void *dequeue(QUEUE qptr)                /* remove first item in queue */
{
  LISTNODE *nptr    = qptr->frontptr;    /* first node */
  void      *dataptr = nptr->dataptr;    /* data in first node */

  if ((qptr->frontptr = nptr->nextptr) == NULL)
    qptr->rearptr = NULL;                /* now queue empty */
  free(nptr);                            /* destroy node */
  return dataptr;
}
```

Figure 19.19 (qs.c) Definitions of queue functions.

Building a Binary Search Tree

Creating an empty tree is easy. An empty tree is really nothing more than a **NULL** pointer, so **tree_create** is just **list_create**: it returns a **NULL** pointer.

Inserting a node into a tree is more difficult. **tree_insert** uses a technique similar to **list_insert** to insert a node into the tree. Again, we use two pointers, **curr** and **prev**. Assuming the tree is not empty, we first set **curr** to its root, and **prev** to **NULL**. We then compare the value with the current node. If the value is less, we set **curr** to point to its left subtree. If the value is greater (or equal), we set **curr** to point to its right subtree. In either case, before changing **curr**, we save its value in **prev**. We keep repeating this process until **curr** becomes **NULL**, at which point we allocate a

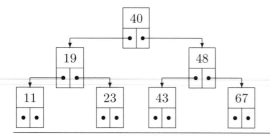

Figure 19.20   An example binary search tree. For every node, all of the items in its left subtree are less than the node, and all of the items in its right subtree are greater than the node.

```
/*
 * Definitions and prototypes for a tree node.
 */
typedef struct treenode
{
  void             *dataptr;
  struct treenode *left;
  struct treenode *right;
}
  TREENODE;

TREENODE *tn_create(void *nodeptr);
void tn_destroy(TREENODE *nodeptr);
```

Figure 19.21   (tnodes.h) Tree node declarations.

new node and make the appropriate pointer field of **prev** point to it. If the tree's empty, it's even easier. The new node becomes the root of the tree.

Suppose we want to insert 27 into our tree. We first compare it with the value at the root; since 27 is less than 40, we move to the left. We then compare 27 with 19; it is greater, so now we move to the right. Finally, we compare 27 with 23 and again find that it is greater. We can't move right, since the right subtree of 23 is **NULL**, so we get a new node and attach 27 as the new right subtree of 23.

tree_update works just as **tree_insert**, except that it updates the node if it's there and inserts it only if it isn't.

```
/*
 * Manage a tree node.
 *   tn_create - create a new tree node.
 *   tn_destroy - remove an existing tree node.
 */
#include <stdlib.h>
#include <stddef.h>
#include "tnodes.h"

TREENODE *tn_create(void *ptr)
{
  TREENODE *nptr = malloc(sizeof(TREENODE));

  if (nptr != NULL)
  {
    nptr->dataptr = ptr;
    nptr->left = nptr->right = NULL;
  }
  return nptr;
}

void tn_destroy(TREENODE *ptr)
{
  free(ptr);
}
```

Figure 19.22 (tnodes.c) Tree node creation.

```
/*
 * Definition of a tree and protoypes for its operations.
 */
#include <stdio.h>
#include <stdlib.h>
#include <string.h>
#include <stddef.h>
#include "tnodes.h"                     /* tree node and prototypes */
#include "ptrfuncs.h"                   /* pointer to function defs */

typedef TREENODE *TREE;

#define tree_create()   NULL            /* create an empty tree */

TREE tree_insert(TREE t, void *dataptr, CMP_FPTR cmp);
void tree_traverse(TREE t, ACT_FPTR action);
void tree_destroy(TREE t);
TREE tree_update(TREE t, void *dataptr, CMP_FPTR cmp, UPD_FPTR upd);
```

Figure 19.23 (trees.h) Tree declarations.

```
/*
 * Manage a binary search tree.
 *    tree_insert - insert a new node in a tree.
 *    tree_destroy - remove all nodes in tree.
 *    tree_traverse - traverse tree in order, doing action.
 */
#include <stddef.h>
#include "trees.h"

TREE tree_insert(TREE root, void *target, CMP_FPTR cmpfptr)
{
  TREENODE *curr = root;                    /* current node in tree */
  TREENODE *prev = NULL;                    /* parent node in tree */
  TREENODE *temp = tn_create(target);       /* new node */
  int cmp;                                   /* result of comparison */

  for (; curr != NULL; curr = cmp < 0 ? curr->left : curr->right)
  {
    cmp = cmpfptr(target, curr->dataptr);
    prev = curr;
  }
  if (prev == NULL)                          /* node is parent of tree */
    root = temp;
  else if (cmp < 0)
    prev->left = temp;                       /* left child */
  else
    prev->right = temp;                      /* right child */
  return root;
}

void tree_destroy(TREE root)
{
  if (root != NULL)
  {
    tree_destroy(root->left);
    tree_destroy(root->right);
    tn_destroy(root);
  }
}

void tree_traverse(TREE root, ACT_FPTR fptr)
{
  if (root != NULL)
  {
    tree_traverse(root->left, fptr);
    fptr(root->dataptr);
    tree_traverse(root->right, fptr);
  }
}
```

Figure 19.24   (trees1.c) Constructing, destroying, and traversing a tree.

```
/*
 * A function to update a node or insert a new node.
 */
#include <stddef.h>
#include "trees.h"

TREE tree_update(TREE root, void *target, CMP_FPTR cfptr, UPD_FPTR ufptr)
{
   TREENODE *curr = root;                    /* current tree node */
   TREENODE *prev = NULL;                    /* parent tree node */
   TREENODE *temp;                           /* new tree node */
   int cmp;                                  /* result of comparison */

   for (; curr != NULL; curr = cmp < 0 ? curr->left : curr->right)
   {
     if ((cmp = cfptr(target, curr->dataptr)) == 0)
     {                                       /* found match, so update */
       curr->dataptr = ufptr(curr->dataptr, UPDATE);
       return root;
     }
     prev = curr;
   }
   temp = tn_create(ufptr(target, CREATE));
   if (prev == NULL)                         /* insert new node, like before */
     root = temp;
   else if (cmp < 0)
     prev->left = temp;
   else
     prev->right = temp;
   return root;
}
```

Figure 19.25   (trees2.c)   Updating a tree.

Traversing a Binary Search Tree

`tree_traverse` tackles the hard job of running through the tree in sorted order. Once we've created a binary search tree, it isn't obvious how we can retrieve the values in a useful way. But we can do so by traversing the tree in a systematic way that corresponds to the way we constructed the tree. The idea is that, since all of the nodes in the left subtree of any node are less than its value, and all of the nodes in its right subtree are greater than its value, we can process the tree in sorted order by processing a node's left subtree, then processing the node, and then processing its right subtree. So `tree_traverse` calls itself recursively on the left subtree, executes its action on the current node's data, and then calls itself recursively on its right subtree (processing those values). The traversal is called "inorder" because accessing the value at a node comes in between the traversals of the subtrees. There are also postorder (the node is processed first) and preorder (the node is processed last) traversals.

tree_destroy traverses the tree, but does it in a slightly different order than **tree_traverse**. That's because it can't destroy a node until it has destroyed both its subtrees. So it first calls itself to destroy the node's right subtree, then the node's left subtree, and then finally the node itself.

A Tree Sort Program

Figure 19.26 uses tree sort to sort its input. As it reads each value, it calls **tree_insert** to place the value in its correct place in the tree. When it has read and inserted all values, it calls **tree_traverse** to display the tree. We use the same comparison and printing functions we used for linked lists of strings.

In general, tree sort is substantially faster than insertion sort. Why? Because assuming that we're lucky and the binary tree is complete—that is, each node has exactly two nonempty subtrees, except for nodes at the bottom level—each comparison of an input value to a tree node reduces the search space by half. As a result, we only have do a few $(\log_2 N)$ comparisons to decide where to put the new node, much less than the $N/2$ comparisons required by insertion sort. For a binary search tree, sorting time for N values averages $N \log_2 N$; for insertion sort, it's N^2. As N gets large, so does the difference in speed between the two sorting methods. Of course, we're not always going to get lucky. In the worst case (already sorted input) the tree degenerates into a list; each node will have, at most, one nonempty subtree. In this case, tree sort is no better than insertion sort. There are ways, however, to modify tree sort to prevent this degenerate case from happening—any data structures book has the details.

19.4

This section is optional!

CASE STUDY—A CROSS-REFERENCE PROGRAM

When debugging, it often helps to have a listing of the program's identifiers and the line numbers on which they appear. Such a listing is called a *cross-reference*, and a program to produce it is called a *cross-referencer*. To give you an idea of what such a program should produce, Figure 19.27 is the output of a cross-referencer run on our earlier interest rate program. We finish this chapter by implementing this cross-referencer.

Basically, all a cross-referencer needs to do is maintain a table of words and the line numbers on which they appear. Whenever the program reads a word, it updates the table. After the program has read all of the words in its input, it prints the table in sorted order. The key question is: How do we organize this table of words?

We've chosen to use a tree, where each node contains a word and a queue of line numbers on which the word appeared (just like our previous trees, except that now we have a queue in the node rather than a string). Why this data structure? We use a tree because we want to be able to store an arbitrary number of words, to quickly locate a particular word, and to easily print the words in order. And we store the line numbers in a queue because we need to print the line numbers in the order they appear.

Figures 19.28 and 19.29 contain our cross-referencer. We've built it on top of our generic routines for trees and queues. All we've had to do is to provide an appropriate definition for the data stored in the trees and queues, and functions for comparing, updating, and printing this data.

```
/*
 * Insertion sort strings using trees.
 */
#include <stddef.h>
#include <string.h>
#include <stdlib.h>
#include "trees.h"                              /* tree type and prototypes */

#define MAXLEN 80

int main()
{
  int  getline(char *line, int len);
  void printstr(void *ptr);
  int  cmpstr(const void *ptr1, const void *ptr2);
  char line[MAXLEN + 1];                       /* input line */
  char *ptr;                                   /* ptr to input line copy */
  TREE st = tree_create();                     /* tree of strings */
  int  len;

  while ((len = getline(line, MAXLEN)) != -1)
    if ((ptr = malloc(len + 1)) != NULL)
      st = tree_insert(st, strcpy(ptr,line), cmpstr);
    else
    {
      printf("Out of memory processing line %s\n", line);
      break;
    }
  tree_traverse(st, printstr);
  tree_traverse(st, free);                     /* not really needed */
  tree_destroy(st);
  return 0;
}
```

Figure 19.26   (tsort.c)   Sort input strings using tree sort.

SUMMARY

- By using structures, pointers, and dynamic allocation, we can implement data structures other than arrays.

- Linked lists consist of a list of nodes. Each node contains a pointer to a data item and a pointer to the next node in the list. The last node in the list contains a pointer to **NULL**.

- Binary trees consists of a set of nodes, each node containing a pointer to a data item and two pointers, one to a node containing a larger item, the other a pointer to a smaller item.

```
Balance                18
Generate               2
Interest               17
INTRATE                7  17 22
PRINCIPAL              6  15
PERIOD                 8  19
Rate                   17
Year                   18
at                     13
accumulation           2
a                      2
balance                13 13 15 21 22 22 22
define                 6  7  8

    . . .

that                   25
table                  2
worked                 25
with                   6
while                  19
year                   8  12 12 13 16 19 21 23 23
```

Figure 19.27   The output of running the cross-referencer on the first version of our Chapter 2 interest rate program. We've elided a little more than half of its output.

```
/*
 * Define cross-referencer tree items and prototypes.
 */
#include "trees.h"
#include "qs.h"

#define MAXWORD 20

typedef struct item                 /* WORD NODE */
{
  char wordtext[MAXWORD + 1];       /* value of the word */
  QUEUE lines;                      /* list of lines numbers */
} ITEM;

void *upditem(void *dataptr, enum status updtype);
int  cmpitem(const void *ptr1, const void *ptr2);
void printitem(void *dataptr);

extern char CurrentWord[];
extern int CurrentLineNo;
```

Figure 19.28   (xref.h) Defines cross-referencer tree items.

```
/*
 * The cross-referencing program.
 */
#include <stdio.h>
#include <ctype.h>
#include "xref.h"

char CurrentWord[MAXWORD + 1];
int  CurrentLineNo = 0;

int main()
{
  int word_get(void);
  TREE words = tree_create();

  while (word_get() != 0)
    words = tree_update(words, CurrentWord, cmpitem, upditem);
  tree_traverse(words, printitem);
  return 0;
}

/* Read next character, updating line count */

int getnextchar(void)
{
  static int lastc = '\n';
  int c = getchar();

  if (lastc == '\n')
    CurrentLineNo++;
  return lastc = c;
}

/* Read next word, storing into CurrentWord */

int word_get(void)
{
  int next;                                  /* next character */
  char *ptr    = CurrentWord;                /* start of word */
  char *endptr = CurrentWord + MAXWORD;      /* end of word */

  while ((next = getnextchar()) != EOF && !isalpha(next))
    ;                                        /* skip non-letters */
  for (; next != EOF && isalpha(next); next = getnextchar())
    if (ptr < endptr)                        /* save up to max chars */
      *ptr++ = next;
  *ptr = '\0';
  return ptr - CurrentWord;                  /* return chars in word */
}
```

Figure 19.29 (xref.c) The cross-referencer program itself.

```
/*
 * The cross-referencer's comparison and update functions.
 */
#include "xref.h"

int cmpitem(const void *xptr, const void *yptr)    /* compare items */
{
  return strcmp((const char *) xptr, ((ITEM *) yptr)->wordtext);
}

void *upditem(void *ptr, enum status todo)             /* update item */
{
  ITEM *iptr = ptr;
  int *lptr = malloc(sizeof(int));                   /* holds line # */

  if (todo == CREATE)
  {                                                    /* new word */
    iptr = malloc(sizeof(ITEM));
    strcpy(iptr->wordtext, CurrentWord);
    iptr->lines = queue_create();
  }
  *lptr = CurrentLineNo;                              /* add line # */
  enqueue(iptr->lines, lptr);
  return iptr;
}

void printitem(void *ptr)
{                              /* write word and count on standard output */
  ITEM *iptr = ptr;                            /* item in current node */

  printf("%-*s", MAXWORD, iptr->wordtext);
  while (!queue_empty(iptr->lines))
    printf(" %i", * (int *) dequeue(iptr->lines));
  putchar('\n');
}
```

Figure 19.30   (utils.c) Some utility functions used by the cross-referencer.

- A stack is a last-in, first-out data structure, easily implemented as a list in which all items are added and deleted to the front of the list.

- A queue is a first-in, first-out data structure, easily implemented as a list in which all items are added to the end and deleted from the front.

EXERCISES

19–1 We can modify our string sort program (Figure 19.8) to sort in descending order simply by changing the comparison function. Add an option, **-r**, to our string sort program to indicate that the values should be printed in reverse order.

19–2 Add the operations **stack_count** and **stack_traverse** to our stack data type (Figures 19.14 and 19.15). **stack_count** returns the number of items in the stack, and **stack_traverse** runs through the stack and executes a function once for each node.

19–3 Add the **list_length** and **list_delete** operations to our list data type. **list_length** returns the number of elements in the list. **list_delete** removes all matching nodes in the list. The function takes a list, a pointer to a comparison function, and a pointer to a function that's called before the node is actually deleted. It's passed the current node's **dataptr**. Typically this function deallocates the node's data item.

19–4 Rewrite Chapter 11's data base program to maintain the data base as a sorted list. Then rewrite it to use a tree.

19–5 Rewrite **tree_traverse** (Figure 19.24) without using recursion. Use a stack to hold pointers to the nodes as you move down the tree.

19–6 xref (Figure 19.29) has a very simple idea of what a word is. It currently restricts words to a sequence of letters. Modify it to treat any legal C identifier as a word. That is, modify it so that it allows a word to begin with a letter or underscore and contain any combination of letters, underscores, and digits.

Of course, this change still won't let it handle file names such as stdio.h correctly. Extend your solution to deal with filenames in **#includes** and quoted strings.

19–7 Modify xref (Figure 19.29) to also include the position of a word on the line.

19–8 Make xref (Figure 19.29) specific to C. That is, have it ignore C reserved words and words inside C comments and strings. Keep the reserved words in a separate table that is searched for each identifier. What is the most appropriate form for this table?

19–9 Rewrite xref (Figure 19.29) to use a different organization for the word table. Have it use an array of linked lists with one array element for each possible first letter of a word.

19–10 Write a function, **list_reverse**, that takes a pointer to a linked list and reverses the order of the nodes. If the list contains nodes with 1, 2, 5, and 7, the list will point to the node with 7, which points to 5, and so on. No data movement should occur, only appropriate alteration of pointers.

19–11 A doubly linked list is one in which each node not only has a pointer to the following node but also one to the preceding node. Rewrite our list-manipulating functions to work with doubly linked lists.

19–12 Write a routine that "visits" the nodes in a binary tree in *level order*. That is, first the value at the root is visited, then all direct "children" of the root, then all their children, etc. *Hint*: Use a queue to hold the pointers to the nodes as you move along a given level.

19–13 Write `tree_delete`. It should take a pointer to a binary search tree and a value. It should remove the first node in the tree containing the value, maintaining the BST property. There are three cases: the node has no children, the node has one child, and the node has two children.

19–14 Write a program that maintains a list of events (event name and date) in sorted order. Rewrite it to use a tree.

19–15 We use stacks to solve some important programming problems. One classic example is a postfix or "Reverse Polish" calculator. In postfix, the values come first, and then the operator. For example, to add 15 and 21, we enter **15 21 +**, and to evaluate $(17+19)\times55$, we enter **17 19 + 55 ***. This last one means "enter 17; enter 19; add the top two values and put back the result; enter 55; multiply the top two values and put back the result." To build one of these calculators, we get each item; if it's an operand, we push it on the stack, and if it's an operator, we pop the items from stack and perform the operation, pushing the result back on the stack. At the end we display the top value. Implement a simple calculator that can do addition, subtraction, multiplication, and division.

20　PORTABILITY

By now you're familiar with C and should feel fairly comfortable programming in it. But what about when you want to take one of your programs and compile it with a different compiler or run it on a different machine or use it with some other operating system? This chapter discusses the problems you're likely to run into and how you can best avoid them. We present a series of problems that arise when porting programs, along with a set of reasonable solutions. The chapter concludes with a case study that develops some portable input and output routines.

20.1　PRINCIPLES OF PORTABILITY

What do we mean by portability? Ideally, a portable program need not be changed to run under a different compiler or operating system, to run on a different computer, or to run with different input or output devices. Unfortunately, however, the ideal is almost always impossible to attain. Compilers differ in how much of the language they implement and which additional features they provide. Linkers differ in the length of variable names they allow. Operating systems differ in the system calls that are available. Computers differ in word sizes, character sets, amount of available memory, available external storage, and in the I/O devices they provide. Input can be typed on the keyboard, entered with a mouse, or selected with cursor input keys. And displays can be black and white or color, and they can be character or bit-mapped. There are so many differences that we must carefully design and code our programs to achieve any degree of portability between different systems.

Since writing portable programs requires extra effort, why do we care about portability at all? If we *always* develop and run our programs using the same compiler on the same machine, we don't. But few of us will write programs that spend their entire lifetime on a single machine. We've found that many programs we've written on the PC are just as useful running on a Macintosh, a workstation, or even a minicomputer or a mainframe. And because we work so hard to write large programs, we want to be able to move them effortlessly from one environment to another.

So, assuming that we care about portability, how can we attain it? By doing two things: avoiding, wherever possible, constructs that are known to be nonportable and, when that's impossible, packaging any nonportable constructs within a portable interface. We can't achieve portability painlessly, but with careful design and an awareness of portable and nonportable constructs, we can at least minimize the changes we have to do when we migrate our code from one platform to another. So now we'll look at some common portability problems and how we get around them.

| 20.2 | **PORTING TO NON-ANSI COMPILERS** |

The C language covered in this text is the "official" C language, as blessed by the American National Standards Institute.[1] One of the biggest portability problems at this time is actually one that will soon go away: not every compiler implements the entire ANSI-standard, but instead implements only the C language as originally defined by Brian Kernighan and Dennis Ritchie in their book, *The C Programming Language*. That leads to problems because programs written using the full range of ANSI features won't compile under "traditional" (K&R) C compilers.

In a few years, these old compilers will gracefully fade away and we'll be able to safely ignore this problem. For now, however, we can't simply bury our head in the sand and assume the programs we write will only be compiled with ANSI compilers. One way to ensure that our programs are portable to these old-style compilers is to avoid completely any special ANSI features. But features like function prototypes and the type checking and automatic conversions they support are extremely useful, and we hate to give them up when they're available on our compiler. What we really want is a way to write our programs so they take advantage of these features when they're present and struggle along without them when they're not.

Dealing with Function Prototypes

How can we use complete function prototypes on an ANSI compiler and avoid them on an old-style compiler? Essentially, we let the preprocessor decide which to use. We illustrate the technique with a new version of **getline** that compiles successfully under both types of compilers. Figure 20.1 contains the header file defining **getline**'s prototype; Figure 20.2 contains **getline** itself.

We start by modifying the header file so that it defines complete prototypes when we're running under the standard C compiler and partial prototypes when we're running on a nonstandard C compiler. To determine which kind of compiler we're running under, we check whether __**STDC**__ is defined. As we saw in Chapter 15, ANSI compilers define __**STDC**__; other compilers don't.

Next, we define a macro **getline** that expands into a call to the function **getline2** with its arguments cast to their proper type. Why do we do that? Because when we provide prototypes, C automatically converts the function's arguments to the types the function expects. The macro allows **getline**'s callers to assume that this is still happening, even if they aren't compiled with an ANSI compiler. But we have to rename the function (here as **getline2**), so that we won't have an infinite macro expansion.

Finally, when we define the functions, we use the preprocessor to select between the old and new styles of parameter declarations.

---

[1]*American National Standard for Information Systems—Programming Language—C*, ANSI X3.159-1989, published by the American National Standards Institute, 1430 Broadway, New York, NY 10018, copyright 1990.

```
/*
 * Defining getline's prototype.
 */
#ifdef __STDC__
int getline(char *, int);
#else
int getline2();
#define getline(l,m)  getline2((char *) (l), (int) (m))
#endif
```

Figure 20.1   (getline.h)   Header file defining `getline`'s prototype.

```
/*
 * Defines a function to read an input line into an array.
 */
#include <stdio.h>
#include "getline.h"

#ifdef __STDC__
int getline(char *ptr, int max)
#else
int getline2(ptr, max)
  char *ptr; int max;
#endif
{
  int  c;                       /* current character */
  char *startptr = ptr;         /* pointer to start of line */
  char *endptr = ptr + max;     /* pointer to end of line */

  while ((c = getchar ()) != '\n' && c != EOF)
    if (ptr < endptr)
      *ptr++ = c;
  *ptr = '\0';                  /* terminate with null */
  return (c == EOF) ? -1 : ptr - startptr;
}
```

Figure 20.2   (getline.c)   A version of `getline` portable to both ANSI and non-ANSI compilers.

```
#ifdef __STDC__
int getline(char *ptr, int max)
#else
int getline2(ptr, max)
  char *ptr; int max;
#endif
```

When we're not compiling under an ANSI compiler, we're actually defining a function

```
/*
 * Definition of generic pointer type.
 */
#ifdef __STDC__
typedef void *GENPTR;                    /* ANSI generic pointer */
#else
typedef unsigned char *GENPTR;           /* no generic pointer */
#endif
```

Figure 20.3 (gens.h) Definition of a generic pointer type.

named `getline2`. But that's OK because its users actually call the `getline` macro, which expands into the appropriate call to `getline2`.

Why are we using `#ifdef` rather than `#if` and `defined`? Because we're now assuming that our program may be compiled on an old-style compiler and `defined` is an ANSI addition.

Generic Pointers

The availability of complete function prototypes is a big difference between ANSI and old-style compilers. But that's not the only difference we need to worry about. Generic pointers are another feature unavailable in many old-style compilers. On these compilers we're stuck with using the type pointer to **char** as a rough approximation to a pointer to **void**. This works reasonably well, as it's usually safe to store any pointer type in a pointer to **char**.

To aid portability, we usually define a type **GENPTR** and use it whenever we need a generic pointer. Figure 20.3 shows its definition. On old-style compilers, we define it as a pointer to **unsigned char**, and on ANSI compilers we define it as a pointer to **void**.

Unfortunately, that's not all we have to do to write portable code. The one big problem is that there are no automatic conversions to and from pointers to **unsigned char**, as there are with pointers to **void**. That means that on old-style compilers we have to do these casts ourselves. For portability, however, we cast *all* our assignments to and from **GENPTR**s.

We can also increase portability by avoiding direct use of functions that access generic pointers and instead placing them inside macros. On old-style compilers, we define the macros to take care of any necessary type casting. But on ANSI compilers the macros map directly into the low-level call. Figure 20.4 provides an example in a revision of the header file allocs.h we provided in Chapter 15. It defines a set of macros, including **ALLOC**, **ALLOC_ZERO**, and **DEALLOC**, which provide a friendly interface to **malloc**, **calloc**, and **free**, respectively.

Figures 20.5 and 20.6 put all of this advice together in a new version of our set-managing functions that compiles and runs successfully under both types of compilers. We've changed the header file to supply complete prototypes under ANSI compilers

```
/*
 * Useful macros for dynamically allocating things.
 */
#include "gens.h"                       /* for generic pointer */

#ifdef __STDC__         /* ANSI C */

#include <stdlib.h>                     /* for malloc/calloc/free */
#include <stddef.h>                     /* for NULL */
#include <string.h>                     /* for memcpy/memset/strcpy etc...*/

#define ALLOC(n,t)      (malloc((n) * sizeof(t)))
#define ALLOC_ZERO(n,t) (calloc(n, sizeof(t)))

#else                   /* Old-style C */

#include <stdio.h>                      /* for NULL */
extern GENPTR malloc();
extern GENPTR calloc();
extern int free();

#define ALLOC(n,t)      ((t *) (malloc((n) * sizeof(t))))
#define ALLOC_ZERO(n,t) ((t *) (calloc(n, sizeof(t))))

#endif

#define DEALLOC(x)      ((t *) (free((GENPTR) x)))
#define COPY(np,op,n,t) (memcpy(np,op,(n) * sizeof(t)))
#define ZERO(p,n,t)     (memset(p,(n) * sizeof(t),0))
#define STRALLOC(s)     (malloc(strlen(s) + 1))
#define STRDUP(ns,os)   ((ns = STRALLOC(os)) ? strcpy(ns,os) : NULL)

#define TABLEDUP(np,op,n,t) \
        (((np = ALLOC(n,t)) != NULL) ? COPY(np,op,n,t) : NULL)
```

Figure 20.4 (allocs.h) A more portable memory allocation package.

and to supply partial prototypes and macros to handle the argument casting for old-style compilers. And we've made **SET** a **GENPTR**, rather than a pointer to **void**. Within the set operations, we're now using our **ALLOC_ZERO** and **DEALLOC** macros rather than **calloc** and **free**. And anywhere we assign a **SET** to another type of pointer, we're careful to use a cast.

Figure 20.7 is a new version of our program that uses the sets package. It requires far fewer changes than the sets functions—just the minor change to allow both ANSI and old-style function prototypes and definitions.

When we have straightforward, extremely short functions, it's often easier to write them as macros than to try to write them as functions that we can compile and use correctly under both types of compilers. We could, for example, rewrite our set functions

```
/*
 * Improved definitions to use "sets" of integers.
 */
#include "allocs.h"

typedef GENPTR SET;

#ifdef __STDC__              /* ANSI C */

extern SET    set_create(unsigned int n);
extern void   set_add(SET s, int e);
extern void   set_delete(SET s, int e);
extern int    set_member(SET s, int e);

#else                       /* Old-style C */

extern SET    set_create2();
extern void   set_add2();
extern void   set_delete2();
extern int    set_member2();

#define set_create(n)      set_create2((unsigned int) n)
#define set_add(s,e)       set_add2((SET) s, (int) e)
#define set_delete(s,e)    set_delete2((SET) s, (int) e)
#define set_member(s,e)    set_member2((SET) s, (int) e)

#endif

#define set_destroy(s)     (DEALLOC(s))
#define set_switch(s,t,e)  (set_delete(s,e), set_add(t,e))
```

Figure 20.5   (sets.h) More portable set package.

as macros, as we did in Chapter 15's case study. That approach, however, has several drawbacks. One is that macros are usually less readable than the functions, since they are dense and lack type information. Macros are also less modular, and the details of how a set is implemented would no longer be kept hidden from its users.

Missing Header Files

ANSI compilers provide a set of header files with prototypes for all library functions. But old-style C compilers provided only partial prototypes for a small subset of the library functions. That means that with old-style compilers, whenever we use a library function, we're stuck declaring the function's return value ourselves and supplying any casts necessary to guarantee that we're passing it the expected arguments. This problem is solvable using the preprocessor: When compiling under ANSI C, we include the usual

```
/*
 * Functions to handle dynamically allocated sets.
 *    set_create - create an empty set.
 *    set_add - add an element to a set.
 *    set_delete - remove element from a set.
 *    set_member - is item in set?
 */
#include "sets.h"

#define US_BITS 16
#define WORD(elem) ((elem) / US_BITS)
#define BIT(elem)  ((elem) % US_BITS)

typedef unsigned short USHORT;

#ifdef __STDC__
SET set_create(unsigned int n)
#else
SET set_create2(n) int n;
#endif
{
  return (SET) ALLOC_ZERO(n / US_BITS + (n % US_BITS != 0), USHORT);
}

#ifdef __STDC__
void set_add(SET s, int elem)
#else
void set_add2(s, elem) SET s; int elem;
#endif
{
  * ((USHORT *) s + WORD(elem)) |= 1 << BIT(elem);
}

#ifdef __STDC__
void set_delete(SET s, int elem)
#else
void set_delete2(s, elem) SET s; int elem;
#endif
{
  * ((USHORT *) s + WORD(elem)) &= ~(1 << BIT(elem));
}

#ifdef __STDC__
int set_member(SET s, int elem)
#else
int set_member2(s, elem) SET s; int elem;
#endif
{
  return ((unsigned) (* ((USHORT *) s + WORD(elem))) >> BIT(elem)) & 01;
}
```

Figure 20.6 (sets.c) A more portable version of our set operations.

```
/*
 * Identify duplicates in the input (more portable version).
 */
#include <stdio.h>
#include "sets.h"
#include "getline.h"

#define MAXLEN      80
#define ELEMENTS    512

int main()
{
  SET   unique = set_create(ELEMENTS);
  SET   dup    = set_create(ELEMENTS);
  int   value;                                 /* current input value */
  char  line[MAXLEN + 1];                      /* current input line */

#ifdef __STDC__
  void set_print(const char *msg, SET set, int n);
#else
  void set_print();
#endif

  while (getline(line, MAXLEN) != -1)
    if (sscanf(line, "%i", &value) != 1)
      fprintf(stderr,"Skipping bad input item\n");
    else if (value < 0 || value >= ELEMENTS)
      fprintf(stderr,"Out of range item %i\n", value);
    else if (set_member(unique, value))
      set_switch(unique,dup,value);            /* move to dup */
    else if (!set_member(dup, value))
      set_add(unique, value);
  set_print("Unique values\n", unique, ELEMENTS);
  set_print("Duplicate values\n", dup, ELEMENTS);
  return 0;
}

#ifdef __STDC__
void set_print(const char *msg, SET set, int n)
#else
void set_print(msg, set, n) char *msg; SET set; int n;
#endif
{
  int i;

  if (msg != NULL)
    printf(msg);
  for (i = 0; i < n; i++)
    if (set_member(set, i))
      printf("%i\n", i);
}
```

Figure 20.7   (usesets.c)   A new version of our Chapter 9 program using sets.

```
/*
 * Using the math library function to compute exponents.
 */
#include <stdio.h>

#ifdef __STDC__
#include <math.h>                    /* grab prototypes */
#define POW(x,y)    pow(x,y)
#else
double pow();                        /* supply prototypes ourselves */
#define POW(x,y)    pow((double) (x), (double) (y))
#endif

int main()
{
  printf("10^6 = %g\n",    POW(10, 6));
  printf("3.3^-2 = %g\n",  POW(3.3, -2));
  printf("-11.5^3 = %g\n", POW(-11.5,3));
  return 0;
}
```

Figure 20.8 (power.c) A program that uses **pow** to compute exponents and that works appropriately under both old-style and ANSI compilers.

header file, but when compiling under old-style compilers, we declare the return values ourselves.

Figure 20.8 shows a new version of our earlier program to compute powers that can run under both ANSI and old-style compilers. When we're compiling with a standard compiler, we include math.h and define a macro POW that simply expands into a call to the math library's **pow** function. Otherwise we define **pow**'s return value ourselves and define another version of the POW macro that appropriately casts its arguments. In either case we use POW to compute powers and rely on the preprocessor to map it to the appropriate library call.

20.3   PORTING ACROSS ANSI-C COMPILERS

Ideally, any program that compiles successfully under one ANSI-C compiler should compile successfully under any other ANSI-C compiler. But not all ANSI-C compilers are created equal. Although there are certain minimum limits they all must meet, many exceed these limits. Table 20.1 lists these minimums; any conforming ANSI-C compiler may exceed them. However, to be truly portable, our programs can't exceed any of these limits. There may in truth be few "strictly conforming" programs. The limit most likely to be exceeded is the one relating to the number of significant characters in an external name—six. This small size was chosen because C programs, after being compiled, must be linked via a linking loader. Many (older) linkers place this restriction—from

TYPE	LIMIT
Nesting levels of compound statements	15
Nesting levels in conditional compilation	6
Nested declarations for a basic type	6
Expressions nested by parentheses	127
Significant characters in a macro or *internal* name	31
Significant characters in any *external* name	6
External identifiers in a source file	511
Identifiers with block scope in one block	127
Macro identifiers simultaneously defined	1024
Parameters in a function definition or call	31
Parameters in a macro definition or call	31
Characters in a logical source line	509
Characters in a string literal	509
Bytes in an object	32K
Levels of nested **#include** files	8
Case labels in **switch**	255

Table 20.1 Minimum limits for a conforming ANSI compiler.

the FORTRAN days—on the number of characters in an identifier.

These limits are large enough that it's unlikely we'll run up against them—except for the amount of an external name that's significant. The standard states that the first 31 characters in an internal name but only the first 6 characters in an external name are significant (the distinction arises because many linkers weren't written with C in mind and can't be easily changed). This is problematic, because our functions often share common prefixes longer than six characters, as with **stack_push** and **stack_pop**. It's possible that a linker will treat these names as identical.

To ensure portability, we must write our program so that all our external names differ somewhere within the first six characters. When two names are identical in the first five characters, we can rename them slightly so they vary. Renaming **stack_push** as **push_stack** and **stack_pop** as **pop_stack** makes them differ in their second character, rather than their eighth.

The problem is that this approach forces us to use short, often unreadable names, and it flies in the face of our convention of building names that start with the data type and end with the operation. Another solution uses **#define**. We simply redefine the troublesome longer names into short names and place the definitions in a header file included by the program containing the long names. We then go ahead and freely use the long names.

Figure 20.9 is a header file that does that for our stack managing functions. It defines the macros only if the linker doesn't provide long names. How do we test for this situation? We check whether a symbol **SHORTNAMES** is defined. **SHORTNAMES** isn't a built-in name. Instead, we're assuming that we define this symbol ourselves

```
/*
 * Definitions of stack data type and prototypes.
 */
#include "lists.h"

typedef LISTNODE *STACK;

#define stack_create()    NULL
#define stack_empty(s)    ((s) == NULL)
#define stack_top(s)      ((s)->dataptr)

#if defined(SHORTNAMES)

#define stack_push(s,i)   stpsh(s,i)
#define stack_pop(s)      stpop(s)

#endif

STACK stack_push(STACK s, void *dataptr);
STACK stack_pop(STACK s);
```

Figure 20.9   (stacks.h)   The header file for our stack managing routines.

before including this header file, but only if we're compiling in an environment with a linker that can handle only short external names.

There are several potential problems with this practice. The first is that only the preprocessor ever sees the longer names, so that error messages will refer to the shorter names. And the other is that we might accidentally **#define** two long names to the same short name, a mistake that may be hard to detect.

20.4   PORTABILITY ACROSS OPERATING SYSTEMS

Most of the programs we've written are useful running under many different operating systems: UNIX, MS-DOS, VMS, and OS/2, among others. So far, our programs have managed to avoid operating system specific calls. But in the real world that's not so easy, since we have often to go through the operating system to access specialized devices, to communicate over a network, to have one executing program talk to another, and so on.

Obviously, it's not a good idea to simply thread these calls throughout our code, as it makes porting programs much more difficult. We would have to thoroughly examine our code, flushing out these calls and replacing them with the appropriate calls for the new operating system. It's a much better idea to place all system calls in higher-level functions whose names indicate the actual tasks they perform. The idea is that the higher-level function takes account of any operating system dependencies, limiting any nonportable code to a small part of our program.

```
/*
 * Prototype and necessary definition for filesize function.
 */
#include <stdio.h>

#define FILESIZE_UNKNOWN   -1L

long filesize(const char *file);
```

Figure 20.10   (filesize.h) Header file for the function `filesize`.

Figures 20.10 and 20.11 contain a portable function to print the size of a file and its prototypes, and Figure 20.12 contains a main program that uses it. We wrote one version of this function earlier. It computed the length of a file by opening it, seeking to the end, and returning that position. That's a completely portable way of doing it, since it uses only the standard C library functions. But MS-DOS and UNIX provide special system calls that find a file's length in a more efficient way. On these systems we want to use these calls. To keep our program portable, as well as efficient, when we need the length of a file, we don't include direct references to these system calls. Instead we call the function `filesize`. We provide several different versions of `filesize`—one for MS-DOS, another for UNIX, and a default version—and we use `#if` to select the most appropriate version.

This approach relies on the compiler having predefined a name for the operating system it's running under, such as `__MSDOS__` or `unix`. If our compiler doesn't do this, we're stuck with defining the appropriate name ourselves.[2]

Placing all of the operating-system-specific code within the file in which we define `filesize` makes that code harder to read. But the main program itself is actually more readable, since the purpose of the strangely named system calls is now clearer.

There's one other place besides system calls where we frequently run into operating system dependencies: specifying path names. On UNIX, we use a forward slash to separate the different components of a file name. But on MS-DOS, we use a backslash. That doesn't affect us when we read file names from the input, since we can assume the user will provide names in an appropriate form. But it does affect us if we're using absolute file names built into our program. Once again, the trick is to use the preprocessor. Whenever we have a name, we define a constant for it and let the preprocessor select the appropriate value.

---

[2]Some compilers and environments are particularly nasty and go out of their way to undefine symbols that programmers tend to count on. The standard HP/UX include files, for example, undefine `unix`, even if we've defined it ourselves! In order to get around this behavior, on these systems we're forced to define `__HPUX_SOURCE`. Yuck! Be on the lookout for similar behavior on your system.

```
/*
 * Determine the size of the given file.  Returns the special
 * value FILESIZE_UNKNOWN if it can't do so.
 */
#include <stdio.h>
#include "filesize.h"

#if defined(__MSDOS__)
#include <io.h>                      /* MS-DOS specific include file */

long filesize(const char *file)
{
  FILE *fp = fopen(file, "rb");
  long len = FILESIZE_UNKNOWN;

  if (fp != NULL)
  {
    len = filelength(fileno(fp));
    fclose(fp);
  }
  return len;
}
#elif defined(unix)
#include <sys/types.h>               /* UNIX specific include files */
#include <sys/stat.h>

long filesize(const char *file)
{
  struct stat s;

  return (stat(file, &s) != -1) ? s.st_size : FILESIZE_UNKNOWN;
}
#else     /* default version */
long filesize(const char *file)
{
  FILE *fp = fopen(file, "rb");
  long len = FILESIZE_UNKNOWN;

  if (fp != NULL)
  {
    if (fseek(fp, 0L, 2) != -1)
      len = ftell(fp);
    fclose(fp);
  }
  return len;
}
#endif
```

Figure 20.11   (filesize.c)   A function to determine the number of bytes in a file.

```
/*
 * Print size in bytes for each of its arguments.
 */
#include <stdio.h>
#include "filesize.h"

int main(int argc, char *argv[])
{
  long fs;                              /* next file's size */
  int i;                                /* index through args */

  for (i = 1; i < argc; i++)
    if ((fs = filesize(argv[i])) == FILESIZE_UNKNOWN)
      fprintf(stderr,"Can't get size of %s\n", argv[i]);
    else
      printf("Size of %s: %li\n", argv[i], fs);
  return 0;
}
```

Figure 20.12   (testfs.c) A main program using `filesize` to determine the length of a file.

20.5   ## MACHINE DEPENDENCIES

C differs from most high-level languages in that it was designed to help us implement programs efficiently and to let us directly access the underlying machine. Although these are two of its most attractive features, they are also a source of several machine dependencies that lead to portability problems.

Data Type Sizes

Most machines work most efficiently on integers when they are stored in a single word. But the size of a word can differ from machine to machine. This means that `int`s vary in size from 16 bits (as on the PC) to 32 bits (as on VAXs, Suns, and 386-based UNIX systems), to 60 bits (on the Cray). The result is that we must never assume that an `int` can hold a value outside the range of -32768 to 32767.

`char`s also vary in size from machine to machine. They range from 6 bits on older CDC machines, to 7 bits on the PDP-7, to 8 bits on most minicomputers, to 9 bits on many older UNISYS, Honeywell, and DEC machines, to 10 bits on the Cray. How can this cause portability problems? Suppose we're using an `unsigned char` to hold small integers in the range of 0 to 255. That's safe if our characters are 8 bits, but what if we go to a machine with 6- or 7-bit characters? Once again, we're in trouble.

The easiest way to minimize portability problems is to use `long`s for all our integers. But the drawbacks to this approach should be obvious—our programs will run more slowly and take up more space. A better way is to carefully define types that reflect their uses and to define these types differently on different machines.

Suppose, for example, that we want a type for dealing with small counters, that is, counters that range in size from 0 to 255. And further suppose that we have an array of 1000 of these. That means on most machines we can save at least 1000 bytes by declaring these types as **unsigned char**s instead of **short**s or **int**s. But then we would have a problem if we tried to port our program to a machine such as the PDP-7 that has 7-bit characters. So we instead define a new type, **SMALL_CNT**, and use it to declare all our counters. On some machines we can define this type as an **unsigned char**; on others we should define it as a **short**. We decide by examining the maximum value of an **unsigned char**, and if it's not big enough to hold the values we want, we use **unsigned short** instead. This extra work lets us use space efficiently without hurting portability.

Figure 20.13 defines this type, and Figure 20.14 provides an example use of it.

Character Set Differences

Different machines can have different underlying representations for characters. The two most common are ASCII and EBCDIC. This causes problems when we make direct use of the underlying representation. Clearly, it isn't portable to compare a variable directly with 48 to determine whether it holds the character '0'. Although 48 is the ASCII representation for the character '0', it represents a different character in EBCDIC. The solution is to always use the character rather than its integer representation. When we need a nonprinting character, we can use its octal code, but to aid portability, we should define a symbolic name for it.

Not only shouldn't we assume that the integer representation of a character is the same across different character sets, but we shouldn't even assume that a particular group of characters is always contiguous. That assumption shows up in relational expressions such as

```
c >= 'a' && c <= 'z'
```

In ASCII, this assumption holds for lowercase letters, for uppercase letters, and for digits. In EBCDIC, however, the assumption only holds for digits.

The functions in the character-testing library discussed in Chapter 4, such as **islower**, provide a more portable way of making these comparisons. In fact, their use leads to more readable code as well. The only possible sacrifice we may be making is in efficiency. But since these functions are actually macros and they usually expand into an index to a table of information about various characters, they may be at least as efficient as the nonportable comparison.

There are, unfortunately, no library functions for a pair of common tasks: converting a character digit (such as '0') to the digit's underlying value (0) and converting the underlying value to the corresponding character. In Chapter 4's case study, we wrote nonportable functions to perform these tasks: **todecimal** converted a character representing a digit in base 2 through 36 to an integer; **tochar** went the other way. The problem is that these functions relied on both the letters and digits being contiguous. That's a property of the ASCII character set, but not of other character sets. Figure 20.15 shows portable versions of these functions. Our new versions use tables of the digits, lowercase, and uppercase characters, and do the conversions through table lookup.

```
/*
 * Defining a "SMALL CouNTer" type.
 */
#include <limits.h>

#if UCHAR_MAX >= 255
    typedef unsigned char  SMALL_CNT;          /* 8-bit chars */
#else
    typedef unsigned short SMALL_CNT;          /* 7-bit chars */
#endif
```

Figure 20.13   (ourtypes.h) Header file defining names for our types.

```
/*
 * Using the "SMALL_CouNTer" type.
 */
#include <stdio.h>
#include "ourtypes.h"                          /* type definitions */

#define MAXCNT 10

int main()
{
    SMALL_CNT table[MAXCNT];                    /* array of that type */
    SMALL_CNT i;

    for (i = 0; i < MAXCNT; i++)                /* some initial values */
        table[i] = i;
    for (i = 0; i < MAXCNT; i++)                /* print them */
        printf("%u\n", (unsigned int) table[i]);
    return 0;
}
```

Figure 20.14   (ourtypes.c) Using the defined types to isolate the underlying types.

Sign-Related Problems

Another source of portability problems arises when we compare **signed** and **unsigned** values. These problems show up most often when we compare **char**s with integers—but only if we've stored a value in the **char** that's outside the range of values for a legal character in the machine's character set.

Figure 20.16 is a nonportable version of Chapter 4's display program. What's wrong with it? It uses a **char** to hold **getchar**'s return value. The problem is that **char**s are sometimes **signed** by default and other times **unsigned**.

This program works when we have **signed char**s and we're dealing with 7-bit

```
/*
 * Functions to convert digits to and from characters.
 *     todecimal - convert char to equivalent decimal number.
 *     tochar - convert decimal number to equivalent character.
 */
#include <ctype.h>
#include <string.h>

#define OFFSET(c,s) ((const char *const) strchr(s,c) - (s))

static const char *const Digits = "0123456789";
static const char *const LowerCase = "abcdefghijklmnopqrstuvwxyz";
static const char *const UpperCase = "ABCDEFGHIJKLMNOPQRSTUVWXYZ";

int todecimal(int c, int toobig)
{
  int value = -1;                          /* simplify later decimal handling */

  if (isdigit(c))
    value = OFFSET(c, Digits);
  else if (islower(c))
    value = OFFSET(c, LowerCase) + 10;
  else if (isupper(c))
    value = OFFSET(c, UpperCase) + 10;
  if (value >= toobig)                     /* make sure result is legal */
    value = -1;
  return value;
}

int tochar(int value)
{
  return (value < 10) ? Digits[value] : UpperCase[value - 10];
}
```

Figure 20.15 (convchar.c) More portable version of our earlier conversion functions.

ASCII characters. There, the high bit of the character represents its sign, and when we compare a character with an integer, C converts it using sign extension (filling its new high bytes with 1-bits if the value is negative). We need this behavior because we're storing **EOF** (-1) into a **char** and later comparing it with **EOF**.

Unfortunately, our program fails miserably if **char**s are **unsigned**. When we compare an **unsigned char** with an integer, its high bit is part of its value and isn't sign-extended. Instead, C fills the new high bytes with zero bits, which means the test for equality with **EOF** always fails. The solution is simple: store the character into an **int** rather than a **char**.

We can also get into trouble comparing **signed** and **unsigned** values with their integral types. That's because when we compare an **unsigned int** with a **long**, the conversions that take place are machine dependent. If **int**s are smaller than **long**s,

```
/*
 * A nonportable version of our display program.
 */
#include <stdio.h>

int main()
{
  char c;

  while ((c = getchar()) != EOF)
    putchar(c);
  return 0;
}
```

Figure 20.16   (baddisp.c)   A nonportable version of our program to display its input.

the **unsigned int** is converted to a **long**. But if they're the same size both are converted to **unsigned long**s.

Figure 20.17 illustrates the problem. On a machine where **int**s are smaller than **long**s, **-1L** is less than **1U**, just as we would expect. But on a machine where **int**s and **long**s are the same size, we're in trouble: **-1L** is greater than **1U**. That's because both are converted to **unsigned long**s and **-1L** is all bits on, a very large value. The solution, of course, is to cast both operands to a particular type ourselves before doing the comparison.

There's one other related time we can get into trouble: when we do right shifts on negative numbers. That's because some machines fill with zeros and other machines propagate the sign bit. The solution is to do right shifts only on **unsigned** quantities. Luckily we don't have a problem with left shifts, since they always shift in zeros.

Sometimes we want to ensure the machine shifts in zeros. In the days before limits.h, we had to calculate special values such as the largest **int** ourselves. One trick was to fill a word with all 1 bits (with ~0) and then shift it over one bit to the right. On two's complement machines, the leftmost bit is the sign bit and the remaining bits are the value, so as long as a zero is shifted in as the new high-order bit, the result is the largest possible positive value. The problem is that some machines shift in a 1, which results in a word of all 1s, or −1. The way to fix this is to cast the value to **unsigned** before shifting. Figure 20.18 shows correct and incorrect calculations for the largest positive value.

Byte Ordering

Unfortunately, the order of bytes in a word also differs among machines. On some the high byte is most significant; on others the low byte is most significant. Figure 20.19 illustrates the difference.

Figure 20.20 shows how this difference results in a portability problem if we access the individual bytes within a word. This program declares a variable that's a **union**

```
/*
 * Comparing signed and unsigned values.
 */
#include <stdio.h>

int main()
{
  unsigned int i = 1U;
  long l = -1L;

  if (i > l)
    printf("As expected: 1U > -1L\n");
  else
    printf("Unexpected: 1U < -1L\n");
  if ((long) i > l)
    printf("As expected: 1L > -1L\n");
  else
    printf("Impossible: 1L < -1L\n");
  return 0;
}
```

Figure 20.17 (unport.c) An illustration of the problems that arise when we compare signed and unsigned values.

```
/*
 * Computing the largest integer, correctly and incorrectly.
 */
#include <stdio.h>

#define BAD_MAXINT    ~0 >> 1              /* not portable */
#define MAXINT        (unsigned) ~0 >> 1   /* portable */

int main()
{
  printf("~0 >> 1 = %i\n", BAD_MAXINT);
  printf("(unsigned) ~0 >> 1 = %i\n", MAXINT);
  return 0;
}
```

Figure 20.18 (shifts.c) Correct and incorrect calculations of the largest positive int.

1	0
08	*F*0
MSB	LSB

(*a*) On some machines the most significant byte (MSB) is the high byte.

1	0
*F*0	08
LSB	MSB

(*b*) On other machines, it's the low byte.

Figure 20.19 Differences in most significant versus least significant bytes.

```
/*
 * Nonportable program with byte-order assumptions built in.
 */
#include <stdio.h>

union word
{
  short x;                                     /* use as word */
  unsigned char bytes[2];                      /* use as bytes */
};

int main()
{
  union word w;

  w.x = 0x08F0;                                /* 08 F0 */
  printf("LSB=%x, MSB=%x.\n", w.bytes[0], w.bytes[1]);
  return 0;
}
```

Figure 20.20 (bytetest.c) A program with a nonportable assumption about byte ordering.

of a **short** and a 2-byte character array. It assigns the **short** the value 0x08F0 and then prints the values of the two entries in the byte array. On some machines the output will be 0x08 followed by 0xf0; on others the values will be reversed. The solution is to avoid directly accessing bytes within integers.

Byte Alignment Problems

Different machines have different alignment constraints. As we saw in Chapter 11, this can lead to empty space being placed in structures in order to line up fields. That means it's not portable to compute the offset of a field in the structure simply by summing the sizes of the preceding fields in the structure definition. Instead, the system header file stddef.h provides a special macro, **offsetof**, that returns the field's offset in bytes from the start of a structure. It takes two arguments, the structure type and the field name (which shouldn't be the name of a bitfield):

```
size_t offsetof(type,member)
```

Figure 20.21 shows a simple program that uses it to print out the byte offsets for each of the fields in a Chapter 11 **struct employee**. Here's its output when we run it.

```
Offset to number:      0 bytes
Offset to name:        4 bytes
Offset to phone:       44 bytes
Offset to age:         60 bytes
```

Pointer Problems

Pointers are another area where portability problems frequently arise. The problems stem from a pair of common, but false, assumptions. The first is that all pointers are the same size. But on some word-oriented machines, pointers to characters are larger than pointers to other types. That means that, in general, we can't count on assigning a pointer to one type to a pointer to another type without losing information. The only exception is a pointer to **void**: the language guarantees that it's large enough to hold a pointer to any object.

The other assumption is that pointers and integers are the same size. But there are plenty of machines where **int**s are 16-bits and pointers are 32-bits. We get into trouble on these machines if we assign an integer to a function expecting a pointer. Most often, that's because we passed **NULL** to a function expecting a pointer without supplying a prototype. The solution is to either provide a prototype or to cast **NULL** into an appropriate pointer type.

We also get into trouble on these machines if we assume that the difference between two pointers is an **int**. It's entirely possible that it will instead be a **long**. However, the system header file stddef.h defines a type **ptrdiff_t** that's defined as the appropriate type to hold a pointer difference. Using **ptrdiff_t** to store the results of pointer subtractions helps make programs using pointers more portable.

Evaluation Order

Another portability problem results from assuming a particular order of evaluation. This problem is especially noticeable in function calls. Many programs assume that function arguments are evaluated left to right. If that's the case, with **i** equal to 0,

```
#include <stdio.h>
#include <stddef.h>

#define MAXNAME 40

typedef struct employee
{
  long number;                              /* employee number */
  char name[MAXNAME];                       /* first and last name */
  char phone[13];                           /* xxx-xxx-xxxx\0 */
  int age;                                  /* age */
} EMP;

#define display_offset(field, bytes) \
  printf("Offset to " #field ":  \t%li bytes\n", (long) bytes)

int main()
{
  size_t number_off = offsetof(EMP, number);
  size_t name_off   = offsetof(EMP, name);
  size_t phone_off  = offsetof(EMP, phone);
  size_t age_off    = offsetof(EMP, age);

  display_offset(number, number_off);
  display_offset(name,   name_off);
  display_offset(phone,  phone_off);
  display_offset(age,    age_off);
  return 0;
}
```

Figure 20.21   (offset.c)   A simple program showing how to use the `offsetof` macro.

```
        printf("%i, %i, %i\n", ++i, ++i, ++i);
```

prints

```
        1, 2, 3
```

But C makes no such guarantee. It could just as well evaluate the arguments right to left or, in fact, inside out.

The solution is to perform all side-effects before the function call. The correct way to do this would be to assign the various values of `i` to temporary variables and then pass these variables to `printf`. Figure 20.22 shows some example incorrect function calls and how to correct them.

```
/*
 * Portable and nonportable function calls.
 */
#include <stdio.h>

int main()
{
  int func1(void), func2(void);
  int i;
  int tmp1, tmp2, tmp3;

  i = 0;
  printf("%i, %i, %i\n", ++i, ++i, ++i);            /* nonportable */

  i = 0;
  tmp1 = ++i, tmp2 = ++i, tmp3 = ++i;
  printf("%i, %i, %i\n", tmp1, tmp2, tmp3);         /* portable */

  printf("%i, %i\n", func1(), func2());             /* nonportable */

  tmp1 = func1();
  tmp2 = func2();
  printf("%i, %i\n", tmp1, tmp2);                   /* portable */
  return 0;
}

int func1(void)
{
  printf("Called func1.\n");
  return 1;
}

int func2(void)
{
  printf("Called func2.\n");
  return 2;
}
```

Figure 20.22   (funccall.c) Some example function calls and their portable replacements.

Libraries and Machines

One very subtle machine-dependent portability problem can arise from assuming that library calls never fail. It arises most frequently when dealing with dynamic allocation and when opening files.

When we assume that **malloc** (or one of its derivatives) always succeeds, we're making an assumption that there will always be some available memory. This may be reasonable in a small program running on a machine with many megabytes of memory. But it is much less reasonable if the program is running on a machine with 64K. Why is not checking **malloc**'s return value a portability problem? Because our program will usually bomb if it runs out of memory, which will happen on some machines but not on others.

Similarly, we shouldn't assume that a file open or write can never fail. It is possible for a file open to fail if the file doesn't exist, and for a file write to fail if there isn't sufficient room on the disk. And while one machine may have a 100-megabyte hard disk that never fills up, another may be running with a 320K floppy disk that is nearly always full.

Not checking these return values could make our program work fine on one machine but fail miserably on another. We would hate to use a text editor that promptly died if it couldn't open our file or allocate enough space to hold it in memory, or failed to at least warn us if a disk was full and it couldn't write the file. To write portable programs, we must always check the return values of system calls and library functions.

20.6   CASE STUDY—PORTABLE I/O DEVICE HANDLING

This section is optional!

The one major portability concern we've so far ignored deals with I/O. There are a multitude of I/O devices out there, each of which is handled in different ways on different systems. Our problem is that we don't want a program wedded to a particular input or output device. But if we directly call the low-level functions needed to manipulate the keyboard or display, we're going to be in trouble once we change to a different device or to a system with different calls. To avoid this problem, we have to treat keyboards and displays as *virtual* devices. Rather than directly calling whatever low-level functions are required to access the display, we make use of a package of high-level functions that do things such as reading a keystroke or moving the cursor. This gives us the flexibility to reimplement these functions for many different devices on different systems.

This chapter concludes by looking at how we can portably implement several display and keyboard I/O functions that C doesn't naturally provide for us. These include functions for reading a character as soon as it's typed, clearing the screen, and moving the cursor to a particular screen location. We implement these functions for programs compiled with Turbo C and for programs running on the most common versions of UNIX.

Immediate Input

getchar doesn't read characters as soon as they're typed. Instead, it waits until the user has typed in an entire input line. That allows the system to handle backspace characters so our programs don't have to worry about them. But there are times when we want to read characters *immediately*—just as soon as our user types them. Our **yesorno** function, for example, shouldn't wait until the user has typed a whole line, since it really needs only to process a single input character. Unfortunately, C doesn't provide any such mechanism. Instead, we have to rely on special, operating system dependent system calls. The problem, of course, is that our code becomes very operating system dependent.

```
/*
 * Prototypes for read-immediate functions.
 */
#if defined(__TURBOC__)

#include <conio.h>

#define ichar_get()     getche()       /* built-in insta-char */
#define ichar_init()    1              /* fake function return */
#define ichar_done()    1              /* fake function return */

#elif defined(unix)

#define ichar_get()     getchar()

int ichar_init(void);
int ichar_done(void);

#else

#error Can only handle Turbo C (under MS-DOS) and UNIX

#endif
```

Figure 20.23   (ichars.h)   Prototypes for our read character immediately functions.

We take a more portable approach and provide a set of functions that together let us read characters as soon as they arrive on the standard input: **ichar_init**, **ichar_get**, and **ichar_done**. **ichar_init** puts us in a mode where we can read characters as soon as they appear. **ichar_get** reads the next char. And **ichar_done** puts us back in our original mode of reading characters only after the user has entered a complete line. In between calls to **ichar_init** and **ichar_done**, we're not allowed to use any of the other standard I/O functions on the standard input. Figure 20.23 provides their prototypes, and Figure 20.24 provides the functions themselves.

With Turbo C, our job is surprisingly easy, because there is already a library function, **getch**, we can call to read the next character immediately. So **ichar_get** is simply a macro that calls **getch**, and **ichar_init** and **ichar_done** are macros that return 1, since they're not needed here. With UNIX, however, our job is more complicated and we have to use a set of system calls to set things up so we can read one character at a time with **getchar**. These calls involve turning off standard I/O buffering for **stdin**, as well as turning off any internal buffering the operating system does for terminal I/O. And when we no longer want to read characters one at a time, we have to restore the default behavior. Our job is particularly difficult because there are two different flavors of UNIX, and slightly different system calls are needed for both.

Figure 20.25 shows a final version of **yesorno** that uses these functions. Each time we call it, it uses **ichar_init** to obtain the special input processing, **ichar_get**

```
/*
 * Package for reading characters immediately.
 *    ichar_init - set things up for character-at-a-time I/O.
 *    ichar_done - restore things to the normal startup state.
 */
#include <stdio.h>
#include "ichars.h"

#if defined(unix)

#if defined(sys5)                        /* ATT UNIX */
#include <sys/termio.h>
#define GETTERMINFO TCGETA
#define SETTERMINFO TCSETAF

struct termio oldt, t;                   /* old and new terminal status */
#else                                    /* otherwise assume Berkeley UNIX */
#include <sgtty.h>
#define GETTERMINFO TIOCGETP
#define SETTERMINFO TIOCSETN

struct sgtty oldt, t;                    /* old and new terminal status */
#endif

int ichar_init(void)
{
  setvbuf(stdin, NULL, _IONBF, NULL);
  if (ioctl(0, GETTERMINFO, &t) == -1)
    return -1;
  oldt = t;                              /* save terminal settings */

#if defined(sys5)
  t.c_lflag &= ~ICANON;                  /* set up for one char read */
  t.c_cc[4] = 1;
  t.c_cc[5] = 0;
#else
  t.sg_flags |= CBREAK;                  /* set up for one char read */
#endif

  return ioctl(0, SETTERMINFO, &t) != -1 ? 0 : -1;
}

int ichar_done(void)
{
  setvbuf(stdin, NULL, _IOFBF, BUFSIZ);
  return ioctl(0, SETTERMINFO, &oldt) != -1 ? 0 : -1;
}
#endif
```

Figure 20.24   (ichars.c) Immediate character input.

```
/*
 * Program using immediate input to get a yes or no answer.
 */
#include <stdio.h>
#include <ctype.h>
#include "ichars.h"

int yesorno(const char *prompt)
{
  int answer;                             /* user entered character */

  (void) ichar_init();                    /* assume worked */
  for (;;)
  {
    printf(prompt);
    answer = tolower(ichar_get());
    putchar('\n');
    if (answer != 'y' && answer != 'n')
      printf("Please enter Y, y, N, or n.\n");
    else
      break;
  }
  (void) ichar_done();                    /* assume worked */
  return answer == 'y';
}

int main()
{
  if (yesorno("What's your answer? "))
    printf("You answered YES!\n");
  else
    printf("You answered NO!\n");
  return 0;
}
```

Figure 20.25   (yesorno.c) A version of `yesorno` that reads characters as soon as they are typed in.

to read the user's responses, and **ichar_done** to return to normal character-at-a-time input.

Cursor Control

Real-world programs can't get by with the simple or almost nonexistent user interfaces we've so far provided to our programs. They need the ability to manage the screen directly. At the very least, they must be able to clear the screen and to move the cursor around it. The underlying code to handle this stuff is messy and system-dependent, so we'll provide a small set of functions to do the work for us: **display_init**, **display_clear**, and **display_goto**. **display_init** handles any necessary ini-

```
/*
 * Prototypes for direct screen access.
 */
#if defined(__MSDOS__)
#define display_init()     display_clear()
#else
void display_init(void);
#endif

void display_clear(void);
void display_goto(int, int);
```

Figure 20.26   (screen.h) Prototypes for functions implementing screen operations.

tialization, **display_clear** clears the screen, and **display_goto** moves the cursor to a particular x, y coordinate. Figure 20.26 contains the prototypes for our functions, Figure 20.27 contains the functions that work under MS-DOS, and Figure 20.28 contains the same functions written to work under UNIX.

These functions are simply a nice interface on top of system-specific display functions. On MS-DOS, we access the display through a low-level hardware interrupt function, **int86**. Essentially, we pass it a structure that describes the operation we want, and it takes care of the rest for us. On UNIX, it's actually more complicated because we have to handle many different kinds of terminals. There, we access the terminal through a package of library calls.

What we've tried to do here is localize the nonportable code in a few specialized routines. That way, only these routines have to be changed and recompiled to use a different display, not the remainder of our program. Figure 20.29 illustrates their use in a new version of our earlier Life program's output routine.

SUMMARY

- An important goal is to maximize the portability of the programs we write. This involves ensuring that our programs can be compiled under a variety of compilers and run on a variety of different machines, as well as under the control of different operating systems and with different I/O devices.

- When our programs must also compile on non-ANSI compilers, our biggest worries are function prototypes, generic pointers, and missing header files.

- The biggest difference between ANSI compilers is in the lengths of external names that are allowed. We use the preprocessor to define short names for any long, potentially conflicting function names.

```
/*
 * Screen output operations (for MS-DOS).
 *   display_clear - clear the screen.
 *   display_goto - move to a particular x,y location.
 */
#include <stdio.h>
#include "screen.h"

#if !defined(__MSDOS__)
#error This file should only be compiled under MS-DOS
#else
#include <dos.h>
void display_clear(void)
{
  union REGS regs;

  regs.h.ah = 0;                          /* OP: set text mode */
  regs.h.al = 2;                          /* clear as side effect */
  int86(0x10, &regs, &regs);
}

void display_goto(int row, int col)
{
  union REGS regs;

  regs.h.ah = 2;                          /* OP: set cursor position */
  regs.h.bh = 0;                          /* page to move to (always 0) */
  regs.h.dl = col;                        /* row to move to */
  regs.h.dh = row;                        /* column to move to */
  int86(0x10, &regs, &regs);
}
#endif
```

Figure 20.27   (dosscr.c)   Functions implementing screen operations under MS-DOS.

- The biggest difference between operating systems is in the low-level system calls they provide. We need to define higher-level functions that internally use the appropriate low-level calls.

- There are a variety of different machine dependencies that can creep into C programs. But to write portable code we have to be careful to avoid using these troublesome constructs.

EXERCISES

20–1   How portable are the programs in the book? Pick two or three of the case studies and

```c
/*
 * Screen output operations (for UNIX).
 *    display_init - initialize display.
 *    display_clear - clear display.
 *    display_goto - tmove to a particular x, y coordinate.
 */
#include <stdio.h>
#include "screen.h"

#if !defined(unix)
#error This file can only be compiled under UNIX
#else
#include <stdlib.h>                        /* for getenv */

extern int tgetent(const char *, const char *);
extern char *tgetstr(const char *, char **);
extern int tputs(const char *, int, int(*)(int));
extern char *tgoto(const char *, int, int);

static char *tn = NULL;                    /* terminal name */
static char tc[1024];                      /* terminal controls */
static char *ptr = tc;                     /* ptr to terminal controls */
static char *clearscreen;                  /* clear screen chars */
static char *movecursor;                   /* move cursor chars */
static char td[1024];                      /* termcap description */

void display_clear(void)
{
  printf(clearscreen);
}

void display_init(void)
{
  if ((tn = getenv("TERM")) != NULL && tgetent(td, tn) == 1)
  {
    clearscreen = tgetstr("cl", &ptr);
    movecursor = tgetstr("cm", &ptr);
  }
  display_clear();
}

static int putcontrol(int c)
{
  return putchar(c);                 /* need function, not macro */
}

void display_goto(int r, int c)
{
  (void) tputs(tgoto(movecursor, c, r), 1, putcontrol);
}
#endif
```

Figure 20.28   (unixscr.c) Functions implementing screen operations under UNIX.

```c
/*
 * Print generation using direct cursor addressing.
 */
#include <stdio.h>
#include "life.h"
#include "screen.h"

#define HEADER_ROW       0    /* row containing header */
#define BORDER_ROW       1    /* row containing top border */
#define BORDER_COL       0    /* col containing left border */
#define TOP_CELL_ROW     2    /* first row with cells */
#define LEFT_CELL_COL    1    /* first column with cells */

static void display_char(int row, int col, int n, char ch)
{
  for (display_goto(row,col); n-- > 0; putchar(ch))
    ;
}

void PutWorld(PTR_TO_CONST_WORLD world)
{
  int c, r;
  static int printed = FALSE;      /* first printing? */
  extern int Rows, Cols, Gen, EndGen;

  if (!printed)
  {
    display_init();
    display_char(BORDER_ROW, BORDER_COL, Cols + 2, BORDER);
    display_char(BORDER_ROW + Rows + 1, BORDER_COL,
                 Cols + 2, BORDER);
    for (r = TOP_CELL_ROW; r <=  TOP_CELL_ROW + Rows; r++)
    {                                      /* other borders */
      display_char(r, BORDER_COL, 1, BORDER);
      display_char(r, LEFT_CELL_COL + Cols, 1, BORDER);
    }
    printed = TRUE;
  }
  display_goto(HEADER_ROW, BORDER_COL);
  printf("Generation %i out of %i", Gen, EndGen);
  for (r = TOP_CELL_ROW; r < TOP_CELL_ROW + Rows; r++)
  {
    display_goto(r, LEFT_CELL_COL);
    for (c = 1; c <= Cols; c++)
      putchar(world[r][c] ? MARKER : ' ');
  }
  display_goto(BORDER_ROW + Rows + 3, BORDER_COL);
}
```

Figure 20.29   (outworld.c) A new version of Life output routines using our portable display functions.

run them on another machine. Make whatever changes are necessary to guarantee that these programs work on both ANSI and old-style compilers.

20–2 Make the changes necessary to port our display package to a system that supports only five significant characters in an identifier name.

20–3 Find out what the machine-dependent operations (such as right shifts of negative integers) actually do on your machine. Do any of your programs take advantage of them? If any do, can you rewrite your programs to avoid these operations?

20–4 If you have access to more than one machine, take a sizeable program that you have written and used on one machine and port it to another. Where were your portability problems? Does the program have identical run-time behavior on both machines?

20–5 Write `exists`, a function that takes a single file name argument and returns 1 if a file with that name exists, and a 0 otherwise. Write it so that it works with MS-DOS and UNIX. The UNIX version should use `stat`, which returns -1 if the file doesn't exist. The MS-DOS version can simply try to open the file for reading.

20–6 Write a program that prints the contents of a long, one byte at a time, using a `union` as we did in Figure 20.20.

20–7 Write a function that can print the contents of any type, including structures, one byte at a time. What might such a function be useful for?

20–8 Suppose you have to write a program that requires a 100,000 element array of integers and that, in addition, must be able to run on a machine with 16 megabytes of virtual memory and on a machine with only 128K of memory where arrays are limited to 64,000 bytes. Assume that the only operations on the table are to access an element and to store a value in an array element. Write functions for these operations that use an in-memory array if there is enough room or store the array in an external file if there is not. Should the callers of these functions be aware of how the array is actually accessed?

21 EFFICIENCY

This chapter studies program efficiency—how to make our programs run more quickly and use less space. But we don't provide devious machine-dependent tricks that make our code much less portable and only slightly faster. Instead, we simply suggest some likely sources of inefficiencies and show how we can best eliminate them. The chapter concludes with a pair of case studies in efficiency: a simple memory allocator that allocates fixed-size blocks, and a new version of our earlier function for reading integers into an array.

21.1   SOME BASICS

We've tried to show that we get efficient, easily modified programs by designing our programs well and by carefully selecting algorithms and data structures. Usually, in fact, the simplest, most direct method of solving a problem is also the most efficient way, especially when we consider programmer time.

Sometimes, however, we're stuck with having to make a program run faster or require less space. Fortunately, there are many areas that we can attack to make our programs more efficient. But before we do so, we need an idea of what we mean by program efficiency and how we might go about measuring it. One common measure is the time a program takes to run as a function of the size of its inputs. We've used this measure in evaluating the various sorting and searching algorithms we've implemented. Insertion sort, for example, takes time proportional to the *square* of the number of input values. Double the number of values to be sorted and computing time goes up by a factor of 4; triple the input size, time goes up by a factor of 9, and so forth.

This measure is an excellent way to examine an algorithm's performance with average data. But it doesn't tell the whole story. There may be special conditions that make an algorithm particularly good or bad for a special set of values. What happens if the values are already sorted? Or if they are sorted in reverse order? When selecting an algorithm or designing a data structure, we have to take this *asymptotic performance* into account.

This measure also says little about how a particular implementation of the algorithm will run on a particular machine, with its particular operating system and compiler. And how we actually implement the algorithm can have a considerable effect on how fast it runs. Our job is not over once we've selected an appropriate algorithm and chosen our data structures—we still have to worry about how to make the program run as efficiently as possible within its environment. And that's our focus for the rest of this chapter:

given a solution that uses an acceptable algorithm for our problem, how do we make it run as fast as possible on our machine, without hurting portability?

But before diving into your programs and trying to make them as efficient as possible, try to find out which parts of these programs are taking the most time. Those troublesome components are where you should devote the most effort. If one function of your program is taking 90% of the time and several others 1% each, no matter how efficient you make those 1%-ers, it will have little effect on the overall efficiency of the program. Fortunately, most environments provide some tools for displaying the time spent in each function, and the number of times these functions are called.

21.2   COMMON SOURCES OF INEFFICIENCY

Many sources of inefficiency result from sloppy programming. So making a program more efficient is often a matter of going through it looking for unintentional uses of expensive language features. Two of the most common efficiency traps are unnecessary conversions and unneeded arithmetic.

Unnecessary Conversions

Conversions are convenient, but they are also costly, and we want to avoid them wherever possible. Unfortunately, they creep in without our realizing it, unnecessarily slowing down our program. They most often creep in in assignments, parameter passing, and arithmetic expressions.

Consider this assignment, taken from our earlier **table_average** function:

```
sum += a[i];
```

Since **sum** is a **double** and **a[i]** is an array of **int**s, there's a conversion going on in this assignment, which happens to be in a loop we later spend lots of time using pointers to optimize. Each time through the loop, however, we're wasting time converting **a[i]**'s value from an **int** to a **double**. This conversion involves a representation change, which will likely involve at least one extra machine instruction. Ideally, we would like to get rid of this conversion—but how?

We have several choices, each of which has its good points and bad points. One is to make **sum** an **int** and then cast it to a **double** when dividing by the number of elements in the array. This approach not only eliminates the conversion, but also changes from slow floating point addition to faster integer addition. But we're now in trouble if the total ever becomes too large to fit into an **int**. Another choice is to make **a** an array of **double**s rather than an array of **int**s. This eliminates the conversion, while also lessening the changes of overflow. But it has problems too. One problem is that we'll have to change the arrays we pass to **table_average** from arrays of **int**s to arrays of **double**s, which is not only inconvenient but may also increase the amount of space our program requires. The second is that our program may really require the exactness of integer arithmetic. There's one final compromise choice: make **sum** a **long**, as we've done in Figure 21.1. There's still a conversion, but usually converting from one integer type to another is faster than converting from an integral type to a

```
/*
 * Compute average of an array, improved pointer version.
 */
double table_average(int *ptr, int n)
{
  long sum     = 0L;
  int  *endptr = ptr + n;

  while (ptr < endptr)
    sum += *ptr++;
  return (n != 0) ? (double) sum / n : 0.0;
}
```

Figure 21.1   (avg.c)   A more efficient version of our table averaging program.

floating point type. And this way we preserve the exactness of integer arithmetic, while also lessening the chance of overflow.

Eliminating conversions like this one may make no noticeable difference. But we should strive to avoid them anyway, because it's so easy to do and because, in many places, such as within a frequently executed loop, doing so adds up to substantial, and noticeable, savings.

Parameter passing is another likely source of unnecessary conversions. When we supply function prototypes, C automatically converts the actual parameter to whatever type the function expects. Chapter 3's exponent computing program provides an example. The call

```
printf("10^6 = %g\n", pow(10.0, 6));
```

hides a conversion. **pow** expects a pair of **double** arguments, but **6** is an **int**, which is converted to a **double** before the function is called. We can easily eliminate this conversion by using **6.0** instead.

Figure 21.2 is a new version of that program, rewritten without conversions. Eliminating them from this program is not worth the bother—the operations of computing powers and printing results are much more expensive than the few conversions we eliminate. In general, however, the cost of conversions quickly adds up, so it's worth some effort to get rid of as many of them as possible.

Automatic conversions during parameter passing are both good and bad. They're good because we can write a function that handles any numeric data type simply by declaring it to take **double**s and then passing it whatever type we want. But they're bad because expensive conversions take place whenever we fail to pass **double**s.

We can avoid some conversions by writing one version of our function for each numeric data type. The standard libraries, for example, provide several different functions to compute absolute values: **abs** returns the absolute value of an **int**, **labs** returns the absolute value of a **long**, and **fabs** returns the absolute value of a **double**.

In general, automatic conversions take place whenever we have two different data

```
/*
 * Carefully avoiding automatic conversions when computing exponents.
 */
#include <stdio.h>
#include <math.h>

int main()
{
  printf("10^6 = %g\n", pow(10.0, 6.0));
  printf("10^-2 = %g\n", pow(10.0, -2.0));
  printf("10^3 = %g\n", pow(10.0, 3.0));
  return 0;
}
```

Figure 21.2   (pow.c) Using **pow** more efficiently.

types within the same expression. So the obvious solution is to try to limit expressions to a single data type. When that's not possible, the best we can hope for is to minimize the number of conversions that take place, either by rearranging the expression or by making use of explicit temporary variables.

> *Avoid unnecessary conversions.*

Unnecessary Arithmetic

Programs frequently spend much of their execution time doing arithmetic. To make them more efficient, we want to avoid arithmetic whenever we can, and when that's impossible, we want to use integer arithmetic rather than floating point arithmetic. Floating point arithmetic is especially slow, since it must often be emulated in software, rather than directly executed in hardware.

As with unnecessary conversions, unnecessary floating point arithmetic often occurs in expressions involving constants. Consider the following expression, assuming **d** is a **double** and **i** is an **int**.

```
    d = i * 2.0;
```

Here **i**'s value is converted to a **double** and then multiplied by 2.0 using **double** arithmetic, and the result is stored in **d**. That's a lot of unneeded work. We could have written this more simply as

```
    d = i * 2;
```

There's still an automatic conversion, but overall the assignment is faster because we're now using only integer arithmetic.

A single floating point number in an expression can cause the entire expression to be evaluated using floating point. Take an assignment as simple as

```
x = i * j * d * k;
```

and suppose that **d** is a **double** and all the other variables are **int**s. Depending on the order the compiler chooses for evaluating the multiplications, it is possible that all will be done in **double**s, which is highly undesirable. To guarantee that integer arithmetic is used wherever possible, we must use a temporary variable

```
temp = i * j * k;      /* integer arithmetic */
x = d * temp;          /* floating point arithmetic */
```

There are some cases where even integer arithmetic is unnecessary, as in these naive macros for determining whether a particular integer is odd or even.

```
#define ODD(x)  ((x) % 2 == 1)   /* odd integer? */
#define EVEN(x) ((x) % 2 == 0)   /* even integer? */
```

These work by examining a remainder, which requires a division. A better way avoids arithmetic entirely by directly checking whether the rightmost bit has been set.

```
#define ODD(x)  ((x) & 01)       /* odd integer? */
#define EVEN(x) !ODD(X)          /* even integer? */
```

We can also use the bitwise operators to speed up some special case multiplications and divisions. If, for example, we need to compute 2^n and we know that **n** will be a small positive integer, we can use

```
#define TWO_TO_THE(n)  (1 << (n))
```

Unneeded arithmetic often occurs because we do the same computation more than once. Figure 21.3 contains a new version of **table_average**, our earlier function to compute the average of a table of **int**s. This version does some unnecessary arithmetic. What's wrong with it is that it's computing the address of the end pointer every single time it goes through the loop. But, as we saw in earlier versions, it really needs to do so only once. We eliminate the extra computation by computing the ending address before we ever enter the loop. That small change can result in significant savings, especially since the loop is so compact.

We can find ourselves unnecessarily repeating the same computation without even being in a loop. Often we have expressions containing multiple instances of a particular subexpression. These repeated subexpressions tend to show up unannounced in two places.

The first is in expanded macro calls. Suppose we define a macro **SQUARE** as

```
#define SQUARE(x) ((x) * (x))
```

One way to compute a^4 is with

```
result = SQUARE(a) * SQUARE(a);
```

But we do better by computing a^2 once, storing it into a temporary variable, and then multiplying the temporary variable by itself.

```
/*
 * Compute average value in a table of integers.
 */
double table_average(int a[], int n)
{
  int *ptr = a;
  long sum = 0L;

  while (ptr < a + n)
    sum += *ptr++;
  return (n != 0) ? (double) sum / n : 0.0;
}
```

Figure 21.3   (avg2.c) A potentially inefficient pointer version of `table_average`.

```
a_squared = SQUARE(a);
result = SQUARE(a_squared);
```

The other place is in array accesses. What could be wrong with this apparently harmless fragment?

```
a[i][j] = a[i][j] + value;
```

We realize it isn't so harmless once we remember that `a[i][j]` is really a shorthand notation for `*(*(a + i) + j)`, a complex computation involving at least two additions. And it's a computation that we're doing twice. In this case, there's a simple fix: we use an assignment operator.

```
a[i][j] += value;
```

> *Avoid unnecessary arithmetic.*

21.3 C EFFICIENCY AIDS

We've shown how to recognize and remove several sources of unnecessary sluggishness. Now we turn to special features of C that help us write more efficient programs. These features, which aren't available in many other high-level languages, are compile-time initialization, pointers, and macros.

Compile-Time Initialization

Compile-time initialization lets us initialize arrays without having to use a potentially lengthy run-time loop. The obvious way to initialize each element of an array of integers to zero is to run through the array, storing a zero in each element. There's a catch, though:

if we're only initializing the array to make sure its elements start at zero, we can make it a global or a **static** instead, since they start at zero by default.

For this example, it's rather obvious that we can use compile-time initialization. But there are less obvious cases where we can do so as well. Suppose, for example, that our program needs to compute x^y for small integers **x** and **y**. We could use the math library function **pow** to compute them. But **pow** works with **double**s, which means that some conversions are necessary. And in any case, it still has to do some computing. We could write our own version of **pow** that works with integers, but this merely avoids the conversions and not the calculations.

There's one other alternative. We can precompute the necessary powers, using either a calculator or another program, and stick them into a table. Then we can write a function on top of **pow** that first examines a table with these precomputed values and computes the necessary powers only if doesn't already know about them. Figure 21.4 does that for powers of 3. For powers of 2 and 4 it uses bit-shifting operators.

Using Pointers

Throughout this text we've emphasized that we gain efficiency by using pointers instead of array subscripting when we traverse arrays. We'll now provide one final example, three new versions of **table_search**, our earlier sequential search function. Figure 21.5 is a main program that uses these functions.

Our new versions of **table_search** use a special trick to eliminate a comparison. The old **table_search** had two tests to determine whether it could exit the loop used to travel through the array. One checked whether we had found the value we were looking for, and the other whether we had reached the end of the array. Now **table_search** cheats. It expects the array to have an additional empty element at the end, and it assigns this element the value for which it's searching. That guarantees that it will always find the value and eliminates the check for the end of the array.

The first version, Figure 21.6, uses array accessing. And as we're by now well aware, the problem is that each time we access **a[i]**, the compiler has to take **i**, multiply it by the size of an element of **a**, and then add it to **a**.

The second version, Figure 21.7, corrects this problem by using a pointer to traverse the array. But it isn't just using a pointer that improves efficiency. Had we simply used ***(a + i)** to access the array element, we would get no improvement, even though it looks like we're using a pointer. Why? Because the compiler still has to do the address calculation, just as before. What makes it more efficient is our incrementing the pointer each time we go through the loop—we've eliminated much of the address calculation required to locate a particular array element.

The final version, Figure 21.8, is a more compact pointer version. Now we combine dereferencing the pointer with incrementing it, which can often be done in a single instruction. This version is slightly harder to read and has the additional drawback that we can't pass it a constant array, so we use it only when we're trying to squeeze the last ounce of performance from our program.

```
/*
 * Compute powers using table of commonly accessed powers.
 */
#include <stdio.h>
#include <math.h>

#define TWO_TO_THE(x)   (1L << (x))
#define FOUR_TO_THE(x)  (1L << ((x) << 1))

#define MAXTHREES 7

long power(int x, int y)
{
  static long threes[] = { 1L, 3L, 9L, 27L, 81L, 243L, 729L};

  switch(x)                               /* special cases */
  {
    case 0: return 0L;
    case 1: return 1L;
    case 2: return TWO_TO_THE(y);
    case 3: if (y >= 0 && y <= MAXTHREES)
              return threes[y];
            break;
    case 4: return FOUR_TO_THE(y);
  }
  return pow(x,y);
}

int main()                               /*  test program */
{
  printf("2^5: %li\n", power(2,5));
  printf("4^1: %li\n", power(4,1));
  printf("7^3: %li\n", power(7,3));
  printf("3^6: %li\n", power(3,6));
  printf("3^12: %li\n", power(3,12));
  return 0;
}
```

Figure 21.4   (fastpow.c) Efficiently computing powers by precomputing common ones in a table.

Using Macros

Macros are the last performance aid that we'll examine. They allow us to keep the readability of a function call without its overhead.

Figure 21.9 provides a good example of where using a macro can aid efficiency. We replace two functions we wrote earlier with macros: **trunc** and **round**.

```
#define TRUNC(x) ((int) (x))
#define ROUND(x) ((int) (x + 0.5))
```

```
/*
 * Driver program for search routines.
 */
#include <stdio.h>

int main(int argc, char *argv[])
{
  int *table_search(int [], int, int);
  int value, i;
  int table[11] = {10, 24, 7, 34, 87, 56, 45, 1, 9, 20};
  int *ptr;

  for (i = 1; i < argc; i++)
    if (sscanf(argv[i], "%i", &value) == 1)
      if ((ptr = table_search(table, 10, value)) == NULL)
        printf("Value %i not found\n", value);
      else
        printf("Value %i found at %i\n", value, ptr - table);
  return 0;
}
```

Figure 21.5   (search.c)   A main program using the **table_search** functions.

```
/*
 * New linear search function (assumes extra array element).
 * Array subscripting version.
 */
#include <stddef.h>

int *table_search(int a[], int num, int target)
{
  int i;

  for (a[num] = target, i = 0; a[i] != target; i++)
    ;
  return (i < num) ? &a[i] : NULL;
}
```

Figure 21.6   (searcha.c)   Original array-subscripting version of **table_search**, our linear search function.

```
/*
 * New linear search function (assumes extra array element).
 * Pointer indexing version.
 */
#include <stddef.h>

int *table_search(int *ptr, int num, int target)
{
  int *endptr = ptr + num;

  for (*endptr = target; *ptr != target; ptr++)
    ;
  return (ptr < endptr) ? ptr : NULL;
}
```

Figure 21.7   (searchb.c) A pointer-indexing version of `table_search`.

```
/*
 * New linear search function (assumes extra array element).
 * More compact, pointer indexing version.
 */
#include <stddef.h>

int *table_search(int *ptr, int num, int target)
{
  int *endptr = ptr + num;

  *endptr = target;
  while (*ptr++ != target)
    ;
  return (--ptr < endptr) ? ptr : NULL;
}
```

Figure 21.8   (searchc.c) An even faster pointer version of `table_search`.

For readability, we want **TRUNC** and **ROUND** to look like functions. But for performance, we're much better off making them macros.

Since macros are more efficient than functions, why don't we turn every function into a macro? Because there's a trade-off between speed and size. A macro executes faster but takes more space, since the entire code into which the macro expands appears each time we call it. We really only want to turn small functions into macros, those functions for which the cost of the function call and return constitutes most of the cost of using the function. Generally, that means functions like `trunc` and `round` that can be turned into a single expression.

```
/*
 * Defining and using ROUND and TRUNC macros.
 */
#include <stdio.h>

#define TRUNC(x) ((int) (x))
#define ROUND(x) ((int) (x + 0.5))

int main()
{
  double x;

  scanf("%lf", &x);
  printf("value=%f,rounded=%i,truncated=%f\n", x, ROUND(x), TRUNC(x));
  return 0;
}
```

Figure 21.9 (round.c) One more example using macros for efficiency.

21.4   SHRINKING SPACE REQUIREMENTS

Our discussion of efficiency has so far been devoted to making our programs run faster. But when we're writing programs for small personal computers, it also becomes important to use less storage. Usually, we trade off space for time—the less space we use, the longer our program takes to run. Sometimes, however, shrinking a program's storage requirements results in a program that works in a smaller memory model and therefore runs faster.

We have two basic techniques for saving storage: eliminating any unused storage space hidden within a data structure and eliminating any information we store that we really don't need. Both of these techniques are likely to increase the running time of our program, but can lead to substantial space savings.

Eliminating Unused Storage

Many of our programs don't store data as compactly as they could. As a simple example, consider our earlier method for storing a date—we declared a structure with three integers, one each for the month, day, and year.

```
struct date
{
  int month, day, year;
};
```

month, day, and year are all integers, but do they have to be? Since there are only 12 possible values of month, we really only need 4 bits to store it. Similarly, the day can range only from 1 to 31, so 5 bits are sufficient for it. The year is more difficult, but if we assume it's an offset into this century (a value that's added to 1900 before processing it), we can fit it within 7 or 8 bits.

C doesn't have 4- or 5-bit integers, but we can use an **unsigned char** as an 8-bit integer. Keeping this in mind, we can use a more compact structure.

```
typedef unsigned char DATE_PART;    /* part of a date */

struct date
{
  DATE_PART month, day, year;
};
```

Now we use half the storage we used before. If our program stores only a single date, the 3 bytes we save here isn't a big deal. But the savings add up rapidly if our program has a thousand-element array of dates. There is a trade-off here, though. Our program is going to run more slowly. Since C always converts characters to integers before comparing them, every time we use the components of a date to perform arithmetic or as part of a comparison, there is going to be an automatic conversion.

We can actually use even less storage for a date: The 4 bits we need for the day, the 5 bits for the month, and the 7 bits for the year can be packed into a single 16-bit word, using bitfields.

```
struct date
{
  unsigned int day : 4;
  unsigned int month : 5;
  unsigned int year : 16;
};
```

This takes less space, but it also takes takes longer to access the individual fields. The field selection operators tend to be inefficient when dealing with bit fields, since they usually compile into instructions that do some type of bit shifting. It's also now more painful to use, since we have to pay attention to all the restrictions on using bit fields, such as not taking their addresses. Fortunately, our programs using dates are simple enough we don't have to worry—all we have to do is substitute the new definition.

It's easy to revise our earlier programs to use our new **struct date**. We were careful to encapsulate its definition in an appropriate header file, so all we now have to do is change the definition. The programs using **struct date**s don't need to be changed. Figure 21.10 provides the revised header file definition.

Eliminating unused gaps by compressing the data is a generally useful technique for saving space. But beware that it may also slow your program down considerably.

Eliminating Extra Information

We saw earlier that a big advantage of linked lists over arrays is that we can insert and delete items without shifting. But we pay a price, the extra pointer we store with each element and the overhead of each call to **malloc**. That may not seem like it's worth worrying about, but suppose we're keeping a list of integers. Then most of our storage is extra information used solely for maintaining the list (the pointer to the next element and

```
/*
 * Date header file.
 */
typedef struct date
{
  unsigned int day : 4;
  unsigned int month : 5;
  unsigned int year : 16;
}
  DATE;

int date_equal(const DATE *d1ptr, const DATE *d2ptr);
int date_lt(const DATE *d1ptr, const DATE *d2ptr);
int date_gt(const DATE *d1ptr, const DATE *d2ptr);
```

Figure 21.10 (date.h) The most compact definition of a **struct date**.

the pointer to each integer). To save storage, we can eliminate this overhead by using an array—although this brings back our original problems with inserting and deleting values. If storage is crucial, use an array and suffer the cost of slow insertions and deletions. If speed is crucial, use a linked list and try to save space elsewhere.

This sort of choice between finite access and storing less information is hard to avoid. In fact, the language's built-in strings are an example of where this choice was made. Many other languages store a string as a structure containing a length and a pointer to the characters it contains. And doing so makes operations that require the length of a string (such as reversing a string or accessing its nth-to-last character) much faster. Unfortunately, it also makes strings one word longer. By eliminating this extra information we save some additional storage.

21.5 CASE STUDY—REPLACING LIBRARY ROUTINES

This section is optional!

As a general rule, a function to do a specific task is more efficient than one to do a more general task. And since many library routines are written to handle a wide range of situations, we can improve efficiency by replacing them with versions that handle only the single, specific situations that are relevant to us.

We illustrate this principle with two examples. The first is a set of routines for managing a free storage pool. The other is a function that reads an array of integers.

Managing Our Own Free Storage Pool

In Chapter 19, we wrote a linked-list version of insertion sort. Most of its work was done in a routine called **list_insert**. That function took a value and a pointer to an already-sorted list and installed the value in its correct place. It used **malloc** to allocate the node. Since we built the list just once, that was a perfectly reasonable way to implement it.

But suppose that we have a program, such as a linked-list version of our earlier data base manager, that has to repeatedly add and delete items. Then we can do better by managing our own free storage pool. The idea is that we'll build our own free storage pool by calling **malloc** a fixed number of times at the start of our program. And then when we need a node, we'll call our own storage allocation function, which grabs storage off this free storage pool.

Figure 21.11 provides the prototypes for our allocation functions, and Figure 21.12 contains the functions themselves. There are a pair of functions for general use: **fsp_alloc** provides a single node, and **fsp_free** releases a single node. We call **fsp_alloc** anywhere we would have called **malloc** to allocate a node, and we call **fsp_free** anywhere we would have called **free** to throw away a node. The first time we call **fsp_alloc**, it allocates space for a set of nodes. Later, if it finds there are no available nodes, it simply allocates space for a new set of nodes.

Figure 21.13 shows how these routines work. Our free storage pool is a linked list of nodes, pointed to by a global pointer **fsp**. **fsp_init** builds this linked list by allocating nodes with **malloc** and inserting them in the front. **fsp_alloc** simply removes the first node from this list and adjusts **fsp** appropriately. **fsp_free** puts a node back by inserting it on the front of the list.

Why go to all of the trouble of writing these routines? Why not simply use **malloc** and **free** as before? The answer is that our routines are faster than the system-supplied **malloc** and **free**. Our routines deal only with fixed-size blocks, but **malloc** and **free** are general purpose storage allocation routines that must be able to deal with blocks of arbitrary size. This means that they have additional overhead, including searching for a block of the appropriate size and combining adjacent free blocks.

But our handler does have one disadvantage. It allocates all the blocks at one time, at the beginning of the program, much as we would allocate a fixed-size array. In fact, our version is really a compromise between fixed-size arrays and the arbitrary allocation and size of dynamic structures. For insertion sorting, linked lists give us the advantage that we can sort with no data shifting, so linked-list insertion sorting is likely to be faster than array-based insertion sorting.

It's easy to use these routines in our linked-list program. We simply change lnodes.c to change the definitions of the functions we used to allocate and free list nodes, as shown in Figure 21.14. When we made this change to a set of programs using our linked-list functions, we on average achieved a savings of 10-15%.

Writing Our Own Input Handler

scanf is powerful, flexible, and convenient, a function that can read an arbitrary number of values of arbitrary types. But all this power and flexibility produces a problem— **scanf** must process a control string to determine what its input is, an extra step that requires some additional time-consuming overhead. And when we use **scanf** to read an array of values, it must do this additional work once for each array element, not to mention the overhead of one call to **scanf** per element. The result is that we should be able to improve our program's performance by writing our own function to read an

```
/*
 * Prototypes for routines that manage free storage pool.
 */
#include "lnodes.h"

LISTNODE *fsp_alloc(void);
void fsp_free(LISTNODE *ptr);
```

Figure 21.11   (fsp.h) Prototypes for routines that manage our own free storage pool.

```
/*
 * Managing our own free storage pool.
 */
#include  <stddef.h>
#include  "fsp.h"

static const int nodes = 100;        /* allocate 100 nodes at a time */
static LISTNODE *fsp = NULL;         /* our free storage pool */

LISTNODE *fsp_alloc(void)
{
  LISTNODE *nptr = NULL;             /* pointer to new node */
  int      i = 0;

  if (fsp == NULL)                   /* make initial pool */
    for (; i < nodes && (nptr = malloc(sizeof(LISTNODE))) != NULL; i++)
    {
      nptr->nextptr = fsp;
      fsp = nptr;
    }
  nptr = fsp;
  if (fsp != NULL)                   /* pool node from pool */
  {
    fsp = fsp->nextptr;
    nptr->nextptr = NULL;            /* sever connection w/pool */
  }
  return nptr;
}

void fsp_free(LISTNODE *ptr)
{
  ptr->nextptr = fsp;                /* assume legitimate pointer */
  fsp = ptr;
}
```

Figure 21.12   (fsp.c) Routines to manage our own free storage pool.

fsp

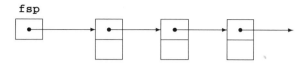

(a) Nodes in free storage pool.

fsp

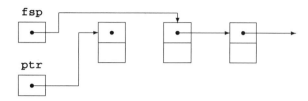

ptr

(b) Allocating a node from the front of the list.

fsp

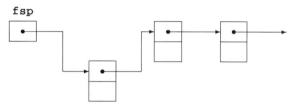

(c) Returning a node to the front of the list.

Figure 21.13   How we manage our own free storage pool.

array of **int**s. And that's exactly what we did. Figure 21.15 contains a new version of **table_fill** that reads the values into the array without using **scanf**.

We recompiled several earlier programs to use our new **table_fill** to read 5000 input values. The version not using **scanf** took approximately one-third the time, a substantial savings.

SUMMARY

- Choose appropriate algorithms and data structures for your task and then forget about efficiency until after you get your program running and it becomes clear that it runs too slowly.

- Before you start trying to make your program more efficient, profile your program to determine which functions are using up the most time and need to be improved. Then concentrate all your energy on the few functions that are the worst offenders.

```
/*
 * Manage linked list nodes using free storage pool.
 *    ln_create - create new list node.
 *    ln_destroy - free space used by existing list node.
 */
#include "fsp.h"

LISTNODE *ln_create(void *dptr, LISTNODE *lptr)
{
  LISTNODE *nptr = fsp_alloc();

  if (nptr != NULL)
  {
    nptr->dataptr = dptr;                    /* points to data */
    nptr->nextptr = lptr;                    /* points to next node */
  }
  return nptr;
}

void ln_destroy(LISTNODE *nptr)
{
  fsp_free(nptr);                            /* destroy node, not data */
}
```

Figure 21.14   (lnodes.c) Revised version of our linked list node creating and destroying functions.

- Two common sources of inefficiency are unnecessary conversions and unnecessary arithmetic. If at all possible, make sure any expression or assignment involves only a single type. And if you have to do arithmetic, try to do integer arithmetic rather than floating point.

- Use pointer indexing rather than array subscripting wherever possible, especially when sequentially accessing elements within higher-dimensional arrays.

- Function calls are another source of inefficiency. For small, frequently called functions, we can usually obtain a substantial speedup by turning them into macros.

- One general technique for speeding up programs is to replace general-purpose routines with specialized versions tuned to the task at hand.

- Two techniques for making programs use less space are eliminating unused storage and choosing the smallest appropriate data type.

```c
/*
 * Read an array of positive integers without scanf.  Assumes one
 * single integer per input line.
 */
#include <stdio.h>
#include <ctype.h>

#define MAX 100

int main()
{
  int table_fill(int table[], int max);
  int table[MAX];

  printf("Read %i values\n", table_fill(table,MAX));
  return 0;
}

int table_fill(int table[], int max)
{
  int *ptr    = table;              /* ptr to next array element */
  int *endptr = ptr + max;          /* ptr to last array element */
  int c;                            /* next character */

  for (*ptr = 0; ptr < endptr; ptr++)
  {
    while (!isdigit(c = getchar()) && c != '\n' && c != EOF)
      ;                             /* find a digit */

    if (isdigit(c))
      do                            /* translate number */
        *ptr = *ptr * 10 + (c - '0');
      while (isdigit(c = getchar()));
    else
      *ptr = -1;                    /* -1 indicates bad number */

    while (c != '\n' && c != EOF)   /* skip rest of line */
      c = getchar();

    if (c == EOF)                   /* reached EOF */
      break;
  }

  return ptr - table;               /* # of values read */
}
```

Figure 21.15   (tabfill.c)   A fast function to read an array of ints.

EXERCISES

21-1 Take a program you've written, perhaps a solution to one of the more complicated exercises you encountered earlier in the text, and find three places where you can improve its efficiency.

21-2 Make the improvements you suggested in the previous exercise. Do they result in a noticeable speedup?

21-3 What's the drawback to defining **BOOLEAN** as an `unsigned char`? How can we get around this?

21-4 Pick one of the larger programs in this book and see if you can improve it by eliminating unnecessary conversions or arithmetic.

21-5 Modify our most efficient search function (Figure 21.8) to save the position and value of the last few items it looked up. Whenever the function is called, it should check this list before searching the larger table. Of course, this technique only pays off when there are certain items that we frequently search for.

21-6 Rewrite Chapter 10's string-handling functions (Figure 10.15) as concisely as possible, making sure that pointers are incremented only when they are used within an expression. Are the resulting functions faster? Are they harder to read?

21-7 Rewrite Chapter 12's Game of Life program so that it increments pointers only when it uses them in expressions.

21-8 What functions throughout this book could have been better written as macros? Start by examining the larger programs, such as the cross-referencer.

21-9 Implement the basic string library functions on strings as structures consisting of a length and a pointer to the first character, with no null character terminating the string. What functions can be improved if we keep the string's length handy?

21-10 Suppose we have a program with a number of boolean variables that we use as flags. What's the most space-efficient way to store them?

21-11 Modify our earlier linked-list routines to keep a count of the number of times a value appears, rather than having separate nodes.

21-12 Rewrite Chapter 9's program that reversed all the numbers on each of its input lines (Figure 9.18) to use our storage pool manager.

21-13 Modify Chapter 11's data base program to use a linked list to store its items and to use our storage pool routines to manage its storage. Is there a noticeable performance improvement when dealing with many additions and deletions?

21-14 Our free storage pool manager (Figure 21.12) is slow to start up. After all, it has to allocate a bunch of nodes right at the start. It can be improved by initially parceling out storage from a preallocated array of nodes. That saves the initial call to `malloc`. Make this improvement.

21-15 `printf` is a complex, general purpose output formatting routine. Write an output converter that prints a single floating point number. That is, it takes a `float` as input and writes its value a character at a time to the output. Compare its running time with that of **printf** in writing 5000 **float**s.

21–16 Write a function that writes an array of **floats** without calling **printf**. Is this function faster than the one you wrote in the previous exercise?

21–17 In this book we've usually focused on readability rather than efficiency. That means that most of the programs in the book can be made to run somewhat faster. Pick one of the larger case studies in the text and try to make it run faster.

22   FROM C
TO C++

C++ is an extension of C designed to support object-oriented programming. There are many definitions for object-oriented, but it's generally agreed that it encompasses data abstraction and encapsulation, inheritance, and polymorphism. This chapter describes these terms and shows how C++ supports these important programming notions. It also introduces several important procedural extensions to C. Since C++ compilers will successfully compile almost any C program, knowing even a few C++ features will prove useful, even without learning the entire C++ language. This chapter is a gentle, and obviously limited, introduction to C++. But our hope is that it will get you started in understanding and using the language and tease and taunt you enough with the language's capabilities that you'll want to explore further.

22.1   INTRODUCTION TO C++

C++ expands on the C language by providing these important concepts in program organization: *data abstraction* and *encapsulation*, *inheritance*, and *polymorphism*. But what do we mean by these terms, and how are they provided in C++?

Data Abstraction And Encapsulation

We've used the notion of *Abstract Data Types* (ADTs) in several places throughout this book. In Chapter 19, for example, we developed a collection of functions for managing stacks and queues. The functions for stacks were **stack_push** and **stack_pop**, for queues they were **enqueue** and **dequeue**. All the programmer had to do to use one of these things was create and initialize it and then call the appropriate functions to access or update it. Our stacks and queues are *abstract* data types in the sense that we don't say, and the programmer doesn't care, how they are represented—we could use an array, a linked list, or even file reads and writes. This property—the hidden nature of the underlying representation, along with the appropriate access functions—is what we mean by an abstract data type.

C gives us most—but not quite all—of the tools to do this right. One problem is that when we create a new stack or queue, the stack or queue variable knows absolutely nothing about how to access its members. We can't, for example, just tell a stack or

553

queue to print itself or free the space it uses. Instead we're stuck with writing functions that take a queue or stack as an argument and then using these routines to access the internals. That means we wind up providing a different print routine for each kind of data structure we have, rather than having a single print that knows how to print any kind of object.

Another problem is that the internals of these data structures really aren't hidden. When we declare a **QUEUE** variable, for example, we also have to include **queue.h**, which defines the internal fields of a **QUEUE**. This is troublesome, since even though we think the only access to the queue's internals is through **enqueue** and **dequeue**, there is nothing but good coding practice preventing the programmer from accessing the internals directly! Although we can get around this problem by using **void** pointers and lots of casting, that's really a messy approach.

C++ provides a mechanism for enhancing data type abstraction and reducing the likelihood of inadvertent messing around with a variable's privates. It involves two closely related features. First, we're allowed to define *methods* or functions inside a structure or class. And second, we have the ability to specifically tag data fields or member functions as **private**, forbidding access to anyone and everyone except internally defined methods and listed exceptions. The name *encapsulation* is also given to this notion of combining in one place both a data type's internal representation and its access functions.

Inheritance

Many abstract data types are merely slight variations of each other. Stacks and queues can be thought of as specialized variants of lists, but with slightly different access methods. Similarly, squares are specializations of rectangles (with the restriction that their height must equal their width), circles are specializations of ellipses, and all four are specializations of planar geometric objects.

Ideally, this similarity should minimize the amount of code we need to write. If we've written code to compute the area of a rectangle, for example, we should be able to use it to compute the area of a square. Or if we've written code to determine whether a list is empty, we should be able to use the same code to determine whether we have an empty stack or queue. In C++, we obtain this type of reuse by defining high-level general classes (that is, storage and access routines for abstract data types) and then creating derived classes that *inherit* properties from their *parent* classes. Once a new class is defined this way, we can add additional access methods or redefine (in C++ terms, *overload*) various access routines to apply to the new object. That is, if we say that a stack is a class derived from lists, we automatically inherit all of the operations on a list. So to create a stack, we'll by default use the existing operation to create a list. And to check whether a stack is empty, we'll use the existing operation for checking for an empty list. But with stacks we can define additional specialized operations, such as **push** and **pop**, that aren't available on lists.

Polymorphism

The term *polymorphism* comes from the Greek and means "many shapes." In programming terms, it's essentially the idea that a single variable can hold many different data types or that a single function can be applied to many different types of objects.

C++ supports this notion by allowing the *overloading* of operators or functions and by allowing *virtual functions*. Overloading an operator involves taking an existing operator and extending it to apply to new data types. For example, we can take the familiar **+** for numerical addition and extend it to apply to strings (where it performs concatenation), to complex numbers (where it performs complex addition), or to lists (where it appends lists together). C++ also lets us apply this notion to functions, allowing us to write a single function that can be applied to many different data types.

Virtual functions are ones whose exact applicability may not be determined until run time. Nonvirtual functions, on the other hand, are bound to an object at compile time. When we apply a virtual function to a particular object, which instance of the function is actually called depends on the data type the object actually refers to at run time. This allows us, for example, to apply a print function to a list of objects and have the right print function executed for each individual object.

22.2   C++ PROCEDURAL EXTENSIONS TO C

Without using any of C++'s class- and object-oriented facilities, the language adds useful capabilities to the way we already do business. In this section, we'll run through some of the more important ones and provide simple examples of their use by rewriting some of our earlier C programs.

References

C's argument passing method is always "call by value." C copies the actual arguments, and the copies are accessed within a function. As we saw in Chapter 14, actually changing a value in the caller requires passing its address and dereferencing that pointer within the function body. C++, however, allows us to have reference variables, which we can use to extend the calling method to include "call by reference." We obtain a reference parameter by prefixing the variable's name with a **&** when we declare it. A reference parameter indicates that a reference to the object is passed, not the object itself. Within the function, we access the object in the usual way, but any changes are propagated back to the referenced object.

Figure 22.1 shows how to rewrite our **swap** function to take advantage of this feature. In its header we declare the parameters **x** and **y** as references.

```
void swap(int &x, int &y)
```

Within **swap**, we just exchange **x** and **y**, using a temporary variable but no pointers. Finally, when we call **swap**, we just pass it **s** and **t**.

```
swap(s, t);
```

```
//
// C++ program using a swap function to exchange two int values.
//
#include <stdio.h>

int main()
{
  void swap(int &xptr, int &yptr);
  int s = 10, t = 20;

  printf("Before swap, s=%i, t=%i\n", s, t);
  swap(s, t);
  printf("After swap, s=%i, t=%i\n", s, t);
  return 0;
}

void swap(int &x, int &y)
{
  int temp;

  temp = x;  x = y;  y = temp;
}
```

Figure 22.1   (swap.C) A C++ function to exchange two values using references.

The result is that **x** becomes a reference to **s** and **y** a reference to **t**, so exchanging **x** and **y** is really exchanging **s** and **t**.

Another use for references is to pass large structures. In C, to avoid copying a large structure, we often pass an address. We have to write the call carefully so that we don't neglect the address-of operator, and to make sure we dereference the structure pointer in the function body. Passing a reference saves this hassle, although we still have to be careful to make it a **const** reference so that the compiler will catch inadvertent changes to the referenced structure. Figure 22.2 provides an example, in a simplified version of Chapter 11's program to print an employee's number, name, phone, and age.

This program takes advantage of one other C++ feature. When we declare a structure, such as **struct employee**, the structure tag becomes a type name we can use to declare variables. In this case, we use it to declare the variable **emp**:

```
        employee emp;
```

Function and Operator Overloading

C++ lets us write multiple versions of a function, each taking different types of arguments, a technique known as function *overloading*. We can, for example, write a single function, **display**, that writes any sort of object on the standard output. To do so, we write one version to handle an **employee**, another a string, another an **int**, and so on.

```
//
// C++ program to display employee information.
//
#include <stdio.h>

struct employee
{
  long number;                    // employee number
  char *name, *phone;             // name and phone
  int age;                        // employee age
};

int main()
{
  void print_emp(const employee &emp);
  employee emp;

  emp.number = 1001;              // fill in employee info
  emp.age    =   23;
  emp.name    = "borromeo, daphne";
  emp.phone   = "310-555-2042";
  print_emp(emp);                 // write our employee
  return 0;
}

void print_emp(const employee &e)       // reference to employee
{
  printf("Employee: %li\n", e.number);
  printf("Name:     %s\n", e.name);
  printf("Age:      %i\n", e.age);
  printf("Phone:    %s\n", e.phone);
}
```

Figure 22.2   (prstruct.C)   A C++ function to print a structure using references to pass the structure.

Figure 22.3 rewrites our employee printing program to provide three different versions of **display**: one takes an employee, another a string, and the last an integer. When we call **display**, the compiler decides which version to call by examining the types of the parameters we're passing. With **display(emp)**, for example, we're passing an **employee**, so we execute the version of **display** that expects an **employee**. But with **display(e.age)**, we're passing an **int**, so we execute the version of **display** that expects to be passed an **int**.

C++ also allows us to overload operators so that they will apply to new user-defined types. In fact, the C++ library overloads the **<<** operator to perform output and so eliminates much of the need for **display**. Similarly, the **>>** operator is overloaded to perform input. Let's take a look at using these operators and how we can redo our employee printing program to use them.

```
//
// C++ program using overloaded functions to display employee info.
//
#include <stdio.h>

struct employee
{
  long number;                          // employee number
  char *name, *phone;                   // name and phone
  int age;                              // employee age
};

void display(const employee &e);        // display prototypes
void display(char *s);
void display(int i);
void display(long l);

int main()
{
  employee emp;

  emp.number = 1001;                    // fill in employee info
  emp.age    =   23;
  emp.name   = "borromeo, daphne";
  emp.phone  = "310-555-2042";
  display(emp);                         // write our employee
  return 0;
}

void display(const employee &e)         // display an employee
{
  display("Employee: ");  display(e.number);  display("\n");
  display("Name:     ");  display(e.name);    display("\n");
  display("Age:      ");  display(e.age);     display("\n");
  display("Phone:    ");  display(e.phone);   display("\n");
}

void display(char *s)                   // display a string
{
  printf("%s", s);
}

void display(int i)                     // display an integer
{
  printf("%i", i);
}

void display(long l)                    // display a long
{
  printf("%li", l);
}
```

Figure 22.3   (prstrct2.C)   A version of our employee printing program using function overloading.

```
//
// C++ Program using the math library to compute exponents.
//
#include <iostream.h>
#include <math.h>

int main()
{
  double x,y;                          // user-supplied base and exponent

  while (cin >> x && cin >> y)
    cout << x << '^' << y << " = " << pow(x,y) << '\n';
  return 0;
}
```

Figure 22.4 (power.C) An exponent computing program written in C++.

Input and Output Operators

The standard I/O library is available in C++, but we're not supposed to use it, as the basic C++ mechanism for performing most operations is to use an *operator*. We can do all input and output using the *extraction* and *insertion* operators: >> and <<, respectively. We use >> for input and << for output. Since these are just the left and right shift operators (overloaded to perform I/O), we can also overload these operators to work on user-defined data types.

For output, the left operand is a file (called a *stream* in C++ terms) and the right is a value or expression. C++ writes the value to the stream, based on its type, using a default format, so we no longer need formatting codes. For input, the left operand is an input stream, and the right operand is a variable. The input is read and converted into the proper form for the variable; again we don't need any formatting codes. << returns a 0 if there was an error in the input or **EOF** was reached.

Our programs start with one input stream and three output streams already open. The input stream is **cin**, which corresponds to **stdin**. The output streams are **cout**, **cerr**, and **clog** (corresponding to **stdout** and **stderr**; **clog** is fully buffered).

Figure 22.4 rewrites Chapter 3's exponent computing program to use these operators to request x, y pairs from the user and then display x^y. We include the header file iostream.h to define these overloaded I/O operators. We don't include stdio.h because we no longer use any standard I/O functions. Because << is defined to return an output stream, we can display a series of items by using it more than once in a single expression.

C++ overloads << and >> to handle its basic data types. But we're forced to overload them ourselves to handle other types, such as structures that we define. Figure 22.5 does so in a final version of our program to print employee information.

The first thing we do is provide a prototype for our overloaded operator:

```
ostream& operator<<(ostream& output, const employee &e);
```

```
//
// C++ program using an overloaded operator to display employee info.
//
#include <iostream.h>

struct employee
{
  long number;                          // employee number
  char *name, *phone;                   // name and phone
  int  age;                             // employee and age
};

ostream& operator<<(ostream& output, const employee &e);

int main()
{
  employee emp;

  emp.number = 1001;                    // fill in employee info
  emp.age    =   23;
  emp.name   = "borromeo, daphne";
  emp.phone  = "310-555-2042";
  cout << emp;                          // write our employee
  return 0;
}

ostream& operator<<(ostream& output, const employee &e)
{
  output << "Employee: " << e.number << "\n";
  output << "Name:     " << e.name   << "\n";
  output << "Age:      " << e.age    << "\n";
  output << "Phone:    " << e.phone  << "\n";
  return output;
}
```

Figure 22.5   (prstrct3.C) A program that overloads the output operator.

This prototype is actually much less complex than it looks. It simply says that << is an operator that takes references to an output stream and an **employee** and returns a reference to an output stream. Since it's a binary operator, when it's called, its first argument will be the operand on the left (typically, **cout**) and its second argument will be the operand on the right (the **employee** to display). It returns a reference to an output stream so that we can chain output operators together to write a set of values. We obtained this declaration simply by modifying one of the declarations in iostream.h that overloads << for the basic data types.

The other thing we have to do is provide a definition for the operator. But that's straightforward, since it looks like any normal function definition. All it does is use << to display each of the structure fields, and then return the output stream it's passed.

```
//
// C++ program to print an array, several elements per line.
//
#include <iostream.h>

int a[10] = {81, 78, 45, 78, 91, 45, 76, 87, 54, 99};

main()
{
  void display(const int a[], int n, int count = 1);

  cout << "Here's the array, one per line.\n";
  display(a, 10);           // one per line
  cout << "Here's the array, three per line.\n";
  display(a, 10, 3);        // three per line
  return 0;
}

void display(const int a[], int n, int count)
{
  int i;

  for (i = 1; i <= n; i++)
  {
    cout << a[i - 1];
    if (i % count == 0 || i == n)
      cout << "\n";
    else if (i != 0)
      cout << " ";
  }
}
```

Figure 22.6   (array.C)   A C++ program using default function arguments.

Default Function Arguments

Many times we write a function with one or more parameters that will almost always
be the same value. We still require these parameters, though, for those times when
the function's caller may want to provide a different value. In C++ we can write such
a function by specifying default arguments. When we call the function with those
arguments missing, it uses their default values. Otherwise, it simply uses the values we
provide in the call. The default arguments must come after all required arguments.

Figure 22.6 uses default arguments in a function to print an array, with a specified
number of elements on each output line. The first (required) argument is the array to
print; the second (also required) is the number of elements in that array. The third and
final argument is the number of items to print on each line, for which we provide a
default value of 1.

We're only allowed to specify the default values in one place, which usually is in the function's prototype, not its header.

```
void display(const int a[], int n, int count = 1);
```

We usually place the prototype in a header file, which ensures that all callers who include it will have access to the default value.

This program shows one of the few places C++ doesn't allow a C feature: In C++ we're not allowed to initialize local arrays or structures when we declare them. To get around this restriction, we've made the array we display a global.

Inline Functions

In C, we often write short functions as preprocessor macros. Unfortunately, there is no type checking of macro arguments, and macro names are not available at runtime, making it difficult to track down error messages or to use a symbolic debugger. In C++, we can preface short function definitions with **inline**. This asks the compiler to insert the function's body into the code each time the function is called. As with **register**, **inline** is a request to the compiler and may be ignored. We save the expense of function calls and returns, at the cost of increased code size. Inline functions are statically scoped and so must be repeated in each file where they're used (the definitions had better match, too, or the result is *undefined*). We'll use **inline** shortly.

Storage Allocation and Deallocation

Storage allocation is handled through two *operators* (they're operators even though they have names): **new** and **delete**. They function much like C's **malloc** and **free**. Since they are operators, though, the programmer may overload them for user-defined types. We can use **new** in two ways. One is to allocate a single item:

> **new** *type*

The other is to allocate an array:

> **new** *type* [*number of items*]

new returns 0 if it can't allocate the requested space.

There are also two forms of **delete**. The simplest is:

> **delete** *ptr-to-space*

where *ptr-to-space* is a pointer to a single object that had previously been allocated with **new**. The other form of **delete** is

> **delete** [] *ptr-to-space*

We use this form only if the pointed-to space is an array (which was allocated with the second form of **new**).[1] As with **inline**, we'll soon use **new** and **delete**.

---

[1] Older C++ compilers require us to place the number of elements in the allocated array inside the square brackets.

```
//
// Simple stack definition, with operations.
//
const int MAXSTACK = 100;        // default stack size

struct stack
{
  private:
    int count;                   // # of elements on stack
    int items[MAXSTACK];         // the stack itself
  public:
    stack();                     // initialize stack!
    void push(int item);         // add element to the stack
    void pop();                  // delete top element from stack
    int top();                   // return top element of stack
    int isempty();               // is stack empty?
};
```

Figure 22.7 (stack.h) A C++ definition of a **stack** data type.

22.3	OBJECT-ORIENTED PROGRAMMING

In C++, object-oriented programming is about defining different kinds of objects (or *classes*). This requires defining their *instance data* and their *operations*. To illustrate how to define and use objects, we'll rewrite our earlier input reversal program to reverse its input using a stack.

Defining a Stack Class

The first step in using objects is to define a class. This is done by defining a structure for the object, which is usually placed in a header file so that it can be used by other programs. The class definition is called the "interface specification," since it defines how other functions or objects can interface with (or use) this class. It typically includes the data types for any private instance data within the class, and function prototypes for public access methods.

Figure 22.7 is the header file defining the **stack** type. Our implementation of stacks uses an array **items** to hold the stack elements, and an integer **count** to keep track of how many elements are actually on the stack. These fields are the *instance data* of a **stack** object. As in our C implementation, we define a **stack** structure containing these fields. We want to keep these fields hidden from the stack's users, so we tag them as **private**. The reserved word **private** tells the compiler to forbid any nonmember function from accessing these values.

As before, our implementation also provides several functions that access a stack: **push**, **pop**, **top**, and **isempty**. These are the operations that we want to be available to stack users. But now we provide prototypes for each of these functions *in the* *definition of the* **stack** *structure*. This makes them member functions and lets them access the **private** fields within a stack. In addition, we tag these functions as **public**. The reserved word **public** tells the compiler to allow direct access to the members following it. That means any stack user can call the various member functions implementing the stack operations.

With **struct**s, the default is **public** access for all of its members. But allowing direct access to a **stack**'s internals violates a basic tenet of object-oriented programming: the details of an object's implementation should be kept hidden and only made accessible by the object's operations. That way we can change the object's internal representation without affecting the way the object is used. The ability to have public member functions (accessible outside the structure) and private fields (accessible only within the structure) allows the compiler to enforce the separation of an object's implementation and its use.

There's actually one special prototype in the definition of a **stack**:

```
stack();
```

Any member function with the same name as the data type is a *constructor*. A constructor is automatically called whenever we create an *instance* of a particular data type, as by declaring a variable or dynamically allocating an object with that type. Its job is to initialize the data fields within an object, saving the programmer the bother of calling a specific initialization routine. Similarly, we can specify a *destructor*—a member function with the same name as the class, with a ~ in front. It's called whenever an object goes out of scope or is deallocated. We can't call constructors and destructors directly, so they have no return type, not even **void**. They're also optional, but used in almost every data type we create.

Defining the Stack Operations

Once we've defined the stack object, we need to provide the code for the stack operations. This corresponds to providing code for the member functions. We usually place these in a separate source file, which we compile separately and then make available in object or library form to programs that need the class.

Figure 22.8 contains the **stack** operations. Implementing **push**, **pop**, and their comrades is surprisingly simple. One catch, however, is that we need to realize that other objects might also have similarly named member functions. That means we need to tell the compiler we're defining member functions for the **stack** class. We do this with a new C++ operator, called the *scope resolution operator*, two colons preceded with the name of the class and followed by the name of the routine. For example, here's the header for **push**:

```
void stack::push(int item)
```

Look closely at the definitions for the **stack** operations. Do you notice something strange? You should—they refer to **items** and **count** without declaring them and without preceding them with any kind of field selection operator. That seems very wrong! But by default the compiler assumes undeclared variables in a member function refer to the instance data for that class. So when we refer to **items** inside a member

```
//
// Simple stack definition, with operations.
//
#include "stack.h"

stack::stack()
{
  count = 0;                          // stack starts off empty
}

void stack::push(int item)          // add element to stack
{
  items[count++] = item;
}

void stack::pop()                   // delete top element from stack
{
  count--;
}

int stack::top()                    // return top element of stack
{
  return items[count-1];
}

int stack::isempty()                // is stack empty?
{
  return count == 0;
}
```

Figure 22.8   (stack.C)   The C++ definition of the **stack** operations.

function such as **push**, we're referring to the **items** in an instance of the **stack** structure.

Using the Stack

Figure 22.9 is the reversal program using stacks. To create a stack, we simply declare a variable with that type.

```
stack s;
```

This invokes the constructor function, which in this case initializes **s**'s **count** field to 0. In C++ terms, this declaration creates an *instance* **s** of a **stack** object.

To use the operations, we access them in the same way we would access member fields. For example, to push **i** onto **s**, we use:

```
s.push(i)
```

This invokes the push operation on the object **s**, placing **i**'s value into the appropriate

```
//
// Use stack to reverse stream of integers, no error checking.
//
#include <iostream.h>
#include "stack.h"

main()
{
  stack s;                            // create a stack
  int    i;

  while (cin >> i)                    // push inputs onto stack
    s.push(i);
  for (; !s.isempty(); s.pop())       // display stack
    cout << s.top() << "\n";
  return 0;
}
```

Figure 22.9   (rev.C)   A C++ input-reversal program using a **stack**.

place in **s.items** and incrementing **s.count**. This type of call is often referred to as sending a message to an object. In this case we're sending the "push" message to **s**. What could be simpler?

When we defined a **stack**, we were careful to make its instance data **private**. The result is that we can't directly access **s.items** and **s.count**. We can only access them indirectly through the **stack** member functions. But if we tagged these functions as **private** too, we'd be in big trouble, because then there would be no way to access that data. The call to **s.push** above would be illegal.

An Improved Stack Class

We'll now make a pair of improvements to our stack class. First, we are going to use a **class** rather than a **struct**. A **class** is exactly like a **struct**, with one difference. By default, **class** fields and member functions are *private* rather than **public**. Essentially, this saves us the effort of preceding the data fields with the keyword **private**.

Second, we'll now dynamically allocate the **items** array, providing a constructor that allows the user to optionally specify the size of the stack, and providing a destructor that frees up the stack when we no longer need it.

Figure 22.10 shows our new stack definition using **class** rather then **struct**. One difference is that the fields are different: **items** is now a pointer, and we have an additional field **size** that records the maximum size of a given stack.

Another difference is that we've changed the prototype for the constructor. It now takes an optional argument. If we declare a stack in the old way

```
stack s;
```

```
//
// Revised stack definition, with operations.
//
const int MAXSTACK = 100;         // default stack size

class stack
{
    int count;                    // # of elements on stack
    int *items;                   // the stack itself
    int size;                     // the size of a stack
  public:
    stack(int n = MAXSTACK);      // create stack
    ~stack();                     // get rid of a stack
    void push(int item);          // add element to the stack
    void pop();                   // delete top element from stack
    int top();                    // return top element of stack
    int isempty();                // is stack empty?
};
```

Figure 22.10   (stack2.h) The new definition of our **stack** class.

we're specifying no arguments to the constructor, so it will be invoked to create the default 100-element stack. But declaring the stack as

```
stack s(50);
```

causes a 50-element stack to be created instead. The idea is that the values for the argument to the constructor follow the variable's declaration. This actually is quite sensible, since the constructor is automatically invoked whenever we declare a variable.

The last change is that we have added a prototype for a destructor. We need it to free up the space dynamically allocated in the constructor.

Figure 22.11 contains our revised **stack** operations. Most of the definitions are the same, except for some additional error checking in **push**, **pop**, and **top**. Now **push** refuses to add to a full stack, **pop** refuses to delete from an empty stack, and **top** returns zero if the stack was empty.[2] We've also modified the constructor to dynamically allocate the stack using **new**, and have the destructor free up that space using **delete**. We can't call the destructor directly. Instead, it is automatically called whenever we exit the block in which a stack has been created.

One nice thing about C++ is that even though we've completely changed the implementation of a stack, we don't have to make any change to the programs using it. Any main program using the new stack will run exactly as before—although we have have to recompile it and link it with the new implementation of the stack routines.

---

[2]Of course, zero is a valid integer, so it may seem strange to return it when the stack is empty. But we aren't returning zero to indicate an error. Instead, we're returning zero simply because **top** has to return something, even if it's invoked incorrectly.

```
//
// Simple stack definition, with operations.
//
#include "stack2.h"

stack::stack(int n)
{
  items = new int[n];                // make stack
  count = 0;                         // stack starts off empty
  size = n;                          // elements in stack
}

stack::~stack()                      // free up stack
{
  delete [] items;
}

void stack::push(int item)           // add element to stack
{
  if (count < size)
    items[count++] = item;
}

void stack::pop()                    // delete top element from stack
{
  if (count != 0)
    count--;
}

int stack::top()                     // return top element of stack (or 0)
{
  return count > 0 ? items[count-1] : 0;
}

int stack::isempty()                 // is stack empty?
{
  return count == 0;
}
```

Figure 22.11   (stack2.C) Our new stack operations.

22.4   USING BUILT-IN CLASSES—FILE I/O

C++ file input and output differs somewhat from C. In C, all files were handled through a variable of type **FILE *** and were opened and closed with calls to special library functions. But in C++, we use different *objects* for input files and for output files, and their constructors and destructors take care of opening and closing the files for us. We use the classes **ifstream** for input files and **ofstream** for output files.

Figure 22.12 illustrates their use in a C++ program to copy one file into another. It takes the names of the files from the command line, so

    filecopy *file1* *file2*

copies from *file1* to *file2*. The program is superficially similar to the C version. First we open *file1* for reading and then *file2* for writing. If both opens succeed, we continue and copy *file1* into *file2*, one character at a time.

We open a file for reading by giving its name along with the variable that we declare to be of type **ifstream**.

```
ifstream f1(argv[1]);                    // Open input file
```

This declares **f1** to be an **ifstream** and also attempts to open the file named in **argv[1]** for reading. It does that by invoking the constructor for **ifstream**, which takes as its argument the name of the file to open.

We determine whether the open succeeded by testing **f1**:

```
if (!f1)
    open_error(argv[1], "reading");
```

And we do a similar declaration and test for **f2**:

```
ofstream f2(argv[2]);

if (!f2)
    open_error(argv[2], "writing");
```

We're careful to attempt to open the second file for writing only if we can open the first for reading. That way we don't wipe out an existing file if the source file can't be opened.

The main loop just reads a character at a time from *file1* and writes it to *file2*. In C++, file objects contain operations for reading and writing a character at a time, called **get** and **put**, respectively. **get** reads a single character from the input file into its argument and returns 0 on end of file or read failure. **put** takes the character and writes it to the file. So the main loop is just

```
while (f1.get(ch))
    f2.put(ch);
```

22.5   INHERITANCE

Often we have an existing data type that's just about, but not quite, what we need. In C, we're stuck with having to create a new data type and providing definitions for its functions, even if they're identical to those for the existing type. C++, however, allows us to define classes as *derived classes* of other classes. These derived classes, or *subclasses*, are said to *inherit* all of the members—data members and function members—of another class. We're allowed to add new members and methods (functions), and we can even *overload* members from the *parent* or *base* class.

```
//
// Copy one file to another.  First argument is source file, and
// second argument is destination.
//
#include <iostream.h>                       // For basic I/O
#include <fstream.h>                         // For file I/O

inline void usage_error(char *progname, char *arguments);
inline void open_error(char *filename, char *access_type);

inline void usage_error(char *progname, char *arguments)
{           // error message for bad program usage
  cerr << "Usage: " << progname << " " << arguments << "\n";
}

inline void open_error(char *filename, char *access_type)
{           // error message for failure to open files
  cerr << "Can't open " << filename << " for " << access_type << "\n";
}

int main(int argc, char *argv[])
{
  char ch;
  int  status = 1;                          // default is failure!

  if (argc != 3)                            // two files required
    usage_error(argv[0], "file1 file2");
  else
  {
    ifstream  f1(argv[1]);                  // open input file

    if (!f1)
      open_error(argv[1], "reading");
    else
    {
      ofstream  f2(argv[2]);                // open output file

      if (!f2)
        open_error(argv[2], "writing");
      else
        while (f1.get(ch))                  // do the copy
          f2.put(ch);
      status = 0;
    }
  }
  return status;
}
```

Figure 22.12   (filecopy.C) Copy from one file to another.

```
//
// Simple linked list class.
//
#include <iostream.h>

struct node
{
  node *next;
  int item;
};

class list
{
  protected:
    node *first, *last;                         // ptrs to front/back
    int items;                                  // number of values
  public:
    list() {first = last = 0; items = 0;}       // initialize list
    ~list();
    void insert_front(int value);
    void insert_rear(int value);
    int  isempty() { return first == 0;}        // is list empty?
    int  length() { return items; }             // # of items in list
    friend ostream& operator<<(ostream &output, const list &l);
};
```

Figure 22.13 (lists.h) A C++ implementation of a linked list.

One fundamental data type we've used throughout the text is a list—a collection of values with operations for putting values in and getting values out. If we restrict the access methods on a list to adding and removing only from one end, we have a stack; if we restrict the access in a slightly different way—adding at one end and removing from the other—we have a queue.

Let's use this idea, that a stack or a queue are just variations on a list, and define a *base class* `list` and a *derived class* `stack`. We define the base class in the usual way: we put the class definitions in a header file lists.h and any member functions not defined in line in an appropriate source file. Any program that needs a `list` class can just include lists.h at the beginning and then link in the object module containing the list operations.

Figure 22.13 contains a definition for the `list` class. Our implementation is a linked list, so `list` has several fields: pointers to the first and last elements of the list, and a count of the number of elements on the list.

This header file makes use of several new C++ features. The first is that we've changed the protection specification for these internal variables from the default **private** to **protected**. **protected** members are visible in derived classes, but still remain inaccessible outside the class; **private** members are not accessible to derived classes. This means operations implementing stacks will be able to access these member functions, but general user functions won't.

The second is that we've included the body of several of the members inside their definitions, rather than placing them in a separate source file. C++ automatically treats these operations like **inline** functions. We can do so only if they're simple, usually just a few lines of code that don't involve loops. For example, the class definition contains the entire **list** constructor, which simply initializes the list pointers to **0** and sets the initial length of the list to zero.

```
list() {first = last = 0; items = 0;}
```

The third change is the addition of a special prototype declaring a **<<** operator for printing the list items.

```
friend ostream& operator<<(ostream &output, const list &l)
```

What's this **friend** business? In general, when we want an operator or function to have access to the private members of the class, we make it a **friend**, declared within the class. **friend** functions are nonmember functions that are allowed to access private class data. We're stating that the overloaded **<<** operator, though not a member function, will be able to get to the private **list** data and functions.

Why declare it as a **friend** and not just make it a member function? Because member functions take a default argument, the unspecified first argument, that is a pointer to the object on which they're called (that's how we can get to member data without specifying to which object we're referring). However, for output, we want the left argument to be the stream and the right argument to be the class, so that the overloaded insertion operator will have the same order of arguments as the ones for the built-in types. So we write it as a friend taking two arguments: the output file (type **ostream&**) and the **list** (except we make the second argument a reference to a constant **list** to avoid copying and to allow the compiler to protect against accidentally changing the list).

Figure 22.14 defines the other list functions. **insert_front** and **insert_rear** allocate space for a new node and hook it into the list as the first or last element, respectively. **~list** is a destructor that runs through the list, using **delete** to deallocate space for the list nodes. And **<<** runs through the list, printing each list element.

Now that our base class is set up, we can define our **stack**, based on the **list** class. The syntax for defining a derived class is

```
class Name :   public Base-Class
{
    Members
};
```

This says that *Name* is a new class that *inherits* all members from another class, *Base-Class*. The word **public** says that the inheritance follows these rules: all **private** members remain **private** and are not accessible to the derived class; all **protected** members are available and are **protected** in the derived class; and all **public** members are available and are **public**.

Figure 22.15 contains our header file defining the **stack** class in terms of lists. By

```
//
// Simple linked list class.
//    ~list - free up list by deleting all elements.
//    insert_front - insert new item at front of list.
//    insert_rear - insert new item at end of list.
//
#include <iostream.h>
#include "lists.h"

list::~list()
{
  node *ptr;

  for (ptr = first; ptr != 0; ptr=ptr->next)
    delete ptr;
}

void list::insert_front(int value)
{
  node *temp = new node;

  temp->next = first;                   // create and fill node
  temp->item = value;
  first = temp;                         // hook into list
  if (!last)                            // only last if empty
    last = temp;
  items++;                              // new node
}

void list::insert_rear(int value)
{
  node *temp = new node;

  temp->next = 0;                       // create and fill node
  temp->item = value;
  last->next = temp;
  last = temp;
  items++;
}

ostream& operator<<(ostream& output, const list &l)
{
  node *ptr;

  for (ptr = l.first; ptr != 0; ptr = ptr->next)
    output << ptr->item << "\n";
  return output;
}
```

Figure 22.14 (lists.C) The definitions of the list operations.

```
//
// Stack class implemented as derived class.
//
#include "lists.h"

class stack : public list
{
  public:
    void push(int value) { insert_front(value); }
    void pop();
    int  top()  { return first ? first->item : 0; }
};
```

Figure 22.15   (stack3.h) Defining **stack** as a derived class of **list**.

defining **stack** as a subclass of **list**, we make all of the **list** functions available to **stack** users. That means we inherit **isempty**, among others. So if we apply **isempty** to a stack:

```
        s.isempty()
```

we automatically use the **isempty** defined for lists.

The header file declares three public operations: **push**, **pop**, and **top**. **push** and **pop** are simple enough that we include their complete code rather than providing a prototype. **push** adds an element by using **insert_front**:

```
        void push(int value) { insert_front(value); }
```

There's no **insert_front** defined for the **stack** class, so the call to **insert_front** will automatically execute the version defined for the **list** class.

top makes use of internal **list** fields. It can do that because a **stack** object automatically inherits those fields.

```
        int top() { return first ? first->item : 0; }
```

All that's left for us to define is the **pop** operation, which is shown in Figure 22.16. It deletes the first element from the list representing a stack.

You might be wondering where the constructors and destructors for a **stack** are. We didn't define them because if we don't define them for a derived class, we automatically use those for the parent class. So here when we declare a stack, the list constructor is automatically called for us. Similarly, when we get rid of a stack, the list destructor is called.

There's actually one problem with our **stack** definition. Because a **stack** inherits all of the **list** operators, there's nothing to prevent a user from using those operations, as in

```
        s.insert_front(100);
```

```
//
// Definitions of stack operations in terms of lists.
//
#include "stack3.h"

void stack::pop()
{
  node *temp = first;

  if (first)
  {
    first=first->next;
    delete temp;
  }
}
```

Figure 22.16   (stack3.C) A definition of the stack operation `pop`.

That's bad. We would like to be able to change a stack's implementation without affecting its users. But if its users write code using those operations directly, they're going to be affected. So what we'd like to do is somehow prevent users from accessing the inherited list functions.

Figure 22.17 is a new **stack** definition that gets around this problem. It provides prototypes for each of the **list** operations (**insert_front**, **insert_rear**, **length**, and **<<**) and labels them as **private** member functions. That means these can be accessed only from member functions for **stack**, which prevents users from applying them to stacks directly. We do this because we want the only publicly available **stack** functions to be **push**, **pop**, and **top**. That way we can later change the internal implementation of **stack**s without worrying that some program depends on them being internally implemented as a **list**.

But there's a catch. Because we provide these prototypes, the C++ compiler now assumes that we'll implement these operations for the **stack** class. As a result, it will no longer allow us to inherit them automatically from the **list** class. That's a problem for us in **push**, which used inheritance to automatically use the **insert_front** for the **list** class. Fortunately, there's an easy way to fix this:

```
void push(int value) { list::insert_front(value); }
```

The **list::** forces **push** to invoke the **insert_front** member function for the **list** class.

We've only scratched the surface of what we can do with inheritance, and we've glossed over many of the difficulties with using it. Our main goal is to get you interested enough to explore it in more detail in the future. The exercises will suggest other classes you can define to see even more of the power of C++!

```
//
// Stack class implemented as derived class.
//
#include "lists.h"

class stack : public list
{
  private:                              // stack users can't get at these
    void insert_front(int value);
    void insert_rear(int value);
    int length();
    friend ostream& operator<<(ostream& output, const list &l);
  public:
    void push(int value) { list::insert_front(value); }
    void pop();
    int  top() { return first ? first->item : 0; }
};
```

Figure 22.17   (stack4.h) A final version of our stack header file.

SUMMARY

- C++ is one implementation of object-oriented programming, which has been around for quite some time and is here to stay.[3]

- C++ is built on C. It provides a variety of features that are nice to have, even without knowing all of its object-oriented capabilities. But C++'s powerful object-oriented features allow us to easily write clear, reuseable code.

- C++ provides references, which we can use to simulate call-by-reference parameter passing and to efficiently pass large structures.

- C++ provides function and operator overloading, which allows us to have the same functions and operators work with a variety of different types.

- C++ provides **inline** functions, which allow us to trade size for speed with small functions.

- C++ allows us to provide functions as structure and class members. These functions then become the operations that we can apply to objects of that class.

- C++ lets us define classes that are derived from other classes. These derived classes automatically inherit instance data and member functions from their base classes.

---

[3]The language is still evolving. There is now an ANSI standard for the C language; no such standard exists for C++, and the differences between AT&T's versions 1.2, 2.0, 2.1, and 3.0 have been substantial. At this time, the language is actively being worked on, and there could be major changes in new versions.

■ We really like C++. It's an elegant extension to C that opens the door to the strengths, advantages, and conveniences of object-oriented programming. But like C before it, it is hardly a panacea for all programming woes, and it brings along its own potential problems and pitfalls.

EXERCISES

22–1 Rewrite Chapter 14's **minmax** function (Figure 14.5) to use references rather than pointer parameters.

22–2 Rewrite Chapter 9's group reversal program (Figure 9.18) to use **new** and **delete**.

22–3 Redo Chapter 8's set functions as a **set** class. Assume that sets are created with a fixed maximum size. The constructor should take care of initializing the set.

22–4 Redo Chapter 9's set functions as a **set** class. The constructor should take care of dynamically allocating the set elements. The constructor should be passed the requested size of the set and should use a reasonable default value if no requested size is provided. Also provide a destructor that frees up the space when the set goes away.

22–5 Rewrite Chapter 11's data base program in an object-oriented style.

22–6 Rewrite Chapter 12's Game Of Life in an object-oriented style.

22–7 Provide suitable definitions for an overloaded function named **fetch**, that takes as arguments a prompt and a reference to a value to read. Here's the prototype for a version of **fetch** to read an **int**.

```
int fetch(int &x, char *prompt);
```

Define versions of **fetch** for reading an **int**, a string (which should be an entire input line), and an **employee**. Allow the **prompt** to default to the string "**Enter Value:**".

22–8 Overload the equality operator **==** to determine whether two **employee**s are the same. Also overload the **!=** operator.

22–9 Define a class **string_table** that maintains a sorted array of strings. It should be represented as an array of pointers. Provide a constructor that allows the user to specify the size of this array, provide a reasonable default, and allocate the desired-size array dynamically. Provide operations to add and delete items and to search for a particular item. Overload **<<** to print the table. Finally, provide a destructor that frees the space allocated for the array table.

22–10 Use the class defined in the previous exercise to sort its input lines.

22–11 Redefine **string_table** to use a linked list rather than an array.

22–12 Create a **queue** class, a derived class of the **list** class. The operations are **enqueue** (add a new element at the end of the list), **dequeue** (remove the element at the front of the list), and **isempty** (returns nonzero if the queue is empty).

22–13 Use the `queue` created in the previous exercise to redo Chapter 8's bus simulator.

22–14 Provide a `date` class. Provide operations for comparing `dates` and for computing the difference between two `dates`.

Part VI

APPENDIXES

A COMPILING AND LINKING

This appendix discusses the actual command sequences necessary to compile, link, and execute run programs under several of the most common C programming environments. In particular, we examine how to use the standard UNIX C compiler, the MICROSOFT C compiler for MS-DOS, and the the TURBO C and QUICK C programming environments for MS-DOS. We also show how to separately compile files and link them together, and we discuss the most commonly used compiler options.

A.1 USING COMMAND-LINE ENVIRONMENTS

C programming environments fall into two general categories. The first uses the traditional command-line approach. With these compilers, such as with the standard C compiler on UNIX or with Microsoft C on MS-DOS, we use separate commands to edit, compile, link, and run our programs. Usually, these compilers provide a single command shortcut that combines the compiling and linking. On UNIX, for example, we use

    cc welcome.c

to compile and link Chapter 1's first program. The result is an executable file named a.out. If we want the resulting executable file to have a more reasonable name, we need to use the -o option:

    cc -o welcome welcome.c

This command results in an executable file named welcome. With Microsoft C, we use

    cl welcome.c

to compile and link our program. This results in an executable file named welcome.exe. That's all there is to it!

Sometimes, however, we want to build an executable program out of a set of source files. Suppose, for example, we want to build Chapter 2's final interest rate program, which consists of two files: irmain.c, which contains the main program, and irfuncs.c, which contains the functions to display values and calculate the year's ending balance. We need to first compile each of our programs into an object module, and then later link all of these object modules together to form the executable. On UNIX, we can do this easily with a single command:

```
cc irmain.c irfuncs.c
```

This command automatically compiles the source files and links the resulting object modules together to create an executable. In this case, it creates an a.out by compiling irmain.c into an object module irmain.o, and irfuncs.c into irfuncs.o and then links the two object modules together. That command is even nice enough to get rid of object modules for us when it's finished. Of course, we could use

```
cc -o ir irmain.c irfuncs.c
```

to create an executable with a more pleasant name, ir, in this case.

As an alternative, we can compile each source file separately and then explicitly link the object modules together.

```
cc -c irmain.c
cc -c irfuncs.c
cc -o ir irmain.o irfuncs.o
```

The first two commands create the necessary object modules, and the last command links them together. The -c option tells the compiler to create the object module but not to invoke the linker. On UNIX, the compiler automatically invokes the linker after compiling any .c files (unless we gave it the -c option).

A.2   USING INTEGRATED DEVELOPMENT ENVIRONMENTS

It's easy to learn how to use these compilers; they provide fast compilation, and let us use our favorite editor to enter our programs. But they have several major drawbacks: incremental program development is time-consuming, and correcting errors is a potentially painful process. Before we can compile our program, we usually have to save our file and leave the editor. If our program contains errors, the compiler provides us with a list of error messages, which we need to record somewhere. To make changes, we have to reenter the editor, reload our file, and work our way through it, trying to find and correct all of our mistakes.

The other approach is to provide an integrated development environment. These systems, such as Turbo C and Quick C on MS-DOS, or Saber-C on UNIX, integrate the editor, compiler, and linker under a single easy-to-use interface. They let us compile and execute our programs with a single keystroke—without leaving the editor. But more importantly, we can also more easily correct our errors. If the compiler detects any errors, it places us in the editor at the location where the first error occurred, with a message on the screen that describes our mistake. After fixing this error, a single keystroke takes us to the location of the next error, and another keystroke to the error after that, and so on. These integrated environments make learning C a much less painful process, and we highly recommend them. These environments are usually menu-driven, which makes learning how to use them extremely simple. In Turbo C, for example, we simply start the development environment with the command tc and follow the menus from there.

Separately compiling files in Turbo C is also easy. There's a menu option for compile-only, rather than compile and link. We can use that entry to compile each of the source files. Linking files together is a bit trickier. We have to create a *project* file (a file with the suffix .prj). In its simplest form, a project file contains a list of source files. When we select the make-executable menu entry, it'll compile all of these files (if they're not already compiled) and then link the resulting object modules together. The result is an executable named *project*.exe, where *project* is the name of the project file (without the .prj).

A.3   COMMON COMPILER OPTIONS

In addition to the standard options for naming the executable and not invoking the linker, most compilers have several other frequently used options. Here we list them by function and show their usual values on UNIX compilers. The integrated development environments have most of these features too, but there we obtain them by selecting a menu entry.

- Display the preprocessor's output rather than passing it on to the compiler (-E). This option allows us to see the result of the preprocessor's substitutions. Some compilers also have an option to place this output in a file (usually with the same name as the source file, except with the suffix .i).

- Invoke the optimizing compiler (-O). This usually leads to somewhat faster code but slightly slower compiles.

- Specify a library that should be linked with the program (-lx), where the x is replaced by a one-letter code indicating the library we want to use. We use this option most frequently to link in the math library, usually -lm.

- Add a location for the preprocessor to look for include files (-I*directory*). We use this when we're providing our own include files, but they're in *directory* rather than in the directory in which our source files reside.

- Define a name to the preprocessor, as if by **#define** (there are two forms, either -D*NAME* or -D*NAME=DEFINITION*). We use this option most often to define symbols, such as **DEBUG**, that we're testing within our program.

- Include profiling code in the resulting object module and executable program (-p). When we run the object module, this extra code automatically keeps track of how much time is spent in each function. After we're done running our program, we can run a utility (prof on UNIX) which prints a nice report of where our program spent its time. This information is valuable when we're worried about where to concentrate when improving the efficiency of our programs.

B   INPUT/OUTPUT REDIRECTION

Most programming environments now provide a mechanism by which we can change where the program's input comes from and where its output goes to. This ability makes many programs much more useful than they might at first appear. This appendix shows how to accomplish this redirection on both UNIX and MS-DOS.

B.1   INTRODUCTION

This text contains many programs that initially don't appear to be very useful, since they don't explicitly deal with external files. Chapter 4's display program is an example. Of what use is a program that simply reads and displays the characters we type? It would be more useful if it read its input from a file or wrote its output to a file. Luckily, most operating systems provide us with a way to redirect a program's standard input and output. Of course, the actual details vary from system to system but the principles are the same. Here we show how to do redirection in two of the most popular systems: UNIX and MS-DOS.

B.2   THE COMMANDS

Suppose we've successfully compiled and linked Chapter 4's display program, display.c, and obtained an executable named display. When we execute it, normally by typing display at the command interpreter's prompt, it sets things up so that the program's standard input comes from our keyboard and so that its standard output goes to the terminal or display. But if we follow the command with a < and a file name, the program's standard input is the named file rather than the keyboard. That means we can use

> display < *somefile*

to display the contents of *somefile*. This command executes display so that every time it reads a character with `getchar`, it is reading from somefile rather than the keyboard.

Similarly, following a command with a > and a file name causes the program's standard output to be the named file rather than the console monitor. So the command

585

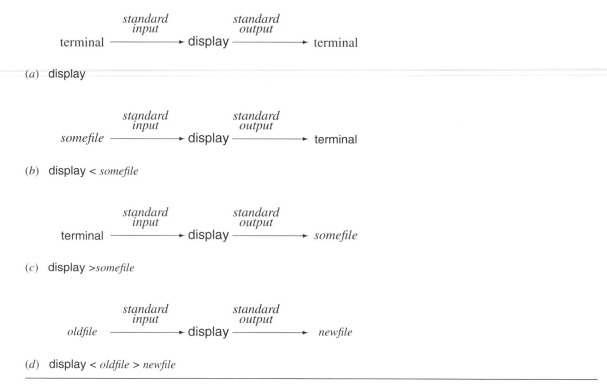

Figure B.1 How input/output redirection works.

display > *somefile*

will cause whatever we type at the keyboard to be entered into *somefile*, rather than being displayed on the screen. That's because now whenever we use **putchar** to write on the standard output, we're really writing onto *somefile*. When we're all done entering our input, we need to hit the end-of-file character.

We're allowed to combine both input and output redirection when invoking a command. So we can use display to copy oldfile into newfile with

display < *oldfile* >*newfile*

Figure B.1 further illustrates what happens when we redirect display's input and output.

C LIBRARY DETAILS

There are a variety of different library functions and header files that come with any ANSI-C compiler. Throughout the text we've discussed the most important of these. This appendix provides pointers to these earlier discussions and discusses the details of the header files and library functions we ignored.

C.1 THE STANDARD HEADER FILES

Table C.1 lists the header files in the standard library, their purpose, and where, if anywhere, we've already discussed them in the text. Each header file provides prototypes for a different set of library functions, as well as definitions of other useful macros and types. Most systems have all of these header files in a standard location, and there's usually nothing to prevent you from examining them. You'll find doing so quite helpful when you need to know exactly what types a particular library function takes or returns, or are curious about how a particular constant or type is defined.

C.2 ERROR HANDLING

The header file errno.h contains the symbolic names and values for a global integer errno that's set when various library functions fail. These library functions indicate errors in two ways: they set errno to a value that indicates what type of error occurred, and they return a failure indication, such as -1. That means when a function fails, we can test errno's value and write an appropriate error message.

There are a couple of cautions. Library functions don't automatically set errno to 0 (no error), so we need to to do that ourselves before calling them. Furthermore, not all library functions set errno; only the functions in the math library and a few others.

Figure C.1 provides an example that uses errno to determine whether the natural logarithm function (log) succeeded or failed. The next section describes more about the particular error codes that the math library functions, such as log, can return.

There are two functions from the standard libraries that are often useful in error handling. The string library provides strerror.

```
char *strerror(int errnum);
```

587

HEADER FILE	ITS USE	WHERE DESCRIBED
assert.h	debugging aid	Chapter 15
ctype.h	character-testing macros	Chapter 4
errno.h	error handling	Appendix C
float.h	floating point ranges	Chapter 3
limits.h	integral ranges	Chapters 3, 4
locale.h	locales	Appendix C
math.h	mathematical functions	Chapter 3, Appendix C
setjmp.h	nonlocal gotos	Appendix C
signal.h	interrupt handing	Appendix C
stdlib.h	generally useful functions	Chapter 16, Appendix C
stdarg.h	variable arguments	Chapter 14
string.h	string manipulation	Chapters 9, 10
stddef.h	useful types and constants	Chapter 9, Appendix C
stdio.h	performing I/O	Chapters 1, 2, 3, 4, 18, Appendix C
time.h	dealing with time	Appendix C

Table C.1   The standard header files.

```
/*
 * A program checking for errors in using the math routines.
 */
#include <stdio.h>
#include <math.h>
#include <errno.h>

int main(void)
{
  double  d, x;

  while (printf("Value: "), scanf("%lf", &x) == 1)
  {
    errno = 0;
    d = log(x);
    if (errno == EDOM)
      fprintf(stderr, "Domain error (bad argument) with log(%g)\n", x);
    else
      printf("log(%g) = %g\n", x, d);
  }
  return 0;
}
```

Figure C.1   (uselog.c) An example using **errno**.

`strerror` returns a pointer to a string containing an *implementation-defined* error message corresponding to its integer parameter, normally `errno`. The standard I/O library provides `perror`.

```
void perror(const char *string)
```

It writes its string parameter to the standard error output (`stderr`), along with a message describing the most recent system error (corresponding to the global variable `errno`). The output format is

> *string*: *system error message*

It terminates its output with a new line.

C.3   THE MATH LIBRARY

Chapter 3 discussed most of the functions in the math library. To use them, we saw that we had to include math.h and request that the math library be linked with our program. What we haven't discussed is the errors these functions can return. We also skipped a pair of math library functions that require an additional pointer argument.

Many of the math routines require that their argument be in certain ranges. If an argument is out of the specified range, the math routine sets the global variable `errno` to `EDOM` (defined in errno.h) and returns an *implementation-defined* value. The call `log(-1)` is a domain error, since the natural log of a negative number isn't defined.

If the value computed by a math library function is outside the range that can be represented as a `double`, the function sets `errno` to `ERANGE`. In addition, on underflow it returns a 0.0, and on overflow it returns `HUGE_VAL` (a constant defined in math.h) with its sign set correctly. The call `exp(x)`, with a large enough `x`, will result in a range error.

The two math library functions we skipped are `frexp` and `modf`. `frexp` breaks the floating point value `val` into a *normalized* fraction and an integer power of 2.

```
double frexp(double val, int *exp);
```

It stores the power of 2 in the location pointed to by `exp`. If `val` is zero, it sets both the fraction and the power of 2 to zero. A *normalized* fraction means that the leading bit is one. That is, the fraction is in the range $[\frac{1}{2}, 1)$ and is exactly zero if `val` is zero. Figure C.2 is an example program using `frexp`. For the input:

```
-123 123 0.5 2 4.0 78.0
```

it produces the output:

```
-123.000000 = -0.960938 x 2^7
 123.000000 =  0.960938 x 2^7
   0.500000 =  0.500000 x 2^0
   2.000000 =  0.500000 x 2^2
   4.000000 =  0.500000 x 2^3
  78.000000 =  0.609375 x 2^7
```

```
/*
 * Using the frexp math library function.
 */
#include <stdio.h>
#include <math.h>

int main()
{
  int     exp;
  double  val, x;

  while (printf("Value: "), scanf("%lf", &val) == 1)
  {
    x = frexp(val, &exp);
    printf("%f = %f x 2^%i\n", val, x, exp);
  }
  return 0;
}
```

Figure C.2   (usefrexp.c) An example program using `frexp`.

The other math library function, **modf**, returns the integer and fractional parts of its first parameter.

```
double modf(double val, double *iptr);
```

It stores the integer part as a **double** in the location pointed to by **iptr**. And it returns the fractional part as the value of the function. Both ***iptr** and the value returned from the function will have the same sign—the sign of **val**.

C.4   THE STRING LIBRARY

Chapter 9 describes all of the string library functions for manipulating byte arrays, and Chapter 10 describes almost all of the library functions for manipulating null-terminated character strings. As we saw earlier, we need to include string.h to use any of these functions.

There are only a few functions we haven't discussed. **strcoll** compares the two strings **s1** and **s2** and returns an **int** with the same interpretation as for **strcmp**.

```
int strcoll(const char *s1, const char *s2);
```

strcoll differs from **strcmp** in that it bases the comparison on the collating sequence in the current locale (discussed later in this appendix). Since many compilers only support the **"C"** locale, these two functions are often identical.

strxfrm transforms up to **n** characters from string **s2** into the space pointed to by **s1**.

```
size_t strxfrm(char *s1, const char *s2, size_t n);
```

strtok

The transformation depends on the current locale. Since many compilers only support the "C" locale, **strxfrm** is often identical to **strncpy**. It returns the same value as for **strncpy**.

strtok is a complex function used to break up a string into *tokens*.

```
char *strtok(char *s1, const char *s2);
```

Tokens are groups of characters in **s1** terminated by any of the characters in **s2**. When **strtok** is first called, it returns a pointer to the first token in **s1** and places a null character at the end of the token (actually modifying **s1**). On subsequent calls, token scanning begins at the place it left off. Second and further calls to **strtok** should pass the null pointer as the first argument. The second argument need not be the same between calls. **strtok** returns a null pointer when there are no more tokens in **s1**.

strtok has many uses. One is to simplify what would otherwise be a rather difficult job: breaking an input line into individual numbers. Suppose that we have a series of input lines, each consisting of a name and zero or more scores, and that we want to break out the name, sum up the scores, and print a total for the name. This task is surprisingly messy for **scanf**, since we don't know how many values appear on each line. Figure C.3 is a program that does this task using **strtok**. With this input:

```
Miller, Larry 89 123
Grant, Rita 105 88 60 70
Quilici, Alex 12 55 23 123 87
Borromeo, Daphne 84 20 6
Cohen, Danny 61 8 9
```

it generates this output:

```
Name                N         Sum
Miller, Larry       2         212
Grant, Rita         4         323
Quilici, Alex       5         300
Borromeo, Daphne    3         110
Cohen, Danny        3          78
```

C.5   THE STANDARD C LIBRARY

The standard C library contains a set of macros and function declarations for a hodge-podge collection of generally useful functions that don't seem to fit well in other libraries. We've already examined some of these functions. Chapter 9 presented its memory management functions, and Chapter 16 discussed its generic searching and sorting functions. However, there are also string conversion functions, random number generators, functions for interfacing with the environment, and functions for manipulating multibyte and wide characters. As we saw earlier, we need to include the header file stdlib.h to use any of these functions. That file also defines the macros and types listed in Table C.2.

```c
/*
 * Break a line into individual integral values.  The input file
 * format is (0 or more values on each line).
 *    Last-Name    First-Name    n1  n2  n3 ...
 */
#include <stdio.h>
#include <stdlib.h>
#include <string.h>
#include <ctype.h>

#define   MAX     256                 /* max input line length */
#define   SEP     " \t"               /* blank or tab--for strtok */

int main(void)
{
  int       getline(char *buf, int max);
  int       count;                    /* number of values on this line */
  long      lno = 0;                  /* current line number */
  long      sum;                      /* total for this line */
  char      line[MAX];                /* current line */
  char      *p;                       /* token pointer from strtok */

  puts("Name                 N               Sum");
  while (getline(line, MAX) != -1)
  {
    lno++;
    if ((p = strtok(line, SEP)) != NULL)
    {
      printf("%s ", p);               /* print last name if there */
      if ((p = strtok(NULL, SEP)) != NULL)
      {
        printf("%s\t", p);            /* print first name if there */
        sum = count = 0;              /* sum and values for this line */
        while ((p = strtok(NULL, SEP)) != NULL)
          if (isdigit(*p) || *p == '-' || *p == '+')
          {
            count++;
            sum += atol(p);           /* atol is a library function */
          }
          else
            fprintf(stderr, "Line %li: %s not a number\n", lno, p);
        printf("%4i\t%10li\n", count, sum);
      }
      else
        fprintf(stderr, "Line %li: no name found\n", lno);
    }
  }
  return 0;
}
```

Figure C.3   (strtok.c) Using strtok to parse simple input lines.

MACRO OR TYPE	FUNCTION
size_t	type returned by **sizeof**
wchar_t	type to hold a wide, or multibyte character
div_t	type of structure returned by **div**
ldiv_t	type of structure returned by **ldiv**
RAND_MAX	maximum value returned from **rand**
NULL	the null pointer
EXIT_FAILURE	argument for **exit** indicating failed return
EXIT_SUCCESS	argument for **exit** indicating successful return
MB_CUR_MAX	number of bytes in a multibyte character

Table C.2   The macros and types defined in stdlib.h.

String Conversion

The standard library provides two sets of string conversion functions. The first set takes a string **s** and converts it to a number.

```
double atof(const char *s);
int    atoi(const char *s);
long   atol(const char *s);
```

atof (ASCII to floating point number) returns the value of the string **s** converted to a **double**. The results are undefined if the conversion can't occur. **atoi** and **atol** are similar, but they convert **s** to an **int** or **long**, respectively. All assume that **s** contains a set of characters representing an appropriate base 10 value.

The other set allows us to determine whether errors took place and to handle values in other bases.

```
double strtod(const char *s, char **endp);
long   strtol(const char *s, char **endp, int base);
unsigned long strtoul(const char *s, char **endp, int base);
```

strtod converts the string **s** to a **double**, just as **scanf** using the %g format. That is, it skips leading space characters (any character for which **isspace** is true) then reads an optional sign (+ or −), digits, an optional decimal point followed by more digits, and an optional exponent (letter 'e' or 'E') followed by a signed integer. It stops converting on the first character that's not part of a floating point number. If **endp** is not **NULL**, it points to this character.

strtod returns the converted number; if it encounters an unrecognized character before the first digit, it returns a 0. If conversion causes overflow, it returns **HUGE_VAL** with the correct sign. If the conversion causes underflow, it returns 0. On either overflow or underflow, it sets **errno** to **ERANGE**.

strtol and **strtoul** convert the string **s** to a **long** or **unsigned long**, respectively. Both skip leading space characters (any character for which **isspace** is true) and then expect an optional sign (+ or −) followed by digits. Both stop converting on the first character that cannot be part of a signed `long`. If `endp` is not `NULL`, it points to this character.

Both of these functions use `base` as a base of conversion. Valid values are 0, or 2 through 36. For a `base` of 0, a base 10 integer is assumed, base 8 if there is a leading `0`, or base 16 if there is a leading `0x` or `0X`. For `base` greater than 10, the letters 'a' through 'z' (or 'A' through 'Z') represent the values 10 through 35, respectively. Any character that is greater than or equal to `base` terminates conversion. If `base` is 16, a leading "0x" or "0X" is allowed.

Both functions return the converted value or zero if the first nonspace character cannot be part of a number. If conversion causes overflow, they both set `errno` to `ERANGE`, and `strtol` returns `LONG_MAX` or `LONG_MIN` and `strolul` returns `ULONG_MAX` or 0, as appropriate.

Random Number Generation

There are two functions that deal with random numbers, `rand` and `srand`.

```
int rand(void);
void srand(unsigned seed);
```

`rand` returns a random number in the range 0 to `RAND_MAX`. We often use `rand() % n` to obtain a random number between 0 and `n`. `srand` "seeds" the random number generator. Calling a sequence of `rand`s after `srand` with the same seed produces the same sequence of random numbers. We can use the `time` function (discussed later in this appendix) to produce a unique seed.

Environment Communication

There are several functions we can use to communicate with a program's environment. The first two, `exit` and `abort`, terminate our program, although they do it in very different ways.

```
void exit(int status);
void abort(void);
```

`exit` returns `status` to the calling environment and does not return to its caller. An exit status of `EXIT_SUCCESS` (or 0) implies successful termination; `EXIT_FAILURE` implies unsuccessful termination. Other return values are *implementation defined*.

Before terminating the program, `exit` does several tasks. First, it calls the functions registered using `atexit` (discussed below) as if they were called from the host environment. Second, it flushes all output buffers and closes all open files. And third, it removes all files created via a call to `tmpfile`.

`abort` generates the signal `SIGABRT`.[1] If this signal is not being caught or ignored, the program's execution terminates with an unsuccessful exit status. The handling of open files, removing temporary files, and flushing output buffers is *implementation defined*.

---

[1]This is similar to the call `raise(SIGABRT)`. We discuss these signals and how to handle them later in this appendix.

```
#include <stdio.h>
#include <stddef.h>
#include <stdlib.h>

int main(void)
{
  void adios(void);
  void goodbye(void);

  if ((atexit(adios) != 0) || (atexit(goodbye) != 0))
    fprintf(stderr, "Can't register both functions!\n");
  return 0;
}

void adios(void)
{
  fprintf(stderr, "Adios and goodbye.\n");
}

void goodbye(void)
{
  fprintf(stderr, "About to rejoin the real world.\n");
}
```

Figure C.4   (useatex.c) An example use of `atexit`.

The closely related function `atexit` "registers" the function pointed to by `f` to be called when the program terminates (either through a specific `return` from `main` or a call to `exit`).

```
int atexit(void (*f)(void));
```

`atexit` returns zero on success and nonzero otherwise. If we register a function more than once, it will be called more than once.[2] Upon termination, the functions are called in reverse order of registration. An implementation must be able to register at least 32 functions. Figure C.4 provides an example. Here's its output:

```
About to rejoin the real world.
Adios and goodbye.
```

The next function, `system`, allows us to execute operating system commands from within our C program.

```
int system(const char *s);
```

It passes the command `s` to the operating system to be executed. The return value is *implementation defined* but generally corresponds to the exit status of the called command `s`. Figure C.5 shows a simple program using `system` to execute the ls

---

[2]This implies `exit` can be called more than once. If that happens, the result is *undefined*.

```
/*
 * Using system to list a directory's contents.
 */
#include <stdio.h>
#include <stdlib.h>

#if defined(unix)
#define DIRECTORY_LISTER "/bin/ls"
#elif defined(__msdos__)
#define DIRECTORY_LISTER "dir"
#else
#error "Don't know how to list directories on this system."
#endif

int main()
{
  printf("Contents of current directory:\n");
  return system(DIRECTORY_LISTER);
}
```

Figure C.5   (usesys.c)   Using **system** to print the contents of the current directory.

command on UNIX or the dir command on MS-DOS, both of which by default list the contents of the current directory.

Finally, **getenv** obtains the value of the environment variable corresponding to **name**.

```
        char *getenv(const char *name);
```

Environment variables are stored in lists provided to the program by the host environment and are generally of the form **name=value**. The **name** argument must match a name in the environment list exactly. If it does, **getenv** returns a pointer to the corresponding value; otherwise, it returns **NULL**. The particular variables supported by an environment are *implementation defined*.

Integer Arithmetic

The standard library contains a small set of functions that perform integer arithmetic (the math library functions all perform floating point arithmetic). The first two compute absolute values:

```
        int  abs(int i);
        long labs(long i);
```

abs returns the absolute value of **i**. The result is *undefined* in the rare case that the result is too large for an **int** (for example, on a 16-bit PC, the largest negative value **INT_MIN** is -32,768, while the largest positive value **INT_MAX** is 32,767). **labs** is similar, except that its argument and return values are **long**s.

There are two other functions that perform integer division:

```
div_t div(int n, int d);
ldiv_t ldiv(long n, long d);
```

div computes both the quotient and remainder of **n** divided by **d**. It stores the result in a **div_t**, a structure defined to have these fields (in either order):

```
typedef struct
{
    int quot, rem;
} div_t;
```

ldiv is the same as **div**, except the arguments are **long**s and the return type is type **ldiv_t**, a structure with the same named fields as a **div_t**, but with **long** types. Their result is *undefined* if we try to divide by zero, so we need to do a check on **d** before calling **div** or **ldiv**.

The library provides these functions for two reasons. One is that division in C produces *implementation-defined* results if one of the operands is negative (that is, -9/5 could evaluate to –1 or –2). The result of **div(-9, 5)** always has a quotient of −1 and a remainder of −4. The other is that they provide a convenient way to obtain the quotient and remainder simultaneously, rather than with two separate arithmetic expressions.

Multibyte Characters

The C library provides a set of functions for converting back and forth between multibyte and wide characters.

```
int    mblen(const char *s, size_t n);
int    mbtowc(wchar_t *p, const char *s, size_t n);
int    wctomb(char *s, wchar_t w);
size_t mbstowcs(wchar_t *p, const char *s, size_t n);
size_t wcstombs(char *s, const wchar_t *p, size_t n);
```

Multibyte characters are of necessity *implementation defined* and depend on the current locale. Since many compilers only support the **"C"** locale, multibyte characters may not be supported on your compiler.

mblen returns the number of bytes required for the multibyte character pointed to by **s** (but only up to **n** bytes). If **s** is **NULL**, **mblen** returns nonzero or zero indicating that multibyte characters do or do not have state dependencies, respectively. If **s** points to an invalid multibyte character, **mblen** returns −1.

mctowc ("multibyte to wide character") is similar to **mblen**, except that it stores the encoding for the multibyte character pointed to by **s** into the space pointed to by **p**.

wctomb ("wide character to multibyte") is the inverse of **mctowc**. It takes a wide character **w** and stores the corresponding multibyte character into the space pointed to by **s** (up to a maximum of **MB_CUR_MAX** characters). It returns the number of bytes required for the wide character **w**, or −1 if **w** isn't a valid multibyte character.

CONSTANT/TYPE	DESCRIPTION
NULL	*null* pointer
_IOFBF	argument to **setvbuf** requesting full buffering
_IOLBF	argument to **setvbuf** requesting line buffering
_IONBF	argument to **setvbuf** requesting no buffering
BUFSIZ	size of **setbuf**'s buffer
EOF	return value indicating end of file
FOPEN_MAX	minimum number of files that can be open simultaneously (at least 8)
FILENAME_MAX	longest file name
L_tmpnam	length of a file name generated by **tmpnam**
SEEK_CUR	tells **fseek** to seek relative to the current position in a file
SEEK_END	tells **fseek** to seek relative to the end of a file
SEEK_SET	tells **fseek** to seek relative to the start of a file
TMP_MAX	minimum number of file names that **tmpnam** can generate (at least 25)
FILE	type used for file access
fpos_t	type used to indicate a position within a file

Table C.3   Macros defined in the header file stdio.h.

mbstowcs converts up to **n** multibyte characters from **s** into wide characters and stores them in **p**. Conversion stops after **n** characters or an all-zero byte. It returns the number of characters converted, not counting the null character, or −1 if **s** contains an illegal multibyte character.

wcstombs is the opposite of **mbstowcs**: it converts up to **n** wide characters into multibye characters. It returns the same value as **mbstowcs**.

C.6   THE STANDARD I/O LIBRARY

Chapters 1, 2, 3, 4, and 18 have described functions in the standard input/output library. To use any of these functions, we need to include the file stdio.h, which defines the macros and types listed in Table C.3.

Removing and Renaming Files

There are a pair of functions for removing and renaming files.

```
int remove(const char *name)
int rename(const char *old_name, const char *new_name)
```

remove removes the named file, so it can no longer be accessed by the name. A call to **remove** on an open file produces *implementation-defined* behavior. **remove** returns 0 on success and nonzero on error.

rename changes the name of an existing file **old_name** to the new name **new_name**. If a file with **new_name** already exists, the behavior is *implementation defined*. **rename** returns 0 on success and nonzero on error. If **rename** fails, the original file with its original name is still accessible.

Temporary Files

There are pair of library functions that deal with temporary files.

```
FILE   *tmpfile(void)
char   *tmpnam(char *name)
```

tmpfile creates a *temporary* file preopened for reading and writing (opened for **"wb+"**). It's just like **fopen** in that it returns a **FILE *** or **NULL** if it can't create and open the temporary file. The file is temporary in the sense that it will be automatically removed when it's closed (either by a call to **fclose** or normal program termination). On abnormal program termination, however, the file may or may not be removed: the action is *implementation defined* (abnormal termination includes a call to the function **abort**, an uncaught signal, and so on).

tmpnam generates a new, unique name that can be used as the name of a temporary file. Each call, up to **TMP_MAX** times, generates a new name; after that, the result is *implementation defined*. The name is unique in the sense that each call produces a new name that is guaranteed not to be the name of any existing file. We can call **tmpnam** in two ways. If we pass it a null pointer, **tmpnam** returns a pointer to the new name. If we pass it a nonnull argument, it places the name in that character array (which must be at least **L_tmpnam** characters long) and also returns a pointer to that space.

Since **tmpnam** only generates a string, it is necessary to open and close the file in the usual way. Despite the implication in the function's name that it gives the name of a *temporary* file, any files opened with names generated by **tmpnam** must still be removed via calls to **remove**, or they will continue to exist after the program terminates.

Error Detection

There are three functions we can use to detect and clear errors.

```
int   feof(FILE *stream)
int   ferror(FILE *stream)
void clearerr(FILE *stream)
```

feof tests the stream for end-of-file indication. Subsequent reads will continue to return end of file until a call to **rewind**, **clearerr**, or the file is closed. **feof** returns nonzero if end of file was detected on the last read on the stream.

ferror tests the stream for a read or write error. Once an error occurs, **ferror** remains true until a call to **clearerr** or **rewind**, or the file is closed. **ferror** returns nonzero if any error was detected on the last read or write on the stream. Errors can occur if the file becomes full, if a read operation cannot be performed because some other operation has changed the permission on the file, and so on.

clearerr resets the end of file and error indicators to 0.

Input/Output Redirection

Usually, we redirect I/O before starting the program, but we can also redirect the input or output from within the program with **freopen**.

```
FILE *freopen(const char *name, const char *mode, FILE *stream)
```

freopen creates a new file pointer for an already opened file. It returns a file pointer or **NULL**, as with **fopen**. The old file is closed, even if **freopen** fails. We use **freopen** most often for associating **stdin**, **stdout**, or **stderr** with another named file. The following call causes all reads involving **stdin** to come from a file named **data.txt**.

```
FILE  *stdin_ptr = freopen("data.txt", "r", stdin);
```

We need **freopen** because even though we think of the names **stdin**, **stdout**, and **stderr** as being type **FILE ***, we can't assign to them.[3] The following is illegal:

```
stdin = fopen("data.txt", "r");
```

Moving the File Pointer

The functions **fgetpos** and **fsetpos** are used to get and set the internal file position when we're manipulating files that are longer than can be represented in a **long**.[4]

```
int fgetpos(FILE *stream, fpos_t *where)
int fsetpos(FILE *stream, const fpos_t *where)
```

fgetpos gets the current position of the file, in a form suitable for a subsequent call to **fsetpos**. The location is returned in the space pointed to by **where**, a pointer to an **fpos_t**. This type could be a simple type on systems incapable of supporting very large files, or it could be a structured type. **fgetpos** returns 0 on success and nonzero on error.

fsetpos positions the file pointer to the location in the file, as specified by the value pointed to by **where**. This value must have been set by a previous call to **fgetpos**. As with **fseek**, a call to **fsetpos** erases the end-of-file indication on the file and any memory of pushed-back characters. **fsetpos** returns 0 on success, nonzero on error. On error, both set **errno** to indicate the error.

Putting Characters Back

The function **ungetc** pushes its character parameter back to the stream (after first converting it to type **unsigned char**).

```
int ungetc(int c, FILE *stream)
```

---

[3] On many systems, these are defined using **#define** as addresses of operating system buffers associated with the appropriate files.

[4] Both **ftell** and **fseek** return and use **long**s for reporting the size of a file. With very large files this is inadequate.

If **c** is **EOF**, **ungetc** fails, and no character is pushed back. The size of the push-back buffer is at least one character. Subsequent reads on the file will return the pushed-back characters in reverse order of being pushed. **fseek** and **fsetpos** erase the pushed-back characters. It's an error if the stream isn't open for reading. **ungetc** returns **c**, the pushed-back character; on failure, it returns **EOF**.

Controlling Buffering

There are several library functions we can use to control the size of input/output buffers and when they're actually written out to the file.

```
int   fflush(FILE *stream)
void  setbuf(FILE *stream, char *buf)
int   setvbuf(FILE *stream, char *buf, int type, size_t size)
```

fflush causes a file's buffer to be written out. It returns 0 on success.

setbuf and **setvbuf** cause a named buffer to be used for input or output buffering on an open file, instead of a system-allocated buffer. In **setbuf**, if **buff** is **NULL**, I/O will be unbuffered. If it's not, the named buffer is used, which must be at least **BUFSIZ** bytes (given in stdio.h). For **setvbuf**, a buffer will be automatically allocated using **malloc**, requesting **size** bytes.

In **setvbuf**, **type** controls the type of buffering we have. There are three choices. **_IOFBF** causes the file to be *fully* buffered. The next input operation on an *empty* buffer will attempt to fill the entire buffer. On output, the buffer must be completely filled before the file is actually written. **_IOLBF** causes the file to be *line* buffered. If the buffer is empty, the next input will attempt to fill the entire buffer. On output, the buffer is written to the file when a newline character is written. **_IONBF** causes the file to be *unbuffered* and both **size** and **buffer** to be ignored. **setvbuf** returns 0 if successful and nonzero otherwise.

Formatted Output

We've seen an entire collection of functions that perform formatted output, but we've left out lots of gory details.

```
int printf(const char *format, ...)
int fprintf(FILE *stream, const char *format, ...)
int sprintf(char *string, const char *format, ...)
int vprintf(const char *format, va_list param)
int vfprintf(FILE *stream, const char *format, va_list param)
int vsprintf(char *string, const char *format, va_list param)
```

Each of these functions takes two sets of parameters. The first is the format specification given in the **format** parameter. The other is a list of expressions to print. All **printf** family routines return the number of characters printed or, if an error occurs, a negative value. The functions differ as to where output goes (standard output, a file, or another string) and whether or not they're provided expressions to display directly or through variable argument lists.

The format string in the **printf** family indicates how a value or expression is to be formatted. It's usually a constant string (provided in double quotes). Characters in the format string are written as is, except for those beginning with the percent character (`'%'`). The format string thus consists of two types of objects: *plain characters* and *format specifiers*.

format specifiers begin with the percent character (`'%'`); for each format specifier there must be one value or expression in the comma-separated expression list or variable argument list. One expression is "consumed" for each format specifier. The syntax of a format specifier is

% [flags] [width] [.precision] [size] type

flags is an optional list of flag characters indicating justification, plus or minus sign, decimal point, trailing zeros, or octal or hex prefix.

width is an optional value that indicates the *minimum* number of characters to print (more characters are printed if a value is too large for the given width). Padding is done with blanks or zeros depending on an appropriate flag character. If no width is specified, a default width is used.

precision is the *maximum* number of characters to print. Again, padding is done with blanks or zeros depending on an appropriate flag character.

size (**h**, **l**, or **L**) overrides the default size of an argument. The size characters are **h** for a **short int**, **l** for a **long int**, and **L** for a **long double**. To print a short hex integer, use `%hx`; a long octal, use `%lo`; and so on.

type indicates the type of the expression or value. Table C.4 lists the various legal types (although many compilers have extensions to this table—see your compiler writeup for details). Most of the various formatting types have defaults associated with them; these are described in Table C.5.

A *flag* is one of the characters **-**, **+**, blank, or **#**. Any combination and order of flag characters is allowed (but **+** will take precedence over a blank if both are given). A minus-sign flag left justifies the value or string, padded to the right with blanks; otherwise the value is right justified and padded on the left with 0s or blanks (0s for numerical values or blanks for strings). A plus-sign flag uses a plus sign for positive values (default is a blank) and a minus sign for negative values (signed expressions). A blank flag uses a space instead of a plus sign for positive values; negative values still have a minus sign. Finally the **#** flag uses an alternate output format, as described in Table C.6.

The width specifier sets a minimum width for the output field. If the expression requires more than the minimum, it overflows the output field (that is, truncation does not occur nor is the output marked with special "field too small" characters as in FORTRAN). The width is given as a number of characters, such as `%10i` or `%010i`, indicating that if the value requires less than 10 characters, it is padded on the left with blanks in the first case and zeros in the second. The width can also be specified as the special character *****: `%*i`. For the ***** width, the expression list provides the width. It is taken from the next argument in the list, which must be an integer preceding the argument being formatted. This call

TYPE	EXPRESSION	OUTPUT FORMAT OR ACTION
d	integer	signed decimal integer
i	integer	signed decimal integer
u	integer	unsigned decimal integer
o	integer	unsigned octal integer
x	integer	unsigned hex integer (uses a—f for the values 10 through 15)
X	integer	unsigned hex integer (uses A—F for the values 10 through 15)
f	floating point	signed value in form [-]dddd.ddd
e	floating point	signed value in form [-]d.dddd e [+|-]ddd (scientific notation).
E	floating point	same as e but prints E instead.
g	floating point	signed value using either e or f form, based on value and precision, with trailing 0s and decimal point only if necessary
G	floating point	same as g but prints E instead
c	character	single character (the integer argument is converted to unsigned char, then printed)
s	pointer to char	characters in string up until a null character or until precision number of characters have been printed
%	none	single percent character
n	pointer to int	stores count of characters written so far in the location pointed to by the next argument (which must be the address of an int)
p	pointer	address is an *implementation defined* format

Table C.4 `printf` format types and their meaning.

TYPE	DEFAULT FORMAT
e or E	Prints a minus sign for negative numbers, and a plus or minus sign for the exponent. Prints one digit before the decimal point. The number of digits after the decimal point is given by the precision (default six). The exponent contains at least two digits.
f	Prints a minus sign for negative numbers, and a blank for positive. The number of digits after the decimal point is given by the precision (default six).
g or G	Uses the default style of e, E, or f. The precision indicates the number of significant digits (default 6). Removes trailing 0s and includes the decimal point only if needed.
x or X	Uses the letters a—f for the x format, and A—F for X.

Table C.5 Default formats for the `printf` format types.

Type	Effect of #
c, s, d, i, u	no effect
o	0 is prepended to a nonzero value
x, X	0x or 0X is prepended to a nonzero value
e, E, f	output always contains a decimal point
g, G	same as e and E, except trailing 0s are not removed

Table C.6 Alternate `printf` format using the # alternate format specifier.

Type	Effect of Precision Specifier
d, i, o, u, x, X	Prints at least n digits. If the value has less than n digits, it pads the output on left with 0s. If the value has more than n digits, it doesn't truncate.
e, E, f	Prints n digits after the decimal point; rounds the least significant digit.
g, G	Prints at most n digits.
c	No effect.
s	Prints no more than n characters. (This is how we print long strings in a short field.)

Table C.7 Effect of *precision specifier* on `printf` formats.

```
printf("Val: %*i", width, val);
```

prints the value of **val** (an integer) using the width given as the value of **width** (also an integer).

A *precision* specifier is used to indicate the amount of space for the decimal part of a floating point value or for zero padding for integers. If no precision or a precision of **.0** is given, the default is used (1 for **d**, **i**, **o**, **u**, **x**, and **X**; 6 for **e**, **E**, and **f**; all significant digits for **g** and **G**; and all characters up to the null for **s**). If the precision is **.n** (where **n** is a constant), n characters or decimal places are printed as specified in Table C.7. Finally, if the precision is *****, the next value in the expression list specifies the precision (this must be an integer expression). If a ***** is used for both the width and the precision, the width expression precedes the precision expression and the value to be printed:

```
printf("Val: %*.*f\n", width, precision, val);
```

There is one oddity for values whose precision is stated as **.0**: if the format specifies one of the integer formats (**d**, **i**, **o**, **u**, **x**, or **X**) *and* the value is 0, then no numeric characters are printed: the field will contain blanks.

Table C.8 shows some examples of the various formatting strings, assuming the following declarations and values:

FORMAT STRING	EXPRESSION	OUTPUT
"[%15i]"	val	[-14]
"[%-15i]"	val	[-14]
"[%15i]"	val2	[87]
"[%+15i]"	val2	[+87]
"[%-15i]"	val2	[87]
"[%-+15i]"	val2	[+87]
"[%f]"	fval	[43.717999]
"[%15.0f]"	fval	[44]
"[%-15.0f]"	fval	[44]
"[%+15.0f]"	fval	[+44]
"[%10.5f]"	fval	[43.71800]
"[%.5f]"	fval	[43.71800]
"[%30s]"	s	[I love rock and roll]
"[%-30s]"	s	[I love rock and roll]
"[%-10.6s]"	s	[I love]
"[%10.6s]"	s	[I love]
"[%15x]"	val	[fff2]
"[%#15x]"	val	[0xfff2]

Table C.8 `printf` format strings, expressions, and output.

```
int    val = -14;
int    val2 = 87;
float  fval =  43.718;
char   *s = "I love rock and roll";
```

Formatted Input

We've also seen a variety of functions for performing formatted input.

```
int scanf(const char *format, ...)
int fscanf(FILE *stream, const char *format, ...)
int sscanf(char *string, const char *format, ...)
int vscanf(const char *format, va_list param)
int vfscanf(FILE *stream, const char *format, va_list param)
int vsscanf(char *string, const char *format, va_list param)
```

Each of these functions takes two sets of parameters. The first is a formatting string, describing the types and number of input values to be read (in a manner similar to the `printf` family). The second set is a list of *addresses* where values are to be stored. As with `printf`, input formats are indicated using a % format code. For each % format of the appropriate type, one address from the address list is used to store an input value.

Type	INPUT TYPE	ADDRESS TYPE
d	integer	`int *`
D	long integer	`long *`
o	octal integer	`int *`
O	long octal integer	`long *`
i	decimal, octal, or hex integer	`int *`
I	decimal, octal, or hex long integer	`long *`
u	unsigned integer	`unsigned int *`
U	unsigned long integer	`unsigned long *`
x	hexadecimal integer	`int *`
X	hexadecimal long	`long *`
e	floating point	`float *`
E	floating point	`double *`
f	floating point	`float *`
F	floating point	`double *`
s	string	`char []` (array of `char`)
c	character	`char *`
%	character	no input (% symbol stored)
n	no input is read	`int *` (number of values successfully stored)
p	hex number in address form	implementation-defined pointer

Table C.9   `scanf` variations and what they do.

The options available for **scanf**'s formatting codes are lengthy and rather complex. Table C.9 summarizes their use.

The conversions in Table C.9 also have certain conventions associated with them. The **%c** code reads the next input character, including whitespace (blank, tab, or newline). An optional count can be used with the **%c** format; in this case, the indicated number of characters is read, and the variable to which characters go should be an array of **char**, rather than pointer to **char**. For example, **%c** reads a single character, **%10c** reads 10 characters.

String input using **%s** requires that the array have enough space for the input. Reading continues until a space (blank or tab) or a newline. This often leads to confusion; if you really don't want to stop reading on a space, but only on a newline, use **gets** or **fgets** instead (or the **getline** function we wrote in Chapter 10).

The **scanf** input formats allow for integer and long types. **short**s can be read using the **h** modifier. Similarly, **long**s can be read by using either the **l** modifier (**%li**) or the uppercase form (**%I**). Here are some examples.

```
scanf("%i", &a);              /* read an int */
scanf("%I", &a);              /* read a long */
scanf("%li", &a);             /* read a long */
scanf("%hi", &a);             /* read a short */
scanf("%lx", &a);             /* read a long hex integer */
```

The **scanf** functions return the number of input values successfully scanned and stored or **EOF** if end of file is read. Scanning will terminate if the input does not match the type of the **%** format specifier. This typically occurs when a numeric input format is specified, but the input contains invalid alphabetics.

The general form of the format control string is

% [*] [width] [size] type

The ***** is an *assignment suppression* character, which we use most often when we know that input meets a rigid format and we don't need to keep all values. As an example, if the input consists of blank-separated fields containing last name, first name, and three values and we only want the last name and the third value, we can read and throw away the unwanted ones like this:

```
scanf("%s %*s %*i %*i %i", lname, &v3);
```

Here we read two string values and three decimal integer values, but we only store two values: the first string into **lname** and the third decimal integer into **v3**. We expect **scanf** to return 2.

The *width* is used to indicate the maximum number of characters to read. **scanf** will read fewer values if it reaches a character for which **isspace** is true, end of file, or a character it can't convert. With the input abcdefghijklmnopq, the call

```
scanf("%6s%6s", s1, s2);
```

will read and assign the string **abcdef** to **s1** and **ghijkl** to **s2**. Similarly, the input 123456789123456 and the program

```
scanf("%6li%6li", &v1, &v2);
```

will assign the value 123456 to **v1** and 789123 to **v2** (assuming **v1** and **v2** are **long**s).

The **%n** format does not consume input; instead it assigns to the next address in the address list, the number of items successfully converted and stored up to, but not including, this **%n**. So

```
scanf("%d %d %n %d\n", &v1, &v2, &how_many, &v3);
```

should store 2 into **how_many**. Since **scanf** returns as its value the number of items correctly read from the input, converted, and stored, it does not count any of the **%n** conversions. **scanf** should return 3 in the above example.

A format specification given in brackets will match any character between the brackets: **%[***list***]**. *list* can be a list of individual characters, a range of characters separated by a dash (the first character must be smaller than the second in the local character set collating sequence), or a list beginning with a caret (^). If the list *begins*

FORMAT	MATCHES
`%[abc]`	any string made up of the characters *a*, *b*, or *c*
`%[a-z]`	any string made up of the lowercase alphabetic characters
`%[A-Z]`	any string made up of the uppercase alphabetic characters
`%[a-zA-Z]`	any string made up of alphabetic characters
`%[0-9]`	any string made up of numeric characters
`%[0-9a-fA-F]`	any string made up of numeric characters, or *a* through *f* or *A* through *F*
`%[^0-9]`	any string made up of nonnumeric characters
`%[^a-zA-Z]`	any string made up of the nonalphabetic characters
`%[0-9^]`	any string made up of the numeric characters or carets

Table C.10 `scanf` string matches.

with a caret, then the meaning is reversed: we match only the characters *not* in the list. If the caret appears other than at the start of the list, then it is part of the *matching set*. Matched characters are assigned to an array of characters, which should be large enough to hold the largest possible match. So

```
scanf("%[a-z]", s);
```

will store "now" into **s** if the input is "now is the time." Table C.10 provides some additional examples.

If the format string contains a character other than a **%** format code or a blank, the character must match exactly in the input. To read two integer values separated by a colon, use

```
scanf("%i:%i", &v1, &v2)
```

Here the first value must be immediately followed by a colon (no intervening spaces). Compare this with:

```
scanf("%i :%i", &v1, &v2)
```

Now the first value must be followed by a colon, but there may be zero or more spaces before the colon.

C.7   LOCALES

The header file locale.h helps a program tailor itself to the individual system or *locale*. A *locale* means a set of capabilities in reading and printing numbers and money that is specific to a country or region. In the United States, we use a comma to separate thousands, and a period for the fractional part of floating point numbers. We use a negative sign or parentheses for negative dollar amounts, and a dollar sign for money. But some other countries use a comma for fractional amounts and place the minus sign after the monetary amount for negative values.

CATEGORY	AREAS FOR WHICH LOCALE IS SET
LC_ALL	all areas
LC_COLLATE	strcoll and strxfrm
LC_CTYPE	*ctype* character testing routines
LC_MONETARY	monetary conversions (from localeconv)
LC_NUMERIC	type/placement of decimal point in formatted input and output
LC_TIME	only for strftime type

Table C.11   The possible categories and their effect on locales.

There are two functions dealing with locales. The first is setlocale:

```
char *setlocale(int category, const char *locale);
```

It sets the program's locale in one of the areas specified by the **category** to the value specified by **locale**. That value is either **"C"**, **""**, or an *implementation-defined* specification. **"C"** is the default and indicates that the source and execution locales are the same. The equivalent of

```
setlocale(LC_ALL, "C");
```

happens automatically before the program starts. A null string for **locale** indicates an *implementation-defined* local environment. Figure C.11 lists the possible values for the **category** and their meaning. These values are defined in locale.h.

On success, setlocale returns a pointer to a string associated with locale information for the given **category**; otherwise the null pointer is returned.

We can also use setlocale to determine what the current **locale** is. We do this by providing **NULL** as its second argument. setlocale then returns a pointer to a string associated with locale information for the given **category**. The information in this string is *implementation defined*, but must be in a form appropriate for a subsequent call to setlocale with the string as the second argument and the same first argument.

The information on setlocale is of necessity hazy, since the meaning of a locale argument other than **"C"** is *implementation defined*. You're stuck scanning your compiler documentation for the specifics for your implementation.

The other locale-related function is localeconv.

```
struct lconv  *localeconv(void);
```

It returns a pointer to a structure describing how numbers are formatted for reading and printing, the separator between thousands, the decimal point, the monetary symbol, how negative monetary values are formatted, how time is formatted, and on and on. These values are all set in terms of the current locale. The name stands for *locale convention*.

Table C.12 lists the fields in a **struct lconv** and what they're used for. By default, **decimal_point** is **"."**, the other strings are null strings, and the **char** fields are **CHAR_MAX**. If any field is the null string or has the **char** value **CHAR_MAX**,

610   **LIBRARY DETAILS**

Field and Type	Meaning
`char *decimal_point;`	Decimal point for *nonmonetary* quantities in formatted I/O.
`char *thousands_sep;`	Separator between groups of digits for *nonmonetary* quantities in formatted I/O. Only used before the decimal point. The number of digits in a group is given by `grouping`.
`char *grouping;`	String indicating the number of characters in each "thousands" grouping for nonmonetary quantities.
`char *int_curr_symbol;`	*International* currency symbol for the current locale. It consists of three symbols for the currency symbol specified in *ISO 4217 Codes for the Representation of Currency and Funds*. Its fourth character separates the currency symbol from the monetary amount (usually a blank or period). For the US, this string is `"USD "`; for Italy, `"ITL."`
`char *currency_symbol;`	*Local* currency symbol. For the US, this is `"$"`; for Italy, `"L."`.
`char *mon_decimal_point;`	Decimal point for monetary quantities. For the US, this is `"."`; for Italy, `""`.
`char *mon_thousands_sep;`	"Thousands" separator for monetary quantities (before the decimal point). `mon_grouping` determines the number of digits grouped as "thousands."
`char *mon_grouping;`	Same as `grouping`, but applied only to monetary quantities.
`char *positive_sign;`	Sign used for nonnegative monetary quantities in formatted I/O (usually the null string). The `p_sign_posn` field describes where the `positive_sign` goes.
`char *negative_sign;`	Sign used for negative monetary quantities in formatted I/O. Usually `"-"`; for Switzerland it is `"C"`. The `n_sign_posn` field describes where the `negative_sign` goes.
`char int_frac_digits;`	Number of digits to the right of the decimal point in a monetary quantity displayed in *international* format. For the US, this is two; for Italy, zero.
`char frac_digits;`	Number of digits to the right of the decimal point in a monetary quantity display in *local* format. For the US, this is two; for Italy, zero.
`char p_cs_precedes;`	One or zero, depending on whether the currency symbol *precedes* or *follows* a nonnegative monetary quantity. For the US and most other countries, this is 1.
`char n_cs_precedes;`	Same as `p_cs_precedes`, but for negative quantities.
`char p_sep_by_space;`	One or zero, depending on whether the currency symbol is, or is not, separated by a space from a nonnegative monetary quantity. For the US, this is 1; for Italy, zero.
`char n_sep_by_space;`	Same as `p_sep_by_space`, but for negative quantities.
`char p_sign_posn;`	Describes formatting of positive sign for nonnegative monetary values. Values given on previous page.
`char n_sign_posn;`	Same as `p_sign_posn`, but for negative monetary values.

Table C.12   The fields in a `localeconv` and their meaning.

nonnegative numbers.

A few fields need additional description. The **grouping** and **mon_grouping** fields describe the size of "thousands" groups in a tricky way. If an element of the string is **CHAR_MAX**, no more grouping occurs; if **0**, then the previous value is repeated for all remaining groups; otherwise, the character is interpreted as an integer, and is the number of characters to be grouped. For example, the value `"\0\3"` indicates that grouping is by threes. `"\0\2\3"` indicates that grouping is by twos, except the rightmost, which groups by threes:

    12,45,89,999.903232

This is certainly odd, but the locale mechanism supports this if such a method is supported in the local environment (through an appropriate call to **setlocale**).

p_sign_posn and **n_sign_posn** are also somewhat tricky. Depending on their value, different methods are used to display the positive or negative sign with monetary amounts. A 0 causes parentheses to surround the value and the currency symbol. A 1 causes the sign to precede the value and the currency symbol. A 2 causes it to follow them. A 3 causes the sign to precede the currency symbol. And a 4 causes the sign to follow it.

C.8   SIGNAL HANDLING

The standard C library provides a function, **signal**, to allow us to handle interrupts and other asynchronous events. Our programs are informed of these events, such as a user hitting the interrupt key, by being sent a signal. These signals may be generated by system, hardware, or software methods or by calling the **raise** function.

C allows us to do one of three things when a signal occurs. The first is to simply ignore it. Our processing continues as if the signal never occurred. The second is to let the system handle the signal in its default way. Each signal has some default action associated with it that is established at the beginning of program execution.[5] The last is to provide a piece of code (called a *handler*) to be executed when the signal occurs. When the signal happens, our program is interrupted and control is automatically transferred to this handler. When the handler returns, control automatically goes back to the place where our program was interrupted.

In general, to process signals, we need to include signal.h. We specify the behavior we want for a particular signal by calling **signal**.

    void (*signal(int sig, void (*f)(int)))(int)

It takes an integer identifying a particular signal and a pointer to a handling function. The integers are constants defined in signal.h and are listed in Table C.13. The language requires that at least these six be available, but most environments provide additional

---

[5]The specific default action for any given signal is *implementation defined*. Operating systems and compilers vary substantially on this, and the documentation for **signal** in the local environment should be examined carefully. Under both UNIX and MS-DOS, most—but not all—signals cause our program to terminate.

SIGNAL	SIGNAL DESCRIPTION
SIGABRT	abnormal termination has occurred
SIGFPE	arithmetic error (floating point exception) has occurred
SIGILL	illegal instruction has occurred
SIGINT	interactive interrupt (attention) has occurred
SIGSEGV	invalid access to data has occurred (called a *segmentation violation*)
SIGTERM	termination request has been sent to the program

Table C.13 Constants for signals that every implementation must provide.

implementation-defined ones. The handling function must take an **int** argument and return **void**.

To ignore subsequent occurrences of a signal, we pass the special constant **SIG_IGN** as the handler. To restore the default action for subsequence occurrences of a signal, we pass **SIG_DFL** as the handler. The only other choice is to pass the name of a function to be used as a handler. This requests that this handler be invoked for the *next* occurrence of the given signal. The handler takes an **int** and returns **void**. It's automatically passed the number of the signal that caused it to be invoked (so we can have the same function handle more than one signal). As soon as the handler is invoked, the action for the signal is automatically reset to **SIG_DFL** (except for a **SIGILL**, for which the reset to **SIG_DFL** is *implementation defined*). If it exits via a call to **return**, execution continues at the exact point at which the signal occurred (except for a **SIGFPE**, where a **return** will cause *undefined* behavior).

signal returns the value of the function from the previous call or if it fails, the special pointer, **SIG_ERR**.

Figure C.6 provides a simple program that shows how to ignore signals and supply handlers. It ignores **SIGTERM** and catches **SIGINT**. The result is an infinite loop that we can stop only by hitting an interrupt three times.

If you look at our handler for **SIGINT** closely, you'll see that the first thing it does is ignore the signal that caused it to be invoked. User-supplied handlers generally don't want the signal handler to be reset to **SIG_DFL**, since receipt of the same signal while in the handler will invoke the default action—usually terminating the program. Usually we reset the action for the given signal to **SIG_IGN** at the start of the handler (leaving only a tiny bit of vulnerability) and then set it back to call our own handler just before exiting.

Since a signal can occur anywhere, including system or library routines, resuming in the middle of what we were doing when the signal occurred may cause unexpected results. In this program, for example, it's possible for the **printf** in **main** to be interrupted in the middle before writing all its output. On some implementations, it may start writing its output again; on others, it may ignore the unwritten output. The most appropriate, safe, portable behavior for a user-supplied interrupt handler is to ignore subsequent occurrences of the signal, do its task, and then call **exit** or perform a **longjmp** (discussed in the next section), bringing the program to a known state.

```c
/*
 * Only way to kill this program is to send it three interrupts!
 */
#include <stdio.h>
#include <signal.h>
#include <stdlib.h>

#define REALLY_QUIT   3                  /* 3 interrupts kill it */

int main(void)
{
  void     int_handler(int);
  unsigned sleep(unsigned);             /* non-standard but portable */

  signal(SIGTERM, SIG_IGN);             /* ignore termination signals */
  signal(SIGINT, int_handler);          /* provide interrupt handler */
  for (;;)                              /* infinite loop */
  {
    printf("Stop me before I print again!\n");
    (void) sleep(1);
  }
}

void int_handler(int sig)
{
  static int count = 0;

  signal(SIGINT, SIG_IGN);             /* turn off interrupts */
  fprintf(stderr,"That's %i interrupts (signal %i).\n", ++count, sig);
  if (count >= REALLY_QUIT)
    exit(EXIT_FAILURE);

  fprintf(stderr,"I'm not quitting until you hit three interrupts\n");
  signal(SIGINT, int_handler);         /* reset interrupt handling */
}
```

Figure C.6 (catchsig.c) A signal handling example.

We can use **raise** to generate a signal from our program:

```c
int raise(int sig);
```

raise sends the signal **sig** to the program, returning zero on success, nonzero otherwise. So **raise(SIGINT)** is suicide, unless we have a handler set up for **SIGINT**. We often use **raise** to test our program's behavior when it's sent different signals.

The header file also defines a special type, **sig_atomic_t**, which is a synonym for an object of integral type that can be accessed *atomically*. This means that any object of this type will be completely accessed even during a signal.

Programs written using interrupts will of necessity be system specific, and will likely need at lease some recoding when they're moved to a different system. But we can minimize the damage by localizing signal handling in a few specific modules. Ideally, only those modules will need to be converted to match the requirements of a new environment.

C.9   NONLOCAL GOTOS

The library provides a pair of functions, `setjmp` and `longjmp`, that let us portably jump out of one function and into another.

```
int setjmp(jmp_buf state);
void longjmp(jmp_buf state, int val);
```

We use these functions most frequently to have an interrupt handler jump back to the main program, rather than return to the function that was interrupted by the signal. To use them, we need to include setjmp.h, which also defines the `jmp_buf` type.

The idea behind `setjmp` and `longjmp` is actually quite simple. Most C implementations use a *stack* to store information about a called function and its caller. As functions are called from within other functions, the stack grows deeper and deeper. In order to jump to an earlier function, we need to restore the stack to the way it was when we were in that function. `setjmp` provides a way of saving the information necessary to restore the stack to a particular state. `longjmp` provides a way to exit a function and request the change to the stack to a previously saved state. A `jmp_buf` is usually an array of `int`s used to contain the registers or other structures necessary for restoring the stack.

`setjmp` saves the current state so that a later call to `longjmp` restores it. Its return value depends on how `setjmp` was called. It turns out that `setjmp` can be called in two ways: directly or through a `longjmp`. If called directly, `setjmp` returns zero. If called through `longjmp`, it returns the value of the `longjmp`'s second argument.

We should only call `setjmp` in the context of a direct comparison with an integral expression (such as in a **switch** statement or relational test). The allowability in any other context is *implementation defined*.[6]

`longjmp` restores the state given in the argument **state**, which must have been previously stored into by a call to `setjmp`. We're usually in big trouble if **state** has not been set with a call to `setjmp` or if the routine that called `setjmp` has returned before the call to `longjmp`. We also may get strange results if we call `longjmp` in a nested signal handling function. A nested signal handler is one that is called on receipt of a signal while in a routine that was called via another signal.

After the return from `longjmp`, all variables have values as of the time of the call to `longjmp`. But automatic variables that are not **volatile** and that have been changed between the call to `setjmp` and `longjmp`, have *indeterminate* values.

---

[6]This is because using `setjmp` in a more complex expression may involve optimizations that can affect the success of what a `setjmp` is trying to do.

longjmp does not return a value, but the result of a **longjmp** is the same as if the corresponding **setjmp** had just returned with the value of the second argument to **longjmp**. However, if **val** is 0, **setjmp** will return as if it were 1. **longjmp** can be thought of as a goto to the corresponding **setjmp**. The effect is as if **setjmp** returns with value **val**.

Figure C.7 is an example. It's a simple loop that requests file names from the user and displays those files. If an interrupt happens at any time during that loop, the program uses **longjmp** to exit a signal handling routine.[7] We're careful to make **fp**, the file pointer, a global variable, since we need to know its value after the **longjmp** in order to close the file.

C.10   TIME FUNCTIONS

The standard library provides a rich and a somewhat strange collection of time-related functions. They're a bit bizarre because they are mainly adopted from UNIX and don't necessarily follow the conventions of other operating systems. To use these functions, we include the header file time.h. It defines the "broken down" time structure **struct tm**, the **time_t** and **clock_t** times, and a constant, **CLOCKS_PER_SEC**, the number of "clock ticks" equal to 1 second.

There are a pair of functions that return a time, **clock** and **time**.

```
clock_t  clock(void);
time_t   time(time_t *t);
double   difftime(time_t t2, time_t t1);
```

clock returns the time (in units of **CLOCKS_PER_SEC**) since some initial time. We use it when we need a relative time but not an absolute one. If the processor time can't be determined, **clock** returns -1.

Figure C.8 uses **clock** to compute a program's total execution time. It calls **clock** at the start and at the end, subtracts the two times, and divides the result by **CLOCKS_PER_SEC**.[8]

time gets the absolute time. Due to the historical association with UNIX, **time** often returns the time in seconds since some distant past. In UNIX, this is midnight, January 1, 1970 (GMT). But there's no guarantee that a **time_t** will be a time in seconds. As a result, if we want portable code we need to use the library functions discussed below to manipulate **time**'s return value. If the time is not available, **time** returns **(time_t)(-1)**.

What about **time**'s argument, the **time_t ***? That's another historical artifact. If the argument is nonnull, just for the heck of it, **time** also stores the result in the pointed-to location. Just call **time** with a null pointer and forget this oddity.[9]

---

[7]Control C is the usual keyboard character for sending interrupts on many interactive systems.

[8]This program calls **sleep**, available in many systems but not part of ANSI C, to suspend execution (but keep the clock ticking) for the specified number of seconds.

[9]It stems from prehistoric times, back when C had no **long**s and the time had to be represented as an array of two **int**s.

```
/*
 * Print files, going to next file at interrupt.
 */
#include <stdio.h>
#include <stddef.h>
#include <signal.h>
#include <setjmp.h>

jmp_buf      state;                    /* for setjmp and longjmp */
FILE         *fp = NULL;               /* currently open file */

int main(void)
{
  int  getline(char *buf, int len);
  void display_file(FILE *fp);
  void intr_handler(int sig);
  char name[BUFSIZ + 1];

  setjmp(state);                       /* return here on longjmps */
  signal(SIGINT, intr_handler);        /* catch interrupts */
  while (printf("File: "), getline(name,BUFSIZ) != EOF && name[0] != '\0')
  {
    if (fp != NULL)           /* close file that may still be open */
    {
      fclose(fp);
      fp = NULL;
    }
    if ((fp = fopen(name, "r")) != NULL)
      display_file(fp);
    else
      fprintf(stderr,"Can't open %s\n", name);
  }
  return 0;
}

void intr_handler(int sig)
{
  signal(SIGINT, SIG_IGN);             /* ignore interrupts */
  fprintf(stderr, "Interrupted (by signal %i)!\n", sig);
  signal(SIGINT, intr_handler);        /* ignore interrupts */
  longjmp(state, 1);                   /* now back to a known state */
}

void display_file(FILE *fp)
{
  int c;

  while ((c = getc(fp)) != EOF)
    putchar(c);
}
```

Figure C.7   (jump.c)   An example of `setjmp`/`longjmp`.

```
/*
 * Print amount of time program takes to run.
 */
#include <stdio.h>
#include <time.h>

#define   DEFL_SLEEP_MAX       10u
#define   SLEEP_MAX            100

int main(void)
{
  unsigned    how_long;
  clock_t     t1;
  unsigned    sleep(unsigned);                    /* nonstandard */
  int         status = 1;

  if ((t1 = clock()) == (clock_t) -1)
    fprintf(stderr, "Can't get processor clock.  Exiting...\n");
  else
  {
    printf("Sleep time: ");
    if (scanf("%u", &how_long) != 1 || how_long > SLEEP_MAX)
      fprintf(stderr, "Time in error.  Defaulting to %u secs.\n",
              how_long = DEFL_SLEEP_MAX);
    (void) sleep(how_long);                       /* nonstandard */
    printf("Program took %.2f seconds to run.\n",
           (double)(clock()-t1)/CLOCKS_PER_SEC);
    status = 0;
  }
  return status;
}
```

Figure C.8   (timeprog.c) Program that prints the execution time.

---

difftime returns the difference (in seconds) of **t2–t1**. **time_t** is usually a **long**, so we could do this ourselves. But it's conceivable that it could be implemented as a structure, in which case we couldn't do direct subtraction.

Another UNIX carryover—**ctime** (for "character time") takes a **time_t** returned from **time** and returns a pointer to a string with the time formatted nicely and neatly.

```
char *ctime(const time_t *when);
```

This string is the current date and *local* time, accounting for time zone and daylight savings time. The string returned from **ctime** is always exactly 26 characters, like this:

```
DDD MMM dd hh:mm:ss yyyy\n\0
```

Notice that it sneakily stuffs a newline at the end of the string.

```
#include <stdio.h>
#include <time.h>

int main(void)
{
    time_t   now = time(NULL);

    printf("Today's date: %s", ctime(&now));
    return 0;
}
```

Figure C.9   (dumpdate.c)   Print today's date.

Figure C.9 uses these functions to nicely print today's date. Here it's output:

```
Today's date: Mon Aug 31 14:01:55 1992
```

There are also a pair of library functions for converting time in seconds into a structure.

```
struct tm *gmtime(const time_t *tp);
struct tm *localtime(const time_t *tp);
```

gmtime takes a **time_t** and returns the current Greenwich Mean Time (now called Coordinated Universal Time). The type returned is a pointer to a **struct tm**. **localtime** is similar, but it converts the time to the local time, accounting for time zone and daylight savings time. The structure they return looks like this:

```
struct tm
{
    int   tm_sec;   /* 0 .. 61 (leap seconds too) */
    int   tm_min;   /* 0 .. 59 */
    int   tm_hour;  /* hours since midnight: 0 .. 23 */
    int   tm_mday;  /* day of month: 1 .. 31 */
    int   tm_mon;   /* month: Jan = 0, etc. */
    int   tm_year;  /* year since 1900 */
    int   tm_wday;  /* Sunday = 0, Monday = 1, etc. */
    int   tm_yday;  /* day of year (Jan 1 = 0, through 365) */
    int   tm_isdst; /* daylight savings time */
};
```

tm_sec ranges from 0 to 61 to account for leap seconds added from time to time; tm_isdst is zero if daylight savings time is not in effect, positive for daylight savings time, and negative if the time in effect can't be determined.

The last thing we may want to do is take one of the structures and turn it into a string. To do that, we use **asctime**, which is similar to **ctime**.

```
char *asctime(const struct tm *tp);
```

It takes a pointer to a **struct tm** and returns a pointer to a string.   In fact,

```
/*
 * Print current local time and Greenwich Mean Time.
 */
#include <stdio.h>
#include <string.h>
#include <time.h>

int main(void)
{
  time_t      now;
  struct tm  *tp;
  char        *p;

  now = time(NULL);

  *(strchr(p = asctime(tp = localtime(&now)), '\n')) = '\0';
  printf("%s", p);
  if (tp->tm_isdst > 0)
    printf(" DST");
  putchar('\n');

  *(strchr(p = asctime(gmtime(&now)), '\n')) = '\0';
  printf("%s GMT\n", p);
  return 0;
}
```

Figure C.10 (currtime.c) Program that prints the time and adds DST for daylight savings time and GMT for Greenwich Mean Time.

`asctime(localtime(&now))` gives the same string as `ctime(&now)`.

Figure C.10 is a little program to print the current time in both GMT and local versions, adding the suffix DST or GMT. Rather than decoding the parts of the **struct tm**, we'll use the string from **asctime**, remove the trailing carriage return, and then append DST or GMT as appropriate. Most of the program is straightforward except for the statement

```
*(strchr(p = asctime(tp = localtime(&now)), '\n')) = '\0';
```

This grungy mess assigns the result of **localtime** to **tp**, passes this value to **asctime**, and saves the result in **p**. Finally, since **asctime**'s string ends with a CR, we use **strchr** to replace it with the null character. The output, run during daylight savings time, was

```
Mon Aug 31 15:44:16 1992 DST
Mon Aug 31 22:44:16 1992 GMT
```

There are only two functions left. **mktime** converts the time components in the structure pointed to by **tp** into a **time_t**.

```
/*
 * Determine day of the week for December 7, 1941.
 */
#include <stdio.h>
#include <time.h>

char *days[] = {"Sun", "Mon", "Tues", "Wednes", "Thurs", "Fri", "Sat"};

int main(void)
{
  struct tm   any_day =   /* 7th of December, 1941 */
    { 0, 0, 0, 7, 11,  1941 - 1900, -1 };

  if(mktime(&any_day) == -1)
  {
    fprintf(stderr, "Can't convert given date.\n");
    return 1;
  }
  printf("Dec. 7, 1941 occurred on a %sday\n", days[any_day.tm_wday]);
  return 0;
}
```

Figure C.11   (usemktim.c) Example program making use of `mktime`.

```
        time_t mktime(struct tm *tp);
```

It sets the values of `tp->tm_wday` and `tp->tm_yday` to correspond to the converted time. It returns the converted time or -1 if conversion cannot be accomplished. Figure C.11 is an example.

The last function is `strftime` (for "string format time"), which convents the time in the structure pointed to by `tp` into a locale-specific representation, according to the format string `format`.

```
        size_t strftime(char *s, size_t n, const char *format,
                        const struct tm *tp);
```

It writes the characters into the string `s` as with `sprintf`. Characters in the format string are copied as is into `s`, except for `%` format characters. For format characters from the table in Table C.14, it uses the appropriate field in the `struct tm` pointed to by `tp`.

The function returns the number of characters stored into `s`. The second argument, `n`, is used by the routine so that no more than `n` characters are stored. However, if the conversion requires more than `n` characters, zero is returned and the contents of `s` are not specified.

Figure C.12 uses it to print when a famous event took place at Pearl Harbor. Here's its output:

FORMAT	COPIES
%a	abbreviation of the weekday name
%A	full weekday name
%b	abbreviated month name
%B	full month name
%c	date and time
%d	day of the month (01–31)
%H	hour in 24-hour notation (00–23)
%I	hour in 12-hour notation (01–12)
%j	day of the year (001–366)
%m	month as a number (01–12)
%M	minute (00–59)
%p	AM or PM designator for a 12-hour clock
%s	seconds (00–61)
%U	week of the year (00–53), based on week 0 starting on a Sunday
%w	weekday as a number (Sunday = 0, Monday = 1, and so on)
%W	week of the year (00–53), based on week 1 starting on a Monday
%x	date
%X	time
%y	year with only two digits (00–99)
%Y	year with all four digits
%z	time zone name if the time zone can be determined
%%	% sign

Table C.14   Format codes and their meaning for the format string in the `strftime` routine.

```
/*
 * Display in a nice format when Pearl Harbor was bombed (12/7/1941).
 */
#include <stdio.h>
#include <time.h>

int main()
{
  char       s[BUFSIZ];
  struct tm day = { 0, 0, 0, 7, 11, 1941-1900, 0, 0, -1 };

  if (strftime(s, BUFSIZ, "Pearl harbor day: %A, %B 7, %Y (%x)", &day))
    puts(s);
  return 0;
}
```

Figure C.12   (pearl.c)   Using `strftime` to print when a famous event took place at Pearl Harbor.

```
Pearl harbor day: Sunday, December 7, 1941 (12/07/41)
```

And that's finally it for C's large collection of library functions.

D NUMBERING SYSTEMS

A value can be represented in any number of different base systems. This appendix discusses some of the more common ones: binary (base 2), octal (base 8), decimal (base 10), and hexadecimal (base 16). We focus on how to understand values in different bases, and how to convert from one base to another.

D.1 INTRODUCTION

In a base system, a value is represented by a string of symbols. In base 10, the base you're most familiar with, we build numbers out of the digits 0 through 9. In binary, however, we can only use the digits 0 and 1. Similarly, in octal, we can only use the digits 0 through 7. But in hexadecimal, not only can we use the digits 0 through 9, as in base 10, but also the letters A through F. Those letters represent the values 10 through 15, respectively. Each of these base systems is centered on an integer, called the *base* or *radix*. For binary it's base 2, for octal it's base 8, and for hexadecimal it's base 16.

Each place occupied by a symbol corresponds to a power of the base. The rightmost place corresponds to base raised to the 0 power (which is 1 for any choice of base). Each move to the left multiplies the current place by the value of the base. In decimal, that means the rightmost place corresponds to 1s, the next place to the left to 10s, the place to left of that to 100s, and so on. In octal, the rightmost place corresponds to 1s; the next place to the left to 8s, the one after that to 64s, and so on. In hexadecimal, the rightmost place also corresponds to 1s, but the next place on the left to 16s, the one after that to 256s, and so on. Table D.1 shows the correspondence between position and value in binary, octal, decimal, and hexadecimal:

We compute the base 10 value of a number $a_n a_{n-1} \cdots a_1 a_0$ in base B by computing $\sum_{i=0}^{n} a_i \times B^i$. For example, to convert 724_8, we need to compute $(7 \times 8^2) + (4 \times 8^1) + (2 \times 8^0)$, which gives us 482_{10}. To convert $A2C_{16}$ to base 10, we evaluate $(10 \times 16^2) + (2 \times 16^1) + (12 \times 16^0)$, which evaluates to 2604_{10}.

BASE		POSITION				
	n	4	3	2	1	0
binary	2^n	16	8	4	2	1
octal	8^n	4096	512	64	8	1
decimal	10^n	10000	1000	100	10	1
hexadecimal	16^n	65536	4096	256	16	1

Table D.1 The correspondence between position and value in various bases. Positions are numbered starting from zero, going from right to left (this way the position's value is equal to the power of the base).

D.2 **CONVERSIONS**

There's a simple and direct relationship between binary, octal, and hexadecimal numbers. To convert from binary to octal, group the number from the right in three-bit units and convert each group to an octal number. To covert to hexadecimal, group the number from the right in four-bit units and convert each group to a hexadecimal number (for hexadecimal, remember that 10 converts to A, 11 to B, 12 to C, 13 to D, 14 to E, and 15 to F). Here's an example:

Binary	0	100	001	110	111	010
Octal	0	4	1	6	7	2

Binary			0100	0011	1011	1010
Hex			4	3	B	A

To convert a number X from base 10 to base B, divide X by B. The remainder becomes the leftmost digit of the converted number. The quotient becomes the next X, and is divided by B, with the process completed when the new quotient is finally zero.

E CHARACTER SETS

Each implementation uses some underlying representation for characters, called a character set. The two most common character sets are ASCII and EBCDIC. This appendix provides a pair of tables that you can use to determine a character's integer representation in either of these sets. Given a character, first locate it in the appropriate table, then add its row number to the number at the top of its column. For example, the ASCII representation for the character 'A' is 64 plus 1, or 65.

E.1 THE ASCII CHARACTER SET

	0	16	32	48	64	80	96	112
0	^@	^P	space	0	@	P	'	p
1	^A	^Q	!	1	A	Q	a	q
2	^B	^R	"	2	B	R	b	r
3	^C	^S	#	3	C	S	c	s
4	^D	^T	$	4	D	T	d	t
5	^E	^U	%	5	E	U	e	U
6	^F	^V	&	6	F	V	f	v
7	^G	^W	'	7	G	W	g	w
8	^H	^X	(	8	H	X	h	x
9	^I	^Y	)	9	I	Y	i	y
10	^J	^Z	*	:	J	Z	j	z
11	^K	escape	+	;	K	[	k	{
12	^L		,	<	L	\	l		
13	^M		–	=	M	]	m	}
14	^N		.	>	N	^	n	~
15	^O		/	?	O	_	o	del

E.2   THE EBCDIC CHARACTER SET

	0	32	64	96	128	160	192	224
0	NUL	DS	SP					
1	SOH	SOS		/	a		A	
2	STX	FS			b	s	B	S
3	ETX				c	t	C	T
4	PF	BYP			d	u	D	U
5	HT	LF			e	v	E	V
6	LC	ETB			f	w	F	W
7	DEL	ESC			g	x	G	X
8					h	y	H	Y
9					i	z	I	Z
10	SMM	SM	¢					
11	VT	CU2	.	'				
12	FF		<	%				
13	CR	ENQ	(	~				
14	SO	ACK	+	>				
15	SI	BEL	|	?				
16	DLE		&					0
17	DC1				j		J	1
18	DC2	SYN			k		K	2
19	TM				l		L	3
20	RES	PN			m		M	4
21	NL	RS			n		N	5
22	BS	UC			o		O	6
23	IL	EOT			p		P	7
24	CAN				q		Q	8
25	EM				r		R	9
26	CC		!	:				
27	CU1	CU3	$	#				
28	IFS	DC4	*	@				
29	IGS	NAK	)	'				
30	IRS		;	=				
31	IUS	SUB	corner					

INDEX

We've tried to be as complete as possible in creating our index. It not only contains all the usual key terms and topics, but also every type, macro, function, and header file that appears in the standard libraries or that we defined in the text. Those that we've defined are followed by a †. In addition, C++-related terms are followed by a ◊. Finally, italic page numbers indicate interesting examples of various language concepts that occurred away from where we discussed the concept in detail.